INVESTIGATING COMMUNICATION

AN INTRODUCTION TO RESEARCH METHODS

SECOND EDITION

LAWRENCE R. FREY

The University of Memphis

CARL H. BOTAN

Purdue University

GARY L. KREPS

National Cancer Institute

ALLYN AND BACON

Boston • London • Toronto • Sydney • Tokyo • Singapore

Series Editor: Karon Bowers
Vice President, Editor-in-Chief: Paul A. Smith
Editorial Assistant: Jennifer Becker
Marketing Manager: Jackie Aaron
Production Editor: Christopher H. Rawlings
Editorial-Production Service: Omegatype Typography, Inc.
Composition and Prepress Buyer: Linda Cox
Manufacturing Buyer: Megan Cochran
Cover Administrator: Jenny Hart
Electronic Composition: Omegatype Typography, Inc.

Copyright © 2000, 1991 by Allyn & Bacon
A Pearson Education Company
160 Gould Street
Needham Heights, MA 02494

Internet: www.abacon.com

Library of Congress Cataloging-in-Publication Data

Frey, Lawrence R.
  Investigating communication : an introduction to research methods.
— 2nd ed. / Lawrence R. Frey, Carl H. Botan, Gary L. Kreps.
    p.   cm.
  Rev. ed. of: Investigating communication / Lawrence R. Frey . . .
[et al.]. Englewood Cliffs, N.J. : Prentice Hall, c1991.
  Includes bibliographical references and index.
  ISBN (invalid) 0-205-19826-0
    1. Communication—Research—Methodology.   I. Botan, Carl H.
II. Kreps, Gary L.   III. Title.
P91.3.F74 2000
302.2'07'2—dc21   99–34444
                                                               CIP

Printed in the United States of America

10 9 8 7 6 5 4 3 2 1   04 03 02 01 00 99

CONTENTS

PART TWO
PLANNING AND DESIGNING
COMMUNICATION RESEARCH   79

PART FOUR
ANALYZING AND INTERPRETING
QUANTITATIVE DATA   287

R*esearch methods*—two little words that seem to intimidate even the best college student. Indeed, when we asked a group of students the first thought that came to mind when they heard these words, they said, "Difficult," "Time consuming," "Worth the effort?" "Boring," and "C" (as in grade). Faculty members, in contrast, responded with, "The pursuit of truth," "Planned investigation," and "Proof."

To quote the boss of the labor camp (an unfortunate analogy, we know!) in the movie *Cool Hand Luke,* "What we have here is a failure to communicate." Students don't understand the full value of learning about research methods. They see research as the province of the elite, as difficult or even impossible to master. Unfortunately, this attitude is often reinforced by how research methods are taught. Research methods courses can become a battle or proving ground, with students wishing merely to survive and then forgetting about what they learned as soon thereafter as possible.

In short, the gap between the attitudes of teachers and students is an obstacle to learning about research methods that must be overcome. To that end, our goal has been to write a text that encourages you as a student to become excited about studying research methods. Call us optimistic, but we seek to make research methods accessible rather than impossible to learn and, hopefully, to encourage you and your teachers alike to have fun in the process.

One way we attempt to do this is by framing research methods in some potentially helpful ways. First, we equate learning about research methods with learning about a new culture. Like a foreign culture, research methods have their own languages, rules, and social customs. Learning about a foreign culture takes time and patience, and learning about research methods is no different. We, the authors, remember what our entry period into the culture of research was like; indeed, some of us did not do all that well in our first research methods course! Yet here we are today teaching and writing about communication research methods. Understanding the maturation process firsthand and being sensitive to the difficulty of learning this new culture, we start at the very beginning and proceed slowly, making sure that everyone is with us along the way.

Second, in line with a communication perspective, it is helpful to think about the research methods culture as a series of conversations that take place among and between its members and constituents. There is, for example, the conversation that goes on between a researcher and the people he or she studies. There is also the conversation that goes on between a researcher and his or her colleagues in the form of journal and book publications and convention presentations. Both conversations, and a number of others, although they are quite different in purpose and nature, are part of the research process. The value of such a perspective, then, is that it grounds the research process in communication acts and processes—something you, as a communication student, already understand.

Third, within any culture there are subcultures where members carry on conversations using particular words and phrases; in some cases, these subcultural conversations are not understood easily by members of other subcultures or by members of the larger culture. For example, if you are a surfer, you know that words like *hollow, closed-out,* and *sucking* describe types of waves, while *drop-in, cut-back,* and *off-the-lip* describe surfing maneuvers (see Scheerhorn & Geist, 1997). The research methods culture also has subcultures within it; as one example, subcultures are represented by the different methodologies that researchers use to study communication, such as experimental, survey, textual analysis, and naturalistic inquiry. Hence, researchers who conduct experiments believe in and understand the importance of *randomization,* which refers to the process of assigning research participants to the different conditions that are part of an experiment (such as treatment and nontreatment conditions) in such a way that each person has an equal chance of being put into each condition so as to rule out the possibility of initial differences between the conditions (see Chapter 7). Each method, thus, has its own terminology and rules about how researchers converse with the people being studied, with colleagues in the discipline and other fields, and with the press and general public. We seek to teach you about these subcultures and the conversations that occur therein.

Finally, we see researchers as being similar to detectives. Like a detective trying to solve a crime, a researcher is trying to uncover new knowledge. The researcher-detective starts with a topic worth studying, poses questions that need asking, and then attempts to find the answers in a systematic manner. Research methods are, thus, the strategies researchers use to solve puzzling questions. Like a detective, a researcher searches for evidence as carefully and as systematically as possible, sorts the meaningful from the trivial, and adopts the most likely solution or answer.

Learning about the conversations that take place in the research methods culture, in general, and the various methods subcultures, in particular, is helped by exposure to the ways other social detectives do it. For that reason, we provide you with many examples of real-life communication research. By the time you finish this text, we are sure you will agree that there are many exciting topics studied in the communication discipline and intriguing ways in which research is done. And while we review many classic examples of research, communication is a young and growing field that seems to change almost daily. For that reason, we concentrate on sharing with you the latest, cutting-edge research studies conducted during the 1990s.

Although a number of good research methods textbooks are available, our approach is particularly helpful in learning this subject in five ways. First, we aim at students with little or no familiarity with research methods. We know that research methods and findings are often steeped in mystery and obtuse language, making it difficult for new learners (and even seasoned veterans), so we try hard to demystify the research process, making it accessible instead of esoteric. This does not mean that we do not deal with important, substantive, and, at times, difficult material; we do, but we never forget that you are an introductory student. Instead of throwing you into the deep end of a pool and seeing whether you swim or drown, we prefer to take you into the water slowly, first getting your feet wet and then immersing yourself in the pool at a comfortable rate.

Second, the primary goal of this text is to enable you to become a more knowledgeable and critical consumer of research. We are not trying to train you as a professional researcher; this is more appropriate for graduate education. Indeed, the primary difference between undergraduate and graduate education is the extent to which students learn to engage in original research as part of their graduate coursework (both in terms of taking a number of methods courses and as the basis for a thesis or dissertation). We are aware that you may not have to conduct research in your professional life, but, as we show in the very first chapter, you most certainly will have to be able to find, read, understand, and evaluate research as part of your work life and as an informed citizen who is called on to make important decisions, such as voting for political candidates or serving on juries. Understanding the research process, of course, is the first step toward becoming a producer of research, so if you choose to go on to graduate school or if you are asked to conduct research as part of this or another course during your undergraduate career, this text will prove invaluable.

Third, we have written this textbook explicitly for students who wish to understand how research methods are used to study communication behavior. This approach prepares communication majors to study, research, and analyze the real-world communication issues they encounter in the various careers they pursue. Most of the principles we talk about, however, cut across disciplines; thus, this text also helps you to become a knowledgeable and critical consumer of many other types of research, such as psychological, sociological, business, and medical research.

Fourth, in a national survey about the teaching of undergraduate communication research methods, Frey and Botan (1988) found that most professors who teach this course require students to read and report on communication research published in scholarly journals. Many other communication courses, as well as courses in other fields, also require students to read journal articles. If you are to remain current and make use of primary source material in this field, you must be able to find and understand the information generated by scholars. Doing so, however, is far more difficult than merely obtaining the leading scholarly journals and reading them. Few research reports are written clearly and in the standard way described in research methods textbooks. The prose is usually inflated, using words not found in everyday language. Students often feel bewildered by what they encounter in these scholarly academic journals, so they just skim the contents of articles, and vow to avoid all further contact with them.

To combat these feelings, we provide you with the "code" in which scholarly research articles are written. Once you know the purpose and the meaning of each section in research articles, the internal logic and value of an article emerges more clearly. Accordingly, this text mirrors the format of a traditional scholarly journal article by proceeding in the following logical manner:

1. Introducing you to the research process
2. Sharing with you some of the topics communication scholars consider worth studying and how research questions and hypotheses are posed
3. Showing you how to find and read previous research
4. Examining how researchers plan and design studies
5. Explaining how researchers conduct studies using various methodologies
6. Understanding how the information collected is analyzed
7. Discussing how results from research are interpreted in a meaningful manner

We also provide you with the code by bolding key terms throughout the text and listing them at the end in one of the most extensive and detailed glossaries you are likely to see. We've even cross-listed these terms, using "see" so that you can find other similar or related terms and "compare" to enable you to compare how the term differs from other related terms.

If you still find yourself having difficulty understanding primary source materials, you may wish to consult our other text, entitled *Interpreting Communication Research: A Case Study Approach* (1992, also available from Allyn and Bacon). In that text, we use the case study method to walk students through actual communication research articles selected from scholarly journals and books. Questions are posed to consider prior to reading an article, the lines of the article are numbered, and we then analyze the article by referring to specific line numbers and discussing the decisions the researcher(s) made. We also cite additional reference material that explains in greater depth the specific methodology being examined, and give an annotated bibliography of five additional research articles that use that methodology.

Finally, the field of communication is fragmented into many subspecialties. Diversity, though rich, also means the possibility of losing sight of what others in the field are doing. Too often textbooks aim at one particular subspecialty of the discipline (such as mass communication) or promote one kind of research method (such as experimental) while giving only lip service to some of the other research methods.

We believe that understanding various research methods fosters the complementary integration of these various subspecialties. Each of the authors of this text has extensive experience in both teaching introductory communication research methods courses and conducting research. Our various research efforts have spanned the major areas of the communication discipline (i.e., speech communication, mass communication, and journalism), the four methodologies we cover (experimental, survey, textual analysis, and naturalistic inquiry), and the two ways of analyzing data (quantitative and qualitative). We believe that this diversity of interest and experience has resulted in a balanced approach to this textbook that could not possibly have been achieved had any one of us written it alone.

We have also grown in our understanding of research methods since the first edition of this book was written. The present edition, consequently, represents a substantive revision of the original text. We were not content merely to change a few things around and put a new cover on it, but instead, took the time necessary to do a thorough job. Virtually every chapter has been significantly revised, mostly by adding new material that makes these entirely new chapters (plus an entirely new chapter in the analyzing and interpreting quantitative data section), by improving the discussions in material retained from the previous edition, and, of course, by including the most up-to-date information about the research studies conducted in the field of communication.

In the final analysis, we encourage you to approach this textbook and this course with an open mind. Preexisting attitudes too often obstruct learning new ones, and this certainly can be the case with learning about communication research methods. So expose yourself to research; as the saying goes, "Try it, you might like it!"

ACKNOWLEDGMENTS

Writing and/or revising a book involves an incredible number of people. We are indebted to those who helped shape both the first edition and the present edition, and would like to express our sincere thanks to these colleagues and friends.

We would like to thank Steve Dalphin, our first editor at Prentice Hall, for his faith in this project from the very start; Joe Opiela, Editor-in-Chief of Humanities at Allyn and Bacon, who inherited this text and placed his trust in us; Paul Smith, Editor-in-Chief of Education, Communication, and Health; and Karon Bowers, Acquisitions Editor at Allyn and Bacon, who helped produce this edition. We also thank the superb team selected to review the first edition for their insightful comments, criticisms, and suggestions: Mark E. Comadena, Illinois State University; Michael E. Mayer, Arizona State University; Robert D. McPhee, Arizona State University; Marshall Scott Poole, Texas A&M University; and Brian J. Spitzberg, San Diego State University.

We also want to express our sincere appreciation to Paul G. Friedman, University of Kansas, one of the authors on the first edition of this textbook. Paul's help on the first edition, as well as our other methods text, was immeasurable, and although he decided for personal reasons not to be a coauthor on this second edition, he still graciously agreed to review material and provided detailed feedback. There is no doubt that this textbook is substantially better because of the help he offered.

We are also indebted to a number of colleagues who wrote research overviews of some areas covered in the first and/or present edition and allowed us liberal use of their material: Richard L. Johannesen, Northern Illinois University, for help with rhetorical criticism; Dawn Kahn, The John Marshall Law School, for help with communication issues related to the law; Kathleen E. Kendall, State University of New York at Albany, for help with political communication; Leah A. Lievrouw, University of California, Los Angeles, for help with bibliometrics; W. Barnett Pearce, Fielding Institute, for help with framing research methods as conversation; Ronald J. Pelias, Southern Illinois University, for his contribution about performance studies; Nancy L. Roth, for help with electronic searches; Thomas J. Socha, Old Dominion University, for help with interaction analysis; Myoung Chung Wilson, Rutgers University Library, for help with online databases and CD-ROMs; and Diane F. Witmer, California State University, Fullerton, for her contribution about Internet and World Wide Web resources for research.

We want to thank all the students in our research methods courses over the years at Illinois State University, Loyola University Chicago, Northern Illinois University, Purdue University, Rutgers University, and University of Nevada, Las Vegas, who provided us with feedback about the first edition of this text. We are also deeply indebted to JoAnn Fricke of Loyola University Chicago for her wonderful secretarial help with the first edition.

The authors extend special thanks to Sandra Metts of Illinois State University. Sandra's only formal commitment for the first edition was to write the instructor's manual, but she went over each draft of that manuscript with a fine-toothed comb and offered wonderful suggestions and rewrote much of the material. Her instructor's manual for the first edition is one of the best ones we've seen.

We were, indeed, fortunate, then, when Jim Query, Loyola University Chicago, agreed to do the instructor's manual for this edition. He has produced an exceptional manual, one that we know instructors will appreciate very much. Thanks, Jim, for your excellent work.

In revising this text, we solicited feedback via a questionnaire from colleagues in the communication discipline. They offered many excellent suggestions that we incorporated into this edition. Special thanks for taking the time to help is extended to (in alphabetical order): Dennis C. Alexander, University of Utah; E. James Baesler, Old Dominion University; Thomas N. Baglan, Arkansas State University; James Barushok, Northeastern Illinois University; Julie M. Billingsley, Rutgers University; Joseph C. Chilberg, State University of New York College-Fredonia; Mark E. Comadena, Illinois State University; Judith M. Dallinger, Western Illinois University; Susan Fox, Western Michigan University; Philip Gray, Northern Illinois University; Stephen C. Hines, West Virginia University; Ann House, Santa Clara University; Lawrence W. Hugenberg, Youngstown State University; Jerry M. Jordan, University of Cincinnati; Richard A. Katula, Northeastern University; Dean Kazoleas, Illinois State University; Sandra M. Ketrow, University of Rhode Island; Ana Kong, Governors State University; Charles U. Larson, Northern Illinois University; Gail Mason, Eastern Illinois University; Michael E. Mayer, Arizona State University; Paul A. Mongeau,

Miami University; Mary Beth Oliver, Penn State University; Ben L. Parker, Boise State University; Marshall Scott Poole, Texas A&M University; Kathleen M. Propp, Western Michigan University; Stephen J. Pullum, University of North Carolina at Wilmington; R. Jeffrey Ringer, St. Cloud State University; William L. Robinson, Purdue University, Calumet; Randall Rogan, Wake Forest University; L. Edna Rogers, University of Utah; Anthony B. Schroeder, Eastern New Mexico University; Dave Schuelke, University of Minnesota; Timothy L. Sellnow, North Dakota State University; Edward Sewell, Virginia Tech; John C. Sherblom, University of Maine; Christine B. Smith, University of Southern California; Roger Smitter, North Central College; Thomas J. Socha, Old Dominion University; Brian H. Spitzberg, San Diego State University; Anita Taylor, George Mason University; K. Phillip Taylor, University of Central Florida; David Vest, Colorado State University; Michael R. Vickery, Alma College; Deborah Weider-Hatfield, University of Central Florida; Richard L. West, University of Southern Maine; Lawrence R. Wheeless, University of North Texas; Gordon Whiting, Brigham Young University; and Maggie A. Wills, Fairfield University.

We would like to dedicate this text to all our colleagues who teach communication research methods. We know this is not the easiest material to teach or the most popular with students, but your dedication to helping students understand communication research does make a difference in their lives.

Finally, each of us would like to thank the following people:

One of the persons to whom I dedicated the first edition was Elaine Bruggemeier, my Chairperson at that time. Elaine has since passed away, but not a day goes by in teaching my methods course that I don't think about her. I especially want to thank Carl and Gary, my coauthors and friends. I have been involved in many group projects, but none has sustained itself so well over time. I also want to thank my colleagues in the Department of Communication at Loyola University Chicago from which, at the time of this publication, I am on leave, especially (in alphabetical order) Bren, Craig, Dan, Elizabeth, Hannah, Jeff, Jim, Lee, Mark, Mary Pat, and Virginia for their support; they make my professional life so much easier and so enjoyable. Special thanks to W. Barnett Pearce, a mentor if ever there was one, for broadening my horizons (he might say showing me the errors of my ways!) about communication and research methods. I also want to thank my family for their love and support, and my Chicago-based friends (especially Mark and Jill and Mike and Heidi) for once again putting up with me during the work on this second edition. This book, as before, is dedicated to Marni Cameron with all my love. —L. R. F.

Any undertaking of this size intrudes on family life and requires that some things be put on hold. I would like to thank my wife, Jennifer McCreadie, for her comments, support, and patience throughout, particularly in reminding me that qualitative methods hold up half the [research] world. I also want to dedicate this book to my father John Botan, mother Julia Tyrrell, and brother Ronald Botan, the reluctant politician in the group. —C. H. B.

I owe a great debt of gratitude to my coauthors on this book, Larry and Carl (as well as Paul Friedman), who supported me and patiently waited for my late-arriving chapter drafts through my moves from one end of the country to the other (and back again). I also sincerely thank my loving family, Stephanie, Becky, and David, who loyally followed me from one job to another and know that they are the ultimate source of my affection. My hope is that this book will encourage rigorous, pluralistic, and socially informed communication inquiry. —G. L. K.

PART ONE

CONCEPTUALIZING COMMUNICATION RESEARCH

CHAPTER 1

INTRODUCTION TO THE RESEARCH CULTURE

We live in an "information society" with a wealth of information at our fingertips. All we have to do is flick on the television with the remote control to see the latest events transpire, even as they happen, or turn on the computer, click the mouse, and cruise the "information highway" in search of the many Internet and World Wide Web sites, databases, and information services offered. A good portion of our life is now spent initiating, processing, arranging, transmitting, disseminating, retrieving, receiving, and/or reprocessing information.

Information is no longer a luxury; it is a necessity on which we depend for survival. The economy of the United States, once driven by agriculture and later by service, is now based on information. And at the global level, "[h]alf of all workers in the industrial world are employed by the rapidly growing information industries" (Dordick & Wang, 1993, p. 2). This means that more people are employed in the information sector than in any other sector of the world's industrial economies. In the United States, 45% of the gross national product is attributable to the value of information products and services, and across the world, the information industry will top $500 billion before the turn of the century (Dordick & Wang).

While there certainly is more information available than ever before, there is a downside: It's getting more and more difficult to distinguish "good" information, that which is valid (or accurate), from "bad" information, that which is not. Not all information is created equally; some information is better than other information because it has been tested and shown to be valid. The key word here is "tested," which means that some *research* has been conducted about it.

If we are to distinguish good from bad information, we need to become competent consumers of how information is produced. In this chapter, we first explore the importance of knowing research methods, for it is absolutely crucial that you be convinced of the need to have a basic understanding of research methods. We then examine some common, everyday ways of knowing and distinguish these from the research process. After exploring some characteristics of the research culture, we return to a discussion of the importance of being a knowledgeable consumer of research, this time in terms of distinguishing good research from pseudoresearch and bad research.

THE IMPORTANCE OF KNOWING RESEARCH METHODS

Can there be any doubt that we value information obtained on the basis of research? Just pick up a newspaper or turn on the television and you will see how much we have become a "research-based" culture. We are bombarded every day with information derived from experiments, surveys or polls, or other research methods about what is good and bad for us (which seems to change daily!), what we value as a society, and even what we are being exposed to by the media (such as reports about the amount of violence on television). And advertising messages designed to get us to purchase products and services are quick to tell us what the "latest research shows." Research has become perhaps *the* most important stamp of approval in our society.

The value of information acquired from research is readily apparent in the world of business.

Virtually all major corporations use research to decide whether and how to launch new products or services, assess their effectiveness, and make changes in what they offer. Research has become part of the ongoing business of doing business.

Even the film industry has jumped on the bandwagon. Movies are now tested at every stage of development, from conception to final product. Roger Birnbaum, president of production at 20th Century-Fox, admitted that every movie produced by his studio is tested with preview audiences (see N. Koch, 1992). The company holds what it calls *research screenings,* where people selected on the basis of important demographics assist the final edit (called *content test screening*) or help the marketing campaign by offering their opinions and suggestions (N. Koch). The original ending to the movie *Patriot Games,* for instance, was found to be confusing to members of a test audience. They preferred an alternative ending mentioned in the questionnaire they were asked to complete, so the director reshot additional footage in line with the preferred ending (N. Koch). While we will never know whether and how much this new ending helped, the movie was a box-office success.

Knowledge of research methods is, thus, of critical importance for success in today's business world. In fact, a 1991 publication by the United States Department of Labor, entitled *What Work Requires of Schools: SCANS* [Secretary's Commission on Achieving Necessary Skills] *Report for America 2000,* identifies ability in "information-acquiring and evaluating data" as one of the five competencies necessary for performing most jobs. (The other four competencies are ability to allocate resources, good interpersonal skills, understanding of systems, and knowledge of technology.) Understanding research-based information, therefore, is an essential business survival skill.

But don't just take our word or the government's word for it; consider what people working in the business world said when we asked them whether the communication research methods course they took in college helps them in their daily work (see Figure 1.1). As their statements show, it was one of the most important—if not *the*

most important—courses they took in terms of being successful in their professions. Ask other people you know in the business world and see what response you get.

The use of research, however, is far more pervasive than simply in the business world; it pervades all aspects of our society. Policy decisions made by community organizations, educational institutions, and federal, state, and local governments, to name but a few, are now made, in part, on the basis of original research conducted and/or extensive reviews of what the available research shows.

And for those of you who might be thinking about going on to graduate school, consider the following testimonies from two former students. The first one is by Joy Cypher, a communication graduate student at the time this was written:

> *On entering graduate school, I quickly learned how valuable a good understanding of research methods was for success, not only in my own research, but even in studying the research of others in the communication field. Taking a rigorous methods course during my undergraduate program prepared me to jump into the complex academic conversations of the graduate classroom, the journals, and even the conventions, as a participant and not simply a befuddled observer. Few other things facilitated my success as a graduate student more than a basic knowledge of communication research methods and the theoretical assumptions therein. Such knowledge enabled me to comprehend course material more readily and bolstered my confidence in my own scholarly research—two fundamental building blocks for a successful graduate career.*

The second statement is from Dawn Kahn, who was a law student at the time this was written:

> *In the first few weeks of law school, we were bombarded with reams of material on numerous perplexing topics and given little—if any—instruction as to what we should do with it. It soon became apparent that the Socratic method was code for "teach yourself." Fortunately, the skills I acquired from my undergraduate communication research methods course helped me to do just that. Those*

Maeve Connell-Lucas, Director of a Mediation Center: As the director of two mediation centers, and as a mediator, my goal is to facilitate communication between disputing parties in reaching a mutually acceptable agreement. It is imperative for communication professionals like me to be well-versed in proper research methods. A colleague, for example, recently tried to convince me that one of our programs was not serving clients appropriately. He pointed to a phone survey he had completed as proof that our clients were less than satisfied with our service. I asked to see the survey questions he had used, and saw that they all were slanted to give the answer he wanted (i.e., "What about the mediation service made you feel uncomfortable?"). I suggested to my colleague that we interview a group of previous clients in a focus group. Together, using a list of open-ended, neutral questions, we interviewed the group. Much to his surprise, the clients stated that they actually were very satisfied with our service. My position, thus, calls for accurate information, and research is the key to obtaining it. Even if a communication professional does not do original research, he or she better be able to spot faulty methods used by someone else.

Gary M. Ruesch, Attorney at Law (a nationally known speaker and author on legal issues involving children with disabilities): Lawyers are in the business of persuasion. In the present-day age of information, persuasion more often takes the form of statistics, analysis of studies, and quantifiable research results. As an attorney, I must present information, evidence, and statistics in the most persuasive format possible. In this regard, the communication research methods course I took as an undergraduate provided me with some important tools that I use every day to effectively represent my clients.

Gregg D. Smith, Gangs and Weapons Counselor, Juvenile Center: As a juvenile probation officer working with high-risk youth and their families, case research and planning is an integral part of both my planning and day-to-day operations. The intensity of this job causes great emphasis to be placed on acquiring background data, interpreting documents, and formulating treatment plans. Many of the skills learned in my communication research methods course have been invaluable in my chosen field. In addition, while serving as program coordinator for a gangs and weapons program grant, I used many tools learned in the research methods course to monitor the control and experimental components of this program. I would strongly recommend this course to students, for it gives them a solid foundation in research.

Nancy Tuma, Director, 1010 WallStreet.com: I remember sitting in my college communication research class and thinking that I would never apply any of the material to my everyday life, but I was wrong. As director of a financial news company, research is the lifeblood of much of the work I do. Every morning, I page through research report after report on various stocks, so I know what stocks will be important to watch that day. These research reports help us to develop news stories and to create the groundwork for what our broadcasters will cover every day. Research also gives us an idea of what may happen in the market on various days, as many times the past tells us about the future. There is no way that I could produce my best work without knowing how to effectively use research reports.

John Zorbini, Vice President of Human Resources, Community Memorial Hospital: I consider my coursework in research methods to be of utmost value as I perform my responsibilities as vice president of human resources. Frankly, I would be greatly disadvantaged without it. As a human resource executive, I am entrusted with the most valuable resource of my organization—its people! To make my hospital a desirable place to work, I continuously propose new programs/processes to senior administration and the board of directors. At this level, expectations for flawless, quality work are high, and research is the key. Every proposal I prepare begins with asking the key questions worth answering and then providing the answers. Literature reviews, questionnaire/survey construction, and data analysis are all vital elements of the process. They are expectations of my job. I'm one of those who wondered why I needed coursework in research methods. It only took me as long as my first job to find the answer—success!

skills gave me an almost unfair advantage in Legal Research and Writing, one of the most dreaded courses in the first-year curriculum. While others struggled to understand research methods and were doing rewrite after rewrite of their papers, I was getting "As" on my first drafts. Being able to understand the scientific concept of reliability was invaluable in the course on Evidence. After we learned that the court's primary concern in determining the admissibility of a piece of evidence is whether it is reliable, I was coming up with innovative objections that used principles from the methods course to attack the reliability of evidence, while others limited the bases of their objections to the strict wording in the rulebook. I can honestly say that the communication research methods course was one of the most important courses that helped prepare me for the particular demands of law school and put me far ahead of those who had not taken such a course.

Finally, understanding research methods might help one's personal life. While it may not save a troubled romantic relationship from ending, knowing research methods can and does make a difference in some cases. For example, being able to read and understand research reports that compare products, such as those published in the magazine *Consumer Reports,* can help people make better choices about the products they buy.

And, as a dramatic example of the personal importance of knowing research methods, consider the following story written by Nancy Tuma:

On a personal level, knowing how to comprehend research reports "saved my life." When I was 24, I was diagnosed with cancer and told by my doctors that I would not live to see 33. After reading the research reports that my doctors used to make their diagnosis and prognosis, I was not convinced that what they were telling me was accurate. Since I now knew how to read the reports, I was able to see that the scientific basis used in the reports did not relate to me. I went to medical libraries and researched the situation myself and determined, much to my relief, that the doctors were basing their decisions on research that dealt with women twice my age and who had pathology reports with abnormal cell counts much higher than mine. In fact, I did not even have cancer! For that reason

alone, I will always be grateful that I spent the time and energy to learn what research really is and how to use the reports to my advantage.

We hope that you or those you care about will never be in such a position, but if you are, you too should be able to understand the research-based information you are given.

But being a knowledgeable consumer is difficult because, as Nancy Tuma's experience shows, we don't always get accurate information and conclusions, even from people we trust. Let's take a closer look at the process by which people make claims and offer evidence.

MAKING CLAIMS AND OFFERING EVIDENCE

If there is one thing that researchers, common folk, politicians, educators, top-level corporate executives, journalists, television tabloid reporters, priests, mystics, fortune-tellers, and snakeoil salespeople have in common, it is that they all make **claims,** that is, assertions or conclusions. Opinions, as they say, are a "dime a dozen"; if only we had a dime for every dozen claims, we would be rich beyond our dreams.

Most claims are supported with some form of **evidence,** or reason, although notice how we just got away with asserting a claim without offering any evidence. That is, some reason(s) typically is offered for why a person believes that a claim is true or false.

The validity of a claim obviously is related, to a large degree, to the validity of the evidence in its favor. Of course, the validity of the evidence offered also depends to some extent on the situation. "Because I said so" is not a very good reason for arguing that the Sun travels around the Earth, or vice versa, but it may be a very good reason for engaging in some behavior that your parent, boss, or relational partner wants you to do.

The validity of a claim and the evidence offered for it also depends on the validity of the often unarticulated **warrant,** a statement (another claim) that logically connects the claim and evidence. And some evidence or backing must be given for the warrant as well. The warrant is particularly important, for if it is not valid, then the argument advanced by the claim and evidence usually falls apart.

Let's take the example of your university deciding to raise its tuition, an example with which you might be all too painfully familiar (see Figure 1.2). Your university might claim that it must raise tuition because it is operating at a deficit, as documented, let's say, by an independent audit. Underlying this claim and the reasons offered for it is some warrant that connects the claim and the reason. For instance, the warrant could claim that raising tuition is the primary means by which the university improves itself, and some backing (evidence) would then be offered for that warrant, such as profit/loss balance sheets that show that tuition is a primary source of income for the university. If that warrant (or others offered) is not valid, the original claim might be able to be rejected. Thus, for example, if one wanted to attack this argument, it could be done both by challenging the evidence on which the claim is made, but more likely by challenging the warrant that connects the claim and evidence. For instance, the university could look for alternative sources of income, such as financial gifts, to offset the deficit.

In this text, we are primarily concerned with understanding and evaluating the claims, evidence, and warrants that are made by researchers about what people do, why they do it, what influences them to do it, and what effect it has on them and others. That is, we teach critical thinking skills for evaluating research-based arguments. Our specific focus is on research about people's communication behavior, but for now, let's keep the discussion at a general level.

Let's start by taking a short true-false test:

1. True or False: Breakfast is the most important meal of the day.
2. True or False: Reading in the dark will ruin your eyes.
3. True or False: Crackling knuckles causes arthritis.
4. True or False: Carrots are good for the eyes.
5. True or False: Chocolate causes acne.
6. True or False: An apple a day keeps the doctor away.

If you are like most people, you probably judged at least some of these statements to be true. But none of these common beliefs is actually supported by science (Kohn, 1990).

These are relatively harmless beliefs, but there are far more scary ones that are potentially harmful. Consider Eve and Dunn's (cited in McCarthy, 1989) survey of 190 high school biology and life science teachers, people we trust to educate young adults. They found that 19% believed that dinosaurs and humans lived at the same time, 20% believed in black magic, and, in the scariest belief of them all, 26% believed that some races were more intelligent than others. Schick and Vaughn (1995) also report a 1990 Gallup poll that shows, among other things, that 49% of U.S. citizens believe in extrasensory perception (ESP), 46% believe in psychic or spiritual healing, 27% believe that extraterrestial beings have visited the Earth, 21% believe in reincarnation, 17% feel they've been in touch with someone who has died, and 14% have consulted a fortune-teller or psychic.

Although we don't have the time to debate these beliefs with those who adamantly hold them, let's think about some typical ways in which people might come to believe these claims and the

---

FIGURE 1.2   A model of argument

Evidence ——————————— Claim

The university is operating at a deficit.

The university must raise tuition.

Warrant

Tuition is a primary means by which the university improves itself.

Backing

Profit/loss balance sheets show that tuition is a primary source of income for the university.

supposed evidence on which they are based. Let's look, therefore, at some everyday ways of knowing.

EVERYDAY WAYS OF KNOWING

Let's call the acceptance of information at face value **everyday ways of knowing.** When we rely on knowledge that we have not questioned or tested, we are using everyday ways of knowing. Five common, everyday ways of knowing are: personal experience; intuition; a uthority; appeals to tradition, custom, and faith; and magic, superstition, and mysticism.

Personal Experience

One way we come to know things is through **personal experience,** experiencing something firsthand. Personal experience certainly serves us well in many instances; many of us probably learned as children not to touch a hot stove after getting burned—a valuable lesson, indeed. Personal experience can also be an excellent starting point for the testing of knowledge. For example, Archimedes, a Greek mathematician, physicist, and inventor, regarded by some historians as the founder of experimental science, was asked by King Hiero of Syracuse, Sicily, to determine whether his crown was made of pure gold or, as he suspected, a mixture of gold and silver. Just when Archimedes was about to give up, he stepped into the bathtub and noticed that the water ran over the edge. He reasoned that the spilled water equaled the volume of his body. At that moment, he realized that he could submerge both the crown and a piece of pure gold that weighed the same and observe whether both objects displaced the same amount of water. Legend has it that he was so excited about his discovery that he ran down the street naked shouting, "Eureka [I have found it]!" The crown did, indeed, displace more water than the same weight of pure gold, which meant that the crown was not made of pure gold, a finding later confirmed by the goldsmith's confession.

Personal experience, however, does not always serve us well. We often believe that what's in

our minds and social encounters is generally true. Hence, if someone fears public speaking, that person assumes that most people are judging his or her performance critically. Many police officers who deal frequently with criminals believe that most people are dishonest, while many psychologists who deal primarily with mentally ill patients believe that most people are neurotic. Their opinions are influenced by their personal experience.

Some research indicates that we form inaccurate opinions about everyday events because we are limited in our ability to think about the information available to us. We need to simplify the complexities of life to cope with all the information to which we're exposed. One way we do this is by jumping to conclusions on the basis of very limited knowledge. Nisbett and Ross (1980) found that when making judgments, most people ignore sound generalizations (e.g., what's reported in research from studies of large numbers of people) and give preference to vivid personal experiences. For instance, when presented with two pieces of information—(a) that a valid national poll of 10,000 Volvo owners certified that the car was perfectly reliable, and (b) yesterday you saw your neighbor's Volvo stranded on the road because of engine failure—Nisbett and Ross found that people ignored the first piece of information in favor of the second piece. People, thus, tend to trust firsthand, concrete, and vivid experiences (anecdotal evidence) more than abstract generalizations made on the basis of research, which Nisbett and Ross called the "Volvo fallacy." Although information derived from the study of many people's lives is more trustworthy, it is also remote and pallid and, therefore, easily ignored. Consequently, although research on a large cross section of people indicates that those with a university bachelor's degree are likely to earn 65% more than high-school graduates of the same age (Lauden, 1997), someone invariably argues something like, "I know someone who dropped out of school in the tenth grade, and is a millionaire." While there certainly are exceptions to a general rule, the exception doesn't negate the rule.

Some of the beliefs reported in the Gallup poll given earlier undoubtedly were formed from personal experience. People who believe in the paranormal, for example, according to Schick and Vaughn (1995), cite personal experience as the most important reason for their belief. Even many of the skeptics in the survey put a high premium on personal experience; they said they didn't believe in ESP because they hadn't yet experienced it!

Intuition

Closely related to personal experience is **intuition,** believing something is true or false simply because it "makes sense." We generally accept love and friendship as valuable goals of communication because people simply sense their value intuitively. Intuition also refers to leaps of insight that we can't explain rationally. When you suspect someone is lying, but can't explain why, you're using intuition.

Intuitive hunches sometimes pay off in useful ideas. J. P. Campbell, Daft, and Hulin (1982) asked well-known scholars of organizational behavior to trace the origins of their most successful projects. Several attributed their ideas to thinking intuitively about promising ideas. The investigators summed up one scholar's comments this way: "I threw out an idea in [a] doctoral seminar to which a student responded. Sense of great excitement—continuous interaction to test ideas against one another—couldn't let go" (p. 98). From this and subsequent exchanges, a pioneering research project was born.

Intuitive reasoning, however, is often just plain wrong. One area where it typically leads people astray is with regard to calculating statistics (see Kahneman & Tversky, 1972, 1973, 1982), especially the probability of the occurrence of events. People are notoriously bad at calculating such odds, typically underestimating the probability of what appear to be highly unlikely coincidences. For example, what are the chances that 2 out of 23 people attending a dinner party have the same birthday: (a) 1/365, (b) 1/183, (c) 1/46, (d) 1/23, or (e) 1/2? The correct answer is (e): there is a 50% chance that two of the people will share a birthday. Because we now suspect that you are starting to become a competent consumer who isn't willing to

take our word for it but wants valid evidence for such a claim, here is Paulos's (1988) explanation:

> By the multiplication principle, the number of ways in which five dates can be chosen (allowing for repetitions) is ($365 \times 365 \times 365 \times 365 \times 365$). Of all these 365^5 ways, however, only ($365 \times 364 \times 363 \times 362 \times 361$) are such that no two of the dates are the same; any of the 365 days can be chosen first, any of the remaining 364 days can be chosen second, and so on. Thus, by dividing this latter product ($365 \times 364 \times 363 \times 362 \times 361$) by 365^5, we get the probability that five people chosen at random will have no birthday in common. Now, if we subtract this probability from 1 (or from 100 percent if we're dealing in percentages), we get the complementary probability that at least two of the five people do have a birthday in common. A similar calculation using 23 rather than 5 yields ½, or 50 percent, as the probability that at least two of the twenty-three people will have a common birthday. (p. 36)

Common, everyday intuitive thinking, then, often results in mistaken perceptions and judgments. One reason is that people often perceive what they expect to perceive. We even perceive meaning in the face of meaningless objects or stimuli, such as discernible images in clouds, a type of misperception or illusion called *pareidolia*. People in the United States, for example, tend to see the figure of a man in the moon, but Samoans see a woman weaving, and Chinese see a monkey pounding rice (Schick & Vaughn, 1995). Piatelli-Palmarini (1994) uses the term *tunnel effect* to describe this and other perceptual tricks of the mind that accompany intuitive reasoning. As he explains:

> Against our will, our mind enters a tunnel in its reasoning. A pound of feathers weighs as much as a pound of lead. Well, which would you rather have fall on your head from a second floor? There's the bias. (p. 23)

Seeing images in clouds or not equating a pound of feathers and lead are relatively harmless examples, but as Schick and Vaughn point out, such reasoning led German Nazi scientists to believe that they could see nonexistent physical differences between the blood particles of Aryan men and those of Jews.

Perhaps most problematic of all, once people form an intuitive perception or judgment, they often cling to it and pay selective attention only to evidence that confirms it. Schenkler (1985) identifies a proclivity called *cognitive conservatism,* whereby we hold onto conclusions we reach even when presented with contradictory information. One reason is that we identify with our ideas; to accept that our ideas have been inadequate is to admit, in a sense, that we ourselves have been inadequate. We want to feel good about ourselves, so we resist and tend to deny indications that we might be wrong. It's threatening to our self-esteem to acknowledge that we've been misguided, even when evidence suggests that is the case. Social interaction also reinforces cognitive conservatism. People prefer us to be consistent in thought and deed, so they can predict how we will respond to them. Frequently changing our mind or actions makes others uncomfortable; people flexible in thought are often accused of being unstable, wishy-washy, or fickle. We also use our ideas to guide our actions. Since action choices about communication often must be made instantaneously, we prefer to keep our ideas about communication simple and consistent. We don't have much time to think in everyday interactions, so we tend to avert or deny information that contradicts what we already believe to avoid confusion and uncertainty. To preserve consistency, we sometimes perpetuate fallacious beliefs. Albert Einstein may have said it best when he noted, "Common sense is the collection of prejudices acquired by age 18."

Authority

A third everyday way of knowing is relying on **authority,** believing something because of our trust in the person who said it. Numerous studies of the persuasive effects of source credibility, the characteristics that make a person believable, show that who says something may be even more important than what is said. You may, for example, have learned that carrots are good for the eyes because authority figures, such as your parents, told you this was true.

There are certainly many cases in which we must rely on authorities. We assume that doctors know how to diagnose diseases, that mechanics know how to fix cars, and that pilots know how to fly airplanes. But as Nancy Tuma's experience, shared previously, demonstrates, even doctors, and other respected authorities, make mistakes. Indeed, a study by Kronlund and Philips (cited in Paulos, 1988) showed that "most doctors' assessments of the risks of various operations, procedures, and medications (even in their own specialties) were way off the mark, often by several orders of magnitude" (p. 10).

Some people also claim and/or are assumed to be experts simply because they hold positions of power, like the boss of a company, although we all probably know instances in which the boss simply is wrong. In other cases, determining who is and isn't an authority can be quite problematic. Not all certified secondary educators are equally informed or trustworthy. And this is even more difficult to judge when talking about "communication experts." For example, what criteria should be used to judge who is an interpersonal communication expert: a person who has a problem-free, long-term romantic relationship or someone who has gone through a divorce?!

Appeals to Tradition, Custom, and Faith

A fourth everyday way of knowing is based on *appeals to tradition, custom,* and *faith.* **Appeals to tradition** and **custom** involve believing something simply because most people in a society assume it is true or because it has always been done that way. Some customary beliefs we now know from research make very good sense, such as cuddling babies and playing word games with them.

But custom can also lead to cognitive conservatism that ultimately cuts off the inquiry process and subsequent growth of knowledge, and leads us to cling tenaciously to the beliefs we hold. Consider how tradition and custom affected the reaction to Galileo's work on astronomy. Aristotle argued that one should be a "passive observer" in learning about the world because he believed that people's preconceptions distort what is learned (Wolf, 1986). Two thousand years later, when Galileo invited his inquisitors (professors at the nearby university, no less) to look through his telescope at the moon, they "refused to do so, arguing that whatever might be visible through the telescope would be a product not of nature but of the instrument" (Lincoln & Guba, 1985, p. 45).

Custom may also lead people to cling to racist or sexist stereotypes, such as "Women are less capable than men of being top managers." When pressed about why they hold this belief, prejudiced people might respond, "Because it's always been that way." Even if that claim were true, which we don't think it is, the world changes and so should our beliefs. We should remember that some of the ancient practices allegedly tested and found useful by generations of healers include such things as bloodletting and purging; George Washington actually died as a result of bloodletting. Other habits continued because of custom are less problematic but still reflect unquestioned beliefs. Should people touch glasses when making a toast? Most people in the United States seem to think so, but they can't necessarily say why. In Italy, the opposite is true; people tend to avoid touching glasses when making a toast, but they too can't necessarily say why they do this.

Somewhat related to tradition and custom are **appeals to faith,** which involve a belief that does not rest on logical proof or material evidence. Asking someone to accept something because of the person who says it or because it has always been done that way in the past are two types of appeals to faith. There are other types as well. Religions often ask for people's faith, such as faith in a supernatural being. While the authors of this text would be the first to defend people's right to their religious faith, religious appeals to faith have, at times, stood in the way of the progress of knowledge. Going back to Galileo again, for centuries, the Catholic Church argued that the Earth was the center of the universe and the Sun rotated around the Earth. Galileo's theory that the Earth revolved around the Sun was condemned by some Catholic religious leaders (including the Pope), and his case

was remanded to the Inquisition, which put Galileo on trial and found him guilty of heresy for believing something that was false and contrary to the Holy Scriptures (see Biagioli, 1993), although he never was sent to prison, contrary to many accounts (see Lessl, 1999). Being told essentially to accept the status quo position on the basis of faith, Galileo replied, "I do not feel obligated to believe that the same God that has endowed me with sense, reason, and intellect has intended us to forgo their use."

Recognizing that mistakes have been made in the past, many contemporary religious leaders understand the importance of aligning their faith with empirical knowledge. Gejong Tezin Gyatsho, the 14th Dalai Lama, "supreme teacher" of Tibetan Buddhism, and winner of the 1988 Nobel peace prize, remarked, "If there's good, strong evidence from science that such and such is the case, and this is contrary to Buddhism, then we will change" (Weintraub, 1990, p. 88).

Magic, Superstition, and Mysticism

A final everyday way of knowing is **magic, superstition,** and **mysticism,** as when we use the word *mystery* to explain an otherwise unexplainable event. Perhaps you remember the television show *That's Incredible!,* where people were shown doing "incredible" things, such as firewalking, walking across beds of burning coals that register more than 1,300 degrees Fahrenheit (Grosvenor & Grosvenor, 1966) without getting burnt.

Many of these so-called mysteries, such as firewalking, are actually easily explained. Although many have claimed that a mystical reason accounts for why people don't burn their feet (such as entering another dimension where the laws of physics don't apply), in fact, it's possible because charcoal, especially when coated with ash, does not transfer heat rapidly to other objects. It's similar to sticking your hand in a hot stove. As long as you don't touch the metal, you can stick your hand in for a short time. If you touch the metal, however, or if you keep your hand in there too long, you will get burned. (We don't, of course, recommend playing with hot stoves; we suggest you remember that early childhood personal experience of getting burned.) The same is true for firewalking. As long as one walks quickly across the coals, a person won't get burnt, as each foot is only in contact with the heat for about a second before being lifted. But if a firewalker stops to "smell the coals," he or she will get badly burnt.

The mystical/superstitious belief that appears to have caught hold the most in the general public is *astrology,* the "study" (and we use that term loosely) of the positions and aspects of heavenly bodies in the belief that they have an influence on the course of human affairs. Have you ever looked at your horoscope in the newspaper? If so, you're certainly not alone; a 1990 Gallup poll showed that 52% of adult Americans believe in astrology (Gallup & Newport, 1991). Even Nancy Reagan consulted her astrologer before making important decisions about former President Ronald Reagan's speaking schedule!

The problem is that there is absolutely no scientific basis or evidence for astrology. Zusne and Jones's (1982) review of the many statistical attempts to verify the predictions of astrology revealed that not one succeeded. And after a review of 700 books and 300 scientific works on astrology, Dean (1977) was forced to conclude that there was no scientific basis for it. But scientific findings haven't stopped a great many people from believing in astrology. Such widespread belief led a group of 186 scientists in 1975 to write a letter that implored the public to reject astrology:

> We the undersigned—astronomers, astrophysicists, and scientists in other fields—wish to caution the public against the unquestioning acceptance of the predictions and advice given privately and publicly by astrologers. Those who wish to believe in astrology should realize that there is no scientific foundation for its tenets.... It is simply a mistake to imagine that the forces exerted by stars and planets at the moment of birth can in any way shape our futures. Neither is it true that the position[s] of distant heavenly bodies make certain days or periods more favorable to particular kinds of action, or that the sign under

> which one was born determines one's compatibility or incompatibility with other people. ("Objections to Astrology," 1975, pp. 4–6)

So the next time you are tempted to consult your horoscope, think twice about it. The Cosmic Muffin summed it up best: "A wise [person] rules the stars; only a fool is ruled by them" (cited in Schick & Vaughn, 1995, p. 122).

THE RESEARCH PROCESS

Everyday ways of knowing can certainly lead to valid knowledge, and it surely is impossible to question and test *every* piece of knowledge we hear or possess. The problem with everyday ways of knowing, however, occurs when we should question what is assumed to be true but do not because we accept things simply at face value. In effect, this cuts off the inquiry process, making people passive receivers of apparent truths instead of active pursuers of knowledge. That's unacceptable; after all, don't "inquiring minds want to know"?

So while personal experience, intuition, authority, appeals to tradition, custom, and faith, and magic, superstition, and mysticism may be good starting points for the systematic pursuit of knowledge, they don't necessarily lead to valid knowledge about the world. When we go beyond these particular ways of knowing to question and test what we know and don't know, we engage in *research.* Archimedes, for example, went beyond his personal bathtub experience to systematically test whether the king's crown was made of pure gold. And his tests could be reproduced by anyone else who wanted to see whether his conclusions were valid. **Research** is what we call the form of disciplined inquiry that involves studying something in a planned manner and reporting it so that other inquirers can potentially replicate the process if they choose.

Characteristics of Research

Research has a number of important characteristics, but before explaining them, we should differentiate two types of research: proprietary and scholarly research. **Proprietary research** is conducted for a specific audience and is not necessarily shared beyond that audience. For example, a radio station might conduct research about its listeners' music preferences and use that research to shape its play list. **Scholarly research,** in contrast, is conducted to promote public access to knowledge, as when researchers conduct and publish studies about the effectiveness of various means of persuasion or new vaccines for treating diseases. Although the methods examined in this text generally apply to (good) proprietary research, we are interested primarily in scholarly research. For the sake of convenience, however, we use the term *research* as the primary referent.

Research has the following characteristics:

1. *Research is based on curiosity and asking questions.* Research starts with a person's sense of curiosity, a desire to find an answer to a puzzling question posed. These questions are posed at various levels of abstraction, such as asking people what they do, why they do it, or what effect behavior has on them. These questions might spring from observed theoretical inconsistencies or gaps in what is reported in scholarly literature or from a practical concern, such as the effects of television on children or how people communicate as leaders. At the heart of all research is a question worth asking and answering.

Too often, researchers are portrayed as dispassionate scientists in white coats handling test tubes in a laboratory. This image omits the curiosity, creativity, and sense of excitement that characterize researchers. A more apt metaphor might be a detective searching for clues to a crime. As Poole and McPhee (1985) explain:

> Like a good detective, the researcher is confronted by a confusing pattern of clues that is meaningful in both an immediate and a deeper, sometimes hidden sense. To get at this deeper meaning and unravel the mystery, the detective (researcher) must probe and order this "reality," often relying on improvisation, inspiration and luck. Once things fall into place there is the possibility of true understanding and in-

sight, but there is also the danger of misinterpreting the multitude of available signs.... [Research] requires the capacity to ask the right questions as well as a sense of what form the answer should take. Detective novels are replete with devices and strategies for attaching a mystery, and this is no less true of social scientific writing. (p. 100)

Research methods, therefore, may be viewed as the strategies researchers use to solve puzzling mysteries about the world; they are the means used to collect evidence necessary for building or testing explanations about that which is being studied. Like good detectives, researchers want to make sense of the unknown, and their methods are the means by which they do this. This text, then, explains the methods researcher-detectives use to satisfy their curiosity and answer the questions they have about communication phenomena.

2. *Research is a systematic process.* Research depends on a planned, systematic process of investigation. Research proceeds in a careful step-by-step manner, employing an ordered system of inquiry. Research is not conducted for the purpose of proving the preconceptions of researchers. Rather, systematic procedures are used to ensure that researchers find and report what is accurate.

Figure 1.3 provides a working model and explanation of the systematic nature of communication research. This model, which we use to organize the sections of this text, views communication research as an ongoing cycle of five interrelated phases of research activities: (a) conceptualization, (b) planning and designing research, (c) methodologies for conducting research, (d) analyzing and interpreting data, and (e) reconceptualization.

3. *Research is potentially replicable.* Because research follows a systematic plan, other scholars can potentially replicate, or reproduce, the entire inquiry process. Research leads to reliable conclusions precisely because it can potentially be replicated. Replication ensures that the idiosyncrasies in the context of any one study, which can produce distorted results, don't lead to inappropriate generalizations. For example, only after

FIGURE 1.3   A working model of communication research

The communication research process can be viewed as an ongoing cycle of five interrelated phases of research activities: (a) conceptualization, (b) planning and designing research, (c) methodologies for conducting research, (d) analyzing and interpreting data, and (e) reconceptualization.

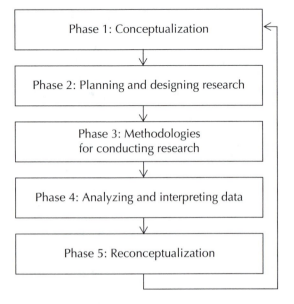

Phase 1: Conceptualization

Phase 2: Planning and designing research

Phase 3: Methodologies for conducting research

Phase 4: Analyzing and interpreting data

Phase 5: Reconceptualization

Phase 1: Conceptualizing Communication Research
Conceptualization, the first phase of research, involves forming an idea about what needs to be studied. Researchers begin communication inquiry by engaging in such conceptualizing activities as identifying a topic worth studying, reviewing the relevant literature to learn what is already known about the topic, and phrasing the topic as a formal research question or hypothesis (prediction).

Researchers establish a field of inquiry by narrowing their focus to a particular topic worth studying and a specific question worth asking. That topic may result from a theoretical proposition that needs testing, a practical problem that needs solving, or an experience that needs explaining. To select such a topic, the appropriate boundaries for communication research must be established. These principles of communication then can be used to pose a formal research question or hypothesis. Chapter 2 explains some fundamental principles that help define the concept of communication and parameters for communication research, as well as how researchers pose formal research questions and hypotheses.

A research study does not exist in isolation. To understand fully and accurately any particular research topic, research question, or hypothesis, it is necessary to know what scholars in the discipline have found by reviewing previous research. Reviewing the literature demands a working knowledge of what are the best sources to consult, where to find those sources with a minimum of effort, and how to read and use them. Finding, reading, and using research is the focus of Chapter 3.

Phase 2: Planning and Designing Communication Research
Good research projects are thought out carefully in advance. Once a topic has been selected, the available information on it has been found, and a formal research question or hypothesis has been posed, researchers need a systematic plan for conducting their study.

Moving from the conceptualization phase to planning and designing research demands that researchers transform abstract concepts into operational, or measurable, terms. **Operationalization** is the process of determining the observable characteristics associated with a concept or variable. Chapter 4 examines this process by showing how researchers develop strategies for observing and measuring the variables they study.

Measurement techniques, of course, need to be valid, or accurate. Validity, however, is not just important for the purposes of measurement; it affects the entire research plan and design. The internal validity of a study has to do with whether the procedures researchers use are accurate. As we shall see, researchers must try to rule out a number of important threats to designing internally valid research. The external validity of a study is concerned with the extent to which researchers can generalize findings to people/texts, situations, and time periods not studied directly in the research. Chapter 5 examines the process of designing internally and externally valid research.

FIGURE 1.3

Planning and designing communication research involves a number of ethical decisions. Ethics affects each stage of the research process: how researchers choose research topics and frame research questions/hypotheses, how the literature is reviewed, how research is designed and conducted, how data are analyzed, and how the findings are interpreted and used. It is also impossible to separate ethics from politics. Chapter 6 explores some important political issues and ethical decisions that confront communication researchers.

Phase 3: Methodologies for Conducting Communication Research

Once the topic has been chosen, the research question or hypothesis posed, the review of the literature conducted, and the research designed, researchers are ready to conduct their studies. Conducting careful research demands understanding and adhering to the specific assumptions and requirements of the methodology chosen. These methods tell researchers what evidence to look for and how to look for it. Chapters 7 through 10 examine four major methodologies available to communication researchers.

Chapter 7 explains experimental research. Experimental research applies principles about causation developed from the physical sciences to the study of human beings. Because of its emphasis on prediction and control, the experimental method is a powerful technique for examining how one variable produces changes in another variable.

Chapter 8 examines survey research. Survey research is used to discover the self-reported characteristics of a relatively small number of people, a sample, for the purpose of generalizing those characteristics to the population from which the sample was drawn. It is a popular method used by scholars and practitioners alike.

Chapter 9 focuses on textual analysis, which is used to analyze spoken, written, electronic, and visual texts, or documents. Four forms of textual analysis are considered. The first is rhetorical criticism, which scholars use to understand and evaluate texts. The second, content analysis, focuses on identifying patterns in the communication content of mass-

mediated and public texts. The third is interaction analysis, which analyzes the nature of messages exchanged during dyadic and group interaction. The fourth, performance studies, involves the analysis and oral performance of texts.

Chapter 10 explores naturalistic research, the study of people in their natural settings. Researchers use this method to probe for people's interpretations of the world and how they see themselves making choices, particularly with regard to their communication behavior.

Try to keep in mind throughout our discussions of these four methodologies that no one methodology is inherently better than another. The use of a particular methodology must always be guided by the nature of the topic chosen and the research question/hypothesis posed. Fitting the method to the topic and the research question/hypothesis, rather than the other way around, avoids the "law of the hammer," the tendency to hit everything in sight with a favorite tool, in this case, a research method. Researchers must, thus, ask themselves whether the topic and research question/hypothesis are best addressed by experiments, surveys, some form of textual analysis, or naturalistic research. Answering complex questions about communication also sometimes necessitates using multiple methodologies in a complementary manner within a single study.

Phase 4: Analyzing and Interpreting Data

Once data, or evidence, have been gathered through the use of the methodologies discussed in phase 3, they need to be analyzed and interpreted. For a number of methods, particularly experimental, survey, content analysis, and interaction analysis, this means processing quantitative (numerical) data through the use of appropriate statistical procedures. For that reason, Chapters 11 through 14 examine how quantitative data are analyzed and interpreted.

Quantitative analytic procedures can be used to describe data, called descriptive statistics, as well as infer meanings from them, called inferential statistics. Chapter 11 explains how researchers describe quantitative data, while Chapter 12 focuses on the theory underlying two types of inferential statistics:

(continued)

FIGURE 1.3   *Continued*

estimation, generalizing the findings from a sample to the population from which it is drawn, and significance testing, assessing whether there are significant statistical differences between groups (such as differences between men and women with regard to listening behavior) or relationships between variables (such as whether age and listening behavior are related). Chapters 13 and 14 then examine specific statistical techniques used in difference and relationship analysis, respectively.

Stage 5: Reconceptualizing Communication Research

Every individual study conducted is part of a larger body of related research. Relevant studies conducted prior to the present study being conducted provide theoretical, conceptual, and methodological foundations from which a researcher can build the current study. What is more, new research waiting to be conducted in the future is very likely to build on the research foundation created by the current inquiry. The research enterprise is a collective, collaborative, building process whereby the studies researchers conduct today are intimately connected to research conducted in the past and research to be conducted in the future. Research is not a disconnected individualistic process. No one study by itself, no matter how compelling it may be, is likely to make major advances in knowledge alone. Collectively, however,

a group of related studies that build on one another help to reach major conclusions, test and refine theories, and extend the expanding body of current knowledge about communication phenomena.

The reconceptualization phase of research is the part of the research process in which researchers formally connect their studies with preceding studies on a specific topic and set the stage for future related research. **Reconceptualization** occurs when researchers rethink the topic of inquiry as a result of the systematic processes associated with conceptualization, planning and designing research, using methodologies to gather data, analyzing the data, and, finally, interpreting research findings.

Reconceptualization involves explaining the meaning and significance of the research findings. Researchers try to explain how the results of a study answer the research questions posed, confirm or disconfirm the predictions made, and support or refute previous theory and research. Researchers also identify any difficulties encountered in conducting the research and how these problems may limit the validity and application of the findings. Finally, researchers address the implications of their findings for future research. Identifying implications from a research study for future communication theory, research, and practice completes the full cycle of the research process. Chapter 15 examines this important concluding phase of the research process.

---

repeated testing is a new drug allowed to be released on the market.

Note, however, that we use the words "potentially replicable," because scholars who wish to reproduce another's research study need to have the appropriate resources to do so. In some cases, such as experimental research, survey methods, or some forms of textual analysis, this may not pose a problem. The exact same procedures can be followed, with the exception that different research participants would be studied in experimental and survey research. In other cases, such as naturalistic research, scholars may find it difficult to replicate a study because of lack of available resources. For example, if one wanted to replicate the naturalistic

research that Dollar and Zimmers (1998) have done on social identity and communication boundaries with homeless street youth, one would need access to homeless street youth. Assuming that one had such access and developed sufficient relationships with those individuals, Dollar and Zimmers's findings are potentially replicable.

4. *Research is reflexive and self-critical.* Research is reflexive in that researchers explicitly examine their methods to discover and report flaws or threats to the validity of any findings from a study. Pick up any scholarly journal article and you will typically find a discussion in the concluding section about the potential problems that may have affected the study and limit the findings. Scholarly researchers openly evaluate the strengths and weaknesses of their own research studies. They don't wait to be criticized; they beat people to the punch by being their own best critics.

5. *Research is cumulative and self-correcting.* By being open to one and all, research creates a shared history. The accumulation of information from research allows for knowledge to evolve and grow. Old beliefs are discarded when they no longer hold true, and new beliefs emerge from the process, only to be challenged once again. Research, thus, leads to more research. Not only is research part of the broader community but it also creates a community of inquirers. Scholars meet regularly at conferences to share, discuss, and critique one another's work.

6. *Research is cyclical.* Research proceeds in stages and ends up back where it started. A researcher begins with a sense of curiosity and a topic worth studying, asks questions and/or makes predictions, plans research carefully, carries out the planned research, analyzes the data to provide tentative answers, and starts all over again by posing new topics and questions worth asking. Scholars, thus, provide feedback to themselves; new questions emerge from answers to previous questions.

Research as Culture

These characteristics make information acquired from research potentially fundamentally different from that obtained from the everyday ways of knowing examined previously. In fact, it is helpful to think about the research community as a distinct type of *culture.* And like any culture, research has its own language, rules, and social customs.

Learning about any new culture takes time and patience. When we first enter a new culture, we feel awkward because we do not know what the cultural members are saying or how to engage in appropriate behavior. We must start by becoming familiar with the language used and the conversations that take place there. Barnlund (1988) notes that "every culture attempts to create a 'uni-verse of discourse' for its members, a way in which people can interpret their experience and convey it to one another" (p. 11). Once we know the "code" and the "ropes," we feel more comfortable and competent within that culture. Our goal in this text is to give you a feel for the culture of research, which we hope will help you to understand its value and, most important, learn to live comfortably and profitably within it.

Research Cultures. Even though researchers generally agree on the six characteristics of research identified above, they do not necessarily all share the same worldview or the same assumptions about how people and communication should be studied. Just as there are different subcultures in any society, there are different research cultures.

At the most general level, we might distinguish three such cultures: (a) the **physical sciences,** in which scholars study the physical and natural world, as represented by such academic disciplines as physics, chemistry, and biology; (b) the **humanities,** in which scholars produce creative products and study the achievements of creative people, such as in the academic disciplines of music, art, and literature; and (c) the **social** (or **human**) **sciences,** in which scholars apply scientific methods to the study of human behavior, such as the disciplines of anthropology, psychology, and sociology.

Communication overlaps, in part, each of these three research cultures. Biologists, for example, sometimes talk about cells "communicating" with one another. The speech sciences, such as audiology (the study of hearing), are also tied to biology, chemistry, and physics. Communication is also associated with the humanities, since art, music, and literature are fundamentally forms of communication, and some communication scholars, such as those in performance studies, perform their work. And perhaps most important for the issues discussed in this text, communication is a social science, since communication researchers, like their colleagues in psychology, sociology, and anthropology, use scientific methods to study human behavior, in this case, communication behavior.

Positivist versus Naturalistic Paradigms in the Social Sciences.   If we examine the social sciences for a moment (although what we say certainly applies to the physical sciences and humanities as well), there are two major **paradigms,** or worldviews, that characterize social-scientific research. They go by many different names, but here we identify them as the *positivist* and *naturalistic paradigms.* The **positivist paradigm** (or **positivism**) can be defined as the "family of philosophies characterized by an extremely positive evaluation of science and scientific method" (W. L. Reese, 1980, p. 450). The positivist paradigm, as applied to the social sciences, is essentially concerned with how to apply some of the methods used in the physical sciences to the study of human behavior. The **naturalistic paradigm** can be defined as the family of philosophies that

focus on the socially constructed nature of reality. The naturalistic paradigm, again as applied to the social sciences, is essentially concerned with the development of methods that capture the socially constructed and situated nature of human behavior. Perhaps the best way to think about the difference between these paradigms is that while the positivist paradigm stresses the word *science* in the term "social science," the naturalistic paradigm stresses the word *social.*

These are paradigms in the sense that they are sets of basic assumptions or beliefs to which their proponents subscribe (see Guba & Lincoln, 1994). As Figure 1.4 shows, there are key differences between these paradigms in terms of five basic assumptions that have important implications for the research process, including communication research.

FIGURE 1.4   Positivist paradigm versus naturalistic paradigm

ASSUMPTION	QUESTION	POSITIVIST PARADIGM	NATURALISTIC PARADIGM
Ontological Assumption	What is the nature of reality?	Singular Objective	Multiple Intersubjective
Epistemological Assumption	What is the relationship of the researcher to that being researched?	Independent	Interdependent
Axiological Assumption	What is the role of values in the research process?	Value-free Unbiased	Value-laden Biased
Methodological Assumption	What is the process of research?	Deduction	Induction
		Search for cause and effect relationships between variables	Wholistic understanding of patterns of behavior
		Static design	Emergent design
		Researcher-controlled setting	Natural setting
		Quantitative methods	Qualitative methods
		Context-free generalizations	Context-bound findings
		Goals of explanation, prediction, and control	Goals of understanding and social change
Rhetorical Assumption	What is the language of research reports?	Formal Impersonal voice	Informal Personal voice

Source: Adapted from John W. Cresswell, *Research Design: Qualitative & Quantitative Approaches,* p. 5, copyright © 1994 by Sage Publications, Inc. Adapted by Permission of Sage Publications, Inc.

The first difference between these paradigms is with regard to the *ontological assumption* about the nature of reality. Proponents of the positivist paradigm see reality as *singular* and *objective;* that is, there is one reality out there that exists apart from any particular individual(s). In contrast, proponents of the naturalistic paradigm contend that there are *multiple realities* that are constructed between and among people (intersubjective).

Closely related to the ontological assumption is the *epistemological assumption* concerning the relationship of the researcher to that which is being researched. Proponents of the positivist paradigm see this relationship as *independent,* in the sense that what is to be known is independent of any researcher per se. In contrast, proponents of the naturalistic paradigm believe that the researcher is *interdependent* with that which is being studied; that what can be known depends on who's doing the knowing.

The differences just explained between these paradigms relate to that age-old philosophical question, "If a tree falls in the forest and no one is around, does it make a sound?" For proponents of the positivist paradigm, it sure does, because that's what happens when trees fall, they make sounds. For proponents of the naturalistic paradigm, sound is dependent on having a hearer, so the tree makes a sound only when someone is there to listen to it.

The third difference is the *axiological assumption* of the role of values in the research process. Proponents of the positivist paradigm believe that research can be *value-free* and *unbiased.* Indeed, the goal is to keep the researchers' values out of the research process. In contrast, proponents of the naturalistic paradigm argue that research is inherently *value-laden* and *biased.* As Lincoln and Guba (1985) explain, research is influenced, by, among other things, the inquirer's values (e.g., what the researcher thinks is important to study), the paradigm that guides the research (e.g., positivist or naturalistic), and the values that inhere in the context being studied.

The fourth difference is the *methodological assumption* concerning the process of research. We will focus the remainder of this text on methodological practices, so we won't spend a long time talking about these issues here. But knowing some of the basic issues involved is helpful at this stage, and we'll identify some chapters where you will find more discussion of these issues.

Research conducted from the positivist paradigm generally tends to use *deduction,* moving from the general to the specific. Researchers often start with a tentative explanation, such as a theory, and proceed to test it by collecting evidence (Chapter 2). One central purpose of such research is the search for *cause and effect* relationships (Chapter 7), or at least statistical relationships, between variables (Chapters 13–14). To discover such relationships, researchers typically use a *static design* in which the specific research procedures are all worked out ahead of time and the researcher sticks to that plan carefully and conscientiously. This type of research is most often conducted within a *researcher-controlled setting,* a setting created and controlled by a researcher (e.g., a laboratory), because it is easier to control for all the potential elements in a study in such a setting (Chapters 5 and 7). Positivist research typically uses *quantitative methods,* research methods that focus on the collection of data in the form of meaningful numbers (Chapter 4), such as the type of data often acquired from experiments (Chapter 7), surveys (Chapter 8), content analysis (Chapter 9), and interaction analysis (Chapter 9). Indeed, some scholars (e.g., Cresswell, 1994), use the term "quantitative paradigm" to refer to the positivist paradigm. By following these procedures, this research yields *context-free generalizations*—conclusions that can be generalized to people, situations, and time periods other than the ones studied (Chapter 5). For instance, researchers seek to discover drugs that cure a large number of people, not just those who were studied. Such generalizations allow researchers to *explain, predict,* and *control* phenomena, for once something is explained, it can be predicted and often controlled (in the positive sense, such as controlling the spread of disease).

Research conducted from the naturalistic paradigm tends to use *induction,* moving from the specific (the evidence) to the general (tentative explanations; Chapter 2). The goal is to gain a *wholistic understanding* of the patterns and behaviors that characterize human beings. To accomplish this goal, researchers use an *emergent design,* planning out their research, but then taking advantage of opportunities that present themselves during the research process. They conduct their research in the *natural setting,* where people normally behave, rather than a setting created and controlled by a researcher; that's why this type of research is called "naturalistic inquiry." And researchers tend to rely primarily on *qualitative methods,* research methods that focus on the acquisition of data that take the form of symbols other than meaningful numbers (although these are sometimes used as well; Chapter 4), such as data acquired from participant observation and in-depth interviewing (Chapter 10), performance studies (Chapter 9), and some forms of rhetorical criticism (Chapter 9). In fact, some scholars (e.g., Cresswell, 1994) use the term "qualitative paradigm" to refer to the naturalistic paradigm. By following these procedures, research studies yield *context-bound findings,* findings that apply to the particular people, situation, or time period studied; provide a rich *understanding* of that social context; and, in some cases, serve the purpose of promoting *social change* (Chapter 10).

Finally, positivist and naturalistic paradigms differ with regard to the *rhetorical assumption* of how research reports are to be written. Positivist research reports tend to have a *formal structure* and are written in an *impersonal (third-person) voice* in line with the view of research as an objective endeavor (Chapter 3). In contrast, naturalistic research reports tend to have an *informal structure* and include the *personal (first-person) voice* of the researcher (Chapter 10).

As you see, there are many important differences between these two paradigms that relate to research. Of course, we've been talking about the extreme positions here, and there are many scholars who work more in the middle ground. We would like to position this book toward the middle of the spectrum. However, we would be remiss if we didn't say that this text focuses mainly on the practices related to positivist research in the sense of studying relationship between variables. But we do try to give you a flavor of some of the issues and methods associated with the naturalistic paradigm. Two of the authors have conducted a number of naturalistic research studies, one has an edited text, which currently is being revised, about qualitative methods in the study of organizational communication (Herndon & Kreps, 1993), and another is planning to write a textbook about such methods. So even though this text leans toward positivist research methods, it is certainly informed by our experiences with using naturalistic methods.

Research as Conversation

We just talked about two very different paradigms for research, and you can imagine the conversations, or lack thereof, that go on between proponents of these two paradigms whenever they get together and discuss research methods. In fact, research itself, Pearce (1996) argues, can be thought of as a complex communication act, that is, as a form of conversation.

First, there are the conversations that take place between researchers and the people (or texts) they study. Most research, at least that which deals with human beings, involves researchers conversing with those they study, if only for a short period of time. The nature of that conversation, as we've just explained, is shaped, in part, by the paradigm that researchers adopt and the specific method(s) they employ. So, for example, a naturalistic researcher who wants to acquire a deep, wholistic understanding of a particular group of people and their communication behavior might use the method of in-depth interviewing and spend a significant amount of time conversing with a relatively small number of people, probing them for insights about their communication behavior. This type of conversation is very different from the one that occurs when a researcher wants to find out what a lot of people think and, therefore, uses a survey questionnaire that asks a large number of people to check off one of several possible choices for each question asked. And these conversations are very different from ones held by a researcher who wants to find out whether exposure to some stimulus leads people to behave in a certain way and, therefore, uses the experimental method to manipulate some variable and observe research participants' behavior. Each of these methods is a type of conversation between researchers and research participants. So part of what we are trying to teach you in this text is how the various methods structure the conversations that take place between researchers and research participants.

Second, there are the conversations that take place between researchers and a variety of other audiences. One important audience is other colleagues in the field. In fact, what makes something scholarly research is that it is intended for other scholars in the field. So researchers try to publish their studies in scholarly journals and texts and present their work at professional conferences. These conversations, of course, are very different in purpose and form from the conversations that take place between researchers and research participants. Researchers have their own language and ways of talking about research practices, including ways of talking about the conversations between researchers and research participants. So another part of what we are trying to teach you in this text is the conversations that take place among communication researchers.

There are also a number of other conversations that researchers can and do have. For instance, many researchers apply for grants to fund their research and these conversations have their own set of rules and procedures. There are the conversations that researchers have with gatekeepers of publication outlets, such as journal editors and reviewers. And sometimes researchers converse with the general public by giving open lectures to community groups and at bookstores or through the mass media, such as when they are interviewed by a newspaper or television reporter about their research. Much of what we have to say is relevant to understanding those conversations.

And let's not forget about research participants as part of the research conversation. They, too, have their own needs and goals in interacting with researchers, and in the case of community, business, and governmental organizations, they often set rules and procedures that must be followed by researchers who wish to do business with them. Research participants also sometimes converse with other research participants as part of a study, such as when they are asked to interact with another participant or group of participants and their behavior is observed, or when researchers put people together in a group, such as a focus group, and probe for information.

Finally, there are the conversations about research that take place at the public level, ranging from research reported by the mass media to discussion of the latest research findings among friends at the dinner table. We started this chapter by calling attention to the importance of understanding "research conversations," and we are now going to conclude by returning to the theme of becoming a competent consumer of these conversations, this time directed toward the importance of distinguishing research from pseudoresearch conversations.

THE IMPORTANCE OF DISTINGUISHING RESEARCH FROM PSEUDORESEARCH

We just explained many of the features of the research culture and how it differs from everyday ways of knowing. We are, then, almost ready to delve into the details of the communication research process. But before doing so, we need to examine one final issue: the importance of learning how to differentiate (good) research from pseudoresearch and just plain bad research. If we are to become competent consumers of research, we must be able to do this, because, as we stressed in the beginning of this chapter, we are being exposed every day to more and more research findings, and it's getting hard to separate the valid information from that which is not. One reason is that many people, recognizing the persuasive value of the term research, are cloaking their non–research-based claims and evidence using the label of research. So let's explore this issue for a moment. We start with a story.

For some years, Iben Browning had been predicting a 50–50 chance of an earthquake registering 6.5 or greater on the Richter scale somewhere along the New Madrid Fault, which runs from Marked Tree, Arkansas, to Cairo, Illinois, on or about December 3, 1990. A 72-year-old climatologist with no formal training in seismology (the geophysical science of earthquakes and related phenomena) or geology, Browning based this prediction on his belief that tidal waves, which would be at a 179-year peak on that day, can cause earthquakes.

Scientists agree, however, that there is absolutely no relationship between tides and earthquakes (the warrant is, thus, false), and they condemned Browning's prediction. Prominent researchers specializing in earth and atmospheric sciences at St. Louis University and the Center for Earthquake Research and Information at The University of Memphis issued a news release on July 29, 1990, rebuking Browning's methods and predictions, while another group of seismologists and geologists reviewed his methods and concluded that Browning's projection "appears theoretically implausible" (Tackett, 1990, p. 20)

Not surprisingly, the media focused on Browning's claims while giving almost no coverage to the scientists' critique. After all, earthquake predictions make "good copy." The result, as might be expected, was widespread panic in the areas that supposedly were affected. Many people left the areas, sporting events and conferences in the St. Louis area were canceled or postponed, and school officials throughout southeastern Missouri and parts of Arkansas, Illinois, Kentucky, Tennessee, and Indiana canceled classes for two days, affecting 150,000 students. The earthquake, of course, never did occur. Tidal waves don't cause earthquakes.

This example, and others like it, illustrates how quickly false information can spread, like a forest fire out of control, and how powerfully it can affect people. The media are partly to blame by lending credence to outrageous predictions and findings. Douglas Wiens, an expert on earthquakes at the University of Washington, in talking about the Browning case, said, "Initially, the media presented this prediction as though it was a valid scientific theory and something that was being put forward by an expert" (Tackett, 1990, p. 20). Jim Mauk, business manager for the New Madrid County Schools, said, "I think they [the media] got snowed. Browning made the projection, but he's not the one who hyped it" ("Who's Fault?" 1990, p. 22).

The media have definitely affected how scientists conduct the business of science. Everyone wants his or her 15 minutes of fame, and scientists are no different. A. Marcus (1991) contends that "competition for public attention encourages scientists to dramatize and popularize their views. The more catastrophic a prediction or conclusion, the more likely it will score newspaper and television coverage" (p. 23). Some scientists now rush to the media to report conclusions from preliminary research, instead of engaging in conscientious efforts to recheck their findings.

The controversial case of fusion (or what might better be called "confusion") in the laboratory a few years back is a classic example of a "rush to print." On March 23, 1989, two respected chemists, B. Stanley Pons, Chairperson of the Chemistry Department at the University of Utah, and Martin Fleischmann, of England's University of Southampton, called a press conference to announce several "table-top" experiments they claimed had generated nuclear fusion—the force that powers the sun, stars, and hydrogen bombs—in a test tube of water at room temperature. The story was picked up by newspapers and television around the world, and rightly so, for their discovery held the promise of solving the world's energy problems for all time.

Unfortunately, efforts to replicate their discovery proved futile, and it became clear after a while that Pons and Fleischmann had employed faulty research methods. They inferred that fusion had taken place because they measured its "symptoms"—additional neutrons and heat produced when an electric current was sent through a palladium rod immersed in heavy water. Their critics questioned this conclusion. They maintained that the two indicators of fusion were more likely outcomes of other processes, and that the two researchers could have determined this if they had conducted controlled experiments, such as using other chemicals under the same conditions to learn whether the same results would occur.

But Pons and Fleischmann did not conduct such controlled experiments. Concerned that their work would leak out and be usurped by others, they rushed to report their findings and, thereby, created excitement about the promise of their "discovery" and enormous disappointment when its significance was deflated. Frank Close, a top physicist at Oak Ridge National Laboratory and Britain's Rutherford Laboratory, and author of the book, *Too Hot to Handle: The Race for Cold Fusion*, believes that Pons and Fleischmann's data "had been obtained more by enthusiasm than by careful science" (D. Burns, 1991, p. 4).

Sloppy research methods might be forgiven, but what cannot be are attempts to mislead people purposely about research findings. Pons and Fleischmann, for example, altered some crucial evidence in their original publication, leading Frank Close to conclude that "how they represented it was a clear violation of how science should be done" ("Top Physicist," 1991, p. 16).

The sad part is that this case is not unique. Newspapers are filled these days with instances of scientific fraud. Dr. Robert C. Gallo, the United States government's top AIDS researcher at the National Institutes of Health, for example, was found guilty of scientific misconduct for falsifying an article to cover up his use of a French virus in establishing the cause of AIDS (Crewdson, 1992). For more than a decade, a doctor falsified and fabricated data in cancer research, including a landmark study that supposedly had established the safety of the common operation of lumpectomy (Crewdson, 1994a, 1994b). What makes these cases so intolerable, as Warren (1993) explains, is that "few groups are as closely associated in the public mind with the pursuit of objective truth as scientists. The notion that they might be venal, money-obsessed careerists is hard to fathom" (p. 2).

In the worst case scenario, falsifying data and research findings amounts to "disinformation." For example, research conducted in the early

1960s at Brown & Williamson Tobacco Corporation, which makes Kool, Viceroy, and other brands of cigarettes, revealed that nicotine was addictive and that cigarettes caused lung cancer, contributed to heart disease, and might cause emphysema ("Tobacco Firm," 1994). Executives at this company, however, chose not to reveal these findings when the United States Surgeon General was preparing the first report in 1963 about the health hazards of cigarettes. Worse, these findings "contradict the tobacco industry's contention during the past three decades that it has not been proved that cigarettes are harmful or that nicotine is addictive" ("Tobacco Firm," p. 7). There is even an Institute for Tobacco and Health, an oxymoron if ever there was one, at the University of Kentucky, where the sole purpose is to conduct research that shows the health benefits of tobacco! It is this kind of systematic disinformation that led to the lawsuits in which the tobacco companies are being forced to pay a lot of money.

While it may not surprise some, even the United States government engages in disinformation with respect to research. In the case of Dr. Gallo, a report to the House Subcommittee on Investigations revealed that "senior U.S. government officials colluded in the misrepresentation and may actually have organized and promoted a cover-up [of the facts]" (Crewdson, 1991, p. 1). Consumer groups in the early 1990s accused the Department of Transportation of manipulating car crash tests and sharing only the results of tests that showed that larger cars were more safe than smaller cars, while not publicizing the many tests that showed otherwise, thereby lending support to the automobile industry's claim that stricter fuel economy standards would produce more dangerous cars ("Auto Safety Tests," 1991).

The examples given above are not meant to depress you (although they should!); they are intended to show how difficult it has become to evaluate the validity of the research findings to which we are exposed on a daily basis. Individual researchers and groups of scientists are to blame in many cases for using faulty methods or engaging in blatant falsification and misrepresentation, and the media feeding frenzy over outrageous predictions and findings only makes things worse.

But let's also lay some of the blame on us—the general public. Let's face it, to the extent that we are ignorant of the way research is produced, and the many potential problems that can jeopardize the validity of research findings, we have no basis for accepting or rejecting research-based claims and evidence. This puts us in a position to be taken advantage of by scientists, the media, the government, and snakeoil salespeople alike.

Being taken advantage of by others because of a lack of knowledge is a common occurrence. If you know little about auto mechanics and take your car into the shop and the service person says you need a new transmission, how do you know whether he or she is telling the truth? You don't—you literally have to take this claim on the basis of faith. Now we are not saying you are being lied to, but there have been times when customers have been charged for work that was not needed, as documented by such television investigative news programs as *Sixty Minutes.*

People who know about cars, however, are not fooled so easily; they can ask good questions and discuss the problem in an intelligent manner. They demand proof before they pay all that money for a new transmission. The same is true with regard to research findings in that people who know how research is conducted and how data are analyzed are able to understand and evaluate research-based information. Unfortunately, most people simply don't know about research methods and, thus, can't differentiate between valid and invalid research-based claims.

The inability to differentiate valid from invalid research-based information is having some terrible effects at the societal level. Take the legal system, where research plays a crucial role in deciding many cases, especially those involving liability claims. Huber (1991) maintains that juries and judges alike are having problems differentiating science from **pseudoresearch,** or what he calls **junk science,** which he describes as "claims dressed up in the form of serious science but lacking serious empirical and conceptual credentials"

(p. 223). Junk science looks, smells, and tastes like real science, but it isn't.

How has junk science infected the courtroom? In 1923, the federal courts adopted what became known as the *Frye* rule, which "allowed experts into court only if their testimony was founded on theories, methods, and procedures 'generally accepted' as valid among other scientists in the field" (Huber, 1991, p. 14). In 1975, however, in the Federal Rules of Evidence, the courts allowed expert testimony if "scientific, technical, or other specialized knowledge will assist the trier of fact to understand the evidence or to determine a fact" (Huber, p. 15).

This ruling essentially opened the door for anyone with some minimum qualification, such as a college degree, to be an expert. While we all know there is a big difference between a general practitioner and a brain surgeon, the two are now treated equally with respect to testifying about brain surgery. No longer is one required to be a specialist in the area under consideration. Worse yet, so-called junk scientists, whose theories, methods, and procedures sound valid to the naive listener but are not considered so by scientists in the field, can now be hired to testify (some have even said "hired to lie") as expert witnesses.

Unfortunately, junk scientists have had some success. For example, the drug Bendectin, which was used to treat women for "morning sickness," which in some cases can be so severe that it threatens the health of both mother and child, was pulled from the market because of a few lawsuits in which supposed medical experts, whose credentials and theories were later discredited, testified that the drug caused birth defects. The parent company actually lost only one of the cases brought against it, due no doubt to jurors' inability to recognize an expert from a junk scientist. After all, each trial is a brand new ball game in which science must prove itself all over again. The trials, however, cost the company upward of $100 million for its vindication, so it decided it was easier to pull the drug from the market than continue fighting a legal battle (Huber, 1991).

Another example is that of Audi, whose car sales plummeted after the media's coverage of the

Audi 5000's problem of "sudden acceleration," where the car supposedly lurched forward even though a person's foot was on the brake. After numerous research studies, including three independent government investigations, the problem was shown to be due to people having their foot on the accelerator, not the brake! But this didn't stop so-called experts from testifying and winning a couple of lawsuits.

The consequences of such lawsuits are, indeed, costly. In the two examples cited above, pregnant women lost a valuable drug to aid in the fight against morning sickness, and what was widely regarded as one of the safest cars on the road disappeared virtually overnight.

But the problem of junk science isn't limited to civil suits against companies with "deep pockets"; it is also affecting criminal trials as well. In what must surely be one of the most bizarre examples of junk science, consider the case of Michael H. West, a forensic dentist who matches bite marks with the teeth that made them, wounds with weapons, and so forth. Matching such things makes some sense, but it is West's methods that raises concerns. He uses a special blue light to study wound patterns, and claims to be able to see things that are invisible otherwise. Now that isn't particularly startling, as blue lights have been used for quite some time to look for clues at the scene of a crime. What is startling, as M. Hansen (1996) explains, is that

> according to his scientific counterparts, West sees things under [the blue light] that he cannot document and that nobody else can see.... [He has] failed to follow generally accepted scientific techniques, and testified about his findings with an unheard of degree of scientific certainty—"indeed and without a doubt"—is his standard operating opinion. (p. 51)

West has been suspended from the American Board of Forensic Odontology because he "misrepresented evidence and testified outside his field of expertise," and he resigned from the American Academy of Forensic Sciences after "its ethics committee recommended that he be ex-

pelled for allegedly failing to meet professional standards of research, misrepresenting data to support a general acceptance of his techniques, and offering opinions that exceed a reasonable degree of scientific certainty" (M. Hansen, p. 52). And in 1993, faced with growing concern over expert testimony, the United States Supreme Court ruled that expert testimony must be validated scientifically, which clearly rules out West and his methods. But none of that has stopped West from serving and being in high demand as an expert witness. He has testified about 55 times, half of them capital murder cases, in nine states over the past decade or so, and with the exception of his first trial, he has not been on the losing side in a single case, helping to put dozens of defendants in prison, some for life and two on death row (M. Hansen, 1996).

Stopping the spread of false information is not just the responsibility of individual scientists, the media, the government, and the courts (which, in many trials, is decided by a group of common citizens)—it is everybody's business. It is, thus, incumbent on us to learn the difference between astronomy and astrology or between chemistry and alchemy so that we are not taken advantage of by those who would deceive us while cloaking themselves in the mantle of "research." We must become knowledgeable and critical consumers if we intend to separate the valid and valuable information from that which is invalid and useless. Rather than giving the benefit of the doubt to any research finding that comes along, we must, instead, seriously question that information and accept it only after it is shown to be true beyond a reasonable doubt.

The problem is that most people have a way to go to become knowledgeable and critical consumers of research, for they are starting out almost from scratch. When you walk into a history, science, or mathematics course, you have studied these topics throughout your educational careers. While there are other college courses for which you have not studied the material previously in a formal manner, you have, in many cases, been studying the topic informally for years. For example, you have been involved in intimate interpersonal relationships all your life and have undoubtedly drawn conclusions on the basis of these experiences that may serve you well in an interpersonal communication course.

In the case of a communication research methods course, however, the odds are that you have no previous experience, or only limited experience, at best. Some of you may have taken a methods course in another discipline, but many have not. This means that most students start off with virtually no knowledge about the nature of the research process.

Don't panic, however, for this book is designed exactly for such students. We are going to walk you through the process step-by-step, sharing with you the excitement of research, the discipline required for rigorous research, and common errors that impede researchers' progress. You will learn characteristics of high-quality research and what it takes to achieve them, and you will learn about the shortcomings in research and what it takes to avoid them. By the end of the text, we promise that you will be a more knowledgeable and critical consumer of research than you are now.

CONCLUSION

We are confronted by research findings every day. If we are to be knowledgeable and critical consumers of this research, we must understand the processes used to conduct it. To do that, we have to learn about the research culture—its assumptions about how the world works, the various methods employed, and the rules of conduct to be followed. Once we know the code of research conversations, we have a better chance of distinguishing valid from invalid information. Our goal is to teach you how to understand and take part in these conversations.

CHAPTER 2

ASKING QUESTIONS ABOUT COMMUNICATION

Research begins with curiosity. Researchers notice something about communication and wish to learn more about it. That moment might occur in the midst of the give-and-take of social interaction in a family, business, or community, or it might occur while perusing the published literature in communication journals and books.

Researchers move from that sense of curiosity to formulating a question that can be answered by engaging in a research project. The articulation of such "researchable" questions is a primary and essential step in the research process. As the saying from the world of computers goes: "Garbage in, garbage out." The questions we ask suggest what information we will gather (the "in"-put of a research study), and the conclusions we will draw (the "out"-put of the study) are based on that information. So phrasing worthwhile questions is a key turning point in the research process. The research question outlines the framework on which the entire research project will be built.

In this chapter, we examine the process of asking questions about communication. We start by describing the domain of human behavior examined in communication research. We then explore commonly studied areas of communication research, two important starting points for communication research, and some ways to justify the selection of particular topics. We conclude this chapter by examining the ways researchers phrase topics and ideas in formal research questions and hypotheses.

DEFINING COMMUNICATION

Defining the term *communication* is like trying to describe a three-ring circus to a child—how can

we put into a sentence or two everything that goes on when so *much* goes on? Indeed, over 20 years ago, Dance and Larson (1976) had already found (in a survey of the literature) that there were 126 different definitions for the word communication!

You've probably noticed that a variety of images come to mind when you tell people you are studying communication. Some assume you're studying public speaking, others think of organizational communication, and still others picture journalism, electronic broadcasting, telephone technology, and who knows what else. They react so variably because communication is an umbrella term that covers numerous, apparently disparate, activities.

But all these activities do have important elements in common. In fact, the term communication, historically, is derived from the Latin word, *communis,* which means "to make common." Today, most definitions of communication emphasize one of two different views about making things common. As Pearce (1995) explains:

> There is a difference in the connotations of communication depending on whether the emphasis is on that which is made common (shared meanings, cultural symbols, traditions, common ground, understanding) or on the process of making *things common (the transmission of messages from place to place; the languages in which things are framed; the patterns of action in which they occur; the things that people actually do and say to each other). (p. 7)

Those who focus on the process of *making* things common adopt what can be called an *information exchange perspective;* they are primarily concerned with how communication can be used as a tool to transfer information from one person or place (a source) to another (a receiver). In contrast, those who emphasize that which is made *common* adopt what can be called a *meaning-based* or *constitutive perspective;* they are concerned with how "our experiences of reality are a product of communicative activity" (Mokros & Deetz, 1996, p. 32).

In this text, we acknowledge these two views on "making things common" in the following definition: **Communication** refers to the processes by which verbal and nonverbal messages are used to create and share meaning. This definition acknowledges that communication is both a meaning-based, creative process, as well as a tool used to exchange information.

WHAT CONSTITUTES COMMUNICATION RESEARCH?

We admit that this is a broad, abstract definition of communication. To better help you understand what is done in the communication discipline, we need to divide it into more concrete parts. A traditional model of communication—*people exchanging messages through channels within a context*—provides a useful way to focus on the types of research done by communication scholars.

This model contains four important components: people, messages, channels, and contexts. The pivotal element of the four is *messages.* Messages are the usual target of communication researchers—messages we send to ourselves, to others, within small groups or organizations, via the media, or within and between cultures.

The other three components of the model—people, channels, and contexts—are usually studied only as they influence messages. We depend on scholars in other disciplines to study the psychological, biological, and many other dimensions of human life. For example, studying how people's self-esteem changes as they grow older is more appropriate for psychology researchers than for communication researchers because the focus isn't on message behavior. However, studying how self-esteem affects communication apprehension (fear

of communicating, such as fear of public speaking) is appropriate for communication research because the focus is on message behavior and not just on psychological variables. Similarly, studying how electronic signals travel through a television cable (a channel) is within the domain of physicists, not communication researchers. Studying whether people acquire more information from messages received via mass-mediated or face-to-face channels, however, certainly is relevant communication research. In the same way, studying how much business organizations (a context) spend on computers is important to accountants and/or computer consultants, but not to communication researchers per se. Studying how new technologies affect the flow of information within business organizations, however, is a concern of communication research.

Communication research, thus, focuses primarily on messages—messages sent intrapersonally, interpersonally, or within and between groups, organizations, and cultures/societies. To make the other elements of people, channels, and/or contexts relevant to communication interests, researchers must relate them to message behavior.

AREAS OF COMMUNICATION RESEARCH

Because message behavior covers such a large array of processes, little can be said about "communication in general." In fact, researchers' first step involves carving out and defining the precise slice of the big communication pie they will investigate. They identify the **research topic,** the novel idea they consider worth studying and hope to understand better. Their goal is to be able to say with some certainty a few specific things about that slice. They also want to compare and contrast what they've learned with what others have discovered about that slice and with what is known about the slices studied by other researchers. Over time, as researchers describe more pie slices more accurately, the communication pie gradually takes on new meaning.

The communication realm can be divided in many ways. One way is to look at the institutional structure of the discipline. Scholars affiliate with colleagues studying similar topics within the professional associations in the communication discipline. The National Communication Association (NCA), the International Communication Association (ICA), and the Association for Educational Journalism and Mass Communication (AEJMC), for example, are major associations for those who study communication. There are also four regional associations (the Central States, Eastern, Southern States, and Western States Communication Associations) and many state associations, as well as other associations that represent more specific communication interests, such as Women in Communication (WIC), or specific interests communication scholars share with those in other disciplines, such as the Public Relations Society of America (PRSA).

Professional associations are themselves organized into different interest areas, each of which addresses the common concern(s) of a group of scholars. These interest areas are often labeled according to their *size* (e.g., NCA "divisions" have at least 300 members, while "commissions" have at least 100 members) or *mission* (e.g., NCA "caucuses" represent the interests of members in specific demographic or socially defined groups—united by gender and race, for instance—who seek to realize the objectives specified in NCA's Affirmative Action Statement) (see Figure 2.1).

Professional associations often publish academic journals (see Chapter 3). Several journals are oriented toward scholars who study particular interest areas (e.g., the journal *Health Communication*). Professional associations also hold conventions where scholars present their work. To make a presentation, scholars send their papers and panel proposals to an elected officer (typically, the chair or vice-chair) of that interest area. These officers are

---

FIGURE 2.1   Divisions, commissions, and caucuses of the 1999 National Communication Association

A. Divisions
Applied Communication
Argumentation and
    Forensics
Asian Pacific American
    Communication Studies
Basic Course
Critical and Cultural Studies
Ethnography
Family Communication
Feminist and Women Studies
Gay, Lesbian, Bisexual/
    Transgender
    Communication Studies
Group Communication
Health Communication
Instructional Development
International and Intercultural
    Communication
Interpersonal Communication
Language and Social
    Interaction
Latina/Latino Communication
    Studies
Mass Communication

Organizational
    Communication
Performance Studies
Political Communication
Public Address
Public Relations
Rhetorical and
    Communication Theory
Theatre
Training and Development

B. Commissions
African American Communi-
    cation and Culture
American Parliamentary
    Practice
American Studies
Communication and Aging
Communication and Law
Communication Apprehension
    and Avoidance
Communication Assessment
Communication in the Future
Communication Needs of
    Students at Risk

Environmental
    Communication
Ethics Communication
Experiential Learning in
    Communication
Freedom of Expression
Human Communication and
    Technology
Intrapersonal Communication/
    Social Cognition
Peace and Conflict
    Communication
Semiotics and Communication
Spiritual Communication
Visual Communication

C. Caucuses
Asian/Pacific American
Black
Disability Issues
Emeritus/Retired Members
Gay and Lesbian Concerns
La Raza (Chicano/Latino
    culture and communication)
Women's

themselves scholars who have devoted some of their own work to that area.

The interest areas of the communication discipline are reflected in the courses taught at universities and colleges, and, in some cases, in the concentrations offered for communication majors (e.g., public relations or mass communication). The material taught within your communication classes is, in this way, defined by the areas scholars in the communication professional associations choose to study.

Within each interest area, several general topics attract scholars' attention. For example, M. W. Allen, Gotcher, and Siebert's (1993) review of journal articles published between 1980 and 1991 identified 18 general topic areas of organizational communication research (see Figure 2.2). Within each of those general areas, many specific topics interest scholars. For example, how superior-to-subordinate feedback affects subordinates' levels of satisfaction and performance has received much attention within the general area of interpersonal relations within organizations.

Existing interest areas within the communication discipline suggest fruitful directions for research. Some journal articles and chapters in scholarly texts, such as the one by M. W. Allen et al. (1993), provide an overview and critique of available research in an area. These publications are an excellent starting point for discovering what is known about an area and what needs to be investigated next (see Chapter 3 about reviewing the research literature).

Officially designated interest areas are not mutually exclusive compartments within which all communication research can be neatly classified. In fact, research, and especially cutting-edge research, is often concerned with the intersections of interest areas, such as the effects of the mass media on interpersonal interactions or rhetorical analyses of organizational communication. As Zarefsky (1993), then President of NCA, noted, "Some of the most exciting recent developments in communication not only have occurred in total disrespect of our disciplinary substructure but make much of that structure irrelevant" (p. 2).

Perhaps different structures for organizing communication scholarship and pedagogy will emerge in the future.

BASIC VERSUS APPLIED COMMUNICATION RESEARCH TOPICS

Another distinction communication scholars make is between: (a) research designed to test and refine theory, referred to as **basic research,** and (b) research designed to solve a practical problem, referred to as **applied research.**

Basic Communication Research

People often misinterpret the word *theory,* sometimes contrasting it negatively with practical knowledge, such as in the cliche, "It may work in theory but not in practice." People, therefore, sometimes distrust theory. The 1930s movie detective Charlie Chan once said, "Theories are like the mist on the eyeglasses: They tend to obscure one's vision."

This caricature of theory is misleading. A **theory** is simply a generalization about a phenomenon, an explanation of how or why something occurs. It is, as Kaplan (1964) explains, "a way of making sense of a disturbing situation" (p. 295). Looked at from this perspective, "Everybody uses theories; we cannot live without them" (Littlejohn, 1996, p. 2).

There is, however, an important difference between "commonsense" theories and "scientifically tested" theories. An example of a commonsense theory is what H. H. Kelly (1950, 1967) called "implicit personality theories." He discovered that people have implicit theories about which personality characteristics go together. For example, many people believe that writing ability and oral communication competence go together. If someone says that his or her friend, Jack, writes well, many people would expect Jack to also be good at social interaction. But this isn't necessarily so. Implicit personality theories are an example of how we use a commonsense assumption or theory to form impressions of others.

FIGURE 2.2   Areas of organizational communication research in journal articles, 1980–1981

1. Interpersonal Relations within Organizations (233 articles): Articles that investigate superior-subordinate relationships, additional interpersonal relations (e.g., expressions of emotions at work), interviewing, interpersonal communication and stress, and issues of gender and race.

2. Communication Skills and Strategies (120): Articles that focus on a wide variety of communication skills in the workplace, including persuasion and influence strategies, listening, self-presentation, and feedback seeking and delivery, as well as the outcomes associated with skills.

3. Organizational Culture and Symbolism (99): Articles that analyze the symbolic aspects of organizational life (e.g., metaphors and rituals) or that discuss organizational culture.

4. Information Flow and Channels (74): Articles that identify issues affecting information flow in organizations (e.g., structural characteristics of organizations).

5. Power and Influence (67): Articles that conceptualize and assess the effects of power and influence in organizations.

6. Positive Outcomes Associated with Communication (67): Articles that assess the effects of organizational communication processes on a variety of outcomes, such as performance, productivity, and employee commitment.

7. Decision Making and Problem Solving (67): Articles that study decision making and problem solving either as outcomes or as processes, and identify constraints on, and prescriptions for improved, decision making.

8. Communication Networks (57): Articles that identify antecedents and outcomes associated with network membership, links between technology and networks, measurement-related issues, and interorganizational networks.

9. Cognitive, Communication, and Management Styles (57): Articles that examine possible relationships between communication/management styles and outcomes.

10. Organization—Environment Communication Interface (53): Articles that address an organization's external communication, such as image-related communication, corporate communication, and boundary spanning.

11. Technology (45): Articles that study how technological advances (e.g., computer-assisted communication) affect organizations and employees.

12. Language and Message Content (41): Studies that concentrate on language as a means of shaping or framing ideas of reality and/or message content.

13. Structure (42): Articles that explore relationships between an organization's structure and communication.

14. Uncertainty and Information Adequacy (40): Articles that focus on interorganizational uncertainty, information adequacy, and information search.

15. Groups and Organizational Effectiveness (41): Articles that focus on the outcomes associated with group interactions in organizations.

16. Ethics (28 articles): Articles that deal with ethical issues associated with the strategic use of communication, as well as information flow issues.

17. Cross-cultural Research (24): Articles that focus on crosscultural and intercultural organizational communication research, including communication patterns and managerial communication.

18. Climate (18): Articles that investigate the determinants or components of organizational climate.

Source: Adapted from Allen, M. W., Gotcher, J. M., & Siebert, J. H. (1993). A decade of organizational communication research: Journal articles 1980–1991. In S. A. Deetz (Ed.), *Communication yearbook 16* (pp. 252–330). Newbury Park, CA: Sage.

Scholars are more systematic in the way they develop and test theories. The purpose of **basic communication research** is to increase our knowledge about communication phenomena by testing, refining, and elaborating theory.

Numerous theories have been developed to explain a wide array of communication events and processes, far too many for us to catalogue in this chapter. (For specific examples, see communication theory textbooks by Baran & Davis, 1995; E. Griffin, 1997; Infante, Rancer, & Womack, 1996; Littlejohn, 1996; Severin & Tankard, 1992; Trenholm, 1991.) But if you pick up almost any issue of a scholarly communication journal, you will see that many of the articles propose and/or test the validity, or increase the precision and scope, of particular theories.

Not all theories proposed by scholars are equally worthwhile. The value of a given theory is judged by the extent to which it explains an important phenomenon satisfactorily, organizes knowledge, predicts certain outcomes, focuses research efforts, and excites inquiry (see Figure 2.3).

The process of testing a theory scientifically is relatively straightforward (see Figure 2.4). The first step involves the selection of a research topic. The next step is the choice of an appropriate theory to help explain important aspects of the research topic. A hypothesis (or hypotheses) is then derived from the theory, and the accuracy of that prediction is tested in a study. Data are collected and analyzed, and they are used to gauge the merits of the prediction. If the findings confirm or support the hypothesis, the theory has one more piece of support. If the findings do not support the hypothesis, more research may need to be conducted, the hypothesis may need to be revised, and/or the theory may need to be revised or rejected.

As an example, many researchers who study interpersonal communication (an area) are interested in communication behavior during initial interactions (a topic). One theory that is especially useful for explaining communication during initial interactions is Berger and Calabrese's (1975) Uncertainty Reduction Theory (URT), a theory that describes the relationship between uncertainty and communication. The theory starts with the premise that people experience a lot of uncertainty during initial interactions (e.g., about the other person, how to behave, etc.) and that they engage in communication to reduce their uncertainty. Berger and Calabrese subsequently derived a number of hypotheses from this theory. For example, they hypothesized that "High levels of uncertainty cause increases in information-seeking behavior."

This hypothesis, among others derived from URT, was tested by W. Douglas (1994). His study involved several steps. He first told research participants that they would be interacting with another person whom they didn't know. They then completed a questionnaire that measured how uncertain they typically are when meeting new people (called "global uncertainty"). Participants then interacted in dyads for 4 minutes and their conversations were tape-recorded. After interacting, they filled out another questionnaire that measured how uncertain they were about their conversational partner. The conversations were transcribed and coded with respect to information-seeking behaviors, such as the number of questions people asked of one another. The results showed that high levels of global uncertainty on the preconversation measure were associated with high levels of question asking, a finding that supported the hypothesis and, consequently, the theory. However, postconversation uncertainty was consistently unrelated to the number of questions asked, a finding not predicted by the hypothesis. This finding calls into question another prediction implied by URT, and Douglas proposed a modification of that theory to account for it.

This research study shows that a theory is really never complete. Theorists are trying to explain an ever-widening range of communication behavior, and always fall a little short of their goal. Their reach always extends beyond their grasp. They continually try to describe, explain, understand, predict, and control more communication phenomena than anyone could before. Theories, like communication, are ongoing and ever-changing, and can always benefit from further refinement and elaboration.

FIGURE 2.3 Evaluating theories

The following is a synthesis of some of the most important functions that theory serves, functions that can be used to evaluate any theory. This synthesis is based on work by Barnlund (1968), Bross (1953), Dance (1982), Hall and Lindzey (1970), Hawes (1975), Kaplan (1964), Kuhn (1970), Littlejohn (1996), and Poole (1990).

1. Explanation: Theories clarify, make sense of, and account for a subject matter. Theories help us understand what something involves by organizing and summarizing knowledge into a system. To the extent that a theory explains something, it is considered to have explanatory power.
   a. Theoretical Scope: The explanatory power of any theory is limited by its boundary—the behavior, people/texts, or contexts it covers. A theory might explain many things or something specific.
   b. Validity: A theory must be internally valid, or consistent, being free from contradiction. A theory also needs to be externally valid, being consistent with observed facts and common everyday experiences.
   c. Simplicity/Parsimony: A theory should be as simple, or parsimonious, as possible. Generally, the fewer the number of propositions, the better the theory. The desire to simplify theories and explanations is known as *Ockham's Razor,* named after William of Ockham (1285–1349).
2. Prediction: Theories foretell what will happen before it does happen. They provide informed guesses about what will occur and when. To the

extent that a theory provides testable predictions about something, it is considered precise.
   a. Focusing: A theory focuses attention on the most important variables and the expected outcomes.
   b. Observational Aid: A theory tells what to look for in observing and measuring important variables and their effects.
   c. Open to Falsification: A theory is open to falsification, or corroboration. It must be able to be tested to determine the extent to which it is true or false.
3. Control: To the extent that a theory explains and predicts something, some measure of control can often be gained over that phenomenon. Such control allows the object to be produced and directed in meaningful ways, by setting up the necessary conditions for causing or inhibiting its occurrence.
4. Heuristic: A theory should generate scholarly research. Theory serves as an impetus for testing its concepts and predictions. Scholars usually devote their energies to testing the most promising theories. Thus, theories that have been examined widely are usually deemed most noteworthy.
5. Communicative: A theory serves as an important focus for discussion and debate. It is a public message about a phenomenon that scholars argue for and against.
6. Inspiration: A theory ought to be exciting, catch the imagination, and teach people something. It ought to help solve important puzzles and intriguing mysteries and should address important and meaningful concerns.

Applied Communication Research

Applied communication research is conducted for the purpose of solving a "real-world," socially relevant communication problem. As Cissna (1982), the first editor of the *Journal of Applied Communication Research,* explained:

> *Applied research sets out to contribute to knowledge by answering a real, pragmatic, social ques-*

> *tion or by solving a real pragmatic, social problem. Applied communication research involves such a question or problem of human communication or examines human communication in order to provide an answer or solution to the question or problem. (Editor's note)*

Applied communication research, thus, seeks to demonstrate the relevance of communication knowledge to a particular event or challenge of

FIGURE 2.4 The process of basic communication research

1. Select Topic of Interest
   Example: Communication behavior during initial interactions
   ↓

2. Select Appropriate Theory
   Example: Uncertainty Reduction Theory: People experience uncertainty during initial interactions and seek to reduce it by engaging in communication behavior (Berger & Calabrese, 1975)
   ↓

3. Derive a Hypothesis
   Example: "High levels of uncertainty cause increases in information seeking behavior" (Berger & Calabrese, 1975, p. 103)
   ↓

4. Design Study and Test Hypothesis
   A. If hypothesis is confirmed, study provides support for the theory
   B. If hypothesis is not confirmed:
      1. Conduct additional research
      2. Revise hypothesis
      3. Revise or reject theory

everyday life. Applied researchers start with a communication problem in a specific context and conduct a study to lessen its intensity and/or prevalence. Hopefully, the study yields valid generalizations about, and potential solutions to, the problem.

Many important problems experienced by individuals, couples, groups, organizations, and societies have attracted the attention of communication scholars. Figure 2.5 provides some recent examples of applied communication research. As you see, communication researchers have channeled their energies and resources toward helping to solve some very important problems.

One type of applied research that has important consequences for the study of communication is **action research,** "a collaborative approach to *inquiry* or *investigation* that provides people with the means to take systematic *action* to resolve specific problems" (Stringer, 1996, p. 15). Action research stresses *participative inquiry,* that is, communication and collaboration with community group members throughout the course of a research study. Working with a researcher, stakeholders define a problem in their community, determine the methods to be used to collect, analyze, and reflect on the data, and use their new understandings to design action steps to resolve and manage the problem (see Argyris, Putnam, & Smith, 1985; Heron & Reason, 1997; Reason, 1994).

One important type of applied communication research that lends itself well to action research methods is **social justice communication research.** This research deals with and contributes to the well-being of people who are economically, socially, politically, and/or culturally underresourced and disenfranchised (see Ray, 1996a, 1996b; Swartz, 1997a). One way researchers do this is by identifying and critiquing dominant structures that underwrite inequality. Clair and Thompson (1996), for example, interviewed 50 working women to describe how pay inequity articulates patriarchical conditions. They found that pay inequity is viewed as a sign of oppression, a symbol of privilege to some groups and marginalization to others. Sometimes social justice communication researchers go beyond identification and critique to actively change an oppressive situation. Schmitz, Rogers, Phillips, and Paschal (1995), for example, conducted a 6-year study of the Public Electronic Network (PEN), a free, computer-based electronic communication network designed by one of the authors and used by over 5,000 Santa Monica, California, residents. The study showed how PEN spurred participation in confronting the problem of homelessness by persons not customarily given "voice." As another example, Hartnett (1998) not only critiqued the "correctional-industrial-complex" (the interlocking interests of police/correctional organizations and industrial corporations that profit from the symbolic construction of racism, fear of crime, and law and order that lead to the solution of prisons), as an activist teaching in a prison, he had his

---

FIGURE 2.5   Examples of recent applied communication research

1. R. J. Adams and Parrott (1994) studied pediatric nurses' communication of role expectations to parents of hospitalized children. Both nurses and parents were more satisfied and perceived a reduction in role ambiguity when nurses communicated rules in writing and/or orally, as compared to no formal communication.
2. Dillard, Plotnick, Godbold, Freimuth, and Edgar (1996) investigated the extent to which public service announcements on the topic of AIDS/HIV evoked emotional responses and the degree to which those feelings predicted receivers' reactions to such messages.
3. Ferguson and Dickson (1995) examined children's feelings and expectations regarding their single parents' dating behavior. They found that children's connectedness, informational certainty, openness, interpersonal acceptance, emotional security, and boundaries were related to their perceptions of this aspect of their parents' lives.
4. Henriksen (1996) studied what skills underlie children's comprehension of advertisements' intent. The results suggested that how well they understand that selling implies an exchange of money for goods influences how young viewers interpret advertisers' motives.
5. Manusov, Cody, Donohue, and Zappa (1994) investigated the frequency, type, and sequence of accusations made during child custody mediation sessions. Accusations were found to be detrimental. Couples were more likely to reach custody agreements when mediators intervened after accusations and when discussion of specific offending behavior was avoided.
6. M. Miller (1995) explored messages across four generations of six women in one family who had engaged in nonfatal suicide behaviors. She discovered recurrent patterns of communication that may have put the female members of this family at risk for suicide.
7. Olson and Olson (1994) studied how judges' statements and decisions in jury trials, through both their trial-management approaches and the accounts of law and justice embedded in their comments during trials, influence jurors' verdicts.
8. T. R. Peterson et al. (1994) conducted a field study of Texas farmers to identify persuasive strategies (such as following a narrative format and avoiding the appearance of relying on technical expertise at the expense of common sense) that work to reduce injuries involving use of farm equipment.
9. Stamp and Sabourin (1995) collected and categorized accounts of 15 abusive males to understand violence between spouses and to design effective treatment programs for them.
10. Vangelisti (1994a) studied marital and relational counselors and found that many focus on individual, rather than interpersonal and relational, factors when conceiving and treating the cause of communication problems.

---

communication class reenact the 1858 Lincoln/Douglas debate over slavery, and added the voice of the black abolitionist David Walker. The research report documents how this public speaking exercise transformed the class into a workshop for democracy, teaching these students/prisoners and invited guests—guards, administrators, other prisoners, and members of the press—about the complicated systems that then supported and contested slavery, many of which still exist today in the fight for racial equality and social justice. As Hartnett explains, "The debate, therefore, enabled us to stage an empowering *counterpublic,* in which a marginalized and viciously stereotyped group of men were able to construct the shape and texture of their own voices while engaging in thoughtful, serious political debate" (p. 237). As L. R. Frey, Pearce, Pollock, Artz, and Murphy (1996) contend, these and other communication scholars (see, for example, Artz, 1998; Crabtree, 1998; T. S. Jones &

Bodtker, 1998; Ryan, Carragee, & Schwerner, 1998; Varallo, Ray, & Ellis, 1998) "have channeled their energies and resources toward challenging the norms, practices, relations, and structures that underwrite inequality and injustice" (p. 110).

An Integrated Model of Basic and Applied Communication Research

Although there are some important differences between basic and applied communication research (see Figure 2.6), these should not be treated as unrelated endeavors. Theory and practice are inherently intertwined. K. Lewin (1951) argued that "there is nothing so practical as a good theory" (p. 169), and Levy-Leboyer (1988) later added that "there is nothing so theoretical as a good application" (p. 785). "Theory and practice," Boyer (1990) concluded, "vitally interact, and one renews the other" (p. 23).

The interrelationship of theory and application is especially important in a "practical discipline" such as communication that has enormous potential to make a difference in people's lives (see R. T. Craig, 1989, 1995; R. T. Craig & Tracy, 1995). As Craig (1995) claims, "All research in a practical discipline is ultimately pursued not for its own sake but for the sake of practice" (p. 151). Moreover, a practical field is inherently theoretical. Wood (1995) contends that there is a dynamic interplay between theory and practice that characterizes what is typically called "applied" communication research: "Applied communication research is practicing theory and theorizing practice" (p. 157). Hence, any strict distinction between "basic" and "applied" communication research, according to G. R. Miller (1995), is "more an intellectual and professional liability than an asset" (p. 49).

FIGURE 2.6 Some differences between basic and applied communication research

DEFINING CHARACTERISTIC	BASIC COMMUNICATION RESEARCH	APPLIED COMMUNICATION RESEARCH
Nature of the problem	Seeks to establish general principles about communication.	Seeks to understand an important communication problem.
Goals of the research	To produce theoretical principles that simplify and explain apparently complex or related communication processes.	To provide knowledge that can be immediately useful to a policymaker who seeks to eliminate or alleviate a communication problem.
Guiding theory	Other scholars' theoretical perspectives.	Any idea, including lay theories or other scholars' theoretical perspectives, that holds promise of changing an unsatisfying situation into a more desirable one.
Appropriate techniques	Theory formulation, hypothesis testing, sampling, data collection techniques (direct observation, interview, questionnaire, scale measurement), statistical treatment of data, validation or rejection of hypothesis.	Observe or ask actors about events leading up to current situation; trial and evaluation of proposed solution.

Source: Adapted from Miller, D. C., *Handbook of research design and social measurement*, p. 4, copyright © 1991 by Sage Publications, Inc. Adapted by Permission of Sage Publications, Inc.

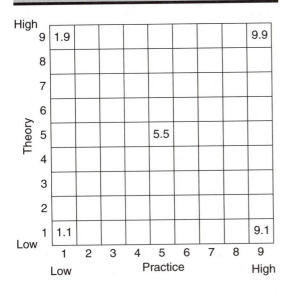

FIGURE 2.7   Basic/Applied Research Grid

Source: Gary L. Kreps, Lawrence R. Frey, and Dan O'Hair, "Applied Communication Research: Scholarship That Can Make a Difference," *Journal of Applied Communication Research,* 19(1/2), p. 74. Copyright © 1991 by National Communication Association. Reproduced by permission of the publisher.

Kreps, Frey, and O'Hair (1991) advanced a conceptual model that integrates concerns for theory with concerns for practice (see Figure 2.7). This model employs two axes: one axis describes the relative emphasis of a particular study on theory and the other axis references the relative emphasis on application/practice.

This model is useful for assessing the potential benefits of research studies. A study low on both theory and application (1/1) is rarely worth doing. For example, many scholars bemoan what they call "variable-analytic research," in which aspects of a communication process are related for no apparent purpose, not because they can potentially advance theory or solve a real-world problem. It might be easy and fun to study whether people born under different astrological signs speak faster or use longer sentences, but this find-ing would have little theoretical or pragmatic significance. (When lots of variables are studied for no apparent reason, this is called a "shotgun approach," because a researcher essentially aims a gun, metaphorically speaking, in a general direction and hopes to hit something.)

A study may have relatively high theoretical interest but little apparent practical application (1/9), at least in the short run. For many years, former U.S. Senator William Proxmire of Wisconsin presented a dubious achievement award called the "Golden Fleece" to what he thought were wasteful federally funded research projects. Senator Proxmire may have had good intentions, but he seemed to assume that the only standard for evaluating research was obvious and immediate economic or practical value. However, theoretical research often concerns phenomena that do not seem immediately relevant to the citizens funding it with their tax dollars. In fact, the more developed a science is, the less laypersons can judge what will eventually be important if it is pursued. We must, therefore, be very careful about dismissing this type of research, because sometimes practical benefits are not immediately apparent. For example, it may seem frivolous to fund a study of conflict styles based on how people compete in a table game, such as the Prisoner's Dilemma, "a mixed-motive game or simulation which forces two sets of players to make a choice in a situation where the outcome or payoff is a function of the interaction between the decisions of the players" (Ashmore, 1987, p. 117). But if the styles identified in that study are later used in another study to reveal how the arguments of couples who get a divorce differ from the arguments of couples whose marriages last, or how the arguments evidenced in successful organizational work teams differ from those in teams in organizations that go bankrupt, the first study proves to have practical value after all.

A study rated high on applied value but low on theory (9/1) is one in which the research solves an important problem in a particular context, but the findings can't be generalized to other contexts (see Chapter 5). For example, say a communication consultant is called in to study a problem of information flow in a company. After conducting extensive research in that organization, the consultant finds that the problem is due to a particular individual and recommends that this individual be fired. In this instance, the company gained valuable information and solved its problem, but that single case does not appear to yield a generalization that can be applied in any other context.

Many studies fall between the extremes, of course (5/5 studies, for example), but communication scholars should aim to do research that has high concern/potential for both theory and practice (9/9). Many 9/9 communication research studies have been done. For example, K. Miller, Birkholt, Scott, and Stage (1995) studied the relationship between emotional communication and job burnout for human service workers. Their study of workers who provide services to the homeless extends the Empathetic Communication Model of Burnout (see K. I. Miller, Stiff, & Ellis, 1988), which explains how different types of empathy are related to communicative effectiveness and subsequent burnout. Their 1995 study includes three important concepts not discussed in the original theory/ model: job involvement, organizational role, and attitude regarding service recipients. This study, thus, not only provided support for a modified version of this model, but offered a more full understanding of, and ways of managing, emotional communication—an important cause of burnout, which is a significant problem for many human service workers.

JUSTIFYING COMMUNICATION RESEARCH TOPICS

R. K. Tucker, Weaver, and Berryman-Fink (1981) argue that all researchers should be prepared to answer the questions: "So what?" and "Who cares?" Researchers, therefore, must develop a clear rationale for why their research topic is worth studying.

We have said that the best topics have the potential to both extend theory and help solve important social problems. Research should, thus, contribute to the "conversation" between those who conduct research and those who might use their research findings. In that light, research can be addressed to three primary audiences, each of which has slightly different needs: scholars, practitioners, and the general public.

A research project is important to communication scholars when it investigates an important communication phenomenon/problem, extends previous research by providing a more complete understanding of that phenomenon/problem, tests and refines theory, and suggests directions for future research. A communication research project valuable to scholars contributes to a better understanding of the significance of previous investigations and suggests directions for subsequent research endeavors.

A second audience is practitioners who apply the knowledge that scholars produce. Practitioners include educators who translate research findings for students, communication consultants who help organizations solve communication problems, counselors who help couples communicate better, and executives who produce television shows. The best practitioners who use communication to carry out their work try to keep informed about the latest research so that their practice is up-to-date. They value communication research projects that help them do their job better.

A third audience is the general public, nonprofessionals who want to know what messages will help them handle their everyday communication challenges better. Occasionally, books about "how to communicate better with your partner" or "how to dress for success," which essentially translate communication-related research findings into easily understood prescriptions (although some don't seem to rely on research at all), have become best-sellers. A communication research project, therefore, is important to the members of the general public to the extent that it helps them live a more fulfilling life.

Some communication research has utility for all three audiences. For example, studying the effects of media violence on children potentially benefits all three audiences. This type of research has a long history, dating back to the 1920s (see Gunter, 1994) and has contributed substantially to theories about relationships between messages and behavior. Understanding these effects is also important to practitioners, such as producers of television shows (e.g., the recent decision by television executives to increase the number of hours per week devoted to nonviolent, family-oriented shows) and doctors who treat aggressive children (the American Medical Association recently issued guidelines about counteracting such effects). And, of course, such effects are important to parents concerned about their children's television-viewing habits. Thus, while any particular research study may benefit some audience(s) more than others, the best communication research potentially benefits all three audiences.

RESEARCH QUESTIONS AND HYPOTHESES

In research articles, researchers first explain why they chose their topic, review the relevant literature (see Chapter 3), and then they articulate the research question or statement that guided their investigation. These questions and/or statements usually are designed to accomplish one of two goals: (a) to describe communication behavior, or (b) to relate communication behavior to other variables.

Describing Communication Behavior

One important purpose of communication research is to describe the nature and characteristics of a particular communication behavior or sequence of communication behaviors. A **research question,** a formal question posed to guide research, of this type essentially asks, "What is the nature of communication behavior 'X'?" For example, consider the following research questions that scholars have asked about communication behavior:

RQ: What receiver behaviors trigger perceived suspicion? (J. K. Burgoon, Buller, Dillman, & Walther, 1995)

RQ: What topics do recipients report being teased about? (Alberts, Kellar-Guenther, & Corman, 1997)

RQ: What are the types of interpersonal rituals reported in friendships and marital relationships? (Bruess & Pearson, 1997)

RQ: What supervisor communication occurs during the dismissal process? (Cox & Kramer, 1995)

RQ: What is the structure of memorable support and nonsupport messages? (L. A. Ford & Ellis, 1998)

RQ: How do able-bodied instructors communicate with students with disabilities? (R. D. Hart & Williams, 1995)

RQ: What are the rules those sexually abused report using to disclose about this crime? (Petronio, Reeder, Hecht, & Ros-Mendoza, 1996)

RQ: What do the emotional experiences of 911 call-takers and citizens look like? (Tracy & Tracy, 1998)

RQ: What are adolescents' motivations for viewing graphic horror? (Johnston, 1995)

RQ: What is the global structure of international news flow? (K. Kim & Barnett, 1996)

These questions are descriptive—much like the who, what, where, when, and why questions journalists ask when covering a news story. But these questions also do something very important: They attempt to categorize a concept and, thereby, measure it and turn it into a variable (see Chapter 4 for a fuller discussion of measurement). A **variable** is any concept that can have two or more values. A single object, therefore, is not a variable; it becomes a variable only when it exists in different types or in different amounts and we understand those different states. A particular make of car, such as a Honda, would not be a variable if all Hondas were identical or we didn't know how to differentiate them. Once we learn that Hondas are divided into such categories as "Accord," "Prelude," and "Civic," we are talking about "types of Hondas," which can be a variable.

To illustrate the process of turning a communication behavior into a variable, take the research question posed by Cox and Kramer (1995) about supervisor communication during the dismissal process. Before they did this study, supervisor communication during this process was talked about as a global, single concept. To turn it into a variable, the researchers asked managers what they said during termination meetings with employees. They discovered that supervisors engaged in a number of specific communication behaviors, such as asking employees about their performance or conduct, explaining the problem and/or reviewing the documentation, and offering some assistance or advice to the dismissed employee. With this information, we can study more precisely how particular behaviors affect the outcome of the process. Therefore, these categories show how supervisor communication behavior during the dismissal process varies in meaningful ways. Describing communication behavior by showing how it varies by type or amount and, thereby, turning concepts into variables, is, thus, important research.

Relating Communication Behavior to Other Variables

Turning a communication concept into a variable makes it possible to examine the relationship between that communication behavior/variable and other important variables. Researchers can answer specific instances of the general research question, "How is communication variable 'X' related to other variables?" Consider, for example, the following research questions:

RQ: Is affective orientation related to the reported use of specific types of nonverbal comforting behaviors? (Bullis & Horn, 1995)

RQ: Is the sex of the siblings related to the amount of verbally aggressive messages? (Teven, Martin, & Newpauer, 1998)

RQ: Are there associations between a woman's surname and men's and women's perceptions of a woman's commitment to the relationship or love for her partner? (Stafford & Kline, 1996)

RQ: What role will gender and psychological type play in conflict style preference for experi-

enced managers? (Sorenson, Hawkins, & Sorenson, 1995)

RQ: To what extent is perceived nonverbal immediacy of teachers related to the students' evaluations of those behaviors? (McCroskey, Richmond, Sallinen, Fayer, & Barraclough, 1995)

RQ: To what degree do international students' frequency of interaction with American students and lengths of time in the United States, the local community, and attending the university increase their perceptions of adaptation to American culture? (S. Zimmermann, 1995)

RQ: How does technology affect the interactions in the classroom? (McHenry & Bozik, 1995)

Each of these questions asks about the relationship between a communication behavior that varies in measurable ways (e.g., nonverbal comforting behavior, verbally aggressive messages, etc.) and other variables.

To understand more fully how scholars pose research questions involving relationships between variables, we must make several more distinctions between: (a) independent and dependent variables, (b) ordered and nominal variables, and (c) research questions and hypotheses.

Independent versus Dependent Variables. When researchers study how two variables are related, they often assume that one of them influences the other. They call the variable that is thought to influence changes in another variable an **independent variable (IV)** (sometimes called an **explanatory variable;** in nonexperimental research, a **predictor variable**). They call the variable thought to be changed by another variable a **dependent variable (DV)** (in nonexperimental research, sometimes called the **criterion variable** or **outcome variable**), because changes in it are dependent on changes in the other variable. For example, in the hypothesis, "If you say 'please,' people are more likely to do what you ask," "saying please" is the independent variable and "people doing what you ask" is the dependent variable. These labels distinguish variables that are thought to influence other variables (independent variables) from variables thought to be influenced by other variables (dependent variables).

Sometimes researchers suspect a **causal relationship** between variables, believing that changes in the independent variable *cause* observed changes in the dependent variable. For example, many researchers believe that smoking cigarettes (the independent variable) causes cancer (the dependent variable). Researchers sometimes study independent variables that are not about messages, but are thought to influence people's communication behavior. For example, the attractiveness of people's appearance may influence how others talk to them, television or radio may influence the comments political candidates make, and newspaper editorials about the bombings of Iraq may be different depending on whether the editorial is published in a United States or Middle Eastern newspaper. These suspected relationships focus on how independent variables (such as the person, channel, and context variables discussed earlier in this chapter) that precede, or exist prior to, communication (called *input variables*) cause changes in a dependent variable that concerns some aspect of communication behavior.

Communication behavior, of course, can also be studied as an independent variable that causes changes in a dependent variable. For example, researchers may suspect that certain messages designed to get other people to comply with a request may actually cause people to *resist* doing what was asked rather than agreeing to it. Researchers may also believe that exposure to violent television messages causes children to tolerate violence on their playgrounds. In such instances, communication is the independent variable that is thought to cause changes in the dependent, or *outcome,* variable.

It should be pointed out that causality is very difficult to establish. We would not want to conclude that a drug cured a disease on the basis of a single study, or two or three, and the same is true when attempting to establish causal principles for communication behavior (see Chapter 5 regarding

the replication of studies). Careful design of studies that yield ample evidence must be obtained before a causal relationship between variables can be inferred. We will examine how to design such studies in Chapter 7 when we explore experimental research.

There are also various models of causal relationships between variables. For example, in some models of causality, called **recursive causal models,** the causal relationship is one way—one variable influences another but not the other way around, that is, one is the cause and the other is the effect. For example, age may influence the amount that people self-disclose about themselves, but self-disclosure can't influence people's age. In other models, called **nonrecursive causal models,** the causal relationship is reciprocal or two way, in that a variable can be both a cause and an effect. For example, studying may lead to better grades, but better grades may well make it more likely that a person studies.

At other times, researchers assume a **noncausal relationship** between variables, meaning that the variables are associated, or occur together, without one necessarily causing changes in the other. A study may discover, for example, that people like people they know more about; that is, self-disclosure and liking are related. But the causal relationship may well remain a chicken-and-egg question. Changes in self-disclosure *may* cause changes in liking and not the other way around, but it could just as easily be that changes in liking cause changes in self-disclosure and not the other way around. Of course, it could also be a nonrecursive causal model, with one variable causing changes in the other that then lead to changes in the first variable. In cases where a relationship between two variables is suspected, but it is not clear which is the cause and which is the effect, a noncausal relationship is assumed.

When posing formal research questions for a study that assesses noncausal relationships, researchers typically designate one variable as the independent variable and the other as the dependent variable, depending on their primary interest. For example, if they are most interested in how changes in self-disclosure relate to changes in liking, then they should designate self-disclosure as the independent variable and liking as the dependent variable. If they think changes in liking are related to changes in self-disclosure, then liking would be viewed as the independent variable and self-disclosure would be the dependent variable.

Ordered versus Nominal Variables.   Variables can also be differentiated with regard to the values researchers assign to them or the kind of "scale" used to measure them (see Chapter 4). **Ordered variables** can be assigned numerical values that indicate how much of the concept is present. Variables such as age, weight, temperature, and income are ordered variables. Being 10 years old, for example, is less than being 20 years old, which is less than being 30 years old, and so forth. We can measure how much older or younger one person is than another. The numerical value, in this case, indicates how much age a person possesses, so age is an ordered variable.

Nominal variables (also called **categorical, classificatory,** or **discrete variables**), by contrast, can be differentiated only on the basis of type (nominal means "in name only"). Variables such as gender (male and female), race (e.g., Caucasian, African American, Hispanic, and Native American), and political affiliation (e.g., Democrat, Republican, and Independent) are nominal variables since they identify different types. No meaningful quantities can be assigned to the categories of a nominal variable. Although numbers are sometimes used to represent nominal categories, for example, we can call males "1" and females "2," we don't mean that females have twice as much of something as males. (A nominal variable such as gender that can only be divided into two categories is called a **dichotomous** or **binomial variable;** if there are more than two categories, such as the many categories used to reference ethnicity, it is called a **polytomous variable.**) License plates are another good example. If you have license plate F1000 and your friend has license plate F3000,

that doesn't mean your friend has more license plate than you! Nominal variables, therefore, indicate what something is or whether an attribute is present or absent, not how *much* of a concept is present.

In some cases, a potentially ordered variable is treated as a nominal variable. Instead of being measured on an ordered scale, it is divided into categories along an ascending or descending range (such as low, medium, or high on communication apprehension). One can easily transform any ordered variable into a nominal variable. We could, for example, say that temperatures of 50 degrees or above constitute warm weather whereas temperatures below 50 degrees constitute cool weather. (An ordered variable that is divided into two categories like this is called a **dichotomized variable.**) But note how much information we have lost in the process. There is, after all, a big difference between 50 degrees and 120 degrees, but both get classified as warm weather in this particular example. Because of this loss of important information, researchers typically don't turn ordered variables into nominal variables.

It is also sometimes possible to turn a nominal variable into an ordered variable. Bem (1979), for example, studied gender as an ordered variable by using numerical values to measure the psychological orientations of men and women regarding traditionally feminine and masculine traits, which she called "psychological gender orientation." Her research participants indicated on a 5-point ordered scale their agreement with many statements representing these male-associated/female-associated traits and were then given a total score for each type of trait. An imbalance of male and female traits signifies whether one has a traditionally male or traditionally female psychological gender orientation; if the scores are relatively equal, people are considered androgynous in their psychological gender orientation. In contrast, biological gender can only be treated as a nominal variable.

Research Questions versus Hypotheses.   Research studies usually are designed to answer research questions or test hypotheses about relationships between variables. Questions typically are posed when researchers don't have enough evidence, on the basis of the literature reviewed (see Chapter 3), to predict the nature of that relationship. They may, for example, be studying variables that haven't been related before. Therefore, they have little information on which to base a claim about the nature of the relationship. It might also be the case that the literature has revealed conflicting evidence, with some studies showing a relationship between two (or more) variables and others showing no relationship. In such cases, researchers typically pose a research question about the relationship between the variables.

At other times, however, researchers have a hunch or tentative answer about the nature of the relationship between an independent and dependent variable. This tentative answer usually is derived from a theory or from the available body of literature about the variables, and sometimes from logic and/or observations of how the variables interact in everyday life.

When researchers feel confident enough to make a prediction, they advance a **hypothesis** (H_a is the general symbol for a research hypothesis; H_1 is used to refer to a specific research hypothesis), a tentative statement about the relationship between the independent and dependent variables. It may simply predict a relationship between variables without specifying the nature of that relationship, called a **two-tailed hypothesis** (sometimes called a **two-direction hypothesis** or, less accurately, a **nondirectional hypothesis**), or it may predict the specific nature of the relationship, called a **one-tailed hypothesis** (sometimes called a **directional hypothesis**) (see Chapter 12).

Posing Research Questions and Hypotheses about Relationships between Variables. How the research question or hypothesis for a communication study is phrased usually depends on two things: (a) whether the independent variable is nominal or ordered, and (b) whether a researcher wishes to pose a research question or a hypothesis

about the relationship between the independent and dependent variables. We will use two hypothetical examples—the effects of gender on self-disclosure and the effects of age on self-disclosure—to explain the general form that research questions and hypotheses take (see Figure 2.8), and along the way, we will take a look at some actual examples as well.

When the independent variable is *nominal,* divided into categories, the research question asks whether there is a *difference* between *a* (the first category of the nominal independent variable) and *b* (the second category of the nominal independent variable) with respect to *c* (the dependent variable). For example, in studying the effects of gender (the independent variable) on self-disclosure (the dependent variable), the research question asks whether there is a difference between males (*a,* the first category of the nominal variable) and females (*b,* the second category of the nominal variable) with regard to self-disclosure (*c,* the dependent variable).

What we just described is a template for how researchers pose a research question when the independent variable is nominal. In actual practice, this form may differ slightly, as the following research questions from actual studies show:

RQ: Will females provide more sensitive comforting messages than males? (Hoffner & Haefner, 1997)

RQ: How do doctors and patients differ in their covert responses during the medical interview? (Cegala, McNeilis, McGee, & Jonas, 1995)

RQ: Do program enrollees and nonenrollees [in a Breast and Cervical Cancer Control Program] differ in their preference for persuasive messages delivered through mass media, one-to-several interpersonal channels, or one-to-one interpersonal channels? (A. A. Marshall, Smith, & McKeon, 1995)

RQ: Do individuals exhibiting high, moderate, and low Adventurousness, Impulsiveness, and Disinhibition, respectively, differ in reported condom use behavior? (Sheer & Cline, 1995)

FIGURE 2.8   Research questions and hypotheses for nominal and ordered independent variables

NOMINAL INDEPENDENT VARIABLE

A. Research Question

  1. Form

  RQ: Is there a difference between *a* (the first category of the independent variable) and *b* (the second category of the independent variable) with respect to *c* (the dependent variable)?

  2. Example: Effects of Gender on Self-disclosure (*a* = Males; *b* = Females; *c* = Self-disclosure)

  RQ: Is there a difference between males and females with respect to self-disclosure?

B. Hypothesis (One-Tailed)

  1. Forms

  H: *A* (the first category of the independent variable) is greater on *c* (the dependent variable) than *b* (the second category of the independent variable).

or

  H: *A* (the first category of the independent variable) is lower on *c* (the dependent variable) than *b* (the second category of the independent variable).

  2. Examples: Effects of Gender on Self-disclosure (*a* = Males; *b* = Females; *c* = Self-disclosure)

  H: Males self-disclose more than females.

or

  H: Males self-disclose less than females.

ORDERED INDEPENDENT VARIABLE

A. Research Question

  1. Form

  RQ: Is there a relationship between *x* (the independent variable) and *y* (the dependent variable)?

  2. Example: Effects of Age on Self-disclosure (*x* = Age; *y* = Self-disclosure)

  RQ: Is there a relationship between age and self-disclosure?

B. Hypothesis (One-Tailed)

  1. Forms

  H: There is a positive relationship between *x* (the independent variable) and *y* (the dependent variable).

or

  H: There is a negative relationship between *x* (the independent variable) and *y* (the dependent variable).

  2. Examples: Effects of Age on Self-Disclosure (*x* = Age; *y* = Self-disclosure)

  H: There is a positive relationship between age and self-disclosure.

or

  H: There is a negative relationship between age and self-disclosure.

RQ: Compared to Caucasian students will Native American students perceive their teachers to have less communication competence? (Bolls, Tan, & Austin, 1997).

A hypothesis for a nominal independent variable predicts the nature of the difference between the two (or more) categories of the independent variable. It takes the form: *a* (the first category of the nominal independent variable) will be greater (or less) on *c* (the dependent variable) than will *b* (the second category of the nominal independent

variable). Regarding the effects of gender on self-disclosure, the hypothesis might state that "Men self-disclose more than women" (or "Men self-disclose less than women"). (Note: Like most research hypotheses, this statement is one-tailed; a two-tailed hypothesis would state: "Men and women self-disclose differently." A difference is still predicted, but investigators are unsure of its direction or location.)

In actual practice, this form varies somewhat. The following hypotheses provide illustrations of its use:

H: Women report more than men that verbal interactions contribute to their relational closeness. (Floyd & Parks, 1995)

H: Employees provided with justifications will perceive the manager's actions as fairer than employees provided with excuses or no social accounts. (Tata, 1996)

H: Older people will evaluate their communication with young family adults more positively than young people in general. (Cai, Giles, & Noels, 1998)

H: Concrete news items will have better recall than abstract news items. (David, 1998)

H: Group members from individualistic cultures will initiate more conflicts than group members from collectivist cultures. (Oetzel, 1998)

When the independent variable is *ordered,* measured in sequenced numbers, the research question asks whether there is a *relationship* between *x* (the independent variable) and *y* (the dependent variable). Say we want to know how age (*x,* the independent variable) affects self-disclosure (*y,* the dependent variable). Because age is an ordered variable, the research question asks whether there is a relationship between the variables of age and self-disclosure.

In actual practice, of course, this basic template is varied quite a bit, as the following research questions reveal:

RQ: How are proportions of argument complexity associated with perceptions of communication satisfaction? (Canary, Brossman, Brossman, & Weger, 1995)

RQ: What is the association between leadership evaluations and specific types of leadership-relevant talk? (Pavitt, Whitchurch, McClurg, & Petersen, 1995)

RQ: What is the relationship between perpetrator message affect and negotiator affect behavior? (Rogan & Hammer, 1995)

RQ: What is the relationship of patients' perceptions of physician communicator styles to patient satisfaction? (Cardello, Ray, & Pettey, 1995)

RQ: Is there a relationship between the length of the answering machine message and the caller's message? (Buzzanell, Burrell, Stafford, & Berkowitz, 1997)

Finally, a hypothesis for an ordered independent variable specifies the nature of the relationship between the independent and dependent variable. While independent and dependent variables may be related in quite a few ways (see Chapter 14), we focus here on two types of relationships: (a) a **positive relationship** (also called **direct relationship**), in which increases in an independent variable are associated with increases in a dependent variable (e.g., the more hours one spends studying before an exam, the higher one's exam scores will be); or (b) a **negative relationship** (also called **inverse relationship**), in which increases in an independent variable are associated with decreases in a dependent variable (e.g., the more hours one spends "partying" the night before an exam, the lower one's exam scores will be). A hypothesis, thus, takes the form: *x* (the independent variable) is positively (or negatively) related to *y* (the dependent variable). For the effects of age on self-disclosure, the hypothesis might be either "Age is positively related to self-disclosure" or "Age is negatively related to self-disclosure." (A two-tailed hypothesis would simply state: "Age and self-disclosure are related.")

Once more, as actual examples of research hypotheses show, this format is sometimes changed slightly:

H: Cognitive efficiency will be positively related to interaction involvement (Jordan, 1998)

H: Increases in the amount of gaze, smiles, head nods, and forward lean will be positively correlated with increases in amount of liking toward the actor. (Palmer & Simmons, 1995)

H: Frequent viewing of nonviolent children's programs leads over time to an increase in children's positive-intense daydreaming. (Valkenburg & van der Voort, 1995)

H: Electronic mail usefulness perceptions will be positively related to frequency of media use. (Fulk, Schmitz, & Ryu, 1995)

H: A positive relationship exists between students' reports of teacher content relevant communication and students' stated motivation to study. (Frymier & Shulman, 1995)

You now have the basic form for posing formal research questions and hypotheses. Before leaving this discussion, however, let us point out two things. First, some independent variables are obviously nominal or ordered, such as the variables of gender and age used above, but others can be treated as either nominal or ordered. For example, are intelligence, self-esteem, and communication apprehension nominal or ordered variables? They could be either, depending on how they are defined and measured. As a general rule, if a variable can be measured either way, it should be treated as ordered and a scale should be used to measure it. As we discussed previously, meaningful numbers give us more information than general categories.

The examples given so far also only refer to one independent and one dependent variable. Researchers, however, are often interested in the effects of *multiple* independent variables on a dependent variable (and even multiple dependent variables). In such situations, researchers are especially interested in **interaction effects** (also called **conditioning, contingency, joint,** and **moderating effects;** sometimes known as **multiplicative relations** in nonexperimental research)—effects due to the unique combinations of the independent variables that make a difference on the dependent variable(s). Interaction effects are due to the effects of multiple independent variables working together, in contrast to the effects of each independent variable working alone (called **main effects**) that we focused on before. For example, people lose weight by dieting (a main effect) and they also lose weight by exercising (another main effect), but when people both diet and exercise, they lose the most weight. The effects due to the combination of dieting and exercising are an example of an interaction effect.

As we will see later in this text, many communication researchers study interaction effects to capture the complex ways in which variables are related. For now, just be aware that some research questions and hypotheses ask about or predict interaction effects. Here are some examples:

RQ: Do argumentativeness and verbal aggression interact to predict an individual's reported use of evidentiary appeals to respond to refusal of a request? (Ifert & Bearden, 1998)

RQ: What are the differences, if any, between the expressed attributions put forth by adolescents and those put forth by young adults in (a) success situations and (b) failure situations? (Roghaar & Vangelisti, 1996)

RQ: What are the effects of sex of subject, sex of partner, and the interaction of sex of subject and partner on the following 11 verbal communication behaviors: number of words spoken, vocalized pauses, verbal fillers, interruptions, overlaps, justifiers, intensifiers, qualifiers, questions, tag questions, and agreement? (Turner, Dindia, & Pearson, 1995)

RQ: Does vividness interact with story or statistical evidence to produce a more persuasive type of evidence? (Baesler & Burgoon, 1994)

H: The combination of interpersonal communication apprehension and receiver apprehension is more strongly associated with sexual communication satisfaction for women than men in sexually intimate, heterosexual relationships. (Wheeless & Parsons, 1995)

H: There will be an interaction between the biological sex of the introducer of an item of information and the level of redundancy of that item of information in its usage. (Propp, 1995)

H: There will be an ordinal interaction between efficacy expectations and relational commitment such that the relationship between efficacy expectations and relational satisfaction will be of greater magnitude at high rather than low levels of relational commitment. (Makoul & Roloff, 1998)

H: There will be an interaction between conflict situation and nationality such that Japanese subjects will equivocate more in avoidance–avoidance conflict situations, relative to non-conflict situations, than will American subjects. (Tanaka & Bell, 1996)

CONCLUSION

Communication scholars study varied and complex phenomena. There is still much we don't know about communication behavior. The first step researchers take is making sure they select a topic appropriate for communication research. Through careful consideration, they narrow their focus from a general topic to a specific research question or hypothesis.

But researchers don't work without guides. Throughout the process of narrowing their focus, researchers consult what their colleagues in the field have reported in the research literature. To learn what else is known about the topic, they need to know where to find and how to read relevant publications. We explain how they do this in Chapter 3.

CHAPTER 3

FINDING, READING,
AND USING RESEARCH

Doing good research requires being able to get the information we need, when we need it, and being able to understand and use it. Most readers of this textbook are probably already comfortable working on a computer, getting information off CD-ROMs or through the Internet. In fact, it's not uncommon for readers like you to be much more at home in the age of electronic information than many of your teachers or textbook authors. One of the authors of this text spent his early childhood in the backwoods of Canada. There were no electric lights in the house until he was 6, the only radio was powered by a car battery that had to be recharged by running a gasoline engine, and television didn't come to his house until his teenage years (and then it had only one channel). Imagine the difficulty he had at first learning the new electronic forms of communication and information acquisition.

Your comparatively greater skill in handling information is a result of being the first true generation of the Information Age. Hence, you undoubtedly already have some skills in acquiring and understanding information. Therefore, we will assume a certain familiarity with various popular sources of information, and focus attention in this chapter on how the information needed for good research differs from other kinds of information with which you are already familiar, as well as how to find, understand, and use this research-relevant information. The information of which we are speaking, which should come as no big surprise, is previous research studies. We'll start by exploring some reasons for reviewing previous research and then examine in some detail the search for research.

REASONS FOR REVIEWING
PREVIOUS RESEARCH

Researchers don't work in a vacuum; their research is a result of previous work done on a topic. A researcher may start, for example, with the tentative idea of studying the difference between using promises and threats to gain compliance, but this idea didn't just appear out of thin air. Compliance-gaining strategies, including promises and threats, have been researched before. Thus, after coming up with a tentative idea, the next step a researcher takes is to review the relevant literature about it.

Knowing what others have done and found helps to avoid "reinventing the wheel." This is true whether one is conducting scholarly research (public knowledge) or proprietary research (research for a private company or organization; see Chapter 1). If, for instance, as a communication expert, you are asked by your boss to conduct a survey of employees regarding their perceptions of the flow of information within the organization, it makes sense to start by looking at what other organizational communication researchers have studied about information flow. Your employer is likely to be quite upset if you use many thousands of dollars to conduct a survey that yields poor information because the relevant literature wasn't consulted and, therefore, the right questions weren't asked.

Even those who don't conduct research per se often need to know what the findings from relevant research show. Suppose an organization is considering implementing a total quality management (TQM) program, a popular management philosophy and practice—affecting 180,000 participants across a wide variety of industries in the United

States (Fairhurst, 1993)—that focuses on customer satisfaction, employee fulfillment, visionary leadership, process management, and continual improvement (see M. W. Allen & Brady, 1997; J. C. Anderson, Rungtusanatham, & Schroeder, 1994; Dean & Bowen, 1994). Before implementing it, decision makers would want to see what the research shows about the effects of TQM, or other programs like it, on such outcomes as worker satisfaction and productivity. They aren't going to adopt the program without some assurance that it works.

Competent consumers also find that reviewing relevant research proves quite helpful. Prior to buying items, especially major purchases, many people consult the popular magazine *Consumer Reports,* which conducts research on consumer products.

Regardless of the communication topic of interest, it's likely that there is some relevant research that has been conducted in the past. In fact, as you pore through research reports and see the references contained within, you're likely to be amazed at the breadth and variety of topics communication scholars explore.

Even for brand new topics that have not been studied before, researchers still consult the literature, searching for sources that can help them to understand the new topic. Botan (1996), for example, was interested in the effects of electronic surveillance on workplace communication. Given that an estimated 26 million workers in the United States are electronically monitored by organizations (Alder & Tompkins, 1997), and that number is growing every day, this is clearly an important topic. But it is such a new topic that there isn't much, if any, published research on it. To provide some frameworks for understanding electronic surveillance, Botan used English philosopher Jeremy Bentham's (1995) notion of the *panopticon* (a prison, workhouse, school, or medical facility in which cell occupants are always exposed to observation, isolated from each other, and unable to know whether they are being observed); French philosopher Michael Foucault's (1977) work on the effects of the panopticon in prisons; and Social Power Theory, which focuses on various types of power, such as reward

and coercive power (see French & Raven, 1959). None of this work actually addressed electronic communication or even workplaces, but Botan drew on it to propose an electronic panopticon metaphor to explain surveillance technology in the workplace. He then surveyed workers to assess the effects of such surveillance. Reviewing previous research, thus, helps scholars discover conceptual and theoretical underpinnings for the new topic(s) they investigate.

Reviewing previous research is bound to shape a new study in a number of ways. The purpose of one's study may be affected. Researchers start with a tentative idea, but as they explore the relevant literature, they discover not only what has been done, but also what has not been done and what might be worth doing. Scholarly studies typically end with suggestions for future research (see the discussion later in this chapter and in Chapter 15); a researcher may adopt one of them and, thereby, extend that work in a very direct way.

Previous research invariably is used to provide support for, or shape, the formal research question or hypothesis posed. Teven and McCroskey (1997), for example, were interested in the effects of perceived teacher caring on students' learning and teacher evaluations. Their review of traditional rhetorical theory, as well as contemporary social-scientific research findings, showed that perceived ethos (source credibility) was associated with other positive attitudes toward a source. Because they viewed "perceived caring" as similar to the theoretical dimension of ethos/source credibility called "good will" or "intent toward receiver," they argued that previous research supported advancing the hypothesis that "teachers who are perceived as more caring by their students will also be evaluated more positively by their students" (p. 3).

As researchers review relevant literature, they also look at how those studies were conducted, gathering ideas for the design of their own study. They look at how the variables of interest were defined and measured, how the data were collected, and possible ways of analyzing the data.

Prior work, thus, provides the foundation on which researchers build. A metaphor for this is standing on the shoulders of those who have gone before. Building on the knowledge and accomplishments of previous scholars is a crucial part of the research process. Anyone interested in studying communication phenomena, whether as a producer or a consumer, should find out what has already been done and learned about the topic(s) of interest. Of course, this means knowing how to conduct an effective search for the available research.

THE SEARCH FOR RESEARCH

The search for previous research (see Figure 3.1) begins by understanding the types of research reports available and where they can be found. Once they have been found, the information contained within them needs to be understood and evaluated. This requires knowing the standard way in which such information is reported.

Finding, reading, and evaluating research usually leads researchers to rethink and revise the original topic they considered worth studying, and this often makes it necessary to find additional, more focused, research. This cyclical process of finding, reading, and evaluating research enables researchers to select and review the most appropriate research until they are ready to pose a formal research question or hypothesis. At that point, researchers are ready to write a review of the literature. Let's examine this search process in some detail.

Types of Research Reports

We have emphasized the importance of knowing what previous researchers discovered about a topic of interest. There are two general types of reports about previous research: primary and secondary. A **primary research report** is the first reporting of a research study by the person(s) who actually conducted the study. A **secondary research report** is a report of a research study by someone other than the person who conducted the study or a later report by the person who conducted the study that cites or uses the primary report that has already appeared elsewhere.

Secondary Research Reports.   We're starting with secondary research reports because what you know about most topics comes from them; that is, from someone other than the person(s) who actually conducted the study. You undoubtedly know that smoking causes cancer, but how many of the actual research studies about that causal relationship have you read? If you are like most people, the answer is "None." Most of what you know about the findings from this and other research has been learned "second hand," analogous in a way to "second-hand smoke."

Secondary research reports are presented in a variety of forms. Textbooks, like this one, are the main way college students learn about course-relevant research findings. Textbook authors essentially summarize what researchers have found about the topic being covered. Notice, in this textbook, how we walk you through communication research studies, often explaining what the researchers did and found. But we didn't conduct all those studies, and even when we did (such as Botan's, 1996, study discussed earlier), we are explaining a study that has already been reported elsewhere. Hence, the studies you read about in textbooks and any other books that review previously published research are secondary research reports.

Most people's exposure to secondary research reports comes from the mass media— the newspapers and magazines they read, the radio programs they listen to on the way to school or work, the television news programs they watch during dinner, and/or the Internet they surf at night. Media reports frequently reference research studies, such as studies of health published in the *Journal of the American Medical Association* or *New England Journal of Medicine.* These secondary research reports may lead people to start eating a particular food (e.g., the oat bran craze) or avoid another altogether (e.g., the red meat scare).

Secondary research reports are quite adequate most of the time. We simply don't have the time or desire to read the research reports on all the things we hear about from the media, our physicians, teachers, or family and friends.

FIGURE 3.1   The search for research

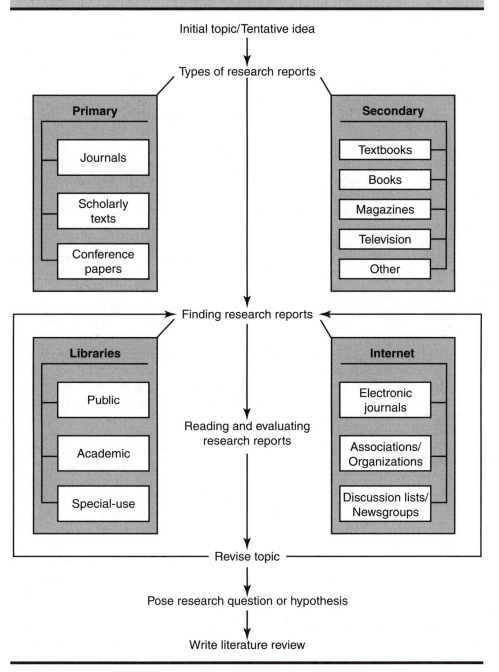

Scholars, too, frequently find secondary research reports helpful. For example, starting in 1996 with Volume 19, the *Communication Yearbook* series, an edited text published annually by the International Communication Association, became exclusively an outlet for state-of-the-art literature reviews. That volume contains reviews, among many others, of the literature on communication and older adults (Nussbaum, Hummert, Williams, & Harwood, 1996), intercultural communication competence (G-M. Chen & Starosta, 1996), and sexual harassment (Keyton, 1996). Scholars studying these areas would want to first read these reviews, for well-written reviews help researchers understand the work done in an area and formulate ideas about what needs to be done, and provide them with valuable reference sources to find and read. As Burleson (1997), editor of Volumes 19 and 20, explained:

> *First and foremost, the good literature review contains a wealth of factual information. That is the primary purpose of a literature review, of course—to synthesize what is known about a particular topic so that it becomes possible to state what is the case and what remains to be determined. Good reviews organize information and answer questions. In so doing, they teach us how to think about an area of study, what questions are important, how those questions can be addressed fruitfully, what we know about a topic, and what we yet need to learn.... These are familiar and important functions of the literature review—but good reviews do even more.*
>
> *Good literature reviews focus on questions of enduring significance and, in so doing, help us refine our sense about those issues that matter and those that do not. (p. ix)*

Primary Research Reports.   Scholars and conscientious individuals, however, aren't content to rely on secondary research reports. They know that such reports, and we're now talking especially about those presented by the media, too often give only a brief overview of a research study, simplify complex findings into a "sound bite," or, worse, report inaccurate findings. Therefore, they read primary research reports—actual studies as reported for the first time by the person(s) who conducted the research. They prefer to get the information straight from the "horse's mouth."

There are three general sources that provide primary research reports: scholarly journals, scholarly texts, and conference papers.

Scholarly Journals.   The most important source for locating primary research reports is a **scholarly journal,** a periodical publication (often called *periodicals* and/or kept in that section of libraries) that prints scholarly essays and research studies. Some journals also have a dialogue section where scholars exchange views on a topic, and some publish book reviews (see Lindholm-Romantschuk, 1998, regarding book reviews as a significant indicator of scholarly communication). While their frequency of publication varies, quarterly publications, with issues published four times a year, are quite common.

Scholarly journals date back to the creation of the *Journal des scavans* in January, 1665, in France, and shortly thereafter, in March, 1665, the *Philosophical Transactions* in England, both regular publications that contained descriptions of research (see Gaines, 1996). Hundreds of scholarly journals flourished during the eighteenth century (Guedon, 1996), and today, there are well over 100,000 scholarly journals around the world, publishing more than six million articles each year (Shermer, 1997). Each academic discipline has many journals devoted to the topics that interest those scholars. Journals are published by the professional associations of each discipline (see Chapter 2) and by independent publishing companies.

The field of communication is no exception; there are a great many journals that report original communication research studies (see Figure 3.2). Some communication journals publish research that cuts across the discipline (such as *Communication Monographs*), whereas others are devoted to particular areas of the discipline (such as *Journal of Broadcasting and Electronic Media*) or topics (such as *Health Communication*).

Communication researchers also frequently find relevant articles in journals from related fields,

FIGURE 3.2   Scholarly communication journals

The following journals frequently publish primary research reports about communication. Name(s) in parentheses are the previous title(s) of the journal.

American Journalism Review
*Argumentation and Advocacy (Journal of the American Forensic Association)
Asian Journal of Communication
Australian Journal of Communication
Canadian Journal of Communication
Columbia Journalism Review
Communication and Cognition
Communication and the Law
*Communication Education (Speech Teacher)
*Communication Monographs (Speech Monographs)
*Communication Quarterly (Today's Speech)
*Communication Reports
*Communication Research
*Communication Research Reports
Communication Review
*Communication Studies (Central States Speech Journal)
*Communication Theory
Convergence: The Journal of Research into New Media Technologies
*Critical Studies in Mass Communication
Discourse & Society
Discourse Processes
European Journal of Communication
Health Communication
*Howard Journal of Communications
*Human Communication Research
Intermedia
International Journal of Listening (Journal of the International Listening Association)
*Journal of Applied Communication Research (Journal of Applied Communications Research)
*Journal of the Association for Communication Administration (Bulletin of the Association for Communication Administration, ACA Bulletin)
*Journal of Broadcasting & Electronic Media (Journal of Broadcasting)
Journal of Business Communication
Journal of Business and Technical Communication
*Journal of Communication
*Journal of Communication and Religion (Religious Communication Today)
Journal of Communication Inquiry
Journal of Development Communication
Journal of Educational Television
Journal of Health Communication
Journal of International Communication

Journal of Language and Social Psychology
Journal of Mass Media Ethics
Journal of Newspaper and Periodical History (Journal of Newspaper History)
Journal of Personal and Social Relations
Journal of Popular Culture
Journal of Public Relations Research
Journal of Radio Studies
Journalism History
Journalism & Mass Communication Educator
Journalism & Mass Communication Quarterly
*Journalism Quarterly
Journalism: Theory, Practice & Criticism
Language & Communication
Management Communication Quarterly
Mass Comm Review
Mass Communication & Society
Media & Methods
Media, Culture, & Society
Media Studies Journal (Gannett Center Journal)
National Forensic Journal
New Media & Society
Newspaper Research Journal
*Philosophy & Rhetoric
Political Communication (Political Communication and Persuasion)
Public Relations Journal
Public Relations Review
*Quarterly Journal of Speech (Quarterly Journal of Public Speaking , Journal of Speech Education)
Research in Language and Social Interaction (Papers in Linguistics)
Rhetoric and Public Affairs
Rhetoric Review
*Southern Communication Journal (Southern Speech Communication Journal, Southern Speech Journal)
Studies in Communication
Technology and Culture
*Text and Performance Quarterly (Literature in Performance)
*Western Journal of Communication (Western Journal of Speech Communication, Western Speech)
*Women's Studies in Communication (ORWAC Bulletin)
World Communication (Communication, The Journal of the Communication Association of the Pacific; Communication)
Written Communication

*Journal included in *CommSearch* (2nd ed.) and Matlon and Ortiz (1997), two reference sources discussed later in this chapter.

such as (in alphabetical order) advertising (e.g., *Journal of Advertising Research*), anthropology (e.g., *Anthropology Quarterly*), business and management (e.g., *Academy of Management Review*), film (e.g., *Film Quarterly*), library and information sciences (e.g., *Information Society*) linguistics (e.g., *Journal of Linguistics*), political science (e.g., *Political Science Quarterly*), psychology (e.g., *Journal of Personality and Social Psychology*), sociology (e.g., *Social Science Quarterly*), and speech and hearing disorders (e.g., *Journal of Speech and Hearing Research*). There are also many interdisciplinary journals that cut across disciplines (e.g., *Public Opinion Quarterly*), some of which publish studies that use a particular methodology (e.g., *Journal of Contemporary Ethnography*), collect certain types of data (e.g., *Qualitative Health Research*), or focus on a specific type of behavior (e.g., *Journal of Nonverbal Behavior*).

The main advantage of scholarly journals is that, unlike some other sources, the importance and accuracy of the reported results have been reviewed by experts in the field before being published. To get an article published in a journal, a scholar submits a manuscript to the journal editor, an appointed position held by a highly respected scholar in the field. On judging the manuscript appropriate for the journal (e.g., the topic or methodology is relevant to the journal's mission), the editor sends it out for review to a panel of experts (other scholars in the field who serve on the editorial board and regularly review manuscripts for the journal or, because of relevant expertise, serve as consulting reviewers for that particular manuscript). Reviewers typically are asked to make a decision about whether to publish the manuscript, rate various aspects of the manuscript (e.g., its quality and contribution to the field), write comments intended for the person(s) who submitted the work, and write comments intended solely for the editor. Reviewers usually make one of four decisions about a manuscript: (a) publish as is, (b) publish with specified minor revisions, (c) revise in line with major suggestions and resubmit it for another round of reviews, or (d) reject it. The majority of manuscripts submitted are rejected; for instance, Eadie (1999)

reported that across the six journals published by the National Communication Association, the mean acceptance rate, calculated on the last completed three-year editorial term for each journal, was 18.3%. One reason for the high rejection rate is the sheer number of manuscripts submitted; Bracey (1987) estimated that a manuscript is submitted to a journal every 30 seconds! And seldom is a manuscript ever accepted without some revision; Chesebro (1993) reported that 95% of manuscripts were revised before being published (see also Knapp & Daly, 1993; Standing Committee on Research, 1993).

This **peer-review** process of having colleagues in a field evaluate manuscripts submitted for publication in scholarly journals became institutionalized in the mid-twentieth century (Burnham, 1990), and today, most scholarly journals use a **blind-review** process, whereby reviewers are not told the name or institutional affiliation of the person(s) who submitted the manuscript. The goal is to judge the work on its merits, not on the reputation or the institutional affiliation of the researcher(s). Choosing competent and conscientious journal reviewers is, of course, key to the review process. In Ziman's (1968) words, the reviewer is the "lynchpin about which the whole business of Science is pivoted" (p. 111).

The peer-review process, thus, tries to ensure that high-quality research is published in scholarly journals. As Thyer (1994) explains, "The peer-review system employed by most journals acts as a brake to the injudicious dissemination of faulty scholarship, at least in the long run" (p. 4).

This is not to say that there aren't problems with the system; there are instances of fraud, plagiarism, misconduct, and other problems in scholarly publications and in the peer-review process itself (see Altman, 1981; Chubin & Hackett, 1990; Cicchetti, 1991; Coughlin, 1989; Eberley & Warner, 1990; LaFollette, 1992; Spencer, Hartnett, & Mahoney, 1985), problems we take up again when we look at research ethics (Chapter 6). And, at a more macro level, there are those who critique the dominant ideologies and disciplinary practices that inform the journal publishing system (as applied to communication journals, see Bach, Blair, Nothstine, & Pym, 1996; Blair, Brown, & Baxter, 1994; Schwartzman, 1997; Swartz, 1997b). However, these important problems and critiques notwithstanding, scholarly journals remain the most important source of primary research reports. As LaFollette (1992) claims, "Journals represent the *principal* means of *formal* communication among scientists and social scientists through which research is made public and through which it is evaluated and authenticated by other experts, before and after publication" (p. 75).

Scholarly Texts.   A second source of primary research reports is a **scholarly text,** a text authored or edited by a scholar that is intended primarily for other scholars to read. Some authored scholarly texts report original research; sometimes as part of a series. The "Everyday Communication Series," for instance, is a collection of authored texts "devoted to the publication of case studies concerning patterns of human communication behavior placed within relevant cultural and social contexts" (Leeds-Hurwitz & Sigman, 1996, p. ix). The texts in this series, in order of their publication appearance, have reported original research studies on: the linguistic performance of auctioneers and sportscasters (Kuiper, 1996); Karaoke (the prerecorded musical accompaniments designed for amateur singing) and the construction of identity in Chinese America (Lum, 1996); arguments, asymmetries, and power on talk radio (Hutchby, 1996); family conversations about bulemia (Beach, 1996); communication and community building in an AIDS residential facility (Adelman & Frey, 1997); Puerto Rican discourse in a New York suburb (Torres, 1997); Israeli settlement museums (Katriel, 1997); the social production of identity among older women (Paoletti, 1997); and dilemmas in the courtoon trials of violent crime in the Netherlands (Komter, 1998).

A common type of scholarly text that features primary research reports is *edited texts*. Here, a scholar, serving as an editor, collects original research studies about a particular topic and puts them together in a book, typically with an introduction that frames the studies and perhaps a concluding chapter or epilogue that comments on them. L. R. Frey's (1994c, 1995, in press) edited texts, for example, feature original studies of communication in natural groups. Many edited texts contain both primary and secondary research reports. Socha and Stamp's (1995) state-of-the-field scholarly text on parent-child communication is like that; about half the chapters present original research studies, while the other half offer theoretical perspectives and/or overviews of research on relevant topics.

Conference Papers.   The final source of primary research reports we want to direct your attention to is a **conference paper,** a manuscript presented at a scholarly conference/convention. In Chapter 2, we explained how scholars submit their work for presentation at professional conferences. Many of these manuscripts are selected through the same type of competitive, peer, blind-review process described for manuscript submissions to journals; however, the percentage of papers accepted for presentation at conferences is much higher than the percentage of articles selected for publication in scholarly journals. Other conference papers are selected as part of a submitted panel and, in some cases, as invited presentations. Hence, conference papers do not have the same prestige, or "stamp of approval," as scholarly journal articles, but they can still be a valuable source of primary research reports. In fact, many scholarly journal articles start life as a conference paper.

Obtaining copies of conference papers cited in research reports, however, can be difficult. Fortunately, many communication conference papers can be obtained through the National Library of Education's Educational Resources Information Center (ERIC) (http://www.accesseric.org/), an informational resource center that selects and stores on microfiche conference papers (sometimes rewritten and polished versions). When conference papers from this and other outlets are not available, it is necessary to write directly to the author for a copy. Addresses for authors who are members of the National Communication Association, for example, are listed in the *NCA Directory,* published annually by NCA (5105 Backlick Road, Building

E, Annandale, VA 22003; 703-750-0533; http://www.natcom.org/).

Finding Research Reports

Primary and secondary research reports may be found in many places and in many forms. Here, we identify two primary places: in libraries and via the Internet.

Libraries.   **Libraries,** as we all know, are locations set aside specifically to store knowledge in an organized fashion. The knowledge stored in libraries can take the traditional form of printed books, journals, magazines, and newspapers on shelves, photographic reproductions of existing print pages on microfilm and microfiche, audio reproductions on audiotape, and other electronic forms, such as databases accessed via computers.

Libraries have a long and rich tradition. The great library in Alexandria, Egypt, which was mysteriously destroyed, contained about 700,000 scrolls, supposedly every scroll in existence at that time; the first public library opened in Athens around 500 B.C.; and by the time the Roman Empire fell, there were 26 public libraries in Rome (Bolner & Poirier, 1997). The prototypes for the modern library were the university libraries that sprung up after the Dark Ages (about 1100 A.D.), and the 1600s and 1700s were known as the "Golden Age of Libraries" (Bolner & Poirier). In the United States, Harvard University opened its library in 1638; the first subscription library open to the public was founded by Benjamin Franklin; and in 1800, Congress established the Library of Congress, a collection that now contains over 100 million items (Bolner & Poirier). The first tax-supported library opened in New Hampshire in 1833, and in the late 1800s, industrialist Andrew Carnegie donated money to help build 2,500 libraries and, in the process, "helped to foster the notion that libraries are a necessary public service" (Bolner & Poirier, p. 5).

There are many types of libraries that differ in terms of purpose, content, and access. Here, we examine three relevant types: public, academic, and special-use libraries.

Public Libraries.   **Public libraries** are municipal libraries operated by a city, town, or local government that are accessible to members of the general public. One might need to be a member of a particular town to check out books and other materials, but most public libraries allow anyone to come in and use the facility. With the exception of big-city public libraries, most public libraries are relatively small. The materials contained within them are those that appeal to the general public, such as nonfiction and fiction texts, popular periodicals (such as *Time* and *Newsweek*), newspapers, and perhaps recorded materials, such as audiotapes and compact disks. Seldom do public libraries stock scholarly journals and texts that report original research studies. Hence, while public libraries are sufficient for the needs of the general public, they are of limited use to scholars, including any scholarly work you intend to do that necessitates reading original research reports. For that, you need to go to academic libraries.

Academic Libraries.   **Academic libraries** are attached to universities/colleges and support their research and teaching needs. These libraries stock both primary and secondary research reports, in addition to some nonfiction texts, popular periodicals, newspapers, and recorded materials. Entrance requirements and policies for checking out materials vary (e.g., some only allow access to students enrolled in that university; others set aside hours for use by the general public). Academic libraries typically do not allow people to take home journals; these are *noncirculating* materials.

Academic libraries are where scholarly journals and texts are housed. Not every scholarly journal or text is housed in every academic library, but the odds are you can find most of the sources you seek in this type of library, such as the one at your university or college. If something is not there, most academic libraries have interlibrary loan agreements with other academic libraries and can acquire the information relatively quickly.

Special-Use Libraries.   **Special-use libraries** contain materials that meet specific needs. A city museum devoted to natural history, for example, may have a library that houses relevant materials. Many of these special-use libraries are operated by private organizations, such as historical societies, religious societies, and even business corporations. Access to these libraries varies widely, but typically is restricted to those who have established a need for the materials and have proper credentials (as determined by those who operate the library). The materials are typically noncirculating and must be requested from an archival curator and returned within a certain period of time.

Some special-use libraries are or contain **archives,** where **primary source materials,** original records and documents, are housed. As M. R. Hill (1993) explains:

> *These facilities are storehouses of rare, often unique materials that were created over time by individuals, organizations, and social movements. Such materials include letters, diaries, confidential memos, lecture notes, transcripts, rough drafts, unpublished manuscripts, and other personal and organizational records. (pp. 2–3)*

Primary source materials should not be confused with *primary research reports;* the first term means any original records and documents, whereas the latter term references reports of original research studies. Primary research reports are, thus, technically a subset of primary source materials.

There are thousands of archival facilities throughout the United States, such as the Walter Reuther Labor Archives (located on the campus of Wayne State University in Detroit, Michigan). Many academic libraries also have an archive section. For a complete listing, consult the *Directory of Archives and Manuscript Repositories in the United States,* published by the National Historical Publications and Records Commission.

While archives present unique challenges and protocols that are different from academic or public libraries, they are often invaluable to communication scholars, especially to those who conduct textual analysis (see Chapter 9). Many of the original texts these researchers wish to analyze are housed in archives.

Finding Research Reports in Academic Libraries. It should be apparent from the discussion above that academic libraries are the primary place where researchers spend their time. Now we know that, for some people, going to any library is like going to the dentist—a real pain. For others, it's like shopping in a great department store of ideas, an absorbing search for products (in this case, research reports) to enrich their minds. Most academic libraries actually contain many more items than even the largest of shopping malls. To enjoy the resources of such a library—rather than wandering around in confusion or searching futilely down blind alleys—you need to know where to find what you're there to obtain. The trick lies in conducting an efficient search.

When you walk into a large, unfamiliar shopping mall with a specific purpose in mind, you usually stop in front of a directory to learn where you're likely to find that for which you're looking. Libraries are also organized in some consistent ways. You may know much of the following information, your library undoubtedly has handouts on it, and the staff at the reference desks are ready to assist you in finding your way around the library, but we want to cover it as part of explaining a library search, and a quick review may help fill in any gaps in your knowledge.

Library Cataloguing Systems.   Libraries organize their holdings using some type of **cataloguing system.** Books in most academic libraries are categorized using the *Library of Congress System,* which uses letters to designate major categories and a combination of letters and numbers to subdivide each category so that each book is assigned a unique **call number** (see Figure 3.3). Public libraries, on the other hand, most frequently use the *Dewey Decimal System* (originated in the nineteenth century by Melvil Dewey), which employs 10 numbered categories as general headings,

---

FIGURE 3.3 Library cataloguing systems

LIBRARY OF CONGRESS SYSTEM

A	General Works
B	Philosophy/Psychology/Religion
C	History-General
D	History-World
E	American History
F	Local American History
G	Geography/Anthropology/Sports
H	Social Sciences
HA	Statistics
HM	Sociology
J	Political Science
K	Law
L	Education
M	Music
N	Fine Arts
P	Language/Literature
PR	English/Literature
PS	American Literature
Q	Science
R	Medicine
S	Agriculture
T	Technology
U	Military Science
V	Naval Science
Z	Bibliography/Library Science

DEWEY DECIMAL SYSTEM

000	Generalities
100	Philosophy/Psychology
200	Religion
300	Social Sciences
400	Language
500	Natural Science/Mathematics
600	Technology
700	The Arts
800	Literature/Rhetoric
900	Geography/History

---

subdivided as many times as necessary to assign a unique call number to each book.

Now in the "old days" (although keep in mind that wasn't so long ago), libraries kept a central-

ized file, called a **card catalogue,** which contained cards for each book in the holdings that were cross-referenced in three ways: by author, title of work, and subject area. You would go to the library, find the appropriate card, and locate the book by its call number. Some libraries still have a card catalogue, but today, most tend to have all this information filed electronically in a **database,** information stored in machine-readable form that can be retrieved by a computer located in the library or elsewhere (Bolner & Poirier, 1997). In fact, you don't even need to physically go to the library any more to find the call number for a book; you can simply dial the library from your home or elsewhere using a computer modem and find this information. And this electronic library information service will even tell you whether the book is checked out. (There was nothing more frustrating than going to the library and discovering that the book you wanted was checked out, although there still are problems with the electronic catalogue saying that the book is not checked out, but finding it missing when you go to the library.)

Electronic Library Searches.   Let's say, for example, that you've been reading a basic interpersonal communication textbook and have run across a citation for the text *The Dark Side of Interpersonal Communication,* edited by William R. Cupach and Brian H. Spitzberg (1994), which you now want to find via an electronic library search. Each academic library has its own electronic information service, so the specific search procedures will vary, but let's illustrate it using the service at Loyola University Chicago.

After sitting down at one of the library's computers and logging onto Loyola's library information service (LUIS), users are presented with a screen that allows them to search for a book or journal by title, simply by typing the letter "t" followed immediately by an equals sign "=" and then followed immediately by the title of the book. One can also search for a book by author (a = name of author), and/or call number (c = call number). If more general searches are desired, users can enter a keyword (k = keyword) or a subject (s = subject). Explanations of all these commands are easily obtained by following the instructions.

Given that we know the title of the book, we type (leaving off the word "The"):

t = Dark Side of Interpersonal Communication

The next screen indicates whether the book is listed. Given that it is, entering the number corresponding to that record leads to a new screen that offers a "brief view" of the book, giving the title, publisher, location, call number, and whether or not the book is checked out. If we type "lon" (for "long view"), the next screen provides even more information about the book (such as its Library of Congress subject categories).

Finding the location of scholarly journals is accomplished in a similar manner. For example, if we wanted to find the location of the journal *Communication Quarterly,* we type:

t = Communication Quarterly

The next screen gives the title, publisher, location, call number, and status. Because scholarly journals are noncirculating materials, status here refers to what volumes the library has and other pertinent information (e.g., bound versus unbound issues and/or whether it is on microfilm). If you prefer to find this information the "old-fashioned" way, your academic library is bound (pun intended) to have a hardcopy version of its current periodicals in alphabetical order with their call number.

As you see, finding the location of scholarly books and journals using an electronic library information service is easy and user-friendly. Locating articles in scholarly journals, however, demands a little more effort.

Let's say we read *The Dark Side of Interpersonal Communication,* found it useful, and now wanted to see what journal articles William R. Cupach has written. The best way of finding these articles is by locating an appropriate database from among the many available ones. For example, a very useful database of journal articles published in the social sciences is PsycINFO, copyrighted by the American Psychological Association, which references scholarly psychological works published in psychology, pharmacology, physiology, linguistics, anthropology, law, and social work. It also references many communication scholarly sources as well. As of August 1999, PsycINFO contained more than 1.5 million references to psychological literature spanning 1887 to the present day, including journal articles, books, book chapters, dissertations, reports, and other scholarly documents (American Psychological Association, 1999a).

PsycINFO can be accessed in a number of ways. At Loyola University Chicago, the best way to access it is through the InfoTrac database, an **online database,** copyrighted by Information Access Company, that is stored on the mainframe of Loyola's computer center. InfoTrac can also access a number of other databases, such as Expanded Academic ASAP, which references research published in astronomy, religion, law, history, psychology, humanities, sociology, and communications. (It's always best to check a number of relevant databases when trying to find scholarly journals and books, because databases often contain different records.) There undoubtedly is a similar system at your university (e.g., FirstSearch).

Hence, when we entered PsycINFO through InfoTrac on June 8, 1999, and conducted an author search for William R. Cupach, we found 28 citations that included 3 books (1 authored and 2 edited), 10 book chapters, and 15 journal articles. What's more, in addition to providing pertinent information about each entry (e.g., author and title), this database also contains a short summary of each record and, depending on the library's service, the full text sometimes can be retrieved electronically or in hardcopy. InfoTrac also has an advanced PowerTrac system that can be used to conduct more focused searches in 20 different ways (e.g., by journal name or date of the article's publication).

Many databases, including a smaller version of PsycINFO, called PsycLIT (containing 1.2 million references with abstracts, American Psychological Association, 1999b), are available on **CD-ROMs,** which stands for "compact disk-read-only memory." These disks are similar to the audio compact disks with which you undoubtedly are familiar. One disk holds approximately 250,000 printed pages, or about 300 books (Bolner & Poirier, 1997). There are thousands of CD-ROMs, so the key is finding the best one to access.

The best CD-ROM for locating articles in communication journals is *CommSearch* (2nd ed.), a database copyrighted by the National Communication Association, that contains: title, keyword, and author indexes for 24 communication journals from inception through 1995 (see Figure 3.1 for a listing of the journals referenced); the full text of NCA journal articles from 1991–1995; and abstracts of articles published between 1972–1995 in six NCA journals (*Communication Education, Communication Monographs, Critical Studies in Mass Communication, Quarterly Journal of Speech, Journal of Applied Communication Research,* and *Text & Performance Quarterly*). Unfortunately, many academic libraries don't have *CommSearch* available; therefore, it must be purchased directly from NCA (address given previously). This database is constantly being updated, and NCA will make arrangements to provide you with upgrades. (Note: In early 1997, the Speech Communication Association changed its name to the National Communication Association. Many older printed reference sources and some electronic reference sources use the initials SCA. The reader should remember to use both names when searching for references.)

If you can't afford *CommSearch,* the most important printed source for finding communication journal articles is Matlon and Ortiz's (1997) text, *Index to Journals in Communication Studies Through 1995* (published by NCA). The text provides a complete listing of articles in those same 24 communication journals from inception through 1995, listed issue by issue. Each journal is assigned an alphabetical code (e.g., CM = *Communication Monographs*), and each article is numbered consecutively (e.g., CM1 is the first article published in Volume 1, 1934, and CM1496 is the last article published in Volume 62, December, 1995, of *Communication Monographs*). The text

contains author and keyword indexes that help to locate articles written by particular scholars or about particular topics, respectively. Hence, when we looked up William R. Cupach in the author index of this reference text, there were eight entries (e.g., CM1270 and CM1334) that correspond to the alphabetical and numerical articles listed in the front part of the text for these communication journals.

This text is an indispensable tool for communication researchers. However, it only references communication journal articles through 1995, and does not include books or book chapters. Researchers, therefore, must use other resources to find more recent articles, as well as books, book chapters, and other scholarly documents.

One final print resource helpful to communication researchers, especially for locating journal articles published between 1991 and the present—which may be available electronically in your academic library through the FirstSearch database—is *Communication Abstracts.* This quarterly publication prints abstracts (one-paragraph summaries) of communication-related articles published in various journals and books over the previous 90 days. The research reviewed is organized according to areas within the communication discipline. There are keyword descriptors that accompany each abstract so that the topic(s) can be easily identified, and there are author and subject indexes that accompany each issue of this publication.

Being able to conduct electronic library searches has certainly made the search for research much easier. One of the main advantages, in comparison to print searches, is the ability to engage in **free-text searching** (or **keyword searching**), searching for key words, regardless of where they appear in a record. Of course, the downside is that such searches often result in numerous *false hits* or *false drops.* So, for example, if you type "apple" in a search, looking for information about the fruit, it is likely that you will get a whole host of records, such as Apple computers, that are not relevant to your interests. To take care of this problem, you need to learn and use various commands that help focus an electronic search.

One useful set of commands are **Boolean operators,** words that allow one to narrow or broaden a search or to link related terms. Three Boolean operators are used in most databases: *and, or, not.* Using *and* in a command—such as "television and children"—results in a search for any occurrence of those words together, that is, any records containing *both* television and children. Using *or* in a command—"television or children"—creates a search for *all* records that contain either the first term (television) or the second (children). Using *not*—"television not children"—searches for records containing the first term (television), *but not* the second (children). Which Boolean operator(s) you use depends on whether you need to broaden or narrow a search.

There are also **positional operators** that can be used to make sure that records are searched with regard to particular word orders. For example, using *adj*—such as "television adj children"—preserves the exact order of those command words when searching for records. This is actually the default system on many databases, so check to see whether that is the case. Records can also be searched in the order of the command words within a specified number of words of each other: "television adj5 children" yields any records that contain the word television within five words of the word *children* (for other useful search terms and strategies, see Bolner & Poirier, 1997; McGuire, Stilborne, McAdams, & Hyatt, 1997).

Finally, although electronic searches are tremendously helpful, they are not without their problems. In addition to learning the set of commands for conducting such searches, there is a lack of standardization of commands across databases. Hence, the commands that work on one database don't necessarily work on another. In addition, many databases only contain relatively recent information; the version of PsycINFO that we accessed through InfoTrac, for instance, covers works published between 1984–1999. If older articles are desired, print resources or other electronic databases must be consulted. Finally, some databases, especially those on CD-ROMs, may only be available for use inside the library. They cannot be

accessed through the Internet, an important resource to which we now turn.

Internet Resources. The **Internet,** as Courtright and Perse (1998) explain, is a conjunction of two words that also explains a little bit of its history:

> *"Net" is an abbreviation for "network," which refers to any number of computers that are linked or connected and, thus, able to share information. In the early days of networking, there were several unconnected networks such as **BITNET** (for universities) or **MILNET** (for the military). The Internet, and thus the prefix "inter," arose when these several independent networks were joined through high-speed phone lines into a single worldwide network of computers. (p. 2)*

This worldwide network of computers offers many exciting and useful features, such as electronic mail (e-mail). But the option that seemingly has created the most excitement among the general public is the **World Wide Web** (**WWW** or **the Web**), a portion of the Internet that uses hypertext language to combine text, graphics, audio, and video (Courtright & Perse, 1998), and which owes its existence to a single person:

> *Tim Berners-Lee was working at the Swiss-based European Particle Physics laboratory (CERN) when, in an astounding burst of creativity, he sat down in 1990 and wrote the specifications for a global hyper-media system, using the innocuous acronyms HTTP, HTML, and URL. Originally designed to let far-flung researchers collaborate on large problems, [it resulted in a] universal information space.... For good measure Berners-Lee even gave his creation a name: the World Wide Web. ("The Father of the Web," 1997, p. 140)*

The growth of the Web during the 1990s was nothing short of astounding. By 1997, there were about 150 million Web pages in existence, and by the year 2000, there will be about a billion ("Kiss Your Browser Goodbye," 1997). Today, you can do everything on the Web from reading the morning newspaper to ordering plane tickets for your next trip. Of course, the Internet and Web are also useful for doing something else—finding research reports and other research-relevant information. Indeed, from a scholar's perspective, the main advantage of the Internet and Web is the ability to locate primary and secondary research reports quickly and efficiently. Since finding such information is most relevant to our purposes, we'll concentrate on that and leave you to surf the Net and Web to discover their other uses and resources.

It should be pointed out right from the start that although the Internet and Web offer vast resources relevant to research, they also create new challenges for finding reliable, accurate, and specific information. Because people move from place to place, and organizations add new computers, Web-based resources sometimes disappear as quickly as they surface. Information quality also varies widely, because anyone with access to a server can create a Web page, regardless of his or her other qualifications. Therefore, it's important to check the veracity of resources acquired through the Internet and Web whenever possible. As Courtright and Perse (1998) warn: "You should never assume that information is accurate or credible just because you found it on the Internet" (p. 105). Perhaps most important, Internet and Web resources should constitute only *part* of your total search. They are best used in conjunction with library searches of electronic databases, many of which can be accessed through the Internet, and relevant print resources. And one final point, as the American Psychological Association (1994) suggests, "If print and electronic forms of material are the same, a reference for the print form currently is preferred" (p. 218).

With those precautions in mind, we asked our colleague in the communication discipline, Diane F. Witmer (California State University, Fullerton), who has extensive experience using and teaching about Internet- and Web-based research resources, to provide an overview of some valuable resources that you might consult. These resources fall into three general categories: (a) electronic journals (and other such sources); (b) academic and professional associations and public and private organizations whose Web pages provide information about accessing their archives, publications, conferences, and other research-related resources; and (c) listserv discussion groups, which promote the exchange of dialogue and information about research by delivering messages to all subscribers, and newsgroups, "bulletin boards" where users go to read messages placed by other users.

Internet and World Wide Web Resources for Research

Diane F. Witmer
California State University, Fullerton

The following lists provide only a few starting points for conducting research via the Internet and, especially, the World Wide Web. The resources listed here have demonstrated reasonable stability over time, but all URLs (Uniform Resource Locators, or World Wide Web "addresses") are subject to change.

Most Web resources have clear instructions and simple menus for online help. To access a Web page, simply type the URL into your Web browser, taking care to type it *exactly* as shown, including capitalization and punctuation marks. Once you enter the correct URL, your browser will link you directly to the resource. To reach the Web page of the United States Census Bureau, for example, type into your browser:

http://www.census.gov/

Your browser will then display the "home" page for the United States Census Bureau, which includes directions on how to find information at that site.

One way to begin your online research is with a Web-based search engine. If you know how to conduct a simple search, these engines can point you to both primary and secondary resources that

Internet and World Wide Web Resources for Research

may not be available in traditional libraries, including working papers, conference proceedings, conference papers, and archives of professional associations and universities. Each search engine has its own cataloging system and search strategies, so it's best to use a combination of several. Four of the best-known search engines are:

Alta Vista Conducts automatic searches in an effort to index all pages on the Web.

> http://www.altavista.com/

Infoseek Uses a "spider" to index Web sites, and reviews selected sites for inclusion in a variety of categories.

> http://infoseek.go.com/

Lycos Maintains a huge database of URLs and periodically visits the listed Web sites to index the content.

> http://www.lycos.com/

Yahoo! One of the most popular search engines, it displays a categorical listing of links to Web pages by title and description. Each one listed is checked and approved.

> http://www.yahoo.com/

A variety of online journals (e-journals), magazines, "e-zines," newspapers, and news media appear on the Web. Of particular importance to communication researchers are the following e-journals:

The American Communication Journal Published by the American Communication Association, this journal is dedicated to the conscientious analysis and criticism of significant communicative artifacts.

> http://www.americancomm.org/~aca/acj/acj.html

EJC/REC: Electronic Journal of Communication/La Revue Electronique de Communication Published by the Communication Institute for Online Scholarship, this journal reports original research, methodologies

relevant to the study of human communication, critical syntheses of research, and theoretical and philosophical perspectives on communication.

> http://www.cios.org/www/ejcmain.htm

Journal of Computer-Mediated Communication Published by the Annenberg School of Communication at the University of Southern California, this journal is devoted to the study of new media.

> http://www.ascusc.org/jcmc/index.html

M/C A journal of media and culture created at the University of Queensland (Australia) that is concerned with the phenomena in today's media and culture environments.

> http://english.uq.edu.au/mc/

A variety of services exist for finding the many other e-journals now published in virtually every discipline. Some of these services are free; others require becoming a member. These services include:

Committee of Institutional Cooperation (CIC) Electronic Journals Collection An academic consortium of the members of the Big Ten athletic conference and the University of Chicago, this collection aims to be an authoritative source of electronic research and academic serial publication—incorporating all freely distributed online scholarly electronic journals (138 at last count).

> http://ejournals.cic.net/

Blackwell's Electronic Journal Navigator Provides full text and abstracts of 565 (as of June 1999) peer-reviewed scholarly electronic journals. A guest pass enables one to try the service free for 3 months.

> http://navigator.blackwell.co.uk/

Ingenta Offers a range of full-text electronic journals from leading publishers, allows a search and browse of the database of articles free of charge, and displays bibliographic information and abstracts. About 120,000

(continued)

Internet and World Wide Web Resources for Research   continued

full-text articles from over 800 journals currently are available.

http://www.ingenta.com/

University of Houston Libraries   Maintains an extensive listing of "Scholarly Journals Distributed Via the World Wide Web" that offers access to article files without requiring registration or fees.

http://info.lib.uh.edu/wj/webjour.html

Many academic and professional associations and public and private organizations provide help in locating research studies, have their own archives of specialized research information, or offer other resources useful when conducting research (as well as many other services and products). The following organizations are particularly helpful for the study of communication:

American Communication Association (ACA)   Created to enhance and promote the academic and professional study, research, knowledge, criticism, teaching, exchange, and application of the basic principles of human communication.

http://www.americancomm.org/

Association for Education in Journalism and Mass Communication (AEJMC)   The oldest and largest association of journalism and mass communication educators and administrators at the college level, AEJMC features online information about the many journals it publishes, as well as its conventions and meetings.

http://www.facsnet.org/cgi-bin/New/facs/4149/

CARL Corporation   A provider of library management tools that offers a variety of online databases, including Uncover, which is a searchable database and delivery service that indexes over 18,000 multidisciplinary journals containing brief descriptive information for over 8,800,000 articles that have appeared since Fall, 1988.

http://www.carl.org/ (Carl Corporation)
http://uncweb.carl.org/ (Uncover)

Communication Institute for Online Scholarship (CIOS)   CIOS supports a searchable resource library, electronic white pages for the communication field,

bibliographic indexes to the professional literature in communication, and abstracts of articles (ComAbstracts). Offers extensive searches of many communication journals and annual scholarly texts for institutional affiliates and associated individuals, as well as limited searches for others.

http://www.cios.org/

December Communications   Specializes in publications, presentations, and consulting related to the Web- and Internet-based computer-mediated communication.

http://www.december.com/

Educational Resources Information Center (ERIC)   Presented by the National Library of Education, this information system, through its 16 subject-specific clearinghouses, associated adjunct clearinghouses, and support components, provides a variety of services and products on a broad range of education-related issues, including research summaries, bibliographies, computer searches and document reproduction.

http://www.accesseric.org/

European Speech Communication Association (ESCA) Promotes speech communication science and technology in a European context, in both industrial and academic areas. Its publications include a journal (*Speech Communication*) with articles written by students and an online newsletter.

http://www.esca-speech.org/

International Association of Business Communicators (IABC)   Provides products, services, activities, and networking opportunities to help people and organizations achieve excellence in public relations, employee communication, marketing communication, public affairs, and other forms of communication. Offers an online magazine (*World Communication*) for members.

http://www.iabc.com/

International Communication Association (ICA)   Brings together academicians and other professionals whose interests focus on human communication. Publishes a number of journals and has a fully searchable online program of its annual conference.

http://www.icahdq.org/

Internet and World Wide Web Resources for Research

Library of Congress   This searchable list of databases includes online documents, photographs, movies, sound recordings, and library catalogues.

> http://lcweb.loc.gov/

National Communication Association (NCA)   Offers a wide range of information, including upcoming conferences, archived files, news, resources, online supplements, highlights of its print publications, information about communication graduate programs, and links to other communication online resources.

> http://www.natcom.org/

Public Relations Society of America (PRSA)   The world's largest organization for public relations professionals provides a forum for addressing issues affecting the profession. It has an online resume service, information on and highlights from its print publications, and links to resources on public relations.

> http://www.prsa.org/

Western States Communication Association (WSCA)   A regional communication association that publishes the *Western Journal of Communication* and has online searchable indexes of abstracts and articles and the table of contents of the current issue.

> http://www.cios.org/www/western.htm

World Communication Association (WCA)   In addition to information on its journal and conferences, this site has "Internet Resources for Communication Studies" that include information on study, research, and writing skills.

> http://ilc2. doshisha.ac.jp/users/kkitao/organi/wca/

In addition to Web-based journals and organizational databases and archives, free Internet-based discussion lists offer opportunities to exchange information, debate topical issues, and find other research resources. Many list administrators also maintain archived files for research purposes. New users, however, should be cautious in posting superficial questions to these lists. Both good "netiquette" and the expectations of members dictate that questions and comments reflect basic back-

ground research and an understanding of list norms. The following are of particular interest for conducting communication research:

CRTNET News (Communication and Theory NETwork)   A daily electronic newsletter service by the National Communication Association, CRTNET is probably the most widely read list for discussion about communication. To subscribe, send an e-mail to:

> listserv@lists.psu.edu

Leave the subject line blank and write in in the body of the message:

> Subscribe crtnet <your name>
> quit

Comserve Hotlines   CIOS offers a variety of discussion lists that pertain to specialties in communication, including interpersonal (INTERPER), mass (MASS-COMM), and organizational communication (ORG-COMM), to name a few. One hotline is provided free of charge. For a complete listing of hotlines and how to join, send an e-mail to:

> Comserve@CIOS.org

Leave the subject line blank and write in the body of the message:

> SHOW HOTLINES

METHODS. A discussion list about topics related to research methodology. To join, send an an e-mail to:

> listserv@vm.its.rpi.edu

Leave the subject line blank and write in the body of the message:

> sub METHODS your name

In addition to the resources listed above, there are literally thousands of newsgroups and Internet discussion lists. Three final Web sites are particularly useful for finding and accessing online discussions that focus on specific topics:

Deja News   A Web site where one can read, search, participate in, and subscribe to more than 80,000

(continued)

Internet and World Wide Web Resources for Research   continued

---

discussion forums, including Usenet newsgroups. Allows search messages dating back more than two years.

http://www.dejanews.com/

ONElist   A free, user-friendly, searchable service that lists e-mail "communities" and facilitates creation and management of new lists.

http://www.onelist.com/

Tile.Net   A comprehensive Internet reference source for discussion/information lists, Usenet newgroups, ftp sites, and more.

http://tile.net/

In addition to the resources Dr. Witmer cites, we want to direct you to a very important Web resource: the Communication Ring (http://nonce.com/commring/). A ring organizes a group of Web sites, and this ring is dedicated to the study and teaching of communication. Sites chosen for inclusion on this ring (many of which are on Dr. Witmer's list) tend to be either a department's or organization's site, an individual's personal/professional home page, or a project site. Once you enter the ring and arrive at a site, you can then go to other sites by clicking the "next site" command or you can tour the ring in a random manner by clicking the "random" command, and you can always return to the site you just visited by clicking the "previous" command. It is a ring, so if you kept going long enough, you eventually would come to the site where you first started.

HOW RESEARCH IS PRESENTED: READING SCHOLARLY JOURNAL ARTICLES

Scholarly journals present the most current research in the field, research that has passed the test of review. Journal articles, therefore, are the bread and butter of communication researchers. For that reason, the remainder of this chapter concentrates on how to read and use scholarly journal articles effectively.

Scholarly journal articles report the results obtained from the methodology employed in a particular study. Thus, there are articles about experiments performed, surveys taken, texts analyzed,

and research conducted in natural settings. As will be explained in some detail in Chapter 4, experimenters, survey researchers, and sometimes textual analysts tend to collect **quantitative data,** numerical data, while other textual analysts and naturalistic researchers collect **qualitative data,** data using symbols other than numbers.

Journal articles that analyze qualitative data are so varied that it is difficult to discuss a single model for how these articles are written. In Chapter 10, we identify some of the strategies used to analyze and write about qualitative data (see also Milinki, 1999). It also should be pointed out that, as previously explained, some articles are state-of-the-art literature reviews. Still other articles are methodology pieces that develop and test an instrument. Some features of how articles are written are the same for all research (e.g., an explication of the methods used), but one particular format is well established for presenting the results obtained from analyzing quantitative data.

A Typical Quantitative Scholarly Journal Article

A typical quantitative scholarly journal article contains a number of important subheadings (see Figure 3.4). Students often find these articles difficult to read, but understanding the accepted format will help you to know where to look in an article for the information you need and to avoid wasting valuable time. (We also refer you to our other text by Frey, Botan, Friedman, & Kreps, 1992, entitled

FIGURE 3.4 Format of a typical quantitative scholarly journal article

The following format typically is used to report the results of a quantitative research study in a scholarly communication journal.

TITLE

ABSTRACT

INTRODUCTION

REVIEW OF THE LITERATURE

Research Question/Hypothesis

METHODOLOGY

Research Participants/Texts

Procedures

Data Treatment

RESULTS

DISCUSSION

REFERENCES

Interpreting Communication Research: A Case Study Approach, in which we examine actual scholarly journal articles that employ various methodologies. In each chapter of that text, we pose a series of questions to keep in mind when reading the article, present the article and number its lines, and then walk through the article and discuss the decisions made by referring to the numbered lines. At the end of each chapter are reference sources for understanding the methodology discussed, as well as annotated communication journal articles that use that methodology. Other helpful texts for reading and understanding journal articles are Girden, 1996; Lombard, 1999.)

Title. The most straightforward title presents the topic and, specifically, the variables studied by the researcher. Ragsdale's (1996) article, for example, is entitled, "Gender, Satisfaction Level, and the Use of Relational Maintenance Strategies in Marriage." Most journal article titles, we dare say, have two parts: The first part might specify the general topic and the second part the specific variables studied. For instance, Floyd and Morman's (1997) article is

entitled, "Affectionate Communication in Nonromantic Relationships: Influences of Communicator, Relational, and Contextual Factors." Quite often, researchers use a catchy phrase in the first part, and then a more straightforward title in the second part, such as Rintel and Pittam's (1997) article, "Strangers in a Strange Land: Interaction Management on Internet Relay Chat." There is a lot of variation in titles, including ones that don't provide a straightforward account of what the authors were after in the study. In such cases, the information contained in the abstract clarifies the nature of the research.

Abstract. Most journal articles start (either in the article itself or in the table of contents for that issue of a journal) with a summary of the important points in that article. This summary, typically one paragraph long, is called an **abstract.** An abstract can be a researcher's best friend because it encapsulates the most important information contained in an article, such as the purpose of the study, methods used, key findings from the study, and/or contribution the study makes (see Figure 3.5). This condensed summary of the entire article, therefore, can establish whether the article is relevant and should be included in a literature review. If the abstract indicates relevance, the researcher then goes on to read the entire article.

Introduction. The introduction begins the actual body of a journal article. This section, frequently no longer than a page or two, orients the reader to the topic and why it is important that it be studied. The author often starts with an introduction to the general area of research under which the specific topic falls, then explains the specific purpose/focus of the research (but not phrased as a research question or hypothesis), and concludes by pointing out the significance/importance of the research for communication scholars, practitioners (including educators), and/or the general public (see Chapter 2). The introduction, thus, establishes the purpose and significance of the study.

Review of the Relevant Literature. The literature review is one of the most crucial sections of a

FIGURE 3.5 Sample abstract

This study investigates the features of an individual's preference for certain kinds of narratives and the resulting shared fantasies. We studied the following features of narratives, whether the stories were happy or sad, set in the past or the present, implied moral or immoral values, and were bizarre or realistic. Fifty-four dramas were created using different combinations of four characteristics and were presented to American subjects in an interview situation with a Q-sort methodology. The Quanal factor analysis revealed five different subject types. Members within each subject type exhibited similar fantasy sharing and rejecting patterns. These findings help fill in an important gap in the symbolic convergence theory by addressing the question of why people share fantasies.

Source: Ernest G. Bormann, Roxann L. Knutson, and Karen Musolf, "Why Do People Share Fantasies? An Empirical Investigation of a Basic Tenet of the Symbolic Convergence Communication Theory," *Communication Studies,* *48,* p. 254, copyright © 1997 by the Central States Communication Association. Used by permission of the Central States Communication Association.

journal article. Here, a researcher identifies the previous work done by scholars that is relevant to the topic. Understanding what needs to be done next in an area of research can only be achieved after a comprehensive and clear review of what has been done, since knowing what has been done directs researchers to topics and questions they now consider worth studying.

Each literature review reflects many factors, including the author's personal style. If the research blazes a new path in the discipline, probably little specific research will be cited. In such a case, the review of the literature might frame the topic being studied within the broader goals of the discipline, some conceptual or theoretical perspectives (such as Botan, 1996, did in his study discussed earlier in the chapter), and/or its applied value. By contrast, some research projects build on topics that have received considerable attention. In such cases, the literature review is targeted

specifically to the research that addresses that topic directly. Sometimes a study seeks to test whether previous research was conducted properly or whether the obtained results are accurate. In such cases, the literature review concentrates on examining the methods used in previous research. Hence, the literature review section varies quite a bit in terms of how it is constructed and what types of sources are reviewed. In all cases, however, the literature review section is meant to provide a coherent and comprehensive understanding of the relevant research previously conducted, so that the author can confidently advance the research question or hypothesis.

Research Question/Hypothesis. At the end of the literature review, either as part of that section or in a separately titled section, the author poses a formal research question or hypothesis (see Chapter 2). The author explains, either before posing it or immediately after doing so, how the research question or hypothesis grew out of what was learned from the literature reviewed. Because communication researchers often examine multiple independent and dependent variables, it is not unusual to have multiple research questions and/or hypotheses posed, with explanations of them in-between.

Methodology. The methodology section (often called "Methods") is where the author explains exactly how the research was conducted. This section usually contains three formal subheadings: "Research Participants/Texts," "Procedures," and "Data Treatment."

Research Participants (Subjects)/Texts. The methodology section typically starts by describing the **research participants** (or **subjects,** designated *Ss*), the people who participated in the study, and/or the **texts,** the recorded or visual messages studied. The author provides all relevant information about the research participants or texts studied, such as their total number, important characteristics, and how they were selected.

Procedures. The second part of the methodology section explains the specific procedures used to conduct the research. This section is a straight-forward account of what was done with the re-search participants/texts. The author explains exactly how the independent and dependent vari-ables were operationalized (put into observable terms) and measured (see Chapter 4), and, if rele-vant, manipulated (such as exposing some but not other research participants to a persuasive mes-sage; see Chapter 7). The goal is to provide enough concrete information that another researcher could reproduce the study if so desired.

Data Treatment.   Some methodology sections in-clude, as a final part, an explanation of the ways in which the quantitative data were analyzed. But sometimes this material is presented in the results section, often at the start of it.

Results.   The results section of a journal article explains what was found. This section is typically a short, straightforward account of the findings without attempting to interpret or discuss them. The author remains objective, not allowing per-sonal interpretations or feelings to color the report-ing. You may find this section difficult to read because of the use of statistics, tables/figures, jar-gon, and abbreviations. However, by the time you complete this textbook, you should be able to read and understand the gist of these data analyses.

Discussion.   In this section, the author interprets the results reported in the preceding section. This is where the author explains the significance of the results and what they mean. The discussion section typically involves three things (see Chap-ter 15). First, the meaning and importance of the findings are examined. The author might discuss, for example, how the findings support or refute a theory and/or previous research and what recom-mendations might be offered from the findings to practitioners and the general public. Second, the problems and limitations of the study are identi-fied on the basis of hindsight. Third, the findings are used to suggest new topics worth studying, new questions worth asking, and new procedures worth trying.

References.   Because scholarly research is cu-mulative (see Chapter 1), readers have a right to know two things: who should get credit for each idea presented and what is the track record of each idea. It is the author's responsibility to identify fully, honestly, and accurately all the research re-ferred to in the article. This disclosure of indebt-edness takes the form of **references,** a complete and accurate list of all sources cited in the text. All good research cites relevant references.

In addition to references, an article may con-tain **footnotes** that provide explanations of mate-rial mentioned in the article that is elaborated on for interested readers. For example, footnotes might explain the history of a term or provide the statistical formulas employed to analyze the data.

WRITING A LITERATURE REVIEW

Once researchers have located and synthesized rel-evant research, they use that information to revise the topic they are studying. This process of find-ing, reading, evaluating, and revising may be nec-essary several times until researchers are ready to pose a formal research question or hypothesis. They then write the literature review section that summarizes and organizes the research findings with respect to the topic being studied.

Because many of you will be asked by your professor to conduct and write a literature review (either as part of a prospectus and/or final paper, or as a stand-alone assignment) similar to those you have read in scholarly journal articles, we outline the steps involved. In fact, we'll cover five things that typically are part of a research prospectus: the title, introduction, literature review, research ques-tion/hypothesis, and reference sections. Again, we point out that we are talking about a quantitatively oriented piece (see also Pyrczak & Bruce, 1992, for additional suggestions). Most important of all, if you are asked to write any of these sections, make sure to check with your professor about ex-actly how he or she wants it done.

A. Title: Construct a clear title for the paper that captures the essence of your intended research study. Most projects examine either *differences between groups* (such as "Male and Female Compliance-Gaining Strategies," or "The Effects of Gender on Compliance-Gaining Strategies") or *relationships between variables* (such as "The Relationship Between Intelligence and Communication Competence," or "The Effects of Intelligence on Communication Competence"). Think about constructing a creative title that starts with a catchy first part, followed by a colon and a second part that specifies the variables of interest (e.g., "Birds of a Feather Flock Together: The Effects of Communicator Style Similarities on Interpersonal Attraction").

B. Introduction: This is a relatively short part of the paper (about a page to a page and a half) that establishes the purpose and significance of the study. You can include a centered, upper- and lowercase heading (i.e., Introduction) if you like, but it isn't mandatory. Start with an introduction to the general area of research under which the specific topic you are examining falls (but avoid making this too general, e.g., "Communication is important in our lives"), followed by a paragraph that explains the specific purpose of your research (do not, however, phrase the purpose as a formal research question and/or hypothesis; instead, explain the specific purpose of the research). This section concludes by pointing out the potential significance/importance of your research study for communication scholars, practitioners, and/or the general public.

C. Literature Review: The literature review section, as discussed above, varies a great deal depending on how much specific information there is on the topic you are studying. Here, however, are some helpful general and specific suggestions for writing this section:

1. To write a good review of the literature, you must first understand the two purposes that this section should serve. One purpose is to summarize what is known about the research in the area that interests you. Hence, you need to provide enough information so that the reader understands what has been studied and found about the topic. The

reader must be convinced that you have conducted a *comprehensive* review of the literature. But this comprehensive review really serves the second purpose of using the previous research as evidence for the argument that you are going to make by posing a research question or hypothesis. That is, your task is to convince the reader that, on the basis of the literature reviewed, it makes sense to ask a research question that links the independent and dependent variables being studied or that there is enough evidence to justify advancing a hypothesis (prediction) about those variables. You should keep these dual purposes in mind as you write the literature review.

2. Use a centered, upper- and lowercase heading (i.e., Literature Review) to separate this section from the introduction. Introduce the literature review by pointing out the directions in which the review will proceed. In other words, establish the organizational scheme for this section (see comments below), so the reader knows how the review is being organized.

3. Not everything written on the topic can be covered. Many students fear that they will not find enough material, but the more typical problem is separating the wheat from the chaff. Your job is to pick out the research that is most relevant to the topic (variables) you are studying and the research question/ hypothesis you will pose, and then to pull out of each piece the ideas that are most useful. Of course, the best possible literature to review is found in studies in scholarly journals and books, especially communication journals. Information obtained from textbooks, magazines, and newspapers may sometimes be useful as general orienting material in the introduction to the paper, but it typically has no place in a literature review. Instead, review the actual research studies that have been conducted.

4. You must cover research relevant to all the variables being studied. The best possible

research to review, of course, is studies that link the specific variables that interest you. If there are a number of these studies (say, five or more), you can restrict the review solely to them. If there are only a limited number of these studies (say two or three), you should provide a more general overview of what is known about each variable and then focus in some detail on the studies that examine them together. If there are no studies about the relationship between the specific variables you are investigating, review what is known about each of these variables separately and then make the link between them yourself when posing the research questions and/or hypotheses. If there are no studies about the specific variables that interest you, review studies that are the most relevant to those variables. So, for example, if there were no studies of the effects of some particular compliance-gaining strategies that interest you, you would review what is known about the relevant effects of other compliance-gaining strategies, and then make the inferential connection when summarizing the literature and introducing the research question or hypothesis. But say there were no studies of compliance-gaining strategies. Then you should review the relevant effects of other persuasion strategies that are most similar to compliance-gaining strategies. In such cases, however, make sure to point out the relevance or similarity of that material to your interests, so that the reader understands that this is, in fact, the most appropriate material to review. Hence, the amount of literature reviewed depends on how many studies there are that directly focus on the variables that interest you. If there are a lot of studies, then your task is choosing the most relevant ones to include and focusing on them in some detail; if there are only a few or none, then you need to review more studies in the most relevant areas in a slightly less detailed manner.

5. Keep your eyes open for any *meta-analytic studies* about the topic being investigated. **Meta-analysis** (also spelled **metaanalysis**) is a procedure used to identify patterns in findings across multiple studies that examine the same research topic or question. It is a way of summarizing, synthesizing, and integrating various research findings for that topic or question (see Glass, McGraw, & Smith, 1981; Hunter & Schmidt, 1990; Rosenthal, 1984; Wolf, 1986). Meta-analysis can show, for example, "the average effect of the independent variable on the dependent variable, as well as the effect of methodological and other features of the study" (Schutt, 1999, p. 390). Because effects across multiple studies are assessed, a meta-analytic study may potentially be more accurate than any single study. As Hamilton and Hunter (1998b) explain, "The purpose of meta-analysis is to use the data from multiple studies to generate a more accurate interpretation of findings than is possible by considering the studies one at a time" (p. 2). Meta-analytic studies, therefore, are valuable sources for understanding the results acquired from numerous communication studies and for setting the agenda for what now needs to be done (see Hale & Dillard, 1991). However, you should keep in mind what Vogt (1999) calls the **file drawer problem,** a potential problem affecting meta-analyses and literature reviews that occurs because studies that yield nonsignificant results are often not published (they're put in researchers' drawers), so the significant effects found may seem to happen more often than they actually do. Some recent examples of the topics examined in meta-analytic studies in various areas of the communication field are presented in Figure 3.6.

6. If you review a specific study in detail (as opposed to discussing general findings from numerous studies), make sure to explain the purpose of the study (including, perhaps,

---

FIGURE 3.6 Recent communication meta-analyses

A. Intrapersonal Communication: Communication apprehension and cognitive performance (Bourhis & Allen, 1992); communication apprehension and communication behavior (M. Allen & Bourhis, 1996); cross-situational consistency of communication apprehension (S. Booth-Butterfield, 1988b); social and communicative anxiety (M. L. Patterson & Ritts, 1997)

B. Interpersonal Communication: Nonverbal behavior and compliance-gaining (Segrin, 1993); reducing dating anxiety (M. Allen, Bourhis, Emmers-Sommer, & Sahlstein, 1998)

C. Persuasion: Attitude-behavior relations (M. Kim & Hunter, 1993a, 1993b; Sheppard, Hartwick, & Warshaw, 1988); effects of distraction during persuasion (Buller & Hall, 1998); explicit versus implicit conclusions in persuasive messages (Cruz, 1998); fear-arousing persuasive appeals (Mongeau, 1998); effects of forewarning (W. L. Benoit, 1998); incentives and counterattitudinal advocacy (Preiss & Allen, 1998); language intensity effects (Hamilton & Hunter, 1998a); narrative versus statistical persuasive evidence (M. Allen & Preiss, 1997); one-sided versus two-sided persuasive messages (M. Allen, 1991, 1998); persuasiveness of rhetorical questions (Gayle, Preiss, & Allen, 1998); powerful/powerless language and attitudes and source credibility (Burrell & Koper, 1998); sleeper effect (M. Allen & Stiff, 1998)

D. Mass Communication: Cultivation research (M. Morgan & Shanahan, 1997); effects of exposure to sexual content/pornography (M. Allen, D'Alessio, & Brezgel, 1995; M. Allen, Emmers, Gebhardt, & Giery, 1995; Paik & Comstock, 1994); effects of foreign (cross-border) television (Elasmar & Hunter, 1997); television effects (Hearold, 1986); television programming and sex stereotyping (Herrett-Skjellum & Allen, 1996)

E. Organizational Communication: Gender differences and similarities in management communication (Wilkens & Andersen, 1991)

F. Communication Education: Correspondence of college textbooks with persuasion research literature (M. Allen & Preiss, 1990); impact of forensics and communication education on critical thinking (M. Allen, Berkowitz, Hunt, & Louden, 1999); impact of student race on classroom interaction (Cooper & Allen, 1998)

what research questions and/or hypotheses were advanced), the methods, findings, and the significance/implications of those findings (including how they relate to your own research interests), in that order.

7. When reviewing studies, write in the past tense, except when discussing their significance/implications, which should be written in the present tense.

8. Use some organizational scheme to review the selected research studies. An organizational scheme helps to provide a coherent explanation of the body of literature included, leads to helpful transitions between studies, and shows relationships among the studies more clearly. In other words, avoid writing a literature review that takes the form of "Here's one study, here's another study, and, oh, here's another." Instead, structure the review so that the studies are presented as an organized and coherent package that flows smoothly from one study to another. There are many organizational schemes that can be used to structure the literature review section; Rubin, Rubin, and Piele (1990) mention the following:

   a. Topical order: Organizes by main topics or issues and emphasizes the relationship of the issues to the main concern/problem.

   b. Chronological order: Organizes by historical progression in terms of time.

   c. Problem-cause-solution order: Organizes so that the review moves from a problem to a cause to a solution.

   d. General-to-specific order: Examines broad-based research first and then focuses on specific studies that relate to the topic.

   e. Known-to-unknown order: Examines current literature about the problem and then identifies at the end what still is not known.

   f. Comparison-and-contrast order: Shows how research studies are similar to and different from each other.

g. Specific-to-general order: Tries to make sense out of specific research studies so that general conclusions can be drawn.

D. Research Question/Hypothesis: The posing of the formal research question or hypothesis comes either at the end of the literature review section or in a separate section that has a centered, upper- and lowercase heading (e.g., Research Question). Here are some suggestions for this material/section:

1. Start by summarizing what the reviewed literature showed in terms of what has been done, what has not been done, and what needs to be done. Remember that the literature review functions as an argument, so this is your chance to present arguments and evidence about what the previous research found and what now needs to be investigated, as represented by your research question or hypothesis. This discussion should, thus, provide a clear transition from the literature reviewed to the research question or hypothesis posed. If there was plenty of research in the areas of interest, show how your study is an extension of this research. If there was limited prior research available, create a link between that material and your interests.

2. It is preferable to advance a hypothesis as opposed to a research question, because statistical procedures, in a sense, make it somewhat easier to find support for a hypothesis (see Chapter 12). However, a hypothesis should be advanced only when there is sufficient previous research to justify it. If there is not enough knowledge available about the topic to make a prediction or when previous research findings are equivocal (e.g., 50% found one thing and 50% found the opposite), then a research question probably should be posed.

3. Phrase research questions or hypotheses with regard to (1) *description* (e.g., RQ1: What compliance-gaining strategies do males and females use?), (2) *significant differences between groups* (e.g., H1:

Males use significantly more threats as a compliance-gaining strategy than females), and/or (3) *relationships between variables* (e.g., RQ1: Is there a relationship between intelligence and communication competence?). The particular phrasing depends on the purpose of the research (describing communication behavior versus relating communication behavior to other variables), the type of independent variable studied (nominal versus ordered), and whether you advance a research question or hypothesis (see Chapter 2).

4. If there is more than one independent variable being studied, one option is to put them together in one research question or hypothesis (e.g., RQ1: Is there a relationship between age, intelligence, and communication competence?; or RQ1: Adult males use significantly more compliance-gaining strategies than adult females or male and female children). Another option is to pose separate research questions or hypotheses for each independent variable (e.g., H1: Males use significantly more threat and promise compliance-gaining strategies than women; H2: Adults use significantly more threat and promise compliance-gaining strategies than children). The choice depends on whether you anticipate interaction effects between the independent variables (see Chapters 2, 7, and 13).

5. Indent a formal research question or hypothesis to the start of a new paragraph (six spaces from the left margin). Start with RQ or H, followed by a number, then a colon, and then the research question or hypothesis. Align the second and third sentences with the beginning of the actual research question or hypothesis. For example:

RQ1: Is there a significant difference between men and women in their use of threats to gain compliance?

H1: Men use more threats to gain compliance than do women.

E. References: On a separate page, with a centered, upper- and lowercase heading (i.e., References), list all the sources cited in the literature review in alphabetical order by the first author's last name. Only include those sources actually cited in the text itself. Quantitative research reports typically use the stylesheet recommended by the American Psychological Association (APA) (see Figure 3.7). In addition to its *Publication Manual,* you can also purchase and download the APA-Style Helper from the APA's website (http://www.apa.org/apa-style/), which provides information needed to compose reports according to APA style guidelines, including a reference builder that features 77 types of citations. There is also an interactive Web site called "APA Wizard" (http://www.stylewizard.com/), operated by Lyle J. Flint (Ball State University), to which you can submit bibliographical information and the appropriate APA reference citation will be built from it. There are, however, a number of other stylesheets, such as the one recommended by the Modern Language Association (and for additional information about citing electronic sources, see Li & Crane, 1993), so ask your professor which one is preferred, and then consult it on how to cite reference material properly.

CONCLUSION

Research does not take place in a vacuum. Communication researchers must, therefore, examine the extant literature to learn what is already known about the topic that interests them. Because time is valuable, the search for research must be as efficient and fruitful as possible, which means doing it in a logical, step-by-step manner.

The search for research requires you to understand the lay of the research land: how to find your way around academic libraries, conduct electronic database searches, and obtain relevant information via the Internet and World Wide Web. The most important source of information for any researcher, as we have stressed time and again in this chapter, is the primary research report—the first reporting of a research study by the person(s) who actually conducted the study. And the most important source of primary research reports is the scholarly journals. Understanding the format of a typical scholarly journal article enables the relevance of each piece to be evaluated. This evaluation process leads researchers to revise the topic being investigated and helps them to select the most appropriate research articles to include in a review of the literature.

Finding, reading, and evaluating relevant literature is a cyclical process, engaged in until researchers are confident enough to pose a formal research question or hypothesis and write a literature review. Once that process is complete, they are ready to plan and design their research study, a topic we examine in Part Two.

FIGURE 3.7   American Psychological Association (APA) style for citing sources

---

A. In the Body of the Text

 1. Direct Quote (A): According to C. R. Scott, Corman, and Cheney (1998), "Although none of the existing identification research appears to operationalize identification in a way that allows for a more changing (situationally dependent) view of the construct, several scholars suggest it should" (p. 320).

 [Note: If two or more first authors listed in the references have the same last name, include the authors' initials when mentioned in the text, such as we did here because there are two first authors with that last name in the references for this text.]

 2. Direct Quote (B): The researchers expected to find that "the greater the consistency between expectations and actual job experiences, the more rewarding an individual will find his or her job" (Kalbfleisch & Bach, 1998, p. 380).

 3. Acknowledging Research (A): Sias and Cahill (1998) found that physical proximity between people in the workplace was perceived as leading to friendship development.

 4. Acknowledging Research (B): A number of researchers have found that significant symbols, especially metaphors, help newcomers to understand an organization's culture and their role in it (see Donnellon, Gray, & Bongon, 1986; S. Koch & Deetz, 1981; Riley, 1983, 1985; Sackmann, 1989; Trujillo, 1985; Vaughn, 1995).

 [Note: One can use "e.g.," in place of "see."]

 5. Citing Secondary Research: Mosteller (cited in Webb, Campbell, Schwartz & Sechrest, 1973) studied which sections of the *International Encyclopedia of the Social Sciences* were read most often by examining the wear and tear of the pages of each section.

 [Note: Provide both the original source, without the publication year, and the secondary source in the text, but list only the secondary source in the references.]

B. In the References

 1. Book by a Single Author

 Spicer, C. (1997). <u>Organizational public relations: A political perspective.</u> Mahwah, NJ: Lawrence Erlbaum.

 [Note: Indent the first line of all references six spaces from the left margin; all subsequent lines are flush left. Capitalize only the first letter of the book title and the first letter following a colon. Underline the book title through the period following it.]

 2. Second and Subsequent Editions of a Book

 Garrison, B. (1998). <u>Computer-assisted reporting</u> (2nd ed.). Mahwah, NJ: Lawrence Erlbaum.

(continued)

FIGURE 3.7 *Continued*

3. Book by Two or More Authors

> Grossberg, L., Wartella, E., & Whitney, D. (1998). <u>Mediamaking: Mass media in a popular culture.</u> Thousand Oaks, CA: Sage.

[Note: If there are six or more authors, in the text, use the first author's last name and then "et al.," such as (Grossberg et al., 1998); this also applies to citing chapters in edited texts and journal articles with six or more authors.]

4. Chapter in an Edited Book

> Horvath, C. W. (1998). Biological origins of communicator style. In J. C. McCroskey, J. A. Daly, M. M. Martin, & M. J. Beatty (Eds.), <u>Communication and personality: Trait perspectives</u> (pp. 69–94). Cresskill, NJ: Hampton Press.

[Note: If the edited text is a second or subsequent edition, give the edition number inside the parentheses with the page numbers, such as (2nd ed., pp. 101–145).]

5. Journal Article by a Single Author

> Fabj, V. (1998). Intolerance, forgiveness, and promise in the rhetoric of conversation: Italian women defy the mafia. <u>Quarterly Journal of Speech, 84,</u> 190–208.

[Note: Capitalize the first letter of each term in the journal name and underline through the comma following the volume number; for journals paginated by issue, rather than volume, give the underlined volume number immediately followed by the issue number in parentheses and then the comma, followed by the page numbers, such as <u>84</u>(2), 190–208.]

6. Journal Article by Two or More Authors

> Barnhurst, K. G., & Wartella, E. (1998). Young citizens, American TV newscasts and the collective memory. <u>Critical Studies in Mass Communication, 15,</u> 279–305.

7. Magazine or Newspaper Article

> Kleiman, C. (1999, January 5). Working at home a "right solution" for more families. <u>Chicago Tribune,</u> Sect. 3, p. 1.

[Note: If there is no author, use the title of the article in its place and in the text, use a shortened version in quotation marks followed by the publication year, such as ("Working at Home," 1999).]

FIGURE 3.7

8. Paper Presented at a Conference

House, A. (1998, November). Naming our relationships: The struggle of fitting language to social experience. Paper presented at the meeting of the National Communication Association, New York, NY.

9. Online Journal

Kayany, J. (1998). Instructional uses and effects of World Wide Web course pages: A review of instruction experiments. American Communication Journal [On-line], 3(1). Available Internet: http://www.americancomm.org/~aca/acj/acj.html

10. Online Web Site Information

The NAMES Foundation Project (1999, January 9). The quilt: All about the AIDS memorial quilt [On-line]. Available Internet: www.aidsquilt.org/quilt/

Source: Based on the *Publication Manual of the American Psychological Association, 4th edition.*

PLANNING AND DESIGNING COMMUNICATION RESEARCH

CHAPTER 4

OBSERVING AND MEASURING COMMUNICATION VARIABLES

If you meet an old friend after a long separation, and ask, "How ya' doin'?" you're likely to get the bland and disappointing answer, "Fine." That answer tells you nothing about what's really happening in your friend's life, and might even leave you feeling rebuffed. But if that were the only question you asked, that would be the kind of answer you would deserve. Vague questions most often yield uninformative responses.

So how might you learn more about your friend's life? You would, of course, ask pointed questions about specific issues, such as "How's your job?" "How are things going with your sister?" "What's new at school?" and "How's your love life?" In so doing, you're taking the overall goal, "learning about your friend's life," and dividing it into some of its main components. You would also probe further about details within each area to learn yet more.

By inquiring about more precise dimensions of your friend's life, you're doing, in a sense, what researchers do—finding out what you want to know about a general issue by identifying, and then getting a reading on, component variables that especially interest you. The process of variable identification and measurement in the work of communication researchers has a similar goal—learning about particular elements of communication in people's lives. They, too, pursue what interests them via questions that target precise kinds of information. Identifying and determining how to measure the observable, or empirical, characteristics of whatever concepts or variables researchers wish to study is called *operationalization*. This chapter examines the process of operationalization, showing how researchers develop strategies

for observing and measuring the variables they study.

CONCEPTUAL VERSUS OPERATIONAL DEFINITIONS

When researchers start to operationalize an abstract term, they take word definition a step beyond our commonsense view of it. We usually define a term by its "conceptual" meaning. A **conceptual definition** describes what a concept means by relating it to other abstract concepts. This is the kind of definition given in dictionaries. For example, one dictionary defines the term "love" as "a deep and tender feeling of affection for or devotion to a person or persons." Notice how this definition uses other abstract concepts—"deep," "tender," "feeling," "affection," and "devotion"—to define the central concept of love.

An **operational definition,** in contrast, describes a concept in terms of its observable and measurable characteristics or behaviors, by specifying how the concept can be observed in actual practice. When we asked a group of students what observable characteristics are associated with "love"—that is, the behaviors enacted by two people who love each other—they mentioned: (a) saying "I love you" to the other person, (b) staring into each other's eyes, (c) holding hands, and (d) smiling at one another. If we put these characteristics together, we have observable, measurable indicators of love—that is, an operational definition for the term love.

Notice that we've also focused on communication-related indicators of love. Had we been psychologists, we might have operationalized love in terms of cognitive or emotional states, such as how much a person reports feeling close, physically attracted, and committed to another person. But because communication scholars are interested in communication behavior, we selected communication indicators of love.

It is theoretically possible to operationalize any abstract concept. The example of "love" is a particularly multifaceted concept, one that has filled the pages of many books, love-advice columns, and therapy sessions. Many concepts of interest to researchers are much easier to operationally define; for example, one's age is defined rather easily in operational terms as the number of years since the time one was born.

Second, while simple concepts, like the volume or pitch of a voice, may be operationally defined by a single observable characteristic (e.g., decibels or frequency of recorded sounds), no single characteristic stands very well for complex concepts. Even a long list of characteristics may not capture the concept fully, as the example of love illustrates. An operational definition represents the most readily available way of specifying the observable characteristics of an abstract concept that we currently know, but operational definitions rarely capture completely all the dimensions of sophisticated concepts. Researchers simply can't specify all the observable characteristics of concepts such as love, wisdom, maturity, evil, or even communication competence, but they never cease trying to devise useful, working operational definitions for conducting research about such complex concepts.

Third, when many observable characteristics are included in an operational definition, researchers must decide which ones are more essential than the others for defining the abstract concept. For example, lots of people smile at each other, but this doesn't necessarily mean they love each other. Saying "I love you" is probably a better indicator of love, although it probably isn't sufficient. After all, people have been known to say this to another without necessarily meaning it!

The first step in research, then, is moving from the abstract, conceptual level to the concrete,

operational level. Only after defining a concept operationally can researchers measure it. In fact, we would argue that abstract concepts depend on their observable characteristics to exist. When we say, for example, that a "paranoid person" is walking down the street, we really mean a person who behaves in ways we associate with being paranoid (e.g., looking over his or her shoulder every few steps) is walking down the street.

Evaluating Operational Definitions

Researchers use a conceptual definition as the basis for devising a good operational definition. As G. R. Miller and Boster (1989) explain, "The conceptual definition contains the seeds of clear, useful ways to operationally define the construct so as to bridge the gap between the verbal and operational universes" (p. 23). Good conceptual definitions describe the primary elements of the research topic being investigated, and researchers often refer back to them to assure that the behaviors they observe and measure in their studies actually reflect the conceptual components of their research topic.

Researchers try to retain in the operational definition the essential meaning of a conceptual definition. This strong linkage between a conceptual and an operational definition is referred to as **conceptual fit.** The closer the conceptual fit, the more likely it is that researchers are observing the phenomenon they intend to study. The looser the conceptual fit, the greater the danger that researchers are observing a phenomenon different from the one they intended to study. Obviously, a poor conceptual fit seriously jeopardizes the theoretical and practical utility of the entire research process.

For example, some people are clearly more humorous or funny than others, but what makes them so? S. Booth-Butterfield and Booth-Butterfield (1991) sought to answer that question by studying individual differences in the encoding of humorous messages. They started by conceptually defining the concept of humor as "intentional verbal and nonverbal messages which elicit laughter, chuckling, and other forms of spontaneous behavior taken to mean pleasure, delight, and/or surprise in the targeted receiver" (p. 206). They then generated a list of behaviors that can be observed when someone is humorous in interpersonal situations. These behaviors included "regularly tells jokes," "has friends who say he or she is funny," and "people usually laugh when he or she tells a joke or funny story." Would you agree that these behaviors characterize a person you find humorous? By putting these, and other, characteristics together, these researchers attempted to construct an operational definition with a close conceptual fit to what we think of as a person with a good sense of humor.

Of course, researchers may differ about how a concept should be operationally defined and measured. In fact, S. Booth-Butterfield and Booth-Butterfield (1991) thought previous ways of operationalizing one's sense of humor—such as Feingold's (1983) method, which assesses how well people complete the punch line of familiar jokes, such as "Take my wife, _____"—did not capture very well how people encode and enact humorous messages, so they constructed their own operational definition.

How do we know whether an operational definition is a good one? L. L. Barker (1989) suggests keeping the following questions in mind when evaluating researchers' operational definitions:

1. Is the definition or operationalization *adequate*? That is, does it provide a complete description of all important dimensions of the variable?
2. Is the definition or operationalization *accurate*? Is it a valid and universally agreed-on way of viewing a variable?
3. Is the definition or operationalization *clear*? Are the terms of measurement devices described and defined familiar to the majority of report readers and future researchers? (p. 71)

MEASUREMENT THEORY

After researchers specify the observable characteristics of the concepts being investigated, they must determine ways to record and order in a systematic way observations of those behavioral characteristics. **Measurement** is the process of determining the existence, characteristics, size, and/or quantity of changes or differences in a variable through systematic recording and organization of the researcher's observations.

Some form of measurement, DeVellis (1991) believes, "has been a part of our species' repertoire since prehistoric times. The earliest humans must have evaluated objects, possessions, and opponents on the basis of such characteristics as size" (p. 3). Even the Bible, as Duncan (1984) points out, references measurement: "A false balance is an abomination to the Lord, but a just weight is a delight" (Proverbs 11:1). Increasingly precise measurement and statistical analysis of behavior, however, are relatively recent developments, pioneered in the nineteenth century and refined in the twentieth century. The following sections examine three important aspects of measurement advances: (a) quantitative and qualitative measurements, (b) levels of measurement; and (c) measuring unidimensional and multidimensional concepts.

Quantitative and Qualitative Measurements

One way measurements are distinguished is with respect to whether they employ meaningful numerical symbols. **Quantitative measurements** employ meaningful numerical indicators to ascertain the relative amount of something, whereas **qualitative measurements** employ symbols (words, diagrams, and nonmeaningful numbers) to indicate the meanings (other than relative amounts) people have of something. For example, saying someone weighs "250 pounds" is a quantitative measurement; saying someone is "heavy" is a qualitative measurement.

Quantitative and qualitative measurements provide researchers with different but potentially complementary ways of measuring operationally defined concepts. Suppose, for example, that the editors of a magazine want to know whether their magazine appeals to readers. One way they could do this is to count how many copies of each issue are sold. The more issues sold, the more appealing the magazine must be. They could also ascertain this qualitatively, by asking a group of readers to express their feelings about the magazine. Positive terms would indicate its appeal, too. From the readers' comments, they learn how appealing the magazine is and *why*. As this example shows, quantitative measurements provide numerical precision about such properties as amount and size, whereas qualitative measurements provide useful information about people's perceptions.

There has been much debate in communication research about whether quantitative or qualitative measurement is more persuasive. Baesler and Burgoon (1994), for example, exposed people to one of four messages about juvenile delinquency that were constructed on the basis of evidence type (story or statistical) and vividness (vivid or nonvivid), and they also had a control group that received no such message. The message was either a story about a particular juvenile delinquent or numerical information (e.g., simple percentages) about the typical pattern for delinquents noted on the basis of several hundred people. Message vividness was manipulated with regard to emotiveness, concreteness, and imagery to form vivid and nonvivid messages. Beliefs about juvenile delinquents (e.g., "they grow up to become criminals") were measured immediately after reading the message, 48 hours afterwards, and 1 week later. The findings showed that all forms of evidence were initially persuasive when compared with no evidence. Statistical evidence, however, was more persuasive than story evidence, and this held constant at 48 hours and even 1 week for the vivid statistical evidence. Baesler and Burgoon believe the vividness of the evidence is most important; when vivid quantitative measurements are presented, people can be "moved" and persuaded by them.

The persuasiveness of statistical evidence is also supported by M. Allen and Preiss's (1997) meta-analysis, which showed that across 15 investigations, statistical evidence was more persuasive than narrative evidence. But there are some studies that support the persuasiveness of other forms of qualitative evidence besides narratives. Kazoleas

(1993), for example, conducted an experiment in which people in the treatment conditions were told that they were reading a transcript from an official congressional forum that advocated the use of seat belts. He used two identical messages, except that one contained quantitative evidence comprised of statistical/numerical information, whereas the other message consisted of qualitative evidence in the form of examples, anecdotes, and analogies. Kazoleas also included another condition with an irrelevant message and a no-message control group for comparison purposes. All participants then immediately completed a posttest (see Chapter 7) that measured their attitudes toward seat belt usage, and half the participants completed it again two weeks later. The results showed that while both types of evidence were equally effective in changing attitudes, the qualitative evidence was significantly more persuasive over time. People also recalled the qualitative evidence better than the quantitative evidence.

It could be that quantitative and qualitative measurements affect people in different ways. For example, in a study of persuasive health messages about organ donation, Kopfman, Smith, Ah Yun, and Hodges (1998) found that quantitative evidence produced greater results on cognitive dependent variables (such as a higher number of total thoughts produced about organ donation), whereas qualitative evidence produced greater results on affective variables (such as the amount of anxiety experienced).

The debate between quantitative and qualitative measurements is by no means settled. Ultimately, the choice of one or the other depends on the purpose of the research, the type of research question or hypothesis posed, the ways in which concepts are conceived and operationalized, and the methodology thought to produce the best results.

Many researchers and practitioners actually use both types of measurements to enhance both the precision of the data gathered (via quantitative measures) and an understanding of contextual influences on those data (via qualitative observations). Using the magazine example above, combining the number of issues sold (quantitative data) with readers' comments (qualitative data) would assess the magazine's appeal more effectively than relying on either type of information alone.

Studying something in multiple ways within a single study is called **triangulation.** The term actually comes from trigonometry, where it means calculating the distance to a point by looking at it from two other points. In social-scientific research, according to N. K. Denzin (1978), there are at least four types of triangulation. **Methodological triangulation** involves the use of and comparisons made among multiple methods to study the same phenomenon. A second type is **data triangulation,** where a number of data sources are used. A third type is **researcher triangulation,** in which multiple researchers are used to collect and analyze data. The fourth type is called **theoretical triangulation** and involves using multiple theories and/or perspectives to interpret the same data.

Communication researchers often use triangulation to increase their understanding of the phenomenon of interest, and one way to methodologically triangulate research findings is to combine quantitative and qualitative measurements. Eaves and Leathers (1991), for example, seeking to understand the effects of the physical environment on people, compared and contrasted the interior environments at McDonald's and Burger King's suburban restaurants. Part of their study involved observing customers' involvement and comfort at these two fast-food restaurants. One of the behavioral indicators of involvement was smiling behavior, operationalized as "any apparent smile on the customer's face for at least two seconds, regardless of the context of the smile" (p. 274). They observed the behaviors of seated customers and counted their number of smiles (a quantitative measurement). But Eaves and Leathers were also interested in what design choices and physical features of the environments at McDonald's and Burger King might contribute to customers' smiling behavior. One of the variables they selected was the color

choices made by designers at these two restaurants. They observed that McDonald's consistently used colors that are known to be "stimulating" and "emotionally arousing" (see L. J. Smith & Malandro, 1985), such as eye-catching wallpaper hues of pure white and yellow; in contrast, Burger King used rustic colors to relax customers and put them at ease. Eaves and Leathers used these qualitative observations to help explain why people smiled more at McDonald's than at Burger King.

Levels of Measurement

In Chapter 2, we described a variable as an observable concept that can take on different values. These different values are measured by using a **measurement scale,** "a specific scheme for assigning numbers or symbols to designate characteristics of a variable" (F. Williams, 1986, p. 14). Stevens (1958) identified four levels of measurement scales used to describe the type, range, and relationships among the values a variable can take: nominal, ordinal, interval, and ratio.

These levels of measurement are arranged hierarchically—each level has all the characteristics of the preceding level, and each provides increasing measurement precision and information about a variable. The choice to use a particular level of measurement depends on the purposes of the research.

Nominal Measurement Scales. Nominal variables are differentiated on the basis of type or category; hence, **nominal measurement scales** classify a variable into different categories. The term "nominal" is derived from the Latin *nomen,* meaning "name," and the categories of a nominal scale may be named by words (such as *male* and *female* or *yes* and *no*) or by numbers (such as phone numbers or license plate numbers on cars). As we explained before, numbers used in this way reference different categories, not the degree or amount of a variable. The categories of a nominal measurement scale (whether words or numbers) are, thus, not arranged in any particular order, from highest to lowest or from best to worst; they simply represent different categories.

A variable measured at the nominal level must be classifiable into at least two different categories. These categories must exhibit three qualities. First, the categories must be mutually exclusive; otherwise, comparisons between them are misleading. The mutually exclusive biological categories of male and female that comprise the variable of gender are a good nominal measure, for a person cannot be classified as both.

Constructing mutually exclusive categories is not always easy, as a federal task force discovered when it reexamined the United States government's official racial designations (see Citro, 1997; James, 1997). The choices offered in the past were White, Black, Asian–Pacific Islander, American Indian–Alaskan Native, and other. The dramatically changing demographics of the United States population, however, called into question the exclusive nature of these categories. Golfer Tiger Woods, for example, calls himself "Cablinasian" to recognize his Caucasian, American Indian, Black, and Asian heritages. The task force considered, but rejected, adding a category of "multiracial." Some argued that this category would be more accurate and inclusive, whereas others argued that it would be confusing, would not provide specific enough information, and might hurt minorities that need help remedying past discrimination. The task force did, however, recommend that the category of "other" be dropped and that people be allowed to check as many categories as needed. Tiger Woods, therefore, would check all four categories that applied.

With regard to communication research, the problem of constructing mutually exclusive categories is illustrated in Christenson and Peterson's (1988) study of college students' perceptions of "mapping" music genres. After consulting music publications and talking with radio music directors, as well as conducting a pretest with 110 undergraduate students, these researchers classified music into 26 categories (see Figure 4.1). But there is undoubtedly some overlap among these categories, which Christenson and Peterson recognize: "We readily acknowledge that no 'perfect' list of music types is possible, because boundaries are in constant flux and open to considerable argument. Indeed, the use of labels at all is probably best considered as a necessary evil" (p. 291).

Second, the categories must be equivalent; otherwise, we will be comparing apples and oranges. For example, classifying prime-time television shows into drama, comedy, half-hour-long, and hour-long categories mixes two different types of categories—type of show (drama and comedy) and length of show (half-hour-long and hour-long). (These also are not mutually exclusive categories, since a drama or comedy show is sometimes a half-hour or an hour long.) Christenson and Peterson's (1988) list of music genres appears to contain two different types of categories—genres (e.g., blues and reggae) and years (e.g., 50s rock and 60s rock). Christenson and Peterson admit that the four categories corresponding to years are "not strictly genre labels," but decided to include them because they "still describe meaningful historical patterns and are terms used by college audiences" (pp. 289–290).

Third, the categories must be exhaustive; otherwise, they will not represent the variable fully. Christenson and Peterson's (1988) list may have been exhaustive when they created it, but does it still fulfill this criterion? Are there other music genres you know of that were not included, perhaps due to changes in music since this study was conducted in 1988? While some categories of nominal measurements don't change over time (e.g., male and female), others (such as music genres) can and do.

Many communication researchers measure variables, especially independent variables, using nominal measurements. For example, studies of differences between people who have and have not been exposed to an experimental treatment (see Chapter 7) measure the independent variable (treatment condition) at the nominal level. Many **background variables** (also called **classification, individual-difference, organismic,** or **subject**

FIGURE 4.1   Nominal-level classification of music genres and examples of artists

MUSIC CATEGORIES	EXAMPLE OF ARTISTS
Contemporary rhythm and blues	Vanity, Shalimar
Blues	Howlin' Wolf, Little Walter, Muddy Waters
Jazz, in general	
Jazz fusion	Weather Report, Return to Forever
Reggae	Jimmy Cliff, Dennis Brown, Burning Spear
Heavy metal	Motley Crue, Iron Maiden, Krokus
Hardcore punk	Sex Pistols, Dead Kennedys
Late 70s disco	BeeGees, Donna Summer, Trammps
Soul	Aretha Franklin, James Brown, Percy Sledge
70s funk	Parliament, Funkadelics, George Clinton
Southern rock	Allman Brothers, Lynyrd Skynyrd
Art rock	King Crimson, Emerson, Lake and Palmer
Folk	Pete Seeger, Joan Baez, Tom Paxton
60s Motown	Four Tops, Temptations, Gladys Knight
Country pop	Willie Nelson, Oak Ridge Boys
Black gospel	Andre Couche, Mahalia Jackson
Christian rock/pop	Amy Grant, David and the Giants
Psychedelic rock	Jimi Hendrix, Jefferson Airplane
Older new wave	B-52s, Elvis Costello, English Beat
Classical, in general	
Post-new wave "new music"	Aztec Camera, Depeche Mode
Mainstream pop	Billy Joel, Fleetwood Mac
50s rock, in general	
60s rock, in general	
70s rock, in general	
80s rock, in general	

Source: Peter G. Christenson and Jon Brian Peterson, "Genre and Gender in the Structure of Music Preference," *Communication Research, 15*(3), p. 290, copyright © 1988 by Sage Publications, Inc. Used by Permission of Sage Publications, Inc.

variables), "aspects of subjects' [research participants] 'backgrounds' that may influence other variables but will not be influenced by them" (Vogt, 1993, p. 16), such as one's nationality and ethnicity, are measured using nominal scales.

Researchers also sometimes measure dependent variables nominally. The most basic way is asking people to answer "yes" or "no" to questions. Alcalay and Bell (1996), for example, examined the use by poor minority women of a health promotion booklet, the *Wellness Guide.* They asked **respondents,** people who answer survey

questions, to use the nominal categories of "yes," "no," or "not sure" to answer such questions as, "Have you ever called any of the phone numbers listed in the *Guide*?"

Another nominal form of measurement is asking people to choose between two or more responses from a checklist. In their study of community life, McLeod et al. (1996) learned how people think about their environment by asking such questions as: "People differ in how strongly they identify with different types of communities and organizations. Which of the following do you identify most closely with? Responses of 'neighborhood' or 'local community'" (p. 205).

Researchers also sometimes measure a dependent variable nominally by first asking people to respond to open-ended questions and then classifying their responses into categories. For example, to study the "rituals" people use to dissolve relationships or to cope with relationship disengagement, Emmers and Hart (1996) asked people to list and describe what they did when (a) they wanted to end a relationship and (b) their partner initiated the termination. Their open-ended responses were coded into seven nominal categories, such as: (a) directness (directly addressing the partner and/or relationship, such as writing and sending letters), (b) avoidance (avoiding the partner and/or relationship, such as not telephoning), and (c) cost-escalation/self (engaging in self-destructive thoughts and behaviors, such as listening to sad music). They counted the number of times one of these behaviors was mentioned, and compiled data about how frequently each nominal category was used by "leavers" and "lefts" at the end of relationships.

Counting the frequency of use of nominal categories may reveal important findings, but it also limits the quantitative data analyses that can be performed and the conclusions that can be drawn. For this reason, researchers often use ordinal, interval, and ratio measurement scales, scales that have meaningful numbers.

Ordinal Measurement Scales. **Ordinal measurement scales** not only classify a variable into nominal categories but also rank order those categories along some dimension. The categories can then be compared because they are measured along some "greater than" and "less than" scale. For example, if you pick out five of the music genres from Figure 4.1, and rank order them from most liked (1) to least liked (5), you have measured your liking for these music genres on an ordinal scale. An ordinal scale in which a particular rank can only be used once (as opposed to allowing ties) is referred to as an **ipsative scale;** a scale that allows ranked ties (as well as interval and ra-

tio rating scales, see below) is called a **normative scale.**

Ordinal measurements provide more information about a variable than nominal measurements because they transform discrete classifications into *ordered* classifications. That is, they not only classify a variable into categories but also arrange these categories in numerical order along a dimension. For example, Zorn and Violanti (1996) studied the relationship between individuals' communication abilities and their achievement in organizations. The research participants were 394 employees of three kinds of organizations. People were ranked according to their position in the organizational hierarchy. For example, six levels were identified in one organization, and each person received a rank order, from the president (6) to non-supervisory nonprofessionals (1). This 6-point rank ordering of organizational position was, thus, an ordinal measurement scale.

Ordinal measurements, however, are still quite limited, for they only rank order a variable along a dimension without telling researchers *how much* more or less of the variable has been measured. We know that the president of an organization is higher in the organizational hierarchy than a vice president, who is higher than a manager, and so forth, but the differences between each consecutive level (e.g., in income or decision-making power) are not likely to be equivalent, and mere ranking does not tell us about this.

A horse race provides a good example of what can and cannot be ascertained from an ordinal scale. It is easy to see which horse finished first, second, and third (an ordinal measurement). However, the first-place finisher may have been ahead of the second-place finisher by one-tenth of a second, while the third-place finisher may have been a full second behind the second-place finisher. The points on an ordinal scale are, thus, arranged in a meaningful numerical order (first, second, third, and so forth), but there is no assumption that the distances between the adjacent points on that scale are equivalent. For that, researchers must use interval and ratio measurement scales (a variable measured by an interval or ratio scale is sometimes called a *continuous, metric,* or *numerical variable*).

Interval Measurement Scales. Interval measurement scales not only categorize a variable (as in nominal measurements) and rank order it along some dimension (as in ordinal measurements) but also establish *equal distances* between each of the adjacent points along the measurement scale. The interval between the measurement points on a Fahrenheit or Celsius temperature scale, for example, is a standard distance; 10 degrees warmer is the same size increase between 20 and 30 degrees as it is between 40 and 50 degrees. Pan and Kosicki (1996), in fact, used a thermometer rating scale from 0 to 100 in their study of how news media influence Whites' racial policy preferences regarding Blacks, with larger numbers indicating more positive feelings.

Interval measurements also include an *arbitrary zero point* on the scale. A zero rating on such a scale does not mean that the variable doesn't exist. For example, a zero degree rating on the Fahrenheit or Celsius scales doesn't mean there is no temperature! Interval scales, therefore, can potentially have both positive and negative values (such as in temperature readings).

Interval measurements provide more information than nominal or ordinal measurements. Different amounts of information are conveyed when one says, "It's a nice day outside" (a nominal measurement), "Today is nicer than yesterday" (an ordinal measurement), and "It's 82 degrees Fahrenheit outside" (an interval measurement). The equal distance between the points on an interval scale also allows the scores or ratings to be manipulated mathematically (added, subtracted, multiplied, or divided).

There are a number of scales used in the social sciences for measuring variables at the interval level. Among the most popular are the Likert and Likert-type scales, the semantic differential scale, and the Thurstone scale.

Likert and Likert-Type Scales. **Likert scales,** developed by psychologist Rensis Likert (1932),

identify the extent of a person's beliefs, attitudes, or feelings toward some object. The traditional Likert scale asks people the extent to which they agree or disagree with a statement by choosing one category on a 5-point scale that ranges from "strongly agree" to "strongly disagree" (see Figure 4.2). For example, M. M. Martin, Anderson, Burant, and Weber (1997) studied the effects of verbally aggressive messages—messages that are sent with the intent of hurting someone (Infante, 1995; Infante & Rancer, 1996)—on sibling relationships. One of the dependent variables was "trust with sibling," which was measured using Larzelere and Huston's (1980) Dyadic Trust Scale. This scale asks siblings to respond to such statements as "I feel that I can trust my sibling completely" and "My sibling is truly sincere in his/her promises" using the 5-point Likert scale ranging from, in this case, (5) strongly agree to (1) strongly disagree.

Researchers often use different answer categories than agree–disagree and sometimes a different number of answers (e.g., 7-point scales), depending on the purpose of the research and type of question(s) asked. Any adaptations that resemble, even superficially, the Likert scale are loosely referred to as **Likert-type** (or **Likert-like**) **scales.** For example, McCroskey, Sallinen, Fayer, Richmond, and Barraclough (1996) measured students'

FIGURE 4.2 A Likert scale

Instructions: Indicate on the scale below, choosing one answer only, how strongly you agree or disagree with the statement.

Listening to heavy metal music makes one prone to violent acts.

_____ Strongly agree

_____ Agree

_____ Neither agree nor disagree

_____ Disagree

_____ Strongly disagree

---

perceptions of their teachers' nonverbal immediacy—the degree of physical or psychological closeness (J. F. Andersen, 1979)—by having them respond to 14 behavioral items that best described their teacher (such as "gestures while talking in class") using a 5-point Likert-type scale: 0 = never, 1 = Rarely, 2 = Occasionally, 3 = Often, and 4 = Very often. O'Mara, Allen, Long, and Judd (1996), on the other hand, measured students' gen-

eral perceptions of their nonverbal immediacy with fellow students and with university instructors on a Likert-type scale ranging from (1) high immediacy to (7) low immediacy. Figure 4.3 provides some additional examples of Likert-type scales used recently by communication researchers.

Most Likert and Likert-type scales include a middle neutral point because sometimes people legitimately neither agree nor disagree or don't

FIGURE 4.3   Examples of Likert-type scales in communication research

RESEARCHER(S)	VARIABLE	SAMPLE QUESTION/ LIKERT-TYPE SCALE
Baron (1996)	Subordinates' perceptions of managers' success in encouraging upward feedback	(1) Low to (7) High
J. K. Burgoon, Buller, Guerrero, Afifi, & Feldman (1996)	Senders' ratings of information during deceptive interviews	(1) Sufficient to (7) Insufficient
Dillard, Kinney, & Cruz (1996)	Affective reactions to watching a videotape of an actor enacting a message varying in explicitness and dominance	"Surprise (surprised, startled, astonished)": (0) None of this feeling to (9) A great deal of this feeling
Fontaine (1996)	Reactions to experiences as participants in intercultural experiential training activities	"During my experience I felt in control of the situation": (1) Very true of my experience to (5) Not true of my experience
Gudykunst et al. (1996)	Ratings of 44 individualistic and collectivisitic cultural values	(1) Not important to (7) Of supreme importance
Kellerman & Shea (1996)	Perceived politeness of threats, suggestions, hints, and promises in seeking to gain another person's compliance with a request	(1) Impolite method for gaining compliance to (7) Polite methods for gaining compliance
M. M. Martin, Anderson, & Hovarth (1996)	Degree of psychological pain/mental hurt experienced by being the target of types of verbally aggressive messages	(1) Almost no hurt to (7) The greatest degree of hurt
Moon & Nass (1996)	Personality ratings of computers by users	"Indicate how well 'friendly' describes the computer you just worked with": (1) Describes very poorly to (10) Describes very well
A. Williams & Giles (1996)	Young adults' perceptions of interactions with older adults (aged 65–75)	"I felt treated like a typically young person": (1) Totally agree to (7) Totally disagree

know how they feel. However, offering a middle point increases the proportion of respondents who use the middle category by 10 to 20% on most issues (Schuman & Presser, 1996). Some researchers, therefore, force respondents to choose whether they agree or disagree, without giving them a neutral option. Lewis and Seibold (1996), for example, in studying how employees responded to a quality program in four organizations, asked them about such things as their uncertainty about it, its effects on their work, and how much they liked it. In each case, they used a 6-point Likert-type scale: strongly disagree, disagree, moderately disagree, moderately agree, agree, and strongly agree.

Some researchers use visual Likert-type scales to measure people's attitudes or feelings. W. S. Z. Ford (1995), for example, studied the influence of cashiers' service behaviors on customers' feelings and behaviors. After interacting with cashiers, customers' mood was measured using a 5-point Likert-type visual scale. Customers were shown a card illustrating various facial expressions (see Figure 4.4), and asked, "Which face most closely represents your mood right now?" (p. 74). Ford justified this scale, inspired by Kunin's (1955) research on "faces," by arguing that it assessed attitudes "without distortion that invariably results from persons translating their 'feelings'

(Kunin's term) into others' words or phrases, as well as by research demonstrating a strong association between persons' moods and their facial expressions" (p. 74).

Finally, researchers also use Likert and Likert-type scales. to rate/evaluate people's behavior. Menzel and Carrell (1994), for example, examined the relationship between preparation and performance in public speaking. To assess performance, students' final videotaped persuasive speech in a course were evaluated by the researchers with regard to four characteristics of thought content (introduction, conclusion, overall organization, and structure of arguments) and four speech delivery behaviors (eye contact, gestures and movement, voice, and energy and enthusiasm) on a 5-point scale for each: (5) "done exceptionally well," (4) "done well," (3) "average," (2) done poorly," and (1) "not done well at all."

Likert and Likert-type scales typically are scored by assigning the number 1 to the category at one end of the scale and consecutively higher numbers to the next categories, up to the number 5 (or 7, etc.) at the other end of the scale. These numbers can then sometimes be summed. Menzel and Carrell (1994), for example, added the values of the four items to arrive at a thought-content score, added the other four to arrive at a speech delivery

---

FIGURE 4.4 Visual Likert-type scale

Source: Wendy S. Zabava Ford, "Evaluation of the Indirect Influence of Courteous Service on Customer Discretionary Behavior," *Human Communication Research, 22*(1), p. 74, copyright © 1995 by Sage Publications, Inc. Used by Permission of Sage Publications, Inc.

score, and added both scores to arrive at a total score.

Semantic Differential Scales.   **Semantic differential scales** were developed by Osgood, Suci, and Tannenbaum (1957) to measure the *meanings* people ascribe to a specific stimulus. Semantic differential scales present a stimulus item (a word, phrase, sentence, etc.) at the top of a list of (usually) 7-point scales representing polar opposites. Respondents choose a single point on each scale that expresses their perception of the stimulus object (see Figure 4.5).

Semantic differential scales are used frequently in communication research. Pfau and Eveland (1996), for example, assessed the influence of traditional and nontraditional forms of news media in the 1992 presidential election campaign on prospective voters' perceptions and attitudes. The information utility of various media sources (e.g., newspapers and television news) was measured using 7-point Likert-type scales, while the dependent variable of candidate competence was measured using three 7-point semantic differential scales: qualified/unqualified, competent/incompetent, and intelligent/unintelligent. The results showed that nontraditional news media exerted more influence than traditional news media on prospective voters' perceptions of candidates' competence.

The selection of the bipolar adjectives for semantic differential scales is not arbitrary or random. Most measure three dimensions: evaluation (e.g., pleasant-unpleasant), potency (e.g., strong-weak), and activity (e.g., fast-slow). Researchers must also make sure that the bipolar adjectives are understood by the research population being studied. For example, in assessing whether workers trust their labor union and its messages, Botan and Frey (1983) used a standard semantic differential scale, the Giffin Trust Differential (see Giffin, 1968, 1969), to measure trust. They found from pretesting the instrument that workers had difficulty understanding the word "extroverted" (which was paired with "introverted"), so they substituted the word "outgoing." The research population must also see the paired adjectives as opposites, which may be problematic, even in apparently simple cases. McCroskey and Richmond (1989) give the following example: "What is the opposite of hard? To a researcher concerned with rocks, it might be 'soft.' To a student who has just completed an exam in another class, it might be 'easy'" (p. 160). The construction of effective semantic differential scales, therefore, requires careful pretesting.

FIGURE 4.5   A semantic differential scale

Instructions: Indicate how you feel about the referent by placing a single check along each scale. For example, on the first scale, if you feel the referent is extremely pleasant, place a check at the extreme left side of that scale. If you feel the referent is extremely unpleasant, place a check at the extreme right side. If you feel somewhere in the middle of these two extremes, place a check at the appropriate place.

Rap Music

Pleasant ___: ___: ___: ___: ___: ___: ___ Unpleasant

Weak ___: ___: ___: ___: ___: ___: ___ Strong

Fast ___: ___: ___: ___: ___: ___: ___ Slow

Like Likert and Likert-type scales, semantic differential scales are scored with numbers 1 through 7 assigned to the points on each scale. When adding up the ratings, researchers make sure that the scoring for each scale is consistent in terms of 1 given to items phrased, for example, in a positive manner and 7 given to items phrased in a negative manner (or vice versa). A respondent's scores on all the scales can then often be summed to produce an overall score for that attitude object (see the discussion of unidimensional scales later in this chapter).

The Thurstone Scale. Although Likert, Likert-type, and semantic differential scales are used extensively in social-scientific research, many scholars question whether the distance between the points on these scales actually are equivalent (e.g., whether the distance between "strongly agree" and "agree" is actually equal to the distance between "agree" and "neither agree nor disagree"). One type of scale that attempts to ensure that the distances are equal is the **Thurstone scale,** named after L. L. Thurstone (1929, 1931).

To construct a Thurstone scale, a researcher first generates many statements, usually several hundred, related to the referent being investigated. A large number of judges, usually 50 to 300, then independently categorize the statements into 11 categories, ranging from "extremely favorable" to "extremely unfavorable." The researcher selects those statements, usually about 20, that all judges code consistently into a particular category. Each statement is assigned a value on the basis of the judges' mean ratings. The instrument that incorporates these statements is then assumed to provide interval measurements, such that a score of 4.2 is assumed to be the same distance from a score of 4.3 as it is from a score of 4.1.

While the Thurstone scale is superior to Likert, Likert-type, and semantic differential scales, and, in fact, is the method from which these scales are descended (see Emmert, 1989), it takes a lot of time and energy to construct. This is probably why it is seldom used in social-scientific research. One

can also never be absolutely sure that these scaled items actually represent equal intervals; indeed, Thurstone called them "equal-appearing intervals." Therefore, in actual practice, researchers use Likert, Likert-type, and semantic differential scales, and assume that the distance between adjacent points on these scales is equivalent. This assumption allows them to use advanced statistical procedures that require interval-level data (see Chapters 13 and 14).

Ratio Measurement Scales. **Ratio measurement scales** not only categorize and rank order a variable along a scale with equal intervals between adjacent points but also establish an *absolute,* or *true, zero point* where the variable being measured ceases to exist. Because of the absolute zero point, ratio measurements cannot have negative values, since the smallest value on a ratio scale is zero. Examples of ratio measurement scales that have absolute zero points are age (you can't be zero years old), weight (you can't weigh zero pounds), and height (you can't be zero feet tall). Because of the absolute zero point and the equal distance between points on a ratio scale, one can say that someone who is 240 pounds weighs twice as much as someone who is 120 pounds.

Ratio measurements are common in the physical sciences, but rare in the social sciences. But some communication variables can be assessed with ratio measurements. For example, in Menzel and Carrell's (1994) study of preparation and public speaking performance, cited previously, ratio measurements were made of several speech preparation variables, including the amount of time spent in audience analysis and adaptation, preparation of speaking notes, and preparation of visual aids; the number of times people rehearsed their speech out loud; and how many of the oral rehearsals were in front of an audience. Other examples of ratio measurements in communication studies include: (a) frequency of nonverbal behaviors (e.g., head movements, gestures, and hand/finger movements) (Vrij, Semin, & Bull, 1996), (b) number of words conveyed and number of speaker turns per group participant (Hollingshead, 1996), (c) number of citations in the *Social Sciences Citation Index* and the *Arts and Humanities Citation Index* (Funkhouser, 1996), (d) number of hours per week people typically watched particular types of television shows (e.g., soap operas, sports, or game shows) (Shrum, 1996), and (e) frequency of various sexual behaviors shown on television soap operas (Lowry & Towles, 1989).

Measuring Unidimensional and Multidimensional Concepts

Many concepts/variables can be measured by asking only one question on a single-item scale. We don't have to ask 20 questions to determine someone's gender, the temperature, or for whom someone will vote. Each of these can be determined by a single question on a measurement scale.

Measuring complex concepts, however, requires multiple items. These several indicators are then combined in some manner to yield the desired measurement. When all those indicators relate to one concept, that concept is called *unidimensional.* When indicators relate to several subconcepts, the concept that unites them is call *multidimensional.* The statistical procedure that reveals whether a concept is unidimensional or multidimensional is called **factor analysis** (see Chapter 14). Here, we comment briefly on the measurement of these two types of concepts.

Unidimensional Concepts.   **Unidimensional concepts** are measured by a set of indicators that can be added together equally to derive a single, overall score. A scale comprised of such items is called a **summated scale.** For example, S. Booth-Butterfield and Booth-Butterfield (1991) took 17 observable characteristics associated with the variable of humor orientation (HO), and asked 275 people to indicate on a Likert scale the extent to which each one applied to themselves. A factor analysis revealed that responses to these 17 items were related to each other and, therefore, they were measuring a unidimensional concept. In other words, those 17

items can simply be summed to obtain a person's overall humor orientation score (see Figure 4.6).

Take a few minutes to complete the HO instrument, and total your score. Make sure you reverse the scoring for items marked with an asterisk; for those items, $5 = 1$, $4 = 2$, $3 = 3$, $2 = 4$, and $1 = 5$. (We will see later in the chapter why researchers do this.) Since there are 17 items on the questionnaire, scores can range from 17 (the highest HO score possible) to 85 (the lowest HO score possible).

Multidimensional Concepts.   Many communication concepts are composed of a number of different subconcepts, called **factors.** These factors can vary relatively independently, so that people's scores (or answers on questionnaire items) on a measure of one factor are not related to their scores (or answers) on another factor. Alternatively, the factors can be related in complicated ways. Concepts that incorporate more than one factor and, therefore, must be measured by more than one set of scale items (each set of scale items, of course, is a summated scale that can be added together), are called **multidimensional concepts.**

For example, a number of researchers (Berlo, Lemert, & Mertz, 1971; E. W. Miles & Leathers, 1984; Teven & Comadena, 1996) have found that credibility (believability) is a multidimensional concept composed of three independent factors: authoritativeness, trustworthiness, and dynamism. Each of these factors has been measured by six 7-point semantic differential scales:

(a) Authoritativeness: qualified/unqualified, informed/uninformed, authoritative/unauthoritative, trained/untrained, experienced/inexperienced, skilled/unskilled
(b) Trustworthiness: agreeable/unagreeable, kind/cruel, pleasant/unpleasant, safe/dangerous, congenial/quarrelsome, friendly/unfriendly
(c) Dynamism: empathetic/hesitant, active/passive, aggressive/meek, bold/timid, frank/reserved, forceful/forceless.

The six items (semantic differential scales) used to measure each factor are added together to produce

FIGURE 4.6   Humor Orientation Scale

Indicate the degree to which you agree or disagree with the statements given below using the following scale:

1 = Strongly agree
2 = Agree
3 = Neutral
4 = Disagree
5 = Strongly disagree

_____   1. I regularly tell jokes and funny stories when I am in a group.

_____   2. People usually laugh when I tell a joke or story.

_____ *3. I have no memory for jokes or funny stories.

_____   4. I can be funny without having to rehearse a joke.

_____   5. Being funny is a natural communication style with me.

_____ *6. I cannot tell a joke well.

_____ *7. People seldom ask me to tell stories.

_____   8. My friends would say that I am a funny person.

_____ *9. People don't seem to pay close attention when I tell a joke.

_____*10. Even funny jokes seem flat when I tell them.

_____ 11. I can easily remember jokes and stories.

_____ 12. People often ask me to tell jokes and stories.

_____*13. My friends would not say that I am a funny person.

_____*14. I don't tell jokes or stories even when asked to.

_____ 15. I tell stories and jokes very well.

_____ 16. Of all the people I know, I'm one of the funniest.

_____ 17. I use humor to communicate in a variety of situations.

_____ Total Score (17–85) (Add numbers, making sure to reverse the scoring for those items marked with an * [e.g., if you answered 1, give yourself a 5, etc.])

Source: Steven Booth-Butterfield and Melanie Booth-Butterfield, "Individual Differences in the Communication of Humorous Messages," *Southern Communication Journal, 56*(3), p. 207, copyright © 1991 by the Southern States Communication Association. Reprinted with permission of the Southern States Communication Association.

a separate score for (a) authoritativeness, (b) trustworthiness, and (c) dynamism. These three scores might simply be summed into a single score, or they might be related in more complicated ways that require differential weighting.

MEASUREMENT METHODS

Let's assume a researcher has taken the steps we've covered so far in this chapter. An abstract concept has been operationalized by specifying the concrete characteristics/behaviors to be observed, a scale has been selected to measure it, and it has been determined whether the scale is unidimensional or multidimensional. The researcher next decides on a method for measuring the extent to which people demonstrate those characteristics. Researchers use three general measurement methods: self-reports, others' reports, and observing behavioral acts. The strengths and weaknesses of each method influence whether it is the best approach in a particular situation.

Self-Reports

Most researchers use **self-reports** to measure their target characteristics/behaviors. They ask people to comment on themselves. The answers are taken as a reading of the operationally defined concept. For example, the answers you gave on the humor orientation instrument (Figure 4.6) are a self-report measure of how humorous you are.

There are both advantages and disadvantages to using self-reports like the HO instrument. On the one hand, self-reports are an efficient way to ascertain respondents' beliefs, attitudes, and values. These are psychological characteristics that exist inside of people's heads, which makes them impossible to observe directly, so asking people what they think, like, or value makes sense. After all, people's self-report is the best way to learn how much they like an activity, such as working out at a health club. Inferring what's in their mind from actual behavior may be misleading. A person who works out regularly at a health club doesn't necessarily *like* working out; he or she may simply believe in a "no pain, no gain" philosophy.

Self-reports can also sometimes be a good measure of how people behave. The researcher asks them how often they do something. Some social scientists distrust self-reports of behavior and believe that observations of behavior are more accurate (see G. S. Howard, Maxwell, Wiener, Boynton, & Rooney, 1980). They fear there may be little relationship between what people say they do and how they actually behave, captured in everyday discourse by the adage "Do as I say, not as

I do." Records at a health club, for example, are probably a better indicator of how many times a person worked out over the past year than his or her self-reported exercise schedule. But behavioral measures aren't always superior to self-reports for assessing behavior. In a series of studies, G. S. Howard et al. (1980) found that self-reports of behavior were as good as or significantly superior to behavioral measures. It is not the measurement method per se that is better, it is a matter of which method yields the most valid information about people's behavior (see Chapter 5, where we examine measurement validity in some detail).

Self-reports don't yield valid information when people aren't able and/or willing to provide complete and accurate information. Sometimes accurate answers are just too difficult to provide. For example, you probably can't recall accurately how many long-distance phone calls you made last year. Your phone records would yield a more accurate measure.

People also may provide inaccurate information when asked to step outside themselves and comment on behaviors they might not normally think about or remember. For example, most people can recall only a small fraction of the things they've said. You've probably met people who don't remember what they said two minutes before, let alone what they said last week, last month, or last year. You've probably also met people who can remember many past conversations almost verbatim. Those people pay more attention to their verbal and nonverbal behaviors, a practice called *self-monitoring* (see Snyder, 1974, 1979). We would expect high self-monitors to provide more complete and accurate information about their behavior than low self-monitors.

Sometimes people don't report the truth. For example, alcoholics asked about the number of drinks they have each day may not be honest, and people with racist ideas may not readily admit them to researchers. Self-reports about controversial issues or deviant behavior are questionable, due, in part, to a **social desirability bias,** the tendency for people to answer in socially desirable ways (see A. L. Edwards, 1953; Furnham, 1986).

A social desirability bias potentially compromises the validity of many self-reports (see Lineham & Nielsen, 1981). For example, Nicotera (1996) assessed whether a social desirability bias affected males' and females' responses to the argumentativeness instrument, which measures the tendency to "advocate positions on controversial issues and to attack verbally the positions which other people take on these issues" (Infante & Rancer, 1982, p. 72). Previous research showed that males score higher than females on this instrument (see Infante, 1981; Infante & Rancer, 1982; Infante, Trebing, Shepard, & Seeds, 1984; Nicotera & Rancer, 1994; Nicotera, Smilowitz, & Pearson, 1990), but Nicotera suspected that this finding might be because arguing is more socially acceptable for men than for women. If that is the case, a social desirability bias would lead women to be more reluctant than men to rate themselves as argumentative.

Nicotera first had a sample of men and women indicate the social acceptability of the 20 items on the argumentativeness instrument. She found that males judged the items to be more socially desirable than did females. She then had a second sample complete the original argumentativeness instrument, and then rate the items' social acceptability. The results showed a positive, but not particularly strong, relationship between argumentativeness and judgments of the instrument's social desirability. Although Nicotera's findings were not strong enough to warrant a revision of the argumentativeness instrument, the findings alert researchers to consider a social desirability bias due to gender when interpreting data acquired from this instrument.

Others' Reports

A second general method for measuring how much people demonstrate particular characteristics/behaviors is through **others' reports,** that is, asking people to describe other people. For example, spouses may be asked to comment on their partner's communication skills, managers may be asked to describe their subordinates' information-seeking behavior, and parents may be asked about their children's aggressive behavior.

In some cases, others' reports may be more accurate than self-reports. For example, if you want to know which professors give clear lectures, it makes less sense to ask professors (after all, the lectures are clear to them) than to ask professors' former students. Others often are more appropriate judges of a person's behavior than the person is himself or herself.

But others' reports can be as susceptible to inaccuracy as self-reports. Some people have insufficient observations on which to draw a conclusion. Managers who travel a lot may not be able to describe their subordinates' behavior accurately. Some people may be biased in favor of or against other people. Asking former students to judge their professors' lectures may be influenced by how well the students did in the class. Observers may also be less motivated than participants to recall or provide information, which may affect the accuracy of their responses. W. J. Benoit, Benoit, and Wilkie (1988), for example, showed that conversational participants remember more than observers, even after a short delay of 5–10 minutes, and P. J. Benoit and Benoit (1994) showed that after a week, memory traces of conversations are substantially stronger for participants than for observers.

To compensate for the strengths and weaknesses of self-reports and others' reports, researchers sometimes use both procedures to develop a triangulated measurement. In Wanzer, Booth-Butterfield, and Booth-Butterfield's (1996) study of humor orientation, for example, both self-reports and other people's reports were used to measure humorousness. Participants first completed the HO instrument. They then asked two acquaintances to complete an adapted version of the instrument that contained identical items, modified to read, for example, "This person regularly tells jokes and funny stories when in a group." They found moderate agreement between how individuals reported their own tendency to be funny and how their acquaintances viewed them, although the higher the individual's self-reported HO score, the more others viewed him or her as humorous. When respondents and others agree that they behave in particular ways, researchers have more confidence in the accuracy of their measurements. When these responses conflict, researchers have less confidence in the accuracy of either measurement.

Behavioral Acts

Researchers needn't rely solely on reports from respondents or from others. They themselves can sometimes observe a person's *behavior* to assess an operationally defined concept.

Shrum (1996), for example, studied psychological processes underlying cultivation effects, a theory that asserts that television programs bias viewers' perceptions of reality to mirror what they see on television (e.g., it predicts that those who watch a lot of crime shows will overestimate the amount of real-life crime). Shrum reasoned that heavy viewers of daytime soap operas (5 or more hours per week) would respond faster to cultivation questions (e.g., "What percentage of women are raped in their lifetime?" or "What percentage of Americans have been the victim of a violent crime?") than those who did not watch such shows, based on the assumption that a shorter reaction time indicates less need to think or greater certainty about these matters. To measure reaction time, participants answered the questions on a microcomputer. When the space bar was pressed, a question appeared, and respondents answered by pressing keys labeled from 0 to 9, with each key corresponding to an intuitive percentage response range (e.g., a response of 6 indicated 60% to 69%). Response time was measured in milliseconds. Sure enough, heavy viewers did respond significantly faster than those who did not watch the shows.

S. W. Smith, Morrison, Kopfman, and Ford (1994) also operationally assessed concepts by studying behaviors. They investigated the influence of prior thought and intent on the impact of messages designed to get people to donate their organs. Respondents first rated their attitudes about donating organs and then were presented with one of two persuasive messages (positive statements only or positive plus refutational statements) regarding organ donation. Two days later, they were given other tests and told they could take a brochure that contained further information and an actual organ donor card. The number of persons who took the brochure containing the donor card was used as a behavioral indicator of the intent to donate organs.

Most researchers believe that direct measures of a person's behavior are more accurate than self-reports or others' reports. Someone may say he or she works out at a health club every day, and his or her friends may concur, but what if we followed that person to the health club every day for a month and found that he or she spent most of the time in the health club bar?! We probably would conclude, in this case, that "actions speak louder than words."

Some communication research shows that what people say they do is often not what they actually do. Carrell and Willmington (1998), for example, had people fill out a self-report instrument that measured their communication apprehension about giving a public speech. These individuals then gave an informative public speech, and behavioral indicators of public speaking competence (such as vocal usage) and anxiety (such as verbal fluency) were rated by two trained observers. The results showed few meaningful relationships between self-reported communication apprehension and the behavioral indicators of public speaking competence.

In two instances, however, behavioral acts aren't as useful to researchers as self-reports or others' reports. First, behaviors show what people do, not what they believe or feel. Scholars studying persuasion know that *compliance,* performing a behavior, differs from *internalization,* valuing a behavior. For example, a person may comply with a spouse's request to go shopping for a number of reasons, but that doesn't necessarily mean the person wants or likes to go shopping. Second, researchers must be sure the behaviors observed accurately represent the concept of interest. The comedian Henny Youngman humorously illustrates the limitations of relying strictly on behavior when he quoted a mother who bragged about her child: "He plays just like Paderewski—he uses both hands."

We would, of course, have the most confidence in the accuracy of behavioral acts that match self-reports and/or others' reports. Wanzer, Booth-Butterfield, and Booth-Butterfield (1995), for example, conducted another study to check whether people who self-report a higher humor orientation actually are more funny in terms of behavior. They measured whether humorous people have a better memory for jokes (one of the items on the HO self-report instrument) by having high- and low-HO people complete Feingold's (1982) measure, mentioned previously, which requires people to complete well-known joke fragments. They found that high HOs did not differ from low HOs on the number of correct answers. This surprising finding led Wanzer et al. to question Feingold's instrument and coding procedures. They argued that his list of answers didn't allow for responses that were funny but not technically "correct." They also argued that some of the items were dated and, therefore, unfamiliar to current college students (e.g., "Did you hear about the David and Goliath cocktail? _____ " [Two sips and you're stoned.]).

In that same study, Wanzer et al. also behaviorally assessed participants' ability to tell a joke. They gave all participants a card with three jokes to tell (e.g., "Why did the Cyclops quit teaching? He only had one pupil."). After participants told the three jokes to two other participants, the two listeners rated the perceived funniness of the person. The performances were also audiotaped and played to trained raters who evaluated them on six scales that assessed funniness (e.g., "This person was skilled in telling jokes"). The results showed that high HOs did, in fact, receive higher ratings of "funniness" than low HOs. This consistency between scores on their self-report scale and a behavioral measure increased the researchers' confidence that each method measured humor ability accurately.

MEASUREMENT TECHNIQUES

Three specific measurement techniques are used in conjunction with self-reports, others' reports, and behavioral acts: (a) *questionnaires,* the presentation of written questions to evoke written responses from people, (b) *interviews,* the presentation of spoken questions to evoke spoken responses from people, and (c) *observations,* the systematic inspection and interpretation of behavioral phenomena. Questionnaires and interviews are used with self-reports and others' reports, while observations are used by researchers to assess behavior. Researchers have developed many **instruments** for using these measurement techniques; that is, specific, formal measurement tools used to gather data about research variables. (For a sourcebook of some available communication research instruments, see Rubin, Palmgreen, & Sypher, 1994.)

These measurement techniques are employed within the guidelines and goals of the four specific research methodologies we discuss later in this text. Many of the same measurement techniques are used to gather data in these four methodologies. Here, we discuss the general use of questionnaires, interviews, and observations *across* the four methodologies, and focus on their specialized uses in Chapters 7 through 10.

Questionnaires and Interviews

Questionnaires, which ask people to write their answers to questions researchers pose, are probably the measurement technique used most frequently in communication research. Scholars often use them in experimental studies to measure independent and dependent variables, and they are the primary tool used in large-scale surveys. Questionnaires can also be used to elicit messages that textual analysts study, and some naturalistic researchers use questionnaires to elicit critical incident reports of respondents' experiences in particular contexts and their interpretations of such experiences.

Interviews, exchanges in which people provide information orally, are also common in communication research and are employed in many of the same research situations as questionnaires. Both are self-report measures that ask respondents to provide information about their own and/or other people's beliefs, attitudes, and behaviors. Researchers using questionnaires and interviews employ many organizational, presentational, and questioning strategies. We examine these in more detail when we discuss survey research (Chapter 8). Here, we focus on three important issues in the use of questionnaires and interviews as measurement techniques: closed versus open questions; question strategies and formats, and the relative advantages and disadvantages of questionnaires and interviews.

Closed versus Open Questions.   Two general types of questions are used in questionnaires and interviews: closed and open questions. **Closed questions** (also called **closed-ended questions**) provide respondents with preselected answers from which they choose or call for a precise bit of information. The Likert and Likert-type scales (see Figures 4.2, 4.3, 4.4, and 4.6) and the semantic differential scale (see Figure 4.5) discussed earlier in this chapter used closed questions. For example, a researcher seeking to measure public speaking apprehension might ask the following closed question using a Likert-type scale:

"To what extent are you comfortable giving a public speech? (Choose one)

____ Very comfortable

____ Comfortable

____ Neither comfortable nor uncomfortable

____ Uncomfortable

____ Very uncomfortable

Another closed question is, "How many public speeches have you given in the last 12 months?" Another is, "Have you given a public speech in the last 12 months? Yes or No."

Open questions (also called **open-ended questions** and **unstructured items**), in contrast, ask respondents to use their own words in answering questions. An example of an open question that might be used to measure public speech apprehension is, "How do you feel when giving a public speech?"

Because closed questions provide limited options or seek quantitative responses, respondents answer using terms *researchers* consider important and, thereby, give direct information about researchers' concerns. Answers to closed questions are also usually easier and less time-consuming for respondents to provide, and are easier for researchers to compile and compare. Closed questions, therefore, are more likely to be used with large samples because of the ease of administration, response, coding, and analysis. A. Fink (1995a, 1995b) also suggests that closed questions are more effective when respondents are unwilling or unable to provide the desired information in their own words.

Open questions are more time-consuming for researchers to administer and for respondents to answer. They also typically provide verbal data that are more difficult to categorize and analyze because respondents' answers can vary widely. (There are some computer software programs, such as TextSmart, that can facilitate the analysis of open survey questions.) Open questions, however, can provide more information than closed questions about the particular perspectives of individual respondents and, thereby, allow people to respond with what is on *their* mind. They do not lead respondents to answer in any preconceived way and they allow wide latitudes regarding the depth of information respondents can give. Open questions, therefore, typically are used with small samples about whom a researcher wants to know a great deal. A. Fink (1995a, 1995b) also suggests that open questions are more useful when researchers are exploring a little-understood issue, want unanticipated answers, and are studying respondents who may resent preselected answers. Sudman and Bradburn (1974) and Bradburn, Sudman, and Associates

(1979) also found open questions to be preferable when asking about sensitive topics. Schuman and Presser (1996) recommend that researchers beginning a research program should first develop open questions to learn what people say spontaneously about them, and then turn those responses into closed questions that are administered to larger, more carefully selected respondent groups.

Researchers sometimes use both open and closed questions in the same study. Gilsdorf (1992), for example, employed the Delphi technique (developed by Dalkey, Rourke, Lewis, & Snyder, 1972, and refined by Delbecq, Van de Ven, & Gustafson, 1975; see also C. M. Moore, 1987), to analyze written corporate policies about communication. The Delphi technique gives a sequence of questionnaires to a group of people. The first instrument contains open questions to which people respond. Answers are distributed back to that group of people and they are asked additional, narrower, closed questions. This practice is repeated until the group achieves consensus.

Question Strategies and Formats. Questionnaires and interviews are *structured* in a variety of ways, depending on the type and arrangement of questions. First, researchers present questions to respondents in a more or less *directive* or *nondirective* way. **Directive questionnaires and interviews** present respondents with a predetermined sequence of questions. In **nondirective questionnaires and interviews,** respondents' initial responses determine what they will be asked next. Directive strategies typically are used to gather easily comparable information from many people; nondirective strategies often are used to let respondents tell their unique stories in their own way.

The list of questions that guide an interview is referred to as the **interview schedule,** or **protocol. Structured interviews** list all the questions an interviewer is supposed to ask, and interviewers are expected to follow that schedule consistently so that interviews conducted by different interviewers and with different respondents are all done in the same way. This approach is, thus, an oral counterpart of a printed questionnaire. In **semistructured interviews,** interviewers ask a set of basic questions on the interview schedule, but they are free to ask probing follow-up questions as well, usually to gather specific details or more complete answers. In **unstructured interviews,** interviewers are provided with a list of topics but have maximum freedom to decide the focus, phrasing, and order of questions.

Which format is used depends on a researcher's intent. If making generalizations about many respondents is most important, structured interviews tend to be used. If determining fully what particular individuals think is most important, semistructured or unstructured interviews are used.

The strategic *sequence* of queries on questionnaires and interviews is referred to as the **question format.** Three common question formats are the tunnel, funnel, and inverted funnel formats.

The first format is called the **tunnel format** because respondents are asked a straight series of similarly organized questions. The tunnel format provides respondents with a similar set of questions to answer and researchers with a consistent set of responses to code. An example might be asking people to identify the television shows they typically watch each night of the week.

Another common sequence is the **funnel format,** in which broad, open questions are used to introduce the questionnaire or interview, followed by narrower, closed questions that seek more specific information. Comer (1991), for example, used this format to study how organizational newcomers acquire information from their peers. Interviews with 30 junior professional staff in their fourth month at a service organization started with broad, open questions (e.g., "What kinds of information have you needed as a newcomer there?") and proceeded to more targeted items to determine type and channel (e.g., "Can you tell me about an occasion when you got information from a peer about the tasks of your job?").

The **inverted funnel format** is the opposite of the funnel format: It begins with narrow, closed questions and builds to broader, open questions.

This question format is often used in interviews to elicit specific data from respondents about the research topic before asking more open questions. If researchers asked people to explain each of their television show choices, they would be using an inverted funnel sequences (going from narrow to broader questions). Some researchers suggest using the inverted funnel format with very personal or taboo topics, because one can pose low-risk, closed, fixed-choice questions first and, after respondents are comfortable with the topic, move on to more probing, open questions. Thus, it might be better to ask people about their participation in specific religious observances *before* asking them to describe their religious beliefs.

Researchers try to structure their question format to avoid **question order effects,** which occur when responses to earlier questions influence how people respond to later questions. J. H. Frey and Oishi (1995) identify three common question order effects: (a) **consistency effect**—respondents believe that questions answered later must be consistent with answers to earlier questions, (b) **fatigue effect**—respondents grow tired after answering many questions and don't provide accurate information to later items, and (c) **redundancy effect**—respondents breeze over questions that appear to repeat previous questions.

Researchers also try to structure their question format to avoid a **response set (response style),** the tendency for respondents to answer questions the same way automatically (such as using only one side of a scale) rather than thinking about each individual question. This is why researchers often used a *balanced-scale approach* (Oskamp, 1991), switching (or "flipping") the wording of questions likely to elicit positive or negative responses (as was done in the humor orientation instrument in Figure 4.6). This forces respondents to react to each individual question. It also helps researchers to catch people who didn't respond authentically; if they see that a person just checked one side of the scale for all answers, that questionnaire usually is discarded. And to take care of an **acquiescent response style,** the tendency of some respondents to be agreeable and

say "yes" to whatever question is asked, or the reverse, a **quarrelsome response style** that leads people to disagree or say "no," researchers will compose scales so that respondents have to use both yes and no responses to express their beliefs in a consistent manner.

Relative Advantages of Questionnaires and Interviews. The most obvious *difference* between questionnaires and interviews is the communication channel used. Researchers using questionnaires communicate via written messages and usually do not converse with respondents. Researchers using interviews interact with respondents.

This difference between mediated versus direct interaction between researchers and respondents provides questionnaires and interviews with respective advantages (see Figure 4.7). Questionnaires are less expensive than interviews. They reach large or dispersed audiences and allow them to respond at their convenience. They require fewer personnel and can be administered consistently by different researchers, since the same written form, asking the same questions, may be used in exactly the same way time after time.

From what we know about the idiosyncratic and processual nature of communication, not even the best-trained interviewers using a structured interview could ask questions with equivalent consistency, as can be done with questionnaires. A number of researchers report that even in structured interviews, interviewers vary their interviews by skipping questions, changing the way they ask questions, and engaging in discussions with respondents that depart from the interview format (see Cannell & Kahn, 1968; M. H. Hansen, Hurwitz, Marks, & Maudlin, 1951; Hyman, 1954; Kish & Slater, 1960).

Giving questionnaires to respondents in groups also minimizes the possible influence of external events on people's responses. Questionnaires also increase respondents' anonymity, because instead of answering an interviewer's questions directly, they can turn in their questionnaire answers without identifying themselves. Finally, questionnaires preserve people's responses exactly as presented, be-

---

FIGURE 4.7 Relative advantages of
questionnaires and interviews

QUESTIONNAIRES

1. Lower cost compared to other methods
2. Reach large or dispersed audiences and allow them to respond at their convenience
3. Require less personnel to administer
4. Can be administered consistently by different researchers
5. Minimize potential influence of outside events as all people receive questionnaires at the same time
6. Increase respondents' anonymity
7. Encourage responses from people who are reluctant to talk with interviewers
8. Increase accuracy of data because respondents record their own data
9. Can use computer-coded forms to facilitate data entry
10. Electronic surveys eliminate need for face-to-face contact and paper exchange

INTERVIEWS

1. Telephones reach respondents quickly
2. Can clarify questions that respondents do not understand
3. Can gather observational data by noting verbal and nonverbal behavior
4. Provide greater depth of response
5. Encourage full participation by establishing rapport
6. Can probe for more information
7. Can be more effective for collecting information about sensitive topics
8. Enhance response rate through personal contact and, thereby, produce more representative samples
9. Computer-assisted telephone interviewing (CATI) and computer-assisted personal interviewing (CAPI) can facilitate survey administration and data entry

---

cause respondents record their own data and, thus, eliminate the interviewer as an intermediary. Furthermore, analysis of responses from questionnaires using computer-coded forms can be accomplished quickly and efficiently. And because the number of people with electronic mail is growing every day, researchers are experimenting more and more with electronic surveys in which "respondents use a text processing program to self-administer a computer-based questionnaire" (Kiesler & Sproull, 1986, p. 402).

An advantage of telephone interviews, on the other hand, is the ability to reach people in a hurry. In both face-to-face and telephone interviews, interviewers can clarify questions respondents do not understand and gather observational data by noting their verbal and nonverbal behavior. Interviews typically provide greater depth of information than questionnaires, especially if interviewers establish rapport and ask respondents probing questions to clarify their answers, such as "Can you elaborate on that answer?" or "Can you give me an example of that?" Interviewers can often encourage more full and honest answers from respondents, especially with regard to sensitive topics. In their study of sex in the United States, Laumann, Michael, Gagnon, and Michaels (1994) got people to talk about very intimate details of their sexual behavior (such as extramarital affairs). Laumann said, "Our feeling was that you could get people to talk about anything if you approach them right" ("But Should We Believe It?" 1994, p. 70). The personal contact between interviewers and interviewees also helps to increase the response rate because interviewers can encourage dubious respondents to participate and, thereby, produce a potentially more representative sample. It is far easier to ignore a questionnaire received in the mail than an interviewer at your front door! And computer-assisted interviewing (CATI and CAPI) are making interviews even easier to conduct.

In the final analysis, choosing between questionnaires and interviews (or using both) depends on three factors: the research population, the research questions, and the available resources. First, researchers consider from whom they want to gather information. For a small group of people who are easy to access, personal interviews work well, but for a large group of people spread all over the country, questionnaires or telephone interviews work better. Second, researchers consider the nature of the questions they want to ask. Are they better suited to mailed questionnaires where respondents can think about responses and answer them anonymously, or do researchers have to probe to gather adequate information about these questions? Finally, researchers choose between questionnaires and interviews on the basis of practical considerations. What funds, people, and equipment are available? Is there an adequate budget to hire interviewers, pay their travel expenses (if necessary), print questionnaires, or cover postage costs? Is there access to computer-assisted telephone interviewing or computer-scanning equipment for coded forms? The answers to such questions will determine the best measurement technique to use in communication research.

Observations

Observations, the systematic inspection and interpretation of behavioral phenomena, are also used to gather data about communication variables. In some studies, researchers themselves examine the communication phenomena rather than relying on people to report about themselves or about other people.

Observational measurement techniques are divided into two primary types: direct observation and indirect observation.

Direct Observation.   Researchers who watch people engaging in communication are using **direct observation.** Sometimes the observations occur in a *laboratory setting* in which a researcher gathers people together in a setting constructed for research purposes, gives them a reason to interact, and then observes what they say and do. Guerrero (1996), for example, hypothesized that people with different "attachment" styles (how they deal with intimate others) would use different content depth and nonverbal behaviors when interacting with a romantic partner. Eighty romantic dyads, who pre-

viously had completed a measure of attachment styles, were invited to a laboratory, which was designed as a comfortable apartment-like setting. Guerrero asked them to pick a topic to discuss, and then left the room. She videotaped them talking for three minutes. Undergraduate students then watched the videotapes and rated the partners' relational messages (e.g., amount of depth) and nonverbal involvement behaviors (e.g., number of touches).

Other times, researchers go out into the *field* to observe people as they engage in everyday activities. In some cases, the people know they are being observed. Smith-Dupre´ and Beck (1996), for example, studied how one physician and her patients interacted. Smith-Dupre´ accompanied the physician into the examination room, and the physician asked each patient if he or she would mind the presence of an observer. If the person agreed, she recorded their exchange with a hand-held tape recorder, and later analyzed the interactions between the physician and her patients.

In other cases, people may know that a researcher is present but not know they are being observed. Schommer (1994), for example, studied pharmacist-patient interaction in 12 community pharmacies. Data were collected through observation of the encounters. To prevent them from becoming self-conscious, pharmacists were not told their behavior was being observed, only that the researcher would interview patients once they exited the pharmacy. The interactions, however, were being observed from an area 25 feet behind the patient and to the side of the pharmacist's area of forward vision.

In still other cases, people may not be aware that a researcher is present and observing. There is, for example, a long history of researchers eavesdropping on people's conversations in public for the purpose of noting differences in the topics talked about in same-gender and mixed-gender dyads (see Deakins, Osterink, & Hoey, 1987; Landis & Burtt, 1924; H. T. Moore, 1922). (We examine the ethics of such observational research in Chapter 6.)

In each of the studies just cited, the researchers and/or observers watched people from the "sidelines." In other cases, researchers themselves participate in interactions to observe the behavior of interest. Smythe (1995), for example, studied the role of storytelling in women's conversations at a popular fitness facility. As a member of the facility for many years, she was included in the story exchanges, most of which took place at a small counter where women congregated while waiting for classes to begin or while preparing to leave after completing a workout. She chose not to tell members about her research during the initial phase to ensure that "typical" interaction behaviors were being observed. This type of participant-observation is sometimes characteristic of naturalistic research (see Chapter 10).

Indirect Observation.   When using **indirect observation,** researchers examine *communication artifacts,* texts produced by people, as opposed to live communication events (see Chapter 9). One form of communication artifacts is recordings/transcripts of events, such as written, audiotaped, videotaped, or filmed speeches, conversations, and meetings. These types of artifacts often are the focus of textual-analytic research methods, such as rhetorical criticism and interaction analysis. For example, both Donohue and Roberto (1993) and Rogan and Hammer (1994, 1995) categorized message strategies used in negotiations with hostages. In each case, the researchers obtained audiotapes of actual hostage negotiations from the Federal Bureau of Investigation (FBI). These audiotapes were transcribed and the variables of interest in those conversations were analyzed.

Other communication artifacts include the products people produce, including written material (e.g., books, pamphlets, magazines, and letters), electronic media (e.g., records, films, and television programs), and assorted works of art (e.g., painting and sculpture). These types of texts are also examined by rhetorical critics and content analysts. Schooler, Basil, and Altman (1996), for example, photographed all 901 alcohol and cigarette billboards in areas of San Francisco zoned as neighborhood commercial districts, and examined their content to see how these artifacts used the social aspects of smoking and drinking to promote those products.

An intriguing type of indirect observation of human behavior involves **trace measures,** or physical evidence, such as footprints, hair, ticket stubs, or cigarette butts, left behind. Researchers who use such measures are like detectives who rely on "clues" to draw conclusions. Sherlock Holmes, for example, was a master at inferring what had happened from small pieces of evidence, and used physical traces to identify and track criminals.

Researchers most commonly use two types of trace measures: measures of erosion and measures of accretion. **Measures of erosion** show how physical objects are worn down by use over time. For example, Mosteller (cited in Webb et al., 1973) studied which sections of the *International Encyclopedia of the Social Sciences* were read most often by examining the wear and tear on the pages of each section. Similarly, the wearing down of the fabric on couches might be a good measure of which furniture in a student lounge was used most, while the wearing down of carpet or grass indicates the walking paths people take the most.

Measures of erosion can be *natural* or *controlled.* The examples just mentioned are natural, occurring normally over the course of time. In contrast, controlled erosion measures are set up by people to identify certain behaviors. For example, tickets numbered consecutively to sequence customers' turns in a busy take-out restaurant are a measure of controlled erosion. Sometimes researchers can even speed up the process of erosion by using special materials, such as floor surfaces that wear easily.

Measures of accretion show how physical traces build up over time. Whereas measures of erosion look at what has worn down, measures of accretion look at what is added on. For example, Du Bois (1963) analyzed the number of different fingerprints on a page to determine how often a magazine advertisement was read. Kinsey, Pomeroy,

Martin, and Gebhard (1953), in a study of the sexual behavior of men and women, noted a significant difference between the number of erotic inscriptions in men's and women's public toilets!

An interesting (but messy) measure of accretion involves examining refuse, or what is called *garbology*. In garbology, researchers gather, sift through, identify, and categorize garbage as a way of determining people's behavior. For example, researchers can determine from empty bottles, discarded containers and wrappings, and smudges on paper plates the kinds of food and drinks people ingest. Garbology may actually be one of the most accurate ways of determining some types of behavior, such as alcohol consumption, where respondents typically underestimate their consumption when asked in survey research. In garbology, however, the number of liquor bottles can easily be observed. (Sampling is critical, though: If the person had a wild party the night before, a garbologist might seriously overestimate that person's liquor consumption!)

Measures of accretion can also be *natural* or *controlled*, based on whether the artifacts build up naturally or are set up by a person. An example of a controlled measure of accretion occurs when a marine sergeant dons a white glove while making an inspection of a platoon's barracks. The dirt on the glove is a controlled measure of accretion. Sometimes researchers can also introduce materials to accelerate the accretion process, such as special glues that help detect how many pages in a book were handled.

It should be pointed out that measures of erosion and accretion, whether natural or controlled, only provide a measure of a physical trace. Researchers must interpret what that physical trace means. Just because people turn a page in a magazine, for example, doesn't mean they read it. Thus, while ingenious researchers may well discover valuable information by using trace measures, they also need to be careful in drawing inferences from data gathered by such means. This is certainly true, although, as J. W. Andersen (1989) points out, few communication scholars use such measures.

Both indirect observations and covert direct observations, in which people don't know they are being observed, are considered **unobtrusive,** or **nonreactive, measures** because people don't know they are being studied and/or don't change their behavior to influence a researcher (see Chapter 5). These observational measures don't intrude into people's lives nor influence the behavior being observed, so they may yield more accurate data than can be obtained from asking people questions via questionnaires and interviews.

Methods of Observation. There are many ways observations can be recorded systematically. Researchers interested in physiological behavior, for example, have used a variety of electronic devices (see Riccillo, 1989). Rothschild, Thorsen, Reeves, Hirsch, and Goldstein (1986) determined which kinds of commercials generated the most thought by showing people 18 commercials embedded in a one-hour program and measuring their brain activity during each commercial through an electroencephalogram (EEG), which measures electrical activity in the brain via electrodes attached to the scalp. Beatty and Behnke (1991) studied the effects of public speaking anxiety and the intensity of a speaking task on heart rate during performance. A transmitter (weighing about 20 grams and about the size of two postage stamps) was attached under speakers' clothing, permitting freedom of movement. The speakers' continuous heart rates were relayed via an FM receiver to an adjacent room, where they were measured and recorded by a physiograph.

Other researchers record observations by taking notes and writing down what occurs as they are doing the observation. In Ketrow's (1991) study of how bank tellers' nonverbal communication cues influence customers' satisfaction, observers stood in the public area of the bank lobby and watched tellers from the time customers stepped to the counter to the time they turned or stepped away fully. One observer dictated to the other all discriminable nonverbal communication cues, such as body orientation and eye contact.

Other researchers use electronic means to record communication behavior. In Schommer's (1994) study of pharmacist–patient interaction, the number of seconds pharmacists and patients communicated was recorded with a stopwatch. Researchers frequently use audiotapes, videotape, or time-lapse filming to preserve observational data. And with the advent and use of the information superhighway, researchers are starting to observe behavior that occurs over the Internet. Scheerhorn, Warisse, and McNeilis (1995), for example, studied the functions of the messages sent by hemophiliacs over a text-based, computer bulletin board.

Coding Observations. Observations need to be categorized, or coded, to be analyzed. Researchers, therefore, develop **coding schemes,** classification systems that describe the nature or quantify the frequency of particular communication behaviors. The categorization occurs during or after the observations take place.

The process of coding observations, like types of questions on questionnaires and interviews, ranges from closed to open. Experimental researchers and some textual analysts (e.g., content and interaction analysts) often use checklists with predetermined categories when making observations. In Ford's (1995) study of the effects of cashiers' courtesy on customers' behavior, observers stood two cashier lines away from the cashiers being observed and used a standard observational form to record their behaviors. In addition to such measures as number of direct eye contacts and number of head nods per minute, the observers recorded the facial expression of the cashiers while customers were paying, using the 5-point visual interval scale, ranging from a big frown (level 1) to a big smile (level 5), shown earlier (see Figure 4.4), that customers also were asked to complete when measuring their own moods. Because predetermined categories were used to make the observations, this is an example of a closed coding procedure.

Researchers using closed coding procedures can sometimes enter their observations directly into a computer program. Henderson (1988) de-

veloped a computer program, called EVENT-LOG, by which observers can score, for example, videotapes of married couples discussing a topic about which they disagree. As the tape is shown, the observer easily codes when each person speaks and for how long by pressing a key designated for each individual and holding it down for as long as the person is speaking. The computer records the data for later analysis. Keys can even be designated for particular types of comments or nonverbal behaviors observed.

Developing effective closed coding schemes is a complex task that requires that researchers first determine the type of observation to be coded, the appropriate unit of analysis, and the relevant categories, and then train coders to categorize each unit. We examine these processes in more depth in Chapter 9.

At the other extreme is open coding or categorization made during or after observations have taken place. Ethnographic researchers typically use this procedure when observing people's behavior (see Chapter 10). Conquergood (1994), for example, spent 4 years doing participant-observation fieldwork of the communication practices of gangs in northwest Chicago. As part of his study, he (de)coded and categorized gang graffiti and showed that it was not meaningless gibberish, as middle-class citizens often assume, but a complex, highly structured way of inscribing the urban landscape.

CONCLUSION

Observing and measuring behavior is a central part of many communication research studies. DeVellis (1991) points out that quite often "an investigator will consider measurement as secondary to more important scientific issues that motivate a study and attempt to 'economize' by skimping on measurement" (p. 10). A researcher who skimps on measurement does so with great peril. Once again, as the saying from the world of computers goes: "Garbage in, garbage out."

Just as people in everyday life hate to be misunderstood and described inaccurately to someone else, it is equally damaging to good communication research for researchers to judge hastily or imprecisely what the people they study say or do and then use those inaccurate observations to describe their behavior in journal articles and books. Researchers, therefore, must work diligently to operationalize and measure effectively the abstract concepts they seek to study. Since they can't see these concepts directly, they must devise valid ways to measure the observable characteristics of the concepts of interest. The issue of validity, however, as we will see in the next chapter, is relevant not only to measurement techniques but also to many other research practices.

CHAPTER 5

DESIGNING VALID
COMMUNICATION RESEARCH

Some people say that political candidates who attack opponents in their speeches and ads are more successful; others say that personal attacks backfire and do a vote-seeker more harm than good. Which statement is more valid? Questions concerning validity arise often when communication controversies are discussed.

People frequently refer to the concept of validity in everyday conversation, saying things like, "She has a valid point" or "That's not a valid statement." They are referring to the accuracy of a statement; therefore, the best synonym for the word **validity** is *accuracy.*

Researchers are especially concerned about the validity or accuracy of the conclusions drawn from their investigations. Because validity is so crucial, we devote this chapter to examining how researchers design and conduct communication research intended to yield valid results.

INTERNAL AND EXTERNAL VALIDITY

Two general types of validity are important: internal and external. **Internal validity** concerns the *accuracy of the conclusions* drawn from a particular research study. Internal validity asks whether a research study is designed and conducted such that it leads to accurate findings about the phenomena being investigated for the particular group of people or texts studied.

External validity concerns the *generalizability of the findings* from a research study. External validity asks whether the conclusions from a particular study can be applied to other people/ texts, places, and/or times. If a study is externally valid, the conclusions drawn from it are not lim-

ited to the particular people/texts, places, and/or time periods studied.

Is one type of validity more important than the other? Some scholars argue that internal validity is more important; after all, one wouldn't want to generalize a false conclusion to other people. On the other hand, research that is valid only for the particular people, contexts, or time periods studied is of limited use. Thus, the best studies are high on both internal and external validity.

There are, however, times when a researcher must sacrifice a little of one type of validity to boost the other. For example, if tape recordings of what you say for days or weeks were studied, we could describe your vocabulary rather accurately. That study would have high internal validity. However, we would know almost nothing about how well those findings describe the vocabulary of anyone else. Hence, that study would have low external validity.

On the other hand, if we give you and 100 of your peers a vocabulary test, what we learn would have lower internal validity—it would describe that group of people's vocabulary less well than the first study described your vocabulary—but the findings would have higher external validity, since we could use them to make more accurate statements about the vocabulary of other people like you than we could after the first study.

Most studies, of course, aren't as self-evidently valid or invalid as the two in this example. Instead, validity ranges on a continuum from studies that have high internal and/or external validity to those with less. Evaluating the validity of a study is based on whether appropriate and accurate procedures were used to conduct the research and the extent to which potential limitations or "threats" to validity can be ruled out.

As Figure 5.1 shows, internal validity is potentially compromised by three general threats, each of which contains several specific threats: (a) how the *research is conducted,* (b) effects due to *research participants,* and (c) effects due to *researchers.* Because so much communication research involves measuring variables, we first examine measurement validity and reliability and then dis-

FIGURE 5.1   Internal and external validity

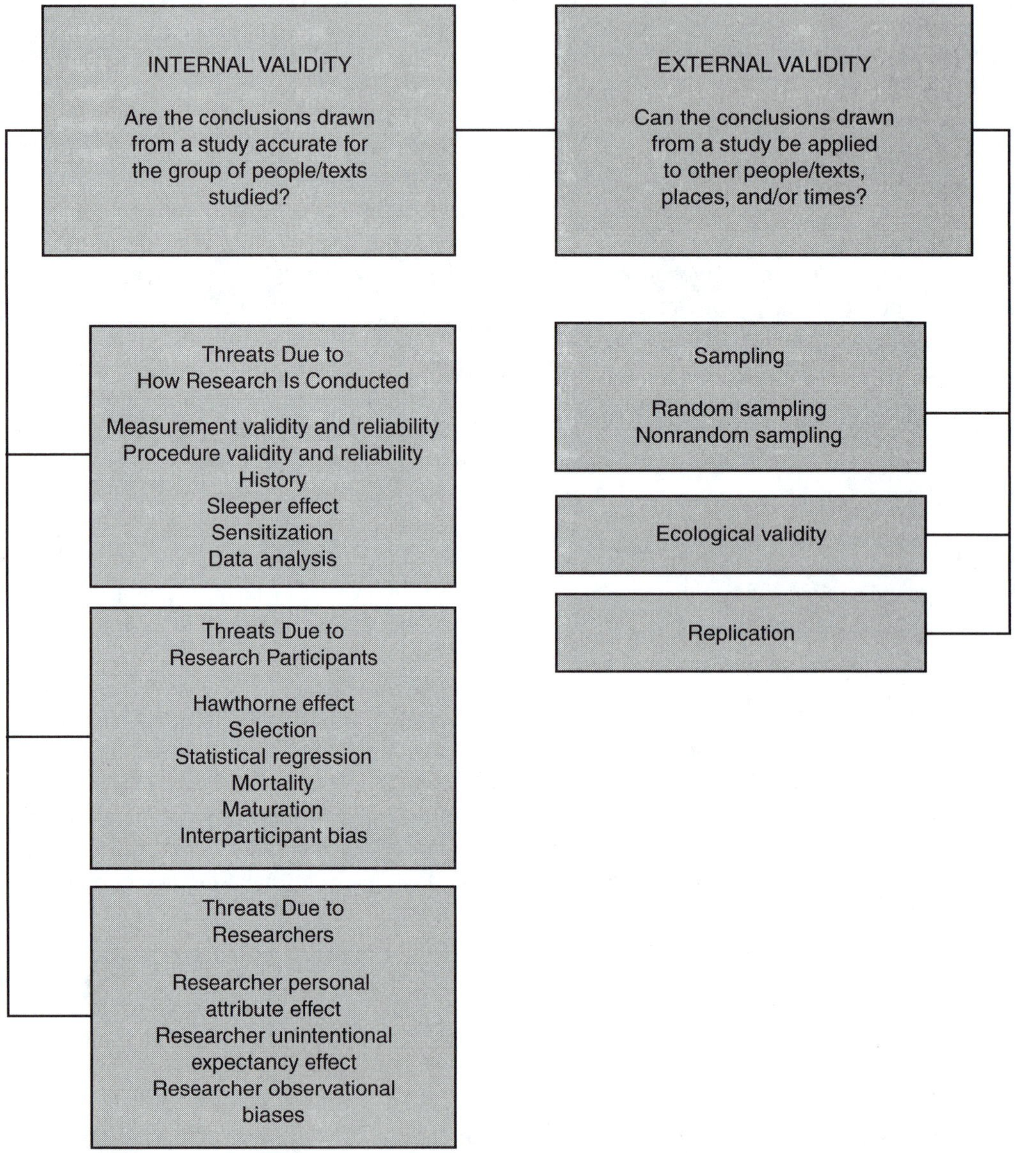

INTERNAL VALIDITY

Are the conclusions drawn from a study accurate for the group of people/texts studied?

EXTERNAL VALIDITY

Can the conclusions drawn from a study be applied to other people/texts, places, and/or times?

Threats Due to How Research Is Conducted

Measurement validity and reliability
Procedure validity and reliability
History
Sleeper effect
Sensitization
Data analysis

Sampling

Random sampling
Nonrandom sampling

Threats Due to Research Participants

Hawthorne effect
Selection
Statistical regression
Mortality
Maturation
Interparticipant bias

Ecological validity

Replication

Threats Due to Researchers

Researcher personal attribute effect
Researcher unintentional expectancy effect
Researcher observational biases

cuss other threats caused by how the research is conducted, followed by threats due to research participants and researchers. We then examine three factors that relate to the external validity of research: (a) how the people/texts studied were selected, called *sampling,* (b) whether the procedures used mirror real life, called *ecological validity,* and (c) the need to *replicate* research findings.

MEASUREMENT VALIDITY AND RELIABILITY

Data collected through questionnaires, interviews, and observations are worthwhile only if they are recorded in accurate ways. Developing valid measurement techniques is, therefore, a primary concern for all researchers.

Measurement validity refers to how well researchers measure what they intend to measure. The more closely the measured data reflect the observable characteristics of the research concepts, the more valid is that measurement technique. Findings from a study that involve measuring the height, width, and depth of a person's physical heart from x-rays, since those dimensions can be assessed so precisely, will have more measurement validity than findings of a study that measures that person's degree of warmheartedness or caring, since that characteristic can't be measured as directly or as precisely.

Measurement validity, thus, refers to the ability of a measurement technique to tap the referents of the concepts being investigated. If researchers wanted to measure how much you like your friends, which of these methods would be most valid: counting how much time you spend with them, calculating how much money you spend on gifts for them, determining how much you tell them about yourself, or simply asking you to rate how much you like them? The measure that yields the most accurate results has the most measurement validity, while the other three are less valid.

For any measurement to be valid, it must first demonstrate **reliability,** a term that implies both consistency and stability. **Measurement reliabil-**

ity, thus, means measuring something in a consistent and stable manner. The more reliable a measurement is, the more dependable it is because it leads to similar outcomes when applied to different people/texts, contexts, and/or time periods. A ruler, for example, is a reliable measurement because it measures the same distances every time a person uses it. Most opinion questionnaires are less reliable, since responses can change depending on, for example, a person's mood.

Measurement validity and reliability go hand in hand; neither is meaningful without the other. However, a measurement can be reliable but not necessarily valid. For example, a measurement scale that consistently overestimates weight by 10 pounds is reliable, but not valid. A watch set two hours ahead is reliable, in that the minutes still tick by in a consistent manner, but if you turned on your favorite television show at 9:00 P.M. on the basis of this watch, the show wouldn't be on. But if a measurement is valid, it must, by definition, be reliable. An accurate scale or watch is consistent in its measurements (unless its battery runs out between uses). Therefore, reliability is a necessary but not sufficient prerequisite for developing valid measurements. For that reason, we first examine measurement reliability and then consider measurement validity.

Measurement Reliability

Think about a friend you consider to be reliable—someone you can consistently count on. If, for example, the person says he or she will be at your house at 8:00 P.M., he or she is usually on time. (Of course, a consistently late person is also reliable!) The key term in that sentence is "usually." We wouldn't expect that person to *always* arrive at exactly 8:00. There are bound to be some minor fluctuations in arrival time (e.g., due to traffic jams and other circumstances), but generally the person arrives at that time.

So even reliable or generally consistent measurements have some deviation, or error. And the more complex the concept being measured—such as measuring how "persuasive" an advertisement is—the more we would expect deviation in the measurements. We can, thus, say that any:

Observed Measurement = True Score + Error Score

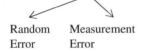

Random Error   Measurement Error

The **true score component** is, in theory, the actual score if researchers could measure something perfectly. But researchers can't measure something perfectly; their measurements always contain some error. The **error score component** (often designated by the letter, upper- or lower-case, E) is, thus, the amount of deviation from the true value.

The error score component is partly due to **random error** (also called **accidental** or **chance error**), error that is not and/or cannot be predicted or controlled, and partly due to **measurement error.** Random error is chance error due to uncontrolled factors and is assumed to equal out over time (Kerlinger, 1986). Measurement error, on the other hand, is due to faulty measurement procedures on the times the behavior *is* measured and, therefore, is more directly under researchers' control. Although researchers cannot completely eliminate measurement error, they can reduce it in several ways, such as by conducting a **pilot study,** a preliminary study that tests the questionnaires, interview protocols, observational techniques, and other methods to make sure they are as effective as possible before the main study starts. If measurement error is reduced, the reliability of a measurement technique is increased.

A perfectly reliable measurement would, of course, be 100% reliable. This may be possible for simple measurements, such as determining biological gender, although mistakes can be made even on this characteristic, such as with infants (Stranger: "That's a beautiful girl." Parent: "She's a boy."). But few techniques are perfectly reliable when it comes to measuring complex variables. The reliability of measurements ranges between 0% and 100%. A reliability assessment, called a **reliability coefficient,** thus, provides a numerical indicator that tells the percentage of time a measurement is reliable, or free of error. Reliability coefficients are phrased as a number equivalent to a percentage, ranging from .00 (no consistency; 0%) to 1.00 (perfect consistency; 100%). While researchers obviously desire the highest reliability possible, they generally accept as reliable a measurement of a complex variable, such as how much an audience member believes a speaker, with a coefficient of .70 or greater. This means that if a person were to hear the same speech on 10 occasions and report the same degree of persuasiveness 7 times, the questionnaire is considered reliable; anything less and that instrument is considered unreliable. The .70 level of acceptability varies depending on the instrument used and how important reliability is in a particular study, so it is a recommendation, not a hard and fast rule.

Several techniques are used to assess the reliability of measurements obtained via questionnaires, interviews, and observations, including: (a) comparing the results from *multiple administrations* of a measurement procedure, and (b) comparing the internal consistency of a measurement procedure administered once, called *single-administration techniques.* Observational measurement techniques are assessed by the amount of *agreement between observers.* In the next few sections, we discuss the reliability of a measurement instrument, such as a questionnaire.

Multiple-Administration Techniques. Multiple-administration techniques involve assessing the temporal stability of instruments at two or more points in time. For example, the **test-retest method** administers the *same* measurement procedure to the same group of people at different times. The measurement is considered reliable if the results are consistent (usually .70 or greater; called the **coefficient of stability**) from one time to another.

Oliver (1993), for example, developed a scale to measure how much people enjoy sad films that asks people to indicate the extent of their agreement with such statements as "It feels good to cry when watching a sad movie" and "Sad movies are too depressing for me to enjoy" (reverse coded). She surveyed 227 college students to see how scores on the Sad-Film Scale were related to a number of other variables, such as their gender and which types of films those people chose to see. She tested the reliability of the scale by asking 40 of them (19 males and 21 females) to complete it again, 45 days after the initial testing session. The test-retest reliabilities were .88 for males and .75 for females, demonstrating sufficient reliability across time.

Just because a measurement varies from one time to another, however, doesn't necessarily mean it isn't reliable. If you step on and off a reliable weight scale 10 times very fast (say within a minute or two), you will get a consistent reading, but if you weigh yourself right after you wake up and again after dinner that night, you probably won't get exactly the same reading, but that doesn't mean the scale is unreliable. As Traub (1994) notes, the shorter the interval of time between measurements, the more consistent readings are likely to be. With longer intervals, whatever is being measured might change for a number of reasons. Sometimes, respondents become familiar with an instrument from one administration to the next (see the discussion of sensitization later in this chapter). In this case, the change is a result of becoming more and more familiar with the instrument. If students take the same examination twice, we would expect them to do better the second time, but that does not negate the reliability of the examination. Its reliability would be better measured by administering it to new groups of students several times.

To help control for this particular problem with the test-retest method, researchers can use the **alternative procedure method,** which involves having the same people complete another, equivalent instrument at the second administration. Statistically comparing scores on these two instruments in the form of a **coefficient of equivalence** is then the basis for making claims about the reliability of the first instrument. This method, however, demands that a valid and reliable alternative instrument be available, which is not always possible. This is especially true in communication research, a relatively young discipline that deals with some complex variables. We have

some, but not a lot of, reliable measurement instruments.

Single-Administration Techniques.   Most researchers don't actually ask people to complete an instrument twice (whether the same or an equivalent one), and, as we have seen, there are some problems associated with multiple administrations. Most measurements are only taken once. The question, then, is how to know whether this is a reliable measurement.

In single administrations, reliability is assessed by measuring the **internal consistency** of an instrument, that is, the extent to which items on a measurement instrument give similar results. Because most instruments are composed of items measuring the same general concept, researchers can examine whether there is sufficient consistency between how people answer the related items. (Multidimensional instruments are composed of unidimensional scales measuring the same subconcept, so this principle can be applied to them as well; see Chapter 4.)

For example, **split-half reliability** is assessed by separating people's answers on an instrument into two parts (half the questions in one part and half in the other) and then comparing the two halves. Their answers will probably not be 100% (1.00) in perfect agreement, but there should be at least 70% (.70) agreement between the halves.

Separating the items on a questionnaire into two halves can be accomplished in a number of ways. For example, the *first-half/last-half split* divides the answers at the midway point of the scale. DeVellis (1991), however, points out that this may be problematic because a number of factors, such as people growing tired or getting better at answering the questions, can potentially make the two halves unequal. A better procedure is to put odd-numbered items in one half and even-numbered items in the other half. Figure 5.2 shows one way of calculating the *odd-even halves* reliability coefficient for a single questionnaire.

Researchers can also create *balanced halves* if they are concerned that an item characteristic might make a difference (e.g., all questions phrased in the

FIGURE 5.2   Split-halves reliability measure

Odd Items	Score	Even Items	Score	x	y	x^2	y^2	xy
Item 1	5	Item 2	4	1	.2	1	.04	.2
Item 3	5	Item 4	5	1	1.2	1	1.44	1.2
Item 5	3	Item 6	3	−1	−.8	1	.64	.8
Item 7	3	Item 8	3	−1	−.8	1	.64	.8
Item 9	4	Item 10	4	0	.2	0	.04	0
	M = 4.0		M = 3.8			$\Sigma x^2 = 4$	$\Sigma y^2 = 2.80$	$\Sigma xy = 3.00$

Pearson Product/Moment Correlation: $r = \dfrac{\Sigma \times y}{\sqrt{\Sigma x^2 \cdot \Sigma y^2}} = \dfrac{3.00}{\sqrt{(4)(2.80)}} = \dfrac{3.00}{\sqrt{11.2}} = \dfrac{3.00}{3.35} = .90$

Split-halves Reliability Coefficient: $= \dfrac{r \times 2}{r + 1} = \dfrac{.90 \times 2}{.90 + 1} = \dfrac{1.80}{1.90} = .95$

Steps:

1. Calculate the mean for each set of scores (4.0 for even items; 3.8 for odd items).
2. For each set of scores, subtract the mean from each score to get the *deviation scores* (columns x and y).
3. Square the deviation scores for column x (multiply them by themselves) and add these squared deviations scores to get the Σx^2 score (equals 4). Square the deviation scores for column y (multiply them by themselves) and add these scores together to get the Σy^2 score (equals 2.80).
4. Multiply each score in column x by its respective score in column y, and add these scores together to get the Σxy score (equals 3.00).
5. Multiply the Σx^2 score (4) by the Σy^2 score (2.80) (equals 11.2), and take the square root of this value (a number which times itself equals that value) (equals 3.35).
6. Divide the Σxy score (3.00) by the result of Step 5 (3.35) to get the *Pearson product/moment correlation* (equals .90).
7. Multiply Step 6 (.90) by the number 2 (equals 1.80).
8. Add the number 1 to the result of Step 6 (.90) (equals 1.90).
9. Divide Step 7 (1.80) by Step 6 (1.90) (equals .95). This is the split-halves reliability coefficient that applies to the instrument.

---

first person can be equally distributed between the two halves). Alternatively, *random halves* can be created, such that items have an equal chance of being assigned to either half. Whichever method is used, DeVellis (1991) says, "What is most important is that the investigator think about how dividing the items might result in nonequivalent subsets and what steps can be taken to avoid this" (p. 35).

Finally, one of the most popular internal consistency methods is **Cronbach's** (1951) **alpha coefficient method (alpha coefficient, coefficient alpha, A, α).** This procedure uses the overall rela-

tionship among the answers as the reliability coefficient for an instrument.

Boosting the Reliability of Measurement Instruments.   When a measurement instrument is found not to be reliable enough, researchers can measure the relation of each single item to the rest of the instrument, called the **agreement coefficient,** and try dropping problematic items. For example, Zakahi and Goss (1995) examined the relationship between loneliness and people's ability to decode verbal and nonverbal messages. They used a 12-item, self-report instrument developed by Goss (1991) to measure listening. Unfortunately, the reliability of this instrument in the new study was only .65. They examined the reliability of each item and found that three were weakly related to the overall score. By dropping those three items, they were able to boost the reliability of the instrument to the .70 level.

Sometimes, however, even this procedure isn't enough. In that same study, Zakahi and Goss used an instrument to measure four dimensions of loneliness: romantic, family, friendship, and group loneliness. Although the other three dimensions were reliable (.90, .85, and .84, respectively), the reliability of the group loneliness dimension was only .66. The researchers tried dropping one problematic item, but this did not improve the reliability of this dimension. Therefore, they dropped this dimension from the study.

Interobserver/Interrater/Intercoder Reliability. In observational research, the most common method for assessing reliability is calculating the percentage of agreement between or among the observations of independent coders, which is called **interobserver, interrater,** or **intercoder reliability.** If the observations recorded by two or more individuals who are not aware of (are "blind" to) the purposes of the study and each other's codings are highly related (showing 70% agreement or more), their ratings are considered reliable. The more trustworthy, or conservative, measures of interobserver reliability also account for agreement due to chance.

For example, suppose two observers are asked to code four instances of facial gestures as either happy (H) or sad (S), and their observations are as follows:

	FACIAL GESTURES			
	1	2	3	4
Observer 1	H	S	H	H
Observer 2	H	S	S	H

In this case, there is 75% agreement between the two observers and, therefore, the observations are deemed reliable. The observers would then be asked to mutually resolve their disagreement on the third facial gesture, or a third observer might make that determination.

If the interobserver reliability score is lower than .70, several options are available. First, researchers can modify the observational system by improving the observation and recording conditions (e.g., schedule shorter sessions or give observers a better viewing position). Second, they can specify more precisely the behavioral categories being observed. Third, they can train the observers better or give them more time to get used to making the desired observations. Fourth, they can increase the length or number of observation sessions or people observed until consistent data are obtained. (For example, the low reliability of the data may have been due to the people being observed reacting initially to the presence of the observers; see the Hawthorne effect discussed later in this chapter.)

All of these methods for assessing measurement reliability are intended to develop a procedure that yields a relatively high consistency between administrations of a measurement technique, between research participants' own scores on a measurement instrument, or between observers. Developing highly reliable measurement procedures is crucial if we are to have confidence in the conclusions researchers draw from studies. For this reason, many scholarly journals will not publish studies that don't report reliability coefficients for new measurement instruments or don't use instruments already determined to be highly reliable. But reliability is only one step in establishing the accuracy of a measurement technique. Researchers must still confront the issue of validity.

Measurement Validity

There is an important difference between measurement reliability and measurement validity. Measurement reliability is assessed by a numerical indicator that ranges from 0 to 1.00. But there is no meaningful number attached to measurement validity: "Validity is not a commodity that can be purchased with [statistical] techniques" (Brinberg & McGrath, 1985, p. 13). Instead, researchers have to argue at the conceptual level that a measurement technique assesses accurately what it is supposed to assess. Arguments at this level are made on the basis of the extent to which a measurement procedure demonstrates content, criterion-related, and/or construct validity.

Content Validity. A measurement instrument, such as a questionnaire, possesses **content validity** if it measures the attributes (or content) of the concept being investigated. For example, an instrument designed to measure communication apprehension should contain items related to fear of communication and not to something else, such as unwillingness to talk about something.

Carmines and Zeller (1979) explain that establishing content validity involves first specifying the full content domain of a concept, selecting specific attributes from this domain, and then putting them into a testable form. Content validity, therefore, is fundamentally concerned with whether aspects of a content domain have been adequately sampled (see DeVellis, 1991).

Specifying the full content domain of some concepts and selecting specific attributes from this domain is relatively easy, if, for example, we're only measuring speed of speaking (e.g., number of words per minute). But specifying the full content domain of the abstract and complex concepts communication researchers often study can be difficult. What items, for example, measure clearly the competence of a communicator?

One way a researcher can establish content validity, although it is the weakest argument for validity, is to make sure that a measurement instrument at least intuitively reflects the construct as it is defined conceptually. The researcher generates items that, "on the face of it," seem to accurately reflect the concept being investigated. This technique, which is based on logical or conceptual validity (Vogt, 1993), establishes what is often called **face validity.**

Although face validity is essential for validity, simply proclaiming that something is valid doesn't make it so. A stronger procedure for establishing content validity is a **panel approach,** where qualified people are recruited to describe the aspects of

that variable or to agree that an instrument taps the concept being measured. C. L. Thompson and Pledger (1993), for example, conducted interviews with 224 people to assess patient knowledge of medical terminology. They first compiled a list of 173 nontechnical terms generated from a family practitioner, a medical dictionary, and a previous study by Samora, Saunders, and Larson (1961). Ten doctors examined the list and indicated which terms they did not use on a regular basis with their patients. If more than five doctors identified a word as one they would not use, it was dropped. This reduced the list to 151 words, and 50 items were then randomly selected and presented to respondents to define. As one can see, the validity of a panel approach depends on the expertise of the panel members selected and the extent to which they agree that items on an instrument are valid.

Criterion-Related Validity. A second form of measurement validity is **criterion-related validity,** which is established when a measurement technique is shown to relate to another instrument or behavior (called the *criterion*) already known to be valid. If scores on a measurement technique are associated with scores on the well-established standard, it is considered valid.

There are two types of criterion-related validity: concurrent and predictive. **Concurrent validity** (also called **convergent validity**) is established when the results from a new measurement instrument agree (concur) with those from an existing, known-to-be valid criterion. For example, if researchers develop a new 5-item instrument to measure humor orientation to replace S. Booth-Butterfield and Booth-Butterfield's (1991) 17-item instrument (see Figure 4.6), the new instrument has concurrent validity (in this case because the instruments overlap or converge) if it is as accurate in identifying people's level of humor as the existing instrument. Of course, this assumes that the original instrument was shown to be valid in the first place.

Concurrent validity can also be established by seeing how a group of experts (called a *criterion group*) perform with respect to a measurement instrument. For example, Booth-Butterfield and

Booth-Butterfield's humor orientation instrument could be given to a group of well-known and successful comedians (e.g., Dana Carvey, Jerry Seinfeld, Robin Williams, and others) to see if they score high on it. If they did not, we would have to question the validity of the instrument.

Predictive validity refers to how well a measurement instrument forecasts or predicts an outcome. For example, most university admissions offices require that students submit when applying for admission their scores on the SAT, GRE, GMAT, and/or LSAT instruments, because these instruments are thought to predict quite accurately how successful college applicants will be on such outcome measures as college grade point average and graduation rate. These scores, thus, are thought to have predictive validity and that's why they are used (along with other criteria) to make decisions about whom to admit.

An example from communication research helps illustrate how the predictive validity of an instrument is established. B. R. Patterson, Bettini, and Nussbaum (1993) developed a 27-item General Inventory of Friendship Intimacy (GIFI) instrument to measure the degree to which two aspects of friendship exist for elderly persons: reciprocation (the extent to which their relationships are characterized by give and take) and absent dysfunction (the social and functional losses they experience due to a lack of friendship). Since it is assumed that the quality of people's friendships is related to their well-being, the researchers argued that the GIFI would be deemed valid if scores on it were related to, or could *predict,* respondents' scores on a test of well-being. In a subsequent article, B. R. Patterson and Bettini (1993) established the predictive validity of the GIFI instrument by showing that elderly respondents' scores on it were, in fact, positively related to their scores on a well-being instrument used extensively in previous research.

Construct Validity. **Construct validity** is the extent to which scores on a measurement instrument are related in logical ways to other established measures (see Cronbach & Meehl, 1955). As Carmines and Zeller (1979) explain, "Funda-

mentally, construct validity is concerned with the extent to which a particular measure relates to other measures consistent with theoretically derived hypotheses concerning the concepts (or constructs) that are being measured" (p. 23). Hence, if a theory suggests that construct A should be positively related to construct B and negatively related to construct C, then a measurement of A is valid if scores on it are positively related to scores on a valid instrument for measuring construct B and negatively related to scores on a valid instrument for measuring construct C.

Say a researcher believes people's politeness will increase how much their coworkers respect them and decrease the number of arguments they have. Perhaps there are journal articles reporting previously validated measures of "coworker respect" and "frequency of arguments," but the researcher must develop a "politeness" measure. The researcher predicts that people with higher scores on this politeness measure will score higher on the "coworker respect" measure and lower on the "frequency of arguments" measure. The researcher tests this hypothesis in a study; if the results support it, the researcher can claim the politeness measure has "construct validity." The difference between construct validity and criterion-related validity is that, in construct validity, theoretically derived relationships between constructs and measurement techniques are being assessed, not just whether a measurement technique is related to a similar measurement technique or outcome, as in criterion-related validity.

The theory of constructivism, for example, asserts that people vary in terms of the number of conceptual categories or constructs they use to interpret the world. The more categories they use, the more complex their understanding. People who have many categories at their disposal are called "cognitively complex"; people with fewer categories are called "cognitively simple." This theory predicts many differences in the communication behavior of people between those who are cognitively complex and those who are cognitively simple.

To measure cognitive complexity, constructivists typically use Crockett's (1965) Role Category

Questionnaire (RCQ). This instrument requires respondents to write a short description of someone they like and someone they dislike. The researcher then counts the number of descriptors used and classifies individuals on this basis as cognitively complex or simple. Some scholars, however, question what this instrument really measures. Some claim it measures loquacity (talkativeness) rather than construct development (see M. Allen, Mabry, Banski, Stoneman, & Carter, 1990; Beatty & Payne, 1984, 1985; Powers, Jordan, & Street, 1979). Hines (1992, 1994, 1995) believes it measures differences in referential communication skill (the ability to construct a message so that another knows to what it refers). Constructivists maintain that RCQ respondents don't have a receiver in mind when they write their answers, so their responses are not related to their loquacity or referential communication skill.

To test these competing claims, Hines conducted two studies. In the first, he found that respondents did, in fact, perceive their RCQ responses as intentional, goal-directed, referential communication. In the second study, he found that the more descriptors people used in RCQ responses, the fewer number of words they used for each descriptor. He interpreted this finding as showing that RCQ responses assess referential communication skill because one element of referential skill is increased verbal efficiency.

Hines, thus, tested the construct validity of the RCQ by assessing relationships among RCQ scores and other variables suggested by constructivists and their critics. While his findings run counter to constructivist reasoning, Hines (1995) is quick to point out that "no single study can firmly establish a measure's construct validity" (p. 22). Nevertheless, his studies raise questions about what this instrument really measures, and suggest that it needs more testing.

Triangulating Validity.   Content, criterion-related, and construct validity are not mutually exclusive. In fact, the best way researchers can argue for the validity of a measurement technique is by trying to establish all three types.

K. Witte, Cameron, McKeon, and Berkowitz (1996), for example, attempted to do that in developing and validating their Risk Behavior Diagnosis (RBD) scale, which is meant to determine what types of health risk messages are most appropriate for particular listeners. The development of this scale was theoretically guided by the "extended parallel process" model, which argues that people who perceive a threat are motivated to control either the *danger* of the threat or their *fear* about it (see K. Witte, 1992, 1994). Individuals' perceptions of (a) the effectiveness of a possible response and (b) the severity of and their susceptibility to the threat determines whether they engage in danger control or fear control.

To establish the *content validity* of the RBD, the researchers conducted a review of the relevant literature and used what they learned to generate items likely to measure people's perceptions of response effectiveness, as well as severity and susceptibility. To further enhance content validity, 10 coders sorted each of their proposed items into one of the four dimensions the instrument measures. Items were classified in ways consistent with what the authors argued 94% of the time. To establish *criterion-related validity,* the researchers showed that the instrument successfully predicted individuals' attitudes, intentions, and behaviors toward a health risk message advocating the use of condoms to decrease the spread of genital warts. Finally, *construct validity* was established by showing, as the theory suggested, that scores on RBD were highly related to other measures of the four dimensions it is designed to measure. Establishing all three forms of validity suggests the researchers can confidently claim that this instrument is valid.

Designing reliable and valid measurement instruments is a crucial part of research that does not come easy. Researchers must engage in a systematic process of constructing and testing instruments (see the guidelines for constructing instrument scales in Figure 5.3). But when done well, the result is a reliable and valid measurement instrument that can be used effectively in research studies.

FIGURE 5.3   Guidelines in constructing scales

1. Determine clearly what it is you want to measure.
2. Generate an initial, large pool of items. Choose items that reflect the scale's purpose. Some redundancy is a good thing at this stage. Both positively and negatively worded items should be included (e.g., items that measure high communication competence and low communication competence).
3. Determine the format for measurement (e.g., binary options, Likert or Likert-type scales, semantic differential scales, etc.).
4. Have initial item pool reviewed by experts.
5. Consider inclusion of validation items (e.g., items to detect flaws or problems, such as social desirability; and items that pertain to the construct validity of the scale).
6. Administer items to a development sample. Nunnally (1978) suggests 300 people as an adequate number.
7. Evaluate the items to see how they perform (e.g., reliability assessment).
8. Optimize scale length. Shorter scales generally are less of a burden to complete, but longer scales may be more reliable.

Source: Based on Robert F. DeVellis (1991). *Scale development: Theory and application.* Newbury Park, CA: Sage.

THREATS TO INTERNAL VALIDITY

Besides measurement validity, many other threats to internal validity may affect the accuracy of the results obtained from a research study. These threats fall into three interrelated categories: threats due to *how research is conducted* (which includes measurement validity), threats due to *research participants,* and threats due to *researchers.*

Threats Due to How Research Is Conducted

A number of threats to the internal validity of a study are due to the way research is conducted. A critical reader will assess a research study with re-

spect to the validity and reliability of the procedures used, history, the possibility of the sleeper effect, sensitization, and data analysis.

Procedure Validity and Reliability.   One aspect of **procedure validity and reliability,** conducting research accurately and consistently, is the one we examined just above—administering accurate measurement techniques in a consistent manner.

A second aspect of procedure validity and reliability is **treatment validity and reliability,** which means making sure that any treatment a study is investigating is what it purports to be every time it is administered. If, for example, researchers intend to study the effects of a frightening film on people, that film must really be frightening to the audience members who see it and not one they think is ludicrous.

To make sure treatments are valid and reliable, researchers conduct **manipulation checks.** For example, Teven and Comadena (1996) examined the effects of office aesthetic quality on students' perceptions of teacher credibility and communicator style. Students first were taken to a professor's office that was either of low aesthetic quality (very disorganized, untidy, and generally unattractive) or high aesthetic quality (a very attractive, clean, and neatly arranged office). They waited there for five minutes and then were told that the instructor would not be able to meet with them at that time. They were taken next to a classroom where they watched a 5-minute videotape of that instructor lecturing to a class. Finally, the students completed a questionnaire that measured the instructor's credibility and communication style. A control group (see Chapter 7) took these last two measures with no prior exposure to the office.

To make sure that the independent variable manipulation was successful, that the students really thought one office was a mess and the other office was attractive, the students rated the aesthetic quality of the office to which they had been exposed on three 7-point semantic differential scales (see Chapter 4): attractive/unattractive, warm/cold, and aesthetically pleasing/aesthetically not pleasing. The manipulation check items had an internal reliability of .90 (Cronbach's alpha); the "treatment," therefore, was reliable.

A third form of procedure validity and reliability is **controlling for environmental influences,** which means keeping the setting in which a study is done as consistent as possible. Communication behavior always occurs in some sort of environment, such as a research laboratory, a living room, or an office. If researchers observe people in varied settings, elements in those settings might affect the participants, so the environment in which the behavior is observed should be kept consistent. In field research involving interviews, for example, people's responses might be influenced by whether they are interviewed at their home or workplace. The more appropriate of the two settings should be selected and then used consistently. This, of course, assumes that the context itself is not a variable being investigated; in such studies, context differences are controlled so that the treatment conditions are reliable and valid.

History.   **History** refers to changes in the environment external to a study that influence people's behavior within the study. Unforeseen events happening in research participants' world may influence the behavior being investigated. For example, a researcher may go into several organizations to measure employees' perceptions of their supervisors' communication style and their satisfaction with that style before and after the supervisors receive special communication training. But suppose, unbeknownst to the researcher at that time but which he or she later discovers after the study is completed, everyone in one organization just got a huge pay raise a few days earlier. If employees' ratings of their supervisor in that organization are extremely positive, that may be due more to the raise (an external variable) than how the supervisor communicated with employees after the training program. The researcher doesn't, of course, know, without additional follow-up (such as interviews with employees) whether this external or "history" factor played a role in employees' ratings, so it is a potential threat to the validity of the findings.

The threat of history is particularly important for longitudinal research that follows people over a relatively long period of time (see the discussion of longitudinal survey research in Chapter 8). Many changes might take place in the environment over the course of that time that could influence the results more than the participants' communication behavior and, thereby, jeopardize the internal validity of the study.

Sleeper Effect.   The **sleeper effect** refers to an effect that is not immediately apparent but becomes evidenced over the course of time. For example, mass communication research shows that some of the effects due to receiving persuasive messages from the mass media do not manifest themselves immediately but, instead, take a while to appear (or that, over time, an event and the identity of those involved in it may become separated). If a researcher only measured people's reactions to a mediated persuasive message immediately after they received the message, the finding of no effect might not be valid over the long run.

Sensitization.   **Sensitization** (sometimes called **testing, practice effects,** or **pretest sensitizing**) is the tendency for an initial measurement in a research study to influence a subsequent measurement. If a study calls for using similar or identical measurement techniques two or more times, the change in people's answers from one administration of that measure to the next may be a result of their becoming "test-wise" rather than whatever the instrument is supposed to measure. Even when two different procedures are used, the first procedure may somehow change people's behavior during the second procedure (perhaps they resent the time taken to fill out *two* questionnaires), and lead them to give different results on the second measure than if it had been the only one administered.

Sensitization is a particularly significant problem that must be ruled out in studies of instructional behavior. For example, Garside (1996) compared the effectiveness of traditional lecture methods of instruction to group discussion methods in developing critical thinking skills. In two conditions of the experiment, students completed a pretest measuring their critical thinking skills; then one group was exposed to a lecture and the other group engaged in group discussion. Everyone completed the critical thinking skills instrument again as a posttest. Significant gains from the pretest to the posttest were evidenced for both instructional strategies. To make sure that these gains were not due to sensitization (learning the posttest by having taken the pretest), there were also four conditions (two lecture and two group discussions) where the pretest was not used. Garside analyzed the data and discovered no significant differences between the conditions in which students were and weren't given the pretest. She then could claim with more confidence that the gain from pretest to posttest was a result of exposure to the instructional strategies and not to people's familiarity with the instrument.

Data Analysis.   An important threat to the internal validity of research has to do with the way in which data are analyzed. Researchers sometimes use improper procedures to analyze data (e.g., procedures that are suited to different kinds of data than the researcher collected), and this may lead to invalid conclusions. We will, however, save this discussion until we have had a chance to examine data analysis in Part Four of this textbook.

Threats Due to Research Participants

All communication research involves a group of *research participants,* particular persons, groups of people, or texts. Threats due to research participants/texts include the Hawthorne effect, selection, statistical regression, mortality, maturation, and interparticipant bias.

The Hawthorne Effect.   How aware people are of a researcher's intent can influence their behavior. People aware that they are being studied often behave differently than they do when they are not being observed. Any change in behavior due primarily to the fact that people know they are being observed is called the **Hawthorne effect.**

The Hawthorne effect is derived from a famous study about the effects of the amount of light in a room on worker productivity, conducted by Mayo, Roethlisberger, and Dickson (as reported by Roethlisberger & Dickson, 1939) at the Western Electric Company Hawthorne Works plant in Chicago. As expected, when illumination was increased, productivity increased. But decreased lighting and even restoring the original lighting resulted in increased productivity as well. The researchers realized eventually that the increases in worker production were not related to the changes in the level of illumination at all. Rather, workers produced more because they knew researchers were studying them! The workers performed in a superior manner because they knew they were being observed, not because the room was lit more or less.

To the extent that people engage in atypical behavior because they know they are being observed, conclusions about their behavior may not be valid. For example, the Nielson company has been experimenting with *peoplemeters,* in which a camera watches people who watch television. People's behavior, such as the frequency of their eye contact with the television set can be assessed. But a critical reader of such research might ask whether the camera affected viewers' behavior. One obvious way to control for the Hawthorne effect is not to let people know they are being observed, but this procedure raises serious ethical concerns (which we examine in Chapter 6). Another control method might be to measure their behavior only *after* they become accustomed to having the camera in their house, hoping that whatever changes they made in their behavior after the camera was introduced have disappeared and they have returned to their normal ways of behaving.

Selection.   **Selection** of people or texts for a study may influence the validity of the conclusions drawn. When different groups of people are studied, such as Republicans and Democrats, for example, researchers must make sure that the research participants actually are members of these groups. When studying the effects of a treatment, however, the results should be due to that treatment and not the type of people examined, so a mixture of people is often recruited for a study.

A particular type of selection problem is **self-selection bias,** which can occur when researchers compare groups of people that have been formed on the basis of self-selection. Comparing undergraduate communication majors with psychology majors, for example, might be difficult because students who choose a communication major may be very different on some important characteristics (e.g., they're smarter, right?) than those who choose a psychology major.

One of the more insidious problems with selection is that it interacts with many of the other internal validity threats to produce unique effects. For example, selection–history occurs when research participants from different settings experience something unique in their local environment over the course of a study that affects the outcome variable. Selection, clearly, influences both the internal and external validity of research, so we will examine it in more depth in the next major section of this chapter.

Statistical Regression.   Another way in which selection can threaten the validity of research findings is **statistical regression** (also called **regression toward the mean**), the tendency for individuals or groups selected on the basis of initial extreme scores on a measurement instrument to behave less atypically the second and subsequent times on that same instrument. Such an effect is called a **regression effect** or **artifact.**

Suppose researchers give a group of people a questionnaire that measures their political opinions. They select people who indicate very liberal and very conservative opinions, expose them to a political speech, and then measure their political opinions again. A critical reader might suggest that changes in their opinions between the first and second measure could have been due more to their tendency to be less extreme in their views over time (regression to the mean) than to the speech they heard.

Statistical regression is a difficult concept to understand, but some examples from the world of sports might help. G. Smith (1997) reports, among other statistics, that only six teams have been able to win a Super Bowl twice in a row, only four baseball world champions have won twice in a row, and

no professional basketball team repeated as champion from 1969 through 1988. As Smith explains:

> *These data are not evidence that champions become complacent or overweight from excess celebration, but are instead an example of regression toward the mean. There are many teams capable of winning a championship, and which of these deserving teams ultimately wins is partly determined by luck—having few injuries and being the beneficiary of lucky bounces and questionable officiating. It is more likely that the winner is an above-average team that experienced good luck than an unbelievable team that survived bad luck. By definition, good luck cannot be counted on to repeat. The next year, another above-average team will have good luck and win the championship.... The statistical fact [is] that those who do exceptionally well are unlikely to continue doing so. (p. 43)*

Of course, the same tendency also is true for those who do very poorly at something, like sports or, to make it relevant to students, scores on examinations; they, too, can be expected to regress toward the mean over time.

Choosing people on the basis of extreme scores also potentially leads to ceiling and floor effects. A **ceiling effect** occurs when people have scores that are at the upper limit ("ceiling") of a variable, making it difficult to tell whether a treatment has any effect. Say the selected research participants are at the top of a communication competence measure. Any treatment designed to increase competence will probably not be able to show that effect. The reverse is a **floor** (or **basement**) **effect,** which occurs when people have scores at the lower range ("floor") of a variable, making it equally difficult to tell whether any treatment has an effect. If selected participants are at the low end of a communication apprehension measure, it will be difficult for any treatment designed to reduce that apprehension to have that effect.

Mortality.   **Mortality** (also called **attrition**) is the loss of research participants from the beginning to the end of a research study. Mortality can be caused by people moving away, losing interest, or even dying. Mortality can also threaten the internal validity of textual analysis, such as when important documents are lost or destroyed (see Chapter 9). Mortality is a potentially important problem for longitudinal research, especially when researchers try to measure the behavior of the same people over a long period of time. A critical reader might suspect that the people who dropped out of the study may be different in some important way(s) than the people who remained; if that were the case, it could threaten the validity of any research findings.

Maturation. **Maturation** refers to internal changes that occur *within* people over the course of a study that explain their behavior. These changes can be physical or psychological and can happen over a short or long time period. A study of a yearlong method for teaching communication competence to teenagers, for example, may seem effective if their competence increases. But their higher scores could also be due to teenagers becoming more mature physically and psychologically. People also often answer the same question differently at the beginning and end of a long experiment or survey interview (e.g., over a two-hour period) simply because they grow tired, resentful, or impatient. Research participants' internal changes over time (their maturation) might, therefore, influence their responses.

Interparticipant Bias. **Interparticipant** or **intersubject bias** results when the people being studied influence one another. The mere presence of other people in a study may influence responses. Seeing a funny movie by yourself and with others can be a different experience. If someone laughs, you may start laughing. Researchers know from studies of groups that people often conform to the way others behave. Suppose someone wants to study how different persuasion techniques influence how willing people are to volunteer to help a charity. Say people in two groups listen to a speech, each using different persuasive methods, and then are asked to raise their hands if they wish to volunteer. If more people in one group raise their hands, a critical reader might ask whether their response was due to the speech they heard or to seeing others raise their hands and feeling compelled to also volunteer (the social desirability bias discussed in Chapter 4).

People who participate in a research study may also communicate with other potential participants before or even during the study itself. If these conversations result in the experimental treatment becoming known, it is called **diffusion of treatment** (or **diffusion effect;** Vogt, 1993). A college student, for example, may inform his or her roommates about the purpose of a study prior to their participating in the study or tell them what is being looked for, even when asked not to do so. Farrow, Farrow, Lohss, and Taub (1975) and Wuebben, Straits, and Schulman (1974) found that many participants renege on their promise not to talk with others about a study they were in before the others have a chance to participate in it.

Threats Due to Researchers

The final major threat to internal validity is **researcher effects,** or the influence of a researcher on the people being studied. Experimental, survey, and naturalistic research, as well as some textual analysis, involves a researcher interacting with people. During this contact, the researcher may obviously or subtly influence their responses. Three types of researcher effects are the researcher personal attribute effect, the researcher unintentional expectancy effect, and researcher observational biases.

Researcher Personal Attribute Effect. The **researcher personal attribute effect** occurs when particular characteristics of a researcher influence people's behavior. Barber (1976) reported a large number of studies that demonstrate how researchers' race, gender, age, ethnic identity, prestige, anxiety, friendliness, dominance, and/or warmth affect research participants' responses. People may answer differently when questions are posed, for example, by a male or a female or by someone warm and friendly as opposed to someone cold and aloof. Yagoda and Wolfson (1964) asked research participants to draw a face and found that their drawings included more mustached men if they were exposed to a mustached researcher.

The researcher personal attribute effect is likely to occur under two conditions. First, when the research task is ambiguous, participants look to the researcher for clues about how to behave. Second, this effect is more likely to occur when the task is related to the personal characteristics of a researcher. For example, interviewers' ethnicity has been found to affect interviewees' responses to questions about affirmative action (Gilbert, Cox, Kashima, & Eberle, 1996).

One way researchers can control for this threat is by employing a variety of research assistants, hoping that any such effect washes out over the many people studied. Or, if it can be determined beforehand which characteristics might affect research participants' responses, researchers can match participants with assistants least likely to influence the results. Power, Murphy, and Coover (1996), for example, in studying the effects of prior exposure to a negative stereotypic or a positive counterstereotypic portrayal of an African American male on the subsequent interpretations by Anglo-Americans of unrelated media events that involve African Americans, had an Anglo male assistant administer the questionnaire to the Anglo participants.

Researcher Unintentional Expectancy Effect.

The **researcher unintentional expectancy effect** (also called the **Rosenthal** or **Pygmalion effect**) occurs when researchers influence research participants' responses by inadvertently letting them know the behavior they desire. Rosenthal (1966) explains that researchers do this by unintentional paralinguistic and kinesic (body language) cues that lead participants to respond in particular ways. Researchers may, for example, smile unconsciously when participants behave in ways that confirm their hypothesis or frown when they behave in ways that don't support the hypothesis. Such behavior is often referred to as *demand characteristics,* as the researcher appears to be "demanding" certain behavior from research participants. (Demand characteristics, however, also apply to any potential cues about the nature and purpose of a study that might influence research participants' reactions, especially their reactions to an experimental treatment.)

To control for this potential threat, some researchers go to great lengths to remove themselves from the actual conducting of a study. This usually is done by employing a research assistant to conduct the study who doesn't know (or is "blind" to) the specific purposes of the investigation and the desired results. Of course, even a "blind" research assistant may still influence research participants' behavior. The most important way to control this threat is to make sure that researchers and/or assistants follow standard (reliable and valid) procedures so that they treat everyone the same.

Researcher Observational Biases.

Researcher observational biases occur whenever researchers, their assistants, or the people they employ to observe research participants demonstrate inaccuracies during the observational process. One such observational bias, called **observer drift**, occurs when observers become inconsistent in the criteria used to make and record observations. This can easily occur when observers are asked to make judgments over the course of a lengthy observational period, either in one sitting or over many observational periods. Obviously, researchers try to control for this by making sure that observers are fresh and not "drifting" (e.g., growing tired and paying less attention) and by checking the consistency of their observations over the course of the observational period.

A second, more insidious bias is called **observer bias** and occurs when observers' knowledge of the research (e.g., its purpose or hypotheses) influences their observations. They may see research participants' behavior as something that it is not. To the extent that such observation supports the hypothesis for a study, this bias is similar to the researcher unintentional expectancy effect, except this time the researcher/observer is the person giving the desired response. Like that effect, this bias can be potentially controlled by employing observers who are blind to the purposes of the study.

A third such bias is the **halo effect,** which occurs when observers make multiple judgments of the same person over time and typically overrate (thus, a "halo" effect, although it can apply to underrating as well) a research participant's performance because that participant did well (or poorly) in an earlier rating. One way to control for this, of course, is to use different observers for each observational period.

EXTERNAL VALIDITY

In addition to knowing that conclusions drawn are valid for the people/texts studied (internally valid), researchers also want to be able to generalize these conclusions to other people/texts, contexts, and time periods. Medical researchers, for example, don't just seek to cure the patients they treat; they want to find cures that will heal anyone with a similar condition. Researchers usually want to apply their findings to people they didn't study directly. Judgments of external validity, the ability to generalize findings from a study to others, are made on the basis of three issues: sampling, ecological validity, and replication.

Sampling

Communication researchers are interested in a **population** (also called a **universe** when applied to texts) of communicators, all the people who possess a particular characteristic, or, in the case of those who study texts, all the messages that share a characteristic of interest. The population of interest to researchers (often called the **target group**) might be members of a business, communication majors at a university, all students at a university, all people living in a city, all eligible voters in the country, or all adult human beings in the world. Similarly, a textual analyst might be interested in a relatively small universe of texts, such as editorials published in a specific newspaper for one week, a relatively large universe, such as every editorial published in every newspaper in the United States, or one still larger, such as all persuasive messages.

The best way to generalize to a population is to study every member of it, or what is called a **census.** If every member is studied, we know, by definition, the population's response at the point in time the study was done.

If the population is small enough, such as a company of 25 employees, a census may be possible. But even here it may be difficult to get everyone to respond. Fulk, Schmitz, and Ryu (1995), for example, wanted to know how perceptions of the usefulness of electronic mail are related to the frequency of this type of media use. They distributed a questionnaire to all 74 electronic mail users within an engineering service and research division of a major petrochemical corporation. Their efforts yielded 65 usable questionnaires, a very high return rate of 87.8%, but not technically a census.

Communication researchers, however, are often interested in much larger populations, where obtaining a census is practically impossible. Sometimes researchers ask everyone in the population of interest and hope for a high response rate. Wicks and Kern (1995), for example, wanted to know what factors influence decisions by local television news directors to engage in coverage of political advertising. They tried to conduct a census of all commercial stations in the United States listed in the *1991 Broadcasting Yearbook.* Of the 1008 questionnaires sent to news directors, 409 were completed and returned, a 40.6% response rate.

Because measuring every member of a population usually isn't feasible, most researchers employ a **sample,** a subgroup of a population. The results from the sample are then generalized back to (used to represent) the population. For such a generalization to be valid (demonstrate **population validity**), the sample must be *representative* of its population; that is, it must accurately approximate the population. In a representative sample, what is characteristic of the sample is characteristic of the population as well. Hence, the most important characteristic of a sample is not its size (although this is important to a certain degree; see Chapter 12) but its similarity to its parent population. There are two general types of sampling procedures, and they differ in terms of how confident we are about the ability of the selected sample to represent the population from which it is drawn: random sampling and nonrandom sampling.

Random Sampling.   **Random sampling** (also called **probability sampling**) involves selecting a sample in such a way that each person in the population of interest has an equal chance of being included. By giving everyone an equal chance, random sampling eliminates the danger of researchers biasing the selection process because of their own opinions or desires. By eliminating bias, random sampling provides the best assurance that the same characteristics of the population exist in the sample, and, therefore, that the sample represents the population.

Of course, no random sample ever represents perfectly the population from which it is drawn. A sample is representative to some degree or within a certain "margin of error." **Sampling error** is a number that expresses how much the characteristics of a sample probably differ from the characteristics of a population. We will explain in Chapter 12 how sampling error is calculated; for now, the important point is that sampling error can be calculated for random samples, but not for nonrandom samples.

There are at least four types of random samples: simple random, systematic, stratified, and cluster.

Simple Random Sample.   To draw a **simple random sample** from a population, we assign each person a consecutive number and then select from these numbers in such a way that each number has an equal chance of being chosen. Numbers are chosen until the desired sample size is obtained.

To conduct a simple random sample, a researcher must first have a complete list of the population. If this is not available, some other random sampling procedure, such as cluster sampling (explained below), must be used. Each population member is then assigned a number, starting with the number 01, if the population is 99 or less (or 001, if there are between 100 and 999 people in the

population; 0001, if there are between 1000 and 9999 people in the population, etc.), to whatever is the last number.

The second step is to use a formal procedure that guarantees that each person in the population has an equal chance of being selected. An important point to keep in mind is that you simply can't pick a random sample by yourself, as you have preferences for certain numbers. You must, therefore, use a formal procedure. For example, you could put all the numbers on different pieces of paper, place them in an urn or a hat, and then pick them until you obtained the desired number of people for the sample. But you would have to make sure that each piece of paper was exactly the same size and folded in the exact same way, and that the urn was well shaken; otherwise, the process would not result in all the pieces of paper having an equal chance of being selected. That's pretty difficult to do, as witnessed by the 1969 military draft lottery, which used this procedure and resulted in a biased selection process because the urn was not sufficiently shaken and, therefore, the numbers put into it last were on top and drawn out first (see Cook & Campbell, 1977; Fienberg, 1971; Notz, Staw, & Cook, 1979).

One alternative to such procedures is to use a random number table (see Appendix A). A **random number table** lists numbers generated by a computer in a nonpurposive way (each had an equal chance of being selected), which means there is no predetermined relationship whatsoever among the numbers on the table. The numbers are truly random.

To illustrate how you might select a simple random sample using a random number table, consult Figure 5.4. It provides a hypothetical population list of 50 members, numbered 01 through 50, and their scores on a communication competence measure (which ranges from a low of 0 to a high of 100). Let's say we want to randomly select 10 people using a simple random sampling procedure. Turn to the table of random numbers in Appendix A at the back of this book, put a pen in your hand, close your eyes (after you read the following instructions!), and put the pen down some-

---

FIGURE 5.4   Selecting a simple random sample

Instructions:

1. Turn to the table of random numbers (Appendix A).
2. Put a pen in your hand, close your eyes, and put the pen down somewhere on the table.
3. Take whatever number is closest to where your pen fell and link it with the very next number. You can link it with the one to the right, left, above, or below it, as long as you continue to do this in a consistent manner. For example, if your pen landed nearest the number "4," and if the number to the right of that is "3," then select the 43rd person from the population list. Then take the next two numbers to the right and do the same thing.
4. Do this until you have 10 people for your sample. If you come across the same number twice, skip it. If you get to the end of a row, start at the beginning of the next row.

Population Members	Communication Competence (0–100)	Population Members	Communication Competence (0–100)
01	50	26	51
02	28	27	19
03	94	28	84
04	78	29	100
05	32	30	24
06	90	31	11
07	12	32	60
08	52	33	91
09	45	34	66
10	81	35	84
11	99	36	36
12	9	37	15
13	69	38	74
14	87	39	59
15	21	40	5
16	98	41	27
17	33	42	98
18	38	43	47
19	44	44	44
20	77	45	86
21	10	46	2
22	83	47	43
23	1	48	50
24	65	49	58
25	63	50	50

where on the table. Take whatever number is closest to where your pen falls and link it with the very next number. You can read this table any way you like—from left to right, right to left, up or down—as long as you are consistent. (Most people like to read left to right, so let's do that.)

Perhaps your pen landed near the number "4." If the very next number to the right of that number is "3," this forms the two-digit number of "43," and you circle person number 43 on the population list. (Because the highest number is 50, we draw two-digit numbers; if the highest number was 100, the numbers would range from 001 to 100, and we would draw three-digit numbers, etc.) Then take the next two numbers to the right of the two-digit number of 43 and select that person (e.g., if the numbers are "2" and "8," the 28th person on the population list is selected). Continue reading across and selecting numbers until there are 10 people in your sample. If you come across the same number twice, skip it. (This is called *sampling without replacement,* in contrast to procedures, like the lottery balls, that use *sampling with replacement,* replacing the number each time so that it has another chance of being selected). If you come to the end of a row, start at the beginning of the next row.

Now calculate the mean communication competence score for the 10 people selected (count up their scores and divide by 10). The actual mean for the entire 50 people is 52.9, so you can see how close or how far away you were from the true mean. Undoubtedly, there will be some difference between your sample mean and the true population mean. That difference is the sampling error.

It is, of course, possible that your sample mean is nowhere near the true population mean. This just goes to show that the accuracy of a single random sample can't be counted on. But try taking 5 samples of 10 people each, and calculate the overall mean of these 5 samples. It is probably closer to the population mean. If you took 10 or 20 samples, you would most likely get even closer still. In fact, given an infinite number of samples, you would eventually get the true population mean. When you have large populations, much higher than 50, you can imagine the efficiency a truly random sampling procedure provides.

Communication researchers often use a simple random sampling procedure because it is an easy way of drawing a relatively representative sample from a population. And many calculators and computers can be used to draw numbers at random. For example, Chaffee, Nass, and Yang (1990) wanted to compare television news with other socialization factors in the acquisition of knowledge by Korean immigrants about United States politics. So they obtained responses to a questionnaire mailed to 1,000 randomly selected addresses from 7,000 listed in the directory of a marketing firm that specializes in the Korean population of central California. C-L. Coleman (1993) used a similar procedure to examine the influence of mass media and interpersonal communication on judgments of environmental and health risks to one's self and to other people. He mailed questionnaires to a simple random sample of 1500 New York State residents supplied by a firm that had combined telephone directories and driving licenses to form the population list.

The biggest difficulty in conducting a simple random sample is obtaining a complete list of a population. To what extent, for example, does a telephone directory provide a complete list of the people living in a town or city? Not everyone has a telephone, and some people have more than one chance of being called if their home has several phones with different numbers. We will look more closely at various ways of identifying populations when we examine survey research in Chapter 8.

Systematic Sample. A **systematic sample** (also called **ordinal sampling**) chooses every *n*th person from a complete list of a population *after starting at a random point.* The interval used to choose every *n*th person is called the **sampling rate.** For example, if every fourth person is chosen, the sampling rate is 1/4, or one in four. The sampling rate chosen must cover everyone in the population. If you wanted to choose 10 people from the list of 50 in Figure 5.4 using this procedure, you would choose a sampling rate of 1/5 to make sure that everyone could potentially be selected. Thus, if you started randomly with person 03, you would also select persons 08, 13, 18, 23, 28, 33, 38, 43, and 48.

Systematic samples are often used with very large populations, perhaps because they are easier to employ than a simple random sample. For example, Salazar, Becker, and Daughety (1994) wanted to assess the impact of social support on smoking cessation and relapse. They used systematic sampling to identify a random sample of 1483 adults, 18 years or older, drawn from three communities in Iowa. Three samples of 500 each were selected from the residential listings in the latest telephone book in each community. The number of residential listings in each book was estimated and divided by 700 (the higher number was used to offset loss due to no answers) to determine the sampling interval. Using a random starting point, that interval was used to select the telephone numbers to which calls were attempted.

Systematic random samples usually produce virtually identical results to those obtained from a simple random sample (see Babbie, 1973). But a systematic random sample would contain more error if the order of the population members were biased in some way, a problem known as **periodicity.** If every *n*th person in a population possesses a characteristic that the other people do not, and these people are selected, this could produce a biased sample. For example, if a systematic random sample of a neighborhood ends up selecting predominately houses on corner lots, this sample may not be representative of the neighborhood, because people who live in corner-lot houses may be different from those who do not (e.g., they may be wealthier).

Stratified Sample.   A **stratified sample** categorizes a population with respect to a characteristic a researcher considers to be important, called a **stratification variable,** and then samples randomly from each category. One popular way of stratifying a population is with regard to demographic variables. For example, to study how members of different races and classes use call-in political television, Newhagen (1994) first divided a suburb of Washington, DC, by race (Black and White) and household income (high and low). Neighborhoods of approximately eight square blocks were then identified, each containing about

2000 residents that fit the four possible combinations (Blacks with high income, Blacks with low income, Whites with high income, and Whites with low income). Equal numbers of households were then drawn randomly from each race-by-class category using a street address-based telephone directory. This procedure assured an equal number of respondents in each group.

In a similar manner, W. J. Brown and Cody (1991) randomly selected 1170 respondents from one city, two towns, and six villages in three distinct geographical regions in India using a stratified sample design in each location conducted on the basis of age and gender. And Barnes and Hayes (1995a, 1995b), in their study of high school instructional practices in language arts employed a professional sampling company to randomly select California high school English teachers, stratified on the basis of school enrollment size.

Stratified samples are used frequently in research, especially in political polling, because they ensure that different subgroups of a population (a subgroup of a population is called a *stratum;* the plural is *strata*) are represented in a sample. This type of random sample is especially important when a researcher wants to include a sufficient number of people from a small subgroup of the population. In such cases, a simple random sample or a systematic sample might not include any members of this subgroup or yield an insufficient number of them.

A population can be stratified along any number of variables, and respondents from these categories can even be randomly selected in proportion to their representation in the population (e.g., if 60% of the students at a university are female, the sample is 60% females), called a **proportional stratified random sample.** However, the more stratification variables there are in a study, the more difficult it may be to obtain a representative sample from a group within the population. The frequency with which respondents can be obtained from stratified populations is called the **incidence.** So, for example, if a high-ability group is defined as students with a grade point average of 3.90 and above (on a 4.0 scale), and 50 students at a university maintain that average, 50 is the incidence of this particular group of potential people in the population. If a researcher were also interested in comparing the communication behavior of other subgroups, say people of different gender, race, and/or other variables, in addition to high ability, it might be difficult to find a sufficient number of respondents who fit each combination of categories.

Cluster Sample.   Each of the preceding types of random samples necessitates obtaining a complete list of the population of interest and then randomly selecting members from it. But obtaining a complete list is not always possible. For example, a researcher interested in studying communication between employers and employees of a large multinational company with many offices, such as IBM, may not be able to obtain a complete list of all employees, but a list of all IBM branch offices would most likely be accessible. The researcher could then study a **cluster sample** by randomly selecting units, or clusters (in this case, branch offices), of the employee population.

Many cluster samples involve **multistage sampling,** a procedure for selecting a sample in two or more stages, in which successively smaller clusters are picked randomly. The simplest example is a two-stage process. In the first stage, researchers select clusters randomly from a population and, in the second stage, they randomly select individuals from within each of those clusters. For example, a researcher wanting to compare the communication skills of public and private high school students in a town may not be able to obtain a complete list of those individuals. But multistage cluster sampling could be used to first select several schools randomly from a list of all public and private high schools in that town and then students at those schools could be randomly selected, too. And because students only attend one high school at any given time, all students would have an equal chance of being selected.

Multistage sampling is particularly appropriate for companies that conduct state, regional, or national surveys, such as the Gallup polls or the Nielsen ratings, where complete lists of the population are not available. To obtain a single respondent, a state is first randomly selected (say Illinois), then a random city (Chicago), then a random street (Sheridan Road), and then a random street number on that road (4201). If that street address is an apartment complex, one of the apartments is randomly selected, and the individual who lives there (or a randomly chosen person from those who live there) is asked to participate. As you see, a study of people selected via this type of sampling would be time-consuming. However, in Chapter 8, we will see how random-digit telephone dialing can be used to speed up the process of obtaining a random sample in cases where complete population lists are not available.

Multistage sampling is perhaps most appropriate for studying large geographical areas, using what is called *area probability sampling* (also called *block sampling*). Whether sampling from a city, rural area, jungle, or desert, as Fowler (1993) explains:

> *The basic approach is to divide the total land area in exhaustive, mutually exclusive subareas with identifiable boundaries. A sample of subareas is drawn. A list then is made of housing units in selected subareas, and a sample of listed units is drawn. As a final stage, all people in selected household units may be included in the sample, or they may be listed and sampled as well. (p. 20)*

To summarize, cluster samples and multistage sampling are used whenever a random sample is desired and a complete list of the population is not available but a complete list of all relevant clusters can be obtained. The reason this is still a random sample is because each cluster sample at each stage of the clustering process is selected in a random manner.

Nonrandom Sampling.   It sometimes isn't possible to sample randomly from a population because neither a complete population list nor a list of clusters is available. This is especially true when studying people with characteristics for which no lists exist. Oppliger and Sherblom (1990, 1992), for example, were interested in what makes late-night talk-show host David Letterman's disparagement humor funny. There is, of course, no master list of people who watch David Letterman, so they selected for their sample any available people who watched that show, showed them an episode of the program, and asked them questions.

It is also acceptable at times for researchers not to sample randomly from a population, even when they could. Exploratory or beginning experimental research is often concerned first with establishing internally valid conclusions and only later with externally valid ones, so researchers don't necessarily take the time and effort needed to study an optimal sample. Many naturalistic researchers doing case studies are concerned with what happens in a particular context that is not easily accessible (such as a street gang). They will be satisfied to rely on any informants who are willing and able to provide them with accurate background information, rather than using any of the random sampling procedures we have discussed (see Chapter 10).

When random samples cannot be obtained for some reason or are not deemed vital, nonrandom sampling is used. **Nonrandom sampling** (also called **nonprobability sampling**) is whatever researchers do instead of using procedures that ensure that each member of a population has an equal chance of being selected. When nonrandom samples are used, researchers cannot compute the amount of sampling error. This doesn't mean that what is learned from a nonrandom sample necessarily isn't representative of its population. A researcher with no way of calculating the amount of bias in the sample does not know if and how a nonrandom sample differs from its parent population. Researchers, therefore, must be very careful in generalizing the results obtained from a nonrandom sample to a population, and must always disclose when they are doing so.

There are at least five types of nonrandom samples: convenience, volunteer, purposive, quota, and network.

Convenience Sample. In a **convenience sample** (also called an **accidental** or **haphazard sample**), respondents are selected nonrandomly on the basis of availability. Market researchers, for example, often go to shopping malls and interview any available people who shop there. Communication researchers, too, frequently rely on convenience samples. For example, to assess the influence of the mass media on young children's general and brand-specific knowledge about alcohol, E. W. Austin and Nach-Ferguson (1995) administered a questionnaire to a convenience sample of 213 children and 276 parents from two rural towns. They simply asked any child they could find between the ages of 7 and 12, as well as his or her parents, to complete their questionnaire.

The most popular type of convenience sample for researchers who teach at universities is one composed of students. Kapoor, Wolfe, and Blue (1995), for example, asked 514 college students attending a university to complete a questionnaire measuring their individualism/collectivism (privileging individuals over the collective, or vice versa). College students are used in numerous studies because they are readily available.

The problem with convenience samples, as with all nonrandom samples, is that there is no guarantee the respondents chosen are similar to the general population they are supposed to represent. The results from convenience samples, therefore, cannot be applied with much confidence to a larger population.

Sometimes researchers can increase that confidence by making the convenience sample similar in some ways to the population that respondents are supposed to represent. Beentjes, Koolstra, and van der Voort (1996), for example, surveyed 1700 students in grades 8 and 10, enrolled in 80 classrooms in 10 urban secondary schools and 10 schools located in rural districts in a province in the Netherlands. The authors argue that this convenience sample is reasonably representative of the national Dutch school population with respect to gender and grade level when compared with the 1993 data from the Dutch Central Bureau of Statistics.

Volunteer Sample. In a **volunteer sample,** respondents choose to participate in a study. Cardello,

Ray, and Pettey (1995), for example, asked patients at both major urban and suburban medical practices in a midwestern metropolitan city to volunteer for their study of the relationship between physicians' communication style and their patients' satisfaction. To study depression and verbal aggressiveness in different marital couple types, Segrin and Fitzpatrick (1992) asked a number of women's business groups in the eastern United States to solicit volunteers to participate in their investigation. And Maibach, Flora, and Nass (1991) recruited volunteers from people who were participating in a Healthy Living Program, one element of the Stanford (California) Five Cities Project, by mailing requests to 30,000 people and distributing 10,000 announcements at various places of work. To enroll, participants tore off and returned an attached postage-paid card. These procedures resulted in the registration of almost 5,000 potential respondents; from these, 10% were randomly selected to evaluate this program.

To recruit volunteers, researchers frequently offer some reward to those people who sign up for studies, especially to university students. Aitken and Neer (1993), for example, studied the relationship between classroom communication apprehension (fear of talking in class) and the motivation to ask questions during class. One hundred fifty-six undergraduates enrolled in a basic communication course volunteered for the study. In return, they received extra credit in the course. Monetary rewards are also sometimes offered to those who volunteer. Adelman and Frey (1997), for example, studied communication and community building at Bonaventure House, a residential facility for people with AIDS, located in Chicago. As part of their research program, residents completed questionnaires at four different points in time. Each time residents volunteered, they were given $10.00. Because many residents have little or no money, this stipend was an attractive reward for participating.

Researchers must be very wary about generalizing the results from a volunteer sample to the population of interest, for research indicates that volunteer respondents often differ from nonvolunteers in important ways that might affect the findings. For example, volunteers tend to have greater intellectual ability, interest, motivation, need for approval, and sociability, as well as lower age and less authoritarianism, than nonvolunteer respondents (see Rosenthal, 1965). A volunteer sample, therefore, like all nonrandom samples, may not be representative of the population from which it is drawn.

Purposive Sample.   In a **purposive sample** (also called a **deliberate,** Vogt, 1993, **judgment,** Honigmann, 1970; Pelto & Pelto, 1975, **purposeful,** Patton, 1990, or **strategic sample,** Hunt, 1970), respondents are nonrandomly selected on the basis of a particular characteristic. Watkins, Lichtenstein, Vest, and Thomas (1992), for example, studied the marketing strategies of a national sample of health maintenance organizations (HMOs). They wanted to study HMOs that had Medicare risk contracts, were planning marketing campaigns designed to attract new Medicare patients, and expected to enroll at least 300 new enrollees during a 3-month period. Cities were chosen in which at least two HMOs had Medicare risk contracts. A final criterion was the need for cooperation by the HMOs because the researchers wanted to obtain proprietary information from them on their marketing activities, advertising, and other sensitive information. The final sample consisted of 23 HMOs drawn from 12 cities.

A purposive sample is similar to a stratification (random) sample in that the characteristic chosen is a stratification variable. But the crucial difference is that a researcher using a purposive sample does not select respondents randomly from each group within the stratification categories. Instead, all available respondents who possess the characteristic(s) are included. The inclusion of any and all such respondents may produce a biased sample and, therefore, limit the generalizability of the findings. That is why Watkins et al. (1992) pointed out in their report, "The fact that the chosen HMOs represent a purposive sample, rather than a random sample, limits the generalizability of results to those cities we selected" (p. 308).

Sengupta (1996) actually makes an argument for using a purposive sample instead of a random sample in a study of factors that affect the quit rate of less educated smokers. As Sengupta explains:

> Collecting data by random telephone survey was ruled out because of the length of the questionnaire…. Because the purpose of this exploratory study was to understand the reason for the difference in quit rate between better educated and less educated smokers and to suggest possible antismoking communication strategies aimed at less educated smokers, it was deemed important to recruit smokers with varying levels of educational attainment. (pp. 61–62)

Sengupta adds, "Although this [the purposive sample] would make the results somewhat less generalizable, such sampling procedures are commonly used by motivation researchers, particularly to generate ideas for communication campaigns" (p. 62)

Quota Sample. To gather a **quota sample,** respondents are selected nonrandomly on the basis of their known proportion in a population. Clair (1993), for example, conducted interviews with 50 working women about sexual harassment. Women were selected to participate on the basis of particular demographic characteristics—such as type of occupation, marital status, and race—in equivalent numbers to match the statistics given by the 1987 United States Bureau of Labor Statistics and the Bureau of the Census. Thus, because 24% of women in the United States at that time held managerial/professional positions, 24% of the women in the sample also held managerial/professional positions.

Network Sample. In a **network sample** (also called a **multiplicity sample**), respondents are asked to refer a researcher to other respondents, and these people are contacted, included in the sample, and, in turn, are asked for the names of additional respondents, who are found and included in the sample (see Granovetter, 1976). This type of procedure is sometimes called the *snowball technique.* Just as a snowball rolling down a hill picks up more and more snow, so too does a network sample become larger as a researcher contacts people who have been referred by other respondents.

Hecht, Larkey, and Johnson (1992), for example, compared African American and European American perceptions of interethnic communication effectiveness. To obtain their sample, the researchers recruited African American and European American students and community members using the snowball technique at a major university, two community colleges, and community groups in a large city in the southwest United States. Individuals were approached and asked to respond to a questionnaire. They were then asked to recruit an additional respondent or to suggest groups to whom the questionnaire could be administered.

The snowball technique is quite popular with naturalistic researchers (see Chapter 10). Sarch (1993), for example, studied how gender and power influence telephone use in dating relationships. She conducted in-depth interviews with 18 women who attended "Single Volleyball Nights," sponsored by a Jewish Community Center in Philadelphia. These women referred Sarch to seven other single women who were actively dating at the time, and she interviewed them, too. Her concern was locating people who would speak to her openly and at length about the topic she was investigating. Sarch argues that

> a goal of qualitative research is not to find lawlike relationships generalizable across a population, but rather to understand specific situations—in this case, of telephone use…. The sample is not random, and, thus, not intended to be representative. (p. 130)

Ecological Validity

Ecological validity refers to research that describes what actually occurs in real-life circumstances. To the extent that research procedures reflect what people do in the contexts in which their behavior normally occurs, confidence in the generalizability of the findings to other people and situations is increased. If, on the other hand, the research setting is artificial or contrived, the study may only assess what people do in those constructed situations and, thus, limit the generalizability of the findings.

One way to increase the ecological validity of communication research is to study message behavior as it occurs in natural settings, which is what naturalistic researchers do (see Chapter 10). For example, to study the communication of gang members, Conquergood (1991a, 1992, 1994; see also Conquergood & Siegel, 1990) moved into Big Red—a sprawling, dilapidated tenement in the heart of "Little Beirut" in Chicago, a neighborhood filled with gangs—and became a part-time substitute teacher in a local school. It took a long time to develop relationships with gang members, but once he did, he was able to experience firsthand their natural communication behavior.

Studying communication behavior in natural settings increases the generalizability of research because communication processes may be thought of as streams of behavior and, like all streams, their course is shaped by the terrain through which they flow. If we ignore the banks and study only the stream or divert the stream into an artificial container and study it there, our knowledge of the stream may be limited. Conquergood would probably not have gotten the same information had he just gone to that neighborhood and tried to survey gang members or asked them to come to a laboratory and studied their behavior.

A critical reader must ask serious questions about the validity of findings from research conducted in controlled settings, such as laboratories. L. R. Frey (1994a, 1994b, 1994d, 1994e, 1996), for example, following in the footsteps of others (e.g., Bormann, 1980), has raised questions about the external validity of much group communication research. Frey's (1988) review of studies published during the 1980s found that the majority of the research involved single observations of student laboratory groups created to undertake artificial tasks assigned by the researcher. The ability to generalize from such groups to real-life groups is limited, he points out:

primarily because students, unlike their real-world counterparts, have little investment in these groups and the tasks they are asked to solve, and because the laboratory/classroom setting hardly mirrors the

significant contextual factors that impinge on groups in the real world. (L. R. Frey, 1994b, p. 554)

This is not to suggest that all research studies conducted in natural settings are more ecologically valid than research conducted in laboratories. Nor are we suggesting that all research conducted in laboratories is ecologically invalid. Ecological validity depends on the procedures used. The point is that researchers conducting laboratory studies must make an effort to assure that their research participants behave as they would in other, natural contexts if they wish to claim that the laboratory results are generalizable to those other contexts.

One way to enhance the generalizability of laboratory findings is to replicate them in natural settings. A good example is the studies by Berger, Knowlton, and Abrahams (1996) that were conducted to test the hierarchy principle in strategic communication. This principle claims that when individuals fail to achieve social goals but continue to pursue them, their initial tendency is to alter the lower level communication elements, such as speech rate and vocal intensity (speaking slower and louder), rather than higher level elements, such as the structure and sequencing of their message content, which are more demanding of cognitive resources.

Berger et al. first conducted a laboratory study in which students were asked to give another student directions to a well-known bank a few blocks away. The other student was actually a **confederate** (a person who pretends to be a research participant to help a researcher) who responded either by expressing general difficulty in understanding the directions, asking the person to slow down and give the directions again (the lower level condition), or asking people to provide an alternative route (the higher level condition). To measure the amount of cognition required, the researchers measured the time that elapsed between the point at which confederates finished indicating they didn't understand and the point at which the research participants began to give the second version of the directions. The results supported the hierarchy principle, as respondents who were asked to alter routes spent significantly more time formulating an alternative set of directions than those asked to speak more slowly or those not given specific information about the failed attempt at giving directions. Berger et al. then replicated this laboratory experiment in a second study, reported in the article, which also supported the hierarchy principle.

But Berger et al. didn't stop there. They wanted to know whether these results could also be observed in the natural environment. So they conducted two more studies, reported in the same article, in which two confederates approached naive pedestrians at a busy intersection and asked for directions. In both studies, after the pedestrian gave directions, the two confederates gave responses identical to those in the second laboratory experiment, and observers used a concealed stopwatch to record the time that elapsed between the end of the confederates' request and the second telling. The results from both field experiments corroborated those obtained from the laboratory experiments, suggesting that the procedures were ecologically valid and providing more confidence in the generalizability of the results.

Replication

Berger et al.'s (1996) study points to the third criterion in establishing external validity—**replication,** conducting a study that repeats or duplicates in some systematic manner a previous study. The results from any single study simply cannot be relied on: "The assumption that a single result can be accepted as valid and replicable is false" (Amir & Sharon, 1991, p. 51). Just as we wouldn't conclude that most horses are Trechainers (a German breed) on the basis of observing horses at an Olympic equestrian event (they are one of the dominant type of horses used in such events), researchers can't conclude on the basis of a single study that a new drug cures a disease or that watching televised violence increases aggression. As Tukey (1969) explains, only when the same, or substantially the same, results are achieved from several replications

of a study can the findings of the original study be confirmed and extended reliably.

Types of Replication.   There is, of course, no way to ever replicate someone else's study exactly, since every investigation involves a different researcher and different research participants. Brogdan (1951) claims that the same study cannot even be repeated by the same researcher, since the research participants are, with few exceptions, different and the researcher himself or herself changes over time. Replication, then, is a matter of degree. Hendrick (1991) delineates three types of replication that differ in terms of degree: exact, partial, and conceptual.

Exact Replication.   An **exact replication** duplicates a research study as closely as possible, with the exception of studying different research participants. Shedletsky (1991), for example, replicated Coltheart, Hull, and Slater's (1975) study of gender differences in verbal and spatial processing, which found that females produced fewer errors on a verbal task, whereas males produced fewer errors on a visual task. Everything done in the original study was replicated with a new group of males and females. Shedletsky found no significant differences between males and females on either task, which called into question the generalizability of the earlier findings.

Exact replications in the social sciences are rare, however (see J. N. Denzin, 1970; Mahoney, 1985; Sterling, 1959). One reason may be that researchers don't always provide clear and detailed information about their procedures. Applebaum's (1985) survey of the communication literature found that the majority of articles provided no information regarding research participant selection procedures. Reinard (1988) reviewed the literature regarding the persuasive effects of evidence. One of his conclusions was that "the failure of many researchers to describe the types of evidence they have used (testimonial assertion, factual evidence, statistics, abstracts and summaries, and the like) had made interpretation of findings difficult at best" (p. 47). How can a study be reproduced or accepted as internally and externally valid if we don't know all the details of how it was done?

Partial Replication. A **partial replication** duplicates a previous research study by changing one procedure while keeping the rest of the procedures the same. For example, the independent and dependent variables and the specific sampling procedure may be kept the same, but the measurement techniques might be changed slightly. Say an interview study reveals that people work harder for bosses who are considerate. If a study measuring work effort on a questionnaire reveals the same thing, researchers can be more sure of this finding. Or, in a partial replication study, everything might be kept the same as the previous study, except that the independent variable is measured in a different way to see if this new method produces the same results. Say employers' level of consideration was measured previously by the "amount of sick-leave benefits" they awarded. If consideration is measured in a replication by employees' perceptions on a Likert-type scale of employers' "willingness to listen to employees' suggestions" and the same results are obtained, that finding is supported. On the other hand, if different measurement techniques yield dissimilar results, researchers are less confident about the external validity of the findings.

Partial replications are the most frequent type employed, for they typically are designed to both retest and extend the findings from a previous study. For example, McCornack (1992) and McCornack, Levine, Solowczuk, Torres, and Campbell (1992) conducted studies to test Information Manipulation Theory (IMT), a theory of deceptive message design based on Grice's (1975, 1989) work on conversational rules. These studies found that deceptive messages violate interactants' assumption that conversation is based on cooperation and rationality.

Jacobs, Dawson, and Brashers (1996), however, argued that deception is tied more to Grice's notion of implicature, that listeners try to "*preserve*

[italics added] the assumption that the message conveyed is a good faith effort to conform to the CP [Cooperative Principle] and its maxims" (p. 71). Jacobs et al. replicated the McCornack studies, using the same independent variables (two hypothetical situations of deceptive communication that involved a relational partner dating someone without telling the other partner) and dependent variables (perceived honesty and competence), but they varied the procedures a little. In the original format, respondents were given full information so they could assess the degree of manipulation involved in the messages. In addition to this "open" awareness condition, Jacobs et al. created a "closed" awareness condition that eliminated the deceptively manipulated "sensitive information" contained in the original hypothetical examples. The findings from this partial replication not only failed to support the basic claims of IMT but also supported the alternative model of deceptive message design based on conversational implicature.

One replication, of course, doesn't prove an alternative model. In fact, in the same journal issue in which Jacobs et al.'s study was published, McCornack, Levine, Morrison, and Lapinski (1996) took exception to this replication. They reanalyzed the data and showed that the data were inconsistent with the premise that deception derives solely from erroneous implicatures. Jacobs, Brashers, and Dawson (1996) then responded to McCornack et al.'s critique, and again challenged the validity of IMT. Although they had the final say in that journal issue, we undoubtedly haven't heard the last word on the subject. More replications will be needed before concluding which model better explains deceptive message behavior.

Conceptual Replication. A **conceptual replication** examines the same issue as a previous study but uses entirely different procedures, measurement instruments, sampling procedures, and/or data-analytic techniques. The goal is to see if the same results can be obtained with very different research procedures (e.g., a survey study is replicated using naturalistic procedures). The use of a

FIGURE 5.5   Effects of success and precision of replication on previous research findings

		Result of Replication	
		Successful	*Unsuccessful*
Precision of Replication	*Fairly precise*	Supports previous findings	Calls into question previous findings
	Fairly imprecise	Extends previous findings	Limits previous findings

Source: Adapted from Robert Rosenthal, "Replication in Behavioral Research," in James W. Neuliep (Ed.), *Replication Research in the Social Sciences,* p. 5, copyright © 1991 by Sage Publications, Inc. Adapted by Permission of Sage Publications, Inc.

very different approach, thus, tests the replicability of the results, not just how they are interpreted.

Evaluating Replications.   While replication is tremendously important, not all studies are worth replicating and not all replications are equivalent; in some instances, replication is more crucial than in others. Rosenthal (1991) argues that

> assuming a constant level of scientific importance, those studies that were better done merit replication more than do those that were poorly done. Studies that were very poorly done in the first place are not so much "done again" as they are "done right" when replicated. (p. 7)

Rosenthal (1991) proposes three criteria for judging the value of a replication: *when, how,* and *by whom* the replication is conducted. First, he argues that earlier replications are more valuable than later ones: "Weighting all replications equally, the first replication doubles our information about the research issue, the fifth replication adds 20% to our information level, and the fiftieth replication adds only 2% to our information level" (p. 2). Second, how "precise" or similar the methodology of a replication is to the original study and how "success-

ful" or similar the findings are determines the type of information gained (see Figure 5.5). A successful and precise (exact) replication "supports" previous findings; a successful but imprecise (conceptual/partial) replication "extends" those findings. An unsuccessful and precise replication "calls into question" the previous findings; an unsuccessful and imprecise replication "limits" those findings. Third, Rosenthal believes that replications by different researchers are more valuable than replications by the same researcher, and that the more the replication researcher is different from the previous researcher (e.g., in philosophical grounding and/or methodological preference), the better. If very different researchers (such as an experimenter and a naturalistic researcher) obtain the same findings, the external validity of those findings is greatly increased because the results have been triangulated.

The case of a successful replication is clear; the similar findings enhance the external validity of the previous findings. The case of an unsuccessful replication, however, poses a dilemma, for we can't be sure whether the previous findings or the replication findings are more valid. To resolve this conundrum, Rosenthal (1991) urges researchers to employ a **replication battery,** which involves multiple replications of a previous study, such as both a replication study that includes an exact replication and one that is a partial or conceptual replication. This is actually what Shedletsky (1991) did in trying to replicate Coltheart, Hull, and Slater's (1975) study of gender differences in verbal and spatial processing (mentioned previously). Shedletsky not only conducted an exact replication; he also conducted four additional partial replications that modified in various ways the variables studied and the procedures used in the original study. In this way, he was able to see whether the previous findings were supported or refuted, as well as how they should be limited and/ or extended in meaningful ways.

In addition to applying the criteria of when, how, and by whom a replication is conducted, we might ask how many replications are enough. In general, the more the better; three replications are better than two, which are better than one, and so forth. But Popper (1962) believes there is a law of diminishing returns. While there isn't a set number, Rosenkrantz (1980) proposes a formula for determining whether a replication is worth doing: The net gain of a replication equals the expected value of the information minus the costs of doing the study. After many replications have been done, the expected value of the information to be gained by another study simply doesn't outweigh the cost of doing it.

The Bias against Replication. There is healthy regard and respect for replication in the physical sciences, where it is a normal part of the way researchers do business, but in the social sciences, including communication research, replication is viewed in contradictory ways. On the one hand, there is widespread agreement that replications are "at the heart of science" (Hersen & Barlow, 1976, p. 317) and "underlie the self-correction that is presumed to be another characteristic of the scientific method" (Lamal, 1991, p. 31). On the other hand, replications are rarely published in social science journals (see Bornstein, 1990, 1991; Bozarth & Roberts, 1972; Greenwald, 1975; Ma-

honey, 1985; Reid, Soley, & Wimmer, 1981). In fact, C. W. Kelly, Chase, and Tucker (1979) found that the leading reason given for rejecting manuscripts for publication in communication journals was that they were perceived to be "mere replications" (p. 341). Perhaps that's one of the reasons that there seem to be so few replications conducted and submitted for publication today. Neuliep and Crandall's (1991) survey of 288 past editors of social and behavioral science journals found that 42% claimed that a replication had never been submitted for publication to the journal they edited, and 18% said they had received only one replication during their editorial tenure.

Another possible important reason for the lack of submissions, however, may be editors' preference for "new" studies over replications, which Neuliep and Crandall's (1991) survey also showed. In addition, there is a tendency to publish research that demonstrates significant relationships between variables, and replications often result in nonsignificant findings. Bornstein (1991) laments that

> conducting a replication study puts the researcher in a difficult, almost paradoxical position. If the original finding is replicated, manuscript reviewers, journal editors, and other researchers are likely to view the results as trivial. (After all, they will respond, you've just discovered something that we already knew; show us something new and different.) On the other hand, if the researcher fails to replicate the original finding, he or she typically will be in the unfortunate position of reporting a nonsignificant (i.e., $p > .05$) result, and social science researchers have traditionally shown a strong distrust of nonsignificant results. (p. 73)

The danger in not replicating research is that invalid results from a single study may end up guiding behavior. Amir and Sharon (1991) point out a number of examples, including Janis and Feshbach's (1953) study of the negative effects of fear-arousing messages, which led advertisers to avoid using them, until a replication by Leventhal (1970) raised serious doubts about the validity of the original findings.

Until replication studies are awarded the respect they deserve, social-scientific research will probably continue to be "perceived by other scholars (and by members of the public) as being less rigorous, less robust, and less replicable and less cumulative than research in other branches of science" (Bornstein, 1991, p. 80).

CONCLUSION

The importance of validity cannot be overestimated, for, as Berlo (1955) maintains, "Poor research is worse than no research, just as false information is worse than no information" (p. 3). Researchers must invest the efforts described in this chapter to produce findings that can be trusted and generalized to other people/texts, situations, and time periods. Evaluating the validity of information obtained from research studies, therefore, is one of the most important tasks confronting researchers.

RESEARCH ETHICS AND POLITICS

Research may appear at first to be a straightforward, value-free activity, one in which a rational, correct way to operate always is evident to anyone familiar with its procedures. But that's just not the case. Research is a human activity guided by value judgments that have serious moral implications. All along the way, choices must be made that can't be decided simply on the basis of scientific logic. Communication research is conducted by human beings, who study human behavior, and often use human beings as participants. Whenever people deal with people, their behavior has an ethical dimension. Thomas Mann wrote, "The great lesson of these times is to discover that the moral and the intellectual are linked." In this chapter, we explore this link, describing some ethical issues and consequences of communication research and identifying some ways to promote ethical communication inquiry.

ETHICAL ISSUES
IN COMMUNICATION RESEARCH

Let's begin by understanding that there is a difference between ethical and legal principles. Laws are usually not universal principles; they are conventions particular to a given culture. It may be acceptable for politicians to defend their behavior with the famous statement, "Nothing illegal was done here," but researchers have an ethical responsibility that goes far beyond not merely breaking the law. Even if it is legal, it's not necessarily ethical.

The word *ethics* is derived from the Greek word *ethos,* meaning "character." An ethical person is a "good" person. In fact, measurements of

communicator credibility and trust often ask for judgments about character. Therefore, an ethical communication researcher is a person whose research activities are guided by larger concerns about fairness, honesty, and public good.

Philosophers generally agree that the closest synonym for the word ethics is *morality,* derived from the Latin word *moralis,* meaning "customs." **Ethics,** therefore, can be defined as moral principles and recognized rules of conduct regarding a particular class of human action. **Research ethics,** consequently, refer to moral principles and recognized rules of conduct governing the activities of researchers.

Two elements in this definition are especially important. The first is "moral principles." To be ethical, communication research should be consistent with fundamental moral principles that apply to all human conduct. Morals inevitably involve values (standards for proper behavior). When researchers confront ethical dilemmas, they are attempting to balance competing values (N. L. Smith, 1985), such as the standards of honesty and courtesy. For example, a communication researcher may want to study very personal intimacy rituals performed by lovers, but the researcher's desire to gather this information must be tempered by the lovers' right to privacy. Even the manner in which a researcher might inquire about such behaviors might lead to embarrassment. Therefore, such research topics must be handled quite delicately, making sure that research participants are willing to share information about the private parts (no pun intended) of their lives. It's sometimes hard to be both honest and courteous simultaneously, so tough choices must be made.

The second element is "recognized rules of conduct regarding a particular class of human action." Communication researchers generally agree that certain forms of behavior are ethically acceptable and others unacceptable when conducting research. Ethical decisions about research are, thus, ones that conform as well as possible to the values and behaviors considered proper by the larger community of researchers. In the case of the earlier mentioned study of intimacy rituals, the researcher would follow the accepted rule of research conduct of requesting "informed consent," asking for research participants' permission to discuss specific topics (examined later in the chapter), before asking any personal questions.

Ethical decisions, however, can rarely be judged simply as right or wrong; they exist on a continuum ranging from clearly unethical to clearly ethical (H. W. Reese & Fremouw, 1984). Therefore, it is virtually impossible to develop a standard checklist that can be used to judge all the ethical decisions made in research studies. As Kimmel (1988) explains:

> The sheer diversity of ethical problems that one might encounter during the various stages of social research seems to have precluded the emergence of a clear typology or set of classifying characteristics by which to describe and contrast particular studies. (p. 26)

Here, we consider ethical issues that affect the treatment of research participants, as well as those related to research findings and their use. But before doing so, we start with a consideration of the politics of academic research, for politics and ethics are deeply connected. And nowhere is this more true than in the academic setting where politics exert substantial influence on professors' decisions to engage in research, what research they might conduct, and the ethical choices they may be forced to make.

The Politics of Academic Research

Each context in which research is a vital component (e.g., government, think tanks, and businesses) has unique political features at work that affect the research enterprise. Because most of the research with which we are concerned in this text is conducted by university professors, and because we too are professors, we focus in this section on understanding the politics of research in the academic context. Specifically, we examine differences between research and teaching institutions, the effects of tenure and promotion on research, and the growing importance of grant money.

Research versus Teaching Institutions. Most students probably don't fully understand the university system, even though they are embedded in it virtually every day for four or more years. They think that professors are hired only to teach courses. That may be true at some schools, but at many, if not most, schools, that's just not the case.

Professors are hired with the expectation that they will engage in three major activities: teaching, research, and service. Universities, however, can be distinguished with regard to how much emphasis is placed on each of these three activities. Some universities are primarily oriented toward research; in fact, they're called *research I institutions.* These universities often have doctoral programs, including one in communication. Professors at these universities are judged first and foremost with regard to the quantity and quality of the research they publish. That's not to say that teaching and service aren't important; they are, but the publication of research is the number one priority. In turn, these institutions often give professors resources to facilitate their research, such as teaching and/or research assistants and reduced teaching loads (compared to other universities). So if you're at one of these research institutions and most of your introductory classes are taught by graduate students, you now know why this is the case—because research is the number one priority. Indeed, at these universities, a great teacher who does not publish enough research typically will not survive, but a great researcher who publishes a lot but is not a great teacher will probably do just fine. That's why these universities are often called "publish or perish" institutions.

At the other extreme are universities and colleges (including junior and community colleges) that primarily privilege teaching. Teaching loads at such institutions are quite high in comparison to research institutions, sometimes two or three times as much (e.g., four versus two courses per semester). At some of these institutions, professors are not expected to engage in research; they are judged solely on teaching excellence and the extent of their service (e.g., to the department, university, community, and/or profession). Research may be considered nice, and even supported in some ways (such as providing travel funds for professors to present their work at conferences), but it isn't mandatory.

Most universities and colleges are somewhere in the middle of this continuum; they promote a balance between teaching and research, with service also considered to be important (although typically less so than teaching and research). Teaching loads (e.g., three courses a semester) may be lighter than those at schools that stress only teaching, but heavier than those at research institutions. And there are appropriate expectations at these institutions for professors to publish research—not as much, of course, as at research institutions, but nearly equal (and, in some cases, more) to the importance given to teaching.

Research, thus, is a vital component of most professors' academic lives. And, in fact, the importance of research is increasing at most universities for a number of reasons. Many universities that previously only stressed teaching or made it their highest priority are focusing more on research. That's because professors' published research enhances the reputation of a university. Indeed, universities are evaluated, on one level, by the impact of their faculty's published research. Think of the top universities in the United States. Why do you suppose such universities as Harvard, Yale, or The University of Chicago spring to mind? That's because these universities have some of the top researchers in the world. The University of Chicago, for example, has more Nobel Laureates on its faculty than any university in the country. Hence, professors' research helps to make these universities

prestigious and, of course, the most prestigious schools attract the best students.

The other reason has to do with the competitiveness of the current job market. There are many more doctoral degrees being granted than ever before, especially in the field of communication. Most of these individuals want to teach at universities, but there are only so many research institutions that can hire new graduates. So schools that had relatively moderate or low research expectations for its faculty are finding that they are now able to hire new professors who are committed to engaging in research. Indeed, in contrast to years past, it now is typical for recent Ph.D. graduates to have already published research. As these individuals enter schools that previously didn't value research that highly, especially schools where communication was seen by administrators and colleagues in other fields as primarily a service discipline (e.g., with the major charge of teaching the core introductory public speaking course), rather than a full-fledged academic discipline that also stresses research, they invariably help to change the culture, making research a more vital component of the mission of the department and/or school. Of course, changing the culture of a department or university is not always easy. There sometimes is tension between senior faculty members who were hired primarily to teach and may not conduct research and the new "kids on the block" who are expected to engage in research as part of their job, with each party not understanding, and perhaps even resenting, the priorities of the other party.

Finally, although we have, to some degree, pitted teaching against research in this discussion, we want to make clear that excellent teaching and excellent research can go hand-in-hand. There is nothing to suggest that these activities work on a teeter-totter principle; that as one goes up, the other must go down. It is the case, however, as you know only too well as a student, that there are just so many hours in the day, so tradeoffs sometimes are inevitable. Perhaps the biggest problem today is not the tradeoffs professors sometimes must make among teaching, research, and service, but the tendency, given the competitive job market, for universities to expect professors, especially new ones, to be "superprofs," demanding that they be excellent at all three activities to receive tenure and promotion.

The Effects of Tenure and Promotion on Research.

To understand the effects of university politics on professors' involvement with research, you have to understand the reward structure universities employ. After all, professors are much like any other worker; they too seek the rewards offered by their workplace system.

Most universities have in place a tenure and promotion (T&P) system. **Tenure** means that a professor is guaranteed a lifetime faculty appointment at a particular institution, except in the most drastic circumstances, such as when a faculty member is convicted of committing a felony or a university must close because of financial reasons. Tenure is awarded only after a faculty member has demonstrated over a number of years (usually seven) competence as an educator and researcher and made appropriate and valuable service contributions, as well as the potential to continue engaging in a high standard of academic performance. The tenure decision is a mandatory "up or out" decision; either a person moves up (is tenured) or he or she must leave that university (typically after a one-year grace period).

Tenure has come under attack as of late, and you might wonder why someone would be granted lifetime employment. After all, most businesses don't offer this to their employees. There are at least two good reasons why universities award tenure.

The first reason has to do with economics. Universities can't afford to pay professors what they are worth on the open market. Most professionals with comparable degrees (e.g., physicians and lawyers) or less (e.g., management consultants) make far more money than do professors. Although universities are not able to pay professors comparably, offering job security (along with other benefits, such as flexible work time) makes the job attractive. Hence, tenure probably prevents some "brain drain" from the university to the private sector, although many people with advanced

communication degrees still go into the private sector.

But there is a much more important reason for tenure, one that bears directly on research: **academic freedom,** the ability to teach and research topics that professors consider to be important. Academic freedom is important for teaching and research because without it, the decision about what to teach or research might be constantly influenced by political pressure. Many people and groups have political agendas to which they are strongly committed and might believe that their tax- or church-supported institution is wrong if professors do not do the type of teaching and research with which they agree. In the case of research, this might mean "finding" the results these people and groups already "know" to be true. Such pressure on researchers to support preestablished findings is clearly unethical. It would cut off the inquiry process—where the data gathered determine the results and not the other way around—that forms the backbone of research. Yet, there are real political pressures put on researchers, and untenured and independent scholars might soon find themselves out of a job if they refuse to give into these demands.

Suppose, for example, that the authors' institutions didn't like our sharing with you all this "backstage" (Goffman, 1959) information about university life. If we didn't have tenure, which two of us have, we could simply be fired. (The third author is the chief of a research branch at a federal agency, an administrative position that doesn't carry tenure, but he's one of the bosses, so to speak, so he's not worried about sharing this information!) The same principle applies to research; if a university didn't like the research a professor conducted—say, at a religious-affiliated university, research on public education campaigns that promote safe sex (see, for example, Maibach, Kreps, & Bonaguro, 1993; Edgar, Fitzpatrick, & Freimuth, 1992)—that professor could be fired. Until a professor has tenure, he or she can be fired at any time, just like employees of any other business.

Tenure guarantees that professors can't be fired from their university for what they teach and research per se. But this doesn't mean that political pressures aren't or can't be brought to bear to affect untenured or even tenured professors' research. As an example of such political pressure, researchers at the University of North Carolina won an award from the United States Health and Human Services to conduct a five-year study of 24,000 junior and senior high school students about their knowledge of sexual practices. The agency wanted to use the results from the survey to combat such problems as teen pregnancy and sexually transmitted diseases. However, conservative and family coalition groups started a campaign to discredit the report, and because of the political pressure they brought to bear on public officials, the survey was temporarily blocked by Health and Human Services Secretary Louis Sullivan. As an anonymous official claimed, "This is one of those times when science and politics cross paths" ("Health Official Blocks," 1991, Sect. 1, p. 18).

Not all people who teach at universities, of course, have tenure or are on tenure-track lines; some teach part-time or even full-time as instructors, lecturers, or under some other title. For those who are on a tenure-track line or have tenure, there are three levels of rank through which they are promoted. A tenure-track person starts off being an assistant professor. Although one can apply for promotion at any time, assistant professors typically work for seven years before they can be promoted to the rank of associate professor. Hence, a person typically goes up for tenure and promotion at the same time. Although it has happened in the past, it is highly unusual in today's competitive market that a person would receive tenure without being promoted to associate professor. Associate professors then typically wait at least five years before being eligible for promotion to the rank of full professor (or simply professor). So although the term "professor" is used in common parlance to describe all university teachers, it technically refers to the highest rank awarded in the university promotion system.

The T&P system directly impacts the research process in at least two ways. Tenure and promotion, of course, are awarded on the basis of a per-

son having accomplished the goals of the university, as judged by a committee in the person's academic department, the department chair, the dean of the college or school in which the department is housed, the university's T&P committee, the senior vice president(s) or provost, and, even in some schools, by the president of the university. Hence, if a university demands substantial research to receive tenure and promotion, a person must demonstrate that this has been accomplished.

The problem is that, given the relatively short time between initial employment and tenure and promotion (essentially five years, as T&P documents are forwarded in the beginning of the person's sixth year), a person doesn't have a lot of time in which to produce a substantial record of research. Moreover, once the tenure and promotion deliberation moves out of the department level, it's doubtful that administrators and those who sit on the various committees understand the candidate's discipline very well. Although external reviewers typically are asked to confidentially judge the quantity and quality of the research produced, it's easier to count the number of published pieces a candidate has than to determine the quality and impact of those pieces on a field. Hence, the T&P system has a tendency to privilege quantity over quality. This may mean, as one example, that new professors do not have sufficient time to conduct longitudinal programs of research that take years to complete. Instead, they may be forced to conduct "quick and dirty studies" that perhaps involve handing out questionnaires to a convenience sample (see Chapter 5) of students in available classes—rather than obtaining a random sample of surrounding community members or even a nonrandom sample of people from outside the academy who may be difficult to access (such as community business leaders)—analyzing the data, writing up the results, and submitting the manuscript for publication consideration. Researchers may also be tempted to study "hot" academic topics that they believe stand a good chance of selection for publication. So publication, more notches in the publication belt, rather than some other criterion, such as serving the public good (not that these are necessarily mutually exclusive), becomes the reason for engaging in research. And given the high rejection rates of most journals (see Chapter 3) and the often substantial turnaround time in evaluating original and revised manuscripts (sometimes as much as a year or more), new professors are forced to do a lot of research quickly in the hopes that some of it will get published.

Thus, until a professor receives tenure, he or she may not be able to engage in certain types of research. For example, one of the authors of this text has an ongoing eight-year longitudinal research program that has been quite productive in terms of yielding publications, but those publications really didn't start to occur until the fifth year of the program. Even though the author worked at the time of tenure and promotion at a university that weights teaching and research about equally, if he had been a new professor when the research program began and placed his hopes on getting tenure and promotion from the publications produced in the first five years, he might not have received them. He certainly wouldn't have been awarded them if he had worked at a research institution.

The second impact has to do with promotion from associate professor to professor. Although those who are promoted to professor are expected to be good teachers and contribute their fair share of service, the primary evaluative criterion for being promoted at most universities has to do with research. Many universities expect that promotion to the rank of professor means the person has obtained a national, as opposed to say a regional, reputation with regard to his or her research. Many associate professors never achieve the rank of professor, which typically means they haven't engaged in the level of research needed for such promotion. Keep in mind, however, that universities differ substantially with regard to their research expectations; an associate professor at a research institution has a much harder time being promoted to professor than a comparable colleague at a teaching institution, at least as far as the research component is concerned.

As you see, university politics play a large role in professors' decisions to engage in research.

Of course, we don't mean to suggest that professors only engage in research because they are required to do so by their university. Personal motivations also play a large role. Most professors enjoy the pursuit of new knowledge and, therefore, engage in research.

There is, however, much pressure on professors to conduct, complete, and publish research. And to be an ethical researcher occasionally slows the process. It requires taking pains to plan and conduct the work carefully and to consider effects that the research project might have on others. Being ethical occasionally forces researchers to choose between the values of quantity and quality. That is, if they choose to do highly ethical research, they may be less productive in the short run. In the long run, however, as we hope to make apparent in the remainder of this chapter, ethical research will be more worthwhile and bring greater respect to professors and the institutions that employ them.

The Importance of Grant Money. A third political influence on professors is the growing importance of acquiring **grant money,** money awarded by public institutions (e.g., government bodies) or private individuals and organizations for the purpose of promoting research. To acquire a grant, a researcher submits, usually in response to an announcement of potential funding (referred to as *RFP,* a request for proposals), a grant proposal or outline for the research, including a complete budget. These grants are extremely competitive, and to succeed in attracting funding, researchers often have to orient their research in particular ways. Equally important, researchers may be tempted to offer more than they can probably deliver. Researchers who are awarded a grant are bound ethically to abide by the provisions of the granting body. If they cannot abide by and meet the needs of the funding agency, they must decide whether to pursue and accept funding.

Applying for a grant is, of course, a choice a professor makes. There is, however, tremendous pressure at universities, especially research universities, for professors to acquire grants. That's because universities receive a portion of every grant, so the more grant money professors bring in, the more money the university makes. Indeed, grants have become such big business that universities usually have an office that informs professors about available grants and helps them write grant proposals. Grant acquisition has become such an important priority that many of the jobs advertised at research universities, especially at the associate professor and professor ranks, require people to have been successful at getting grants. In fact, in certain fields, such as medicine, it is not unusual for professors' jobs to be contingent on receiving grant money.

There is, thus, a lot of pressure exerted on professors to acquire grants. And being awarded a grant also often means that a professor does not teach for a semester, year, or longer. Of course, that person's classes must still be covered. So if you're at one of those research institutions and your courses are being taught primarily by part-time or full-time instructors, it might just be because some of the tenured and tenure-track professors are off playing the "research grant game."

Ethical Issues Involving Research Participants

Communication research projects often intrude into the lives of the people being studied. Communication researchers often send messages to individuals and measure how they react or they observe how groups of people ordinarily exchange messages among themselves and then make their findings known to others. Such investigations can't be conducted without somehow affecting the people being studied.

Up to this point, we have examined the research process from the viewpoints of two participants in the research process: the researcher (the communication scholar) and the audience (the consumers of communication research). We now shift our attention to a third population influenced by communication inquiry, the *participants* studied in communication research.

People don't wake up saying, "Hey gang, let's go out today and be in a research project." Nor do

the people being studied usually participate in planning research projects (with the exception of action, social justice, and other forms of cooperative research; see Chapter 2). Communication researchers intend to answer questions that will ultimately help people communicate more effectively, but this benefit accrues mainly to readers of the investigation's results. The participants of the research project, those involved in the means for achieving this noble end, have an entirely different experience and may even accrue more costs than benefits. Taking the participants' perspective, therefore, shifts the concern from the question, "Is this study worthwhile?" to "Are participants being treated right?" Making this shift refocuses attention on the ethics of studying human beings in communication research.

Although there are no easy answers about how research participants should be treated, some legal guidelines have been established. These guidelines arose primarily in response to serious breaches of ethics evidenced in biomedical research. For example, during World War II, Nazi scientists conducted research on how people are affected by extreme cold weather by subjecting inmates at the Dachau concentration camp to freezing weather and watching them die. This and other unethical research by the Nazis led to the 1949 Nuremberg Code, which established some guidelines for research on humans, including the concept of participants' giving voluntary consent (examined below) (see Wexler, 1990).

Lest it be thought that only Nazis engaged in unethical research, there are a number of examples in the United States. One of the most infamous cases was the Tuskegee syphilis study conducted by the U.S. Public Health Service (PHS). Begun in 1932 and spanning more than 40 years, this study investigated the effects of untreated syphilis in 400 African American men, denying those men available drug treatments such as penicillin and resulting in the death of anywhere from 20 to 100 of them (Brandt, 1978; see also J. H. Jones, 1981). The experiment was reported in at least 13 progress reports in major medical journals between 1936–1973, but only one member of the medical profession (in 1963) voiced an objection to the study prior to the strong objections raised by PHS officer Peter Buxton (M. Solomon, 1985). His response resulted in the press bringing the matter to the public's attention in 1972 (e.g., "An Immoral Study," 1972; "Inhuman Experiment," 1972; "Official Inhumanity," 1972). Even after it was exposed, there were people who defended this unethical study (e.g., Kampmeier, 1972; Seabrook, 1972). After 25 more years of White House silence on the matter, in 1997, President Clinton publicly apologized for the experiment on behalf of the nation, saying that "the United States did something that was wrong— deeply, profoundly, morally wrong" (Neikirk & James, 1997, p. 18). The experiment had the unfortunate long-term effect of leading many African Americans to distrust government-funded research, such as AIDS studies. Clinton acknowledged the racial bias of the study when he said, "To our African-American friends, I am sorry that your federal government orchestrated a study so clearly racist" (Neikirk & James, 1997, p. 18).

The 1960s, in particular, witnessed a number of ethically unjustifiable biomedical experiments (see Hershey & Miller, 1976), including two research physicians in New York City injecting live cancer cells into 22 elderly patients without their knowledge (R. J. Levine, 1986). And it was during this time that Milgram (1963) conducted his infamous study of obedience, in which research participants, role-playing teachers no less (!), were instructed to give electrical shocks to a "student" in another room (a confederate who was in on the experiment) when that person made a learning mistake on a simple word-association task. Participants were told, and most agreed, to increase the intensity of the shock as the number of errors increased, even to the point of the shocks being potentially lethal.

These and other unethical experiments led the U.S. Surgeon General in 1966 to establish a committee to review every proposal that sought PHS funding to make sure that research participants would not be harmed and had been informed of any risks. Other government agencies (such as the Department of Health, Education, and Welfare)

soon adopted this rule and, in 1974, Congress passed the National Research Act, which required all institutions sponsoring research to create **institutional review boards (IRBs).** As Berg (1998) explains:

> *IRBs were expected to ensure that research investigators had considered both potential risks and benefits to subjects, that important scientific knowledge could be derived from the project, that legally informed consent would be obtained from each subject, and that the rights and interests of subjects were protected. (p. 36)*

Today, IRBs are a normal part of doing research, especially in the university context. Most universities require that research conducted by faculty and students, whether externally funded or not, be evaluated by their IRB. IRBs are supposed to consist of "at least five members, with varying backgrounds to promote complete and adequate review of research activities commonly conducted by the institution" (Department of Health and Human Services, 1989, p. 7). Typically, an IRB evaluates a written proposal for a study prepared by a researcher that describes the entire research design. The researcher often has to fill out a questionnaire that asks specific questions about the costs and benefits of the study for participants. In some cases, the researcher may have to appear in person before the IRB to answer specific questions about the study (see Sieber, 1992).

In evaluating a research proposal for approval, an IRB's greatest concern is to ensure that the research study does not cause any undue harm or hardship to the people participating in the study. If it appears that a study may have some harmful effects on research participants, or even those not directly involved (e.g., family members), the IRB will ask for specific modifications of the research design to ensure the safety and comfort of those individuals. Although some researchers see IRBs as "handcuffs impeding their search for scientific answers to social problems" (Berg, 1998, p. 37), sometimes researchers are so eager to study a phenomenon that they don't recognize the potential hardships their studies can cause for research participants. IRBs help make sure that the welfare of everyone connected with the research is taken into account. They also serve as a legal " 'control document'…showing that the research is acceptable to a legally constituted board of reviewers" (Sieber, 1998, p. 129). Once a study has been approved by an IRB, a researcher must, of course, conscientiously follow the agreed-on procedures.

IRBs, then, essentially judge the ethical merits of a research study on a reward/cost basis. If the amount of rewards for conducting the study (such as advancing knowledge and/or solving a social problem) outweigh the amount of potential risk or harm, then the study is ethically permissible (R. B. Taylor, 1994). If the rewards don't outweigh the costs, then the study shouldn't be undertaken. Of course, rewards and costs are in the eye of the beholder; what research participants may perceive to be a cost may not be viewed as such by a researcher (see Sieber, 1993). Therefore, as Bulmer (1982b) argues, reward/cost judgments should always be made in accordance with the principle that the rights of research participants override the rights of research.

To make these judgments, IRBs generally rely on a set of ethical guidelines established by governmental and professional associations. The American Psychological Association (APA), for example, publishes a set of guidelines for research with human participants ("Ethical Principles," 1992; see Figure 6.1). Failure to follow these guidelines can result in censure and even expulsion from the association. In most professions, including academia, peers regulate each other's behavior. Ultimately, however, self-regulation prevails. The final responsibility for conducting ethical research rests with the researcher.

Ethical guidelines for the treatment of research participants are based on four primary moral principles or rules of conduct commonly advocated by scholars: (a) provide the people being studied with free choice; (b) protect their right to privacy; (c) benefit, not harm them; and (d) treat people with respect. However, as the following discussions show, some of these rules are not always easy to fully enact; they often create dilemmas that communication scholars must confront.

Provide Free Choice.   Ethical researchers do not coerce people into contributing to their investigations. Whenever possible, they first provide **voluntary informed consent** by having research participants voluntarily agree to participate only after they have been fully informed about the study. If for legal reasons participants cannot grant consent (such as in the case of children or those who are mentally disabled), consent must be obtained from the legal guardian (e.g., parent) or agency.

The principle of voluntary informed consent is very important; indeed, it is one of the fundamental principles that guide IRBs. IRBs typically will not support research unless it is clear "that the potential research subject understand[s] the intention of the research and sign[s] an 'informed consent' form, which incidentally must specify that the subject may withdraw from the research project at any time" (Weppner, 1977, p. 41). There are, however, exceptions to this rule. For example, obtaining research participants' written consent may not be required for "low-risk" styles of research, such as in large-scale surveys, observation in public places, and archival research (see Berg, 1998). In the case of large-scale surveys, the completion and return of the questionnaire itself is taken as an indication of **implied consent.**

Voluntary informed consent is especially important within the context of research that is designed to be cooperative or empowering. As Ristock and Pennell (1996) explain:

> [C]onsent is part of the contract between researcher and participants that clearly lays out the assumptions, goals, and purpose of the research, the risks involved, participants' rights to confidentiality and anonymity, and the researchers' rights to document their own experiences within the project. (p. 36)

When seeking people's consent, researchers ought to provide them with some important information (see Figure 6.2). As an example, Adelman

FIGURE 6.1   Ethical Principles of Psychologists and Code of Conduct

RESEARCH

6.06 Planning Research

(a) Psychologists design, conduct, and report research in accordance with recognized standards of scientific competence and ethical research.

(b) Psychologists plan their research so as to minimize the possibility that results will be misleading.

(c) In planning research, psychologists consider its ethical acceptability under the Ethics Code. If an ethical issue is unclear, psychologists seek to resolve the issue through consultation with institutional review boards, animal care and use committees, peer consultations, or other proper mechanisms.

(d) Psychologists take reasonable steps to implement appropriate protections for the rights and welfare of human participants, other persons affected by the research, and the welfare of animal subjects.

6.07 Responsibility

(a) Psychologists conduct research competently and with due concern for the dignity and welfare of the participants.

(b) Psychologists are responsible for the ethical conduct of research conducted by them or by others under their supervision or control.

(c) Researchers and assistants are permitted to perform only those tasks for which they are appropriately trained and prepared.

(d) As part of the process of development and implementation of research projects, psychologists consult those with expertise concerning any special population under investigation or most likely to be affected.

6.08 Compliance with Law and Standards

Psychologists plan and conduct research in a manner consistent with federal and state law and regulations, as well as professional standards governing the conduct of research, and particularly those standards governing research with human participants and animal subjects.

6.09 Institutional Approval

Psychologists obtain from host institutions or organizations appropriate approval prior to conducting research, and they provide accurate information about their research proposals. They conduct the research in accordance with the approved research protocol.

6.10 Research Responsibilities

Prior to conducting research (except research involving only anonymous surveys, naturalistic observations, or similar research), psychologists enter into agreement with participants that clarifies the nature of the research and the responsibilities of each party.

6.11 Informed Consent to Research

(a) Psychologists use language that is reasonably understandable to research participants in obtaining their appropriate informed consent (except as provided in Standard 6.12 Dispensing With Informed Consent). Such informed consent is appropriately documented.

(b) Using language that is reasonably understandable to participants, psychologists inform participants of the nature of the research; they inform participants that they are free to participate or to decline to participate or to withdraw from the research; they explain the foreseeable consequences of declining or withdrawing; they inform participants of significant factors that may be expected to influence their willingness to participate (such as risks, discomfort, adverse effects, or limitations on confidentiality, except as provided in Standard 6.15, Deception in Research); and they explain other aspects about which the prospective participants inquire.

(c) When psychologists conduct research with individuals such as students or subordinates, psychologists take special care to protect the prospective participants from adverse consequences of declining or withdrawing from participation.

(d) When research participation is a course requirement or opportunity for extra credit, the prospective participant is given the choice of equitable alternative activities.

(e) For persons who are legally incapable of giving informed consent, psychologists nevertheless (1) provide an appropriate explanation, (2) obtain the participant's assent, and (3) obtain appropriate permission from a legally authorized person, if such substitute consent is permitted by law.

(continued)

FIGURE 6.1   Continued

6.12 Dispensing With Informed Consent
Before determining that planned research (such as research involving only anonymous questionnaires, naturalistic observations, or certain kinds of archival research) does not require the informed consent of research participants, psychologists consider applicable regulations and institutional review board requirements, and they consult with colleagues as appropriate.

6.13 Informed Consent in Research Filming or Recording
Psychologists obtain informed consent from research participants prior to filming or recording them in any form, unless the research involves simply naturalistic observations in public places and it is not anticipated that the recording will be used in a manner that could cause personal identification or harm.

6.14 Offering Inducements for Research Participants
(a) In offering professional services as inducement to obtain research participants, psychologists make clear the nature of the services, as well as the risks, obligations, and limitations.

(b) Psychologists do not offer excessive or inappropriate financial or other inducements to obtain research participants, particularly when it might tend to coerce participation.

6.15 Deception in Research
(a) Psychologists do not conduct a study involving deception unless they have determined that the use of deceptive techniques is justified by the study's prospective scientific, educational, or applied value and that equally effective alternative procedures that do not use deception are not feasible.

(b) Psychologists never deceive research participants about significant aspects that would affect their willingness to participate, such as physical risks, discomfort, or unpleasant emotional experience.

(c) Any other deception that is an integral feature of the design and conduct of an experiment must be explained to participants as early as is feasible, preferably at the conclusion of their participation, but no later than at the conclusion of the research. (See also Standard 6.18, Providing Participants With Information About the Study.)

6.16 Sharing and Utilizing Data
Psychologists inform research participants of their anticipated sharing or further use of personally identifiable research data and of the possibility of unanticipated future uses.

6.17 Minimizing Invasiveness
In conducting research, psychologists interfere with the participants or milieu from which data are collected only in a manner that is warranted by an appropriate research design and that is consistent with psychologists' roles as scientific investigators.

6.18 Providing Participants With Information About the Study
(a) Psychologists provide a prompt opportunity for participants to obtain appropriate information about the nature, results, and conclusions of the research, and psychologists attempt to correct any misperceptions that participants may have.

(b) If scientific or humane values justify delaying or withholding this information, psychologists take reasonable measures to reduce the risk of harm.

6.19 Honoring Commitments
Psychologists take reasonable measures to honor all commitments they have made to research participants.

Source: Reprinted from "Ethical Principles of Psychologists and Code of Conduct," *American Psychologist, 47,* pp. 1608–1609. Copyright © 1992 by the American Psychological Association. Reprinted with permission.

FIGURE 6.2   Information necessary when requesting informed consent

Researchers ought to provide research participants with the following information when requesting their consent to participate in a research study:

1. The purpose of the research phrased in a simple and easily understood manner
2. The procedures to be followed (including identifying those that are experimental)
3. The identities of the individuals conducting the research and their educational and other credentials
4. A description of the immediate and long-term discomforts, hazards, and risks involved and their possible consequences
5. An offer to answer any inquiries concerning the study at any time
6. A means of contacting the principal investigator (address and phone)
7. An instruction that the research participant is free to withdraw consent and to discontinue participation in the project or activity at any time without prejudice
8. Assurance that any information derived from the research project that personally identifies the research participant will not be released voluntarily or disclosed without that person's separate consent, except as required by law
9. Assurance that if the design of the study or use of information is changed, the research participant will be informed and his or her consent reobtained

and Frey (1997) have been involved in a longitudinal cooperative program of research on communication and community building at Bonaventure House in Chicago, a residential facility for people with AIDS. Their studies involved, among other things, having residents and staff complete the same questionnaire at four different times over a two-year period. Before each questionnaire was handed out, residents were asked to read and sign a voluntary informed consent form (see Figure 6.3).

The principle of informed consent, however, often presents a dilemma to communication researchers. Take the case of researchers who wish to study unpleasant phenomena, such as conflict communication or communication designed to embarrass another person, or socially desirable phenomena, such as helpful or cooperative communication. If research participants are warned fully about what is being studied and why, as voluntary *informed* consent insists, that knowledge may distort the data they provide. They might deny or hide socially unacceptable behavior or exaggerate their reports of behavior in which they believe they should be engaging. Or take the case of studies of communication behaviors related to deception. It just isn't possible, without ruining the study, to say to research participants, "The purpose of this study is to deceive you and see whether you can tell you've been deceived." In such situations, Gans (1962) argues that "the researcher must be dishonest to get honest data" (p. 46).

To avoid these problems, researchers often omit information, are vague, or even are deceptive regarding what will occur or be measured in an upcoming study. Several approaches, however, may be employed to approximate voluntary informed consent when foreknowledge must be limited.

Berscheid, Baron, Dermer, and Lebman (1973) suggest that a complete description of the study be given to a sample of the population from which the participants in the study will be chosen (see Chapter 5), while Sieber (1998) recommends conducting focus groups (see Chapter 9) with members of the target population. In both cases, people are asked whether they would volunteer to participate in the study. If most people say they would, researchers may conclude that the study would be acceptable to most participants.

M. Lewin (1979) suggests running a pilot study with just a few people and then discussing the purpose of the study with them. If they don't object and believe that their participation was acceptable, researchers are on firmer ground for inducing others to participate. If they regret their participation, researchers should modify or drop the planned study.

A related procedure is what Sable (1978) calls *prior general consent plus proxy consent.* A

FIGURE 6.3   Voluntary informed consent form for participation in research (Adelman & Frey, 1997)

Purpose

The purpose of this research is to understand residents' and staff's views of personal and community life at Bonaventure House and to evaluate the effectiveness of various services. This material will be used for program evaluation and research on community living.

Procedures

The research involves completing a questionnaire that covers a variety of areas, including background information, your relationships with residents and staff, and your general perceptions of Bonaventure House.

Voluntary Participation & Confidentiality of Information

Participation in this study is *strictly voluntary*. At no time will you be identified by name. Information will be kept confidential, available only to the researchers associated with this study. Information may be reported in materials produced by Bonaventure House, at scientific conventions, or in professional articles. Rest assured, however, that no resident will be identified by name.

Risks

The questionnaire is designed to be nonthreatening. However, if you experience emotional discomfort, please discontinue answering it. Your decision to discontinue will not affect your membership in the House.

Benefits

You will not benefit directly from participating in this study. This information, however, will be used to assist in program development within Bonaventure House. This information will also contribute to better understanding community living. Upon completion of the questionnaire, residents will receive $10.00 in cash. There is no financial compensation for staff. All inquiries regarding this study should be directed to Larry Frey (773-508-3733).

INFORMANT'S STATEMENT

I have read the information above and understand that my participation in this study is voluntary and I am free to withdraw at any time. I agree to participate in this study as described above.

_____   _____
                Signature   Date

researcher first obtains the general consent of a person to participate in a study that may involve extreme procedures. The person then empowers a friend to serve as a proxy—that is, someone who examines the details of the specific procedures in advance and makes a judgment as to whether the person would have consented to it given the choice. If the proxy says yes, the researcher may proceed.

Kelman (1967) suggests role playing as an alternative to the use of deception. A researcher invites participants to be partners in the investigation and encourages them not to behave in ways they think the researcher wants but to conscientiously assume the role and carry out the tasks the researcher assigns.

A particular problem related to voluntary informed consent arises when faculty members or graduate students conduct research that involves students as participants. Should students be *required* to participate in research projects? Some people say yes: Current students benefit from knowledge obtained from studies involving students who preceded them, so they should make a parallel contribution to students who will come after them. Others believe that coercing students yields only contaminated data and damages the teacher–student relationship. Requiring student participation in research is an unresolved issue. What do you think?

Whenever students are required to participate in studies, M. Lewin (1979) suggests several guidelines:

1. [S]tudents should realize how vital their assistance is. The faculty needs their participation. It should not be withheld for minor reasons.
2. Researchers should make participation as educational as possible by devoting adequate time to explanation and providing a meaningful context.
3. An alternative means of satisfying the participation requirement, such as a book review or paper, should be available.
4. A mechanism should be available to review a particular study. This usually means that [a] departmental ethics committee or a designated person is available to subjects who wish to discuss the research. The committee may also be used to review projects before they are used as course requirements. (pp. 28–29)

Another problem arises when conducting field studies. Sometimes researchers wish to manipulate natural settings and observe people's responses without their knowing they are being observed because that knowledge may distort their behavior (the Hawthorne effect discussed in Chapter 5). In such cases, voluntary informed consent is not possible, so researchers involve people in their research involuntarily. Piliavin, Rodin, and Piliavin (1969), for example, studied helping behavior by having a confederate stagger and fall to the floor in a subway car. In some cases, the confederate appeared to be sick; in other cases, he appeared to be intoxicated. They compared how many people helped, and how quickly, in each case. These bystanders did not know they were involved in a research study. Bochner (1979) calls this procedure "street theater strategy"; typically, an incident is staged, and the reactions of people affected by it are recorded.

There is debate about whether such research procedures are ethical. Cook and Campbell (1979), otherwise advocates of unobtrusive research, point out that "from ethical and perhaps legal perspectives, much technically feasible unobtrusive experimentation is not desirable since it violates the ethical requirement of "informed consent" (p. 369). They maintain that research is ethically justified only if what participants are asked to do is innocuous, takes very little time or effort, and is within the range of participants' normal experience.

Sometimes researchers don't manipulate but simply study people's natural behavior without them knowing they are being observed. Some naturalistic researchers "infiltrate" (Punch, 1986) a group or setting and conduct covert research (see Chapter 10). In a controversial study that raised serious ethical concerns, Humphreys (1970) became a "drag queen" and covertly observed interaction between gays in a rest room. He wrote down the men's license plates as they drove away, found their addresses, and visited them as a researcher (in a different disguise) and interviewed them as part of a social health survey.

Many scholars question the ethics of such deceptive practices, although there are some who defend them. As Bulmer (1982a) argued, "Social actors employ lies, fraud, deceit, deception and blackmail in dealings with each other, therefore the social scientist is justified in using them where necessary in order to achieve the higher objective of scientific truth" (p. 10).

There is little doubt that having to obtain voluntary informed consent in this type of "street-style" ethnography (Weppner, 1977) might mean having to forgo doing it. Reiss (1979) also notes that trying to obtain consent often reduces people's participation in research. As Punch (1994) concludes, "In much fieldwork there seems to be no way around the predicament that informed consent—divulging one's identity and research purpose to all and sundry—will kill many a project stone dead" (p. 90). And in some situations, it might even pose a risk to researchers; there are cases where researchers have been threatened with harm, such as Yablonsky (1968) in studying a commune, and even physically harmed, such as H. Thompson (1967) being beaten up by the Hell's Angels.

Even in situations that normally require voluntary informed consent, such as medical research, where the procedures have the potential to significantly affect people and their health, there may be some difficulties in acquiring it. Physicians, for example, must obtain written consent from patients before administering treatment, except in extreme cases, such as an emergency procedure. Obtaining such consent, however, is complicated by a number of factors, one of which is the type of population being studied or being provided with medical treatment. Hines, Badzek, and Moss (1997) studied the problem of obtaining voluntary informed consent among the chronically ill elderly, who may have difficulty understanding the facts needed to make informed choices. They interviewed 142 elderly (people over the age of 64) dialysis patients (chosen because they had agreed to a life-sustaining medical procedure with serious side effects, including nausea, anemia, and infection) to determine whether consent had been obtained, how much information had been provided to them, and the communication choices patients made. They discovered that most patients lacked the information needed to render fully informed consent. They also discovered that the potential causes for the very low levels of information were attributable to patients' educational level, cognitive capacity, and willingness to discuss medical contingency. They suggest that physicians and patients must treat informed

consent as a process rather than as a legal accomplishment, and that physicians should ask explicit questions concerning what patients want to know. This is good advice for all researchers.

Another way researchers deal with the mandate to inform research participants is by providing a **debriefing** session *after* a study is completed. Systematic debriefing involves explaining the full purpose of the study, as well as seeking feedback from participants to learn how they perceived the research (see Kreps & Lederman, 1985). For example, a researcher can try to determine during debriefing whether participants recognized the hidden intentions of the research, whether their responses were due to the intended stimuli or to some uncontrolled artifact, and/or whether there were any other factors that might have influenced their responses. The debriefing session can also explore whether there were any unintended negative influences on research participants and, if so, help them to cope with those negative consequences. And, of course, debriefing should be a form of two-way communication: research participants should be given the opportunity to ask questions and offer unsolicited observations.

Debriefing is particularly important in cases where deception has been used. In fact, the promise of a full debriefing can be used as a way to seek research participants' consent prior to the study being conducted. They can be asked to generally consent to being deceived or can waive their right to be informed prior to the study being conducted on the promise that everything will be explained during the debriefing stage.

Aronson and Carlsmith (1968) recommend the following procedures when conducting research debriefings:

1. Ask the participants whether they have any questions, and answer them honestly and completely.
2. Ask participants if they did not understand parts of the study or whether they were confusing or disturbing.
3. Ask what they thought was being studied and how they felt about the study.

CHAPTER 6 RESEARCH ETHICS AND POLITICS **155**

4. Provide any additional information so that participants are completely aware of all aspects of the study and why deception was necessary.

Two particular forms of debriefing that warrant attention are *desensitizing* and *dehoaxing*. **Desensitizing** is needed when research participants may have acquired negative information about themselves as a result of the research study. For example, people who don't perform well in experiments that require public speaking may need help coping with their poor performance.

In cases where research participants have been deceived, the debriefing involves **dehoaxing,** convincing them that they actually have been deceived and attempting to "eliminate any undesirable effects the deception might have had" (Vogt, 1993, p. 65). For example, people may be told in experimental research that, on the basis of an instrument completed, they are low in communication ability, when, in fact, they are not. An ethical experimenter will tell research participants after the study is complete that they have been deceived, although as Vogt (1993) points out, this might be difficult because the experimenter did just deceive participants and now claims to be telling them the truth. Dehoaxing also needs to considered in naturalistic inquiry when a researcher becomes a complete participant in the natural setting, participating fully in the activities as just another cultural member and not telling people they are being studied and, thereby, deceiving people about his or her true identity.

Being completely open when informing research participants about the results of their investigations during a debriefing is not always beneficial, however. In some studies, participants perform in ways that aren't commendable. For instance, participants were debriefed in Milgram's (1963) infamous study of obedience to authority, described previously, where participants were ordered by an experimenter to inflict what they thought was severe pain on another person by pushing a switch that supposedly sent electrical shocks to the chair located in another room. But

did it help or hinder the participants to learn in the debriefing session that the experimenter who ordered the painful electric shocks was an actor who intimidated them into administering the electric shocks with his white coat, name tag, and authoritative voice?

Baumrind (1979) calls such feedback "inflicted insight" and maintains that it is not necessarily more ethical to reveal negative information about research participants in a debriefing than to refrain from doing so. Dawes and Smith (1985) compare debriefing research participants about deception to adultery and confession in marriage. In both cases, they suggest, "the debriefing may do more harm than the act itself. Besides, it doesn't undo the act" (p. 550). They maintain that if researchers think their deception is wrong in the first place, they shouldn't do it; if they don't think it's wrong, they should shut up about it. So they recommend no debriefing at all and deception only in situations where debriefing wouldn't be necessary.

As you see, what started out as a simple ethical principle—obtaining voluntary informed consent from research participants—can easily become a complicated matter. In the final analysis, in keeping with the view of research espoused in this text as a form of communication, voluntary informed consent "goes beyond the statement that is prepared and administered in the so-called consent procedure. It is an ongoing, two-way communication process between research participants and the investigator" (Sieber, 1998, p. 130).

Protect the Right to Privacy. Researchers study people's behavior and elicit information from them. This information should not be used to violate participants' privacy. Researchers usually protect privacy by assuring their research participants of *anonymity* or *confidentiality*. **Anonymity** exists when researchers cannot connect responses to the individuals who provided them, such as when self-administered, anonymous questionnaires are completed by research participants. **Confidentiality** exists when researchers know who said what, such as in interview research, but promise not to reveal that information publicly. Anonymity usually is ensured by identifying research participants with code numbers rather than their names. Confidentiality usually is assured by publishing **aggregate data,** data about groups, rather than about individuals; if the latter are necessary, names are omitted or disguised (e.g., by using pseudonyms).

Whenever possible, anonymity is preferable, since research data can leak out inadvertently. Babbie's (1967) research provides an example. He studied the attitudes and behavior of church women by asking ministers in a sample of churches to distribute questionnaires, collect them, and return them to his office. One minister read through the questionnaires before returning them and then "delivered a hell-fire and brimstone sermon to his congregation, saying that many of them were atheists and were going to hell" (Babbie, 1992, p. 452). Even though the minister could not identify particular respondents, many of them probably felt that their privacy had been violated.

We have been talking about keeping the information collected from research participants anonymous, but we might also wonder about what happens when research participants interact with one another under conditions of anonymity. Surprisingly, while anonymity is an important consideration in the conduct of research studies, surprising little research has been done on such effects. In a statement that is still true today, R. Williams (1988) argued that "anonymity is a notion that ought to be thought, taught, and written about much more than it is at present" (p. 765). What little research does exist comes from the study of new communication technologies (see Scott's, 1999, review). In some studies, technologies such as group decision support systems, which combine "communication, computer, and decision technologies to facilitate decision making and related activities of work groups" (Poole, DeSanctis, Kirsch, & Jackson, 1995, p. 300), allow participants to work in different locations (see Spears, Lea, & Lee, 1990). In other studies, people work in the same room, but are "hooded" so they can't see one another. In both cases, people are assured of visual anonymity. In still other studies, computer systems allow for written remarks to be made anonymously

(see Hiltz, Turoff, & Johnson, 1989; Olaniran & Walther, 1997). The results from recent studies show both positive and negative outcomes under conditions of anonymity versus identification. For example, in comparison to nonanonymous conditions, anonymity has been shown to encourage greater group member participation (Ahern & Durrington, 1995; Everett & Ahern, 1994; Valacich & Schwenk, 1995a, 1995b), help reduce status perceptions (Pollard, 1996), promote the forwarding of more creative ideas (D. Coleman, 1997; Di Pietro, 1995; Sosik, Avolio, & Kahai, 1998), allow members to discuss sensitive issues, including their feelings toward other group members (Massey & Clapper, 1995), and produce perceived higher quality products (Bikson, 1996). Anonymous groups, however, have also been found to take longer to make decisions (Ahern & Durrington, 1995; Bamber, Watson, & Hill, 1996), do not necessarily lead to stronger member participation (Weisband, Schneider, & Connolly, 1995), and don't necessarily prevent groups from experiencing problematic outcomes, such as choice shifts (Karan, Kerr, Murthy, & Vinze, 1996). As these new communication technologies are used more widely, understanding the effects of anonymity will be even more important.

When conducting research via interviews, it is virtually impossible to guarantee anonymity to interviewees. Researchers usually protect privacy in such cases by being cautious themselves, by recruiting responsible and mature interviewers to assist them, and by training and supervising their interviewers carefully.

In naturalistic research, researchers may well have the right to videotape or photograph people behaving in public places, but there are still questions about the invasion of people's privacy. For example, even though they are performed in a public setting, intimate acts (such as hugs) should be treated as private behavior. In the case where people are videotaped in a private setting, researchers must, of course, obtain participants' permission to have their image recorded. Adelman and Schultz (1991), for example, in filming daily life among the residents of Bonaventure House made sure that those who didn't want their faces shown had their backs to the camera at all times. The film was even delayed from being shown on a PBS-affiliate station for a year because one resident, who had agreed to be photographed, refused to sign the necessary release form to televise the videotape because that person had not told family members about having AIDS. And in the case of people engaged in illegal activities, special care must be taken to assure people's right to privacy. In their videotape of gang members' communication behavior, Conquergood and Siegel (1990) blurred many of the gang members' faces, because belonging to a gang is illegal.

The appropriateness of protecting respondents' privacy is sometimes called into question. Some researchers have found themselves in the dilemma of learning information that might be incriminating to their research participants. Hartman and Hedblom (1979) give the example of a researcher observing a badly battered child in a home where she was conducting the interview. As they ask:

> *In seeking the cooperation of the respondent and promising anonymity, had the interviewer lost the right or the responsibility to report legal violations to the authorities?...The interviewer's presence in the home was contingent on a single role; did the interviewer have the right or the mandate to play another? (p. 345)*

These are difficult ethical questions. In this particular case, fortunately, the interviewer called the mother and guided her subtly toward making contact with a community agency that would help rather than prosecute her.

In such potentially volatile situations, researchers can include as part of a voluntary informed consent form a clause that specifies that all information will be kept confidential, unless the researcher believes the person is in danger of hurting others or himself or herself. One potential problem in legally honoring any such agreement, however, is that researchers are not entitled to professional privilege regarding the disclosure of research information, including research participants' names and

their activities, during criminal proceedings. Unlike lawyers, priests, and physicians, who often are entitled to a privileged relationship with their clients, researchers must reveal this information if required to do so in a court of law, or else risk being held in contempt of court. There has been at least one case in which a judge upheld a researcher protecting suspects by withholding field notes about a suspicious fire at a restaurant (Fried, 1984), but no laws were changed as a result of that case. Researchers can apply for a **Federal Certificate of Confidentiality,** which authorizes the legal withholding of information by researchers conducting sensitive research (regarding the study of sensitive topics, see the essays in Renzetti & Lee, 1993); however, as Berg (1998) points out, few of the many thousands of researchers who apply are awarded this certificate. One other alternative, of course, is to avoid keeping any written records, but this does not prevent researchers from having to verbally testify.

The protection of research participants' privacy also extends to making sure that the data acquired are secure, so that other people do not have access to them, and that accidental disclosure of people's names doesn't happen when the data are discussed with others. Members of a research team can even sign a statement of confidentiality that prohibits them from discussing a study with anybody else unless the other team members agree (Berg, 1998). Exercising such precautions not only protects research participants; it protects researchers as well. For in cases where research participants' right to privacy has been egregiously violated, research participants may sue researchers.

Finally, it should be pointed out that anonymity and/or confidentiality are not always desired by research participants. In naturalistic research, participants sometimes request to be cited by name, expressing the desire to have their "voice" represented (see Morse, 1998). In such cases, it is perfectly appropriate, indeed preferable, for researchers to use participants' real names.

Benefit People, Not Harm Them.   The people being studied should benefit, not suffer, from participating in a research investigation. There are numerous ways in which this precept may be violated, as well as many ways in which researchers can take it into account.

By providing information, participants contribute to researchers' efforts. Ethical researchers, in turn, consider how they might reciprocate. They try to make being a research participant a pleasant or beneficial experience, or at least one participants do not regret afterward. People in stigmatized or oppressed social groups may benefit, personally and as a group, from being the focus of a research study. Varallo et al. (1998), for example, studied the effects of the research interview process on adult survivors of incest who had previously been involved in one of their interview research projects. They found that the research interviews did benefit these survivors by helping them to better understand and make sense of their incest experience.

Some researchers pay people a small fee for their participation. Focus group members, for example, are usually rewarded financially for their time. Other researchers give their participants a copy of the research report and, thus, reciprocate by sharing with them the knowledge obtained. Organizational leaders often encourage their employees to participate in particular research projects because they believe that the results will prove useful to their organization.

The more uniquely and comprehensively the findings relate to particular research participants, the more attention must be given to benefits. For example, Spradley (1980) recalls:

James Sewid, a Kwakiutl Indian in British Columbia, was an excellent informant, and together we recorded his life history about growing up during the early part of this century. When it became apparent that the edited transcripts might become a published book, I decided to safeguard Mr. Sewid's rights by making him a full partner who signed the contracts with Yale University Press. He shared equally in all royalties and had the right to decide with me, on crucial matters of content. I also wanted to safeguard his sensitivities, so before we submitted the final manuscript I read the completed version to both him and his wife. They made dele-

tions and changes that were in their best interests, changes that reflected their sensitivities, not mine. (pp. 21–22)

Research, of course, is ultimately conducted to benefit people, although as Berg (1998) points out, "When researchers vaguely promise benefit to science and society, they approach being silly" (p. 148). Some applied communication research is explicitly designed to benefit people by serving the purposes of social action or social justice (see Chapter 2). Adelman and Frey's (1997) research on communication and community building at Bonaventure House (BH), for example, has been designed to provide a number of tangible benefits to BH members. The concepts and models from their written work, as well as the videotape Adelman and Schultz (1991) made, are used by administrators to help new staff, volunteers, and residents understand BH. The researchers coauthored an article with BH's Executive Director (Adelman, Frey, & Budz, 1994), who very much wanted to see his name in print, and also wrote a chapter in a handbook produced by BH that is designed for practitioners who seek to construct such facilities (L. R. Frey, & Adelman, 1993). Their quantitative studies (e.g., L. R. Frey, Adelman, Flint, & Query, in press; L. R. Frey, Query, Flint, & Adelman, 1998) are potentially useful for justifying external funding for the house, and a portion of the proceeds from the sale of the videotape and the book goes directly to residents (most of whom have little or no money). Most important from Adelman and Frey's (1997) point of view, their ethnographic work "strives to capture members' views of this community from their perspective, giving residents a voice, even in death" (p. 17).

Berg (1998) identifies at least seven ways in which research may potentially benefit any of seven kinds of recipients—research participants, communities, investigators, research institutions, funders, science, and society in general. He uses the example of a community to illustrate these benefits:

1. *Valuable relationships:* The community establishes ties with helping institutions and funders.

2. *Knowledge or education:* The community develops a better understanding of its own problems.
3. *Material resources:* The community makes use of research materials, equipment, and funding.
4. *Training, employment, opportunity for advancement:* Community members receive training and continue to serve as professionals or paraprofessionals within the ongoing project.
5. *Opportunity to do good and to receive the esteem of others:* The community learns how to serve its members better.
6. *Empowerment* (personal, political, and so on): The community uses findings for policy purposes and gains favorable attention from the press, politicians, and others.
7. *Scientific/clinical outcomes:* The community provides treatment to its members (assuming that the research or intervention is successful). (p. 151)

The flip side of benefiting participants is not causing them harm. Suppose a researcher wants to study the effects of a negative condition, such as high stress or pain, on how people communicate, or whether certain messages, such as those contained in violent or pornographic films, cause harm. While studying such conditions, the researcher might exacerbate them.

This danger may be avoided in several ways. One is studying people already in that condition. In studying the effects of stress, for example, instead of creating experimental conditions that frighten participants, researchers can study people who are already experiencing stress, such as patients facing dentistry or surgery or students about to take examinations.

A second approach is studying minimal levels of negative states. Say researchers are studying stage fright. Instead of comparing the behavior of people who feel normal and those who experience high communication apprehension when giving a speech, researchers may be able to study the phenomenon equally well by comparing speakers with low and normal apprehension and, thereby, avoid subjecting highly apprehensive people to an upsetting experience. Or they might require that participants be in the negative state for a minimal amount of time, say, by making the highly apprehensive people speak only as briefly as needed to make the required measurements.

Researchers must be attentive to causing discomfort to their participants inadvertently. Activities that don't disturb most people may be upsetting to a few. Participants whose parents are deceased or divorced, for example, may feel uncomfortable or even angry when asked to provide their mother's age, occupation, or address. Pretesting methodological procedures and consulting with people familiar with the research population help researchers to identify and eliminate or at least reduce instances of avoidable discomfort.

When communication researchers study how well particular treatments alleviate problems and use control groups that do not receive the treatment (see Chapter 7), they face the ethical dilemma of not benefiting their participants as well as they might. Say researchers devise a new way to alleviate fear of public speaking. Is it fair to teach it only to an experimental group and give no help to the control group? One approach some researchers use in such circumstances is to solicit volunteers for the treatment and then select some randomly for the treatment group(s) and some for a "waiting list" control group. They then offer the experimental treatment to the control group at a later date, or they offer the control group some other known treatment rather than no treatment at all.

That may be fine for studying new treatments for alleviating fear of public speaking, but what happens when researchers are dealing with life and death issues? For example, some people have questioned the ethics of a recent study about the ability of the drug AZT (commonly used in the fight against AIDS) to prevent the transmission of the HIV disease from mother to child in pregnant women in the Third-World countries of Ivory Coast, Dominican Republic, and Thailand ("What's Justified," 1997). The debate occurred because, in keeping with standard scientific practice, half the mothers were given a placebo—pills that did not contain the drug. But researchers know what effects occur when AZT is not taken, "and so the women receiving placebos are being used by the researchers the same way the poor black men in the infamous Tuskegee syphilis experiment were used" ("What's Justified," Sect. 1, p. 12). The United States government agencies that sponsored the research were quick to point out that the use of a control group was ultimately chosen by the countries themselves (or at least by the persons/ agencies responsible for approving such research) and the international medical research community. This was done because, given the living conditions in Third-World countries (e.g., diet and environment), it is the only way to obtain valid research information. What do you think: Is it a regrettable necessity or an unethical research practice?

When publishing the results of their study, researchers must also consider whether they are benefiting or harming their research participants. For example, a study of drug use, cheating, or sexual behavior on a college campus that doesn't take into account the effect on trustees, parents, or alumni donors may do much harm. And the research participants may feel that their trust has been betrayed. To minimize harm, ethical researchers might either avoid naming the institution in the publication or make very clear how the behavior they report compares with data from similar institutions.

Treat People with Respect. Most communication research is undertaken in an effort to learn something about how all people (or large groups of people) communicate. Thus, an easy trap for researchers to fall into is forgetting to view and treat research participants as individuals worthy of respect. Garfinkel (1967) reports that when one of his students conducted an ethnomethodological experiment (see Chapter 10) on his family with no advance warning or explanation, his sister said, "Please, no more of these experiments. We're not rats, you know" (p. 49). By the way, a federal judge ruled that even rats, mice, and birds, which previously had been exempt from the U.S. Depart-

ment of Agriculture's policy, were entitled to the same humane conditions required for other research animals, such as dogs and cats ("Judge to Researchers," 1992).

Some authorities disapprove of the term *subjects,* an expression commonly used to describe research participants (although it also can refer to other types of units studied, such as cities and organizations)—a carryover from experiments with animals—because of its dehumanizing implication that human subjects are like rats in mazes. That's why we use the term "research participants" instead of "subjects" throughout this text.

Sexism in research is another manifestation of a dehumanized view of people. Eichler (1988) identifies four major symptoms of sexist research:

1. *Androcentricity,* viewing the world from a male perspective, such as assuming that power over others is something everyone wants.
2. *Overgeneralization,* when a study deals only with one sex but presents itself as applicable to both sexes, such as using the term "parenting" but studying only mothers.
3. *Gender insensitivity,* ignoring sex as a variable, such as not reporting the sex of research participants or studying the speeches of a politician without considering their differential effects on men and women.
4. *Double standards,* treating identical behaviors, traits, or situations in different ways, such as viewing interruptions during conversations by women as demonstrating poor listening ability but expressions of social power when performed by men.

Comparable manifestations of bias, in terms of age or race (see, for example, W. H. Tucker's, 1994, work on the politics of racial research), also violate the principle of respecting people. Researchers must be careful not to assume that their own worldview encompasses all the ways that a research study or its findings may be perceived. Thus, ethical researchers often invite their research participants or at least representatives of the population being studied to provide input on the design of the studies and the interpretation of the results.

Ethical researchers also express their respect for people by using participants' time and energy as efficiently and as effectively as possible. *Efficiency* refers to doing things right; *effectiveness* means doing the right things. Efficient researchers pilot-test their studies to be certain that all the procedures are clear and necessary. Investigators doing survey research, for example, will try out their questionnaire or interview protocol with a small sample of respondents to be sure that the meaning of each question is clear and that questions eliciting redundant information are eliminated. Effective researchers think long and hard in advance about the topic being investigated; they consult with colleagues and review previous theory and research carefully before launching their study. In short, to be ethical, research must be competent.

Besides research participants, other individuals to whom researchers are accountable and must show respect include colleagues in their profession and members of society at large. Researchers who deceive research participants unnecessarily, for example, encourage the stereotype that researchers are not to be trusted and that research is never about what researchers say it is. In such cases, the field is spoiled for others, and the whole research community is tarnished as a result.

In the final analysis, a good commonsense guideline for treating research participants with respect is the golden rule: Researchers should treat research participants as they themselves would like to be treated—or preferably even better.

Ethical Decisions Involving Research Findings

The findings from research are used to make important decisions. Here, we consider ethical issues regarding how data are analyzed and reported, the public nature of scholarly research, and the general use of research findings.

Analyzing Data and Reporting Findings.   As discussed in Chapter 1, research is cumulative and self-correcting, building on itself in a step-by-step process. The findings from research, however, depend on the data collected and appropriate analyses of them. If a study has a weak research design that has low levels of internal and external validity, the findings of that study are of questionable value. Such a study will have minimal value for expanding the body of communication knowledge. That's why scholarly journals in the communication discipline typically use a rigorous process of multiple blind review by experts in the field (review of manuscripts where the identities of the authors of the research report and the individuals reviewing the reports are kept confidential) to determine whether research reports are of high-enough quality to merit publication (see Chapter 3). Only if a majority of the expert reviewers and the journal editor agree that the study has scholarly merit (i.e., is well designed, conducted, analyzed, and written) is the research report published in the journal and, thereby, disseminated to the discipline. The American Psychological Association (1994) has also established several ethical standards for the reporting and publishing of research findings (see Figure 6.4)

Consumers of research rarely see the actual data themselves; instead, they take the findings on faith and read about the conclusions drawn from the analysis of the data. Only researchers see the actual data they collect. Therefore, they have an ethical responsibility to make sure that their data are collected in a reliable and valid manner (see Chapter 5) and, in the case of quantitative data, that they are analyzed using appropriate statistical procedures (see Chapters 11–14). We know, however, that researchers often make mistakes when collecting data. For example, mistakes may occur in counting participants' scores and recording their responses. The majority of the time these mistakes are in the direction that supports the research hypotheses (J. W. Kennedy, 1952; Laslo & Rosenthal, 1971; O'Leary, Kent, & Kanowitz, 1975; Rosenthal, 1976; Silverman, 1968). Ethical researchers, therefore, look closely at their data to catch, for example, skewed responses (such as the response bias of someone answering all the questions using only one end of the scale provided to get through the task quickly; see Chapter 4); incorrect coding, keying, or computer

FIGURE 6.4   Ethical standards for the reporting and publishing of research results

6.21 Reporting of Results

(a) Psychologists do not fabricate data or falsify results in their publications.

(b) If psychologists discover significant errors in their published data, they take reasonable steps to correct such errors in a correction, retraction, erratum, or other appropriate publication means.

6.22 Plagiarism

Psychologists do not present substantial portions or elements of another's work or data as their own, even if the other work or data source is cited occasionally.

6.23 Publication Credit

(a) Psychologists take responsibility and credit, including authorship credit, only for work they have actually performed or to which they have contributed.

(b) Principal authorship and other publication credits accurately reflect the relative scientific or professional contributions of the individuals involved, regardless of their relative status.

(c) A student is usually listed as principal author on any multiple-authored article that is substantially based on the student's dissertation or thesis.

6.24 Duplicate Publication of Data

Psychologists do not publish, as original data, data that have been previously published. This does not preclude republishing data when they are accompanied by proper acknowledgment.

6.25 Sharing Data

After research results are published, psychologists do not withhold the data on which their conclusions are based from other competent professionals who seek to verify the substantial claims through reanalysis and who intend to use such data only for that purpose, provided that the confidentiality of the participants can be protected and unless legal rights concerning proprietary data preclude their release.

Source: Reprinted from "Ethical Principles of Psychologists and Code of Conduct," *American Psychologist, 47,* pp. 1609–1610. Copyright © 1992 by the American Psychological Association. Reprinted with permission.

reading of data; and exceptions to the qualitative generalizations they would like to make about the context they are studying.

Worse yet, instances of outright falsification of data occasionally occur. False data may be given when research assistants are hired who have little commitment to professional ethics. For example, interviewers falsify data if they do not ask a question but record responses anyway or simply do not even conduct the interview but say they have (Andreski, 1972; Guest, 1947; Hyman, 1954; J. A. Roth, 1966; Sheatsley, 1947; Wyatt & Campbell, 1950). In observational research, interrater reliability coefficients have been increased by observers communicating with each other and then changing their coding to reflect greater agreement (O'Leary & Kent, 1973). Azrin, Holtz, Ulrich, and Goldiamond (1961) even found researchers who

reported conducting an experiment that by design was practically impossible!

One of the reasons for having reviewers evaluate research reports submitted for publication in journals is to ensure that proper procedures are used in a study and that the data are analyzed using the most appropriate statistical procedure(s). Occasionally, reviewers find serious mistakes made in analyzing data. For example, researchers sometimes use inappropriate statistical procedures that don't fit the nature of the data (Chapanis, 1963; Wolins, 1962), conduct too many posthoc, or follow-up, analyses that weren't planned (Lipset, Trow, & Coleman, 1970), perform a large number of statistical tests that inevitably make some findings statistically significant and then report only the significant ones (Barber, 1976; McNemar, 1960), report significant findings without indicating that the statistical power of the findings is relatively low (Kish, 1970; see Chapter 12), or simply fail to report data that do not support the hypotheses (Lipset et al. 1970; Selvin, 1970).

Most of the time, these problems are inadvertent and can easily be corrected. Two of the authors of this text, for example, published a study of workers' trust in their labor unions and their messages (Botan & Frey, 1983). The study asked workers to complete a questionnaire that measured three types of trust: expertness, character, and dynamism. In the original submission of the manuscript, these were analyzed as three separate factors of trust. A reviewer, however, questioned treating these as independent, multidimensional factors (see Chapter 4), and suggested that they probably were highly related to one another. If this were the case, then a different statistical procedure for analyzing the data would be necessary. Sure enough, when Botan and Frey checked, the factors were highly correlated. They reanalyzed the data using the proper statistical procedure, which did, in fact, change the nature of the results. This is precisely how the review process is supposed to work, helping scholars publish the highest quality research possible.

Some data-analytic deficiencies may actually be encouraged by the nature of academic publication procedures. Some journals, for example, tend to accept only articles for publication that report significant findings. Rosenthal (1966) argues that research needs to be reviewed on the basis of the importance of the questions it asks, the appropriateness of its design, and how effectively it was conducted, not by the results obtained.

It is also not uncommon for researchers to practice self-censorship, omitting particular facts and features of their research findings for various reasons. Interestingly, according to Adler and Adler (1993), "this usually involves deleting experiences that reveal personal, sensitive, or compromising features about researchers or their subjects" (p. 250). The tendency to omit information or "doctor" research results may also be exacerbated in the case of funded research: "Sponsorship not only influences the formulation

and execution of a variety of researchable issues, but directs the analysis and presentation of findings as well" (Broadhead & Rist, 1976, p. 325). Private sponsors may expect research reports to reflect favorably on their organization or they may have a preferred political agenda that researchers are expected to follow.

Because it is difficult to evaluate the actual research data, researchers need to be as clear as possible when reporting what they were looking for, how they got the data they did, and how the data were analyzed. After all, the conclusions drawn from data are only as worthwhile as the data themselves and the analyses performed on them.

Researchers must also be careful when presenting the results from research, especially in a public forum. Part of the reason people believe that statistics lie is that researchers with vested interest can present them in manipulative ways (see Chapter 11). For example, one of the authors of this text served for a time as a research methods consultant and media contact person to a reputable "watchdog" group that investigates social issues. One project involved examining the effects of riverboat gambling on small businesses in towns in which the boats were located. The watchdog group had already surveyed owners of local small businesses about these effects. A representative from the group approached the author and asked him to analyze the data. The representative admitted that the watchdog group was against gambling, but wanted to work with a researcher who would analyze the data objectively. The author admitted that while he personally favored riverboat gambling, he did not know whether it helped or hindered local businesses. The author looked over the questionnaire, found it to be acceptable (e.g., it was not biased in terms of using leading questions; see Chapter 8), and agreed to help analyze the data, and to receive no compensation.

The data showed that 50% of shop owners said that riverboat gambling had significantly increased their business, while the other 50% said it had no effect, positive or negative, on their business. The author reported these and other findings to the watchdog group representative, who stated that his group had also gone over the data numerous times and analyzed them in different ways, but could find no negative effects of gambling.

A short time later, the author, who expected to serve as the media contact person for this study, as he had in past projects, saw that the watchdog group's study was reported on the local television evening news. To his dismay, the lead-in to the story was, "Survey finds that 50% of shop owners claim riverboat gambling doesn't help their business at all," and went on to disparage riverboat gambling on the basis of this "evidence." While this claim was technically true (half of the shop owners did say it didn't help or hinder their business), the author objected to the "spin" given to the survey results. He resigned from the project and never worked with that group again.

The Public Nature of Scholarship.   Fundamentally, the type of research with which we are concerned in this text, scholarly research, is public research. Accordingly, researchers should not withhold the results of their research unless they honestly believe that releasing the results could be damaging or misleading. Professional ethics require that scholars be free to examine each other's research. This principle does not always apply to privately funded research. Private research may be proprietary—firms may withhold findings, particularly from competitors. Laws exist to protect original discoveries, usually in the form of a patent or copyright.

One way researchers can subject their work to public scrutiny is to save their data and make them available to fellow researchers who have an honest need for them. Wolins (1962), wanting to see how well scholars abide by this standard, asked to see the original data from articles published in psychology journals. Fully 70% of the authors either did not respond or claimed that their data were lost. J. R. Craig and Reese (1973) also found that half of the authors they contacted did not supply their original data or a summary of them.

Researchers certainly have the right to protect themselves from having the fruits of their labor stolen under the guise of a request to examine data. However, if a researcher's results are ever challenged by a competent authority, such as a colleague, he or she should be able to substantiate the findings. So data generally should not be destroyed. Research is a collaborative process that requires that data, and the findings obtained from them, be made available as public information.

The desire to make research public knowledge should not, however, compromise the pledge of privacy that researchers make to research participants. That is, the identity of an individual respondent should not be compromised by the desire to share information. That is why agencies that collect data that will be shared with the public—such as the United States Census Bureau, which has a Confidentiality Research Group housed in the Bureau's Statistical Research Division—often restrict the amount of information that they make public, even when giving summary statistical information in visual tables (see Chapter 11). There are a number of common statistical methods used to limit disclosure of such information; these techniques are called **statistical disclosure limitation methods** (in the United States; **statistical disclosure control procedures,** in Europe) ("Statistical Disclosure Control," 1998). For example, if the number of respondents in any particular category or cell is less than some specified number (e.g., 10), agencies will define that category as *sensitive* and not publish information about sensitive cells to protect the identity of these respondents; this process sometimes is called **cell suppression** ("Statistical Disclosure Control," 1998). University researchers and public research agencies, therefore, often walk a fine line between the need to protect research participants' privacy and the public's need to know.

The Use of Research Findings.   Research findings are often used by people taking actions that affect society as a whole, such as advertisers, government officials, and business managers. Researchers, therefore, have the potential to affect the lives of many people. Kimmel (1988) believes that "many individuals within the scientific community would argue that research ethics become increasingly important as the results of investigations acquire policy, professional, and personal implications outside the social science professions" (p. 12). In fact, Baumrin (1970) and M. Weber (1949) have argued that it is unethical not to use research findings to improve society.

Researchers, therefore, need to consider the effects of their research on the people who use them or are affected by them. K. Lewin (1947) argued that researchers can be both scientists and practitioners simultaneously; the roles are not mutually exclusive. Although some researchers prefer to view themselves as testing theories and the hypotheses derived from them and don't concern themselves with the practical applications, they need to realize the important relationship between theory and practice, especially in the practical discipline of communication (see Chapter 2).

The potential for the use of research findings to affect people adversely is particularly true for medical research, which is why it is so important to stamp out fraud when it occurs. For example, federal investigators found that, for more than a decade, an important breast cancer research program had been based on falsified research (Crewdson, 1994a, 1994b). The researchers had enrolled cancer patients who were ineligible and then falsified or fabricated their medical records. This research, unfortunately, was subsequently used to help establish the relative safety, and increased use, of lumpectomy.

Of course, not all use of research findings is cut-and-dry in terms of being right or wrong. As a final thought on the public use of research findings, we offer the following case and ask you to be the judge.

For a long time, smallpox was a deadly disease, killing millions of people over the course of history, until a vaccine was discovered in 1790. Two hundred years later, the smallpox virus is the only disease that has ever been eradicated ("Should Science Kill," 1993).

Scientists, however, have kept for study about 600 test tubes that contain the virus, which are sitting in heavily guarded freezers in Atlanta and Moscow. These remaining test tubes have generated an ethical debate about whether they should be destroyed or saved. Some argue that there is still much to be learned by studying the virus. Brian Mahy, of the Centers for Disease Control and Prevention in Atlanta, said, "Smallpox information could add to our understanding of viruses and how they cause disease and how they attack humans. I don't think we should throw away something until we've fully exploited it" ("Should Science Kill," p. 2). The World Health Organization, however, wants the vials destroyed, so that history's deadliest disease will never ravage the world again. As William Shaffner of Vanderbilt University School of Medicine put it, eradication would be an "awesome achievement" that "puts the final period to the sentence" ("Should Science Kill, p. 2). The vials could be destroyed in a moment by a flip of a switch. What do you suggest be done?

CONCLUSION

Ethical research involves important and complicated moral decisions about appropriate modes of conduct throughout the entire research process, including why researchers engage in research, how research participants are treated, what is done with the data collected, and how research findings are reported and used. Ethical research particularly requires taking into account the perspective of research participants, giving them as much information and free choice as possible, respecting their privacy, looking after their interests, and treating them as worthwhile people, not just numbers. And ethical researchers go to great lengths to collect, analyze, and report their findings carefully and to consider the impact of their research on their research participants, their colleagues, and on society at large.

Researchers, of course, confront the ethical issues, dilemmas, and suggestions discussed in this chapter on a case-by-case basis. In the final analysis, then, what makes someone an ethical communication researcher is the desire to thoroughly examine head-on the ethical dimensions of a communication research project, being up-front about what is done and the reasons for the choices made, and welcoming the moral judgment of the research by the community of scholars, sponsoring agencies, members of society, and, most important, by the participants who contributed to the research.

PART THREE

METHODOLOGIES FOR CONDUCTING COMMUNICATION RESEARCH

CHAPTER 7

EXPERIMENTAL RESEARCH

The attribution of causation pervades everyday, commonsense explanations of behavior. People often explain their own or others' behavior by saying "I did this because…" or "If he hadn't done that, it wouldn't have resulted in…." Such causal reasoning also pervades public discourse, as demonstrated in many mass media messages. As Shoham (1990) observed, "All one needs to do is scan a popular publication and verify that causal terms—causing, preventing, enabling, bringing about, invoking, resulting in, instigating, affecting, putting an end to, and so on—appear throughout it" (p. 214). Because of people's tendency to explain behavior in causal terms, Argyris (1995) calls human beings "causality producing organisms" (p. 4).

Many researchers are interested in finding the cause(s) of events and behavior. Who hasn't, by now, heard that smoking causes cancer or that one can catch HIV from unprotected sex with an HIV-infected partner? Some communication researchers also concentrate on understanding the causes of communication behavior. From investigations of which communication acts lead to the most amount of persuasion to the influence of television violence on those who view it, these communication researchers are like detectives hot on the trail of cause-and-effect relationships between variables. Just as a criminal detective looks for the culprit who committed a crime, researchers interested in attributing causation look for the variable(s) that is responsible for an outcome. As discussed in Chapter 2, the variable that is thought to produce the outcome is called the *independent variable;* the outcome variable is called the *dependent variable.*

To assess the causal effects of independent variables on dependent variables, researchers con-duct systematic investigations under tightly controlled conditions where people are exposed to only the independent variable and the effects of that exposure on the dependent variable are observed. These tests of the cause-and-effect relationships that researchers suspect exist are called **experiments,** and are the focus on this chapter.

ESTABLISHING CAUSATION

It should be pointed out, right at the beginning, that many scholars question the application of principles of casuality to explain human behavior, including communication behavior. We do not have the space to review the history of arguments for and against causality; suffice it to say that while causation is a contested concept, most people accept it, and many communication researchers believe in it and investigate the causal features of communication behavior.

One distinction that is useful is between *universal laws* and *statistical laws.* **Universal laws** "suggest that a consequent event or condition will always follow a given antecedent," whereas **statistical laws** "assert that a specified antecedent condition will be followed by a given event a certain percentage of the time, and they predict the percentage within specific limits" (J. W. Bowers & Courtright, 1984, p. 19). This is the difference between something that must happen if something else first occurs (e.g., the universal law that when one jumps in the air on the Earth, one must come down because of the causal effects of gravity) and something that probably happens if something else first occurs (e.g., the statistical probability that listening to a persuasive speech is likely to lead to being persuaded). When we talk about causality in this chapter, we are referring to the probability that one variable influences changes in another variable, not universal laws.

With that in mind, based on philosopher John Stuart Mill's reasoning, there are at least three requirements necessary for attributing a causal relationship between an independent and a dependent variable. All three are necessary for inferring causality, but none is sufficient in and of itself.

First, the independent variable must precede in time the dependent variable. Unless something comes first, it cannot cause something else to occur. Mistakenly believing something that is chronologically impossible, including attributing cause to something that came after an event (e.g., claiming that television influenced the 1928 presidential elections, which is impossible since television didn't debut until the 1940s) is called an *anachronism.*

In experimental research, making sure that the independent variable precedes the dependent variable is accomplished by first exposing research participants to the independent variable and then seeing how that exposure affects the dependent variable. In drug research, for example, people are given a drug thought to cure a disease and researchers then see if the drug works. An analogous communication experiment was conducted by J. Ayres et al. (1993), who were interested in helping people cope with public speaking anxiety. They first selected highly anxious individuals, and one third of them watched a film entitled "Coping with the Fear of Public Speaking." One third watched a film about how to construct standard speeches, but it didn't deal with handling public speaking anxiety and, thus, this third served as a **placebo group** that thought it was getting the independent variable being studied but did not. (The Latin term *placebo* means "I shall please," and placebos typically are thought of in popular culture as sham treatments that physicians hand out merely to "please" or placate anxious patients; any change in a placebo group, which sometimes is as great as 55% of people given it—see Harrington, 1997—is called a **placebo effect.**) Finally, one third did not

view any film (and, thus, served as a **control group** that did not receive any manipulation). All participants then delivered a public speech and were measured afterwards for their level of anxiety (communication apprehension). When compared to the other two groups, the "Coping with the Fear of Public Speaking" film was found to help reduce people's communication apprehension.

Second, the independent and dependent variables must covary, that is, they must go together in a meaningful way. For example, an experiment by Salazar, Hirokawa, Propp, Julian, and Leatham (1994) investigated, among other things, the effects of the quality of group discussion on group decision-making performance. As anyone who has ever worked in a group can attest, it makes sense that a high-quality discussion (e.g., one that explores available options in a systematic manner) should be related to a high-quality group decision. Sure enough, it was.

There are, however, many behaviors, events, and occurrences that go together statistically (in that there is a high probability of them occurring together, even in a consistent order) but are not related in any meaningful manner. It may be the case that almost every night it rains in London, decision-making groups in New York City the next day perform brilliantly. But we know of no logical connection between rain in London and group performance in New York City. Such patterns of statistical but meaningless occurrence are called **spurious relationships** (or **nonsense correlations**). Such "relationships" are the stock-in-trade of many hair-brained stock market and gambling schemes, as well as fringe conspiracy theories.

Researchers, therefore, must have some justification for believing that there is a connection between the variables they study, and this is especially true if causal connections are thought to be involved. There must be a legitimate reason why changes in one variable are suspected of causing changes in another variable. One way of establishing a meaningful connection between variables (as we saw in Chapter 3) is through a conscientious review of the relevant research literature. If previous research shows the variables to be meaningfully related (especially in terms of a causal relationship) or to be related to another, common variable, researchers can feel more confident hypothesizing a (causal) relationship between them. Determining that variables covary is, thus, an argument researchers make on the basis of available evidence.

Third, the changes observed in the dependent variable must be the result of changes in the independent variable and not some other variable. This criterion requires researchers to make sure that the causal relationship is a valid one—that the changes in the dependent variable are not caused by some other variable than what researchers think causes them. If some other variable causes the observed changes, there is an **alternate causality argument** (sometimes called **alternate hypothesis**).

The first two criteria, as we have briefly seen, are met, respectively, by (a) exposing research participants to and seeing the effects of the independent variable on the dependent variable and (b) finding evidence that the variables of interest are related in a meaningful manner. The third is accomplished by designing and conducting experiments in such a way as to rule out alternative explanations that might account for the changes in the dependent variable. Meeting each criterion means that researchers must exercise a great deal of control. Let's take a closer look, then, at how researchers exercise control in experimental research.

EXERCISING CONTROL IN EXPERIMENTAL RESEARCH

To establish a causal relationship between an independent and dependent variable, experimental researchers must exercise a good deal of control. **Control** means that a researcher "tries systematically to rule out variables that are possible 'causes' of the effects he [or she] is studying other than the variables that he [or she] has hypothesized to be the 'causes'" (Kerlinger, 1973, p. 4).

Control is not something that is either present or not. It exists on a continuum, ranging from loosely controlled experiments to those that are very tightly controlled. What distinguishes one

end of the continuum from the other is the way in which researchers: (a) expose research participants to the independent variable, (b) rule out initial differences between the conditions, and (c) control for the effects of extraneous influences.

Exposing Research Participants to an Independent Variable

To be confident that changes in an independent variable cause changes in a dependent variable, research participants' exposure to the independent variable needs to be controlled. Researchers who regulate or manipulate how participants are exposed to an independent variable exercise a high degree of control. Conversely, researchers who only observe, without manipulating, people's exposure to an independent variable exercise a relatively low degree of control.

Manipulating Exposure to an Independent Variable. In highly controlled experiments, researchers *manipulate* an independent variable by controlling when or how much of it research participants receive. When researchers control participants' exposure to a variable, that variable is called a **manipulated** (**active** or **controlled**) **variable.**

There are many ways to manipulate research participants' exposure to an independent variable, from asking participants to read, listen to, or view some stimulus material to having them perform behaviors that then serve as a manipulation for other research participants. Figure 7.1 provides some examples of various stimulus materials that have been manipulated in communication experiments.

These examples also show how experiments typically involve various **conditions** or **groups** that receive differential exposure to the independent variable. The most basic procedure is to divide research participants into two conditions, one that receives a manipulation (called a **treatment** or **experimental group**) and one that does not (the *control group*). Howze, Broyden, and Impara (1992), for example, conducted an experiment about whether informal caregivers, hair stylists, in this case, can increase women's intentions to

FIGURE 7.1   Stimulus materials used in experimental manipulations

1. Written Materials: R. Gibson and Zillmann (1994) investigated the differential effects of exaggerated versus representative news reports on people's perceptions of issues and personal consequences. Research participants read three news stories, one of which, about carjacking (stealing a car while the driver is in it), was manipulated in one of eight ways. One manipulation was with regard to whether the information was presented in a highly precise or comparatively imprecise manner. This was crossed with four versions of the story that differed in terms of representativeness regarding injury vis-à-vis the population of pertinent incidents: no physical harm, slight physical harm, severely injured, and being killed. After reading one of the stories, participants were asked about the severity of carjacking as a national problem and their own personal vulnerability. As expected, those exposed to the most severe condition considered carjacking to be a more serious national problem and overestimated the incidence of being killed as the outcome.

2. Audiotapes: Infante et al. (1992) studied the effects of verbal aggression on perceptions of credibility. Students at a United States university listened to a 14-minute audiotape of two speakers arguing in favor of (pro) or against (con) the Canadian Universal Health Insurance Program. They were randomly assigned to one of five conditions, four of which were based on whether the con speaker demonstrated a high (12 messages) or low (3 messages) level of verbal aggression and whether the pro speaker reciprocated all or none of the verbally aggressive messages; there was also a control group that listened to the discussion, minus any verbal aggression. The five audiotapes were identical, except for the manipulated variables; to control for paralinguistic cues, the high verbal aggression with reciprocity condition was first recorded and the other four versions were created from it by electronic editing. Participants then rated the credibility and the extent to which they agreed with each speaker. The results showed that initiators of verbal aggression were seen as less credible, but targets of verbal aggression were more credible, when they reciprocated the level of verbal aggression.

3. Videotapes: To assess the influence of judges' gender and nonverbal involvement on jury decisions, Badzinski and Pettus (1994) systematically assigned student mock juries to one of eight experimental conditions that involved watching a videotape of a simulated trial. The videotapes were produced by a professional educational television studio and the trials were taped in a law school courtroom. The trial segments were edited from actual trial transcripts and actors were hired to role-play trial participants. The videotaped trial dramatizations were identical, except for differences in the trial judge's gender (male versus female), nonverbal involvement (low versus high), and the type of trial (murder versus marijuana possession). Research participants watched one of the videotapes, assessed individually whether the defendant was guilty or not guilty, and then deliberated as a group until a verdict was reached. They also rated the credibility, attractiveness, and attentiveness of the judges. The results showed that while female judges were perceived similarly regardless of their nonverbal involvement, high-involved male judges were perceived as more credible and attractive than low-involved male judges. Judges' nonverbal involvement, however, had little impact on jurors' verdicts.

4. Scenarios and Role-Playing: Leichty and Applegate (1991) studied the influence of three situational variables and interpersonal construct differentiation (the relative degree of development of a person's construct system) on the use of face-saving strategies (the protection of another from embarrassment or humiliation). Forty-two university residence hall directors first completed a questionnaire that categorized them as either highly differentiated (those with more developed interpersonal construct systems) or less differentiated. Each director was then given a notecard with a description of a compliance-gaining scenario (e.g., obtain student participation in programming events) and role-played what he or she would say to a same-gender listener. Directors were randomly assigned to one of 16 possible situations created on the basis of two levels of speaker power (high versus equal), request magnitude (small versus large), familiarity (close friend versus acquaintance), and two persuasive tasks. Their verbal statements were recorded and coded by observers with regard to level of positive face-saving behavior. The results showed that while interpersonal construct differenti-

FIGURE 7.1

ation did not affect face-saving strategies, situations did. For example, speakers with high power engaged in less positive face-saving strategies than those with equal power.

5. Confederates: J. K. Burgoon and Le Poire (1993) assessed the effects of communication expectations, actual communication, and expectancy disconfirmation on evaluations of communicators and their communication behavior. Research participants first rated themselves on 23 character and personality traits and were led to believe that a person in another room was completing the same self-assessment. A research assistant then showed each participant the other person's (supposed) rating sheet, and commented that it was was either similar (P) or dissimilar (N) to the one completed by that participant, and that, based on an interview with the other person, that person was currently either in a pleasant (P) or unpleasant (N) communicative state. Hence, these procedures created four conditions (PP, PN, NP, and NN). Participants then engaged in a discussion about three dilemmas with that other person, who was actually one of four trained confederates (selected because of their acting ability and physical similarities to one another). Confederates were trained to enact either a highly involved, pleasant nonverbal interaction style or a detached, unpleasant style (e.g., forward versus backward lean, respectively). The

findings showed that expectations and expectancy violations played a significant role in the evaluation of communicators and their behavior.

6. Research Participants as Confederates: Manusov (1995) examined whether relational couples are likely to reciprocate their partners' involvement behaviors, and whether this depends on how satisfied they are with the relationship. On arriving at the laboratory, couples who were married or living together were separated and completed some questionnaires, including a relational satisfaction measure. One member of the pair was trained as a confederate to act "positively" or "negatively" (e.g., expressing positive or negative affect) at certain points in the upcoming interaction. Couples then were videotaped playing a game of *Trivial Pursuit* for 7 minutes; the third and seventh card in the deck told the participant-as-confederate to act positively or negatively throughout his or her turn and then to return to normal behavior. The interaction was videotaped and 17 nonverbal behaviors of the partners were analyzed with regard to reciprocity. The results showed that some adaptation did occur when partners acted uninvolved, used cues signifying low activity, and showed positive affect. Satisfied couples were also more likely than dissatisfied couples to reciprocate their partners' positive affect.

obtain a mammogram (which detects breast cancer). Eight hair stylists at a local salon were trained to give clients in the treatment group information about breast cancer, including the benefits and risks of mammography, and to encourage them to schedule an appointment for a mammogram if they had not had one recently. Clients in the control condition did not receive any information or encouragement. One year later, women in the treatment group were more than twice as likely (44%) to report having had a mammogram during the previous year compared to those in the control group (21%).

A more common and complex way researchers manipulate an independent variable is by ex-

posing research participants to different levels or types. (The term **level** is generally used to indicate a condition of an independent variable in an experiment, both for nominal and ordered variables.) Note that virtually all of the studies reported in Figure 7.1 are like this, such as the eight treatment conditions created on the basis of two levels each of gender, nonverbal involvement, and trials in Badzinski and Pettus's (1994) experiment. Many researchers also add a control group when there are multiple treatment groups, such as in Infante et al.'s (1992) experiment, where, in addition to the four audiotape verbal aggression treatment conditions, a control group listened to an audiotape that did not contain any aggression. (By the way, the term **comparison group** is used in the broad sense to imply any group against which another is compared, such as two treatment groups, whereas the term *control group* refers to a no-treatment comparison group.)

Theoretically, researchers can have as many conditions in an experiment as they like; as an extreme example, Garlick and Mongeau (1993) conducted an experiment that had 32 conditions. Of course, the more conditions comprising an experiment, the greater the number of research participants needed (see the discussion later in the chapter).

Observing Exposure to an Independent Variable. It is not always possible, or even desirable, to manipulate an independent variable. Some variables, like **attribute variables** (traits or characteristics of people, such as age or gender), simply can't be manipulated.

Other variables can theoretically be manipulated, but researchers would never do so. For example, many scholars contend that people's social support systems often collapse when they get AIDS (see Adelman, 1989; Adelman & Frey, 1994, 1997; Cline & Boyd, 1993; Crandall & Coleman, 1992; Scheerhorn, 1990). As Adelman and Frey (1997) contend, "AIDS, unfortunately, is a disease so imbued with fear and contempt that even loving family members are afraid to visit their dying sons and daughters" (p. 8). The suspected causal relationship between acquiring AIDS and loss of social support deserves study, but it would obviously be unethical to conduct an experiment that measured the amount of social support people have, injected half of them with the HIV virus but not the other half, waited for AIDS to develop, and then measured their amount of social support sometime after that. No researcher would ever want to conduct such an experiment, and no Institutional Review Board (see Chapter 6) would approve it.

Unfortunately, however, some people get AIDS while others don't. The former may be thought of (or plays somewhat the same role) as a treatment group and the latter a control group, and their amount of social support can be compared. In this case, exposure to the independent variable

(AIDS) is not manipulated by the researcher, but it can be observed in its natural occurrence (hence, this is sometimes called a **natural experiment**).

An example from communication research helps illustrate how researchers sometimes must be content to observe people's exposure to an independent variable. Ketrow (1991) wanted to assess the effects of various nonverbal communication cues exhibited by bank tellers during banking transactions (e.g., looking at versus looking away, and smiling versus frowning) on the satisfaction of their clients. One way to do this would be to bring people into a laboratory and have them pretend to interact with a bank teller whose behavior was manipulated in consistent ways (e.g., smiling versus frowning the majority of the time). But this procedure (like many conducted in the laboratory) undoubtedly suffers from a lack of ecological validity (see Chapter 5) because it isn't very similar to a real-life banking transaction. One could perhaps train real bank tellers to manipulate their nonverbal behavior in consistent ways, but bank administrators probably wouldn't let a researcher interfere with their business by having some customers treated negatively. Faced with these difficulties in manipulating the independent variable, Ketrow decided to study the effects of bank tellers' naturally occurring nonverbal communication behaviors on customer satisfaction. She obtained permission from bank administrators to have trained observers watch and code tellers' nonverbal behaviors when interacting with clients (without either the tellers or clients knowing they were being observed). As clients left the bank, they were asked to complete a questionnaire about their satisfaction with the bank and their teller's service. The different naturally occurring teller nonverbal behaviors that the observers coded served as the different treatment conditions of the independent variable and they were compared with regard to clients' satisfaction.

A more common case, perhaps, of observing people's exposure to an independent variable occurs when researchers study a treatment manipulated by someone else. For example, in 1989, as part of its efforts to strengthen India's dairy cooperatives, the main channel for marketing milk in India, the National Dairy Development Board launched a Cooperative Development (CD) Program designed to empower women dairy farmers (who make up 85% of dairy farmers in India, but only 16% of whom belong to a dairy cooperative) to have control over their dairy enterprise and other aspects of their lives. As Shefner-Rogers, Rao, Rogers, and Wayangankar (1998) explain, the CD program provided education and organized a women's dairy farmer club in which the women could discuss important issues. By 1995, approximately 250,000 in about 4,000 villages were being reached each year, making this one of the largest women's empowerment programs in the world. To study the effects of the program on participants' sense of empowerment, Shefner-Rogers et al. interviewed 184 female dairy farmers, half of whom had participated in the program and half of whom were from villages where it had not been conducted. They, thus, observed people's exposure to an independent variable manipulation (in this case, resulting in a treatment and control group) that was not designed nor administered by these researchers.

Whenever exposure to an independent variable is not manipulated by researchers themselves, the variable is called an **observed variable.** Studying observed as opposed to manipulated variables, of course, affords researchers less control over an experiment.

Ruling Out Initial Differences between the Conditions

As we have just seen, when researchers manipulate or observe people's exposure to an independent variable, they typically have at least two conditions and usually quite a few more. (Single-condition experiments are discussed later in the chapter.) One of the most important things researchers need to know is that the people in the different conditions were equivalent at the start of the experiment; otherwise, changes in the dependent variable might be the result of such initial differences rather than people's exposure to the independent variable treatment(s). That is, the results may be due to the internal validity threat of *selection* discussed in Chapter 5.

For example, suppose a public relations researcher conducts an experiment to test the hypothesis that "appeal" strategies are more effective than "warning" strategies at gaining compliance, in this case, getting people to sign the backs of their driver's licenses authorizing the donation of their organs. In one condition, people receive an "appeal" message (e.g., "You will feel good about yourself if you donate") and in the other they receive a "warning" message (e.g., "You will feel bad about yourself if you don't donate"). All participants are then given an opportunity to sign the back of their driver's licenses. The findings, as expected, show that people exposed to the appeal message did indeed sign their licenses significantly more than those receiving the warning message. The researcher would be tempted to conclude that the experiment successfully documented the expected effect. But it's possible, however, that the people in the appeal message condition are, for some reason, more "persuadable" in general than those in the warning message condition; that is, they're more susceptible to changing their behavior regardless of the type of message they receive. In this case, the initial difference between the two conditions prior to the experimental manipulation taking place, and not the manipulation itself, may well account better for the observed change in people's behavior. The end result is that the researcher can't be sure whether appeal compliance-gaining strategies are, in fact, more effective than warning strategies.

You see, then, how important it is for researchers to rule out initial differences between the conditions of an experiment if they are to be confident that any observed effects are due to the exposure to the independent variable and not those initial differences. Experiments that rule out initial differences demonstrate high control, whereas those low in control cannot rule these differences out as an explanation for the observed effects. Researchers, thus, strive to create *equivalent* conditions. This is done, as we will see, by using the procedure known as *random assignment.* When this procedure is not possible for some reason, researchers attempt to create *quasi-equivalent* conditions by using what are called *pretests.* When researchers don't use either of these procedures to check for initial differences, they create *nonequivalent* conditions; in such cases, there is no assurance that any observed changes in the dependent variable are the result of the independent variable manipulation, because the alternate explanation of initial differences between the conditions cannot be ruled out. Let's take a look at the two procedures that experimenters use to create equivalent and quasi-equivalent conditions.

Random Assignment.   In any experiment, there are potentially hundreds, thousands, maybe, as scientist Carl Sagan used to say, "billions and billions" of initial differences between the conditions that could account for observed changes in the dependent variable. Fortunately, there is a procedure that attempts to rule out these differences—it's called *random assignment*. **Random assignment** (also called **randomization**) means that each research participant has an equal chance of being assigned to any particular condition of an experiment. For example, a researcher could flip a coin to decide whether each participant is assigned to the treatment or the control group. Or the random number table (see Appendix A and discussion in Chapter 5) could be used. Hence, if there are nine conditions, the researcher might close his or her eyes and puts a pen down somewhere on the random number table. If the number nearest the pen is 6, the first participant is assigned to the 6th condition; if the next number is 3 (reading whichever way as long as it is consistent), the second participant is assigned to the 3rd condition. This continues until all the conditions are filled, usually equally. When a condition is filled with the allotted number of participants, it is no longer included in the random assignment procedure.

Random assignment gives the best possible assurance that the conditions of an experiment start off equivalent because all the initial differences between people that could potentially threaten the validity of the research findings should be distributed evenly across the conditions. As S. R. Wright (1979) explains:

> The advantage of randomization is thus that important variables and processes which can potentially produce the observed differences between experimental and control groups operate as random error. In the vocabulary of statistics, random error has

the characteristic that its expected or long run average is zero—that is, some errors will be positive, some with be negative, but in the long run they average out to zero or cancel out. (p. 38)

Random assignment, thus, is the best assurance of washing out all the initial differences that might make a difference, creating equivalent groups and, thereby, increasing researchers' confidence that any changes in the dependent variable are due to something other than the initial differences between the conditions (hopefully, the independent variable manipulation, although, as explained below, there are all sorts of other potential explanations). The importance of random assignment, therefore, cannot be underestimated. As Bausell (1994) claims:

> Research that does not protect against the possibility that subjects who receive an intervention are systematically different from those who do not produces such weak causal evidence, in fact, that the majority of the scientific community categorically refuses to allow anything approaching the meaning of causation to slip into descriptions of the results. (p. 60)

It should be pointed out, however, that random assignment is not always the perfect solution to ruling out a selection bias. As Cook and Campbell (1979) note, "Though random assignment does serve to make *most* things equal between the different experimental groups…it does not necessarily make *all* things equal" (p. 342). Moreover, as they explain, it "does not guarantee that the initial compatibility between groups will be maintained over the course of an experiment" (p. 342). Mortality (loss of research participants), for instance, may be potentially higher (or lower) for a treatment than a control condition, such as when undesirable treatments lead participants to withdraw from a longitudinal experiment. And random assignment doesn't guarantee the creation of equivalent conditions in any single instance. Suppose, for example, that a researcher wanted to conduct an experiment to find out which of two basketball coaching philosophies (the independent variable) leads to higher scores (the dependent variable).

Random assignment could be used to divide 10 participants into two basketball teams, so that each person has an equal chance of being assigned to either team. Theoretically, then, there should be no initial differences between the two teams (including their varying basketball skills) that might make a difference in the upcoming basketball game. However, if one of the players is basketball superstar Michael Jordan or Shaquille O'Neal and the other nine players are average, school-yard players, random assignment will not result in equally matched teams. Or say there are two relatively good players and the rest are average. It is quite possible that both of the good players might be randomly assigned to the same team (although this can be prevented by using pretests, as explained below). In that way, random assignment is like random sampling (see Chapter 5), in that just as one random sample doesn't necessarily result in a representative sample, one random assignment doesn't necessarily result in equivalent conditions.

Do not, however, confuse *random assignment* with *random sampling*. Random sampling is concerned with how research participants are selected for a study (including experiments) in the first place and making sure that they represent the population from which they are drawn. Random assignment, in contrast, is not concerned with how research participants are selected, but, once they are acquired, with how they are placed into the different conditions of an experiment. Random assignment, thus, increases the *internal validity* of the findings from an experiment by making sure the findings are accurate for those who are studied. Random sampling, in contrast, increases the *external validity* of the findings, so that the findings can be generalized to other people/texts, places, and times. Of course, the best research, as pointed out in Chapter 5, is high in both internal and external validity, so the best experiments use both random assignment and random sampling.

Pretests.   When researchers aren't able to assign participants randomly to the conditions of an experiment or want additional assurance that random assignment was successful in creating equivalent

groups, they can assess whether some initial differences exist between the conditions by using *pretests.* A **pretest** measures research participants on relevant variables that need to be accounted for *before* exposing the treatment group(s) to the manipulation of the independent variable.

Pretests typically are used in one of two ways to rule out initial differences between conditions. The first is when researchers suspect that some important variable(s) that is not the focus of the study might potentially influence people and explain the results better than the independent variable(s) does. Pretests are used in this case to make sure that the conditions are equivalent with respect to that variable. One can then simply remove participants who jeopardize the findings. For example, R. F. Smith (1989) conducted an experiment to determine how design and color affect perceptions of newspaper credibility. He wanted, however, to make sure that research participants were familiar with the newspapers used, so he pretested them, and those who were not frequent readers of the newspapers being used in the experiment were excluded from the study. He was, thus, assured that the conditions started off equivalent with regard to this variable. In the basketball analogy given previously, pretests could be used in this way to remove Michael Jordan or Shaq from the mix and, thereby, try to create equal teams. As Bausell (1994) contends, "Deciding upon exclusion criteria for one's subjects is one of the most crucial decisions a researcher must make in the design of his or her research" (p. 98).

An alternative is not to remove research participants who demonstrate particular characteristics but to simply make sure that there is, as much as possible, an equal number of them in each condition. For example, if intelligence is thought to be an important variable that may influence the results of a study, researchers can pretest participants for intelligence and make sure that each condition contains roughly the same number of intelligent, average, and below-average people. In the basketball analogy, pretests could be used in this way to make sure that the two good players are assigned to different teams. The goal in both cases is to try to create equal conditions.

The second use of pretests in terms of trying to rule out initial differences between the conditions of an experiment is to measure research participants on the dependent variable before the independent variable manipulation occurs. If the conditions generally are equivalent, researchers are more assured that any resulting effects are due to the independent variable manipulation and not the initial differences between the conditions on that variable. For example, in continuing their research, mentioned earlier, on helping people to cope with public speaking anxiety, D. M. Ayres, Ayres, and Hopf (1995) tested the effects of that videotape ("Coping with the Fear of Public Speaking") to reduce public speaking apprehension for "at-risk" grade school students (those from low-income, broken, and/or alcohol/drug–abusive homes and who are likely to drop out of school). Students with high fear of public speaking were first identified using McCroskey, Andersen, Richmond, and Wheeless's (1981) Personal Report of Communication Fear (PRCF) instrument. Hence, all participants were pretested and started off with a similar high fear. Participants then gave a speech about either their favorite sport or their favorite subject in school, after which they were randomly assigned to the experimental (the "Coping" videotape), placebo (a videotape on mass communication), or control (no treatment) group. They then delivered a second speech on the topic not previously chosen, and completed the PRCF again. The results showed that the **difference score** (also called **gain score,** even when referring to the lowering of scores, as in this case), found by subtracting the pretest from the **posttest** (a measurement of relevant variables that occurs after the manipulation of the independent variable), or vice versa (as in this case), was significantly lower in the experimental condition (48.1 to 35.9, a difference score of 12.2) than in the placebo and control groups (2.4 and 1.8 difference scores, respectively).

Using pretests in these ways is not as effective as random assignment for creating equivalent groups because there may be important differences between the conditions that can't be accounted for by pretests. A researcher simply can't pretest all the known, and unknown, initial differences that might potentially make a difference. In addition, pretests of a dependent variable may also create a validity threat due to sensitization (discussed in Chapter 5), such that the change from pretest to posttest is not a result of the experimental manipulation but of having learned the dependent variable. Consider, for example, how much better you would be likely to do on a "second-chance" final examination! A pretest of a dependent variable might also interact with an experimental treatment and cause a change that the treatment alone would not have produced. For these reasons, using pretests to rule out initial differences between conditions, rather than the preferred random assignment, creates what we call "quasi-equivalent conditions."

Controlling for the Effects of Extraneous Influences

As we have seen, experimenters want to show that the independent variable, and not some other, extraneous variable(s) produce the observed changes in the dependent variable. But that's easier said than done. Manipulating/observing the independent variable and attempting to rule out the selection threat of initial differences between the conditions through random assignment and/or pretests are powerful tools researchers use to control for the effects of extraneous influences. But these procedures don't control for all the problems that potentially undermine the findings of an experiment. As Lipsey (1990) notes:

> It takes a considerable amount of skill to design and conduct research sensitive enough to document the existence of a true effect within the stylized confines of an empirical research study. Most of the things that are likely to go wrong with a study (at least one in which random assignment of subjects to treatments is employed) conspire to prohibit the documentation of a true effect, rather than artifactually producing spurious positive results. (p. 50)

Researchers can maximize the probability of finding a true effect by exercising control over (a) the internal validity threats posed by the way research is conducted, researchers, and research participants (discussed in Chapter 5), and (b) other variables that may influence the relationship between the independent and dependent variables studied.

Controlling Threats Due to the Way Research Is Conducted, Researchers, and Research Participants.

In Chapter 5, we discussed these three major threats, as well as some specific types, that potentially compromise the internal validity of the results of a study, and some of the procedures that experimenters and other researchers use to control for them. Many of these threats, such as sensitization (the effects of one measurement on a subsequent measurement), history (changes in the external environment that impinge over the course of an experiment), and maturation (internal changes in research participants over the course of an experiment) are controlled for by the way an experiment is designed, and we'll discuss them in the next section of the chapter. Some threats are particularly germane to experimental research, so we'll focus on these here.

With regard to the way experimental research is conducted, one potential threat is a lack of procedural reliability, which makes it unclear whether any observed difference between conditions is due to the independent variable or the different treatments. Treatment reliability requires that researchers conduct the experiment in as similar a manner as possible with all participants. This includes what is said during an experiment and exposing participants to the experimental treatment in exactly the same way. For example, Tamborini, Stiff, and Zillman (1987) studied people's preference for graphic horror by manipulating whether participants saw a film containing male or female victimization. To make sure that participants in their experiment got precisely the same treatment, they had them listen to tape-recorded instructions.

Researchers must also be wary of **threshold effects,** where changes in a dependent variable may not occur until the independent variable reaches a certain level (threshold). Smoke alarms are like this; it takes a certain amount of smoke before the alarm is set off.

The way in which variables are measured also enhances or threatens the internal validity of an experiment. Experimental researchers, like all researchers, rely on questionnaires, interviews, and observations to measure variables. Whatever measurement technique is employed, it must be reliable if researchers are to establish a high degree of control necessary for ascertaining causal relationships between independent and dependent variables.

There are also some unique threats due to experimenters and those who help them. For example, **experimenter effects** occur when different experimenters consistently administer particular manipulations of the independent variable. If one experimenter always administers treatment A and another always administers treatment B, it won't be clear whether participants' responses are due only to the differences between the treatments or perhaps the way the experimenters administered them. To control for the researcher personal attribute effect, where experimenters' characteristics might influence research participants, participants can be matched with researchers, as Power et al. (1996) did in their experiment when they matched an Anglo research assistant with Anglo research participants. Or they can employ a wide variety of researchers to try to limit the effect to a few participants. The most common procedure for controlling for the researcher unintentional expectancy effect (researchers encouraging participants to behave in certain ways) is to employ an assistant to conduct the research who does not know the purpose of the research or the hypothesized results. Researchers also commonly use a **double-blind procedure** that ensures that those who administer the different independent variable manipulations and those who receive it do not know (are "blind" to) which participants are getting what manipulation. And when researchers want to manipulate a person's behavior, such as lying or self-disclosure, to see its effects on another person's behavior, they typically employ *confederates,* people who pretend to be research participants as part of an experimental manipulation. To control for the unintentional expectancy effect, confederates usually aren't told the goals of the research. In all of these cases, researchers are separated from the actual research conducted so as not to influence participants' behavior.

Experimental researchers also attempt to control for such participant threats as the Hawthorne effect (the tendency for participants to change their behavior because they know they are being observed), mortality (differential participant loss from experimental conditions), and interparticipant bias (participants influencing one another). Researchers control for the Hawthorne effect by not letting participants know they are being observed, perhaps by using a one-way mirror or directing participants' attention away from the true purpose of the experiment or about which part of a multistage experiment is the actual manipulation. Researchers will also conduct **blank experiments,** introducing an irrelevant treatment to keep participants from guessing the true purpose of the experiment or becoming automatic in their responses. Researchers also watch out for the **John Henry effect,** a type of Hawthorne effect that occurs when research participants in a control group take the experiment as a challenge and exert more effort than they otherwise would. Researchers also try to employ many participants to minimize the threat due to participant mortality. Researchers take great care to prevent participants from discussing an experiment. For example, in Perry et al.'s (1997) experiment on the effects of levels of humor in programs on television and perceptions of the commercials and products they advertise, participants were "supervised when entering and leaving the test site to prevent the exchange of information about testing procedures among participants" (p. 26). Researchers also stress during debriefings the importance of not discussing an experiment with future participants.

There are, as you see, a whole host of internal validity threats that potentially affect experiments. In the final analysis, such threats are best controlled for by pretesting experimental procedures and making sure that they work in the ways they are intended. In addition, researchers often conduct manipulation checks using questionnaires, interviews, and observations to make sure that the manipulation of the independent variable was suc-

cessful. The bottom line is that these threats must be controlled for if researchers are to have confidence in the findings from their experiments.

Controlling Other Variables.   There are a number of variables, besides the independent variable studied, that might potentially influence the dependent variable. One such variable, called an **intervening, intermediary,** or **mediating variable,** intervenes between the independent and dependent variables to explain the relation between them or provide the causal link. For example, suppose there is a relationship between amount of communication competence and amount of money made. There must be an intervening variable that explains this relationship, as having communication competence per se doesn't make one money. Some intervening variable, like job position, would explain this relationship, as those with more communication competence probably get higher paying jobs and, thus, make more money (one can only hope!). The effects of an intervening variable can, thus, be diagrammed as:

Independent Variable → Intervening Variable → Dependent Variable

There are also **confounding variables** that obscure the effects of another variable; when the separate effects of two or more variables cannot be determined, the variables are said to be **confounded.** For example, a **suppressor variable** conceals or reduces (suppresses) a relationship between an independent and dependent variable. Communication competence probably increases the number of friends people have, but it may also increase people's tendency to work harder at their jobs, which, in turn, decreases the number of friendships they might have. The tendency to work harder is, thus, a suppressor variable. The effects of such a variable can be diagrammed as:

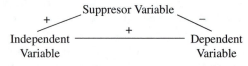

The opposite is a **reinforcer variable,** one that increases a causal relationship between variables. For example, communication competence might increase the number of friendships people have, but perhaps it also increases the number of social functions people are invited to and attend, which increases the number of friendships people form. The number of social functions attended is, thus, a reinforcer variable, and the effects of such a variable can be diagrammed as:

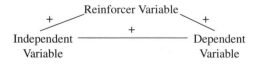

Finally, there are **lurking variables** (a kind of confounding variable), lurking there "like the troll under the bridge, an unpleasant surprise when discovered" (Vogt, 1999, p. 165). There may be a relationship between communication competence and the number of friendships people have, but perhaps there is a lurking variable, such as sociability (the tendency to be sociable), that explains both communication competence and number of friendships. The effects of a lurking variable can, thus, be diagrammed as:

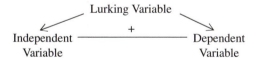

All of these variables are what might be called **extraneous variables,** variables that are not the main focus of attention in an experiment but which can have an effect on the variables being studied and potentially compromise any causal relationship found between the independent and dependent variables. It is, of course, impossible to control for all the extraneous variables that might intervene, confound, or be out there lurking, but experimental researchers try to control for them as much as possible. A variable that researchers try to control for is called a **control** (or **concomitant**) **variable.**

Controlling for Extraneous Variables.   One way researchers control for such variables is to make them another independent variable in the experiment. If, for example, gender is suspected of influencing or explaining the relationship between communication competence and the number of friendships people have, then gender could be included as another independent variable (see the discussion of factorial designs later in the chapter). This is a common procedure with attribute variables, characteristics of individuals, such as gender, that can't be manipulated per se. One strategy, as we have seen, is to equalize the conditions, placing an equal number of males and females in each of the conditions of an experiment, and observing whether the variable makes a difference. As an alternative, researchers can use pretests to assess these variables (such as "need for social approval"; obviously, one doesn't need pretests to determine participants' gender!) and then maximize the differences between the conditions of an experiment. R. A. Bell, Abrahams, Clark, and Schlatter (1996), for example, studied some individual differences that make people susceptible to the "door-in-the-face" (DITF) compliance-gaining strategy, which "is based on the premise that the probability of an individual granting a request for assistance can be elevated by getting that person first to turn down a more costly request for help" (p. 108). One such variable that the researchers suspected made people more susceptible was need for social approval. So they pretested participants and divided them into two conditions on the basis of "low" and "high" need for social approval prior to administering the experimental treatment. In this way, they could assess whether there were differences between those who were high and low on this need.

Another procedure is to use a **matched-pairs design** (also called **participant** or **subject matching**) in which participants are matched in pairs on some important characteristic (such as need for social approval) and then one member of each pair is randomly assigned to the first condition and the other partner is assigned to the second condition. However, as Vogt (1999) points out, "Without random assignment, matching is not considered good research practice" (p. 170).

There are also a variety of statistical techniques that can be used to parcel out the effects of extraneous variables once they have been assessed via pretests (see Chapter 14). Any variable controlled for statistically in this manner is called a **covariate.**

There are clearly many variables that potentially impinge on an experiment and threaten the validity of any findings discovered about the causal effects of an independent variable on a dependent variable. As you've seen, there are many specific procedures researchers use to maintain a high degree of control (such as random assignment) so that the causal effects found are, indeed, valid. Such step-by-step procedures are referred to as the **protocol** for an experiment. But at a larger level, the amount of control exercised and, thus, the degree of confidence that can be placed in the findings of an experiment have to do with the way in which an experiment is designed. We now turn to a discussion of experimental designs.

EXPERIMENTAL RESEARCH DESIGNS

D. T. Campbell and Stanley (1963) identify three general types of experimental designs: (a) full experiments; (b) quasi-experiments; and (c) preexperiments. These designs differ according to whether an independent variable is manipulated or observed, whether random assignment and/or pretests are used to rule out the validity threat due to selection, and what form of equivalence between conditions is created. These three types of experiments, thus, range from highly controlled experiments (full experiments) to moderately controlled ones (quasi-experiments) to ones that demonstrate little or no control (preexperiments; see Figure 7.2). Here's a brief explanation of these three types, and then we'll go through and explain them in some detail.

Full experiments demonstrate the highest degree of control because the independent variable is manipulated by the researcher (as opposed to being observed) and research participants are randomly assigned to create two or more equivalent conditions. Note that full experiments demand two or more conditions; if there is a single condition, only a quasi- or preexperiment can be conducted. If the controls of independent variable manipulation, two or more conditions, and random assignment to create equivalent conditions are not present, it is not a full experiment.

Quasi-experiments either manipulate or observe the independent variable and may have one or more conditions. When there are multiple conditions, research participants are not randomly assigned to them, as they are in full experiments, so full equivalence is not achieved. But quasi-equivalent conditions are created by using pretests to assess whether there are some important initial differences between the conditions. In cases where there is only one condition, quasi-experiments use multiple pretests and posttests as baseline measures to assess changes within those same participants before and after an experimental treatment. Quasi-experiments, thus, exercise a moderate amount of control; indeed, the term "quasi" means "to some degree." Hence, we can be less confident of the conclusions drawn from these experiments than from full experiments, but more confident than in the case of preexperiments.

Preexperiments demonstrate the least amount of control of the three types of experiments. Preexperiments, like quasi-experiments, manipulate or

FIGURE 7.2 A comparison of full experiments, quasi-experiments, and preexperiments

TYPE OF EXPERIMENT	MANIPULATION OF INDEPENDENT VARIABLE	RANDOM ASSIGNMENT	CONDITIONS	CONTROL OF EXTRANEOUS VARIABLES
Full experiment	Manipulate	Yes	Equivalent	High
Quasi-experiment	Manipulate or observe	No	Quasi-equivalent or intragroup baseline	Moderate
Preexperiment	Manipulate or observe	No	Nonequivalent or no comparison group	Low

observe the independent variable and may have one or more conditions. And like quasi-experiments, when there are multiple conditions, research participants are not assigned randomly to them. However, unlike quasi-experiments, initial differences between the conditions are not assessed by using pretests, which means the conditions must be assumed to be nonequivalent. When there is only one condition, preexperiments use a single pretest, at most, and, therefore, do not establish any baseline comparison, as done in quasi-experiments. Clearly, preexperiments demonstrate little or no control, leading to questionable conclusions because of the many threats that jeopardize the internal validity of these experiments.

The three general experimental designs are not hard and fast categories; indeed, what one authority calls a full experiment, another one might label as a quasi-experiment. The important point is to understand how they differ on the amount of control that a researcher exercises. To do this, we'll discuss a few specific designs for each type (for more designs, see, for example, D. T. Campbell & Stanley, 1963; Cook & Campbell, 1979). We'll use the same hypothetical example throughout the discussion so as to compare these designs directly. Accordingly, suppose a researcher is interested in the effects of a communication training program on increasing organizational members' communication skills (which ranges on a valid measurement instrument from a low of 1 to high of 10). The researcher conducts the experiment in a large organization (e.g., 500 employees) and selects about 50 employees to study (nonrandomly, and this raises the threat of validity due to selection, which we will discuss later). So that we can talk about full experiments, let's say that the researcher manipulates the independent variable by designing and administering the training program. We'll now walk through some designs and talk about their strengths and limitations as they apply to drawing conclusions about the effects of the training program on employees' communication skills. We'll start with preexperimental designs and work up to full experimental designs, as this will show the substantial limitations of the least controlled designs and the strengths of the more controlled designs.

Preexperimental Designs

Preexperimental designs, as noted above, manipulate or observe the independent variable. They can involve one or more conditions, but in the case of multiple conditions, there is no random assignment to create equivalent conditions nor use of pretests to create quasi-equivalent conditions. Let's take a look at three such designs: the one-group posttest-only, one-group pretest-posttest, and posttest-only nonequivalent groups designs.

One-Group Posttest-Only Design. The simplest preexperimental design is the **one-group posttest-only design,** in which a single treatment group is exposed to the independent variable and then assessed on a posttest. This design, thus, takes the following form:

$$\text{Treatment} \quad \rightarrow \quad \text{Posttest (PO)}$$

Applying this design to the hypothetical example of the communication training program, the 50 employees go through the program and their communication skills are then measured. Let's suppose their posttest mean (mathematical average) score is 7 (out of the possible 10; from now on, whenever we refer to scores, it is the mean score). At first glance, the treatment may appear to have been successful; after all, the score of 7 is fairly high. But the problem is that we don't know what their communication skills were prior to receiving the program and that makes a big difference. For example, if those employees started with a score of 9, the training program may have actually backfired and decreased their communication skills. The point is that we have no way of knowing what effect the training program had because a pretest wasn't used to assess employees' communication skills prior to receiving the program. Therefore, we have no basis for claiming that the independent variable (the training program) did or did not change the dependent variable (employees' communication skills).

As you see, this is a very problematic design and, therefore, isn't really used in experimental research. But when researchers do a study under unusual circumstances, this may be the only design possible. For example, a researcher may want to know the effects of the *Challenger* space shuttle disaster on the public's attitudes toward space exploration. Say there is no previous measure of those public attitudes, and there really was no way of anticipating this disaster, so no pretest is likely to have been administered (although, as some communication researchers discovered, there was, in fact, evidence prior to the launch that the O-rings were problematic in the type of cold weather in which the launch occurred; see Gouran, Hirokawa, & Martz, 1986; Hirokawa, Gouran, & Martz, 1988). In such instances, the one-group posttest-only design could be employed. Conducting this type of preexperiment might also serve the purposes of exploratory research, with the results from it used to design quasi-experiments and full experiments to assess the effects of interest in a more controlled and valid manner.

One-Group Pretest-Posttest Design. The **one-group pretest-posttest design** is similar to the previous design except that it adds an important feature—a pretest. This design, thus, takes the form of:

$$\text{Pretest (PR)} \quad \rightarrow \quad \text{Treatment} \quad \rightarrow \quad \text{PO}$$

Adding this pretest allows researchers to compute a difference score between the pretest (before) and posttest (after) scores (which is why pretest-posttest designs are sometimes called **before-after designs**). This design, therefore, gives much more information than the one-group posttest-only design.

Applying this design to the hypothetical example means that the 50 employees are pretested on their communication skills, they then go through the training program, and their communication skills are measured again. (In this and future pretest-posttest designs, we discuss the pretest as being the same as the posttest; pretests of other variables, of course, could also be employed in these designs.) Let's say that the pretest score is 4 and the posttest score is 7, producing a difference score of +3. At first glance, the treatment appears to have been very successful; after all, the posttest

score is considerably higher than the pretest score. But there are lots of problems with asserting this claim.

One of the most likely alternative explanations for the increase in communication skills is that of sensitization, that the employees improved on the posttest because they completed the pretest. If that occurred, the increase is potentially due to this internal validity threat, not the training program per se.

Two other alternative explanations are that of history or maturation, changes in the external environment and internal changes in the research participants, respectively. For example, perhaps these employees experienced something in between the time the pretest and the posttest were given that increased their communication skills, such as a new communication technology (e.g., a computer) that helped them become more proficient communicators (history), or maybe they gave a successful public speech that increased their communication confidence and skills (maturation). And if the pretest and posttest are relatively far apart in time, the likelihood that these threats might have had an effect increases. A researcher could potentially control for this by giving the posttest immediately following the training program. But if the posttest showed a score of 3 and, hence, no change, this might be because of the sleeper effect; that is, the changes come later, after they have had a chance to soak in. Such delayed causation is quite typical, for example, in medical research. After all, one doesn't immediately get cancer after smoking a cigarette; it takes some time for that to happen. Without some additional posttests, there is no way of knowing for sure whether there may be a sleeper effect.

History and maturation may not be particularly likely explanations in this example, but you can well imagine other studies where these threats would have a decisive impact. For example, if the researcher were measuring employees' satisfaction with the organization, instead of their communication skills, it is quite possible that something occurred in between the pretest and posttest, which the researcher may never know about, in the environment, such as a substantial pay raise, or inside employees, such as becoming more satisfied with life generally, that would lead them to be more satisfied on the posttest.

Alternatively, the pretest score may be an aberration; that, for some reason (perhaps "waking up on the wrong side of the bed"), employees' "normal" communication skills weren't measured accurately, which, let's say, is typically a score of 7. If that's the case, the training program doesn't seem to have had any effect at all. Without some additional pretests, there is no way of knowing for sure whether this was or was not the case.

It is also possible that statistical regression might potentially account for the results obtained from using this preexperimental design. Suppose the pretest score was 1 and the posttest score was 5. It could be that these extremely low-skilled employees regressed back toward the mean, as would be expected. Again, without some additional pretests and posttests, this will never be known.

But let's say that, somehow, all these problems could be ruled out. There is still one big problem that can't be solved—the fact that there was only one condition studied. There is, thus, no way of knowing how this group of employees compares to another group that didn't receive the training program. What if that other group started off with a pretest score of 4, but then demonstrated a 9 on the posttest? In that case, we might suspect that the pretest sensitized participants to the posttest.

Equally important, the researcher doesn't know whether the pretest is indicative of the population of employees of the organization studied. The researcher would know this if (a) all employees had taken part in the experiment (a census), or (b) the 50 research participants were randomly selected from the population (but they weren't in this example). If there were an additional condition(s), it would at least be possible to see whether the pretest score of 3 is characteristic of this other group as well. If it were not, there might be some important limitations to the findings; perhaps the training program only works for those who start with relatively low scores (like 3). For those who start with higher scores (like 6 or 7), it may not work at all. Unfortunately, we'll never know, as

there is no comparison group in this preexperimental design.

As you see, this design, like the previous one, is fraught with many potential problems. Although it may at times be the only one possible, the validity of the conclusions drawn from it is questionable. Many of the problems with this and the one-group posttest-only design, as we've seen, stem from the fact that there is only one condition in the experiment. The next preexperimental design takes care of this problem, although, as we will see, it too is problematic.

Posttest-Only Nonequivalent Groups Design.
The **posttest-only nonequivalent groups design** (sometimes called the **static group comparison design**) nonrandomly assigns research participants to a treatment or a control group and then measures them on a posttest. (For convenience sake, when we talk about multiple-condition experiments from now on, we use the example of a treatment and control group, but keep in mind that these designs also can have multiple treatment conditions, with or without a control group). This design, thus, takes the form of (the dotted line between the two conditions signifies that they are nonequivalent):

$$\text{Treatment} \quad \rightarrow \quad \text{PO}$$
$$\text{-----------------------}$$
$$\text{No Treatment} \quad \rightarrow \quad \text{PO}$$

Applying this design to the example, 25 of the 50 employees receive the training program while the other 25 do not and all 50 are then measured, at the same time (regardless of the decision about when that occurs), for their communication skills. It is now possible to compare the posttest scores of the two conditions. Suppose those exposed to the program have a posttest score of 7, whereas the control group has a 5. It is tempting to conclude that the program made a difference, but that may just not be the case because the selection bias of initial differences between the conditions cannot be ruled out. There was no random assignment nor pretest given to these two conditions, so we have to assume that the conditions did not start off equivalent with respect to communication skills or anything else for that matter. For example, suppose a pretest had been administered and it showed that the treatment group started with a score of 9 while the control group started with a 5. In that case, it would appear that the training program actually backfired, at least for those who began with high communication skills.

But okay, suppose both conditions started off with a pretest score of 5 and, indeed, the treatment group increased to 7 on the posttest while the control group stayed at 5. Although that would seem to provide some evidence that the program might have made a difference, the problem is that we can't rule out any other initial differences that might have influenced the results. Perhaps the treatment group contained very intelligent people while the control group contained average intelligence people. That could potentially jeopardize or limit the results, as perhaps the training program only works for those who are very intelligent. And that's just one variable that might have made a difference; there are, as we noted earlier, many many more that could influence the results. As such, we can't be sure whether the treatment really did or did not have an effect, and, even if it did, we don't know the extent of that effect.

Although there may be times when this is the only feasible design, as when researchers study how an observed treatment affected two different intact groups (hence, the reason for sometimes calling this the *static group comparison design*), it should be obvious by now that this and the other preexperimental designs demonstrate a very low level of control. Consequently, we lack confidence in the validity of the supposed causal findings obtained from them. Indeed, Huck, Cormier, and Bounds (1974) call these "pseudoexperimental designs" because they do not allow researchers to rule out competing explanations for changes in the dependent variable. They believe that "it is impossible to make completely valid inferences from the results of studies that use pseudoexperimental designs" (p. 227). Hence, researchers try to avoid using these preexperimental designs whenever possible. Indeed, we could not find a single example of such a design in published communication research

(which speaks well of the discipline). Instead, researchers investigating cause-effect relationships conduct quasi- and full experiments.

Quasi-Experimental Designs

Quasi-experiments, like preexperiments, either manipulate or observe an independent variable, and have one or more conditions. However, unlike preexperiments, in both single- and multiple-condition cases, pretests are used (when they would not have been) or used in a fundamentally different way than they are in preexperiments. This difference is like night and day with regard to the degree of confidence that can be placed in the findings.

It should be pointed out that quasi-experiments are most often conducted in the field rather than the laboratory (see the discussion later in this chapter). Researchers conducting field experiments are visitors in the natural setting and must work within restrictions imposed by that setting. These restrictions might mean, for example, that it is not possible to manipulate the independent variable. In our hypothetical example, perhaps the communication training program is designed and administered by someone within the organization. Even when researchers are able to manipulate the independent variable, they may be forced to have only one condition. The president of a small company, for example, may want all employees to go through the training program. Withholding a treatment from a control group may even be viewed as unethical if the treatment is likely to work (see Chapter 6). Even when there are multiple conditions, researchers often aren't able to randomly assign participants to them. The organization may want particular individuals, perhaps only management personnel, to go through the program, while others do not receive it. Thus, many factors may prevent the use of full experimental designs when conducting research in the field.

In such cases, quasi-experimental designs can be used to try and establish at least partial cause-effect relationships by maximizing the real-world transferability of research findings while sacrificing some degree of internal validity as compared to full experiments (although certainly exercising far more control than preexperiments). As Huck et al. (1974) explain:

> *Quasi-experimental and true experimental designs differ in the degree to which threats to internal and external validity are controlled. Generally, true experimental designs can have greater control over internal threats than over external threats, while quasi-experimental designs have greater control over external threats to validity. (pp. 301–302)*

With this in mind, let's look at three quasi-experimental designs: the single-group interrupted time series, pretest-posttest quasi-equivalent groups, and interrupted time series quasi-equivalent groups designs. The first has only a single condition; the other two employ two or more conditions.

Single-Group Interrupted Time Series Design.
The **single-group interrupted time series design** (sometimes called just **time series design**) involves giving a series of pretests to a single group prior to an experimental treatment, followed by a series of posttests. As D. T. Campbell and Stanley (1973) explain, "The essence of the time-series design is the presence of a periodic measurement process on some group or individual and the introduction of an experimental change into this time series of measurements" (p. 37). This design, thus, takes the form of:

$$PR \rightarrow PR \rightarrow PR \rightarrow Treatment \rightarrow PO \rightarrow PO \rightarrow PO$$

Although this design may look superficially similar to the one-group pretest-posttest preexperimental design, it is different in a very important way. Unlike the single pretest used in that preexperimental design, the multiple pretests in the interrupted time series quasi-experimental design (and as many of these as desired can be used) helps to establish an *intragroup baseline comparison,* that is, a way of comparing the same group over time prior to the experimental manipulation. This baseline measure can then be contrasted with the posttest scores following the treatment.

Let's say, using our example, that the following communication skills scores are obtained on three pretests prior to the training program and three posttests that follow it:

$$4 \quad 4 \quad 4 \quad Treatment \quad 7 \quad 7 \quad 7$$

Given that there are no differences between the pretests, but there is a difference between the last pretest and the first posttest, the researcher can be more confident, in comparison to the one-group pretest-posttest preexperimental design, that the training program might have made the difference. In addition, the multiple posttests (and as many of these can be given as desired) help to determine whether the first posttest was an aberration, the long-term effects of the program, or potentially (depending on when they are given) whether there is a sleeper effect.

The single-group interrupted time series design, however, still suffers from a number of potential problems. It is possible that the multiple pretests sensitize participants to the posttests to the extent that, for some reason, three measurements of employees' communication skills may have led to their improvement on the fourth and subsequent measurements. Or what if there is a change in the third posttest, but not in the other two? Can one be sure that this is a sleeper effect or an aberration?

But undoubtedly the biggest problem with this design is the lack of a comparison group. There is no way of knowing whether a group not exposed to the training program would demonstrate the same kind of changes as did the treatment group. To ascertain this, there must be at least two conditions, which the next two quasi-experimental designs have.

Pretest-Posttest Quasi-Equivalent Groups Design.
The **pretest-posttest quasi-equivalent groups design** nonrandomly assigns research participants to a treatment or control condition, measures them on a pretest, exposes one group but not the other to the treatment, and then measures both groups again on a posttest. This design, thus, takes the following form (the broken line signifies quasi-equivalent conditions, unlike the dotted line used

in preexperimental design, which indicated non-equivalent groups):

$$\frac{PR \rightarrow \text{Treatment} \rightarrow PO}{PR \rightarrow \text{No Treatment} \rightarrow PO}$$

This design represents a significant improvement over all the previous designs because of the use of multiple conditions and both pretests and posttests. Not only can we compare the two conditions on the posttest, like the posttest-only non-equivalent groups preexperimental design, but, more importantly, we can compare the pretest-posttest difference scores between the two conditions.

Applying this design to our example, suppose the following communication skills mean scores are obtained on the pretests and posttests:

$$\frac{4 \quad \text{Treatment} \quad 8}{4 \quad \text{No Treatment} \quad 4}$$

In this case, it would appear that the training program had the intended effect. We can certainly be more confident of this claim than with any of the previous designs we have seen so far.

There are, however, potential problems that still are not accounted for by this design. One of the biggest threats is still the potential selection problem of initial differences between the groups. Although the conditions started off equivalent in terms of participants' communication skills (and let's assume that isn't an aberration), we don't know whether they started off equivalent on the many other variables that might make a difference. Once again, perhaps intelligence interacts with the training program to improve employees' communication skills. The researcher could include an intelligence measure as another pretest, but as explained before, researchers cannot use pretests to account for all the known and, of course, unknown initial differences that might make a difference. Only random assignment can potentially equalize conditions on all those variables. This design, therefore, can only rule out those initial differences that are assessed, resulting in conditions that are quasi-equivalent. Cook and Campbell

(1979) explain that this means that "the task confronting persons who try to interpret the results from quasi-experiments is basically one of separating the effects of a treatment from those due to the initial incompatibility between the average units in each treatment group" (p. 6).

It could also be the case that the pretest sensitized the treatment group, but not the control group, to the posttest. Or perhaps history, maturation, or the various selection-interaction effects (see Chapter 5) affected the treatment group but not the control group. To try and rule out these threats, researchers can use the interrupted time series quasi-equivalent groups design.

Interrupted Time Series Quasi-Equivalent Groups Design. The **interrupted time series quasi-equivalent groups design** (sometimes called the **multiple time series design**) combines the previous two quasi-experimental designs by nonrandomly assigning participants to a treatment or control group and measuring them on a series of pretests and posttests. This design, thus, takes the following form:

$$\frac{PR \rightarrow PR \rightarrow PR \rightarrow \text{Treatment} \rightarrow PO \rightarrow PO \rightarrow PO}{PR \rightarrow PR \rightarrow PR \rightarrow \text{No Treatment} \rightarrow PO \rightarrow PO \rightarrow PO}$$

This design contains some important features that increase our confidence, compared to all the previous quasi-and preexperimental designs, in the effects of the treatment. If the pretests for both conditions are not fundamentally different from one another and are similar across the three time periods (in our example, say, a communication skills score of 4 for both conditions on all three pretests), initial differences on this particular variable can be ruled out. And if the scores for the last pretest and the first posttest are statistically significantly different (see Chapters 12 and 13) for the treatment group but not for the control group (e.g., 7 for the training program group and 4 for the control group), we are far more confident about the effects of the treatment than we were with the single-group interrupted time series design. The long-term effects of the training program can also be studied by comparing the multiple posttests for the treatment and control conditions, which represents a substantial improvement over the pretest-posttest quasi-equivalent groups design.

This quasi-experimental design, however, doesn't solve the potential problem of selection that results from a lack of random assignment to the conditions. Once again, pretests can only rule out initial differences on the variables assessed; there still could be lots of unmeasured and unknown variables that make a difference for the treatment, but not the control, group on the posttest. The multiple pretests might also sensitize participants differentially in the two conditions to the posttests. Therefore, while this design is undoubtedly the best of all the designs examined so far in terms of the confidence that can be placed in the validity of the findings, like those other multiple-condition designs, it, too, potentially is problematic because random assignment is not used to equalize the conditions. For that, researchers must use full experimental designs.

Full Experimental Designs

Full experiments are the highest in terms of control because the independent variable is manipulated by researchers and there are two or more conditions to which research participants are randomly assigned, which rules out initial differences and creates equivalent conditions. Here, we examine three full experimental designs: pretest-posttest equivalent groups, posttest-only equivalent groups, and Solomon four-group designs.

Pretest-Posttest Equivalent Groups Design. A traditional full experiment is the **pretest-posttest equivalent groups design** (sometimes called the **pretest-posttest control group design**) that randomly assigns research participants to a treatment or a control group and administers a pretest and posttest. This design, thus, takes the following form (R stands for randomization; the solid line signifies equivalent conditions):

$$R \quad \frac{PR \; \rightarrow \; Treatment \; \rightarrow \; PO}{PR \; \rightarrow \; No \; Treatment \; \rightarrow \; PO}$$

Applying this design to our example, suppose the following scores are obtained:

$$\frac{4 \quad Treatment \quad 8}{4 \quad No \; Treatment \quad 4}$$

Because random assignment was used, the researcher can rule out the selection bias and all the many known and unknown initial differences between the conditions that might have plagued the quasi-experimental and preexperimental multiple-group designs. And notice that a pretest is used to check whether the conditions, in fact, started off equivalent on the dependent variable. After all, remember that random assignment does not guarantee equivalent groups for any single experiment, so the pretests will tell whether it did work.

This design, thus, provides a high degree of confidence that the findings are due to the treatment and not to initial differences between the conditions. However, before concluding that the treatment made the difference, there is at least one glaring alternative explanation. Undoubtedly, after reading about the problems with quasi- and preexperimental designs, you noticed that the pretest might sensitize participants to the posttest. The next design is intended to solve this potential problem.

Posttest-Only Equivalent Groups Design. The **posttest-only equivalent group design** (sometimes called the **posttest-only control group design**) is the same as the previous design, except that a pretest is not used; participants are randomly assigned to a treatment or control group and given a posttest. This design, thus, takes the following form:

$$R \left\langle \frac{Treatment \; \rightarrow \; PO}{No \; Treatment \; \rightarrow \; PO} \right.$$

This is a very powerful design because it not only takes care of the potential selection threat, as does the previous design, but it does not risk the sensitization threat as that design does. Hence, when researchers can use a full experimental design but believe that the pretest may sensitize participants to the posttest, the posttest-only control group design can be used. In fact, Huck et al. (1974) argue that "there is general agreement that, unless there is some question as to the genuine randomness of the assignment, the posttest-only design is as good as, if not better than, the pretest-posttest design" (p. 253).

Of course, it still is possible that there are important initial differences between the conditions on the dependent variable (or other variables) if the random assignment didn't work. For that reason, many scholars still suggest checking whether the random assignment procedure did what it was supposed to do—equalize the conditions. And if researchers really want to control for both selection and sensitization threats in the same design, they can do so by using the Solomon four-group design.

Solomon Four-Group Design. The **Solomon four-group design** literally combines the pretest-posttest equivalent groups and the posttest-only equivalent group designs and, thus, takes the following form:

$$
R \Big\langle
\begin{array}{l}
PR_1 \rightarrow \quad \text{Treatment} \quad \rightarrow PO_1 \\
PR_2 \rightarrow \text{No Treatment} \rightarrow PO_2 \\
\hline
\qquad\quad \text{Treatment} \quad \rightarrow PO_3 \\
\qquad \text{No Treatment} \rightarrow PO_4
\end{array}
$$

By combining those two designs, the Solomon four-group design reveals three valuable things. First, it shows whether random assignment worked and produced equivalent conditions on the dependent variable (by comparing PR_1 and PR_2). Second, it shows whether the pretest did, in fact, sensitize participants to the posttest (by comparing PO_2 with PO_4). Since neither condition received the treatment, as long as their posttests are the same, the pretest had no effect; if the posttests are different, then sensitization has occurred. Third, assuming sensitization did not occur, it reveals whether the pretest combined with the treatment to produce a unique interaction effect that is different from the experimental treatment alone (by comparing PO_1 and PO_3). (Remember from Chapter 2 that any effect that is due to a combination of two or more things, such as a pretest and a treatment or two dif-

ferent treatments, is called an *interaction effect;* this is discussed in the next section of the chapter.)

Although the Solomon four-group design is one of the most powerful experimental designs for determining the causal effects of an independent variable on a dependent variable, it also requires twice as many research participants as the other two full experimental designs. Thus, it tends not to be used too frequently in experimental research.

FACTORIAL DESIGNS

Up until now, we have referred to the independent variable as if there is only one, and participants either do or don't experience it or are exposed to different levels of it. Because communication is such a complex process, researchers usually are interested in examining the effects of more than one independent variable on a dependent variable. In real-life situations, independent variables hardly ever act alone. Using the detective metaphor, sometimes crimes are committed by two (or more) people working together. Neither of the individuals would have done it alone, but together they decide to commit it.

When there is more than one independent variable studied, the independent variables are called **factors,** and the study is called a **factorial design.** Depending on how they are conducted, factorial experimental designs can be full experiments, quasi-experiments, or preexperiments.

Returning to the example of the employees who attend a communication training program to improve their communication skills, suppose there were actually two possible programs: one that stressed public speaking skills and one that stressed interpersonal communication skills. To test which training program was more effective, an experiment (preferably a full experiment) could be conducted by assigning participants to one training program or the other and comparing their improvement. A control group that didn't receive either program could also be included. But what if the company suspected that employees who received training in *both* public speaking and interpersonal communication would show the most amount of improvement? A single independent variable experimental design simply can't test this prediction; a factorial experiment is needed.

For example, a full experimental posttest-only equivalent groups factorial design for such a study would assign participants randomly to one of four conditions. The first condition receives both the public speaking and interpersonal communication programs. The second condition receives the public speaking but not the interpersonal program, while the third condition receives the interpersonal but not the public speaking program. The fourth condition serves as a control group by not being exposed to either program. This design, thus, takes the following form:

$$R \begin{cases} \text{Public Speaking} & \to & \text{Interpersonal} & \to PO_1 \\ \text{Public Speaking} & \to & \text{No Interpersonal} & \to PO_2 \\ \text{No Public Speaking} & \to & \text{Interpersonal} & \to PO_3 \\ \text{No Public Speaking} & \to & \text{No Interpersonal} & \to PO_4 \end{cases}$$

This experimental design reveals two very important things. First, it assesses the effects of each independent variable. To see whether the public speaking program was more effective than no program at all, the posttest for the second condition (PO_2) is compared to the posttest for the fourth (control group) condition (PO_4). Similarly, to see whether the interpersonal communication program was more effective than no program, the third-condition posttest (PO_3) is compared to the fourth-condition posttest (PO_4). Effects due to an independent variable in a factorial study (as mentioned in Chapter 2) are called *main effects.*

Second, this design reveals whether the *combination* of the public speaking and interpersonal communication programs is more effective than the public speaking program alone (by comparing PO_1 and PO_2), the interpersonal program alone (by comparing PO_1 and PO_3), or no treatment whatsoever (by comparing PO_1 and PO_4). Effects due to the unique combination of independent variables (as mentioned in Chapter 2) are called *interaction effects.* Interaction effects are important in communication research because they do some justice to the complex nature of causation in the human

sciences and the complex nature of communication itself.

In theory, researchers can investigate the main and interaction effects of as many independent variables as they deem important. Of course, adding more variables increases the number and type of interaction effects. With three independent variables (A, B, C), there are three two-variable (the term *way* is used, as in two-way) interaction effects (AB, AC, and BC) and a three-way interaction effect of all three variables (ABC). Interaction effects among three or more variables are called **second-order** or **higher-order interaction effects;** an interaction effect between two variables when three or more variables are studied is called a **first-order interaction effect.**) Calculate how many different interaction effects exist with four or five independent variables! Because of the large number of possible interaction effects involved, researchers typically choose only those independent variables they consider most crucial and can be examined reasonably within a single study.

When an interaction effect is found, it typically is considered to be more important than any main effect. That's because either the interaction of the variables makes a difference above and beyond the individual variables themselves or because one independent variable only affects the results under one condition of the other independent variable, so it would be misleading to discuss any main effect for the first independent variable (see Chapter 13). For example, it may be that one can lose weight by dieting or by exercising (two main effects), but one undoubtedly loses the most amount of weight by dieting and exercising (an interaction effect). In our hypothetical example, the public speaking program may work somewhat, as might the interpersonal program, but an interaction effect means that going through both programs works better than the either of them alone. Hence, an organization seeking to improve its employees' communication skills would want them to go through both programs. And, as if we didn't know it already, those wishing to lose weight should diet and exercise.

Factorial Design Statements and Diagrams

Factorial studies may seem complex, but understanding them is not hard. For shorthand purposes, studies with more than one independent variable are summarized with a design statement. A **design statement** is a series of numbers, one number for each independent variable in the study, separated by a multiplication sign (×). The actual numbers represent the number of levels for each independent variable.

The simplest factorial design statement has two independent variables and two levels for each variable, so there are two numbers (because there are two variables); in this case, both numbers are 2s: a 2 × 2 design. As an example from communication research, consider Monahan's (1995) investigation of why conversational participants view their partner more positively than do observers of the conversation. She suspected that two variables accounted for the less positive ratings made by observers: self-presentation concerns (conversational participants are more motivated to like a target than observers) and cognitive load (observers can focus their attention solely on impression formation, whereas participants must also coordinate the interaction). As part of an experiment, Monahan assigned observers to watch a videotape of a brief conversation between two people and evaluate one of them (the target). Observers were assigned to one of four conditions in a 2 × 2 factorial design. The self-presentation variable was manipulated by having an observer watch the videotape either alone or with the target. The cognitive load variable was manipulated by having half the observers in each of the self-presentation conditions being told to memorize as much of the conversation as possible because they would have to repeat it, while the other half were not given this instruction. Thus, there were two independent variables manipulated, each with two levels.

More complex factorial designs, of course, have more than two independent variables (sometimes called **N-by-M designs,** as opposed to the **two-by-two design** just reviewed). For example, Mullin, Imrich, and Linz (1996) conducted a 2 × 3 × 2 factorial experiment to investigate the effects of (A) pretrial publicity exposure to general stories about acquaintance rape and (B) case-specific publicity about a defendant on (C) males' and females' decision making about a rape case. Variable A (with the two levels of exposure versus no exposure) was manipulated by having some participants read articles about a "typical" predatory acquaintance rape occurrence, whereas others read crime stories unrelated to rape. Variable B (with the three levels of negative, neutral, or no exposure) was manipulated by having one group read negative, "highly prejudicial" articles about a specific rape event and defendant (e.g., his prior criminal record and negative assessments of his character made by members of his fraternity), one group read neutral "allowable" information about that incident (e.g., the facts, without information about the defendant's character or prior record), and one group read crime stories unrelated to this case. Variable C was manipulated by assigning males and females in equal numbers to each of the six conditions formed by the first two variables, producing a total of 12 conditions. All participants then watched a 41-minute enactment of an invented sexual assault trial involving that case-specific defendant and rendered a verdict.

Both of the factorial designs just discussed are called **crossed factor designs** because they involve having every level of one factor appear with every level of the other factor. This is the most common factorial design, but in some experiments, the levels of one factor only appear (are "nested") within a single level of another factor, and this is called a **nested factor design.** For example, if there are three levels of one variable (low, medium, and high) and six levels of the second variable (1–6), the second variable can be nested inside the first variable if, say, the low condition was exposed to levels 1 and 2, the medium condition experienced 3 and 4, and the high condition received 5 and 6. And when the number of levels for each factor aren't equal, as in this example, or in Mullin et al.'s (1996) 2 × 3 × 2 experiment, it is known as a **mixed design.**

To understand factorial designs and design statements more fully, it's often helpful to depict them visually in a **design diagram.** In a simple,

---

FIGURE 7.3   A two-factor (2 × 2) factorial design diagram (Monahan, 1995)

		COGNITIVE LOAD VARIABLE	
		Told to Memorize	No Instruction
SELF-PRESENTATION **VARIABLE**	Watched Videotape with Target	I	II
	Watched Videotape Alone	II	IV

---

two-factor design, a design diagram is a box with one independent variable represented on the **abscissa,** the horizontal (or *x*) **axis** (a line used to construct a graph), and the other on the **ordinate,** the vertical (or *y*) axis. Figure 7.3 is the design diagram for Monahan's (1995) 2 × 2 factorial design experiment about the effects of self-presentation and cognitive load on observers' ratings of conversational targets. Notice that the design diagram plots only the independent variables and not the dependent variable(s). For three-factor experiments, two of the variables are reported on one dimension of the diagram. Figure 7.4 shows the design diagram for Mullin et al.'s (1996) 2 × 3 × 2 factorial experiment. Additional subdivisions of the diagram can be used to visually show experiments with more than three independent variables.

A design diagram shows researchers all the possible combinations of the independent variables; each possible combination is called a **cell.**

You can, therefore, always tell how many cells an experiment has simply by multiplying the numbers in the design statement. The experiment, of course, must include research participants for each cell, usually equal numbers (when there are unequal numbers, it is called an **unbalanced design**). A generally accepted rule is that at least five participants are needed for each cell in a factorial design (Kidder, 1981), but typically far more are desired. A 2 × 4 × 5 factorial design has 40 cells and, thus, demands a minimum of 200 participants (assuming equal distribution in the cells, which is probably quite rare). Hence, as more independent variables and/or more levels of them are added, creating more cells in a study, more research participants are needed to fill the cells. At some point, the need to recruit participants becomes a burdensome responsibility for researchers using complex factorial designs. One solution to this problem is to expose the same research participants to multiple

---

FIGURE 7.4   A three-factor (2 × 3 × 2) design diagram (Mullin et al., 1996)

		ACQUAINTANCE RAPE SCENARIO PRETRIAL PUBLICITY VARIABLE			
		Exposure		No Exposure	
		Gender Variable			
		Male	Female	Male	Female
CASE-SPECIFIC PRETRIAL **PUBLICITY VARIABLE**	Negative	I	II	III	IV
	Neutral	V	VI	VII	VIII
	No Exposure	IX	X	XI	XII

treatments. To understand this procedure, we need to talk about between-group and within-group (repeated-measures) experimental designs.

Between-Group and Within-Group (Repeated-Measures) Designs

A **between-group design** (**between-subjects design**) are those in which one group of research participants receives one level of an independent variable (such as a treatment) and are compared to another group that receives another level (such as no treatment). We've already seen quite a few of these experimental designs. A **within-group design** (**within-subjects design**) is one in which a single group of people is tested two or more times. We've already seen examples of this in pretest-treatment-posttest designs. Another type is where the same participants are given multiple treatments of the independent variable and measured after each exposure. This type of within-group design is called a **repeated-measures design.**

Let's say that a researcher wants to see whether people are more effective in presenting three types of speeches (informative, persuasive, and entertainment). One possibility is to use different research participants for each of the three cells, which is a between-group design. Another possibility, requiring fewer participants, is to have all the participants give all three of the speeches. That's a repeated-measures design and, thus, takes the form of:

$$\text{Treatment 1} \rightarrow \text{PO} \rightarrow \text{Treatment 2} \rightarrow \text{PO} \rightarrow \text{Treatment 3} \rightarrow \text{PO}$$

Of course, not all independent variables can be used in this way. People can't experience being both male and female without some radical operation!

Repeated-measures designs allow researchers to use research participants as their own comparison, since the same participants are charted across different treatments. However, a **treatment order effect** occurs if the order in which the treatments are presented makes a difference; earlier treatments might sensitize participants to later treat-

ments. For this reason, researchers randomize the treatment order or **counterbalance** it by making sure that all possible orders are used. If, for example, there are three treatments (A, B, and C), participants will be divided into six groups, and the first group receives the ABC order, the second ACB, and so forth (BAC, BCA, CAB, and CBA). In this way, all the possible orders are included and any treatment order effects can be observed. That's what Brentar, Neuendorf, and Armstrong (1994) did in their study of whether repeated exposure to a stimulus in radio programming results in enhanced positive affect toward that stimulus. They used a repeated-measures design that involved exposing research participants to four different songs (two were high and two were low in subjective complexity), with the number of exposures being either 1, 8, 16, or 24. As Figure 7.5 shows, they designed the study in such a way that "song and exposure level were counterbalanced so that each participant heard only one song at each exposure level and that each song appeared an equal number of times at each exposure level" (p. 166). By the way, the findings showed that the burnout point where listeners start to feel negative toward a song may be earlier than radio programmers realize, as early as between 8 and 16 exposures. The researchers concluded that radio stations should en-

FIGURE 7.5 Example of a counterbalanced experimental design

	NUMBER OF EXPOSURES			
	Song A	*Song B*	*Song C*	*Song D*
Group I	24	16	8	1
Group II	1	24	16	8
Group III	8	1	24	16
Group IV	16	8	1	24

Source: James E. Brentar, Kimberly A. Neundorf, and G. Blake Armstrong, "Exposure Effects and Affective Responses to Music," *Communication Monographs, 61*(2), p. 169. Copyright by the National Communication Association. 1994. Reproduced by permission of the publisher.

gage in less repetition by using a larger selection of songs. Here, here, or should we say hear, hear?

Researchers using the repeated-measures design must also be sure that there are no **treatment carryover effects,** that the effects of each treatment have passed before exposing participants to subsequent treatments. The repeated-measures design, then, reduces the number of participants needed for an experiment, but raises other potential internal validity threats that must be controlled.

We've been talking about repeated-measures designs for a single independent variable, where one group of people are exposed to different treatments, but the more common use is to study multiple independent variables and use repeated measures as part of the factorial design (which is why we're discussing it here under that heading). That is, researchers combine the between- and within-group designs by having two or more different groups exposed to multiple treatments. Going back to the example of the three public speeches, a researcher might wonder whether there is a difference between communication and biology majors in giving these speeches. In this case, there are two independent variables (major and public speech), making this a 2 × 3 factorial design. The researcher could use a between-group design by having one group of communication majors give an informative speech, another group gives a persuasive speech, and still another group gives an entertainment speech, and the same thing would be done with biology majors. However, a repeated-measures factorial design could be used to have all the communication majors and all the biology majors give all three speeches. The order of the speeches could be randomized or counterbalanced so as to control for order effects, and the speeches could be given far enough apart so that there are no carryover effects. Such a design would tell whether there are main effects for major (e.g., communication majors are more effective across all speeches) and type of public speech (e.g., people are better at informative speeches than the other two), as well as whether there is an interaction effect between those variables (e.g., communication majors are better at persuasive

speeches, whereas biology majors are better at informative speeches).

Using repeated measures in this way to combine the between- and within-group designs is very common in communication experimental research. An example is a study by Kopfman, Smith, Ah Yun, and Hodges (1998) that examined people's cognitive and affective reactions to persuasive health messages about organ donation that contained either statistical or narrative evidence. The between-group variable was prior thought and intent concerning organ donation (high versus low) and the within-group (repeated-measures) factor was evidence type (statistical versus narrative). The experimental design involved participants first reading a statistical evidence message and evaluating it (e.g., its credibility) and then reading a narrative message and evaluating it. Participants, thus, evaluated both types of messages, although no mention is made of whether the message order was random or counterbalanced. If the messages were consistently presented in the same order, with the statistical evidence first, this could potentially bias the results, which showed that statistical evidence produced greater cognitive reactions, whereas narratives produced greater affective reactions. In addition, level of prior thought and intent influenced both cognitive and affective reactions, although no interaction effects between level of prior thought and intent and evidence type were found.

LABORATORY VERSUS FIELD EXPERIMENTS

We've been talking about many different types of experiments, and one of the ways in which these experiments have differed is with regard to the setting in which they are conducted. Some are **laboratory experiments** that take place in a setting created by researchers, whereas others are **field experiments** conducted in participants' natural setting. Full experiments, quasi-experiments, pre-experiments, factorial experiments—all can be conducted in the laboratory or the field.

Experimental research, however, typically is conducted in a laboratory because that setting allows researchers to manipulate independent variables easily, randomly assign research participants to conditions, control for the effects of extraneous influences, and measure participants' behavior cleanly, especially their communication behavior. Laboratories, thus, help researchers conduct highly controlled full experiments.

Although people typically picture a laboratory as a place with scientists in white coats, test tubes, and Bunsen burners, a laboratory is actually any research environment that is set up by researchers, including ones created in the research participants' natural setting. For example, when Hoffner, Cantor, and Thorson (1988) studied children's understanding of a televised narrative, they wanted the experiment to take place in a natural but controlled setting, so they used "a quiet room within the child's school building" (p. 233). This laboratory setting maximized both the internal and the external validity of the experiment.

Laboratories allow researchers to exercise high control, but often they can minimize external validity because participants may respond differently in laboratories than in natural settings (the ecological validity issue discussed in Chapter 5). Many experimental researchers, particularly organizational, journalism, public relations, mass media, and political communication researchers, therefore, try to maximize external validity by conducting field experiments in natural settings.

Sometimes field researchers can conduct full experiments. Cappella and Jamieson (1994), for example, conducted a full experiment during 1992 by randomly assigning people in 11 cities to one of six treatment groups or a control group. The six treatment conditions involved different amounts of exposure over varying number of days to "ad-watches," responses by national news networks to misleading political campaign attack ads. A 1-hour videotape was prepared that contained numerous types of early evening television fare and differed only in the number of adwatches inserted. The adwatchs were directed at a Pat Buchannan attack ad against George Bush that aired in Michigan during the 1992 presidential primary campaign. The researchers checked to make sure that the random as-

signment process resulted in equivalent conditions for a number of variables (e.g., race, sex, and age), and deemed it satisfactory. Participants watched the videotapes in their own home over the allotted days and then completed attitude measures toward Pat Buchanan and George Bush. The researchers, thus, conducted a posttest-only equivalent groups full experiment in the field.

At other times, as explained previously, field researchers cannot randomly assign research participants to conditions or manipulate the independent variable(s), so they conduct quasi-experiments. And there are a wealth of other potential problems stemming from a lack of control that may plague field experiments. For example, people working together who are part of an experiment may discuss their different treatments and infer reasons for being treated differently that influence their reactions and confound the results.

Rancer, Whitecap, Kosberg, and Avtgis (1997) experienced some of these problems in their field quasi-experiment. Two hundred and thirty-nine 7th-grade students from one school participated in a 7-day program of instruction designed to enhance their motivation to argue and argumentative skills, while 57 from that same school did not receive the training and served as a control group. Students were not randomly assigned to conditions, but pretests and posttests were used to measure students' argumentative skills before and after the program, making this a pretest-posttest quasi-equivalent groups design. The researchers point out, however, that conducting this experiment in the field setting imposed some limitations:

> The administrators of the school imposed some limitations in the material we were able to present to the participants. For example, we were constrained in the topics we could present to obtain the measure of argumentative behavior.... Conditions imposed by the administration also limited our ability to constitute and gather data from the "control group," including obtaining pre-test data on argumentative behavior. (p. 284)

Had this study been conducted in a laboratory, these problems probably would not have occurred.

Thus, these researchers made a trade-off between the high internal control of a laboratory experiment and the high external validity of a field experiment.

The quality of experimental research is, of course, determined not by where it takes place, but by the amount of control researchers exercise. Whether in a laboratory or the field, experimental researchers exercise high control when they are able to manipulate independent variables, randomly assign participants to create equivalent conditions, and control for the effects of extraneous influences. Typically, however, laboratory experiments maximize internal validity by using full experimental designs whereas field experiments maximize external validity by using quasi-experimental designs.

CONCLUSION

Albert Einsetin once wrote that the "development of Western science is based on two great achievements: the invention of the formal logic system and the discovery of the possibility to find out causal relationships by systematic experiment" (Mackay, 1977, p. 51). That's the purpose of experimental research—to discover causal relationships between variables.

Designing a high-quality experiment is no easy task. As Bausell (1994) points out, "Designing an experiment is like choreographing an intricate mating dance between the intervention [indepen-

dent variable] and the outcome variable" (p. 114). The beauty of the choreography pirouettes on researchers exercising a high degree of control so that alternate causality arguments for the changes in the dependent variable are ruled out. It is the degree of control that ultimately determines whether the findings from an experiment are valid.

Experimenters, like the detectives they are, do all this to discover the reasons for why things are the way they are. As that master detective, Daryl Zero, from the movie *Zero Effect,* said:

> *I can't possibly overstate the importance of good research. Everyone goes through life dropping crumbs. If you can recognize the crumbs, you can trace the path all the way back from your death certificate to the dinner and a movie that resulted in you in the first place. But research is an art, not a science, because anyone who knows what they're doing can find the crumbs, the where's, the what's, and who's. The art is in the why's; the ability to read between the crumbs, not to mix metaphors. For every event, there is a cause and effect; for every crime, a motive; and for every motive, a passion. The art of research is the ability to look at the details and see the passion.*

By bringing their passions to bear to discover the details—the causes and effects of communication behavior—to steal a phrase, communication research takes one small step for the research participants studied, one giant step in helping people.

CHAPTER 8

SURVEY RESEARCH

Communication research concerns a wide range of situations, from intimate exchanges to mass appeals, from one-to-one interaction between members of a family to messages sent from one person to a large audience. Survey research is particularly relevant to the latter end of this continuum. Researchers who want to design a message that will influence a large audience need to first understand the beliefs and behaviors of most people in that group. This is typically done by finding out what some people in that group think or do and then generalizing their answers to the larger group. Thus, researchers use the **survey method** to ask questions about the beliefs, attitudes, and behaviors of respondents for the purpose of describing both the characteristics of those respondents and the population(s) they were chosen to represent.

THE PREVALENCE OF SURVEYS

Surveys have been used almost as long as people have gathered into social groups. The Romans regularly conducted a census to tax people, and in 1086, an English census listed all landowners in the *Domesday Book* (Weisberg, Krosnick, & Bowen, 1996). In the twentieth century, however, surveys came of age. Surveys by major government institutions at the beginning of this century, newspaper polls begun shortly thereafter, the rise of market research, and university-sponsored surveys refined the survey process into an art form.

Survey research is particularly useful for gathering information about populations too large for every member to be studied. For example, it would be impossible to ask all United States citizens who they plan to vote for in the next presidential election, so pollsters ask only a relatively small, representative group of voters before and immediately after they vote, and use their responses to make remarkably accurate predictions about the election's outcome. Similarly, it would be difficult to ascertain the communication competence levels of all undergraduates at a large state university. It would be much more feasible to ask a representative sample of students from that university to complete a communication competence instrument, and then extrapolate from those results.

The survey method also is a relatively straightforward research strategy: You ask people questions and analyze their answers. Surveys, thus, provide researchers with a convenient method for gathering information about a population's beliefs, attitudes, and behaviors from asking questions of representatives of that population.

Applied Uses of Survey Research

Survey research has become a big business; survey research organizations grossed $4.4 billion in worldwide revenues in 1994 (J. K. Stewart, 1996b). Federal, state, and local governments use surveys to learn about many characteristics of their constituents (e.g., health and employment statistics). Lawyers commission research firms to conduct surveys to use as evidence in trials that will decide such issues as whether companies have engaged in misleading advertising. And Hollywood moguls use surveys to test how the public responds to films from their conception to completion.

Surveys are used most often as a tool in **public opinion research.** Three major applications of public opinion survey research deserve some extended discussion: **political polls,** which describe public opinion on political issues and potential voting behavior; **market research,** which describes consumers' attitudes and product preferences; and **evaluation research,** used to assess the performance of specific programs, products, and/or organizations.

Political Polls.   Political polls are one of the most publicized applications of the survey method. Results of political polls are presented to us routinely by the media, especially during election years. Pollsters typically survey a sample of potential voters to measure popular support for political issues or candidates. Many of these polls are designed to predict the results of upcoming elections, providing extremely useful information for political candidates, parties, and speechwriters. In fact, most political candidates at the national level employ their own pollsters, with 2% of the total budget in a presidential campaign being spent on polls, 3–4% for Senate candidates, and 5% for House of Representatives candidates (J. K. Stewart, 1996b).

Decades ago, political polls were held in disrepute after highly publicized election predictions were shown to be inaccurate. In 1936, for example, the *Literary Digest,* a popular national newsmagazine whose surveys were a national institution (Looney, 1991), mailed 10 million questionnaires and asked people who they would vote for in the presidential election between Republican Alf Landon and incumbent Democrat Franklin Roosevelt. On the basis of the 2.3 million responses they received, the newsmagazine predicted a stunning 57% to 43% upset of Roosevelt. Roosevelt, however, actually posted one of the largest victories in presidential elections, winning 61% of the popular vote and 523 electoral votes to Landon's 8. That was the last survey the newsmagazine ever conducted.

Squire (1988) points out that the poll was inaccurate for two reasons. First, the mailing lists were developed from telephone directories and automobile registration lists. At that time, during the Great Depression, phones and cars were luxuries, so these sources disproportionally included wealthy people, likely to vote for Landon, and excluded poor people, likely to vote for Roosevelt's New Deal recovery program (see Babbie, 1995). Second, less than 25% of the people contacted returned the ballot, a group that included a disproportionate number of Landon supporters. Sample selection and response rate are, thus, two important concerns for survey researchers that we address later in this chapter.

George Horace Gallup actually predicted in 1936 the failure of the *Literary Digest* poll and offered, instead, a "scientific" approach to polling (see Hogan, 1997). Today, the Gallup poll, conducted by the American Institute for Public Opinion Research that Gallup founded, is one of the most respected polls in the nation. This and other contemporary polls are more accurate at predicting election results because of the use of representative sampling techniques and the increasingly sophisticated design and administration of surveys. As an example, the average of the final results from the Harris and five other major media polls on the eve of the 1992 U.S. presidential election was 43.8% for Clinton and 36.5% for Bush; the actual vote count was 43% for Clinton and 38% for Bush ("Pollsters Pat Selves on the Back," 1992). However, contemporary polls certainly are not infallible, as witnessed by the 1992 preelection poll results in Britain, which erroneously predicted a Labour victory (see Mitofsky, 1998).

One reason today's pollsters do make more accurate predictions on election days is because of the use of **exit polls,** asking people how they voted just after they cast their ballot. There is, however, some concern that the reporting of results from exit polls may influence potential voters. The 1960 U.S. presidential contest between John F. Kennedy and Richard M. Nixon, one of the closest ever, provides some evidence of such influence. Some people in California did not go to the voting booth after hearing television and radio reports that Kennedy had won, a prediction made only on the basis of exit polls of those who had voted earlier in the day on the East Coast. Because Nixon was from California and had much support there, it is thought that he might have won the election had more Californians voted.

In summarizing studies about the effects of reporting exit polls on voters, Sudman (1986) concludes:

> [T]here is a possibility of a small decrease ranging from 1 to 5 percent in total vote in congressional districts where polls close significantly later than 8 p.m. EST [Eastern Standard Time] in those elections where the exit polls suggest a clear winner when previously the race has been considered close. (p. 338)

Because the reporting of exit polls may sway potential voters, the media typically do not predict a presidential winner in a state until all the voting booths in that state have closed, even though they may well know who won that state long before the polls close.

Political polls have come a long way in a relatively short amount of time. Today, they not only capture what people think, but have become an important form of news that influences public policy making. As Hogan (1997) laments:

> With leaders refusing to lead out of deference to polls, and with references to the polls often supplanting deliberation over the merits of policies, the polls increasingly shape both the agenda and the outcomes of public debate.... Instead of guiding policy makers, polls have become "news events" in themselves that not only substitute for substantive information, but also fuel so-called "horse race" journalism. (p. 162)

This is a far cry from Gallup's original belief that by accessing public opinion, scientific polling could "bridge the gap between the people and those who are responsible for making decisions in their name" and help make "democracy work more effectively" (Gallup & Rae, 1940, pp. 15, 11).

Market Research.   Market research that identifies consumers' preferences for purchasing and using specific goods and services accounts for the lion's share of the money spent on survey research (J. K. Stewart, 1996b). Surveys are used in market research to determine current, and predict future,

levels of consumption of products and services, evaluate consumer satisfaction with the performance of existing products, predict consumer preferences for new products, and identify persuasive strategies for product packaging, pricing, and advertising.

Market research, for example, is used extensively by mass media producers. **Advertising readership surveys** are conducted regularly by such companies as Starch to identify differences in demographic characteristics between readers and nonreaders of a publication and to identify those who read advertisements for specific products (see R. C. Adams, 1989). **Editorial content readership surveys** are conducted to determine which articles newspaper and magazine subscribers like and don't like and what topics they would like to see covered in the publication. These surveys provide editors with important feedback regarding how their audience views the publication, and this information is used to establish publication policies.

Broadcast audience surveys identify the size and composition of the audience that television and radio stations and specific programs reach. A broadcast rating is a measure of the market share, and serves as the major indicator of the relative success of stations, programs, and their staffs. "Research data, reported as 'ratings," provide the institutional knowledge used for the sale of advertising time, the industry's economic base, as well as providing criteria for program selection" (Stavitsky, 1998, p. 521). Consider, for example, that, on the basis of projected ratings, advertisers paid $1.2 million for a 30-second commercial for the 1997 Super Bowl, and Fox network had no trouble selling all the time slots.

A variety of measurement techniques are used by rating services, such as A. C. Nielsen (for television) and Arbitron (for radio) (see Beville, 1988; Webster & Lichty, 1991). For example, some ask people to keep diaries that divide the day into 15-minute blocks between 6 a.m. and 2 a.m. the following morning, and to report for each block whether the television was on, to what channel it was tuned, the name of the program, and who was in the room (see D. R. Anderson, Collins, Schmitt, & Jacobvitz, 1996). Questionnaires are often distributed and telephone interviews conducted—local radio surveys are known as *call-out research* (see Adams, 1989; Balon, 1981; Fletcher & Martin, 1981)—to determine audience viewing and listening behavior. Sophisticated electronic equipment, such as meters attached to television and radio sets, now monitor automatically the programs turned on at any given moment. The "peoplemeter" is a device that has audience members push buttons on a small keypad to register media choices (Beville, 1988). Some peoplemeters contain heat-sensitive devices that determine the number of people in the room (Beniger, 1987). Some firms even use cameras to watch people who are watching television. (Do you think this might produce the Hawthorne effect, discussed in Chapter 5, by influencing how people dress or behave while watching TV?!)

Market research is a dynamic field that is constantly developing new research techniques. For example, two new emerging techniques are usability testing and contextual inquiry (McQuarrie, 1996). **Usability testing** involves watching potential users interact with a new product under carefully controlled conditions, such as in a laboratory (see Chapter 7), while **contextual inquiry** involves studying customers' use of a product at their place of work. As McQuarrie (1996) explains, each technique is "unique relative to traditional marketing research techniques in that it examines the *interaction* between product and user" (p. 132).

Evaluation Research.   Surveys are often used to evaluate the effectiveness of specific programs or products by inquiring about audience members' and customers' experiences and feelings. A **formative evaluation** is conducted while a program or product is in the process of being developed to identify ways to refine it. A **summative evaluation** is conducted after a program or product is completed to learn its overall effectiveness, usually to determine whether to continue or discontinue it.

Surveys also are used in **need analysis** research to identify specific problems experienced by a target group, usually by identifying gaps between what exists and what is preferred, as well as to test reactions to potential solutions to those problems. The data collected in need analysis surveys are used to design new products and programs intended to relieve the identified problems. These interventions are then evaluated by surveying the people who participated in them.

Another type of evaluation research is **organizational feedback surveys and audits,** in which organizational members and representatives of groups those organizations serve, known as "stakeholders," are questioned about current or potential opportunities and constraints facing the organization. The International Communication Association's (ICA) Communication Audit (Goldhaber & Rogers, 1979), for example, uses survey methods to evaluate an organization's communication strengths and weaknesses concerning use of communication channels, information flow, quality and adequacy of information, communication relationships, and communication climate (for a review of this and other audits, see Downs, 1988). J. D. Johnson (1987) also developed and tested a communication and physical environment scale that works well in conjunction with the ICA Communication Audit.

It should be pointed out that the financial cost of conducting even small-scale surveys in an organization can be high. Scarpello and Vandenberg (1991) estimate that a 120-item questionnaire given to 500 employees costs $31,560: $15,000 in direct expenses, approximately $30 per employee to administer, process, and analyze the questionnaires; and $16,560 in indirect costs, $33.12 per employee for two hours of salary and benefits while completing the questionnaire—which equals $63.12 per employee.

While organizations must weigh carefully the benefits versus the costs of surveys and audits, useful information gathered from them allows communication consultants to develop strategies to help organizations meet the challenges that confront them. Brooks, Callicoat, and Siegerdt (1979) reported 16 field tests of the ICA Communication Audit conducted from 1974–1977. They found that audits uncovered problems and helped identify intervention techniques that improved both communication awareness and communication processes in the majority of these organizations.

Network analysis is a type of evaluation research used to identify "structures in social systems based on the relations among a system's components" (Barnett & Danowski, 1992, p. 268). A network is a group of individuals within a social system (a group, organization, or society) whom frequently interact (Kreps, 1986). Network analysts identify the patterns of interaction within a social system by gathering information about whom system members communicate with and how often, either by surveying system members via questionnaires or interviews or by observing them. This analysis is then used to construct a "blueprint" of the communication networks within the social system.

By identifying networks and constructing a blueprint, researchers describe and evaluate communication patterns and information processing within a social system. A communication consultant might examine the general flow of messages within an organization by identifying, for example, the "grapevine" by which rumors are spread or the potential blocks to the exchange of information between interdependent members or departments of the organization. This information is then used to design strategies to improve the flow of communication among people who need to coordinate their work.

Use of Surveys in Communication Research

Groves (1987), a senior study director at the Survey Research Center at the University of Michigan, begins an overview of survey research by pointing out:

> Survey research is not itself an academic discipline, with a common language, a common set of principles for evaluating new ideas, and a well-organized professional reference group. Lacking such an organization, the field of survey research has evolved through the somewhat independent and uncoordi-

nated contributions of researchers trained as statisticians, psychologists, political scientists, and sociologists. (p. S156)

Many contributions to our understanding of people's communication behavior have been made by scholars who use the survey method. Indeed, the survey is *the* method used most often in published communication research (see J. A. Anderson, 1987, 1996; Potter, Cooper, & Dupagne, 1993).

Figure 8.1 presents some recent examples of how researchers use the survey method to study communication. These examples illustrate how that method is used to answer the two primary questions, examined in Chapter 2, that guide communication scholarship: (a) the nature of communication and (b) how communication is related to other variables. Researchers often use survey responses to describe the communication characteristics of a population and to assess relationships between communication and other behavior.

Network analysis, for example, can be used to investigate relationships between organizational members' participation in communication systems and various outcomes. A. A. Marshall and Stohl (1993) used the survey method as part of their network analysis to learn how workers' participation in the communication system at a plant affected their satisfaction and productivity. All workers completed a questionnaire indicating who they talked to about their jobs, issues and concerns in the plant, and the general business of the company. Workers also made some global judgments about their participation (such as their general activity in voluntary groups). The dependent variables were worker satisfaction and performance. In line with the researchers' hypothesis, workers who communicated the most also had the best performance and the highest satisfaction.

When studying relationships between variables, survey researchers rarely exercise the same amount of control as experimental researchers. Instead of using experimental designs to manipulate independent variables to determine their influence on dependent variables, they use a **correlational design;** that is, they use a questionnaire or interview to assess all the variables of interest at one

---

FIGURE 8.1   Some recent examples of communication survey research

---

1. Byerly and Warren (1996) studied the prevalence of activism in mainstream newsrooms by surveying journalists at 18 major United States daily newspapers with circulations between 250,000 and 1.3 million.

2. Fitzpatrick and Ritchie (1994) surveyed parents of children enrolled in the public high schools of Madison, WI, to study the relationships between their schemata about marital and parent-child communication and a number of other dimensions of family life.

3. Gunther (1995) conducted 648 computer-assisted telephone interviews of people selected randomly from the United States population to learn their exposure to and perceptions of the effects of X-rated pornographic media content, as well as to determine the level of public support for the censorship of pornography.

4. Kalbfleisch and Davies (1993) surveyed 431 faculty from a large university to test a model of the relationship between three interpersonal components and involvement in mentoring relationships.

5. Katz (1994) had the Public Opinion Laboratory at Northern Illinois University interview 522 people across the United States, selected by using a random-digit dialing procedure, about the nature of obscene phone calls they had received.

6. Liebes and Ribak (1992) assessed the contribution of family culture to political participation and political outlook by interviewing 400 adolescents (between the ages of 12 and 19) and their parents in Jerusalem, Israel, chosen at random from automatic voting registration lists.

7. Petronio and Bradford (1993) surveyed a simple random sample of 148 divorced, absentee, noncustodial fathers who participated in a nationwide writing program to study issues that might interfere with written communication used as a means of relational bonding.

8. Salwen and Driscoll (1997) conducted a representative telephone survey of 605 United States adults six weeks after the O. J. Simpson jury had been sequestered to test the third-person effect perceptual-bias hypothesis that people perceive news media coverage to exert greater influence on other people than on themselves.

9. Teboul (1995) examined the information-seeking behavior of 281 new hires in organizations (people working in full-time positions for less than six months) on the basis of responses to survey questionnaires.

10. Yum and Kendall (1995) conducted telephone interviews with 567 New York residents to examine and test gender differences in interpersonal political communication during a one-week period prior to the 1988 presidential election.

---

point in time, and then analyze the relationships among them. Although causation can sometimes be inferred from such a study, survey research typically establishes noncausal relationships among variables. For example, if the results from a survey show that respondents like people to whom they self-disclose, a researcher would not necessarily assume that self-disclosure causes liking, or vice versa. Because both variables were assessed at the same point in time, the researcher must assume that these two variables probably mutually influence each other, such that the more of one, the more of the other. In Chapter 14, we examine the data-analytic procedures used to assess relationships between variables.

One survey can sometimes provide data for multiple studies. When survey data are stored in archives, communication researchers can reanalyze them, looking for new relationships among variables. Reanalysis by one scholar of data collected by someone else is called **secondary data analysis,** to distinguish it from primary research conducted by the original researcher (see Chapter 3). Alcaly and Bell's (1996) study of the impact of a health promotion intervention on poor African American, Hispanic, and non-Hispanic White women, for example, reanalyzed survey data collected by earlier researchers as part of their independent evaluation of the effectiveness of a state-funded program. Their reanalysis showed that the original intervention made a significant difference for all three groups, although Hispanics benefited less than the other two ethnic groups.

SURVEY RESEARCH DESIGN

Designing an effective survey study involves a series of challenging decisions. The sample of people surveyed influences the kinds of responses one obtains and the generalizability of those responses; the strategy used to reach survey respondents (e.g., telephone, mail, or personal contact) also influences both response rate and responses; the ways in which survey questions are worded and the order in which they are asked influence respondents' answers, too; and researchers must decide whether the survey will be conducted over a short or a long period of time. Therefore, researchers who use the survey method must establish clear goals and administer these techniques carefully if they are to generate valid data.

Selecting Survey Respondents

Sampling is essential when surveying large populations. It is often unreasonable, as well as unnecessary, to study every member of a large population. Instead, researchers generally select a sample of representative members of a population to survey (see Chapter 5). Responses from this sample are presumed to reflect the characteristics of that population.

Sampling Frame.   To select a sample, researchers first identify the population they want to describe. They then acquire (or develop) a **sampling frame,** a list of the population from which they will sample. Ideally, the sampling frame lists all the members of the population, although in actual

practice the sampling frame is as exhaustive a list of the population as researchers can obtain.

If the population of interest is small enough, researchers can obtain a complete list of all members. Reinking and Bell (1991), for example, investigated relationships among loneliness, career success, and communication competence to see whether people who occupy low positions in organizational hierarchies are more prone to loneliness. Their study targeted one organization, a department within a large agency of the State of California that performs a type of social welfare work. They obtained a list of all personnel employed at the Branch Administration Offices and mailed everyone a questionnaire to complete.

Even if a population is relatively large, it may be possible to obtain a list of all members. For example, in their study of factors influencing decisions by local television news directors, Wicks and Kern (1995) mailed a questionnaire to all 1008 commercial television stations listed in the *1991 Broadcasting Yearbook.*

But when a population is very large—a city, a state, or a country—researchers must use sampling frames that probably do not include everyone in the population. They might use voter registration lists or driver's licences as the sampling frame. Le Poire, Burgoon, and Parrott (1992), for example, studied strategies people use to restore privacy once it has been invaded in their workplace. Their sample consisted of 285 people waiting to be selected for jury duty. Prospective jurors in the United States are selected by local governments using a simple random sample from driver-license and voter-registration lists, so they assumed the jurors constituted a random sample representative of adults in that particular community. Of course, not everyone in that community probably has a driver's license or is registered to vote, so those people were ineligible to be selected for jury duty and, therefore, excluded from the study.

Survey researchers also often use telephone directories as the sampling frame. Dimmick, Sikand, and Patterson (1994), for example, studied the gratifications people obtain from using their household telephone by randomly selecting 382 respondents from the 1991/1992 Columbus (Franklin County), Ohio, telephone directory. Though most people in the United States have telephones, not everyone does; in fact, 12.2% of households in Jersey City didn't have a telephone in 1990, according to Survey Sampling, Inc., a professional sampling firm. Most telephone directories are also slightly out of date and don't include people who have moved recently into and out of the area. And many households that have a phone have an unlisted telephone number. According to Survey Sampling, Inc., in 1990, the total number of unlisted phones across the United States was 31.1%, and in some cities, like Las Vegas, it was as high as 62.3%. So this sampling frame, too, is somewhat flawed.

Random-digit dialing solves some of these problems by having a computer generate randomly all possible combinations of telephone numbers in a given exchange. All telephone numbers within that bank of numbers, thus, have an equal chance of being selected. Hofstetter, Sticht, and Hofstetter (1999), for example, conducted two random-digit-dialed telephone surveys of adults in San Diego, CA, to examine relationships among the amount of general and specific knowledge people have, their literacy practices, and their acquired social and political power. Each telephone number in their survey had an equal chance of being selected, although individuals with multiple telephone lines had a greater likelihood of being selected. Of course, the researchers could simply ask whether the household has been called previously and, if so, not readminister the survey.

Generalizing the findings from a sample to a population requires the use of a full and accurate sampling frame. Using incomplete lists of people living in a specific region potentially produces a biased sampling frame. If that happens, the sample will not be representative of the population from which it is drawn and the findings cannot be generalized with confidence to that population.

Sampling Method.   Once a sampling frame is identified (or created), survey researchers must choose a method for selecting respondents from it. A random sample provides the best guarantee of generating an externally valid sample from a population (see Chapter 5). For this reason, most survey researchers, especially political pollsters who want to predict public attitudes and potential voting behaviors precisely, use a random sampling method (such as a simple random, systematic, stratified, or cluster sample described in Chapter 5).

Because it is often difficult, if not impossible, to obtain a complete list of all the members of a large population, many large-scale surveys use a *cluster sampling* procedure to select respondents. A researcher conducting a national survey, for example, selects states, counties within the state, cities within the counties, streets within the cities, houses on the streets, and, finally, household members, all in a random manner.

Survey researchers also often use *stratified* samples to make sure that individuals with particular characteristics are selected, often in numbers proportional to their occurrence in the actual population. Rothenbuhler (1991), for example, conducted a telephone survey of 400 adult residents of Iowa about the role of communication in community processes. He divided (stratified) the state into nine geographic areas, and selected at least one county in each area. The probability of selecting a county and the number of people sampled within the selected counties were proportionate to the size of their population. He even checked that the urban/rural balance of the sample matched that of the state. This stratification procedure made sure that people from different counties of the state were included and that their representation in the sample was proportional to their representation in the population. This procedure maximized the similarity between the sample and the population and, consequently, increased the external validity of the conclusions drawn from that sample.

Obtaining random samples, especially national random samples, is fraught with problems. Survey Sampling, Inc. (1990) points out some of the problems in conducting a national random sample survey via telephone. We already mentioned the problem of unlisted phones, which random-digit dialing solves, although this method is potentially problematic because the average working phone rate (WPR) of random-digit-dialed (RDD) samples across the nation in 1997 was only 61.4%, and in some places, like Washington, DC, it was as low as 46.3% ("Lower Working Phone Rate," 1997). In addition to these problems, in 1990, the **contact rate,** the percentage of phone calls that result in contact with an English-speaking interviewee, was only 56.4%; the average **cooperation rate,** the percentage of phone calls in which interviewees agree to participate, was only 53.2%; and 26.0% of respondents had been surveyed too frequently, called the **surveyed rate,** and were, therefore, not eligible to participate in the survey. If you compile those figures, only 22.2% of the population of eligible households with telephones would actually have been available to be surveyed.

Many survey researchers, especially market researchers, actually use nonrandom samples. They often identify preferences about a specific product from *purposive* samples of any available consumers who qualify for the survey. You have probably encountered interviewers working for a market research firm in a shopping mall. These interviewers are trained to approach particular individuals on the basis of key *market segmentation* characteristics that can be observed (e.g., age or gender) or asked about (e.g., shopping habits or product use). Qualified respondents are then asked to answer some questions about specific products. These purposive samples, although not random and, therefore, not necessarily representative of the population of interest, do provide market researchers with "quick and dirty," yet reasonably accurate, information for making decisions about products.

Volunteer samples are also used to assess what people think. For example, respondents may be asked to call one of several 900-numbers to register a choice. The first 900-number poll was used to judge the winner of the Carter-Reagan debates on television (Frankel & Frankel, 1987); today, these polls are used extensively by television shows. Their validity, however, is questionable. Researchers know that volunteers differ from non-

volunteers (see Chapter 5) and, therefore, may not represent the population of interest. Schiavone (1984), for example, reported that the ABC program *Nightline* found from a 900-number poll that 67% of more than 186,000 callers wanted the United Nations headquarters out of the United States. A random poll of United States citizens, however, found that 72% wanted the United Nations to remain in the country. Perhaps the real winner of these "pseudosurveys" is the telephone company, which collects a fee for every call made to a 900-number!

Sampling Unit of Analysis.   Survey researchers usually obtain responses from individuals, but individuals are not always the unit of analysis in the survey. Individuals are often asked questions about a larger unit of analysis, such as their family or work unit, and **cross-level inferences** are drawn about this larger unit. The danger in having respondents represent a larger unit of analysis is the chance that these individuals will not portray the larger group accurately.

For example, in some studies of how families communicate about sexuality, college students are asked to describe conversations that occurred in their families. Do you think students' report the same information their parents would provide? If not, an **ecological fallacy** exists, where the data collected from respondents representing one unit of analysis (such as college students) do not describe accurately the larger unit of analysis (such as their families). Researchers may need to gather additional information about the unit of analysis in which they are interested if they are to avoid ecological fallacy errors.

Response Rate.   Regardless of how a sample is obtained and the sampling unit of analysis, survey researchers have to be concerned about the **response rate,** the number of usable responses divided by the total number of people sampled. The response rate is crucial for evaluating survey research, for if there are important differences between those who did and did not respond, the results of the survey may not be valid.

There is no generally accepted minimum response rate. The Office of Management and Budget of the U.S. federal government generally will not fund a survey unless it is likely to yield a response rate in excess of 75% (Fowler, 1993). This is an ideal standard, and probably is possible only if researchers have a lot of available time and resources. Even companies with many resources can't achieve this standard. Richard Morin (1999), Polling Director of the *Washington Post,* noted on a recent television show that the newspaper's (and other pollsters') overall response rate for national random phone samples ranges from about 25–40% and that "40% is very high in our profession." Studies by academic researchers sometimes yield even much lower response rates. Gardner and Gundersen (1995), for example, mailed questionnaires to a random sample of 2600 hotels/motels in the United States to explore the extent to which the hospitality industry employs various information technologies. They received back 240 questionnaires, a very low response rate of 9.2%. They did, however, test for *nonresponse bias* in two ways. First, the data on the ownership structures of both responding and nonresponding units did not differ significantly (i.e., the number of chains and independent hotel/motels). Second, early responses they received did not differ in most respects from later responses; late responders are considered to be similar to nonrespondents, since both appear to be less interested (see J. S. Armstrong & Overton, 1977). These findings led them to argue that, despite the low response rate, the sample was reasonably representative of the hospitality industry, and that the threat of nonresponse rate did not appear to be serious.

Researchers, of course, try very hard to maximize response rates. Bourque and Fielder (1995) suggest a number of ways people can be motivated to respond to a survey. People are more likely to respond if the topic being investigated is important to them or if they believe they are contributing to an important cause. Offering monetary rewards also increases response rates. People also need to be assured that their name and the answers they provide will be kept confidential and reported as **aggregate data** (grouped with responses of many other respondents), especially if they are asked to divulge sensitive information.

Researchers sometimes go to great lengths to get a high response rate. For example, in their recent and quite controversial survey of sex in the United States, Laumann et al. (1994) first randomly selected addresses across the country, and then randomly chose the member of the household to contact. Many people refused to participate at first, but the researchers didn't give up. They kept returning to those homes, making up to 15 visits in some cases. This comes awfully close to making the researchers "stalkers," but it was successful; they ended up getting 79% of the 4,369 in their sample to participate. (We use the word "stalker" loosely; researchers should not in any way be compared, for example, to paparazzi who become stalkarazzi in their attempts to photograph celebrities, and who may have contributed to the death of Princess Diana in Paris by engaging in a high-speed chase with the car in which she was a passenger.)

Despite such valiant efforts, more and more people are refusing to complete surveys. Studies show that about 35% of adults refuse to cooperate with survey researchers (Looney, 1991), which is in sharp contrast to the 90% response rate typical during the 1950s (Weisberg et al., 1996). And fewer than half of United States households are willing to have a meter attached to their television sets, as compared to 68% who said they would cooperate in 1980 (Looney, 1991). Perhaps one reason for this decline in participation is because many telephone salespeople claim they are doing a survey when, in fact, they are selling something. Selling *under* the *guise* of a survey is called **sugging** (Weisberg et al., 1996). Even participation in political polls may be in jeopardy because of certain tactics used. Senator Bob Dole's staff used *push-polling,* "negative polling" in which survey questions were asked in a way that discredited his opponent, Steve Forbes, during the 1996 Republican Presidential Primary in Iowa, and that practice turned many voters off (see J. K. Stewart, 1996a). More and more people use their answering machines to screen calls and may not pick up when they hear a survey researcher on the other end. Perhaps, too, some people are just plain tired of being surveyed!

Cross-Sectional versus Longitudinal Surveys

Some researchers gather information about respondents at one point in time, like a snapshot of a research population. Other surveys are more like a motion picture; they provide data about respondents at several points in time. Surveys that study respondents at one point in time are called **cross-sectional surveys;** those that study respondents at several points in time are called **longitudinal surveys.**

Cross-Sectional Surveys. Cross-sectional surveys that describe the characteristics of a sample at one point in time are relatively easy to do and used most often. They are very effective for describing the status quo. For example, cross-sectional political polls are used to assess respondents' position on a political issue at the time they are asked. A typical cross-sectional political poll might ask respondents the question, "If the election were held today, for whom would you vote?"

When evaluating the results from a cross-sectional survey, it is important to take into account the particular point in time when the survey was conducted. The results of a cross-sectional survey are time-bound in the sense that they may be quite different if conducted at a different point in time, even if the same people were surveyed. People change their mind about who they will vote for, which is why political polls are taken almost daily during an election year, especially as election time draws near. The results of cross-sectional surveys can also be misleading if done at an unrepresentative point in time. Many circumstances, personal as well as environmental, may influence how people respond to a one-time survey. Support for a politician, for example, usually changes radically after it is learned that he or she has engaged in improprieties. The data gathered from a cross-sectional survey apply to that specific point in time but may not capture the enduring or changing characteristics of a research population.

Longitudinal Surveys. Longitudinal surveys help to overcome the limitations of cross-sectional surveys. By gathering data from respondents at several points in time, researchers can assess the enduring beliefs, attitudes, and behaviors of a population, as well as the impact of unusual or unique environmental events on a population. Therefore, longitudinal surveys are much more effective than cross-sectional surveys at capturing the processual nature of communication. Of course, they also take more time to conduct.

Three primary techniques—trend, cohort, and panel studies—are used to conduct longitudinal surveys (for an inventory of longitudinal surveys in the social sciences, see Young, Savola, & Phelps, 1991). A **trend study** measures people's beliefs, attitudes, and/or behaviors at two or more points in time to identify changes or trends. For example, each week, the Centers for Disease Control's National Center for Health Statistics conducts a health survey, interviewing one adult randomly selected from each United States household (see Engelberg, Flora, & Nass, 1995). Changes in people's health behaviors are, thus, monitored over time and long-term trends, referred to as **secular trends,** can be observed.

A second type of longitudinal survey is a **cohort study,** in which responses from specific subgroups of a population, usually divided on the basis of age, are identified and compared over time. Market researchers, for example, might study the consumer preferences of baby-boomers (people born between 1945 and 1960) at various points in time (e.g., during the 1980s and 1990s). Any effects due to membership in this subgroup are called **cohort effects;** the effects due to being a member of the same generation or age group are called **generation effects,** and the effects due to the influence of a particular era or time period are called **period effects.**

The third type of longitudinal survey, and the one used most often by communication researchers, is a **panel study** (also called a **prospective study**), which obtains responses from the same people over time to learn how their beliefs, attitudes, and/or behaviors change. Each session in which responses are obtained from the same individuals is called a *wave*.

Kramer (1995), for example, studied the impact of supervisor communication on transferees during their first year at new locations. Data were collected from new transferees at four times during the year: Time-1 (T1) was prior to or just after the job transfer; T2 was one month after transfer, so that nearly all transferees were still adjusting to their new positions; T3 was 3 months after transfer, to see how transferees varied in their adjustment; and T4 was one year after people had transferred and adjusted to their new positions. These periods represent the loosening (T1), transition (T2 and T3), and tightening (T4) phases in Kramer's (1989) job transfer model. The results showed that transferees' relationships with their supervisor had a significant impact on the feedback and social support messages transferees received and their adjustment to their new role at each of those points in time.

Since panel members cannot be replaced, panel studies are threatened by participant mortality (see Chapter 5), referred to as *panel attrition*. Valkenburg and van der Voort (1995), for example, conducted a one-year panel study to establish relationships between the frequency with which children watch violent and nonviolent dramatic television programs and the kinds of daydreams they have. The study was conducted with students at a sample of 14 primary schools in an urban district in the Netherlands. The researchers surveyed 781 3rd and 5th graders on two occasions. At the second measurement, one year later, 37 children (5% of the sample) were not available because they had moved to other schools or stayed back a grade. This relatively small loss (attrition level) probably didn't affect this study too much.

Compare this to Koolstra and van der Voort's (1996) three-year, longitudinal study of 522 Dutch 2nd graders and 528 4th graders about the effects of television viewing on the frequency with which these children read books and comic books at home. Panel attrition over the course of the study was 21%. Such a substantial loss of respondents can compromise the results of a study, especially if the respondents who drop out are different in relevant ways from those who complete the study. Koolstra and van der Voort did, in fact, investigate whether those who completed their study were different from those who did not. They found no statistically significant differences between the final sample and the participants lost to attrition with regard to reading frequency and a host of other variables (e.g., mental effort and reading concentration). But the children who were lost to attrition did exhibit significantly higher scores for television viewing. A significant difference such as this must obviously be taken into account when explaining the results.

Because of the potential problems due to the loss of respondents, researchers using longitudinal panel designs try to begin with relatively large samples to minimize the panel attrition level. Notice that the two studies cited above began with 781 and 1,050 children, respectively. Researchers also attempt to be diligent in persuading respondents to cooperate over several administrations of the survey instrument.

Finally, researchers can sometimes combine cross-sectional and longitudinal survey designs into an **accelerated longitudinal design** to study individuals over time. Vogt (1999) gives the example of a researcher interested in studying the effects of aging on some variable over the 30 years from age 20 to 50. It would, of course, be too much to expect a researcher to devote 30 years to this study, but it also isn't appropriate to simply conduct a cross-sectional survey of people of different ages. In such a case, the researcher might select respondents who represent different ages (say 20, 25, 30, 35, 40, and 45) and then follow each group for 5 years.

SURVEY MEASUREMENT TECHNIQUES

Questionnaires and interviews are the primary measurement techniques employed by survey researchers. Both are self-report measures (see Chapter 4 about the strengths and weaknesses of self-reports). Here, we first focus on designing questions for survey instruments, and then discuss specific issues related to the use of questionnaires and interviews to gather research data.

Designing Questions for Survey Instruments

The value of survey instruments rests on asking effective questions. Good questions elicit useful answers; poor questions evoke useless information. Researchers consider three things in designing questions for survey instruments: (a) question selection, (b) question phrasing; and (c) question format.

Selecting Questions. Asking the "right" question is always important, as illustrated in the story shared by Crossen (1994): "A young monk was once rebuffed by his superior when he asked if he could smoke while he prayed. Ask a different question, a friend advised. Ask if you can pray while you smoke" (p. 23).

Criteria for good questions in survey research depend on the purpose(s) or objective(s) of the survey. Sometimes the purpose allows researchers to use a set of questions that have been developed and tested previously. Sometimes an earlier set of questions must be adapted, perhaps because the original instrument is too long, a different population is being studied, or the questions must be translated into another language (see Bourque & Fielder, 1995). And sometimes researchers must develop new questions.

Many types of questions can be asked. Figure 8.2 offers two category schemes for the types of questions that appear on survey questionnaires or in interviews. Patton (1980) describes six "generic" types of questions, each of which can be phrased in terms of the past, present, and future—by asking, for example, what respondents did when a certain event occurred in the past, what they do now, and what they expect to do in the future. Schatzman and Strauss (1973) offer a different typology, identifying five categories.

The type of question asked influences the accuracy of people's answers, especially when they call for recall of past events. For example, people tend to think that past events either occurred more recently than they did (called **forward telescoping**) or longer ago than they did (called **backward telescoping**) (Weisberg et al., 1996). Recent and important events, as would be expected, are recalled more easily. To illustrate, Mooney (1962) found that people reported far fewer incidences of illness for the fourth week prior to an interview than for the most recent week. The difference was much lower, however, for important illnesses, those serious enough to restrict activity or require medical attention.

People also tend to report inaccurately incidents that are unpleasant or ego-threatening. Wenar (1963) reported that mothers being interviewed about their children's upbringing usually exaggerate their children's positive traits and underreport their misbehaviors. A. L. Clark and Wallin (1964) interviewed husbands and wives separately about their relationship and found more disagreement about the frequency of sexual intercourse reported by couples who were less satisfied with their sexual relations.

Questions also need to be valid. Some researchers design valid questions by working collaboratively with respondents on what questions to ask. The validity of questions can potentially be enhanced by pretesting them with a relatively small sample from those who will be surveyed. McPhee and Corman (1995) did both in their study of communication networks and practices in a United Methodist church. They first designed a questionnaire in collaboration with several church leaders and conducted group interviews with several adult Sunday school classes to obtain needed information. They then pretested the questionnaire with some church members and revised it before distributing it to 850 adults on the church membership rolls.

Phrasing Questions. The way a question is phrased influences the kind of responses received. Remember from Chapter 4 that two general types of questions can be asked: (a) *closed questions,* which provide respondents with a limited number

---

FIGURE 8.2 Two category schemes for survey questions (A hypothetical study of respondents' reactions to a speech by President Clinton is used to formulate illustrative questions.)

A. Patton (1980)

1. *Experience* and *behavior* questions that elicit what respondents do or have done ("Did you watch President Clinton's speech about treaty X on television last week?")

2. *Opinion* and *value* questions that elicit how respondents think about their behaviors and experiences ("What do you believe was President Clinton's most important argument in that speech?")

3. *Feeling* questions that elicit how respondents react emotionally to their behaviors and experiences ("Did you feel more or less favorable about treaty X after you heard President Clinton's speech?")

4. *Knowledge* questions that elicit what respondents know about their world ("What do you know about the terms of treaty X?")

5. *Sensory* questions that elicit respondents' descriptions of what they see, hear, touch, taste, and smell in the world ("Please describe what you remember about President Clinton when he delivered that speech.")

6. *Background* and *demographic* questions that elicit respondents' descriptions of themselves ("Do you tend to vote for Republican or Democratic candidates?")

B. Schatzman and Strauss (1973)

1. *Reportorial* questions that elicit respondents' knowledge of factors in a social situation, usually preceded by interrogatives, such as who, what, when, where, and how ("Who else in your family watched President Clinton's speech?")

2. *Devil's advocate* questions that elicit what respondents view as controversial ("What issues did President Clinton avoid addressing in the speech?")

3. *Hypothetical* questions that encourage respondents to speculate about alternative occurrences ("How would you have felt about treaty X if Speaker of the House Denny Hastert had made the same speech?")

4. *Posing the ideal* questions that elicit respondents' values ("What else should President Clinton have done to promote Senate approval of treaty X?")

5. *Propositional* questions that elicit or verify respondents' interpretations ("Are you saying that you formed your opinion of treaty X more from newspaper accounts than from President Clinton's speech?")

---

of predetermined responses from which to choose, and (b) *open questions,* which ask respondents to use their own words in answering questions.

Choosing closed or open questions (or both) can influence the results obtained about the topic. Schuman, Ludwig, and Krosnick (1986), for example, in studying what people considered to be the most important problem facing the nation, found that 60% of their respondents chose one of four alternatives presented to them in a closed question, but only 2.4% mentioned any of those four alternatives when asked via an open question.

Whether closed or open, the wording of questions needs to be appropriate for the specific re-

spondents being surveyed. Researchers must take into account respondents' educational levels and cultural backgrounds and pose questions that use language with which they are familiar and, thereby, maximize the chances that the questions will be understood and answered.

Lin (1993), for example, asked 7th and 10th graders to complete a questionnaire about their television-viewing motives, activities, and satisfaction. The questionnaire contained items that had been used in previous research with adults. On the basis of a pilot study she conducted, Lin changed the wording of some items, making them easier for the teen respondent group to comprehend.

Although questions need to be custom-tailored to the particular respondents being surveyed, we offer the following five general guidelines for phrasing effective questions:

1. Good survey questions are straightforward, to the point, and stated clearly. Respondents must understand questions clearly if they are to provide valid and reliable information. Figure 8.3 pokes fun at survey researchers who don't keep questions simple, using language that is easily understood by the intended respondents. J. E. Edwards, Thomas, Rosenfeld, and Booth-Kewley (1997)

FIGURE 8.3

Drawing by Geo. Price; © 1989 The New Yorker Magazine, Inc.
Used by permission of the Cartoon Bank.

"Next question: I believe that life is a constant striving for balance, requiring frequent tradeoffs between morality and necessity, within a cyclic pattern of joy and sadness, forging a trail of bittersweet memories until one slips, inevitably, into the jaws of death. Agree or disagree?"

---

advise those writing survey questions to heed the KISS strategy—Keep it simple, stupid!

One way to keep wording simple, or at least appropriate for the intended audience, is by conducting a **readability analysis** to measure how easy or difficult it is to read a particular passage. This analysis tells the educational grade level needed to comprehend the passage based on such things as word and sentence length. Most word-processing programs now come with this feature built in to the tool used to check grammar. For example, when we analyzed the readability of the previous three sentences in this paragraph, the analysis revealed 23.3 words per sentence and 5.0 characters per word, resulting in a Flesch-Kincaid grade level of 13.1, an appropriate level of readability for our audience of college students. (By adding that last sentence, we just raised the grade level to 15.8!)

2. Good survey questions should ask about one and only one issue. **Double-barreled questions** that ask about several issues at once should be avoided. For example, say a person is asked how much he or she "agrees" (on a 5-point Likert scale) with the statement, "I am uncomfortable giving a public speech, having an interpersonal conversation, or interacting in small groups." The answer will be confusing and difficult to interpret, especially if the person answers "disagrees," because we don't know whether it applies to public speaking, interpersonal conversations, small group interactions, two of these, or all three.

The responses to closed questions should also be limited to a single referent. One wouldn't want to have people report their feelings about public speaking on a five-point scale ranging from "comfortable and rewarding" to "uncomfortable and nonrewarding." Instead, two separate responses should be offered, one about the degree of comfort and one about how rewarding it is.

3. Good survey questions are not **loaded questions**—they don't lead people to respond in certain ways. For example, a question that begins "Don't you think that…" leads respondents to agree with the opinion that follows. Loftus (1979) reports several studies that indicate that eyewitness accounts in interviews vary depending on how questions about an event are worded. Even apparently insignificant words make a difference. For example, Loftus showed people a film depicting a multiple-car accident and then asked them questions about what occurred. The questions posed to half the people began "Did you see a...," as in "Did you see a broken headlight?" The other half were asked, "Did you see the...," as in "Did you see the broken headlight?" Witnesses asked *the* questions were more likely to report having seen that object than witnesses asked *a* questions, regardless of whether the object had actually appeared in the film.

4. Good survey questions avoid using emotionally charged, inflammatory terms that can bias people's responses. For example, researchers inquiring about people's attitudes toward abortion should avoid asking them to agree or disagree with a statement such as "Fetuses should be murdered." The term "murdered" is inflammatory.

5. Good questions avoid using double negatives (e.g., "one should not never..."). Consider, for example, the controversy raised about whether people believe the Holocaust occurred or not. Alarmingly, a 1992 Roper Poll found that 22% of United States citizens said it was possible the Holocaust never happened and 12% percent said they didn't know. These results, however, probably were due to the confusing way in which the question was worded; specifically, as a double negative: "Does it seem possible or does it seem impossible to you that the Nazi extermination of the Jews never happened?" A revised 1994 Roper Poll asked the question this way: "Does it seem possible to you that the Nazi extermination of the Jews never happened, or do you feel certain that it happened?" This time, 91% of those surveyed said they were certain it happened, 8% did not know, and only 1% expressed any doubt that the Holocaust had occurred (see "Few Americans Doubt Holocaust," 1994; Ladd, 1994).

These are merely some things researchers keep in mind when phrasing survey questions. Fig-ure 8.4 offers some additional suggestions that survey researchers try to follow in phrasing effective questions.

Question Format. Questionnaires and interviews are *structured* in a variety of ways, depending on the type and arrangement of questions used. Remember from Chapter 4 that the sequence of queries is called the *question format* and that three common types of question format are the tunnel, funnel, and inverted funnel formats. The *tunnel format* asks a series of similarly organized questions; the *funnel format* begins with broad, open questions followed by narrower, closed questions; and the *inverted funnel format* begins with narrow, closed questions and builds to broader, open questions.

In addition to these general formats, there are many specific guidelines for structuring the format of survey questions. Figure 8.5 offers some important guidelines that J. H. Frey (1983) suggests.

Questionnaire Survey Research

Questionnaires are commonly used in survey research to gather information from large samples. Most are self-administered in that respondents complete the instrument themselves with little or no help from researchers.

Types of Self-Administered Questionnaires. There are two types of self-administered questionnaires: those completed by respondents in the presence of the researcher and those completed outside the researcher's presence.

Sometimes one individual at a time completes a questionnaire in the presence of a researcher. But more commonly, researchers administer questionnaires to a group of people, just as teachers administer exams to all students in their class at the same time. (By the way, written exams may be viewed as examples of questionnaires used in evaluation research; students' performance on them is one gauge of a course's effectiveness.) Group administration of questionnaires is obviously more efficient than individual administration because a large number of respondents can be surveyed in a

FIGURE 8.4 Suggestions for wording survey questions

The following is a synthesis of some suggestions for wording survey questions based on work by Bourque and Fielder (1995), A. Fink (1995a, 1995b), A. Fink and Kosecoff (1985, 1998), Fowler (1993), J. H. Frey (1983, 1989), J. H. Frey and Oishi (1995), Miller (1991), and Patten (1998).

1. Use complete sentences.
2. Use correct grammar and sentence structure.
3. Write questions in a natural, conversational tone, similar to the way people talk.
4. Ask short questions and keep the wording simple; avoid lengthy and overly complex questions.
5. Ask questions to which you need to know the answers; avoid asking questions that are not relevant to the goals of the survey.
6. Avoid slang, jargon, abbreviations, acronyms, vague qualifiers, colloquial expressions, and technical terms (unless you are very sure respondents understand them).
7. Underline, italicize, or bold important terms so people pay attention to them (e.g., How many speeches *in front of an audience of more than 20* did you give last month?). However, don't highlight too many terms as that may distract respondents.
8. Ask sparingly about demographic items, asking only those that are related to the topic being asked, and placing them at the end of a survey. Use standard demographic categories whenever possible. Think carefully, however, about how to phrase questions about race or ethnicity.
9. Avoid all-inclusive terms, such as "always" or "never" (e.g., don't ask, "To what extent do you always feel comfortable giving a public speech?").
10. Avoid phrasing questions in negative terms (e.g., "To what extent are you not comfortable giving a public speech?"), as respondents may read over the negative term.
11. Ask about a specific/precise/limited time period (e.g., "How many public speeches have you given in the past 30 days?").
12. Be specific/precise about the context to which you are referring or the information you are requesting (e.g., "How many speeches in front of an audience of more than 20 have you given in the past 30 days?").
13. Make sure any facts mentioned in a question are correct.
14. Don't assume respondents have particular knowledge.
15. Make sure response categories to closed questions match the dimensions of the question (e.g., "To

what extent are you comfortable giving a public speech? A lot, much, some, a little, or not at all." "Agree-disagree" response categories would make no sense here.).
16. Response categories to closed questions should be mutually exclusive; respondents should be able to indicate only one answer (e.g., don't ask: "Are you a parent or a step-parent?" Someone can be both.).
17. Response categories to closed questions should be exhaustive, covering all the possible anticipated answers. Include an "other" category (and ask people to specify the answer), but the use of this category should be relatively rare. If it is not, it suggests that another category or categories should be provided as an option.
18. List response categories to closed questions in ascending or descending order (e.g., "a lot, much, some, a little, not at all"; not "a lot, not at all, some, much, a little").
19. Typically include a "don't know" or neutral middle category to closed questions (e.g., "neither agree nor disagree" or "don't know" as the middle category on a 5-point Likert scale). However, the number of "don't know" responses should be kept to a minimum; too many probably indicates a bad question. The middle category can also sometimes be removed if everyone probably has an opinion about a well-known topic.
20. Use items that require ranking sparingly. It typically is better to have items rated (e.g., on a 5-point scale) than ranked (see Chapter 4).
21. Use open-ended questions sparingly, as too many may prove too time-consuming for respondents to complete.
22. When asking open-ended questions, let respondents give positive feelings about a referent first and then negative feelings (e.g., "What do you like best about public speaking?" followed by "What do you like least about public speaking?").
23. Phrase questions about personal matters in ways respondents can comfortably respond (e.g., "How much money do you make?" is not answered as readily as giving respondents categories from which to choose, such as "below $10,000," "$10,001–20,000," etc.).
24. Avoid phrasing questions in ways that may embarrass respondents or deflate their ego (e.g., Ask "What is the highest school level you completed?" rather than "Did you graduate from college?").

FIGURE 8.5   Suggestions for arranging the format of survey questions

1. Treat all questions as part of a whole, not isolated or disjointed.
2. Order questions using a logic that makes sense to respondents. Questions should be grouped according to topic; each question is then perceived by respondents to be in a meaningful context.
3. Error is reduced if the questions "flow" easily from one to another.
4. Use transitional sentences freely.
5. Avoid questions that duplicate earlier items or appear redundant.
6. Avoid breaking a question between pages of a questionnaire.
7. Place easy-to-answer items, such as demographic items, at the end to avoid inadequate responses due to respondent fatigue.
8. Place sensitive questions in the middle, after the respondent is comfortable and before fatigue begins to take effect.
9. Response effects, such as fatigue, can begin to affect responses after six or more items of similar interest or form. Thus, it is a good idea to vary response patterns and group topics as often as is practical.

Source: Adapted from James H. Frey, *Survey research by telephone,* pp. 115–116, copyright © 1983 by Sage Publications. Adapted by Permission of Sage Publications.

---

short amount of time. However, group administration can affect the data if respondents' verbal and nonverbal comments influence others' responses.

There are three types of paper-and-pencil, self-administered questionnaires: traditional paper, generic scannable, and customized scannable (see J. E. Edwards et al., 1997). The traditional paper questionnaire is the most common form, but scannable questionnaires, which ask respondents to mark their answers on a special form that is scanned by a computer (see Booth-Kewley, Rosenfeld, & Edwards, 1993), are becoming very popular. A generic scannable questionnaire provides a question sheet and a separate answer sheet, which

is then scanned, while a customized scannable questionnaire provides the questions and answers on the same scannable sheet. While scannable questionnaires may be easier to process than traditional paper questionnaires, one drawback is that scannable questionnaires must rely only on closed questions and limit the number of categories from which respondents can choose.

Mail Surveys.   Using the postal service to distribute questionnaires is a relatively efficient and inexpensive way to reach representatives of large, geographically dispersed populations. Researchers do not have to travel to these people, nor ask them to gather in one place. Mailed questionnaires also afford respondents more privacy and anonymity than questionnaires completed in the presence of a researcher.

But mailed questionnaires must be self-sufficient and "user-friendly." When questionnaires are completed in the presence of a researcher, he or she can give verbal instructions and answer any questions, which helps minimize errors in filling out the questionnaire. Mailed questionnaires, in contrast, must come with clearly written instructions for filling out the instrument correctly. Mail questionnaires, therefore, must be worded in simple and straightforward ways, and be easy to fill out.

The use of mailed questionnaires, in comparison to other methods, potentially jeopardizes the response rate. Mailed questionnaires generally result in a lower response rate than questionnaires completed when a survey researcher is present, for example, because respondents do not feel as obligated to complete them. Indeed, Bourque and Fielder (1995) claim that researchers can expect no better than a 20% response rate when using a single mailing with no incentives to a sample of the general community. Some simply can't read the material sent; the adult rate of illiteracy in the United States is 20% (Bourque & Fielder, 1995). Weisberg et al. (1996) also note that many people are upset about what they call **frugging,** *f*und-*r*aising attempts *u*nder the *g*uise of a survey, and may throw all questionnaires they receive in the trash. Even when questionnaires are returned, the researcher can't be completely sure that they were actually completed by the intended person.

Researchers who mail questionnaires use several strategies to increase response rate. Prenotification of a questionnaire prior to its arrival can increase response rate by as much as 47.4% (R. J. Fox, Crask, & Kim, 1988). It helps to describe the purpose, sponsorship, and importance of the survey research in a cover letter that accompanies the questionnaire, and to promise respondents a summary of the results. Sponsorship of a survey by a university has also been found to increase returns (R. J. Fox et al., 1988; Houston & Nevin, 1977; W. H. Jones & Lang, 1980; W. H. Jones & Linda, 1978; R. A. Peterson, 1975). Some researchers even provide rewards to respondents who complete a questionnaire, such as money, discounts, or presents.

Most mail surveys also provide respondents with an addressed, postage-paid, return envelope to encourage responses. Armstrong and Lusk's (1987) meta-analysis of the literature found that first-class return postage yielded an additional 9% return over business-reply rates. They also found that using commemorative rather than standard stamps increased responses. Even the color of questionnaires has been found to affect response rates, with green questionnaires producing a higher response rate than white ones (R. J. Fox et al., 1988).

Some researchers also attempt to increase response rate by sending people who haven't responded within a few weeks a follow-up mailing that reminds them to complete and return the questionnaire. A follow-up mailing usually includes another questionnaire, as well as a stamped reply envelope. Another follow-up strategy is to telephone reluctant respondents and remind them to return the questionnaire, hoping that personal contact will increase the likelihood of compliance.

Even if researchers encourage many more people to respond to mailed questionnaires, increasing response rate doesn't necessarily result in a more representative sample. Berry and Kanouse (1987) argue that "some methods of boosting re-

sponse rate may do so at the expense of introducing further bias. Because incentive payments may appeal more to some types of respondents than others, they certainly have this potential" (p. 112).

Interview Survey Research

Structured interviews are the other major tool of survey research. Interviews enable survey researchers to question respondents personally about research topics. This personal contact has potential benefits but also potential problems.

Because interviews are interactive, the **interviewer,** the person conducting the interview, and the **interviewee,** the person being interviewed, engage in interpersonal communication and react to one another. The degree to which the interviewer establishes rapport with interviewees influences somewhat how much and what kind of information interviewees offer in response to questions.

The interview process can subtly bias responses. The way respondents view the interviewer may affect what they say, producing the researcher personal attribute effect we talked about in Chapter 5. For example, Hyman (1954) reported on a study of 1000 Black respondents conducted in 1942 by the National Opinion Research Center in Memphis. Researchers compared the information elicited by White and Black interviewers when interviewing Black respondents. Hyman said:

> On almost all the opinion and attitude questionnaires, the white interviewers obtained significantly higher proportions of what might be called by some people "proper" or "acceptable" answers. Negroes were more reluctant to express to the white interviewers their resentments over discrimination by employers or labor unions, in the army, and in public places. (p. 159)

Researchers, therefore, frequently assure that interviewers are similar in crucial ways to the interviewees. W. Douglas (1987), for example, studied how people on dates assess how attractive they are to the other person. Fifty college students were interviewed and asked to "describe, as completely as you can, all the things you do to find out how much somebody of the opposite sex likes you." To ensure frank responses, Douglas reported, "The interviewers met only with subjects of the same sex as themselves. This precaution was taken to maximize subjects' willingness to disclose" (p. 6).

Researchers are also aided in developing rapport if their own experiences are similar to those of their interview respondents. For example, B. S. Lee (1988), who interviewed Holocaust survivors, was once herself a concentration camp inmate. As she put it, "Being a survivor myself facilitated my empathy and the sensitivity to know when not to probe or be too intrusive" (p. 75).

Another limitation of survey interviews is interviewers' ability to record answers accurately while engaging in conversation with respondents. Respondents write their own answers on questionnaires, but when data are collected orally, the interviewer must record interviewees' responses without omitting anything important. Audiotaping or videotaping interviews creates an electronic record of those responses, but the presence of these devices can influence responses of people who become self-conscious about being recorded (the Hawthorne effect).

Training Interviewers.   K. A. Smith (1988) points out that back in the 1930s, most survey interviews lasted only about 10 minutes. Today, surveys take considerably more time to complete and the questions often are more complex. Survey interviews, thus, must be conducted by competent and responsible interviewers, since the quality of the data gathered in the interview is largely dependent on the skills of interviewers. Lofland (1971) notes:

> *Successful interviewing is not unlike carrying on unthreatening self-controlled, supportive, polite, and cordial interaction in everyday life. If one can do that, one already has the main interpersonal skills necessary to interviewing. It is my personal impression, however, that interactants who practice these skills (even if they possess them) are not overly numerous in our society. (p. 90)*

Unskilled interviewers can destroy the validity of a well-designed interview. Weisberg et al. (1996) report a study that found that

> *interviewers performed unwanted behaviors in more than half the questions asked, including asking more than a third of the questions not exactly as written. The specific problems included reading errors, speech variations, improper probes, and unprogrammed feedback to the respondent. (p. 118)*

Ineffective interviewers not only compromise the effectiveness of the specific research project, but can also impugn the reputation of the research organization that sponsors the survey.

Many researchers, therefore, train interviewers beforehand, helping them to become familiar and comfortable with the interview procedure by practicing it in a supervised setting before they use it in the actual study. A discussion of how to train interviewers also appears in Chapter 5. Somers, Mannheimer, Kelman, and Mellinger (1982), for example, studied changes in college students' values and lifestyles between their freshman and senior years. The interviewers they hired were required to participate in "all-day group discussions in which a large proportion of the time was spent on 'mock' interviewing and review and criticism of practice interviews with friends and randomly selected strangers outside the training session" (p. 150).

M. H. Brown (1985) employed three assistants to help her interview employees in a nursing home to see how the use of stories relates to the socialization of members in an organization. To be sure that she and the assistants conducted equivalent interviews, she trained them before the actual study began. She then assessed the effectiveness of her training program by asking five graduate students to rate samples of the assistants' interviews taped during training on "content, style, and strategy" (p. 29). Her training program was effective— the judges all found the taped interviews to be very similar. In fact, four of the five judges thought all the interviews were conducted by the same person.

Although all interviews demand skilled interviewers, different types of interviewing demand different interviewing skills. Remember from Chapter 4 that *directive interviews* use more closed questions and demand only that interviewers read questions to respondents clearly and accurately and record their answers. *Nondirective interviews,* in contrast, use more open questions and, thus, demand added sensitivity, flexibility, and communication skills on the part of interviewers. In nondirective interviews, interviewers must phrase questions appropriately for the specific individual being interviewed, know when to let the respondent speak and when to direct him or her, as well as when and how to probe for more information. These are all skills that interviewers must be trained to perform.

Initially, all interviewers should be educated about the goals and methods of the survey so that they can answer respondents' questions accurately. Interviewers should become familiar and comfortable with the interview schedule and be given opportunities to practice administering the interview in a supervised setting before they actually conduct the interview with respondents. Training programs also help interviewers to develop strategies for establishing rapport with interviewees, which potentially helps encourage fuller answers when those are desired. Billiet and Loosveldt (1988) report that training programs optimally should teach interviewers "to convey to the respondents what is expected of them by means of instructions, to probe, and to give adequate positive and negative feedback" (p. 205). Effective training programs for interviewers help identify and rectify potential problems before they compromise the validity of the interviews. Interviewer training programs, thus, minimize damage that could be caused by unskilled interviewers and increase the likelihood that the interviews will accomplish the goals of the survey.

Some variation, however, among interviewers' personal traits and communication ability is inevitable. Researchers sometimes turn this potential problem into an advantage by having interviewers work in teams. K. Miller, Scott, Stage, and Birkholt (1995), for example, in their study of coordination and communication in agencies that provide services to the urban homeless, put to-

gether a four-person research team to conduct face-to-face, on-site interviews with directors of such agencies. Each interview was conducted by two interviewers. As K. Miller et al. explain:

> *This allowed one interviewer to concentrate on asking questions and eliciting follow-up responses while the other interviewer could take notes and engage in careful observation of the institutional environment. It was hoped that our use of interview teams would enhance the quality of our observations and our ability to interpret interview results. (pp. 687–688).*

Face-to-Face versus Telephone Interviews.   Interviews can be administered in person ("face-to-face"), as well as over the telephone. There are many similarities between face-to-face and telephone interviews, but each has distinct advantages and disadvantages. In face-to-face interviews, interviewers have more cues available for identifying when interviewees do not understand questions, are unsure about their answers, or even when they appear to provide misleading answers. Such immediately available nonverbal feedback is instrumental in helping interviewers to decide when to restate questions or to probe. Interviewers can also make note of some demographic characteristics revealed by respondents' appearance (such as their race, age, and socioeconomic status) and need not ask about these directly.

Portable computers also make it possible to record face-to-face interviews with people in their homes. In **computer-assisted personal interviewing (CAPI),** "the question text appears on the screen, with possible response categories or indication of what sort of answer is required. The interviewer reads out the question and enters the response and the next question appears automatically" (J. Martin & Manners, 1995, p. 52). Varied question sequences also can be programmed, so people are asked questions that appropriately follow-up earlier answers.

Face-to-face interviews also pose several limitations for survey researchers. It takes more time to gather data via face-to-face interviews. If interviewers have to travel long distances to reach interviewees, the time and expense of conducting interviews increase even more. Face-to-face interviews also decrease the privacy and anonymity of interviewees and, thus, make it more difficult to gather valid data about personal, risky, or embarrassing topics.

Telephone-administered interviews overcome some of the time, expense, and reactivity problems of face-to-face interviews. Bourque and Fielder (1995) claim that, given the same length, questionnaires cost about half as much as telephone interviews, but telephone interviews cost about 25% less than personal interviews. The telephone also reaches interviewees over long distances and can increase respondents' privacy and anonymity, especially if they know they were selected through a random-digit dialing procedure. **Computer-assisted telephone interviews (CATI)** further increase interviewing efficiency by selecting and calling respondents automatically, cuing interviewers to the questions to be asked, and providing a simple mechanism for recording, coding, and processing responses (see Saris, 1991). J. D. Johnson and Meischke (1993) and J. D. Johnson, Meischke, Grau, and Johnson (1992) used CATI to conduct interviews with women in their research on cancer-related information seeking and media channel selection. To ensure consistency and quality, their phone interviewers received six hours of training by project staff.

Using the telephone to conduct interviews is convenient, but the amount of nonverbal information available to the interviewer is limited to paralinguistic cues, which may make it more difficult to assess the honesty of respondents' answers. In addition, the telephone obviously limits an interviewer's ability to identify respondents' demographic characteristics. Answering some closed questions over the telephone can also be difficult, especially when using scales with seven points or more. In face-to-face interviewing, respondents can be given cards with the response alternatives on them, but in telephone interviewing, they must remember the responses available to them. To compensate for this problem, Weisberg et al. (1996) suggest using a *branching format,* asking respondents first, for ex-

ample, whether they agree or disagree, and then asking a follow-up question about the strength of their agreement or disagreement (e.g., whether they strongly agree, moderately agree, or only slightly agree) (see also Aldrich, Niemi, Rabinowitz, & Rhode, 1982). Krosnick and Berent (1993) found a branching format to be more reliable than providing respondents with all the options at once.

Finally, two new computer-assisted telephone interviewing techniques don't require a human interviewer at all. **Touchtone data entry (TDE)** and **voice recognition entry (VRE)** are both systems in which a "computer reads questions from a record and the respondent has to answer by use of the telephone" (Saris, 1991, p. 30). They record respondents' numerical answers either by having respondents use a touch-tone phone and punch in the number (TDE) or by allowing respondents to speak directly into the telephone so that the computer then recognizes the numeric answers (VRE) (see Clayton & Harrel, 1989; Winter & Clayton, 1990).

Individual versus Group Interviews.   Survey researchers usually interview respondents individually, unless, of course, their research purpose calls for respondents to be interviewed as a couple or group, such as in studies of marital or family communication. In some situations, researchers use **focus group interviews,** in which a facilitator leads a small group of people (usually five to seven members) in a relatively open discussion about a specific product or program (see Greenbaum, 1997; Herndon, 1993; Kreps, 1995; Krueger, 1994; D. L. Morgan, 1993, 1997; D. L. Morgan & Krueger, 1997; D. W. Stewart & Shamdasani, 1990). The facilitator introduces topics, encourages participation, and probes for information in a flexible, interactive way to elicit people's genuine views. Focus groups also encourage people to "piggyback" on others' ideas, which sometimes makes it easier for reluctant communicators to participate. Kreps (1995) describes the advantages of using focus groups:

Focus group discussions help stimulate the disclosure of information by encouraging a chaining-out of shared perceptions.... The technique produces a wealth of information because outspoken respondents often encourage the more timid respondents to share information. By observing group members' verbal and nonverbal behaviors, the group facilitator can encourage maximum participation, information sharing, and creativity, thus obtaining more relevant information in less time from one focus group discussion than would be possible by conducting personal interviews with each member of the group. (pp. 177–178)

Focus group interviews are becoming increasingly popular for gathering data in communication survey research (see Lunt & Livingstone, 1996). B. H. Ellis and Miller (1993), for example, used them to gather information from nurses about their burnout and commitment. Ferraris, Carveth, and Parrish-Sprowl (1993) examined the processes of organizational identification by conducting focus groups at a worksite when the organization was undergoing a major operational transition. And to understand the communication perspectives of freshmen as they adjust to their role as university students during their first academic term, G. M. Johnson, Staton, and Jorgensen-Earp (1995) held 45-minute focus group sessions with 19 freshmen once a week for 8 weeks of a 10-week term.

Focus groups are also proving helpful for developing survey questionnaires (see D. L. Morgan, 1993). Johnston (1995), for example, was interested in identifying the reasons adolescents watch graphic horror films, such as the "slasher movies" *Halloween* and *Nightmare on Elm Street*. She first conducted a focus group with 12 high school freshmen and sophomores to elicit their views and opinions about slasher movies (e.g., "What characteristics make a good slasher movie?" and "What feelings best describe your mood after watching a slasher movie?"). The 2-hour discussion was videotaped and then transcribed, and their comments were content analyzed (see Chapter 9). This analysis was then used to generate items for a questionnaire that was administered to 220 freshmen and sophomores at that high school.

Focus groups can also help generate information that can be used to design persuasive messages for communication campaigns. Kreps (1995), for example, gathered information from focus groups about the relevant public's perceptions and attitudes toward an urban substance abuse center to identify strategies for increasing public acceptance, support, and utilization of its programs. On the basis of focus groups conducted with teenage tobacco users about smoking and chewing tobacco, Bormann, Bormann, and Harty (1995) offered recommendations about communication strategies likely to be persuasive in an upcoming media campaign to promote a tobacco-free lifestyle being planned by the Center for Nonsmoking and Health of the Minnesota Department of Health. Cragan and Shields (1995) used focus groups to develop a plaintiff attorney's opening and closing statements in preparing a high-profile personal injury case for trial. And A. A. Marshall, Smith, and McKeon (1995) conducted focus group interviews with women enrolled in a breast and cervical cancer screening program and with non-enrollees to determine differences in preferences for sources, messages, and channels used to disseminate persuasive messages about the program.

Beginning the Interview.   How interviews are begun often determines whether, and then how fully, respondents cooperate. Cannell and Kahn (1968) suggest that interviewers begin by identifying themselves, the research agency they represent, the general research topic, how the person was selected to be interviewed, and the amount of time the interview will take. Figure 8.6 is an example of an introduction an interviewer might use when beginning a telephone survey of public reactions to a televised presidential debate.

In-depth interviews may require a great deal of time and disclosure from respondents. In such cases, J. D. Douglas (1985) recommends that researchers make an effort to convince respondents of the importance of the research project and their contribution to it. He believes that research interviewers

FIGURE 8.6 A telephone survey introduction

"Hello. My name is Gary Kreps, and I'm from the National Cancer Institute's Communication and Informatics Research Branch. We are doing a survey about public reactions to last night's television commercial about recommended nutritional guidelines. The study is being conducted across the United States, and the results will be used to increase our understanding of the influence of the media on public health behaviors. Your phone number was chosen at random by a computer from all possible numbers within this area code. The interview will take only about 15 minutes to complete. All information you provide will be kept strictly confidential. May I conduct the survey with you?"

should be "supplicants" and "sell" themselves. Douglas says, in effect, to potential respondents:

The world is a serious place where only people who are directly involved in it can know completely what it's like. You are that expert and I meekly beseech your help in gaining a more complete—never complete—understanding of it. (p. 60)

Planning the Interview Questions.   Cannell and Kahn (1968) provide an overview of interview planning. They recommend conducting the entire interview so as to

make the total experience as meaningful as possible, to give it a beginning, a middle, and an end. More specifically, the early questions should serve to engage the respondent's interest without threatening or taxing him [or her] before he [or she] is really committed to the transaction, and to exemplify and teach him [or her] the kind of task the interview represents. The most demanding of questions might well be placed later in the interview, when respondent commitment can be presumed to have peaked—and fatigue has not yet set in. Sometimes the riskiest of questions may be put very late in the interview, so that if they trigger a refusal to continue, relatively little information is lost. This procedure seems prudent, but it risks also the possibility of an unpleasant leavetaking. (p. 571)

Interviewers usually prepare the major questions they will ask long before they meet the respondents. Miall (1986), for example, studied the social experiences of women who were infertile. She reports that the questions used in her interview "were based on previous research on infertility, over one-and-a-half years of participant observation in an infertility self-help group, discussions with infertile individuals in the community, and popular anecdotal literature on infertility" (p. 271).

A preliminary set of questions is devised and often pretested in some trial interviews. This step is especially important when respondents' verbal abilities differ from the investigator's. D. Hart and Damon (1986), for example, studied how children's "self understanding" develops by interviewing children of several different ages. They first prepared a large number of possible questions that were "pilot-tested extensively, and only the questions that were comprehensible at all age ranges and that were consistently successful in eliciting responses relevant to self-understanding were retained for the study" (p. 393).

The list of questions that guide the interview (as discussed in Chapter 4) is referred to as the *interview schedule* or *protocol*. Structured interviews require the interviewer to follow a preset list of questions the same way each time, *semi-structured interviews* require the interviewer to ask the specific primary questions but then allow for probing secondary questions, and *unstructured interviews* provide interviewers with a set of questions but allow them maximum freedom to decide what questions to ask and how to phrase them. The type of interview schedule employed ultimately depends on the purpose of the research.

Responding to Answers.   Interviews are influenced as much by how researchers respond to the answers they receive as by how initial questions are posed. Whyte (1984) provides this advice:

Like the therapist, the research interviewer listens more than he [or she] talks, and listens with a sympathetic and lively interest. We find it helpful occasionally to rephrase and reflect back to informants what they seem to be expressing and to summarize the remarks as a check on understanding.

The interviewer avoids giving advice and passing moral judgments. We accept statements that violate our own ethical, political, or other standards without showing disapproval in any way. (p. 98)

Such neutrality is not easy to maintain. Interviewers' attitudes may leak through without their awareness. Zaleski (1987) makes this point in analyzing accounts of near-death experiences. She was surprised to find very few negative reports in her review of the literature and suspected that this omission may be due somewhat to interviewers' behavior. She pointed out that even

the most noncommittal line of questioning still falls short of providing sterile laboratory conditions; the mere presence of the interviewer contaminates the data.... The interviewer can unwittingly steer the conversation by subliminal signals more subtle than direct speech or overt body language. Our social experience is a web of such mutual influencing, much of it below the threshold of conscious communication. (p. 149)

To obtain accurate and complete information, interviewers probe for more information when responses at first are too brief or too general. For example, in Wenner's (1983) study, people were interviewed regarding why they watch, or why they avoid watching, presidential campaign coverage on network news programs. Interviewers were instructed "to probe beyond the 'easy answer,' a type of superficial response which is often categorized as 'surveillance' (i.e., 'to find out what is going on in the world,' or 'to keep up with things')" (p. 383). By using probes, Wenner was able to identify 17 distinct categories of responses to his research question.

Probes are often planned in advance, but sometimes they are improvised by interviewers on the spot. Douglas (1985) advocates a strategy of "research opportunism." He suggests being prepared to make

creative adaptations of the plans at all levels and all times, depending on the situations that emerge

and especially on the particular quirks of the always perverse and intriguing human animal you are confronted with...always ready to pounce on any phenomenon that shines with the promise of a new truth-discovery. (p. 69)

USING MULTIPLE METHODS IN SURVEY RESEARCH

We separated questionnaires from interviews and compared them to explain survey research, but questionnaires and interviews often are used together in the same research study. Sometimes interviews are conducted first, and those findings are used to construct a survey questionnaire. Cornett-DeVito and Friedman (1995) did this when they analyzed how managerial communication differed in more and less successful mergers. They first asked managers from eight recently acquired financial institutions to assess the success of the merger, and chose the two rated the highest and the two rated the lowest. They then conducted 30 intensive interviews with respondents from these four institutions about the managers' communication activities during the merger. These communication activities were incorporated into a questionnaire that was then distributed to personnel at several additional sites. The questionnaire data allowed them to quantify and test the inferences they had made from the interviews.

Sometimes researchers conduct interviews *after* asking people to complete a questionnaire. This usually is done when researchers want to learn more from respondents about their questionnaire answers. Theus (1993), for example, was interested in how the openness of newspaper organizations' communication structure is related to discrepancies between the organization and its reporters regarding how they frame and communicate about important issues. In phase 1 of the research, she collected data through mail questionnaires from 155 newspaper executives. In phase 2, she conducted eight pairs of in-depth interviews with organizational spokespersons and reporters, chosen on the basis of what she learned from the questionnaires regarding the level of manager/reporter discrepancy about issues. She used open questions in her interviews to assess the impact of organizational structure on decisions related to those discrepancies.

Survey research also may help to verify findings that have been obtained using other methodologies. J. R. Barker (1993), for example, conducted naturalistic (ethnographic) research (see Chapter 10) for two and a half years, observing and interviewing members of a small manufacturing company as it changed to a self-managing teamwork structure. During that time, Phillip Tompkins, another communication researcher, played a "nonparticipating consultant" role, and helped to analyze the data. He and Barker wanted to study the effect of the change on employees' identification with their teams and the larger organization that created the teams, so they surveyed them using the Organizational Identification Questionnaire developed by Cheney (1982). Their interpretation of the data from that survey draws on some relevant findings from their naturalistic study (see J. R. Barker & Tompkins, 1994).

Finally, researchers, especially those who conduct longitudinal research, sometimes design a study to include both survey and other methods, either at the same time or in different phases of the research project. McMillan and Northern (1995), for example, investigated how communication can create dysfunctional relationships and codependency in organizations. They collected data in three phases over a period of five years in seven different types of organizations. In the initial phase, individual interviews were conducted with 24 employees at one of the organizations. Employees were asked open questions that probed for the presence or absence of codependent behaviors as described in the literature (e.g., excessive helping). On the basis of the responses, expert coders classified the respondents as either "codependent" or "noncodependent." These employees also completed a 70-item, self-assessment questionnaire about codependent behaviors to determine significant differences between the responses of codependents and noncodependents. In the second phase, the researchers conducted 41 interviews in four additional organizations to include more var-

ied organizations and technologies and to probe the significant codependent characteristics revealed from the questionnaire results. During the last three years of the project, both researchers engaged in naturalistic (ethnographic) research in their respective organizations—observing day-to-day work, attending organizational and departmental meetings, and talking with managers and nonmanagers. Throughout their naturalistic work, they collected and analyzed rhetorical artifacts, including organizational documents, annual reports, newsletters, and speeches (see Chapter 9). Their research, thus, combined survey methods (including both interviews and questionnaires), naturalistic inquiry, and textual analysis.

CONCLUSION

What we learn from the survey method may be likened to what we see from the window of an airplane—an overview of a vast territory. From a plane we can see patterns of land use that may not be discernible to someone standing in just one of the many fields or city streets below us. But we must be careful that we record and analyze accurately the terrain we are observing, that we don't mistake cows for cars, that clouds don't obstruct our view, and that we don't assume our generalizations apply to every individual plot of land below us or to other areas that we can't see.

Likewise, with a survey, we get an overview of human behavior—we collect a little information from a lot of people and then analyze the data to identify some patterns among them and others like them. But finding *commonalities* among people, whom we know also *vary* in so many ways, isn't easy. Getting a clear view and making accurate statements about a population, especially one that is large, dispersed, and heterogeneous, can be very challenging, as we've tried to show in this chapter.

Much work has been and is being done to refine survey methodology, as is evident, for example, when pollsters can predict election outcomes within a percentage point of the final results. Consequently, many companies now rely on survey results to make decisions that will influence our lives. As Looney (1991) claims, "Surveys determine what type of car we will drive, the kinds of food we will eat, the pain-killers we take, the deodorants, toothpaste, soap, and perfume we use" (Sect. 5, p. 1).

Despite the best efforts of survey researchers, however, most new products put out on the market don't sell, and many politicians don't win election even when they advocate what polls show that the public wants. So we must be wary of survey findings obtained on the basis of flawed research designs or methods that reveal only a part of the landscape.

Using surveys to measure the subtle, ephemeral processes of human communication taxes their strengths even more—it's worse than trying to capture a swarm of bees in a nest. But many scholars are employing new technologies and more ingenious methodologies to overcome traditional survey limitations. They will be measuring more elusive phenomena and getting more accurate results as social science evolves in the twenty-first century.

CHAPTER 9

TEXTUAL ANALYSIS

Experiments and surveys ask people to respond to situations or answer questions to generate new messages not previously available. Other researchers, however, prefer to study messages that already exist in recorded or visual form. **Textual analysis is** the method communication researchers use to describe and interpret the characteristics of a recorded or visual message. Communication texts can be written transcripts of speeches and conversations, written documents (such as letters, personnel records, newspapers, and magazines), electronic documents (such as audiotapes, films, videotapes, and CD-ROMs), or visual texts (such as paintings, photographs, World Wide Web sites, and architecture). There are, thus, a great many texts; in fact, there are as many kinds of texts as there are communication media. This chapter first examines the purposes of and important considerations in conducting textual analysis and then explores in more detail some specific methods textual analysts use.

PURPOSES OF TEXTUAL ANALYSIS

Textual analysis, like experimental and survey methods, can be used to answer the two major questions posed in communication research: "What is the nature of communication" and "How is communication related to other variables?" In answering the first question, textual analysts describe the content, structure, and functions of the messages contained in texts. For example, K. L. Hacker, Howl, Scott, and Steiner (1996) collected a sample of texts from three computer-mediated communication networks (BUSH-L, CLINTON-L, and PEROT-L) used for political discussion during the 1992 presidential election campaign. Their analy-

sis showed that the messages exchanged over these networks were primarily assertions of personal opinions about the candidates, issues, and the election, followed by talking about one's life experiences, telling others what they should be doing, and posting information for others to read. These researchers, thus, described the functions of the messages within these texts and, consequently, inferred some of the reasons why voters may use computer networks as new channels of political communication.

Describing the communication embedded in a text is not as easy as it might seem because there isn't a single meaning of a text, nor is there a single perspective from which to interpret it. Lindkvist (1981) points out that the "meaning of a text can be identified with the producer, the consumer, or the interpreter of a text" (p. 23). Hirsch (1967), for example, argues that the purpose of textual analysis is to ascertain the meaning intended by the producer of a text. Other scholars focus on how consumers perceive and interpret a text, regardless of the meaning intended by the producer. As a third alternative, the meaning of a text can be assessed by qualified interpreters, those who have the power and/or expertise to interpret its meaning.

The 2nd Amendment of the United States Constitution provides a good example of these three perspectives on the meaning of a text (see Figure 9.1). The 2nd Amendment says: "A well-regulated militia, being necessary to the security of a free state, the right of the people to keep and bear arms, shall not be infringed." The founders who wrote this Amendment had a certain intent in mind, although we can't ask them what it was since they are no longer alive. Today's citizens

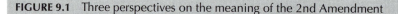

FIGURE 9.1   Three perspectives on the meaning of the 2nd Amendment

interpret this statement in at least two very different ways. Gun-ownership advocates see this it as guaranteeing individuals the right to own a gun, whereas gun-control advocates believe it guarantees a collective right (the right of states to maintain militias) but not necessarily an individual one. Ultimately, however, as Chapman (1997) points out, "[T]he only reading of the 2nd Amendment that matters is the one made by the Supreme Court" (Sect. 1, p. 19). The Justices of the Su-preme Court, being granted the power to interpret the Constitution, are the final arbiters of this issue.

Qualified interpreters of texts are not just those who have been granted the power to inter-pret, but also include those who have specialized training and experience that lead others to see them as expert interpreters of particular texts and types of texts. Well-known film critics, such as (the late) Gene Siskel and Roger Ebert, for instance, have studied and evaluated films ("thumbs up" or "thumbs down") for many years and have achieved a certain status as qualified interpreters of film texts. This doesn't mean their interpretation of a film is "correct"; just because Siskel and Ebert like a film doesn't necessarily mean you will like it. But their expert opinion is highly valued by many filmgoers and may influence whether people go to see a film.

Communication scholars also often function as qualified interpreters of texts. They are trained in the methodologies discussed in this chapter, which means they study texts using rigorous and systematic procedures. Their methods often lead to new insights about texts that are not readily apparent to those not trained in these methodologies.

Besides describing the communication embedded in a text from a chosen perspective, textual analysis can also be used to study how that communication is related to other variables. Some analysts investigate how various factors/variables that precede communication are related to the messages contained in a text. M. P. Moore (1996), for example, showed how increasing levels of cynicism toward government over the past 30 years have influenced recent presidential candidates who run against an incumbent to use irony as a rhetorical strategy in their nomination acceptance speeches.

Some researchers also study relationships between the communication embedded in a text and various outcomes, or lack thereof. McOmber (1996), for instance, analyzed the messages in Sigmund Freud's lecture on "The Etiology of Hysteria," presented in 1896 at the Society for Psychiatry and Neurology in Vienna, in which Freud argued that the sexual abuse of children was the single cause of hysteria in adults. McOmber's analysis of this text argues that Freud's failure to show how psychoanalysis could be compatible with traditional models of medical authority, which considered hysteria a hereditary affliction, led to Freud's inability to persuade a skeptical medical establishment to consider a new explanation. A short while thereafter, Freud renounced what came to be known as his "Seduction Theory."

Finally, some textual analysts (such as rhetorical critics) often go beyond these two questions to *evaluate* texts, pointing out their strengths and weaknesses. K. K. Campbell (1995), for example, analyzed two of the earliest-known speeches by United States women: Priscilla Mason's 1793 salutatory oration and Deborah Sampson Gannett's 1802 lecture tour. Campbell's analysis showed how these women demonstrated considerable rhetorical skill in the face of significant constraints (e.g., being barred from education), and how these speeches emboldened and served as resources for subsequent women speakers.

IMPORTANT CONSIDERATIONS IN TEXTUAL ANALYSIS

Researchers conducting textual analysis must make a number of important decisions. These decisions include the types of texts to be studied, acquiring appropriate texts, and which particular approach to use to analyze them.

Types of Texts

Texts can be divided into two general categories: transcripts and outputs of communication. **Transcripts of communication** are verbatim recordings of actual communication, such as written transcripts of courtroom behavior made by a court stenographer or audio/audiovisual recordings of group meetings. **Outputs of communication** are messages produced by communicators themselves, including written artifacts (such as letters, graffiti, and books), works of art (such as paintings, statues, and films), and other symbolic outputs (such as footprints and refuse).

Both transcripts and outputs of communication range from *scripted* (planned ahead) to *unscripted* (spontaneous) and from *public* (intended for general consumption) to *private* (intended for select individuals or groups). Whereas some scholars argue that all communication is intentional, the amount of preparation varies, as do the purposes and audiences for which the communication is produced. A United States President's State of the Union Address, for instance, is a well-scripted text designed for public consumption and analysis. By contrast, a videotaped recording of a family vacation is representative of a more unscripted, spontaneous text, intended primarily for private viewing only by members of that particular family and perhaps some of their friends. Note, however, how private texts often become available for public consumption. People seem to be fascinated, for example, in reading the private letters, especially the love letters, of celebrities and other famous people.

Studying transcripts and outputs of communication relies primarily on *indirect,* rather than *direct,* observation. Recall from Chapter 4 that researchers use direct observation to examine live communication behavior and indirect observation to examine recordings of communication behavior. The predominant use of indirect observation in textual analysis makes this a relatively *nonreactive* or *unobtrusive* research methodology that, for the most part, does not intrude into people' lives. Many of the analyzed texts are the result of natural communication behavior, as opposed to being generated at a researcher's request. The internal validity of these texts, therefore, is not threatened by the Hawthorne effect or the researcher effects discussed in Chapter 5.

Acquiring Texts

A challenge for scholars is identifying and acquiring the texts most appropriate for the purposes of their research. Outputs of communication are more readily available for analysis than transcripts, if only because some outputs, such as newspapers and books, are stored in libraries, while many other original records and documents are stored in *archives* (see Chapter 3).

Archival communication research involves examining the communication embedded in existing records of human behavior kept in archives. Webb, Campbell, Schwartz, and Sechrest (1973) identify at least four types of public records that are available in archives: (a) actuarial reports, such as births and deaths; (b) political and judicial records, such as the *Congressional Record* and transcripts of court trials; (c) other government records, such as

weather reports, city budgets, and traffic accident reports; and (d) mass media products, such as newspapers and films. Three sources of private records might also be available to researchers in archives: sales records, industrial and institutional records, and personal written documents.

Textual analysts often study archival records. D. C. Gibson (1994), for instance, studied the rhetoric of J. Edgar Hoover by spending two weeks in the Freedom of Information-Privacy Act Reading Room located in the J. Edgar Hoover Federal Bureau of Investigation Building. He sampled files from 17 categories of declassified FBI memoranda; in all, approximately 30,000 pages of memos were used. As another example, Kuypers, Young, and Launer (1994) analyzed the rhetoric of the U.S. government during the 1988 Airbus crisis, in which an Iranian airliner was shot down by a U.S. ship, by examining all written verbatim archived records produced by the U.S. administration within a 30-day period following the crisis. And Vaughn (1995) examined the type of symbols and functions they served in the corporate discourse of a company by analyzing 3,000 archival documents that spanned over 6 years.

In contrast to outputs of communication, transcripts of communication may be much more difficult to acquire. Most communication events are not recorded or available in the form of transcripts. Public speeches by major political figures are often recorded, but most interpersonal, group, and organizational communication is not preserved. Researchers can, of course, record such communication, but this can make people nervous and distort their normal behavior (the Hawthorne effect).

Acquiring a database is a primary consideration in textual analysis, particularly when texts are not readily available, but a second issue concerns how well the texts selected represent the population/universe from which they were drawn (see Chapter 5). Sometimes researchers can conduct a census of all relevant texts if the database is limited. Sellnow (1996), for example, studied the rhetorical strategies of continuity and change on musical artists' appeal over time by analyzing the albums of Bruce Springsteen. It was relatively easy to obtain all nine albums that Springsteen had produced through 1992.

Most of the time, however, it is not possible to obtain a census of all relevant texts, so a sample is studied. In such cases, researchers must strive to have the sample accurately represent the population from which it was drawn. Spirek and Glascock (1998), for example, studied gender portrayals in the visual content of newspaper advertisements for horror films. They selected the *Chicago Tribune* for analysis because of its large circulation as a major metropolitan newspaper. They reasoned that the type of ads that appear in this newspaper probably appear in newspapers throughout the country (a proposition supported by Lees & Berkowitz, 1981), so this newspaper probably was representative of the national advertising area. The researchers then randomly sampled six newspaper issues for each year from 1940–1990, for a total of 300 issues covering a span of 50 years. The specific day and month of each issue selected was generated by drawing a number from 1 to 31 for the day and a number from 1 to 12 for the month. This type of conscientious selection procedure helps to increase the confidence that the results obtained for this sample of texts hold for the population of texts to which the authors wish to generalize.

A third issue in acquiring texts concerns the need for complete and accurate texts. Researchers analyzing historical texts kept in archives, for example, often find that texts are incomplete or, worse, have been destroyed. Webb et al. (1973) point out that archival records are susceptible to the problems of selective deposit and survival. Not all records are kept, and not all survive over the course of time. And sometimes archival records, such as statistical records, are invalid (see J. W. Andersen, 1989). With regard to transcripts, audiotaped or videotaped interactions are not always of sufficient quality to permit understanding of everything recorded. Moreover, audiotapes and videotapes are typically transcribed into written form for analysis, and information can be lost in the process, such as nonverbal communication.

Approaches to Textual Analysis

How a text is analyzed depends on the purposes of the research and the particular method used. Here, we describe four major approaches to textual analysis: rhetorical criticism, content analysis, interaction analysis, and performance studies. These approaches differ in purpose (ranging from descriptive to critical) and type of data analyzed (ranging from qualitative to quantitative), but they all share a common focus on examining the communication embedded in texts.

RHETORICAL CRITICISM

To the average person on the street, the words *rhetoric* and *criticism* conjure up some interesting images. Some people view rhetoric as grammar and syntax, as in, "Oh, I took a freshman English rhetoric course." Rhetoric often carries negative connotations, such as when it is applied to grand, eloquent, bombastic, or verbose discourse—as Shakespeare said, "Full of sound and fury, signifying nothing." Rhetoric is also sometimes viewed as the "prettying up" of an idea, the clothing that surrounds the substance. And it is not uncommon to hear people say, "That's mere rhetoric," which usually means talk without action.

The word *criticism* also carries certain connotations. Andrews (1983) believes that the term typically is associated with tearing down or denigrating comments—we ask people to "stop being so critical." Criticism is also thought of as advice, which when perceived as helpful is called "constructive criticism."

For scholars, the word *rhetoric* is traditionally associated with Aristotle's definition: "the available means of persuasion." And *criticism* is "the systematic process of illuminating and evaluating products of human activity" (Andrews, 1983, p. 4). **Rhetorical criticism,** therefore, is a systematic method for describing, analyzing, interpreting, and evaluating the persuasive force of messages embedded within texts.

Rhetorical criticism serves five important functions, according to Andrews (1983). First, rhetorical criticism sheds light on the *purposes* of a persuasive message. Second, it can be used to understand historical, social, and cultural *contexts* and, thereby, explain how contexts affect and are affected by persuasive messages. Third, rhetorical criticism can be used to evaluate contemporary society, providing a form of *social criticism* by critiquing, for example, stereotypical representations of women or other minorities by the media. Fourth, rhetorical criticism contributes to *theory-building* by showing how theories apply to the practice of persuasive discourse. An example might be applying a theory of emotional arousal to analyze the speeches of a demagogue. Fifth, rhetorical criticism serves a *pedagogical* function by teaching people something about how persuasion works and what constitutes effective and ineffective persuasion.

Rhetorical criticism holds an honored place in the history of communication inquiry, and textual analysis, in particular, since the earliest studies of human communication were rhetorical studies of public discourse. Early rhetorical theory and criticism developed by the Greeks and Romans, referred to as **classical rhetoric,** examined the characteristics and effects of persuasive public speaking, such as how political speeches enlisted support for a specific leader or helped establish and maintain social order.

Contemporary rhetorical criticism has expanded to incorporate a wide range of philosophical, theoretical, and methodological perspectives that are used to study the persuasive impact of many different types of texts and messages. In addition to written and spoken texts, contemporary rhetorical critics analyze mass media messages, such as Hanke's (1998) analysis of the television sitcoms *Coach* and *Home Improvement,* Brookley's (1996) rhetorical critique of the film *Philadelphia,* and Delgado's (1998) investigation of rap music. Other scholars study visual texts, such as the NAMES Project AIDS Memorial Quilt (Foss, 1994), Vietnam Veterans Memorial in Washington, DC (e.g., Blair, Jeppeson, & Pucci, 1991; Carlson & Hocking, 1988; Jurma, 1982), spontaneous shrines constructed at the site of the Oklahoma City bombing (Jorgensen-Earp & Lanzilotti,

1998), and Internet and World Wide Web texts (e.g., Warnick, 1998).

Contemporary rhetorical criticism has also expanded from the traditional public speaking context to other communication contexts. Rhetorical critics now analyze, for instance, organizational discourse, such as D. Johnson and Sellnow's (1995) study of the rhetorical strategies used by Exxon following the *Valdez* oil-spill crisis in Alaska and Violanti's (1996) analysis of the United States Navy's formal response to the 1991 Tailhook sexual harassment scandal. Rhetorical critics have also begun to study intercultural communication, such as Xioa's (1995) investigation of how influential works of one culture (in this case, Darwinism) are adapted to the needs, circumstances, and thought patterns of another (China). Some scholars even analyze the rhetorical practices of disciplinary scholarship, such as the rhetoric of science (e.g., Gross, 1990; Kelso, 1980; Lessl, 1985; Lyne & Howe, 1986, 1990; Prelli, 1990).

Conducting Rhetorical Criticism

According to Foss (1989), rhetorical criticism involves four steps: (a) choosing a text(s) to study; (b) choosing a specific type of rhetorical criticism; (c) analyzing the text(s) according to the method chosen; and (d) writing the critical essay.

The first step involves identifying the text(s) that will be analyzed. Some scholars formulate a research question about the process of persuasion and then choose an appropriate rhetorical text(s) to analyze; others first choose an interesting and significant rhetorical text(s) and then pose questions about it.

The second step involves choosing an appropriate type of rhetorical criticism with which to analyze the text. All rhetorical critics view texts through a method, or "lens," that illuminates the meaning of the text. A critic might choose a method that already exists, modify an existing method, combine elements from different methods, or create an entirely new method.

The third step is the systematic application of the method to illuminate the meaning of the text.

If, for example, the methods call for analyzing the metaphors contained in the text (see the explanation following), then the rhetorical critic looks for these metaphors, describes them, and evaluates their persuasive effectiveness.

The final step is to write the critical essay. Foss (1989) claims that a rhetorical critique should address seven major topics: "(1) introduction; (2) description of the artifact [text]; (3) description of the critical method; (4) report of the findings of the analysis; (5) interpretation of the findings; (6) evaluation of the artifact; and (7) contribution of the study to rhetorical theory" (p. 20).

Types of Rhetorical Criticism

Three general, interrelated research questions are asked by rhetorical critics, according to Foss (1989): (a) What is the relationship between a text and its context? (b) How does a text construct reality for an audience? and (c) What does a text suggest about the rhetor? The first question directs attention to how the elements of a social context (such as the time, place, and occasion) influence the production of a persuasive communication. The second question investigates how persuasive messages influence an audience's conception of reality. And the third question asks how the motives, personality, and other features of a rhetor influence the construction of his or her persuasive message.

Several types of rhetorical criticism may be used to answer one or more of these questions. Here, we review eight types: historical, neo-Aristotelian, genre, dramatistic, metaphoric, narrative, fantasy theme, and feminist criticism.

Historical Criticism. **Historical criticism** examines how important past events shape and are shaped by rhetorical messages. In historical criticism, researchers go beyond merely describing and recreating past events from documents to evaluate the reasons why the past events occurred as they did. And understanding a significant event that occurred in the past can provide a point of comparison for understanding current events.

Historical critics primarily analyze the relationship between a text and its context by conducting four types of studies: oral histories, historical case studies, biographical studies, and social movement studies. Each approach to historical criticism studies the role of communication in historical events and/or the accomplishments of historical individuals/groups (see J. W. Bowers & Ochs, 1971; Riches & Sillars, 1980; C. J. Stewart, Smith, & Denton, 1984).

Oral Histories. **Oral histories** investigate spoken, as opposed to written, accounts of personal experiences to understand more fully what happened in the past. Oral history interviews are conducted between researchers and those who participated in past events to understand the meaning of those individuals' lived experiences (see Chapter 10). In this sense, "oral history is a form of conversation. Its generic function is to transmit a culture by word or mouth" (McMahan & Rogers, 1994b, p. 3).

In the context of historical criticism, oral history interviews are conducted to corroborate, correct, and extend historical inquiry (E. C. Clark, Hyde, & McMahan, 1980). For example, Studs Terkel (1970), a well-known oral historian, extended understanding of the Great Depression by interviewing and analyzing the stories told by people who had lived through it. And D. A. Hacker and Hansen (1974) interviewed Japanese Americans who had been interned at the Manzanar (California) Relocation Center (concentration camp) during World War II, and focused specifically on understanding the riot that occurred on December 6, 1943, which left two internees dead and nine others wounded (also see A. A. Hansen, 1991, 1994; A. A. Hansen & Mitson, 1974).

The strength of oral histories is that researchers study *primary sources* of information—firsthand, eyewitness accounts of historical events—instead of *secondary sources*—descriptions and interpretations of events by people who did not experience them personally (see Chapter 3). Oral historians interview people who lived through a period of time or experienced an event, rather than rely on second hand information, such as media accounts of that period or event.

Historical Case Studies.   **Historical case studies** examine texts related to a single, salient historical event to understand the role played by communication. Rhetorical critics first describe the key factors that precipitated the event (the case) and then analyze the case in light of current communication theory and research. The goal is to identify appropriate strategies that were used or could have been used to solve problems experienced during that particular event.

One landmark text that has been analyzed frequently by rhetorical critics is President Abraham Lincoln's Gettysburg Address, which, as we all know, begins with the line: "Four score and seven years ago our fathers brought forth on this continent, a new nation, conceived in Liberty, and dedicated to the proposition that all men are created equal." Black's (1994) study shows how this address functioned rhetorically within that particular historical context by examining such elements as the audience suggested by the speech and the geographical references Lincoln made. Another example of an historical case study, this time applied to a visual text, is Skow and Dionisopoulos's (1997) analysis of rhetorical strategies used to frame the "Burning Monk" photograph, when, on June 11, 1963, Buddhist Monk Thich Quang Duc sat in a lotus position in a busy street of Saigon and set himself on fire to protest the Vietnam War.

Biographical Studies.   **Biographical studies** examine public and private texts of prominent, influential, or otherwise remarkable individuals. Biographical studies analyze how the messages used by these individuals helped them to accomplish what they did. Many scholars, for example, have analyzed the rhetoric of United States presidents, including recent studies of Abraham Lincoln (Slagell, 1991), Theodore Roosevelt (Dorsey, 1995), Franklin Delano Roosevelt (Houck, 1997), Dwight Eisenhower (Medhurst, 1994; Parry-Giles, 1993, Zagacki, 1995), John Kennedy (Goldzwig & Dionisopoulos, 1995), Lyndon Johnson (G. E. Pau-

ley, 1997, 1998), Jimmy Carter (Bostdorff, 1992; Lee, 1995a, 1995b), Ronald Reagan (Johnstone, 1995), George Bush (German, 1995; Rountree, 1995; Stuckey, 1992, 1995), and Bill Clinton (Stuckey, 1995). Other politicians' rhetoric studied recently include 1950s presidential candidate Adlai Stevenson (J. M. Murphy, 1994), Vice President Dan Quayle (C. R. Smith, 1995), Senator Bob Packwood (M. P. Moore, 1997), and retired General Colin Powell (J. L. Edwards, 1998). Other prominent individuals whose messages have received attention recently by rhetorical critics include: civil rights activists Jesse Jackson (P. Wilson, 1996), Malcolm X (Houck, 1993; Lucaites & Condit, 1990), Martin Luther King, Jr. (Appel, 1997; Johannesen, 1995; R. E. Lee, 1991; Lucaites & Condit, 1990), Louis Farrakhan (J. L. Pauley, 1998), Robert Parris Moses (Jensen & Hammerback, 1998), and Stokely Carmichael (C. J. Stewart, 1997); women activists, such as Mary Wollstonecraft (a British feminist writer in the 1790s) (C. L. Griffin, 1994) and Margaret Sanger (an advocate of birth control in the early 1900s) (Cuklanz, 1995; McCleary, 1994); and many others, including Italian fascist leader Benito Mussolini (Nelson, 1991), Yippie leader Jerry Rubin (Jensen & Lichtenstein, 1995); psychologist Carl Rogers (Cissna & Anderson, 1990); singer-songwriter Madonna (Hallstein, 1996; Schwichtenberg, 1992), and rap artist KRS-One (Aldridge & Carlin, 1993).

Social Movement Studies.   **Social movement studies** examine persuasive strategies used to influence the historical development of specific campaigns and causes. Social movements include the rise (and fall) of religious denominations and cults, political parties and campaigns, and civil rights activism. Critics studying social movements analyze a variety of texts, including movement leaders' speeches, correspondence, and writing, as well as the public relations media campaigns used to promote the movements (see Riches & Sillars, 1980; Simons, 1970; Simons, Mechling, & Schreier, 1984; C. J. Stewart et al., 1984).

Social movements that have received recent attention from rhetorical critics include: the free

Blacks annual commemoration of emancipation in the British West Indies on the first day of August (in lieu of celebrating July 4th) from 1834 until the end of the United States Civil War (D. L. Bowers, 1995); American Female Moral Reform Society (one of the first antebellum reform movements to be founded and controlled by women) (Carlson, 1992); Knights of Labor (a secret labor society founded in 1869 by Philadelphia garment cutters that became one of the most powerful labor reform groups in the world) (C. J. Stewart, 1991b); National Consumer's League (an early twentieth-century organization that fought for improved working conditions and labor laws) (Salvador, 1994); the "Intifada" Palestinian movement (Hasian & Flores, 1997); Students for a Democratic Society (SDSS) (Walsh, 1993); the women's movement (Zaeske, 1995); the Chicano movement (Delgado, 1995); the Mothers of Plaza de Mayo (a group of mothers whose children disappeared under the military dictatorship that ruled Argentina from 1976 to 1983) (Fabj, 1993); gay liberation (Darsey, 1991; Slagle, 1995); the neoconservative movement (Zagacki, 1996); environmentalism (Killingsworth & Palmer, 1992a, 1992b, 1995); the anti-fur campaign (Olson & Goodnight, 1994); Robert Bly's men's movement (Mechling & Mechling, 1994); the political correctness (PC) movement (Bello, 1996); and ACT-UP (AIDS Coalition to Unleash Power) (Christiansen & Hanson, 1996).

Neo-Aristotelian Criticism. **Neo-Aristotelian criticism** evaluates whether the most appropriate and effective means, as articulated in the specific set of criteria given in Aristotle's *Rhetoric,* were used to create the rhetorical text(s) intended to influence a particular audience. Aristotle's inventory for describing and evaluating rhetoric includes five major canons: (a) *invention,* the development of persuasive arguments through *ethos,* the credibility of the speaker, *pathos,* appealing to the emotions of the audience, and *logos,* presenting logical evidence; (b) *disposition,* the organization of a persuasive message; (c) *elocution,* a speaker's style or use of language to express ideas; (d) *delivery,* the

nonverbal manner in which a speaker presents the message; and (e) *memory,* the strategy a speaker employs to recall information for a presentation. The goal of neo-Aristotelian criticism, then, is "to discover whether the speaker makes the best choices from the inventory to get a favorable decision from a specified group of auditors in a specific situation" (F. Hill, 1972, p. 106).

Despite some critics' doubts as to whether this or any particular set of criteria can be applied to all forms of rhetoric, neo-Aristotelian criticism has been a popular method. Indeed, Black (1965) maintains it was *the* dominant mode of rhetorical criticism during the twentieth century (at least the first half) in the United States.

Genre Criticism. **Genre criticism** rejects using a single set of criteria to evaluate all persuasive messages, arguing, instead, that standards vary according to the particular type, or *genre,* of text being studied. Genre criticism, therefore, differs from neo-Aristotelian criticism by applying standards that are intrinsic to the type of rhetorical act being studied, instead of applying a single set of standards to all rhetorical acts.

Aristotle originally argued that there were three genres of rhetoric: forensic, epideictic, and deliberative. *Forensic* rhetoric deals with the past and concerns issues involving legality and justice. *Epideictic* rhetoric concerns the present and is ceremonial. *Deliberative* rhetoric speaks to the future and involves political oratory. Dow (1989), for example, analyzed the function of epideictic and deliberative strategies in presidential crisis rhetoric.

In the years since that classification, scholars have studied a number of other rhetorical genres. *Apologias, image restoration strategies,* and *self-defense rhetoric,* for instance, are attempts to present a public defense of character and restore one's image. Many such studies focus on how organizations explain their actions following disastrous circumstances, such as Ice's (1991) examination of how Union Carbide attempted to apologize and restore its image following a leak of deadly gas on December 3, 1984, in Bhopal India, while Brinson and Benoit (1996) focused on how Dow Corning attempted to repair its image following the breast implant crisis. Other scholars look at individuals' attempts to explain their actions and recoup their image, such as Tonya Harding's defense of her image in her interview on the television show *Eye-to-Eye With Connie Chung* (W. L. Benoit & Hanczor, 1994) or Newt Gingrich's self-defense discourse following his multimillion dollar book deal controversy (J. A. Kennedy & Benoit, 1997). Other scholars analyze *political speeches,* such as campaign speeches or political debates. Clayman (1995), for example, analyzed the famous television interaction episode between vice presidential candidates Lloyd Bentsen and Dan Quayle concerning Quayle's reference during their debate to having "as much experience in the Congress as Jack Kennedy did when he sought the presidency," and Bentsen's response of, "I served with Jack Kennedy. I *knew* Jack Kennedy. Jack Kennedy was a friend of mine. Senator, you're no Jack Kennedy" (p. 121). *Eulogies* are texts written in honor of a deceased person, such as Goldzwig and Sullivan's (1995) analysis of post-assassination newspaper editorial eulogies about John F. Kennedy, Martin Luther King, Jr., and Robert F. Kennedy. As a final example of genre criticism, *jeremiads* are texts that castigate a specific group, blaming the group for current problems and urging the group to remedy its ways. Johannesen (1986), for example, showed how Ronald Reagan's speeches blamed economic woes on the tendency of the general public to be swayed by bad leadership and their easy lifestyles, and urged them to return to the Puritan values of hard work and competition.

Dramatistic Criticism. **Dramatistic criticism** primarily analyzes texts according to philosopher Kenneth Burke's (1945, 1950, 1966) view that all communication can be seen in terms of elements that comprise a dramatic event. The nature of any dramatic event is captured, in part, by five essential elements: *act* (a particular message produced by a communicator); *purpose* (the reason for the message); *agent* (the person who communicated the message), *agency* (the medium used to express the

message); and *scene* (the context in which the message occurs).

Pentadic analysis, as it is called, uses these five elements to isolate essential characteristics of and differences between symbolic acts. Burke contends that within a given piece of discourse, two of the five elements of the pentad should emerge as more important than the others, which is called a *ratio.* A rhetorical act that emphasizes agent and scene, for example, may be contrasted with a rhetorical act that emphasizes agency and purpose. Dramatism, thus, calls for assessing how rhetorical acts highlight a particular ratio of the pentad.

Highlighting particular elements and ratios of the pentad makes it possible to understand, differentiate, and critique the purpose and nature of rhetorical acts. That's what Cooks and Descutner (1993) did in using the pentad to contrast the discourse of two therapies designed to help women cope with eating disorders: a spiritual recovery therapy (SR) and a feminist therapy (FT). They found that SR featured agent-agency as the principal ratio by stressing that women must place their trust in the controlling power of a Higher Power. In contrast, FT featured act-scene and act-purpose ratios that stressed, respectively, understanding weight loss within the context of the way society oppresses women and the need for women to unite their mind and body and reclaim their identity.

It should be pointed out that Burke's dramatistic criticism extends far beyond pentadic analysis. As just one example, Burke focuses on *identification* processes, for the more actors identify with one another, the more effective rhetors are in evoking cooperation. Rhetorical critics using dramatistic criticism, therefore, often seek to "discover and illuminate the strategies operating through language that promote the desired end of identification" (Andrews, 1983, p. 59). Identification leads to coordinated, harmonic understanding, an ideal relational state Burke called *consubstantiality.*

Metaphoric Criticism. **Metaphoric criticism** assumes that we can never know reality directly. Rhetors' language represents reality, functioning as a *metaphor,* likening one thing to another. Metaphors used in persuasive messages, therefore, create visions of reality for receivers. Rhetorical critics, consequently, identify and evaluate how rhetors use metaphors to help create a shared reality for the audience.

Stuckey (1995), for instance, examined some of the ways in which Presidents George Bush and Bill Clinton, in the post–Cold War era, blended the rhetorical forms of the Cold War metaphor with other foreign policy metaphors (such as the New World Order) to publicly justify the actions of the United States in foreign policy. Ausmus (1998) analyzed scientist Carl Sagan's use of a "nuclear winter" metaphor as being instrumental in making the public aware of the potential catastrophic effects of even a limited nuclear war. And Leeman (1995) examined how the persuasive use of relational, locational, and directional spatial metaphors in the discourse of three African American orators' speeches emerged naturally and readily from the African American experience.

Narrative Criticism.   **Narrative criticism** assumes that many (or all) persuasive messages function as narratives—stories, accounts, or tales. Stories embedded in texts provide descriptions of situations, central characters, and action sequences, and often carry implicit or explicit "lessons" that lead an audience to make sense of, or account for, important events. As Kirkwood (1992) explains, "Rhetors may tell stories of deeds which reflect characters' states of mind, or they may enable or challenge people to perform such acts themselves, with striking consequences for their own life stories" (p. 30). Narrative criticism, therefore, involves analyzing the stories rhetors tell and evaluating how effective they are at shaping an audience's perception of reality.

Katriel and Shenhar (1990), for example, explored the narrative construction of Israeli symbolism as demonstrated in the stories told and retold of the heroic saga of Israel's pre-state era, and looked at the rhetorical role these narratives played in the larger cultural conversation. As another example, Clair (1997) showed how the multiple narrative genres of historical, ancestral, personal, and contemporary narratives gave voice to issues that might otherwise have gone unheard in the signing of the Treaty of New Echota, a story of the Cherokee Nation and the events surrounding the Cherokee removal of 1838–1839.

Fantasy Theme Analysis.   **Fantasy theme analysis,** based on the work of Ernest Bormann (1972, 1973, 1982), examines the common images used to portray narrative elements of situations described in a text. Rhetorical critics use fantasy theme analysis to reveal the motives of rhetors and how they shape people's views of social reality by analyzing four symbolic categories: fantasy themes, fantasy types, rhetorical visions, and rhetorical communities. *Fantasy themes* are mythic stories present in communication that involve characters with which people identify. The activities of the dramatic characters (such as "good people" and "bad people") symbolize general moral principles or philosophies. Leaders of a country going to war, for example, tend to portray the enemy as villains carrying out evil deeds or philosophies. Fantasy themes form patterns that recur throughout a text, referred to as *fantasy types.* These recurring types become powerful rhetorical symbols that a rhetor can use to unite an audience in its perception of social reality. Speaking about a "war on poverty" or "the evil empire," for instance, rallies people to support a cause. These fantasy theme types create *rhetorical visions,* interpretive schemes about reality shared by groups of people, who are called *rhetorical communities.* Rhetors who evoke shared rhetorical visions among an audience can transform that audience into a rhetorical community that identifies strongly with specific fantasy themes and types.

As an example, Duffy (1997) used fantasy theme analysis to explain the persuasive strategies of a publicity campaign to persuade opinion leaders and the general public that riverboat gambling should be legalized in Iowa. She examined and noted the fantasy themes contained in planning documents, news releases, agency-produced letters to the editors of newspapers, and agency personnel reactions to the campaign, in addition to all available news coverage of this effort. One of the fantasy themes concerned potential economic development, with the texts frequently citing impressive dollar amounts, while another was the use of a scenic fantasy theme of riverboat gambling as an historical legend. Recurring use of these fantasy themes hardened them into fantasy types and were, in the final analysis, persuasive in leading decision makers and the general public to legalize riverboat gambling in Iowa (and perhaps other places as well).

Feminist Criticism.   **Feminist criticism** analyzes how conceptions of gender are produced and maintained in persuasive messages. Feminist critics argue that people's conceptions of the characteristics of men and women are influenced by rhetoric describing men and women. Feminist critics also argue that a masculine view of the world has traditionally dominated rhetorical criticism and that females' thinking differs fundamentally from males', providing a distinct and valuable perspective from which to understand and evaluate persuasive message.

It is impossible to do justice to the broad range of issues to which feminist rhetorical critics direct attention, but some examples help to suggest this breadth. Some scholars focus on traditional problems faced by women, such as Buzzanell's (1995) critique and reframing of the "glass ceiling" as a socially constructed process that prevents women from attaining high-level status in organizations. Other scholars direct attention to media representations of women, such as Vavrus's (1998) analysis of the way in which the media portrayed women Senate candidates during the 1992 campaign, the supposed Year of the Woman, as being outside the perceived mainstream and how such representations served to comment on feminism in the United States. Other scholars critique what appear at first glance to be pro-women-oriented texts but on closer examination reveal anti-women tendencies. Vande Berg (1993) documented three interrelated strategies through which the prime-time television series, *China Beach,* feminized violence and mili-

tarism and neutralized war and, thereby, showed how the program "uses feminist strategies (e.g., making women and women's concerns central) to articulate a conservative, anti-feminist, pro-war perspective in the name of feminism" (p. 363). Still other scholars study particular women who have experienced problems because of their gender and/or have risen above such problems to be very successful, such as United States House of Representatives member Patricia Schroeder (Sullivan, 1993) and Texas Governor Ann Richards (Dow & Tonn, 1993; S. Miller, 1997), or groups of women who fight together against oppression, such as Fabj's (1998) analysis of how Italian women's testimonies legitimized the fight against the Mafia. Still other scholars focus on understanding texts authored by and for women, such as Hayden's (1997) study of how women's personal experiences are privileged throughout the five editions of the popular book, *Our Bodies, Ourselves,* published by the Boston Women's Health Book Collective.

CONTENT ANALYSIS

How are children portrayed in magazine ads (Alexander, 1994)? What messages do the media give about cancer, heart disease, and AIDS (J. N. Clark, 1992)? How much sexual content is there on television soap operas (S. G. Larson, 1991)? Do billboard advertisements differ depending on where they are located in a city (Schooler, Basil, & Altman, 1996)? Has the proportion of crime content in films changed over the years from 1945–1991 (J. Allen, Livingstone, & Reiner, 1997)?

Each of these research questions, in one way or another, asks about the *content* of messages embedded within texts, such as their characteristics, amount, and so forth. To answer these types of questions, researchers use **content analysis** to identify, enumerate, and analyze occurrences of specific messages and message characteristics embedded in texts.

Content analysis was developed primarily as a method for studying mass-mediated and public messages. Its roots stretch back at least to the eighteenth century, when scholars in Sweden counted the number of religious symbols contained in a collection of hymns to see whether the hymns were preaching against the church (Dovring, 1954–1955). At the end of the nineteenth century, scholars started conducting quantitative content analyses of newspapers. Sneed (cited in Krippendorf, 1980), for instance, counted the number of various types of articles in New York newspapers and showed that the content was changing from a focus on religious, scientific, and literary matters to an orientation toward gossip, sports, and scandals. Content analysis was soon applied to radio and public speeches, such as McDiarmid's (1937) study of the number of symbols used to promote national identity in presidential inaugural addresses.

During the Second World War, researchers content-analyzed music played on German radio stations and compared it with that played on radio stations in other occupied territories in Europe to measure changes in troop concentration on the continent. Increases in the volume of messages exchanged between Japan and various island bases were also found to be associated with new operations launched by the Japanese (Wimmer & Dominick, 1994). After the war, newspaper editors content-analyzed reporters' stories using readability formulas (see Chapter 8), such as Flesch's (1949) formula, to assess whether words and sentences could be understood by a person with an 8th-grade education. Editors still use these formulas today as "fog indexes" to determine whether an article is readable. Content analysis has even been used to determine authorship by comparing the content and structure of new documents with known examples of authors' work. Martindale and McKenzie (1995), for example, showed how content analysis was used to correctly attribute authorship of *The Federalist* papers, whose authorship was once in dispute.

Today, content analysis is one of the dominant, if not the most dominant, methodologies employed in mass communication research, and is widely used in other areas of the discipline as well. G. Comstock (1975) found more than 225 content analyses of television programming, and a survey by Jackson-Beeck and Kraus (1980) showed that content analysis was used in one-third of journal articles published on political communication in 1978 and 1979. More recently, Stroman and Jones (1998) described the broad use of the methodology to analyze television content.

Most content analyses are quantitative in nature, which involves counting the particular instances of certain types of messages in texts. There are, however, **qualitative content analyses,** where researchers are more interested in the meanings associated with messages than with the number of times message variables occur. Researchers use narrative approaches, for instance, to focus on major themes and stories contained in texts. Waitzkin, Britt, and Williams (1995), for example, analyzed the major themes expressed in narratives told about aging and social problems in medical encounters with elderly patients; Kreps (1994) identified sources of satisfaction and dissatisfaction for elderly nursing home residents by analyzing the themes these residents expressed in narrative accounts of their health care experiences; and Berdayes and Berdayes (1998) content analyzed the worldviews that characterized magazine articles about the information highway. Some content analysis blends both quantitative and qualitative analysis of data by combining traditional objective analyses of messages with data interpretation made on the basis of participant observation. Altheide (1996), for instance, described how participant observation of electronic media and analysis of online messages can be fruitfully combined to provide rich interpretations of the uses and functions of new media.

The vast majority of content analyses, however, employ quantitative procedures (although some of the specific procedures used are sometimes also used in qualitative content analysis). For that reason, the remainder of this discussion focuses on **quantitative content analysis,** the

> *systematic and replicable examination of symbols of communication, which have been assigned numeric values according to valid measurement rules, and the analysis of relationships involving those values using statistical methods, in order to*

describe the communication, draw inferences about its meaning, or infer from the communication to its context, both of production and consumption" (Riffe, Lacy, & Fico, 1998, p. 20)

Value of Quantitative Content Analysis

The primary goal of quantitative content analysis is to describe and count the characteristics of messages embedded in public and mediated texts. Krippendorf (1980) identifies four advantages of content analysis that potentially make it a more powerful technique than questionnaires or interviews for describing the nature of communication and for inferring relationships about the effects of input variables on communication content and how communication content may be related to various outcomes.

First, content analysis, like some other forms of textual analysis, such as rhetorical criticism, is an *unobtrusive technique* because researchers study texts that already exist rather than asking people to produce texts. Second, content analysis accepts *unstructured material,* which observers categorize. Structured questionnaires and interviews, by contrast, ask predetermined questions that limit respondents' answers. Third, questionnaires and interviews often obtain data in settings far from the context in which the communication occurs, but content analysts study the data as they appear in a *context.* Krippendorf argues that "content analysis is a research technique for making replicable and valid inferences from data to their context" (p. 21). Consequently, researchers not only examine the content of texts, but can also infer such things as the underlying motivations of the producers of texts and the effects of texts on consumers (Hsia, 1988). Fourth, content analysis is able to handle *massive amounts of data,* especially with the increased use of computers to store information. Kunkel and Gantz (1992), for example, content analyzed more than 10,000 commercials to see what type were shown during children's television programs on broadcast networks, independent stations, and cable networks.

In addition to these advantages, content analysis is a very useful method for studying changes in messages over time. Longitudinal content analyses can be conducted relatively easily, in comparison to experiments and surveys, because researchers work with texts that have already been produced. Some examples of longitudinal content analysis include: Wasserman, Stack, and Reeves's (1994) study of *The New York Times*'s presentation of front-page suicide stories between 1910 and 1920; Trent and Sabourin's (1993) investigation of television political ads during the decade of the 1980s; Chesebro's (1991) analysis of the values contained in 903 prime-time network television series from 1974–1991; and Alexander's (1994) content analysis of the images of children in magazine advertisements from 1905 to 1990. In each case, the researchers were able to show whether there were changes in the content of the texts studied over the course of a relatively long time period.

Content analysis can also be used to investigate the effects of important input variables on the content of messages. For example, the *community structure approach,* developed by Pollock and colleagues (see Pollock, in press), focuses on the ways in which key characteristics of communities (such as cities) are related to the content coverage of newspapers in those communities. In these studies, a content-analytic technique is used to combine the amount of attention a newspaper article about a particular topic receives (e.g., its placement, headline size, story length, and presence of photographs) and the attitudinal direction of the article (e.g., favorable, balanced/neutral, or unfavorable) into a single score for each newspaper selected. The newspapers are then ranked on this score and these rankings are compared with city rankings where the newspapers are published on a variety of relevant demographic characteristics.

Using such statistical procedures as correlation, regression, and factor analysis (see Chapter 14), Pollock has been able to show, for instance, high associations between a large percentage of "privileged" groups in a city (measured as the percent of the population that is college educated or families with annual incomes over $100,000 or with professional occupations) and coverage of three types of issues: (a) favorable media coverage of economic issues affecting the financially privileged, such as NAFTA (Pollock, 1995); (b) favorable coverage of those making human rights claims for equitable treatment, such as Cuban refugees (Pollock, Shier, & Kelly, 1995) and noncelebrities with HIV/AIDS (Pollock, 1997)—and, by extension, negative coverage of countries where human rights are abused, such as China (Pollock, Kreuer, & Ouano, 1997); and (c) relatively unfavorable coverage of issues that threaten biological existence or a predictable way of life, such as Dr. Kevorkian (Pollock, Caughlin, Thomas, & Connaughton, 1996) or the Internet (Pollock & Montero, 1998). Pollock calls the relation of privilege in a city to favorable coverage of human rights claims a "buffer" hypothesis because the higher the relative privilege or more "buffered" individuals are from economic uncertainty in a city, the greater the media sympathy for claimants. Similarly, the relation of privilege to relatively unfavorable coverage of threats to biological or predictable existence is called a "violated buffer" because these associations are found when rapid social and technological changes appear capable of unsettling even the most privileged groups. In addition to city characteristics measuring "privilege," the higher the percentage of "stakeholders" in a city, the more favorable the media coverage of that group's interests. For instance, the greater the proportion of businesses or other institutions marketing goods or services to the gay community in a city, the more likely a city newspaper is to report favorably on legalization of same-sex marriage (Pollock & Dantas, 1998); the higher the percentage of Catholics in a city, the less favorable the coverage of the *Roe vs. Wade* U.S. Supreme Court decision about abortion (Pollock, Robinson, & Murray, 1978); and the greater the proportion of those over 75 in a city, the less positive the coverage of legalization of physician-assisted euthanasia (Pollock & Yulis, 1999).

Finally, once texts have been content analyzed, the effects of exposure to that content can then be studied in conjunction with other methodologies. Lowry and Towles (1989), for example, discovered that there were 7.4 instances of sexual behaviors per hour in the television soap operas they content analyzed in 1987, which, if projected for an entire year of viewing, would result in 20,124 portrayals of sexual behaviors. They also found no treatment in those programs about the prevention of pregnancy or sexually transmitted diseases. They concluded their article by asking about, and calling for other types of research on, the effects of this exposure on young people:

> *Of course, one cannot demonstrate audience effects (especially long-term effects, the most important kind) with content analysis studies alone. What are the cumulative effects, for example, upon a teenage girl or boy who has watched soap operas for three or four years? To what extent does the transcending message about worry-free, promiscuous sex influence that teenager's own perceptions of sex and sexual practice? Such questions highlight the need for large-scale public health surveys and field studies. (pp. 81–82)*

Quantitative Content-Analytic Procedures

Quantitative content analysis is a systematic, step-by-step procedure used to answer research questions and test hypotheses. The procedure involves selecting texts, determining the units to be coded, developing content categories, training observers to code units, and analyzing the data.

Selecting Texts. Content analysts start by choosing appropriate texts to study. A wide range of texts have been content analyzed; some recent examples include: (a) newspapers (e.g., Hertog & Fan, 1995; Imrich, Mullin, & Linz, 1995; Molitor, 1993); (b) magazines (e.g., Alexander, 1994; Basil et al., 1991); (c) books (e.g., Cawyer et al. 1994); (d) television programs (e.g., Hickson, Scott, & Vogel, 1995; Kunkel & Gantz, 1992; M. S. Larson, 1991; Oliver, 1994); (e) public service announcements (e.g., Friemuth, Hammond, Edgar, & Monahan, 1990); (f) transcripts of interviews and similar written documents (e.g., Coffman, 1992; Krizek, Hecht, & Miller, 1993; J. C. Meyer, 1995); (g) brochures (e.g., Perloff & Ray, 1991); (h) job announcements (e.g., Merskin & Huberlie, 1995); (i) comic strips (e.g., Penner & Penner, 1994); (j) billboards (Schooler et al., 1996); (k) songs (e.g., C. J. Stewart, 1991a); and (l) Internet messages (e.g., Newhagen, Cordes, & Levy, 1995).

In the beginning of this chapter, we observed that all textual analysts must acquire an appropriate database of texts. Of course, the best way to do that is to conduct a census of all the relevant texts. Sometimes this is possible in quantitative content analysis; Schooler et al. (1996) were able to locate all 901 billboards in areas of San Francisco zoned as neighborhood commercial districts.

Most often, however, content analysts face the same problem as all researchers, the need to acquire a representative sample, in this case, of texts. Kaid and Wadsworth (1989) explain that researchers using content analysis "must devise a method of obtaining a sample which is (1) representative of the universe from which it comes and (2) of sufficient size to adequately represent that universe" (p. 201).

Content analysts, therefore, first specify the population of texts to which they wish to generalize and then use some procedure for selecting a sample from this population. If they are interested in generalizing from the sample to the population, they should, of course, use a random sampling procedure (see Chapter 5). Thus, whenever possible, content analysts use simple random, systematic, stratified, or cluster sampling techniques to acquire representative samples of texts. For example, to study portrayals of the elderly (characters over 65 years of age) on prime-time television, Robinson and Skill (1995) first videotaped all prime-time (7:00–10:00 p.m., CST) programs appearing on ABC, CBS, Fox, and NBC television networks from October 28, 1990–November 24, 1990, and then randomly sampled for analysis 100 episodes comprising 181.5 hours of programming.

As explained in Chapter 5, however, it often is not possible to use random sampling procedures to select texts for consideration in content analysis. One can't, for example, randomly select love letters people write. When random sampling procedures are not feasible, researchers rely on nonrandom sampling procedures, such as convenience or purposive samples.

Determining the Unit of Analysis.   Quantitative content analysis involves coding messages embedded in the selected texts into descriptive categories.

To accomplish this, researchers first identify the appropriate message unit to code, a process referred to as **unitizing.** While the research question or hypothesis itself ultimately leads researchers to determine the appropriate unit to be coded, a number of different types of units are possible.

Krippendorf (1980) identifies five types of units that content analysts might study: physical, syntactical, referential, propositional, and thematic units. **Physical units** are the space and time devoted to content, such as the number of particular items or amount of space devoted to them in the texts. Hickson, Stacks, and Amsbary (1993), for instance, counted the number of journal articles published by active communication scholars, while Pritchard and Hughes (1997), in their study of the patterns of deviance reported in newspaper crime stories, looked at such physical units as average story length and proportion of items on the front page of the newspapers they studied.

Riffe et al. (1998) point out that physical units differ from the remaining ones because physical units use standardized measurement units (such as a square inch or minute). The other four units are called **meaning units** because they involve symbolic meaning, and, therefore, are less standardized than physical units. **Syntactical units** consist of discrete units of language, such as individual words, sentences, and paragraphs. Lacy, Fico, and Simon (1991), for instance, investigated whether newspaper coverage was balanced by counting the number of words devoted to a particular side of a controversy. This is not the same thing as Hickson et al.'s (1993) counting of the number of published journal articles, because articles differ widely in the number of words they contain. **Referential units** (also called **character units,** Holsti, 1969) "involve some physical or temporal unit (e.g., event, people, objects, etc.) referred to or alluded to within content.... Referential units can be used to measure the meaning attached to a particular person, event, or issue" (Riffe et al., (1998), p. 66). Havick's (1997) content analysis, for instance, focused on national media coverage of women congressional candidates in 1990 and 1992. **Propositional units** place content into a consistent structure, such as assertions about an object. Ruben (1993), for instance, content analyzed 1,125 "critical incidents" collected from patients about their most memorable positive or negative experience while staying at a hospital or visiting a health center. Finally, **thematic units** are topics contained within messages. Oliver (1994), for example, looked at portrayals of crime, race, and aggression in "reality-based" police television shows.

Developing Content Categories.   Once researchers have identified the appropriate unit of analysis, they use nominal measurement procedures to develop categories into which units can be classified. This is a very creative process; theoretically, there are an infinite number of categories into which units could potentially be classified. To illustrate the creativity of this process, think of 10 ways in which the following objects could be divided into two categories. Identify the categories and say which objects are in which categories.

Pen   Gum   Keys   Book

Perhaps, for example, you divided the objects into the categories of edible and nonedible, with the gum in the edible category and the others in the nonedible category. Or maybe you divided them into objects that fit in your pocket (pen, gum, and keys) and those that don't (book). There are undoubtedly many different categories into which these four objects could be classified.

The simplest procedure, of course, is the one that we just used of dividing texts/units into two categories. Content analysts often use a far greater number of categories. Regardless of the number of categories employed, these categories must be mutually exclusive, equivalent, and exhaustive (see Chapter 4). The value of a content-analytic study rests on developing valid categories into which units can be classified. Diligent researchers, therefore, try to follow all the valid measurement procedures discussed in Chapter 5 so that the categories into which the units are coded are, indeed, valid.

Coding Units into Categories.   Once the appropriate units have been determined and the catego-

ries have been developed, researchers train observers, called **coders,** to identify the appropriate category for each unit. Researchers usually use two coders, and preferably more, who independently classify each unit into its appropriate category. Researchers then use a procedure to assess the reliability of these codings. For example, the percentage of agreement between coders can be computed on a unit-by-unit basis. Other formulas, such as W. A. Scott's (1955) *pi,* take into account chance agreements, as well as the complexity of the category system itself. Each procedure yields a coefficient of interobserver reliability. As explained in Chapter 5, a coefficient of .70 or above generally is considered reliable, whereas one below .70 is suspect. Finally, if there is sufficient reliability, coders are asked to work together and reach agreement on coded units about which they disagreed.

As an example of how to code units into categories, consider the content-analytic scheme that Metts (1991) constructed as a pedagogical tool to analyze the types of advertisements that appear in a typical issue of a university newspaper (see Figure 9.2). After identifying the individual advertisements (the unit of analysis), each is placed into one of six mutually exclusive categories on the basis of what it promotes: product, professional service, social/entertainment, recreation, human development, or other. Obtain a copy of your university newspaper and try using the scheme to code the advertisements in the first five pages or so. Then ask a friend to do the same thing. Compare your codings of the individual units with those made by your friend to see the extent to which you agreed or disagreed. If there was less than 70% agreement, perhaps there are some changes you might suggest for the categories of this content-analytic scheme.

It should be pointed out that, to save time, researchers frequently divide the units equally between coders, except for a certain amount (say 20%) that are coded by both observers so that interobserver reliability can be established. Sometimes, however, both observers code all of the units independently, and then they meet, discuss, and reach agreement on all analytic decisions. W. L. Benoit, Pier, and Blaney (1997) used this procedure by

FIGURE 9.2   Content analysis exercise

CONTENT ANALYSIS OF NEWSPAPER ADVERTISEMENTS

PURPOSE: To describe the types of advertisements that appear in a typical issue of a university newspaper.

UNIT OF ANALYSIS: Individual advertisements are the unit of analysis. An advertisement is any published statement by a profit or non-profit organization that endorses, promotes, or encourages a specific behavior on the part of the reader. Excluded from the analysis are any such statements that appear in the "Classified" section of the newspaper.

CATEGORIES: Advertisements must be assigned to one, and only one, of the following categories: product, professional service, social/entertainment, recreation, human development, or other.

CODING FORM

Product—promotes the sale or use of some product or products (e.g., food, film, tires, etc.)

Professional Service—promotes a professional service (e.g., film development, dentist, etc.)

Social/Entertainment—promotes a social event or a form of entertainment (e.g., dance, rock concert, etc.)

Recreation—promotes participation in recreational or physical fitness events (e.g., running program)

Human Development—promotes events for professional, intellectual, cultural, or personal development (e.g., guest lectures)

Other—an advertisement that cannot be placed into one of they above categories

Source: Adapted from Sandra M. Metts, *Instructor's manual*, p. 97, copyright 1991 © by Prentice Hall. Adapted by permission of Allyn & Bacon.

having two of the authors content analyze 206 televised campaign advertisements from the Republican and Democratic general election campaigns for president in 1980, 1984, 1988, 1992, and 1996. Consequently, they did not need to report an inter-observiable reliability coefficient. As they explained, "[W]hen inter-coder reliability is less than 100%, there is no way to tell which coding of the two disagreeing interpretations is preferable. We

know that two authors reached 100% agreement on every analytic decision for every message we studied" (pp. 17–18).

Computer content-analytic programs are also being used to code texts. These programs include: simple word counts; key-word-in-context (KWIC) that lists every word with its content and page number; dictionaries that assign words to groups using some classification scheme; language structure that examines grammar and syntax; and, as mentioned previously, readability formula programs (see Franzosi, 1990, 1995; Riffe et al, 1998; R. P. Weber, 1984, 1990). Computers also are used to conduct "dynamic content analysis," in which people code data in real time into a computer as they watch video (such as a television program).

Analyzing the Data.   Coding units into nominal categories yields qualitative data; counting the number of units in each category yields quantitative data. Knowing the types of categories informs researchers about what is being communicated; knowing the number of units in each category informs them about how often these types of messages are being communicated.

Both types of data are useful for describing, understanding, and critiquing the content of the communication being studied. For example, knowing the types and amount of gender stereotypical themes in books written for children can lead to rich descriptions, interpretive insights, and critiques about what a culture values and is teaching its children about gender. Furthermore, researchers can use this information to hypothesize how input and output variables relate to message behavior. It may be possible, for example, to show how various cultures (an input variable) differ in the gender stereotypes that pervade children's books. It may also be possible to show how such books influence children's thoughts and behaviors (an output variable). Berne (1972) argues that the implicit morals in fairy tales help children develop unconscious "scripts" that influence their behavior later in life. Finally, communication practitioners use these interpretive insights to inform people about appropriate courses of action, such as advising parents about which books their children might read. Content analysis is, thus, a powerful method for analyzing texts that is useful to researchers, practitioners, and consumers alike.

INTERACTION ANALYSIS

People typically view interaction as something they know how to do instinctively. We ordinarily don't pay much attention to routine, everyday ac-

tivities, although we probably pay more attention to talking than walking. From time to time, however, all of us engage in interactions that lead us to pay more conscious attention to what we say and how we say it, perhaps because our apprehension is increased. You probably pay more attention to what you say, for instance, when you are interviewed for a job, confront someone about something bothering you, or talk to a parent while waiting for your date to come downstairs.

Scholars pay a great deal of attention to interaction, believing that much can be learned from what we seem to take for granted (Hopper, 1981). They view interaction as a complex *accomplishment* that requires much knowledge on the part of individual communicators and the ability to coordinate behavior with others. For example, even asking someone the simple question, "Can you please pass the salt?" requires not only knowing rules of grammar and syntax, but also a shared understanding that the question is not meant as a request about the person's *ability* to pass the salt.

The study of interaction, in general, examines messages exchanged during dyadic and group interactions to discover the "systematic and orderly properties which are meaningful to conversants [and researchers]" (Heritage, 1989, p. 23). This involves both description of various features of interaction, as well as an understanding of how those features relate to other variables.

Scholars who study interaction, however, differ in some important ways. One important difference is between those who study interaction using qualitative methods, such as those who conduct **conversation analysis,** and those who use quantitative methods, called **interaction analysis.** The qualitative study of interaction is a form of naturalistic inquiry, so we will discuss it in Chapter 10. Here, we concentrate on interaction analysis.

Describing Interaction and Relating It to Other Variables

The quantitative study of interaction seeks to answer the two general research questions of "What is the nature of communication?" and "How is communication related to other variables?" These are interrelated in the sense that once interaction is described, its features can be related to other variables. For the purposes of discussion, however, we will look at each issue separately.

Describing Interaction.   To describe interaction, researchers focus on a number of things. Some researchers study *linguistic features* of interaction. Such studies range from the analysis of particular words and sentence components (such as verbs; see, for example, Rudolph, 1997), to nonverbal features (from hesitancies and pauses to such things as eye contact and touch; see overview by J. K. Burgoon, 1994), to more interpretive aspects of language (such as powerful versus powerless speech; see, for example, Grob, Meyers, & Schuh, 1997; Hosman, 1997; V. Smith, Siltanen, & Hosman, 1998).

Other researchers study the *content* of interaction by examining, for example, the types of topics people talk about. H. T. Moore (1922) did this by eavesdropping on people in public on the streets of Manhattan and noted the topics they talked about in same-sex and mixed-sex dyads. Moore's study found that the topics talked about most frequently by men (money/business and amusement) and by women (men, clothing, and interior decorating) were the topics talked about the least by the opposite sex. Moore also found that women adapted more to men within mixed-sex dyads by talking about the topics that interested men.

Of course, Moore's study was conducted in 1922, so we would expect that the types of topics discussed would have changed over the course of time, right? Well, a follow-up study by Deakins, Osterink, and Hoey (1987) 65 years later found no change for male and male-female dyads, as money/business and amusement still were the topics talked about most frequently. Female dyads showed one change, as women talked most frequently about women in addition to clothing, interior decoration, and men.

Some researchers are particularly interested in identifying the *purposes* of specific actions and utterances in an interaction. Interactants have general goals in mind when communicating, such as

conveying information to others ("There will be an election Tuesday") and persuading them ("You should vote for candidate X on Tuesday"). Some researchers, therefore, want to know what *functions* messages serve in interactions.

One of the earliest and most influential functional analyses of communication was Bales's (1950) Interaction Process Analysis (IPA) scheme, which examines the communication that characterizes decision-making group interaction. The basic purpose of the IPA scheme is to categorize the purpose, or function, of each person's (and the group's) communication acts forwarded during group discussion into 12 categories: seems friendly, dramatizes, agrees, gives suggestion, gives opinion, gives information, asks for information, asks for opinion, asks for suggestion, disagrees, shows tension, seems unfriendly. A comment such as, "I think we should vote now," for instance, would be categorized using this scheme as "gives suggestion." Notice that the statement is categorized with regard to its function (a suggestion), not its content (about voting).

By studying many decision-making groups, Bales determined a relative range of acts that typically characterize an effective group in each category, and these norms are applied both to individual group members and to the group as a whole. By comparing the interactional patterns of a group and its members to these norms, researchers, practitioners, and group members can infer whether a group is effective and what particular problems are being experienced.

From these early beginnings emerged what is known, today, as Functional Theory (see Gouran & Hirokawa, 1996; Hirokawa & Salazar, 1999; Poole, 1999). The central premise of this theory is that effective group decision making requires that group members satisfy fundamental tasks, called *functional requisites,* and that communication is the means by which this is done. Hirokawa (1985) suggests at least four critical functions that must be met if a group is to be successful:

(1) thorough and accurate understanding of the choice-making situation; (2) identification of a

range of realistic alternative courses of action; (3) thorough and accurate assessment of the positive qualities or consequences associated with alternative choices; and (4) thorough and accurate assessment of the negative qualities or consequences associated with alternative choices. (p. 22)

Many interaction analysts view functional messages that are designed to accomplish particular goals as *moves* or *strategies*. One of the most widely researched interactional strategies, for instance, is compliance-gaining strategies—communication designed to get others to behave in accordance with one's request, such as threats and promises (see, for example, Baglan, Lalumia, & Bayless, 1986; Boster & Stiff, 1984; Dallinger & Hample, 1994; Dillard & Hale, 1992; Levine & Wheeless, 1990; Marwell & Schmitt, 1967; Wiseman & Schenck-Hamlin, 1981). In turn, this has led to an interest in how people use strategies, compliance-resisting strategies, to refuse such compliance (see, for example, Ifert & Roloff, 1996; McLaughlin, Cody, & Robey, 1981; McQuillen, 1986). As Figure 9.3 shows, interaction analysts have studied a wide variety of communication strategies.

Researchers interested in the functional nature of messages exchanged during interaction focus on the purpose of *each* communicator's moves. But other researchers analyze the *structure* of interaction by studying the relationship between conversants' moves. Some do this at the macro level by focusing on the rules people use to guide interactional sequences. Sunwolf and Seibold (1998), for instance, asked people who were waiting in a courthouse—to discover whether they would serve as jurors—to give oral responses to five vignettes that had them imagine themselves as a member of a deliberating jury. The situations were designed to elicit five rules participants brought with them about jury interaction: selection of a leader, how to communicate their opinions on the appropriate verdict, how to communicate with someone outside the group to get information that might affect the group's decision, how to deal with a deviant member, and how long jurors should talk and how they should handle disagreements about this.

Other researchers study the structure of interaction at a more micro level by examining the communication exchanged among interactants. But rather than looking at the strategies that each interactant employs as divorced from the other interactant(s), researchers look at paired sequences of communication behaviors. Jacobs and Jackson (1982) use the analogy of chess to describe this approach, where one person's (communication) moves depends on the other person's (communication) moves. Communication moves that are designed intentionally to be recognized by another as requiring a response or uptake are called *illocutionary acts* (J. L. Austin, 1962).

The combination of an illocutionary act with a meaningful response is called an *adjacency pair.* Adjacency pairs consist of (a) two utterances in length, (b) occurring one after the other, (c) produced by different speakers, made up of (d) a first pair part (such as a question, "What time is it?") that calls out for (e) a second pair part (in this case the answer, "It's 10 o'clock") that has some discernible relationship to the first pair part (McLaughlin, 1984). Examples of adjacency pairs include request-grant or deny, greeting-greeting, compliment-accept or reject, insult-response, and accuse-deny or confess.

The adjacency pair, and other concepts like it, has been used to understand a number of different types of interactional sequences. For example, researchers (many working from a qualitative perspective) have studied the sequences of moves associated with interactional openings (e.g., Hopper, 1992; Krivonos & Knapp, 1975; Nofsinger, 1975; Schiffrin, 1977), arguments (e.g., Alderton & Frey, 1983; Jacobs & Jackson, 1981, 1982), conversational closings (e.g., Knapp, Hart, Friedrich, & Shulman, 1973), and retelling sequences of events stories (e.g., Jefferson, 1978).

Relating Interaction to Other Variables.   While some researchers restrict their focus to describing the various features of interaction, most interaction analysts go beyond description to study the ways in which interaction is related to significant input and output variables. Some researchers, for

---

FIGURE 9.3 Examples of communication strategies studied in interaction analysis

---

Accounts: Communication designed to explain one's behavior (Braaten, Cody, & DeTienne, 1993; Buttney, 1993; McLaughlin, Cody, & O'Hair, 1983; McLaughlin, Cody, & Rosenstein, 1983; Mongeau, Hale, & Alles, 1994; Schonbach, 1980)

Affinity-Seeking: Communication designed to get others to like a person (R. A. Bell & Daly, 1984; R. A. Bell, Tremblay, & Buerkel-Rothfuss, 1987; Buerkel-Rothfuss & Bell, 1987; R. B. Rubin, Rubin, & Martin, 1993; Tolhuizen, 1989a; Wanzer, 1998)

Argument: Communication designed to forward opinions (Alderton & Frey, 1983, 1986; Brashers, Adkins, & Meyers, 1994; Canary, Brossman, & Seibold, 1987; Jacobs, 1989; Jacobs & Jackson, 1981, 1982; R. A. Meyers & Brashers, 1998; R. A. Meyers, Seibold, & Brashers, 1991)

Comforting/Social Support: Communication designed to provide emotional support or help (Albrecht, Adelman, & Associates, 1987; Barbee & Cunningham, 1995; Bullis & Horn, 1995; Burleson, 1984; Burleson, Albrecht, & Sarason, 1994; Burleson & Goldsmith, 1998; R. A. Clark & Delia, 1997; Cutrona & Suhr, 1992; Goldsmith, 1992)

Conflict/Dispute Resolution: Communication designed to manage relational disagreements (Canary, Cunningham, & Cody, 1988; Canary & Spitzberg, 1987, 1989, 1990; Conrad, 1991; Legge & Rawlins, 1992; Marin, Sherblom, & Shipps, 1994; Millar, Rogers, & Bavelas, 1984; Nicotera, 1993; M. J. Papa & Natalle, 1989; Sillars, 1980; Sillars, Coletti, Parry, & Rogers, 1982; Sorenson, Hawkins, & Sorenson, 1995; Witteman, 1992)

Deception: Communication designed to lie or be deceitful (Buller & Burgoon, 1994; J. K. Burgoon, Buller, Guerrero, Afifi, & Feldman, 1996; deTurck, Freeley, & Roman, 1998; deTurck & Miller, 1985; Knapp & Comadena, 1979; Knapp, Hart, & Dennis, 1974; Levine, McCornack, & Avery, 1992; McCornack & Parks, 1990, Metts, 1989; O'Hair & Cody, 1994; Powers, 1993)

Disqualification/Equivocation: Communication designed to answer questions in an ambiguous, indirect, contradictory, or evasive manner (Bavelas, Black, Chovil, & Mullet, 1990a, 1990b; Bavelas &

Chovil, 1986; Bavelas & Smith, 1982; Chovil, 1994; M. L. Williams & Goss, 1975)

Embarrassment/Embarrassment-Reducing: Communication designed to promote or reduce the discomfort associated with embarrassment (Braithwaite, 1995; B. R. Brown, 1970; Cupach & Metts, 1990, 1992; Cupach, Metts, & Hazleton, 1986; Petronio, 1990; Petronio, Olson, & Dollar, 1989; Sharkey, 1991, 1992; Sharkey, Kulp, Carpenter, Lee, & Rodillas, 1997; Sharkey & Stafford, 1990)

Guilt: Communication designed to make a person feel bad about behavior committed (Baumeister, Reis, & Delespaul, 1995; Baumeister, Stillwell, & Heatherton, 1994, 1995; W. H. Jones, Kugler, & Adams, 1995; Vangelisti, Daly, & Rudnik, 1991)

Humor: Communication designed to make other people laugh (S. Booth-Butterfield & Booth-Butterfield, 1991; Graham, Papa, & Brooks, 1992; Wanzer et al., 1995, 1996)

Hurtful: Communication designed to psychologically hurt a person (Vangelisti, 1994b; Vangelisti & Crumley, 1998)

Jealousy: Communication designed to respond to feelings/episodes of jealousy (Afifi & Reichert, 1996; P. A. Andersen, Eloy, Guerrero, & Spitzberg, 1995; Guerrero, Andersen, Jorgensen, Spitzberg, & Eloy, 1995)

Immediacy: Communication designed to decrease physical and/or psychological distance between people (Christensen & Menzel, 1998; Freitas, Meyers, & Avtgis, 1998; McCroskey et al., 1995; A. Moore, Masterson, Christophel, & Shear, 1996; J. Rodriguez, Plax, & Kearney, 1996; Thweatt & McCroskey, 1998)

Information-Seeking: Communication designed to acquire information (Berger & di Battista, 1992; Edgar, Freimuth, Hammond, McDonald, & Fink, 1992; Waldron, 1990)

Interruption/Silence: Communication designed to interrupt another person or to produce silence (Capella & Planalp, 1981; DeFrancisco, 1991; Dindia, 1987; C. W. Kennedy & Camden, 1983; Markel, Long, & Saine, 1976; McLaughlin & Cody, 1982; D. H. Zimmerman & West, 1975)

(continued)

FIGURE 9.3

Opening Lines: Communication designed to express a desire to initiate a romantic relationship or encounter (Levine, King, & Popoola, 1994)

Politeness/Face-Saving: Communication designed to be courteous (Baxter, 1984; P. Brown & Levinson, 1978; R. T. Craig, Tracy, & Spisak, 1986; Leichty & Applegate, 1991; Lim & Bowers, 1991; J. R. Meyer, 1994a; S. Wilson, Aleman, & Leatham, 1998)

Relational Maintenance, Intensification, and Repair: Communication designed to sustain, increase, or repair an interpersonal relationship (Baxter & Dindia, 1990; Baxter & Simon, 1993; Canary & Stafford, 1992; Canary, Stafford, Hause, & Wallace, 1993; Dainton, Stafford, & Canary, 1994; Dindia & Baxter, 1987; R. B. Patterson & Beckett, 1995; R. B. Patterson & O'Hair, 1992; Stafford & Canary, 1991; Tolhuizen, 1989b)

Relational Termination: Communication designed to end an interpersonal relationship (Baxter, 1979, 1982; Cody, Kersten, Braatan, & Dickson, 1992; Cupach & Metts, 1986; Metts & Cupach, 1986)

Self-Disclosure: Communication designed to share information about oneself with others (G. Chen, 1993; Cozby, 1973; Dindia & Allen, 1992; Jourard, 1971; Sanders, Wiseman, & Matz, 1990; Wheeless, 1976; Wheeless & Grotz, 1976; Wheeless, Nesser, & McCroskey, 1986)

Sexual: Communication designed to promote or discuss sexual matters (Egland, Spitzberg, & Zormeier, 1996; Metts & Spitzberg, 1996)

Sexual Harassment and Resistance: Unwelcomed communication designed to request sexual favors from another or to resist such requests (Bingham, 1994; Keyton, 1996; Kreps, 1993; Metts, Cupach, & Imahori, 1992; Motley & Reeder, 1995; Wood, 1992)

Storytelling: Communication designed to share a narrative (M. H. Brown, 1985; Helmer, 1993; J. W. Kelly, 1985; Mandelbaum, 1987; McLaughlin, Cody, Kane, & Robey, 1981; J. C. Meyer, 1995)

---

example, are particularly interested in how the characteristics of interactants influence their behavior during an interaction. The effects of sociodemographic characteristics, such as gender (see Canary & Emmers-Sommer, 1997, for an overview) or race (see Hecht, Collier, & Ribeau, 1993, for an overview of African American communication), have received some attention. Others focus on personality traits, such as: affective orientation (the tendency to use one's emotions as guiding information) (M. Booth-Butterfield & Booth-Butterfield, 1990, 1994, 1998; Yelsma, 1995); anxiety (Shepherd & Condra, 1988); attachment style (the type and quality of relationship one wants to share with another) (Guerrero & Burgoon, 1996; Simon & Baxter, 1993); attributional confidence (confidence in the ability to predict other people's feelings and behavior) (Gao & Gudykunst, 1995); cognitive complexity ("the degree of differentiation, articulation, and integration within a cognitive system," Burleson & Caplan, 1998, p. 233); defensiveness

(Stamp, Vangelisti, & Daly, 1992); depression (Patterson & Bettini, 1993; Segrin, 1990, 1992; Segrin & Dillard, 1991); extroversion (Hecht, Boster, & LaMer, 1989); empathic ability (Stiff, Dillard, Somera, Kim, & Sleight, 1988); locus of control (degree to which people versus the environment are held accountable for enacted behavior) (Alderton, 1980, 1982; Arnston, Mortensen, & Lustig, 1980; Canary, Cunningham, & Cody, 1988; A. M. Rubin, 1993; R. B. Rubin & Rubin, 1992; Steinfatt, 1987); loneliness (C. M. Anderson & Martin, 1995; R. A. Bell, 1985; R. A. Bell & Daly, 1985; R. A. Bell & Roloff, 1991; Spitzberg & Canary, 1985; Spitzberg & Hurt, 1989; Wanzer et al., 1996; Zakahi & Duran, 1985; Zakahi & Goss, 1995); need for privacy (J. K. Burgoon, 1982; Hosman, 1991; Hosman & Siltanen, 1995; L. H. Larson & Bell, 1988); self-efficacy (degree of confidence people have in being able to attain their goals) (R. B. Rubin, Martin, Bruning, & Powers, 1993); self-esteem (Rancer,

Kosberg, & Baukus, 1992; Rancer, Kosberg, & Silvestri, 1992); self-monitoring (the extent to which people pay attention to their verbal and nonverbal behaviors) (R. A. Bell, 1987; Hample & Dallinger, 1987a, 1987b; Snyder, 1974, 1979); and tolerance for disagreement (Teven, McCroskey, & Richmond, 1998).

Of particular interest to communication scholars are *communication predispositions,* traits that relate directly to a person's tendencies toward communication behavior. Figure 9.4 presents some important communication predispositions that scholars have studied. In addition to communication predispositions, scholars working from a cognitive perspective have also studied how people's communication motives (see, for example, C. A. Anderson & Martin, 1995; Graham, Barbato, & Perse, 1993; R. B. Rubin, Perse, & Barbato, 1988; R. B. Rubin & Rubin, 1992; Zorn, 1993) and planning processes affect their interpersonal interactions (see, for example, Berger, 1989; Berger & Bell, 1988; Berger & di Battista, 1992, 1993; Berger & Jordan, 1992; Berger, Karol, & Jordan, 1989; di Battista, 1994; Jordan, 1994, 1998; J. R. Meyer, 1994b; Waldron, 1990).

Many researchers also want to know how various aspects of interaction relate to important outcomes. Researchers might study, for instance, how interactional elements are related to a person being persuaded to a particular point of view, partners being more or less satisfied with their relationships, or group members engaging in higher or lower quality decision making.

Conducting Interaction Analysis

Conducting interaction analysis involves two general tasks: (a) obtaining a sample of interaction, and (b) analyzing that sample of interaction.

Obtaining a Sample of Interaction. A number of ways of obtaining texts were explained earlier in this chapter. In gathering a sample of interaction, researchers make choices that affect both the type and quality of the data obtained. These choices include the type of interactional data required, the

desired location of the interaction, and the appropriate means for gathering the data.

An important consideration is whether *any interaction* may be studied or whether *specific interactions* are required. For example, researchers can study how people take turns talking in any interaction. Researchers interested in how power differences affect interaction, however, must study interactions in which power differs, such as superior-subordinate interactions. And some researchers are interested only in particular interactions, such as physician-patient interactions.

Another consideration is whether the interaction is to be *natural and unstructured* or whether people are asked to engage in a *structured interactional* activity or task. For example, in their research program on negotiation and bargaining during crisis situations, Rogan and Hammer (1994, 1995) analyzed audio recordings of authentic crisis negotiations obtained from the Special Operations and Research Unit of the FBI training academy at Quantico, Virginia. In contrast to this type of natural and unstructured interaction, Solomon (1997) was interested in the explicitness of relational partners' request for a date, so she asked one member of a dating relationship to telephone his or her partner and ask for a date. Participants were seated in a private room with a telephone and tape recorder and received the following instructions:

> *We would like you to call your dating partner with the goal of arranging some kind of date. It's important that you try to talk to your partner the way you normally would. Just consider how you would normally talk to your partner if you wanted to make plans with him or her, and try to talk that way today. It's important that you let your partner know at the beginning of the conversation that you're making the call as part of a study and that your side of the conversation is being recorded. So all you do is (1) call your dating partner; (2) press the record button; (3) explain that you're calling as part of a study in the Center for Communication Research and that your side of the conversation is being recorded, but that your partner is not being recorded; and (4) proceed as you normally would when you want to make arrangements to do something with*

FIGURE 9.4 Examples of communication predispositions

Affirming versus Nonaffirming Communicator Style: "An affirming style supports rather than attacks a person's self concept" (Infante, Rancer, & Jordan, 1996, p. 318).

Alexithymia: "The reticence to communicate affect" (Johnston, Stinski, & Meyers, 1993, p. 149).

Argumentativeness: "A personality trait which predisposes an individual to recognize controversial issues, to advocate positions on them, and to refute other positions" (Infante & Rancer, 1982, p. 68; see also Rancer, 1998).

Communicative Adaptability/Flexibility: The degree to which an individual has the cognitive and behavioral "ability to perceive socio-interpersonal relationships and adapt one's interaction goals and behaviors accordingly" (Duran, 1983, p. 320; see also Duran, 1992).

Communication Apprehension: "An individual's level of fear or anxiety associated with either real or anticipated communication with another person or persons" (McCroskey, 1977, p. 78; see also McCroskey & Richmond, 1987, 1998).

Communication Competence: "The ability of an interactant to choose among available communicative behaviors in order that he [or she] may successfully accomplish his [or her] own interpersonal goals during an encounter while maintaining the face and line of his [or her] fellow interactants within the constraints of the situation" (Wiemann, 1977, p. 198; see also R. B. Rubin, 1990; R. B. Rubin & Martin, 1994; Spitzberg & Cupach, 1984).

Communicative Suspicion: "Predisposition toward believing that the messages produced by others are deceptive" (Levine & McCornack, 1991, p. 328).

Compulsive Communicators/Talkaholics: "A trait that predisposes a person to communicate excessively, even when to remain silent would be in the person's best interest" (McCroskey & Richmond, 1993, p. 109; see also Bostrom & Harrington, 1999; McCroskey & Richmond, 1995).

Conversational Narcissism: The tendency for people to "turn the topics of ordinary conversation to themselves without showing sustained interest in others' topics" (Derber, 1979, p. 5; see also Vangelisti, Knapp, & Daly, 1990).

Conversational Sensitivity: The "ability to detect meanings in what others say, a good memory for conversations, an ability to generate a variety of ways of saying something in a social exchange, an interest in listening to conversations, skill at detecting affinity and power relationships in conversations, and an appreciation for the nuances for what is said in social interaction" (Daly, Vangelisti, & Daughton, 1987, p. 191; see also Stacks & Murphy, 1993).

Humor Orientation: The degree to which people use "intentional verbal and nonverbal messages that elicit laughter, chuckling, and other forms of spontaneous behavior taken to mean pleasure, delight, and/or surprise in the targeted receiver" (S. Booth-Butterfield & Booth-Butterfield, 1991, p. 206).

Interaction Involvement: "The extent to which an individual partakes in a social environment" (Cegala, 1981, p. 112).

Receiver Apprehension: "The fear of misinterpreting, inadequately processing, and/or of not being able to adjust psychologically to messages sent by others" (Wheeless, 1975, p. 263; see also Roberts, 1984).

Rhetorical Sensitivity: The tendency to be "an undulating, fluctuating entity, always unsure, always second guessing, continually weighing" communication alternatives (R. P. Hart & Burks, 1972, p. 91; see also R. P. Hart, Carlson, & Eadie, 1980).

Sociocommunicative Style: A person's image of his or her own...regular communication behavior patterns" (Richmond & Martin, 1998, p. 134).

Unwillingness to Communicate: A "chronic tendency to avoid and/or devalue oral communication" (J. K. Burgoon, 1976, p. 60).

Willingness to Communicate: "An individual's predisposition to initiate communication with others" (McCroskey & Richmond, 1998, p. 120; see also McCroskey, 1992; McCroskey & Richmond, 1990).

this partner. When you're done with the call, stop the recorder and come get me. You can talk for as little or as much time as you like. Again, try to do what you normally would when calling this partner to make some kinds of plans. (p. 104)

Another consideration is whether the conversation needs to be *real* or can be *hypothetical.* For example, if an actual interaction between married couples about purchasing a home is desired, couples who have contacted real estate agents could be asked to tape their interactions whenever they talk about their impending house purchase. However, if researchers are interested in the functional messages husbands and wives use to persuade a spouse to buy a house, people could be told to imagine themselves engaged in an interaction with the spouse and asked to construct a persuasive message. The hypothetical procedure is, undoubtedly, the more common one, but it does not necessarily capture accurately what occurs in actual interaction because it allows people more time to think about their message choices than they have in normal interactions, and it does not account for interactional sequences of actual conversation.

Another consideration is whether the data are to be acquired from *one individual* or *both/all interactants.* For instance, in studying communication strategies, researchers frequently use survey methods that ask research participants to select the strategy they and/or an interactional partner normally use. One problem here concerns the validity of one interactional partner's answers about his or her partner's choice(s). Of course, one solution is to ask both interactional partners. And when interactional features are studied, such as the sequencing of communication moves, clearly, both/all interactants are needed.

The *location* in which an actual interaction is studied also affects the nature of the data. Three locations that differ in terms of the control provided to researchers and the naturalness of the setting for participants are in a laboratory, in interactants' homes or offices, or in some publicly accessible place, such as a shopping mall or on public transportation. Using a laboratory to study interaction certainly provides researchers with the most con-

trol, because they can structure the environment according to their needs (including the use of experimental manipulations), and it makes videotaping easy. Studying interaction in a laboratory, however, may make interactants feel uneasy or overly aware that they are being watched (which can produce the Hawthorne effect discussed in Chapter 5). People may feel more at ease and comfortable in their homes or offices, but researchers have less control over those environments than in a laboratory. Studying interactions overheard in public affords researchers the least amount of control, but is the most natural of these three locations.

Researchers must also consider the *means for gathering the data.* Some current available options include audiotaping, videotaping, observational notes taken by researchers, and questionnaires answered by respondents. Audiotape and videotape recorders are readily available. In a laboratory setting, a camera can be set up so it cannot be seen by research participants (although the taping needs to be done with their permission, of course). Researchers can even set up cameras on tripods in people's homes and leave them simple instructions on recording their interactions. Taking notes while observing interaction is also possible for certain tasks, such as noting the topics discussed or the types of functional messages exchanged. This procedure, however, is open to many problems and biases, since it is very difficult to keep track of all the sequential messages exchanged. Finally, questionnaires are often used when studying hypothetical situations, such as asking people to indicate which compliance-gaining strategy they would use in a hypothetical instance or asking them to write out what they would say in such a situation and then categorizing the message as a particular type of compliance-gaining strategy.

Analyzing the Sample of Interaction.   The specific analysis of a sample of interaction, of course, depends on whether the goal is to describe interaction or relate it to other variables, as discussed previously. But in a broader sense, the analysis also depends on the form the data take. For instance, in cases where people are asked to choose between different types of communication strategies, once the choice is made, the data are ready to be analyzed using appropriate statistical procedures.

In cases where a sample of actual interactions are obtained, researchers have at least two analytic options. First, research participants can be invited to make judgments about their own interactions. Aune, Buller, and Aune (1996), for example, investigated differences between more and less developed couples in the rules they use for the experience and expression of emotion. Twenty-four couples who had been dating between 1 and 3 months and 28 couples who were married or had lived together 1 year or more were invited to a communication laboratory. The couples identified a common problem that was not too severe (rated between 3 and 8 on a 1–10 scale), and discussed the problem for 12 minutes. They were seated side by side in swivel chairs in front of a one-way mirror, behind which was a video camera that recorded their interactions. They were told to act as they would if they were having the discussion at home and were left alone to encourage spontaneous and natural conversation. The researchers then separately showed partners five 1-minute segments of the videotape and asked them to stop it when they recalled an emotion experienced during the discussion. For each instance, participants used Likert-type scales to assess the intensity of the experience, perceived degree of expression, and perceived appropriateness of emotion expression.

In most cases, however, interaction is analyzed by trained observers. J. K. Burgoon et al. (1996) justified their choice of employing observers rather than research participants to analyze the data obtained from mock interviews as follows:

> *Relative to participant receivers, observers represent lesser independence with senders (Surra & Ridley, 1991). They offer a distinct perspective that is relatively free from the perceptual biases, cognitive load, spatial and temporal immediacy, relational engagement, and conversational demands associated with actual participation (Burgoon, 1994). As such, they afford a clear contrast to sender participants and potentially greater ability to make fine discriminations than participant re-*
> *ceivers occupied with their own conversational responsibilities. (pp. 57–58)*

In having observers (or research participants) analyze interactions, the interactions are often first transcribed into a written form. Researchers need to decide how much detail is needed in a transcript to answer their research questions. Labov and Fanshel (1977), for instance, have one of the most detailed transcription procedures, which includes pictures of electronic spectrographic analysis of the pitch waves of the voices of the interactants, times pauses to 1/100 second, and uses a detailed system to categorize audible breaths. Their analysis of 15 minutes of an interaction between a therapist and a client took 9 years to transcribe and analyze! At the other extreme is a simple counting of the number or types of topics people talk about or the verbal moves they make. The rule of thumb in interaction analysis is not to include any more detail in a transcript than is needed to answer the research question(s).

Once a written text is generated, researchers often use the procedures discussed in content analysis to have coders unitize and categorize the types of messages exchanged during the interaction. Sometimes unitizing is relatively easy, such as determining the different topics discussed. At other times, it is very difficult to determine where each interactional unit begins and ends, as in determining meaningful adjacency pairs in a group discussion. To unitize in a reliable manner, researchers assess interobserver reliability. Once reliable units are determined, they are categorized, and reliability coefficients are computed for these codings.

Once the units have been unitized and categorized reliably, they are analyzed through appropriate data-analytic procedures. The analysis may involve counting and summarizing the codes for each interactant, such as the type and number of compliance-gaining strategies each used, or it may involve studying paired sequential messages. Researchers often employ the statistical procedures discussed in Chapters 13 and 14 to analyze differences between groups (such as how males and females might differ in their interactions) or relationships between variables (such as how interactional features are related to group decision-making performance).

Interaction analysts, thus, study what people normally take for granted, viewing interaction as a complex and organized accomplishment that deserves study. By describing interaction and relating it to other variables, researchers make sense of this complex art and skill.

PERFORMANCE STUDIES

The final approach to textual analysis covered in this chapter is *performance studies.* It is quite unique from the three perspectives of rhetorical criticism, content analysis, and interaction analysis described earlier. **Performance studies,** according to Pelias (1992), is "the process of dialogic engagement with one's own and others' aesthetic communication through the means of performance" (p. 15). It combines elements of textual analysis, naturalistic inquiry, and techniques from the oral interpretation of literature (Crow, 1988;

Stucky, 1986). In performance studies, researchers interpret texts by carefully examining their communication nuances and then recreating them through performance. In essence, researchers perform texts as a method of inquiry that enables them and audiences of performances to interpret the aesthetic richness of those texts.

To help explain this type of research, we asked Ronald J. Pelias (Southern Illinois University), a respected scholar who has written extensively about performance studies, including a textbook (Pelias, 1992) and a text on writing performance (Pelias, 1999), to provide an overview of this method. His explanation makes clear how performance researchers use their own voices and bodies as tools of exploration. The process of performance studies demands that the researcher develop understanding and empathy for the communication perspectives being portrayed that enable the intricacies and functions of language patterns to be clearly displayed in performance.

Performance as a Method

Ronald J. Pelias, Southern Illinois University

When most people think of performance, they imagine theatrical presentations, actors on stage, on television, or in films. Performances occur, of course, in other contexts. For instance, when people tell stories of their lives in everyday conversations or participate in religious or public rituals, their communication might best be described as a theatrical performance. Broadly conceived, theatrical presentations might include, then, a wide range of communication practices that are aesthetic, practices that function in the artistic realm. We need not, however, think about performance as solely an aesthetic communicative act. Instead, we can also view performance as a method of inquiry. Thinking this way establishes performance as both an aesthetic *event* for our enjoyment and study, as well as a *method* for examining the communication acts of others.

The belief that performance is a powerful method of inquiry is based on a simple premise: To take on or embody the communication acts of others is a profound way of coming to understand them. More specifically, reaching some level of understanding rests on performance researchers' willingness to work in three particular ways.

First, researchers must be willing to use their own voices and bodies as tools of exploration. When doing so, researchers work *somatically,* a process of thinking, intuiting, and feeling with the voice and body. Performance researchers employ their own voices and bodies as probes, as instruments that examine the intricate workings of others' communication acts. The performance researcher's voice and body, then, are the equivalent of the statistician's computer program—they compute or tally what one has come to discover.

Performance as a Method

Second, performance researchers must be willing to give over or submit to the presence of others. In short, they put themselves aside in order to witness others speak through their own voices and bodies. Coming to understand others through the performance method requires that researchers provide space within themselves for others to speak. They allow their own voices and bodies to take on the qualities of others. Through empathy and trial and error, they work toward becoming others. This holds true even in cases when performers elect to place others' communication acts in dialogue with or in opposition to their own.

Third, performance researchers must be willing to reflect on what their voices and bodies reveal as they go through the process. They must constantly ask, "What is my voice and body saying to me as I enact different behaviors?" Their process is one of listening to themselves, of analyzing what they feel, hear, and see as they speak the words of others.

With these beliefs in mind, we can turn to how performance researchers proceed in generating and reporting their insights. While there are no set fundamental steps that all performance researchers follow, we can identify six fundamental steps that appear common to the work of those researchers who consider performance a method of inquiry. One caution: While the steps are presented in a linear sequence, it is often the case that performance researchers find themselves returning to an earlier stage for further reflection.

Generating and Reporting Insights in Performance Studies

Step One: Selecting. Performance researchers start their work by identifying the communication act or text they wish to examine. At times, they find the text they wish to explore by listening to and recording others' speech. In such cases, they may take a communication act and create a written text that captures the other's utterance with more or less specificity. For example, a researcher might just note what the other person said or transcribe pauses, inflections, emphases, disfluencies, and so on, until the researcher feels that he or she has provided a highly detailed replication of another's speech. At other times, a researcher might begin with written material as the communication act to be examined. From literary texts, to public speeches, to autobiographies, to even scholarly essays, performance researchers find material worth pursuing. Whatever the case, the text that the performance researcher selects may provide minimal or considerable information about the other that the researcher wishes to explore.

Step Two: Playing. Having selected a text, the researcher begins to play, trying on different vocal and bodily behaviors. The researcher experiments with voicing the words with various attitudes, inflections, and motives. The researcher experiments with movement, altering the intensity and range of the actions. In the initial working with the text, the researcher gains some tentative understandings. The researcher starts to make sense of what the other's text is saying. At this point, however, the researcher remains open to numerous readings. Playing allows the researcher to entertain a variety of interpretations, to encounter various possibilities, and to enact multiple explanations. As the process of playing continues, the researcher collects clues and follows hunches, always remaining receptive to the intricacies of the other's text. The researcher resists formulating any definitive understanding in the desire to embrace the complexity of the other's text. The researcher pursues, through voice and body, the possible ways the other's text might be embodied. The task involves both careful attention to the information that the voice and body is generating, as well as a willingness to drop one's own inhibitions as the other's text is explored.

Step Three: Testing. Playing generates understandings; testing establishes the range of legitimate understandings. At its most fundamental level, this step acknowledges that people typically

(continued)

use words in predictable ways. When a word is spoken, it carries a range of denotative and connotative meanings. Testing involves isolating or specifying the range of possibilities. The researcher uses the other's text to guide his or her vocal and body work, and the researcher's vocal and body work help reveal textual dimensions. The movement back and forth between textual evidence (e.g., the actual words, an audio- or videotape, or the speaker's comments about his or her intent) allows the researcher to discover what appears valid. It pinpoints the claims that the researcher is willing to support. In the end, the researcher may feel that there are several permissible interpretations of a given text.

Step Four: Choosing.   Choosing is a question of selecting among those valid interpretations to isolate one possible understanding to pursue. It sets in motion a **performance vision,** a reading that the performance researcher attempts to enact. At this stage, the researcher questions if all the dimensions of his or her interpretation coalesce; if all the parts come together to form a coherent explanation. The researcher also considers whether the chosen textual understanding should be placed in dialogue with other perspectives. In other words, the researcher may elect to simply present the other's utterance or may decide to stage his or her own or someone else's alternative point of view alongside the other's text. In the first case, the performance researcher is giving consent to the other, allowing the other to speak through his or her own voice and body. In the second case, the researcher presents the other's text but not without marking some distance from or opposition to the other's utterance. Whatever the case, choosing involves commitment to a performance concept on the basis of a particular understanding of the other's text.

Step Five: Repeating.   Repeating the words of another, over and over, allows the performance researcher to set and refine his or her chosen inter-

pretation. In this stage, the researcher finds nuances of meaning, subtle distinctions, and fine discriminations. Repetition leads to a depth of understanding. It is a way of making another's utterance one's own. With each repetition, the other's utterance settles more and more comfortably within one's body. As the performance researcher memorizes the other's words, they become natural, as if one's own. At this stage, the researcher becomes another, taking on the other's voice and body, speaking and moving as if he or she were someone else.

Step Six: Presenting.   Once choices are set through successive repetitions, the researcher is ready to report what he or she has discovered through public performance. Public presentation, the final step in the process, puts on display for others' consideration what the performance researcher has come to understand. Performance, then, is a mode of producing one's insights for public assessment. But even in the final stage of public performance, the researcher continues to learn about the text. Lines that the researcher thought would be viewed one way, for instance, may be taken quite another by the audience. As the researcher takes in the audience's responses, certain understandings that he or she once held may be reconsidered. In short, the researcher may return to earlier stages in the process, once again playing, testing, choosing, and repeating until he or she feels confident about the interpretation of the other's utterance.

Following public presentation, the researcher may also elect to write in essay form what he or she has discovered through the performance work. Ideally, the essay captures the sensuousness and power of the artistic event. It reproduces for the reader the aesthetic experience of viewing the public presentation.

Whether the researcher elects to report findings through public performance or written essay, the steps of selecting, playing, testing, choosing,

Performance as a Method

repeating, and presenting are a method for examining the communication acts of others. They position the researcher to learn about others' discourse experientially, to come to know others by becoming them, to live in complete empathy, at least for a time, in the voice and body of others.

As Pelias also points out, performance scholars not only perform texts but also often write about performance from a variety of perspectives and interests. Sometimes they focus on a performance that they gave and what they learned personally from performing. Randall (1993), for instance, vividly describes the complexities she encountered in conducting a performance study:

> I eventually learned that if I am committed to embodying another human, then I must include all the details available. For me it became the ultimate challenge in not only creativity but accountability as well. I was provided with the words and paralinguistic features. But from that I had to create visual, mental, and emotional aspects of the character while remaining true to her real-life experience. (p. 198)

Other researchers focus on interpreting the significance of particular performances and/or those who wrote and/or performed them. L. Papa (1999), for instance, examined how the play *Waiting for Lefty*, written by Clifford Odets and first performed in 1935, indoctrinated United States workers into issues of the labor movement, while Fleming (1999) examined ways in which Argentinean playwright Griselda Gambara used Sophocles's *Antigone* myth to "comment upon the political repression Argentina faced under military Juntas which ruled and terrorized the country from 1976–1983" (p. 74).

Many scholars are interested in the performance of texts acquired through naturalistic inquiry that they or someone else conducted (see Chapter 10). Their report might describe the conclusions reached about performing such a text.

Randall (1993), for example, described the performative decisions she and her partner made in recreating a couple's role-play from a tape-recording and a written transcript. Her report illustrated the intricate process used to develop a communicatively rich and nuanced public presentation.

Other researchers analyze events from the perspective of performance, identifying, for instance, how those events constitute sites of performance. Sometimes researchers focus on explaining events that occurred in the past. Fuoss (1999), for instance, used archival materials—both texts and images—to show how lynchings are "performance-saturated events" and to posit "the concept of a 'performance complex' to describe the entire web of performance woven in and around lynchings" (p. 1). Latham (1997) analyzed displays by female bathers in the 1920s to reveal the performative "ways in which the female body serves as a site where cultural values are exhibited, endorsed, defied, mediated, and transformed" (p. 170).

Many researchers choose to study contemporary events and everyday behavior as performative sites. Brouwer (1998), for instance, analyzed the politically precarious performative phenomenon of individuals who acquire tattoos that proclaim that they have HIV/AIDS, while Nadesan and Sotirin (1998) offered alternative possibilities to "normal" and "moral" conceptions and performances of breast-feeding.

Performance studies is, thus, a type of textual analysis that involves obtaining, analyzing, performing, and writing about texts. This type of research provides a uniquely qualitative perspective for researchers to use in studying and interpreting texts.

CONCLUSION

A famous industrialist once said, "A person's language, as a rule, is an index of his or her mind." This suggests that examining word choices can provide insights into people's characters. The essence of this message is also a basic premise of textual analysts. Their mission is understanding how people think, and consequently act, by studying patterns displayed in their discourse, broadly defined.

Embedded in texts are clues to the regularities in human thought and conduct. Those regularities are like the tracks wilderness scouts use to trace the movements of wildlife. One has to be trained and equipped to discern animals' footprints and other signs of activity and from them to infer predictable behavioral patterns. But once key features are decoded, they become evidence, useful guides to tracing and predicting the animals' future behavior. Texts preserve tracks of people's communication behavior. Analysts sift through them to identify, analyze, and perform the patterns underlying how we act and interact.

CHAPTER 10

NATURALISTIC INQUIRY

Two communication professors, car-pooling to work one day, were listening to the news on the radio. One featured story concerned a teenager who had brought a gun to school the day before and shot several classmates who had been taunting him. The driver shook his head sadly and asked aloud, "What could those kids have been *saying* that would drive that boy to commit murder?" His companion mused, "Perhaps verbal abuse is commonplace at that school. If it is, I wonder why students *there* are so cruel to each other—what's life like at that school? How do those who bully others justify to themselves what they're doing?" "And I wonder how other teasing victims deal with them—without using a gun," the driver pondered, "If we knew, murders like this might be prevented!" His colleague nodded thoughtfully, and they drove on.

Next on the news was a feature story in which the chief executive officer of a new and unusually profitable local business was interviewed. She bragged, "We owe our success to the terrific *teamwork* in our firm. Our competitors' employees don't talk with each other and cooperate the way *our* people do." The driver smiled and turned to his companion and said, "I'd love to find out what she means by 'teamwork,' 'talk,' and 'cooperate'— you know, what *really* goes on in that firm, and why people there work together so effectively. My organizational communication students would eat up that kind of information." "So would managers in *any* company," agreed his colleague.

As they pulled into the campus parking lot, the driver said, "That news report this morning brought to mind some useful research ideas. I wonder, too, how that station decides which events to include in the news." "Hey," exclaimed his col-

league as they entered the building, "that's *another* worthwhile research topic!" The first researcher laughed, "If we follow up on all of them, we'll have a busy year ahead!"

If you were one of those researchers, your first task would be reading this chapter. That's because the methodologies examined so far are based on analyzing texts or measuring how people respond to researchers' cues (e.g., manipulated variables or survey questions). Researchers' concerns predominate in these studies. Other researchers, however, believe that researcher control distorts the inquiry process. They maintain that the social *context* in which people communicate influences what occurs. These researchers want to study people in the situations where they usually interact—at the local high school, successful business, or radio station— behaving as they customarily do when engaged in their everyday activities, without interfering in (or controlling) what they say or do. We call research that focuses on how people behave when they are absorbed in genuine life experiences in natural settings, **naturalistic inquiry.**

Some of these researchers observe (and even participate in) those situations directly; some ask participants to describe in detail what they and others say, do, and/or think in those situations; most do both. Their research reports describe and explain patterns in participants' communication behavior. These reports often include how participants *perceive* their own experiences and how researchers interpret them. They explain to readers commonalities in how people interact in the particular situations the researchers studied. Readers may then apply those insights to comparable situations they wish to understand better. This chapter explores how researchers employ naturalistic inquiry to study communication behavior.

COMMON ASSUMPTIONS GUIDING NATURALISTIC INQUIRY

In Chapter 1, we discussed two philosophical paradigms—the positivist and naturalistic paradigms—that differ with respect to how "reality" is conceived and studied. Naturalistic researchers believe that social events are defined and shaped by people in the "culture" in which the events occur. Research itself is a social enterprise in which the researcher's expectations influence what is inferred. Since culture influences everything that occurs within it, the goal of naturalistic inquiry is to develop context-specific statements (as opposed to universal generalizations) about the multiple, constructed realities of all the key participants (including the researcher) involved in the process being investigated (see Guba & Lincoln, 1994; Lincoln & Guba, 1985).

Potter (1996) identifies some other general assumptions of naturalistic inquiry. While not every naturalistic researcher shares all of them, Potter argues that "most hold almost all of these beliefs, and it would be inconceivable for a…researcher *not* to hold any of them" (p. 45). Three fundamental premises are: naturalism, phenomenology, and the interpretive nature of naturalistic inquiry.

The first assumption is **naturalism,** the belief that phenomena should be studied in their natural context. Naturalistic researchers believe that studying people in a laboratory leaves out important elements, so they study people in the natural settings in which they behave. Furthermore, they rarely manipulate variables to see how people respond; instead, they seek to understand how people usually communicate within particular contexts during the course of their everyday life. In fact, they are often interested in ordinary, undramatic communication behavior that is usually taken for granted, messages that people exchange almost unconsciously.

To understand how and why people behave the way they normally do, naturalistic researchers adopt a second assumption, that of **phenomenology,** which Potter (1996) describes as "the belief

that the object of interest be examined without any preconceived notions or a priori expectations" (p. 43). The goal is to set aside preconceived expectations so as to understand how participants make sense of their behavior. As Guba (1990) argues, the goal of research is to "*reconstruct* the 'world' at the only place at which it exists: in the minds of constructors" (p. 27).

The term *presuppositionless research* is often used to characterize this stance that resists the influence of preconceived expectations, but as J. A. Anderson (1987) explains, this doesn't mean that a researcher is "somehow a cultural blank without norms, values, and ideology. It means that the researcher makes his or her own norms, values, and ideology apparent and does not assume that they are those of the members" (p. 242). According to Potter (1996), researchers *bracket*—acknowledge and then set aside temporarily—their thoughts and expectations about what they will find, so they can "get inside the mind of the actor to see what the actor sees and believes. This understanding leads the researcher to explain how the actor constructs reality and why the actor behaves as he or she does" (p. 43).

Whitbourne's (1986) work on adult identity development shows how researchers put aside their expectations. She interviewed 94 adults regarding the question "Who am I?" To draw conclusions from what she heard, Whitbourne rethought her preconceptions:

> *Countless attempts at numerically based rating systems were tried and discarded progressively, until finally I decided to read all the transcripts in sequence, person by person rather than question by question. What I found…flew in the face of my previous ideas about developmental changes in adulthood. (p. 1)*

In line with a phenomenological approach, Whitbourne set aside what she expected to find so she could understand more fully the data she had gathered.

The third assumption is the **interpretive** nature of this research, described by Potter (1996) as "the belief that the researcher, while trying to see the situation from the point of view of those who are being studied, cannot escape from providing his or her own interpretation of the situation" (p. 43). Rather than ignoring or devaluing researchers' interpretations of participants' behavior, descriptions and interpretations made by participants and researchers are woven together to produce "well-grounded, rich descriptions and explanations of processes in identifiable local contexts" (M. B. Miles & Huberman, 1994, p. 1).

TYPES OF NATURALISTIC INQUIRY

While naturalistic research is generally guided by these assumptions, under this broad umbrella are a number of allied methodologies that place these assumptions into practice differently. Here, we focus on four of these methodologies: ethnography, ethnomethodology, critical ethnography, and autoethnography. The name of each methodology is derived from the Greek word *ethnos,* meaning "tribe, race, or nation," and three of the terms end with the Greek word *graphos,* meaning "something written down." These methodologies, then, involve a report of a group of people based on the principles articulated above (see Philipsen, 1989).

Ethnography

Ethnography was first employed by anthropologists to describe cultures different than their own. They showed that what was assumed to be "human nature" (e.g., war, male dominance, dislike of aging, and so on) actually were cultural traditions. Now, most ethnographers study how specific groups in their *own* society interact. Through immersion in the context, they examine the patterned interactions and significant symbols of specific groups to identify the cultural norms (rules) that direct their behaviors and the meanings that people ascribe to their own and each other's behaviors. As Gephart (1988) explains:

> Ethnography is the use of direct observation and extended field research to produce a thick, naturalistic description of a people and their culture. Ethnography seeks to uncover the symbols and categories members of the given culture use to interpret their world and ethnography thus preserves

the integrity and inherent properties of cultural phenomena. (p. 16)

Ethnographic research, therefore, seeks to "discover and disclose the socially acquired and shared understandings necessary to be a member of a specified social unit" (Van Maanen, 1982, p. 103). Ethnographers want to understand the explicit and implicit tacit assumptions that exist in particular cultural groups that simultaneously enable and constrain interaction among members. They report what people do and don't do, and why people think they should do those things and avoid the others.

A seminal example of ethnographic communication research is Philipsen's (1975, 1976) studies of "talking like a man" in "Teamsterville," a neighborhood of blue-collar, low-income Whites on the near-south side of Chicago. Philipsen spent 21 months in that neighborhood as a social worker, and then came back a year later and spent 9 months devoted to research. He told his "white-collar" readers that the "blue-collar" men he observed and interviewed didn't value speaking (in contrast to other communication strategies, such as silence, physical violence, and other nonverbal behaviors) as much as they did. Philipsen wrote that "talk is negatively valued in many of the very situations for which other American communities most highly prize speaking strategies" (Philipsen, 1975, p. 21). His ethnographic work helps to understand and appreciate, for example, that talking with one's spouse about a problem at work is not what *everyone* values and wants to do—that people in various social milieus view interpersonal communication differently.

Ethnomethodology

In 1967, sociologist Harold Garfinkel and colleagues engaged in a series of studies that were designed to

> treat practical activities, practical circumstances, and practical sociological reasoning as topics of empirical study, and by paying to the most commonplace activities of daily life the attention usually accorded extraordinary events, seek to learn about them as phenomena in their right. (p. 1)

These studies gave rise to **ethnomethodology,** "the empirical study of methods that individuals use to give sense to and at the same time to accomplish their daily actions: communicating, making decisions, and reasoning" (Coulon, 1995, p. 15). Ethnomethodologists, thus, seek to understand the everyday, commonplace talk routines people use to socially construct their world.

According to Coulon (1995), ethnomethodologists first phenomenologically bracket their expectations by adopting a posture of **ethnomethodological indifference** that leads them to abstain from judging people's actions. They then engage in **experimental breaching,** deliberately upsetting patterned routines to reveal the rules participants use to organize experiences. For example, researchers might introduce a conflict into a meeting to reveal the communication rules people use to manage disagreements in everyday life.

Beach (1982) identifies at least two lines of ethnomethodological inquiry that have emerged since Garfinkel's early studies. One line is *conversation analysis,* which, as mentioned in Chapter 9, examines interaction using qualitative methods. The second is *formal ethnomethodology,* which involves "a series of single case studies focusing on the social construction of everyday events within a variety of settings" (Beach, pp. 314–315). In these studies, "researchers examine the relatively unnoticed, routine, informal interactions that take place in human communities, such as how people do their jobs, shop, watch television, talk to other people, cook, eat, and the other practical accomplishments of everyday life" (Potter, 1996, p. 53). Formal ethnomethodology is, thus, "a perspective used by the researcher to view taken-for-granted behavior…and there are numerous techniques by which the researcher can 'get at' the meanings of taken-for-granted behavior" (Hickson, 1983, pp. 187, 188). We examine some of these techniques later in the chapter.

Critical Ethnography

A number of scholars, especially critical-interpretive theorists and feminist scholars, have challenged the "traditional" view of ethnography as an attempt to be a relatively "objective" report about another culture. According to these scholars, description and interpretation are not enough; research must also be directed toward constructive action with and on behalf of the group under study, especially those who are marginalized (see Deetz, 1982). In particular, they believe that research tacitly supports or consciously opposes oppression. Conquergood (1995) argues that

> *We must choose between research that is "engaged" or "complicit."…Engaged intellectuals take responsibility for how the knowledge they produce is used instead of hiding behind pretenses and protestations of innocence.… As engaged intellectuals we understand that we are entangled within world systems of oppression and exploitation.… Our choice is to stand alongside or against domination, but not outside, above, or beyond it. (p. 86)*

These scholars believe that research should serve the purposes of social justice, emancipation, and empowerment (see L. R. Frey et al., 1996; Ristock & Pennell, 1996). These are the goals of **critical ethnography,** a form of ethnography designed to promote emancipation and reduce oppression. As Thomas (1993) explains, "Critical ethnography proceeds from an explicit framework that, by modifying consciousness or invoking a call to action, attempts to use knowledge for social change" (p. 4). Critical ethnographers, thus, seek to give voice to mistreated people and those struggling for social change.

A good example of critical ethnography is Conquergood's (1991a, 1992, 1994) research on gang communication. To understand gang communication, Conquergood moved into Big Red, a dilapidated tenement building in a section of northwest Chicago called "Little Beirut," in the heart of territory controlled by Latin King gang members. He lived there for 20 months, observing and participating in all aspects of daily life (including two break-ins of his apartment). He slowly developed relationships with gang members. He did not at first reveal that he was a researcher until he felt a moral obligation to do so after one member showed him his guns. At the time he revealed his intentions, his relationships with gang members were well developed, so the young men viewed his research efforts as acceptable. He was able to spend significant time observing gang members and their communication, interviewing them, and participating in their activities (including, after 3 years of intense participant observation, being granted access to the carefully guarded underground manifestos and charters that spell out the rules, rituals, and symbolism for the members of this gang).

Conquergood's research shows how gang communication is a complex system that creates both a protective boundary against the outside world and a sense of place—a home, family, and dwelling—for these marginalized members of society. He recognizes that gang members sometimes engage in acts that are violent or illegal, but he seeks to demonstrate that these descriptors do not summarize the total function of the group for its members. His portrayals of gang members, thus, offer an alternative voice to the demonization of them by the mainstream media. He gives them a compassionate "voice" and, thereby, serves the purpose of social justice/action. He also testifies in court on their behalf and helps raise bail money for them. And he has spent countless hours helping with their education, teaching them to read and write, and involving them as camera operators in the making of a documentary film about gang communication (Conquergood & Siegel, 1990).

Autoethnography

Another critique of traditional ethnography is the tendency to see an ethnographer as a neutral, objective self who studies a "strange," subjective "Other" from a position of elitist omniscience (see Dorst, 1989). Such a perspective emphasizes a one-way process: the people being studied need to be "made sense of," while the researcher is immune from sense-making.

But a researcher is a subjective person who must also be accounted for in naturalistic research. As Bird (1992) explains:

Ethnography, once seen as an objective, scientific exercise, is now seen as an interpretive, humanistic enterprise, in which the subjectivity of the researcher is crucial in both fieldwork and writing, and in which the ethnographer's claim to speak in the name of the other is increasingly brought into question. (p. 252)

The recognition of researchers' subjectivity is foregrounded in **autoethnography** (or **personal ethnography**), a form of ethnography in which researchers examine their own life experiences and fieldwork. **Autobiography,** the story of one's own life, has a rich tradition in nonfiction writing, and autoethnography is a form of it. Autoethnographers focus on their own past experiences and how they viewed themselves and others at that time, made sense of people's behavior (including their own), and all the other things ethnographers seek when studying people. Autoethnography, thus, turns "the ethnographic gaze inward on the self (auto), while maintaining the outward gaze of ethnography, looking at the larger context wherein self-experiences occur" (Denzin, 1997, p. 227; also see Communication Studies 298, 1997; Hayano, 1979). Repositioning researchers as the object of inquiry rips away their privileged stance of being beyond the boundaries of a study and, thereby, confronts them with the experience of embodied ethnographic practice (see Crawford, 1996).

A good example of autoethnography is J. L. Jones's (1996) study of herself as an observing ethnographer. Jones conducted fieldwork with the Yoruba of Southwestern Nigeria in Africa and was interested in their cosmology and rituals. Her study focused on the Osun Festival, held in honor of a deity of fertility, sensuality, and creativity. When she returned to the United States, Jones found herself struggling with how to write about her experiences. Before she could write, she felt that she "had to find a way to get perspective on the personal and subjective nature of my fieldwork experience" (p. 131). To continue deepening her understanding of the Yoruba, she created and performed three times a piece entitled *Broken Circles: A Journey through Africa and the Self,* in which she played three Yoruba she had met during her fieldwork while another person played the role of "Joni the Ethnographer." Her performances were dialogues in which people with different voices and worldviews conversed for the purposes of understanding, questioning, and challenging one another. As Jones explained, "As I performed, I was conversing with the Yoruba, negotiating the truths of my cultural reality with the truths of theirs" (p. 132). The performances helped her as an ethnographer to better understand her constructions and representations of herself and those she studied. Although autoethnography need not culminate in a performance piece, "*Broken Circles,*" she wrote, "gave me an opportunity to deepen my understanding of the Yoruba and the particular constructed identity I call Joni" (p. 144) leading to "a more sophisticated understanding of myself as an African American, an academic, and a woman" (p. 131).

THE FLOW OF NATURALISTIC INQUIRY

While there are important variations in the four methodologies, a general method characterizes these lines of inquiry. Lincoln and Guba (1985) identify the following characteristics of the naturalistic research process (see Figure 10.1).

The first step, following the assumption of naturalism, involves studying phenomena *in situ,* that is, in context. Researchers believe that people must be seen behaving in natural settings. Thus, they go to people's homes and offices, streetcorners, and other places where people interact.

Studying people in context makes naturalistic inquiry an *embodied practice:* researchers place their bodies in a context and use themselves as the primary "instrument" to collect data (as opposed to paper-and-pencil questionnaires). Goffman (1989) explains the personal involvement of the researcher in the field:

> It's one of getting data, it seems to me, by subjecting yourself, your own body and your own personality, and your own social situation, to the set of contingencies that play upon a set of individuals, ...so that you are close to them while they are responding to what life does to them. (p. 180)

Conquergood (1991b) argues that embodied practice is especially meaningful to communication scholars because it "privileges the processes of communication that constitute the 'doing' of ethnographic research: speaking, listening, and acting together" (p. 181). In fact, naturalistic research is often judged by the quality of the embodied experience: "Ethnographic rigor, disciplinary authority, and professional reputation are established by the length of time, depth of commitment, and risks (bodily, physical, emotional) taken in order to acquire cultural understanding" (Conquergood, 1991b, p. 180).

Because researchers serve as the instruments through which data are collected, they rely on tacit (intuitive, felt) knowledge in addition to propositional knowledge (expressible in language form), and they primarily use qualitative, as opposed to quantitative (numerical), methods (see Chapter 4). *Qualitative methods* is "an umbrella term covering an array of interpretive techniques which seek to describe, decode, translate, and otherwise come to terms with the meaning, not the frequency, of certain more or less naturally occurring phenomena in the social world" (Van Maanen, 1983, p. 9). Such methods are preferred because they are more likely to access multiple realities, human meanings, and interactions from insiders' perspective.

As we will see later in the chapter, naturalistic researchers' primary data-gathering techniques are observation and in-depth interviewing. As Erlandson, Harris, Skipper, and Allen (1993) explain:

> Through interviews, the researcher often gains a first insight into the constructed realities that are wrapped up in the idiolect [the speech] of the respondent. Through observations, the researcher gains a partially independent view of the experience on which the respondent's language has constructed those realities. The interview provides leads for the researcher's observations. Observation suggests probes for interviews. The interaction of the two sources of data not only enriches them both, but also provides a basis for analysis that would be impossible with only one source. (p. 99)

Naturalistic researchers, however, also use a variety of other methods to gather data. They often use some of the textual-analytic methods discussed in Chapter 9, such as rhetorical criticism and content analysis; they employ unobtrusive

FIGURE 10.1   The flow of naturalistic research

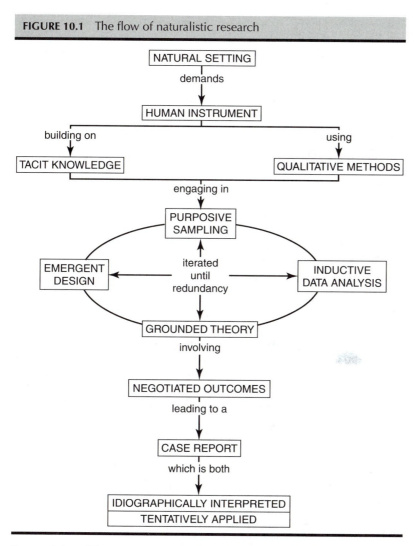

Source: Adapted from Yvonne S. Lincoln and Egon G. Guba, *Naturalistic inquiry,* p. 188, copyright © 1985 by Sage Publications, Inc. Adapted by Permission of Sage Publications, Inc.

measures (see Chapter 5); and even survey questionnaires are sometimes used (see C. Marshall & Rossman, 1989).

Naturalistic researchers usually employ multiple methodological procedures (observation and interviewing, at least), for "the best way to elicit the various and divergent constructs of reality that exist within the context of a study is to collect information about different events and relationships from different points of view" (Erlandson et

al., 1993, p. 31). Levin and Arluke's (1987) research illustrates the variety and creativity of the methods used. To study gossip in contemporary United States society, they: examined the content of several newspaper "gossip columns" over the preceding three decades; interviewed 15 gossip reporters from newspapers, magazines, and tabloids; studied biographies and autobiographies of "legendary gossip columnists"; "spent time observing informally and talking casually with the staff of the *National Enquirer* at its Lantana, Florida, headquarters"; and over an 8-week period spent the hours of 11 A.M. to 2 P.M. coding 194 instances of gossip overheard being exchanged between people sitting in a college student lounge (pp. 199–202).

Naturalistic researchers employ nonrandom, *purposive (purposeful) sampling,* as opposed to the random sampling techniques used by many other methodologists. They select **informants** who can provide unique insight into the culture, people, and communication behavior being studied. As Patton (1990) explains:

> *The logic and power of purposeful sampling lies in selecting information-rich cases for study in depth. Information-rich cases are those from which one can learn a great deal about issues of central importance to the purpose of the research, thus the term* purposeful *sampling. (p. 169)*

Naturalistic researchers use an **emergent design**—they may introduce or change procedures *during* the research process—rather than following a strictly predetermined plan as do experimental and many survey researchers and content/interaction analysts. As already explained, this does not mean that researchers improvise all their activities. They have beliefs and values that direct their observations and use protocols to guide interviews, but they are open-minded and search for profitable paths while observing and interviewing people, and then follow those leads. As discussed later in the chapter, the data collected from this process are analyzed inductively—that is, from the ground up—often with the goal of building a theory (see Glaser & Strauss, 1967; Strauss, 1987; Strauss & Corbin, 1990).

Throughout the process, researchers elicit how people make sense of and interpret their own beliefs, values, and behaviors to construct reality from the participants' point of view. Participants' views are then blended with the researchers' views. Researchers often engage in **member checks,** giving a draft of their research report to participants, or people similar to them, for feedback. Scheibel (1992), for example, studied how

underage females enacted communication performances designed to gain them access to clubs and bars. He hung out at the front door of clubs and watched these interactions unfold. He later conducted interviews with employees who worked the front door, bouncers, and customers whose fake IDs had been confiscated. He showed a draft of the report to undergraduate students who had experience using fake IDs, and their feedback helped shape the final report.

Findings from naturalistic inquiry are reported in the form of a **case study,** a detailed examination of a single subject, group, or phenomenon (Yin, 1994). Case studies tell a lot about the situation or people described (see V. Chen & Pearce, 1995; Hamel, 1993; Stake, 1994), but they must be applied tentatively and cautiously to other, even superficially similar, contexts.

Naturalistic researchers use the aforementioned processes to describe, understand, and interpret the complexity of human behavior as it occurs naturally. These processes are designed to maximize the external validity of researchers' claims, to bolster their "capacity to convince us that what they say is a result of their having actually penetrated (or, if you prefer, been penetrated by) another form of life, of having, one way or another, truly 'been there'" (Geertz, 1988, pp. 4–5). The result is "thick" and richly detailed accounts of people's behavior.

COLLECTING DATA IN NATURALISTIC INQUIRY

While naturalistic researchers employ many methods, two major investigative strategies are almost always used: direct observation of communication phenomena as they occur, and in-depth interviews with cultural informants. We first look at observational methods and then examine in-depth interviewing.

Naturalistic Observational Research

Yogi Berra (a "natural" naturalistic researcher) once said, "You can observe a lot just by watching." Naturalistic researchers go "into the field" to observe people interacting as they ordinarily do while carrying out everyday activities. Fieldwork involves a number of important issues, including what to study, gaining access, what observer role to assume, how long the observational period should last, what to look for while making observations, and how to record observations.

Deciding What to Study.   In the give-and-take of everyday life, all the elements in any situation—the people, setting, and communication activity—are interrelated. For example, to study how people in organizations communicate during a planned change process, one could observe individuals from a number of organizations who are most responsible for and/or affected by a planned change, a particular organization undergoing change, or meetings at which a planned change is discussed. But if a change project were found over time to succeed/fail, where would the responsibility lie? With the behavior of individuals? With the culture of the organization? With the group dynamics at meetings? No one element of a communication event can be singled out as most essential and observed in isolation from others.

Naturalistic researchers, therefore, try to observe as much as possible about the phenomenon of interest. For example, to study how communication practices are affected when an organization moves from a traditionally structured hierarchy to self-directed teams, J. R. Barker, Melville, and Pacanowsky (1993) conducted ethnographic research at XEL Communications, a company that had recently converted to self-directed teams. Their methods included the "observation of day to day work, attendance at team meetings, analysis of company documents, analysis of team experiences, and analysis of taped, in-depth interviews with both workers and management" (p. 298).

Of course, even the most conscientious researchers can't observe everything going on in a setting; they must make choices about what to study. Observations of communication usually focus on one of three interrelated aspects. First, sometimes the primary interest is the communication behavior of a particular *group of people.* Baxter and Goldsmith (1990), for example, were interested in United States high school adolescents' (16- to 17-year-olds) natural language descriptions when talking about the kinds of everyday events they experience. They had unique access to a group attending a 6-week summer residential academic program for college-bound students. One of the researchers was a residence hall assistant in the dormitory in which the students lived, which gave her many opportunities to observe, interact with, and record students' natural language choices about "what was going on there." Their report describes the underlying semantic dimensions by which members of this particular group perceptually organize their everyday life experiences.

Second, sometimes the primary interest is understanding communication among people within a particular *setting.* Adelman and Frey (1997), for example, conducted research and volunteer work at Bonaventure House, a residential facility for people with AIDS. Their research focused on how communication practices help create and sustain community in this compelling setting.

Third, sometimes the primary interest is a particular *communication act.* Braithwaite (1995), for instance, focused on communication designed to embarrass another person and how the receiver responds to it. Previous studies used survey methods to study such behavior (e.g., Cupach & Metts, 1992; Petronio, Olson, & Dollar, 1989; Sharkey & Stafford, 1990), so Braithwaite conducted naturalistic research, attending and videotaping five mixed-gender "coed" wedding showers and seven baby showers, and followed this up with interviews of 20 people who had attended one of those showers. She discovered that women embarrassed men primarily by teasing and causing them to look unpoised, and that men responded by using avoidance, humor, remediation, and justification. This naturalistic study not only extended previous survey findings but also allowed the researcher to "look at embarrassment as an interaction, an opportunity the self-report measures do not well provide" (Braithwaite, 1995, p. 154).

Gaining Access to Observational Settings and People.   Researchers must, of course, have opportunities to observe what they wish to study. Some use what is already available to them; they study communication in settings where they work or socialize. E. Bell and Forbes (1994), for example, studied "office folklore"—cartoons, parodies, and sayings that are photocopied, faxed, and displayed in offices—by walking around their university campus, observing available texts, and talking about them with those who worked in clerical support positions.

Other researchers study settings or people with which or whom they are not affiliated. Gaining access is not a problem when the setting is open to the public. For example, most social support groups that help individuals cope with similar problems welcome newcomers. This is particularly true for social support groups for people with AIDS (see Maione & McKee, 1987). Cawyer and Smith-Dupre´ (1995) wanted to study naturalistically the role of supportive communication for members of an HIV/AIDS support group. They contacted a local AIDS information hotline and found locations and times of support group meetings open to the public. One of the researchers was a caregiver and loved one of a person living with AIDS, so she went to a meeting and was accepted as a new member. She was allowed to take notes, although members did not know she was conducting research. She later contacted one of the group facilitators and asked for and received permission to use her observations as empirical data.

In contrast, when settings are private, researchers must negotiate with "gatekeepers" who have the power to grant or refuse access. Crawford (1986), for example, wanted to study life in a commune. He learned of one headed by an author of books on an Oriental philosophy, Taoism, whom he admired. Crawford called the commune and was invited to come for a preliminary visit for a few days. After deciding that the commune would be a suitable site for his fieldwork, he wrote to the leader, explained his intentions, and was granted permission to join them for the 6-month period needed to conduct his research.

Some private settings are actively kept hidden from the view of outsiders and rarely accept researchers or other observers (see Jorgensen, 1989). Members may even view research about them as offensive (see Hornsby-Smith, 1993). In such cases, access can be difficult. Lesch (1994), for example, studied how spontaneous storytelling episodes facilitated shared consciousness among members of a coven of witches. Before being allowed to study the coven, Lesch had to pass some "tests." She attended a few open meetings where prospective members are interviewed. The witches were then able to know her in much the same way they learn to know others who want to join the coven—by having her share personal stories and answer questions about her religious/spiritual background and beliefs. Satisfied with her sharing, members allowed her to attend their private, sacred meetings.

Lesch's study illustrates an important point about observational research in private and/or guarded settings: while a researcher chooses *whom* to observe, those individuals choose *whether* to allow the researcher to observe. Conquergood's (1991a, 1992, 1994) studies of gang communication, described earlier, are a good example. During the early days of his fieldwork, gang members "scoped him out," thinking he was a "narc" (police informant), and, therefore, wanting nothing to do with him. They spat on him and told stories about narcs when he walked past them on the street. Conquergood contends that they were actually doing a study of him as much as he was doing research about them. He eventually developed a relationship with a 10-year-old "wannabe" who spoke on his behalf to the gang members. The older youths then slowly started talking with him.

Finally, naturalistic research sometimes results from being associated with a group in another role. Adelman and Frey's (1997) research on communication practices at Bonaventure House (BH), mentioned earlier, did not begin as a "research project." Adelman lived in the neighborhood and argued on behalf of opening the house at several bitterly contested neighborhood meetings. Shortly after it opened, she became a volunteer, and spent a lot of time there. "In truth," she wrote, "BH was like my second home" (p. 13). After about 6 months, house administrators, knowing Adelman was a communication professor, asked her to conduct a study of residents' experiences. Many residents also encouraged her to do so, for they felt comfortable engaging with her in formal interviews. After conducting the study and presenting the findings, BH administrators asked her to conduct a longitudinal study, and she asked Frey to join the new study.

Role of the Observer. Naturalistic researchers must decide on the **observational role(s)** to assume vis-à-vis the people being observed. There are a variety of roles, ranging from deeply involved community members to dispassionate observers. Gold (1958) identified four segments of the role continuum that researchers can assume in observing everyday interaction: complete participant, participant as observer, observer as participant, and complete observer. These roles are defined by: how much researchers participate in the activities being observed (from high to low); degree of distance on the part of observers (from relatively close, **emic,** to relatively far, **etic**); and, to some extent, by whether people know they are being observed.

First, a **complete participant** is fully involved in a social setting and does not let people know they are being studied. The researcher is, or pretends to be, a regular member of that milieu and does not acknowledge being a researcher. For example, to study racial prejudice in the United States, J. H. Griffin (1961) darkened his skin color and traveled to public places, experiencing firsthand the reactions his skin color engendered.

The complete-participant role provides researchers with firsthand knowledge about a social context while minimizing researcher effects (see Chapter 5), since the people don't know they are being studied. But there are a number of potential problems with this role. First, it may not be possible to become a complete participant; for example, not many researchers can become astronauts to experience space travel firsthand. It is also easy in this role to become so involved that researchers lose the ability to "see the forest for the trees." This

is called *going native,* which happens when researchers become so close to the people they are studying that they are unable to reflect on experiences from the perspective of a researcher. The complete-participant role also does not allow researchers to engage in formal interviewing, since this would require revealing their research goals.

Perhaps most important, there are significant ethical dilemmas involved in conducting covert participation based on deception (see Bulmer, 1982a, 1982b; Mitchell, 1993; Punch, 1986, 1994). Gold (1958) believes that it is often difficult to continue in this role because researchers may become intimately involved with people, but must continue to deceive them about the true purpose of their involvement. This appears to have happened in Della-Piana and Anderson's (1995) research on how the concept of "community" was central to the discourse and organizing practices of a community service organization. Della-Piana was invited to study a student-oriented community service organization at a public university. Volunteers at the center engage in service projects, and she wanted to experience this firsthand, so she joined the alumni group in cleaning a home for single-parent mothers and engaged in other service activities. She did not, however, reveal herself as a researcher to the other volunteers and recipients of the services. She struggled with this decision and questioned the ethics of her research strategy:

> After working alongside volunteers and recipients who did not know (and would not know) I was doing research, I began to view my own research disguised as community service as a form of exploitation—advancing my own agenda in the name of service to others. (p. 192)

While ethical dilemmas pervade all communication research (see Chapter 6), there are some unique ethical decisions confronting those who participate in the lives of others. Perhaps that's why communication researchers seldom conduct naturalistic inquiry as complete participants.

Second, a **participant-observer** becomes involved as fully as possible in a social situation where people know they are being studied. Similar to the complete-participant role, researchers experience the activities firsthand; however, they reveal their research agenda—usually at the start of the project, but sometimes as it progresses.

In most cases, the people being studied know from the outset that a researcher is a participant-observer. Cherry (1995), for example, conducted ethnographic fieldwork in an apartment building in Florida for persons with AIDS. He wrote a letter to the director of housing asking for permission to conduct a study. The letter was read at the monthly residents' meeting, and the project was accepted. Everyone in the building knew that he was conducting research.

In other cases, a researcher may start off as a complete participant and not tell people they are being observed, but then reveals this information at a later time. This strategy is employed when the researcher first wants to collect data that are not influenced by people knowing that they are being observed, and then follows up those observations with formal interviewing. One exemplar is Smythe (1995), who was a regular member of a fitness facility and, therefore, had no trouble observing the role of storytelling in women's conversations at that site. At first, she conducted covert observation, not telling the women they were being studied, to "ensure that 'typical' interaction behaviors were observed and recorded" (p. 250). She would take extensive notes following each observation and try to reconstruct the conversation she had participated in or overheard. After this initial phase of research, she identified herself as a researcher and conducted interviews with some of the women to listen to their interpretations of their shared experiences.

Participant observation is a popular image of naturalistic inquiry. Through participation, a researcher acquires information firsthand, and then uses interviews to supplement observations. It is, however, sometimes impossible to become a participant-observer without extensive, rigorous training. For example, to study newcomer socialization in a volunteer agency, Travelers Aid Society, located at one of the airports in Washington, DC, McComb (1995) became a volunteer at the agency. She attended 13 hours of classroom train-

ing over a period of 3 months and worked 28 shifts (100.5 hours) as a trainee before being allowed to work a shift by herself. Another potential problem with this role is that researchers' participation might influence people's behavior in the situation. And like the complete participant, a participant-observer runs the risk of taking many subtle but important routines in the research setting for granted (as most members do) and not reporting them.

Third, an **observer-participant** primarily observes and participates only to a limited extent. The researcher attempts to fit into the social setting, perhaps by dressing similarly to the people being studied and recording notes unobtrusively, but does not participate actively in the activities. Trujillo (1992) did this in studying how interactions among employees who worked at a major league baseball stadium helped construct ballpark culture. He attended 67 home games; sometimes as a fan, but mostly as a "ballpark wanderer," just wandering around and observing workers. This role emphasized observation, with just a small amount of participation; he did not, as a participant-observer might, become a hot-dog vendor to experience work-oriented communication at the ballpark.

Observer-participants function as marginal members of the group being studied, neither completely in nor completely out of it. They don't gain the depth of vivid firsthand experience as do complete participants or participant-observers, but because they are less intrusive, researcher effects are reduced. Hollihan and Riley (1987), for example, studied the rhetorical power of "Toughlove," a network of support groups for families with delinquent children that urges parents to use strict discipline. With members' permission, they sat in on four meetings of a group in Los Angeles. Although they didn't participate in the formal discussions, they were concerned that members might have behaved differently due to their presence. So they interviewed the two group leaders and several randomly selected members, who told them that their behavior was not affected by being observed.

Finally, a **complete observer** does not interact with the people being observed. The researcher is concerned with faithfully gathering observational data about people's behavior without influencing them in any way. Some researchers do this covertly by not telling people they're being observed. Deakins et al. (1987), for example, eavesdropped on and recorded dyadic conversations in public places without people's knowledge. In other cases, people may know they're being observed, but the researcher tries to be unobtrusive, like a fly on the wall that's never noticed. Fitch (1994), for instance, conducted cross-cultural research on compliance gaining in the United States and in Columbia. As part of the research protocol, she and her research assistants each "shadowed" another person for a day, recording in a diary as unobtrusively as possible all compliance-gaining attempts uttered and received by the shadowed individual.

Although the complete-observer strategy affords researchers the greatest distance from participants and, therefore, the greatest "objectivity" in recording data, it also reduces their potential insights into the social situation, especially since they do not speak directly with the people being studied to learn their perceptions of the phenomena being observed. And in cases where people know they're being studied, the presence of a complete observer may still influence their responses. For these reasons, few communication researchers adopt this observational role.

Viewing naturalistic observation from a role-taking perspective is helpful, but Adler and Adler (1987) question Gold's (1958) typology because it artificially separates participation from observation. They argue that all naturalistic researchers participate in the sense of placing their bodies in a context and observing others. Therefore, Adler and Adler believe that a more useful distinction is the extent to which a researcher is a committed member of the group being studied. They differentiate three *membership roles* on the basis of degree of committed membership: complete member, active member, and peripheral member. As they explain:

Peripheral-member-researchers participate as insiders in the activities of the group they are studying, but they refrain from engaging in the most central activities.... [Active-member-]researchers participate in the core activities in much the same way as members, yet they hold back from committing themselves to the goals and values of members.... Complete-member-researchers study their topics from the perspective of full members by either selecting groups to study in which they have prior membership or by converting to membership in these groups. (p. 35)

This typology, according to Lindloff (1995), usefully recasts observational roles in terms of researchers' experiential involvement and the social functions membership roles fulfill.

Length of Observations. Naturalistic researchers must decide on the amount of time spent observing in the field. How much time is needed to collect the data necessary for understanding and being able to write about the communication phenomena of interest?

In some select cases, when the phenomenon is a fleeting, one-time performance, only that single observational period is necessary. Trujillo (1993), for example, conducted a critical ethnography of the 25th anniversary of the assassination of President John F. Kennedy (November 22, 1988) by going to Dealey Plaza in Dallas, Texas, where Kennedy was shot. He observed the activities that took place that day and interviewed some of the people who visited the location. He analyzed this one-day event as a site where people came to "commemorate a fallen leader, to mourn the loss of symbolic community, to protest dissatisfaction with the official version of the assassination, and to exchange personal narratives for promoting self-interests and for mediating the ideology of a united America" (p. 463). Thus, a single day of observation was appropriate.

Some naturalistic researchers can acquire sufficient data after only a few observational periods. Bullis (1991), for example, observed three meetings of members of the United States Forest Service to see how communication practices create social reality while emphasizing a control function. One of those meetings, however, lasted for 2 full days spread out over 3 days, and Bullis attended the entire meeting.

Most naturalistic researchers, however, favor *sustained observations,* which means conducting longitudinal research. Novek's (1995) ethnographic study of inner-city youths' communication practices, for example, was based on 6 years of living in that culture, teaching at a weekend education program and a community recreation center, and serving as a literacy tutor (see Figure 10.2 for additional examples). It is this longitudinal, embodied fieldwork that simultaneously makes naturalistic inquiry both worthwhile and daunting.

Long-term research is preferred because it helps establish quality relationships between researchers and research participants. According to Goetz and Le Compte (1984), it also produces more valid and reliable information: "Collecting data for long periods provides opportunities for continual data analysis and comparison to refine constructs and to ensure the match between scientific categories and participant reality" (p. 221). During longer observational periods, people become less self-conscious about a researcher's presence and are more likely to interact the way they usually do, making the research less susceptible to the Hawthorne effect (see Chapter 5) and, thereby, maximizing the internal validity of the findings.

What to Observe.   The stage of a research project influences how observations are made. In the beginning, many investigators just *observe impressionistically,* looking for any clues that help them comprehend what is going on in the setting. According to Lindlof (1995), the general all-purpose question that guides researchers' observations during this early period is, "What is going on here?" As researchers spend more time in a setting, they become more selective about what to observe. And by the time they are ready to leave the setting, they may only be looking for instances that confirm or disconfirm their earlier perceptions and interpretations.

Lindlof (1995) poses six general questions that guide the choices among phenomena that communication researchers can observe. An example from Adelman and Frey's (1997) research at Bonaventure House (BH), with page numbers

cited, illustrates a potential answer to each of these questions:

1. *Who are the actors?* This question refers both to members' formal roles and their relative status, including dominant and subordinate positions. BH members include residents, staff, and volunteers, but some have more influence than others. One resident was nicknamed *La Reina* (The Queen) because of the central mothering role she played in the house.

2. *How is the scene set up?* This question refers to what the physical features of the setting signify to members. BH is modeled after the Alexian Brothers' (a Catholic order) contemplative living arrangement. They designed "a house that ensured small, private quarters for each resident, semiprivate social space, and large public rooms for daily communal meals and leisure" (p. 12). Residents consider their private rooms to be their castles; Clyde described how his door signals social boundaries: "I usually have the door open because we have a very nice floor. It's like a code. If the door's open, you can come and say 'Hi.' If the door's closed that means someone may be ill or sleeping" (p. 49).

3. *How do initial interactions occur?* This question directs attention to the importance of early encounters, such as how new members are socialized into a culture. One of the residents, Terrance, recounted his first day at BH. He was "sitting alone in his new room, wondering if he had made a good choice. Maria, another resident, knocked on the door, poked her head in, and said, 'Well, I hope you came here to live and not to die,' a reassurance that made him realize that things would be OK. This vision is more than a rhetorical veil; it not only emphasizes the importance of remaining active and healthy, it also wards off the shroud of inevitable and imminent mortality" (p. 35). BH veterans, thus, help newcomers construct a rhetorical vision of the house as a place to *live,* not die, with AIDS.

4. *When and how do actors claim attention?* This question refers to how individuals communicate, as well as why some items incite talk and others do not. For example, the only mandatory task for BH

FIGURE 10.2   Examples of long-term naturalistic inquiry

1. Baxter (1993) conducted a two-year ethnography based on participant observation as members of one private United States university revised its system of governance with respect to communication codes of collegiality and professional management.

2. Comeraux (1995) attended two courses once a week during the 1992–1993 academic year, observing 15 of the 20 class sessions for each course, to study the impact of interactive distance learning on classroom communication. This study was actually part of a larger research program in which she examined eight courses, some in high schools, some in community colleges, and some at the university level.

3. Conquergood (1988) spent a year living in Bain Vinai, the largest Hmong refugee camp (about 48,000 people) in Thailand. He worked with refugees to design and direct a health performance education campaign that featured skits and scenarios drawing on Hmong folklore and traditional communication forms (such as proverbs and storytelling) to increase awareness about the health problems in the camp. While other agency workers at the camp commuted from a village an hour away, Conquergood lived in the camp full-time. Since that work, he has lived for short periods of time in 11 refugee camps in Southeast Asia and the Middle East.

4. Fitch (1991) conducted 400 hours of observation during a 9-month period of fieldwork in Bogota, Columbia, obtaining access to schools, a printing plant, hospital, legal aid clinic, family and couples counseling service, and several corporate settings, to elucidate address terms in Colombian Spanish derived from the central term *madre* (mother).

5. Helmer (1993), seeking to understand storytelling in the creation and maintenance of organizational tension and stratification, conducted field research over 7 months at a harness racetrack, acquiring a groom's license and working alongside other grooms—mucking stalls, rubbing and exercising horses, and socializing with the other grooms.

6. Lange (1993) conducted 300 hours of participant observation of strategy and planning meetings, conferences, and other gatherings of environmental and timber industry groups as they engaged in conflict over the Northern spotted owl and "old growth forests" in the Pacific northwest.

7. Schneider and Beaubien (1996) investigated the strategies doctors use to encourage patients to comply with their requests over a 9-month period by accompanying five physicians into examination rooms at various times of the day and night as they treated 105 patients in two health care facilities.

---

residents is dish duty. Once a week, a team of residents sets the tables for meals, cleans up, and washes the dishes. No issue incites more talk among BH residents than dish duty, for this innocuous task is deeply symbolic in that it tests residents' commitment to the collective. Individuals who don't contribute their fair share, consequently, are seen as rebellious and demanding attention. Jason, a resident, noted, "For some people, not doing dishes is a rebellion against their disease. They didn't want to be part of this community. It is their way of fighting the world because you gave me this God-damned disease" (p. 71).

5. *Where and when do principal actors ordinarily congregate and interact?* This question refers to both physical settings and the significant interactions that take place there. At BH, "residents learn quickly that the primary public space for both formal and informal gatherings is the dining room, which consists of approximately 10 round tables that each seat six to eight people. Here, hot coffee, cold drinks, and snacks are available around the clock, and the radio is usually playing. There is no TV (it is located in the family room upstairs), so interactions and conversations abound" (p. 47). In terms of the interactions that take place in the dining room, Edward, a resident, noted, "There's a lot of griping…it seems to me that the gripe is the central expressive genre that a lot of people have, and you certainly find that here just sitting around talking with people. I don't know why that is, except, of course, I guess people have a lot of anger" (p. 72). In their interpretation of this behavior, Adelman and Frey noted that "griping about dish duty offers not only a way of displacing feelings about illness and loss, but also serves—given the unusual and everpresent reality of living with AIDS—as a way of normalizing everyday life; it is a reminder that even in this bizarre trauma, one still washes dishes" (p. 73).

6. *What communicative events are significant?* One of the most significant and poignant events at BH is a balloon ceremony that occurs after a resident passes away. People stand in a circle holding balloons, remembrances of the deceased are spoken, and the balloons are then released simultaneously, typically evoking cathartic laughter and joy. Adelman and Frey see this ritual as a compelling example of symbolic reversal: "the letting go of the balloons symbolically reverses a sad occasion of mourning into a celebration of relief and release" (p. 89). And the symbolism of this ritual is not lost on BH residents; as Randy, said, "It's a letting go of someone who is unique and special. I think the symbolism is very important to the whole process, from birth to death—that we celebrate life and we end life with a celebration" (p. 92).

Recording Observations.   Naturalistic researchers keep track of their observations in the form of **field notes,** written or audiorecorded records of what occurred. Field notes are a "record of what was meaningful…. The goal is not to record everything—that simply creates chaos—but to carefully note those critical moments when some meaning of the social action was revealed, however imperfectly, to the researcher" (J. A. Anderson, 1987, pp. 257–258).

Field notes are taken either while observing events or as soon as possible thereafter. All researchers take *headnotes* (mental logs) while observing, but some are able to take extensive written

notes as interaction unfolds. A case in point is Bullis (1991), who took shorthand field notes of the three meetings of the United States Forest Service she observed, providing near-verbatim transcripts of the meetings. There are even technologies, such as "Stenomask," "a shoulder-shielded microphone attached to a tape recorder on a shoulder strap" (Lindlof, 1995, p. 200), that allow researchers to whisper and record notes while an activity unfolds (see Patton, 1990).

Most researchers write notes as soon as possible after leaving the field. Elwood, Dayton, and Richard (1995) studied how four outreach workers used communication to establish sufficient trust to engage drug users in risk-reduction interventions. Two of the researchers spent 3 months accompanying outreach workers during their daily routines. They jotted down notes between each outreach encounter and wrote additional descriptions as soon as they returned to the office.

In addition to field notes, some researchers create *activity logs,* documenting what happens in the field. Others maintain *journals* of their experiences or *self-observational diaries* (see D. Zimmerman & Weider, 1977). As Sanjek (1990) explains, "Chronologically constructed journals provide a key to the information in field notes and records; diaries record the ethnographer's personal reactions, frustrations, and assessments of life and work in the field" (p. 108).

Observational notes are crucial to describing and inferring patterns in people's communication, but there is little agreement regarding how field notes, activity logs, journals, diaries, and other observational records should be compiled. (For some valuable suggestions on writing ethnographic field notes, see Emerson, Fretz, & Show, 1995.) Essentially, researchers try to construct detailed notes so that they and others can later vividly recall the scene they observed and make sense of what happened.

Finally, researchers can't, of course, observe all the activities in which people engage; lots of activities take place outside their presence. There are some innovative, quasi-naturalistic observational methods that try to use the science of sampling to study people's ongoing experiences and interpretation of them. Kubey, Larson, and Csikszentmihalyi (1996), for example, describe the Experience Sampling Method (ESM), developed at the University of Chicago over two decades ago, which asks respondents to carry around, often for about a week, a paging device (beeper) and a small booklet of self-report forms. The pager signals the person at random times of the day (typically six to nine times per day) and the person must immediately write down on the form the activity in which he or she is engaged and subjective experience of it (typically taking less than 2 minutes to complete). Kubey et al. argue that the EMS "makes possible an ecologically valid assessment of human behavior and experience in real time, place, and social context, and, in so doing, has numerous applications" (p. 103). To date, this quasi-naturalistic method has been used to study, among other things, adjustment to a change in residence (Hormuth, 1986), binge eating (C. Johnson & Larson, 1982), and alcohol and drug use and rehabilitation (Filstead, Reich, Parrella, & Rossi, 1985).

Interviewing in Naturalistic Inquiry

We live in an "interview society," accustomed to interviews being used to acquire in-depth information about people and situations. Interviews help decide whether prospective parents adopt children, which applicants organizations hire, and whether attorneys win or lose cases. And let's not forget, said tongue-in-cheek, the infamous "in-depth" media interviews:

> *Larry King introduces us to presidents and power brokers. Barbara Walters plumbs the emotional depth of stars and celebrities. Oprah, Geraldo, and Donahue invite the ordinary, tortured, and bizarre to "spill their guts" to millions of home viewers, and intimates and experts tell the "O. J. Simpson Story" for TV and the tabloids. (Holstein & Gubrium, 1995, p. 1)*

Naturalistic researchers, too, conduct in-depth interviews to understand people's lived experi-

ence. To understand these interviews, let's first contrast them with survey interviews.

In survey research, interviews are used to obtain information from a relatively small, representative sample so that generalizations can be made about the population of interest (see Chapter 8). Survey interviews proceed in a deductive manner; the questions are prepared ahead of time and tend to be highly structured (all respondents are asked the same relatively closed questions in the same order).

Naturalistic **in-depth interviews** typically proceed inductively, using an unstructured format consisting of open questions. Researchers use interviews to understand *particular* social phenomena by developing "intimate familiarity" (Brenner, 1985, p. 148) and a "detailed, dense acquaintanceship" (Lofland, 1976, p. 8) with interviewees. They want to understand the other person's "inner view," "comprehending the essence of an individual, his or her emotions, motivations, and needs" (Chirban, 1996, p. xi).

An in-depth interview is highly exploratory—researchers learn gradually about participants and events, and modify the interview strategy as they proceed. Expanding on Pool's (1957) metaphor of interviewing as an interpersonal drama with a developing plot, Holstein and Gubrium (1995) liken an in-depth interview to a kind of "improvisational performance":

> *As a drama of sorts, its [an in-depth interview's] narrative is scripted in that it has a topic or topics, distinguishable roles, and a format for conversation. But it also has a developing plot, in which topics, roles, and format are fashioned in the give-and-take of the interview. (p. 17)*

Naturalistic interviews are, thus, more like "guided conversations" (Lofland, 1971) than question-and-answer sequences. G. E. Marcus and Fischer (1986) propose *dialogue* as a metaphor for research, which, as Geist and Dreyer (1993) explain, is particularly appropriate for in-depth interviewing:

> *Taking the dialogic perspective to heart challenges researchers to communicate with research participants*

*in ways that overcome the asymmetry that often un-
dermines the participants' experience and understanding. Dialogic interviewing's primary goal is
to empower respondents by engaging them in dialogue. (p. 245)*

To meet this goal, Chirban (1996) calls for an interactive-relational approach that "invites the
interviewer and interviewee to share their experiences genuinely and to relate to one another"
(p. xiii). Kvale (1996) fittingly calls these interactions "inter views," an "inter-change of views between two persons conversing about a theme of
mutual interest" (p. 14).

In striving to develop meaningful connections
with interviewees, interviewers face a number of
issues, such as whom to interview, where and
when to interview, how to structure interviews,
whether to use specific interview methods, and
how to record and transcribe interviews.

Whom to Interview.   Naturalistic researchers rely
almost exclusively on nonrandom samples, meaning that the people interviewed do not have an
equal chance of being selected from the pool of
possible people, in contrast to random samples
where they do (see Chapter 5). Most select a *purposive sample,* intentionally choosing the people,
on the basis of theoretical and/or experientially informed judgments, who are likely to be the most
willing and able to shed light on what the researcher is studying (Figure 10.3 shows some purposive sampling strategies).

Many researchers begin with and continue to
rely on **key informants**, "well-informed informants" (J. C. Johnson, 1990, p. 31) who can enlighten a researcher on what and whom he or she
should know. Key informants can "judge the reliability of potential interviewees, suggest people to
talk with, make introductions, propose tactics for
collecting information, and react to collected data
and tentative interpretations" (J. T. Murphy, 1980,
p. 78). Consider the plight of Whyte (1955), who
was unable to make headway studying a group of
streetcorner boys until he explained his research to
Doc, a leader of the Norton Street gang, who
agreed to help and became Whyte's key informant.

Reflecting later on the importance of Doc to his research, Whyte (1984) wrote:

> *Doc was an extraordinarily valuable informant.
> Whenever checked, his accounts seemed highly re-
> liable. He was also well-informed about what was
> happening in his own and other groups and organi-
> zations in his district. This was due to the position
> he occupied in the community social structure.
> Other leaders discussed with him what they were
> doing and what they should do.... Because of the
> wide variation in quality of informants, the re-
> searcher is always on the lookout for informants
> such as Doc, who can give a reasonably accurate
> and perceptive account of events. (p. 127)*

Researchers sometimes want to interview
people who possess salient characteristics that, on
the basis of theory and previous research, may
make a difference, so they employ a **theoretical
(theory-based) sample** (see Glaser & Strauss,
1967; Strauss & Corbin, 1990). L. A. Howard and
Geist (1995), for instance, explored how members
of a utility company responded to contradictions
evolving from a merger the company was undergoing. Because members' position in an organizational hierarchy had been found in previous
research to influence their viewpoint, the researchers interviewed employees selected from
three hierarchical levels—managers, supervisors,
and hourly employees—in each department of the
organization.

In cases of difficult-to-reach populations, or
when discussing very sensitive personal topics,
researchers often use *network* (or *snowball*) *sampling* (see Granovetter, 1976; Werner & Schoepfle, 1987). Initial individuals interviewed who fit
the criteria, usually selected because of convenience, are asked to refer the researcher to other
qualified people, who are then asked for the
names of others; the list of respondents grows, or
"snowballs," as the research progresses (see
Chapter 5). Braithwaite (1991) used this procedure to study how persons with disabilities communicate with able-bodied persons who expect or
demand disclosure about their disability in new
relationships. She conducted a pilot study in
1985, recruiting disabled students registered with

FIGURE 10.3   Purposive sampling strategies in naturalistic inquiry

TYPE	PURPOSE
1. Extreme or deviant case sample	People chosen on the basis of extreme characteristics, such as top-of-the-class students.
2. Intensity sample	Information-rich people who manifest the phenomenon intensely, but not extremely, such as good/poor students, above average/below average students.
3. Maximum variation sample—purposefully picking a wide range of variation on dimensions of interest	People who vary in how they adapt to particular conditions; used to identify important common patterns that cut across variations.
4. Homogeneous sample	Similar types of people; used to focus, reduce, and simplify analysis, and facilitate group interviewing.
5. Typical case sample	Typical, normal, or average people.
6. Stratified purposive sample	Particular subgroups that share a characteristic; used to facilitate comparisons.
7. Critical case sample	An exemplar that permits logical generalization and maximum application of information to other people because what is true of this person is likely to be true of other people.
8. Network or snowball sample	Information-rich people referred by other information-rich people.
9. Criterion sample	People who meet some criterion, such as children abused in a treatment facility, to produce a quality assurance sample.
10. Theory-based or operational sample	People who manifest a theoretical construct of interest; used to elaborate and examine the construct.
11. Confirming and disconfirming cases sample	People who can confirm or disconfirm researchers' expectations; used to elaborate and deepen initial analysis and test variation.
12. Opportunistic sample	Following new leads during fieldwork, taking advantage of unexpected opportunities to interview people.
13. Random purposive sample (still small sample size)	Selecting people from a small sample such that each has an equal chance of being selected; used to add credibility to the sample when potential purposive sample is larger than one can handle.
14. Politically important case sample	Politically important people; used to attract public attention to the study (or avoid attracting undesired attention by purposefully eliminating from the sample politically sensitive cases).
15. Convenience sample	People chosen on the basis of availability; used to save time, money, and effort.
16. Combination or mixed purposive sample	Combining purposive sampling methods; allows triangulation and meets multiple interests and needs.

Source: Adapted from Michael Quinn Patton, *Qualitative evaluation and research methods* (2nd ed.), Newbury Park, CA: Sage, pp. 182–183, copyright © 1990 by Sage Publications, Inc. Adapted by Permission of Sage Publications, Inc.

a university disability office. The office would not give out names, so she wrote letters, with a return postcard students could complete if they were willing to participate, and the office put on name labels and mailed them. For the 1991 study, she contacted several adults from the pilot study and asked them for names of others they thought might participate. At the end of each interview, interviewees were asked for names of other disabled individuals who might be willing to be interviewed.

Finally, many naturalistic researchers rely on a *convenience sample,* interviewing whomever is available at the particular place and time the research is conducted. A study by Aden, Rahoi, and Beck (1995) is illustrative, as they developed a theory about interpretive communities from the narratives of 113 visitors to the site of the film, *Field of Dreams.* During the summer of 1992, the researchers went to the site for 3 days and asked individuals whether they had time to answer a few questions. If they did, they were interviewed. The researchers did attempt, however, to include some demographic variation in interviewees' age, gender, and ethnicity.

Interview Logistics. After identifying people to be interviewed, researchers must decide some logistical issues. For one, they must decide where to conduct interviews. Most interviews are conducted in a convenient and comfortable place for respondents, usually in their own homes or at work. Kaufmann (1992), for example, interviewed members of women's cooperative art galleries in New York City and Philadelphia about their social identities as women artists. She wanted to create an equal relationship between herself and interviewees, so she conducted interviews on the women's turf—in their studios.

Sometimes interviews can't be conducted where people live or work because of the need for confidentiality (see Chapter 6). For example, as part of their study of conflict at Disneyland during a 22-day strike in 1984, R. Smith and Eisenberg (1987) interviewed hourly employees. The researchers sought to maximize confidentiality by conducting interviews in a favorite haunt of Disneyland employees—the lounge of a local restaurant.

Most interviews are conducted *one-on-one* between an interviewer and interviewee, but sometimes an interview *team* approach works best (see Erickson & Stull, 1998). In K. Miller et al.'s (1995) study of communication and coordination in agencies that provide service to the urban homeless, two people interviewed directors of agencies. One asked questions and probed for answers while the other took notes and made observations of the institutional environment.

When interviewing people who know each other, such as dyadic partners or group members, researchers must decide whether to interview them *alone* or *together.* Each approach has advantages and disadvantages. C. Surra, Chandler, and Asmussen (1987) studied the effects of premarital pregnancy on the relationships of 36 newlywed couples. They first interviewed both spouses together, asking them to come to an agreement about if and when certain events occurred during their courtship (such as their first date). Partners were then separated for the remainder of the interview. The time spent together clarified some facts and jogged some memories; the time spent apart allowed partners to speak more freely about their private thoughts and feelings.

Sometimes people are interviewed in small groups, including the use of *focus groups* (see Chapter 8). For example, to study television use in a retirement community, Riggs (1996) interviewed residents over a 2-year period singly and in small groups, conducted focus groups with them, and observed residents in their apartments while they watched television.

Research interviews typically are conducted at a time convenient to respondents. But sometimes researchers take advantage of particular moments when people are readily available. Caspi (1984), in particular, wanted to know how politicians—representatives in the Knesset, the Israeli parliament—use various mass media to understand social phenomena. One day, a group of students he had trained "swooped down" on the

Knesset cafeteria during the lunch hour and interviewed 91 of the 120 Knesset members.

Interview Format.   In-depth interviews range in format from unstructured to structured. Schwartz and Jacobs (1979) explain that, in the purest form of an unstructured interview,

> the interviewer does not know in advance which questions are appropriate to ask, how they should be worded so as to be nonthreatening or unambiguous, which questions to include or exclude to best learn about the topic under study, or what constitutes an answer (what the range of answers to any question might be). The answers to these problems are seen to emerge from the interviews themselves, the social context in which they occurred, and the degree of rapport that the interviewer was able to establish during the interview. (p. 40)

The famous journalist and author Studs Terkel conducts this type of unstructured interview: "He simply turns on his tape recorder and asks people to talk" (Holstein & Gubrium, 1995, p. 2).

Most naturalistic researchers, however, conduct semistructured interviews by outlining questions in advance and improvising probing questions on the spot. For example, on the basis of 1- to 2-hour in-depth interviews with 59 adult women, Chatham-Carpenter and DeFrancisco (1997) identified possible strategies women use to maintain and regain self-esteem. They used a semistructured interview guide that asked all the women five open questions, such as "If you could give advice to young girls or parents of girls regarding how to build positive self-esteem, what would it be?" (p. 169).

Some naturalistic researchers include very structured questions within their interviews. In their study of conflict at Disneyland, R. Smith and Eisenberg (1987) conducted three-part structured interviews with employees. Employees first were asked general, open questions, such as "What is it like working at Disneyland?" They then were given a list of metaphors that management had used to describe the park and asked whether they saw the park in each of those ways. The interview concluded by

asking employees to complete, and elaborate on, the sentence, "Life at Disneyland is like...."

Some highly structured in-depth interviews are guided by a questionnaire. For instance, Mc-Cracken's (1988) **long interview** uses a questionnaire to create a "sharply focused, rapid, highly intensive interview process that seeks to diminish the indeterminacy and redundancy that attends more unstructured research processes" (p. 7). Before conducting any interviews, a researcher thoroughly reviews the literature to discover categories familiar to interviewees and uses these to develop a questionnaire. The questionnaire is used during interviews to ensure that the same topics are covered in the same order for each interviewee. T. R. Peterson et al. (1994) used a variation of the long interview with Texas farmers who live in regions associated with high injury and death rates due to farm equipment accidents to identify themes that could be used to construct persuasive safety campaigns. They first conducted relatively unstructured interviews for about an hour, followed by 30-minute structured interviews using a questionnaire regarding safety.

Many in-depth interviews, even those including structured questions, follow a *funnel format,* proceeding from general to specific levels of inquiry (see Chapter 4). Interviewers start with open questions and then ask more narrow and precise questions. For example, in their interviews with teenagers about their natural language descriptions, Baxter and Goldsmith (1990) used the strategy suggested by H. S. Becker (1954) of "playing dumb." They asked teenagers to imagine the interviewer as a foreigner who knew nothing about how United States adolescents spend their typical days. The interviews began with *grand tour questions* (Spradley, 1979) that asked adolescents to describe all the different communication events of a recent typical day. Follow-up questions were more focused and direct, asking for examples or direct language usage (e.g., "How do you refer to that kind of situation?").

Interview Methods.   Even unstructured and flexible interviews are often guided by specific methods that help interviewers to decide what questions to ask and how to conduct the interviews. For instance, some researchers base their interview on a particular philosophical/theoretical orientation, such as *phenomenology,* in which interviews are used to understand how people experience life processes without imposing researchers' preconceptions on them. C. S. Becker (1987) used interviews in this way in her study of women's friendships. She interviewed two sets of women friends separately for a total of 8–10 hours over a 4-month period. The initial interview began with the request: "Please describe as completely as possible your friendship with (friend's name)" (p. 61). Each woman was asked to speak about her everyday experiences of this friendship and to avoid talking abstractly about it. Subsequent questions asked for further descriptions of situations already mentioned. Each additional interview began by asking the woman to describe experiences of the friendship since the last interview. In later interviews, Becker pursued unclear aspects of previous interviews to obtain richer descriptions of those areas. Interviews were discontinued when each woman felt she had communicated a thorough and complete description of that particular friendship.

Other researchers conduct in-depth interviews from a *feminist perspective.* That's what Kaufmann (1992) did in studying the social identities of women artists by using principles from Feminist Standpoint Theory to guide the interviews (see Harding, 1987a, 1987b, 1990). For example, the theory speaks to the unique experiences of women, so Kaufmann focused on issues faced by these women not just as artists but as women artists. Such interviews also strive to create coequal relationships between researchers and research participants, so Kaufmann opened herself up to being questioned about her interview procedures, and she changed her approach during the interviews. As she explained:

> *I learned to understand negotiations over the interview as women artists telling me that my methodology did not fit their experience, indeed, pointing out the presumptuousness of my attempt to set the conditions of our interaction.… To stand on protocol would have been precisely to invalidate myself,*

> *them, our relationship, and the entire project. (p. 195)*

The type of naturalistic inquiry also influences how interviews are conducted. For example, B. C. Taylor's (1992) study of how conversations between older people and college students influence older persons' identity employed an *ethnomethodological interview* procedure. He conducted interviews in line with an expansion model of discourse analysis proposed by Cicourel (1980), a disciple of Garfinkel's. The interviews involved "the use of open questioning strategies that heighten the reflexivity of relational partners concerning their involvement and performances with each other" (p. 497). Interviews routinely started with the questions, "What did you talk about this week?" and "How did you talk about it?" leading both the older people and the college students to reconstruct conversational topics in their evolving relationships.

Many in-depth interviewing methods elicit specific types of discourse from respondents. A variety of methods are used to obtain *personal narratives,* or stories. The **life story interview,** for instance, asks people to construct in their own words their entire life as a story or narrative, starting from the time a person is born to the present day, as well as hopes and visions for the future. As Atkinson (1998) explains, "A life story is a fairly complete narrating of one's entire experience of life as a whole, highlighting the most important aspects" (p. 8).

Narratives about particular past experiences can be obtained via *oral history* (see McMahan & Rogers, 1994a; Yow, 1994; see Chapter 9). Schely-Newman's (1991, 1993, 1995, 1997) oral history research program focuses on Jews who immigrated to Israel between 1948 and 1955 after the State's independence and settled in agricultural communities. The 1995 study used oral history to explore childbearing experiences of women who immigrated to Israel in the early 1950s from Arab countries.

Schely-Newman's (1995) research also reveals how *similarity* between interviewers and interviewees plays a role in shaping in-depth interviewing. Schely-Newman was visibly pregnant when she conducted the interviews, and her pregnancy helped create a context for talking about childbearing. Having grown up in an agricultural community in Tunisia and immigrating to Israel also facilitated establishing a relationship with her interviewees. As she explained:

> Interviewees wanted to establish my identity— where did I reside, from where did my family emigrate, was I married, to whom, and did I have children—before and while addressing issues I raised. [These] elements of identity…are more important in this culture than professional affiliation or research interest. This line of questioning reflects a personal interest in me; the interviewees treated me the same way they would treat their own daughters. (p. 177)

Narratives about especially potent incidents in people's lives can be obtained by using Flanagan's (1954) **critical incident technique,** which asks for "people's most memorable positive and negative experiences within a specific, social context" (Query & Kreps, 1993, p. 64). Orbe (1994) used this technique to collect descriptions of lived experience from 35 African American men so as to understand themes that were central to their communication. The men were asked to describe in detail a positive or negative past incident in which they had interacted with a non–African American person.

Another approach is **episode analysis,** where the interviewer asks a person to reconstruct a scene, complete with lines of dialogue, that represents a recurring pattern in a relationship. Mascheter and Harris (1986), for example, interviewed a couple who had been married and divorced yet maintained a close friendship. In joint interviews, this couple was asked to reconstruct three scenes from their relationship: one from their marriage (past), one from their postdivorce relationship (present), and one depicting how they would resolve conflict should it arise (future). For every line of dialogue, the speaker was asked, "What were you trying to do when you said that?" and the other person was then asked, "Was the speaker effective in carrying off this intention?"

Researchers also often observe what they consider to be critical incidents or important episodes and want to know how the people involved perceive these experiences. They can do this using **account analysis,** asking people to account for what was observed. Accounts provide an "actor's own statements about why he [or she] performed the acts in question, [and] what social meanings he [or she] gave to the actions of himself [or herself] and others" (Harre & Secord, 1973, p. 9). To illustrate, DiSanza (1995) collected accounts from part-time bank tellers of the formal training they had received as part of their assimilation into a large branch banking office.

Finally, researchers who want to know why people respond as they do while an event or activity is taking place can use **protocol analysis,** which asks people to verbalize their intentions, thoughts, and feelings as they engage in that activity (see Burgoyne & Hodgson, 1984). People watching television, for example, can be asked to "think aloud" as they choose a program and react to what is being shown on the screen.

To assist protocol analysis, researchers sometimes use **stimulated recall,** first recording a conversation and then playing back the tape for the conversational partners to stimulate their recall of the episode. As they listen to or watch the tape, researchers ask them to describe what they were thinking and feeling at points throughout the activity. Pomerantz, Fehr, and Ende (1997), for example, studied strategies supervising physicians (called preceptors) use with trainees, especially in difficult situations with patients. Thirty-five patient visits to a general clinic were videotaped, and the majority of perceptors and interns were interviewed using stimulated recall. The preceptor or the intern viewed the videotape of an interaction in which he or she had participated and was asked to provide comments. For example, the instructions given to preceptors were: "Stop the tape when you think the intern needed to be guided, or when you're trying to teach or correct, or for anything else you want to say. The more the better" (p. 592). The researchers analyzed both the videotapes and participants' commentaries to describe strategies supervising physicians and trainees use to manage interactional difficulties.

Recording and Transcribing Interviews. Most in-depth interviews are audiotaped (or sometimes videotaped), but recording interviews might not be possible, in which case interviewers try to take notes as close to verbatim as possible. Audiotaped interviews are typically transcribed, which is a difficult and time-consuming process. Even a 1-hour, two-person interview takes 4–5 hours to transcribe (Lindlof, 1995). And because these are in-depth interviews, many pages of transcripts are often produced.

The amount of detail in the transcripts depends on the purpose of the research. Most transcripts in ethnographic-type research, however, are not as detailed as those used in conversation analysis, where transcripts are marked for many features of conversation, such as the length of pauses and overlaps in talk.

Most important, researchers must make sure that the transfer of dialogue from an oral to a written medium is done accurately. Rawlins and Holl (1987), who interviewed 11th graders about their friendships, handled this process particularly well. They read each transcript repeatedly while the audiotape was played. Doing so ensured accurate transcription, familiarized them with each respondent as an individual, and enabled them to note special emphases that might help them to interpret the written transcript more appropriately.

START MAKING SENSE: ANALYZING AND REPORTING QUALITATIVE DATA

The massive amount of material gathered via naturalistic inquiry has to be made sense of and reported. Before such data can be effectively analyzed, they must, of course, be effectively managed; that is, stored appropriately and able to be easily retrieved. H. G. Levine (1985) proposes five general storage and retrieval processes: (a) formatting (laying out materials, such as putting them into type of files), (b) cross-referral (drawing links across different files), (c) indexing (using codes to

identify specific data), (d) abstracting (condensed summaries of lengthy data, such as interviews), and (e) pagination (using numbers and letters to locate materials). Huberman and Miles (1994) point out that, historically, these functions were performed using index cards, file folders, and the like, but they now can be done much more effectively and efficiently using computer software (see also Weitzman & Miles, 1993). Effectively managing the data makes it much easier to analyze them and report the findings.

Analyzing Qualitative Data

In his introductory comments about **qualitative data analysis,** the analysis of data that indicate the meanings (other than relative amounts) people have of something, Lindlof (1989a) identifies four interrelated principles that should be kept in mind: process, reduction, explanation, and theory. First, data analysis should be viewed as an ongoing *process* that occurs throughout the course of a study. Unlike quantitative researchers, naturalistic researchers don't collect all their data and then make sense of them; they make sense of data as they are acquired, and acquire more data after making sense of earlier data.

Second, the collected data must be *reduced* in some way. It's just not possible to present the large amount of data typically acquired from naturalistic inquiry (e.g., observational notes, interview transcripts, and documents), so the data must be reduced to some manageable amount. Wolcott (1990) claims that the crucial task in naturalistic research is "not to accumulate all the data you can, but to 'can' (i.e., get rid of) most of the data you accumulate" (p. 35)! This means both *physical reduction*—selecting which material is most useful to include in the analyses—and *conceptual reduction*—using a conceptual scheme to help sort and categorize the data.

Third, the goal of data analysis is to *explain* the meaning of the data, but there are at least two types of explanations: first-order and second-order explanations. **First-order explanations** are research participants' explanations of their own attitudes, behaviors, and so forth, whereas **second-order explanations** are explanations of participants' attitudes, behaviors, and other things, as seen through the researcher's eyes. Second-order explanations attempt to "explain the patterning of the first-order data" (Van Maanen, 1979, p. 541). Lindlof (1995) points out that although second-order explanations depend on first-order explanations, they do not always converge. That's because researchers, trained in data-analytic procedures and having read other research studies that influence the way they see the data, approach the data with a different lens than do participants. This doesn't mean their explanations are better than participants' explanations, they're just different.

Fourth, some naturalistic researchers analyze data for the purpose of *theory development.* As Lindlof (1995) explains, "The intensive examination of a single case can certainly test how and where a theory can be applied. It may also aid in the discovery of theoretical possibilities" (p. 218). We'll look first at data analysis directed toward theory development and then consider some other ways of analyzing qualitative data.

Testing Theory and Building Grounded Theory. Some naturalistic researchers engage in something akin to basic research by analyzing data *deductively* to see whether the data conform to theoretical expectations (see Chapter 2). N. L. Roth (1995), for example, explored the influence of social and personal forces on discussions of sexuality in client/provider interactions about HIV/AIDS. She observed interactions at two health clinics where clients were learning the result of their HIV antibody test, and she interviewed service providers after each interaction to clarify observations. She used a theoretical framework suggested by philosopher Anthony Giddens to deductively code the data with respect to acknowledged and unacknowledged personal and social forces (such as societal norms about sexuality and the guilt associated with their violation). The analysis confirmed the theoretical influence of these forces, as many of the interactions reproduced already sedimented social and personal norms. The analysis also re-

vealed how interactions, in turn, can influence the forces and, thereby, identified possibilities for altering the reproduction of societal norms.

Most naturalistic researchers, however, engage in **analytic induction** (Bulmer, 1979), inferring meanings from the data collected, rather than imposing such meanings on the data from another source (such as a theory). They look for emerging patterns in the data and revise their tentative formulations as they proceed to collect and analyze more data. As Huberman and Miles (1994) explain, this is actually a combination of inductive and deductive analysis: "When a theme, hypothesis, or pattern is identified inductively, the researcher then moves into a verification mode, trying to confirm or qualify the finding. This then keys off a new inductive cycle" (p. 431).

A number of naturalistic researchers who practice analytic induction are primarily interested in building what is called a **grounded theory,** in which generalizations are grounded in or inferred from the data collected (see Glaser & Strauss, 1967; Strauss, 1987; Strauss & Corbin, 1990). Developing grounded theory often occurs by using the **constant comparative method** to create and compare exhaustive categories that explain the data. To analyze interviews, for example, using this procedure, all interview responses are recorded and included in the data analysis, often by writing each response on a card. The analysis begins by searching for commonalities among responses. When the content of several cards appears to belong together, those responses are presumed to constitute a category, and a word or phrase is selected to title it—in terms used by the research participants, whenever possible. Gradually, all the data (response cards) are sorted into categories. Each card is copied and placed in as many categories as it fits, to preserve the conceptual richness of the phenomenon being studied.

Stamp and Banski (1992), for example, studied communication management of changes in autonomy during marital couples' transition to parenthood. They interviewed, both separately and together, 10 married couples before and after the birth of their first child. The data were analyzed using the constant comparative method. Each interview was first read thoroughly and relevant statements about incidents were divided into discrete incidents (and printed on separate note cards) and then randomly sorted and compared with one another. As the researchers maintain, "In this way, the subjects' accounts, taken from the interviews, were treated as textual evidence and examined through an ongoing, and emergent, process of comparative analysis with one another for similarities and differences" (p. 285).

Throughout the analysis, the researcher's hunches and theoretical ideas about the structure underlying the phenomenon being studied are recorded as *memoranda* kept separate from the data. This recording of preliminary and tentative inferences is intended to reduce drift away from the grounding of the categories in the data gathered from participants. As the conceptual scheme develops, new respondents may be interviewed who promise to provide further insights into the phenomenon. The initial cycle of data gathering and data analysis is followed by wider ranging data gathering and refined data analysis.

Karp (1986), for example, studied what occurs when people change their social status by interviewing 72 socially mobile people. As he went along, he wrote "numerous theoretical memos on emerging themes in the data" (p. 22). In other words, as he reviewed his interview tapes and notes, he made initial inferences about respondents' careers. In fact, Karp changed his interview guide as he went along to probe more deeply into the issues he uncovered along the way. As he explained, "Unproductive questions have been deleted and other questions have been included in order to obtain systematic data on important themes unanticipated at the outset of the project" (p. 22). He also developed his own set of coding categories after approximately 30 interviews; this enabled him to "stay close to the data and clarify areas of greatest substantive richness" (p. 22).

Eventually, new data (e.g., interview responses from additional respondents) add little to the development of new descriptive categories. At this point, the categories are considered "saturated." The re-

searcher then reviews the theoretical memoranda and conceptualizes higher level (more abstract) generalizations that subsume the initial set of categories yet are grounded in them. If possible, a *core category* is conceptualized that incorporates all others. The conceptual structure is usually hierarchical: lower level categories serve as properties of broader categories, which, in turn, comprise the core category. The resulting grounded theory is a description of this hierarchical category structure, including relationships among the categories and between categories and the data.

Rawlins and Holl's (1987) study of the conceptual structures underpinning teenagers' descriptions of how they manage their friendships illustrates these aspects of grounded theory. As they examined the transcripts, they developed conceptual categories from similar words and phrases used, such as references to "trust, backstabbing, someone you can talk to, keeping a confidence, etc." (p. 348). They also put into a single category statements about friends that seemed similar, even though different words were used. For example, some respondents described what others called "school friends," without exactly using that phrase. The classification scheme was continuously revised as the analysis proceeded. At the end, the researchers recategorized the transcripts using the final category system to ensure accuracy and consistency. They went so far as to develop a core concept encapsulating the most specific categories developed. They point out that "an overarching concern for these adolescents was the preservation or violation of trust in their friendships" (p. 348).

Research that seeks to develop theory from the ground up should meet four criteria. The results from such a study should be *believable,* in that they should seem plausible to the reader; *comprehensive* in accounting for all (or most) of the data; *grounded* or tied closely to the data; and *applicable,* leading to testable propositions and additional investigation.

Qualitative Data-Analytic Techniques. Other naturalistic researchers analyze the qualitative data acquired without intending to test or build a formal theory per se. They too, however, are interested in making larger level claims on the basis of particular features of the data. In this sense, all naturalistic researchers, in one way or another, tack back and forth between specific data and larger themes (such as identity, organization, or community). There are a number of data-analytic techniques used to analyze and make inference about qualitative data, including dialectical analysis, metaphor analysis, and fantasy theme analysis.

Some communication researchers analyze field notes and interview transcripts using **dialectical analysis,** which explores the tensions produced from seemingly contradictory elements within a system. For example, a common tension in many cultures, including the United States, is between the individual and the group, but from a dialectical perspective, these are two sides of the same coin—you can't have one without the other. Dialectical contradictions like these "are not merely different from one another or in conflict with one another; they are the underlying opposing tendencies in a phenomenon which mutually exclude and simultaneously presuppose one another" (Goldsmith, 1990, p. 538). Researchers operating from a dialectical perspective, thus, explicate relevant dialectics and explain how they are managed.

An example of dialectical analysis is Cissna, Cox, and Bochner's (1990) study of the dialectics of stepfamily life. An experienced marital and family counselor conducted semistructured interviews with nine stepfamily couples about their experiences in building a stepfamily. The analysis of their statements revealed a "'relationship dialectic' between the freely chosen marital relationship and the not-so-freely chosen stepfamily relationships" (p. 44). Couples attempted to manage this dialectic in a number of ways, such as by communicating clear statements to children about the importance of the marriage and by maintaining direct communication between the marital partners that helped them to present a "united front" to their children. This research, thus, demonstrates ways in which communication helped to manage a dialectical tension.

Some data-analytic techniques focus on identifying and interpreting specific types of discourse that research participants use. **Metaphor analysis,** for example, looks for participants' use of *metaphors,* figures of speech in which a word or phrase that denotes one object is applied to another. Owen (1990) used this to analyze the data acquired from interviews conducted every two weeks for five months with two female students who were going through a change in a romantic relationship and from the diary they kept over that time period. He wanted to "determine precisely why, how, and at what points a person's changing relational circumstances require changes in metaphorical concepts" (p. 37). He read through the transcripts and diaries in temporal order to identify turning points and the meaning of the main metaphors used by participants to make sense of the relationship at each turning point. For example, when Anna first met Mark, he kept asking her for dates and phoning her, behavior that Anna associated with the metaphor of "relationship as a journey" (e.g., "Mark wanted me to go on a trip with him to a place I'm not ready to go to yet"). After they had dated for about 5 months, Mark proposed marriage, which led Anna to begin using the metaphor of "relationship as a container" (e.g., "I felt trapped"). This study, thus, shows how significant events in a relationship help to change the metaphorical concepts people use to make sense of those events.

Another technique that focuses on a specific type of discourse is *fantasy theme analysis,* which looks at the stories shared among people (see Chapter 9). Putnam, Van Hoeven, and Bullis (1991), for example, studied collective bargaining by observing negotiation sessions, planning meetings, and caucus interactions of two school districts. They adopted the framework of Symbolic Convergence Theory, which explains how group consciousness is created and sustained, to look for fantasy themes in the data. They found that both school districts developed symbolic convergence on common enemies and past negotiations, which instilled similar values and motives for the negotiation process.

These and other techniques are used to make sense of the qualitative data acquired through naturalistic inquiry. The analysis of such data has also been aided recently by a number of computer software programs (see Fielding & Lee, 1998; Richards & Richards, 1994; Weitzman & Miles, 1993). Some programs, such as Ethnograph (Qualis Research Associates, 1990) and ATLAS/ti (Muhr, 1991), even help to build grounded theory by making, respectively, hierarchical (e.g., A is a subset of concept B) or network (A promotes B) links among concepts identified in the data.

Reporting Findings from Naturalistic Inquiry

Naturalistic inquiry needs to be "written up" in one form or another. Doing so requires consideration of some important issues, such as the type of tale being told, writing strategies and techniques, and even other forms a report might take.

Telling a Tale.   A naturalistic research report is essentially a **tale,** a story told by a member of one culture about another culture (or his or her own culture) to the members of his or her own culture. Van Maanen (1988) identified three such tales: realist, confessional, and impressionistic. Perhaps the most common type is the **realist tale,** a story told from the point of view of the people studied. The goal is to capture as fully as possible the ways in which the participants make sense of their world. The researcher, consequently, is removed from the tale and the story is told in a documentary style. A **confessional tale** is somewhat the reverse, focusing primarily on the researcher and his or her experiences during the fieldwork. An **impressionistic tale,** in some ways, blends the realist and confessional tales to provide an account of the participants and the researcher as central characters in an unfolding drama.

In addition to these three tales, Potter (1996) points out that there are **critical** (critiquing problematic social structures through the perspective of those who are disadvantaged), **formal** (those that follow the rules of a particular theory or analytic procedure, such as semiotics or conversational analysis), **literary** (told using a novelist's sense of narration), and **jointly told tales** (told by researchers and research participants working together).

The general type of tale told inevitably influences the way the research is reported.

Writing the Report.   Although there are naturalistic research reports that take somewhat the form discussed in Chapter 3 of first reviewing the literature, followed by the methods, results, and discussion, most naturalistic reports simply don't follow that form. This doesn't mean, however, that there isn't a structure to such reports. Lindlof (1995) identifies a number of structures that can be used to organize the text.

Some scholars use a *thematic* structure to discuss the topics or themes that emerge from the data analysis. Lind (1997) used this strategy to identify and discuss four content dimensions of the ethical sensitivity of television news viewers: story characteristics, ethical issues, consequences, and stakeholders. Other scholars organize the report *chronologically* into phases or stages, like Adelman and Frey's (1997) study of the AIDS residence; the three main chapters of the text follow residents over the course of their life in the house as they "move from being a newcomer, to a community member, to someone the community remembers" (p. 18). Other reports are written from a *puzzle-explication* perspective, treating the phenomenon of interest as a puzzle that needs to be solved. Still other reports adopt a *separate narration and analysis* structure, first describing the situation in rich detail and then, in a separate section, analyzing and explaining what was described. And some scholars use a *narrowing and expanding the focus* structure, which Lindlof likens to a zoom camera lens, in that a topic is introduced, then focused on in descriptive detail, and then is explained from a more distanced perspective (i.e., the larger picture), and this process is repeated for a number of topics.

Each of these and many other organizational strategies include as part of the report verbatim quotes from research participants. For example, to study how abusive males make sense of their acts of spousal abuse, Stamp and Sabourin (1995) collected personal narratives from 15 abusive males. Their report is filled with representative verbatim quotes (including an extended narrative that runs for four pages) to illustrate the themes they identify. To illustrate the act of denial, for instance, the authors included the following narrative:

> *She grabbed my jacket, tore that, tore my, tore the little muff on my ear thing. So then I was still just moving away from her then she punched me in the face and I said, "hold up, hold up" and pushed her back and I said, "don't touch me. Just don't touch me," you know. After that I say, "I'm going to work, just leave me alone." And when I went to work, where I work it was about 3:45 in the morning, next thing I know my supervisor came to me and said, uh, "the police are waiting for you outside." I said, "what's the problem." I said, "what, are you coming to get me because I took my own car?" He said, "No, you assaulted your wife." I said, "Assaulted my wife, in what way?" "She said that you hit her." I said "Hit her? I did everything but hit her."* (p. 296)

Such verbatim quotes, as well as descriptions of critical incidents, episodes, and the like, function as *exemplars* that help illustrate and crystalize the concept(s) being discussed, in this case, the denial of spousal abuse.

Other Forms of Presentation.   We have focused on written reports because that is the form most naturalistic research reports take. However, naturalistic inquiry can also be presented in a number of other visual forms (see D. Harper, 1989). Some communication ethnographers, such as J. L. Jones (1996), described previously, perform their work. Others, for example, Adelman and Schultz (1991) and Conquergood and Siegel (1985, 1990), make ethnographic films. Photographic images are also being incorporated into written reports (see, for example, Conquergood, 1994; L. R. Frey, Adelman, & Query, 1996). These visual forms can be powerful presentations of naturalistic research, although, as Ball and Smith (1992) point out, they are not necessarily more "realistic" than written reports per se.

There are also new forms of writing with which naturalistic researchers are experimenting. These forms, according to Richardson (1994), emphasize writing as a "method of inquiry," a way of knowing, and have in common the "violation of prescribed conventions; they transgress the boundaries of social science writing genres" (pp. 516, 520). Such experimental writing takes the form of narratives of the self (e.g., autoethnographic tales, such as Crawford, 1996), fiction (e.g., Pacanowsky, 1988), poetry (e.g., D. A. Austin, 1996), plays (e.g., Mienczakowski, 1996), multivocalic texts (e.g., K. V. Fox, 1996), and even a "divined" ethnography (M. Meyer, 1997; see C. Ellis & Bochner, 1996, for other examples).

In the final analysis, whatever form it takes, a good naturalistic research report provides thick description, rich interpretation, and a compelling account. There are many excellent examples of such work, including ones cited in this chapter. We'll leave you with this paragraph from Conquergood's (1994) gang communication research, in which he analyzes a mural painted for Negro, a gang member who was killed during Conquergood's fieldwork, in terms of its symbolic features and larger connection to the hood in which Negro lived:

> *In a profound way, this tiny death mural painted on one of the narrow edges of a bridge can be thought of as an enblematic image for the world-making capacities of the hood. It is a miniature, designed to enclose, concentrate, clarify, control, and intensify meaning. All reppin' practices can be thought of as metonymies and condensation symbols for the hood. They represent it in a heightened, stylized, and focused way. The hood that Negro embodies and, paradoxically, enlivens in death is a miniature world excavated and constructed out of subjugated knowledges and marginal materials. At every level of refraction, the hood represents an enclosed space, a microworld, for the nurturance of agency, intimacy, and meaning. The very forces that threaten to rip it asunder—sudden violence and death—are appropriated and absorbed as value-clarifying and community-building moral dramas of heroic sacrifice and solidarity.* (p. 52)

CONCLUSION

As you see, the communication professors whose conversation about a radio newscast they heard while commuting to work, mentioned in the introduction to this chapter, would have a lo-o-ong way to go before they could answer the research questions they raised using naturalistic research procedures. Naturalistic researchers must identify and gain entry to the site they want to study (for those professors, one or more high schools, businesses, or radio stations), determine the role they will take at those sites, what they want to observe and how they will make those observations, whom they will interview and what they will ask, how they will record and analyze the information they acquire, and how to write up or otherwise present the research study.

Naturalistic inquiry may appear to be a daunting task, but this should not hinder one from doing it. Bird (1992) relates a piece of folklore from anthropology, a story about a young graduate student about to embark on her first field research:

> *She knocked on the door of a great master of fieldwork…nervous because she had no training or idea how to do ethnography. The master gave her a notebook and pencil and told her to get out and get on with it. (p. 256)*

In many ways, that's what naturalistic communication researchers do—they get on with the business of studying communication in context as best they can. When they are done, they hopefully have acquired rich, useful information from having interacted in the natural setting with people dealing with genuine communication concerns and issues.

PART FOUR

ANALYZING AND INTERPRETING QUANTITATIVE DATA

CHAPTER 11

DESCRIBING QUANTITATIVE DATA

At the beginning of this textbook, we noted that we live in an "information society," bombarded by information from all sides. Much of the information we see or hear on a daily basis is in the form of "stats," all those numbers people use to describe things. For instance, you wake up to a television weather reporter saying it's 85 degrees outside, and pointing out that it's already 3 degrees warmer than the average for that day. On the way to work, you hear on the car radio that the Dow Jones Industrial Average (DJIA, or Dow) fell 49.23 points yesterday. During a sales team meeting at the office, a colleague displays charts and graphs that describe the amount and type of sales over the past few months. Back at home after work, the anchor on the early evening television news says that the latest poll shows that, unless something dramatic happens in the next few days, the mayoral election later that week is all but decided, as one candidate is preferred 55% to 40% over the other candidate, with only 5% undecided, and the margin of error for the poll is plus or minus 3%. You finally get a chance to read the newspaper, and see an Associated Press release that documents an important difference between women and men in the standard of living in the first year after divorce, with women experiencing a 27% decline while men experience a 10% increase ("Divorce Researcher," 1996). And later that night, while eating one of your favorite "comfort" foods and thinking you are safe from any more "stats," a television program about medicine says there is a substantial correlation—.70 is mentioned, but isn't explained—between eating that very food and heart disease! As these examples, and many others we could have offered, demon-

strate, we are exposed to quite a few statistics every day. Indeed, our society thrives on such information; in the words of the members of Generation X, "Stats rule."

Some of these statistics, like temperature readings and arithmetic averages, are relatively straightforward, easy to understand, and trustworthy. We know how these statistics are produced and what they mean. But other statistics, such as estimating what a population believes from a relatively small sample (as in polling) or statistical tests of differences between groups (e.g., men and women) and relationships between variables (food consumption and heart disease), are more complex and difficult to understand. Most people don't know how these statistics are produced and, therefore, don't know whether they are accurate or the conclusions drawn from them trustworthy.

This chapter, and the subsequent chapters in this section of the textbook, is designed to help you understand various types of statistics used to analyze quantitative (numerical) data. Our goal is to help you become a competent consumer of such information. We start by explaining the nature and purposes of statistical data analysis.

MAKING SENSE OF NUMBERS: STATISTICAL DATA ANALYSIS

Each research methodology we have examined in this text relies on various measurement techniques (e.g., questionnaires, interviews, and observations) to acquire data. A set of acquired data, however, is not very useful in itself; it needs to be analyzed and interpreted. **Data analysis** is the process of examining what data mean to researchers. Data analysis transforms data into useful information that can be shared with others.

Quantitative data lend themselves to data-analytic procedures associated closely with the applied branch of mathematics known as *statistics.* **Statistical data analysis,** therefore, refers to the process of examining what quantitative data mean to researchers.

The word "statistics" comes from the Latin root *status,* which implies that statistics are used to understand the status or state of quantitative data. The earliest forms of organized statistics were of this type. The ancient civilizations of Babylon and Egypt, for example, collected statistics on the number of people and livestock, among other things, for the purposes of taxation and the raising of armies (see M. Cowles, 1989). Today, our society produces a large number of statistics for many different reasons, including trying to count the number of people living in the United States for the purposes of taxation and, when there is a need for a draft, the raising of an army. Used in this sense, then, **statistics** refers to any numerical indicator of a set of data. There are a number of techniques and procedures used to produce such statistics, such as the arithmetic average. Many people, in fact, equate the term *statistics* with these techniques and procedures (Gephart, 1988). Let's call these procedures and the descriptive information they yield "descriptive statistics."

But as M. Cowles (1989) points out, starting in the seventeenth century, another activity was referenced by the term *statistics:*

> *the practice of not only collecting and collating numerical facts, but also the process of reasoning from them. Going beyond the data, making inferences and drawing conclusions with greater or lesser degrees of certainty in an orderly and consistent manner is the aim of modern applied statistics. (p. 6)*

Such inference making was made possible by the development of sophisticated techniques and procedures for analyzing quantitative data, such as estimation procedures, examined later in this chapter, which allow researchers to generalize from a sample to a population. Let's call these procedures

and the inferential information they yield "inferential statistics."

Drawing conclusions and making inferences is part and parcel of how we now process numerical information. In fact, it's doubtful that there is such a thing as a "neutral" statistic, one about which we don't infer something. Even something as simple as knowing the temperature may lead to an inference about whether it's a good day to go to the beach or a good day to stay indoors and get some work done.

Today, statistics are one of the most pervasive and persuasive forms of evidence used to make arguments. In fact, Abelson (1995) believes that "the purpose of statistics is to organize a useful argument from quantitative evidence, using a form of principled rhetoric" (p. xiii). Using some of the examples that opened this chapter, a stockbroker may urge a client to sell some stocks because of a falling DJIA. The colleague at work may use the charts and graphs documenting sales to persuade your team to proceed in a certain way. The television news anchor actually made the claim, on the basis of poll statistics, that the upcoming election was essentially over. Statistics on the effects of divorce rates on standard of living have been used by policymakers to help bring about stricter child-support enforcement and more flexible property-division laws ("Divorce Researcher," 1996). And of the basis of statistical evidence, physicians warn against eating harmful foods.

We are sure everyone, including you, has used statistics at some point to support or refute an argument. Many people, in fact, may be wary of statistical information because it is used so frequently as evidence in arguments. They believe, as Huff (1954) pointed out long ago, that statistics is a way of lying with numbers. (According to Mark Twain, England's Prime Minister Benjamin Disraeli said there were three types of lies: "lies, damn lies, and statistics.") People, thus, doubt the "principled" nature of numerical evidence in arguments. And in many cases, well they should. If you turn on the television and see an advertisement boldly claiming that four out of five doctors recommend a certain headache medicine, you should be wary of the claim. Not only don't we know how this "study" was done, but also we suspect the agenda of selling the medicine had an important effect on how those statistics were produced. (By the way, this claim also means that 20% of doctors don't recommend it—a pretty high figure. Imagine how effective the advertisement would sound if it said, "Twenty percent of doctors do not recommend this medicine.")

We've probably all been guilty of using statistics in a less-than-honest manner, or what Huff (1954) calls "statisticulation," that is, misinforming people by manipulating statistical information. So part of our distrust of statistics may be because each of us has used them as we fear they may be being used on us. But this doesn't mean we should reject statistics whenever we hear them. After all, as Abelson (1995) retorts, "When people lie with words (which they do quite often), we do not take it out on the English language" (p. 1). We don't start to distrust all words.

We think a main reason for people's distrust of statistics, especially complex statistical information, is a lack of knowledge about how such information is produced and whether it is valid. There are also a number of people who suffer from what Paulos (1988) calls "innumeracy," the mathematical equivalent of illiteracy that leads them to be uncomfortable dealing with numbers and elements of chance. These problems mean that people often are not confident that they can understand fully the value, or lack thereof, of particular statistics. As just one example, consider again the Dow Jones Industrial Average. Most people probably don't know that the Dow is simply the total stock prices of 30 representative stocks, not a very large number. And because it gives greater weight to higher priced stocks, the Dow is a notoriously poor gauge of overall stock market activity (Maier, 1991). Stock market experts look more at the New York Stock Exchange Index or the Standard and Poors (S&P 500) Index, which are much better measures because they include many more stock prices and weight them by corporate size (Maier, 1991). For example, on Tuesday, December 15, 1998, the Dow fell 126.16 points, or 1.4% of its market value, but the day was actually much worse, as the S&P 500 declined 25.56 points, or 2.2% of its market value. And on Thursday, January 21, 1999, the Dow dropped 19.31 points while the S&P 500 rose 4.26 points. Most people, however, rely on the Dow, and the media continue to feature it.

The lack of knowledge about statistical information results either in the tendency to reject the information completely or to accept it at face value. Both responses demonstrate a lack of competence and confidence and place people at risk. What people need to do, instead, is to become competent and confident consumers of statistical evidence, so that they can make informed decisions about whether to accept such information when they see or hear it.

The first step, which we've just accomplished, is understanding that the word *statistics* refers to at least two things: (a) products—numerical descriptions and inferential statistics that characterize a set of quantitative data, and (b) techniques—the application of procedures to produce numerical descriptions and statistical inferences. We are now ready to take a look at some of these statistical techniques and products, and the conclusions and inferences drawn from them that comprise the statistics enterprise.

To do so, we focus on the two general purposes of description and inference as reflected in two types of statistical data analysis. **Descriptive statistical data analysis** is used to construct simple descriptions about the characteristics of a set of quantitative data. In this chapter, we explore three ways to describe data: (a) numerical indicators that summarize the data, called *summary statistics,* (b) converting raw scores into what are called *standard scores,* and (c) constructing visual displays of data. **Inferential statistical data analysis** has two interrelated purposes: (a) *estimation*—estimating the characteristics of a population from data gathered on a sample, and (b) *significance testing*—testing for significant statistical differences between groups and significant statistical relationships between variables. In Chapter 12, we cover the general principles of inferential statistical data analysis, while Chapters 13 and 14 examine the specific data-analytic procedures used to test for significant statistical differences and relationships.

DESCRIBING DATA THROUGH SUMMARY STATISTICS

When one has a relatively small data set, such as temperature readings for the previous five days, one can verbally describe the entire data set by referring to each individual entry (e.g., Monday was 70 degrees, Tuesday was 60 degrees, and so forth). But when there is a fairly large data set, it doesn't make much sense to verbally give all the individual entries that comprise the set. For example, the radio announcer doesn't tell how the stock market did yesterday by reading off each and every stock. (If you want that kind of detail, you have to read the newspaper or watch CNN or some other television channel that lists stock prices running across the bottom of the screen during daytime programming.) Nor does the television news anchor, when describing what people said about how they would vote, read off each of the 1600 (or however many there are) individual responses. In both cases, and many others, the sheer amount of information would be difficult, if not impossible, to process.

The data that comprise a relatively large data set, therefore, must be condensed in some way to make sense of them. Hence, the DJIA (despite its flaws) is used to describe how millions of stocks and tens of millions of stockmarket transactions did on any particular day. And the percentage of people who said they would vote for one candidate versus the other is used to summarize people's answers to a poll. In each case, the data have been condensed to a numerical indicator that best summarizes the data set, or what is called a **summary statistic.** Summary statistics, thus, provide an efficient way to describe an entire set of quantitative data.

There are two types of summary statistics that are most important for our purposes: measures of central tendency and measures of dispersion. The first type provides a numerical indicator that describes the "center" of a data set, while the second type provides a numerical indicator of how much the scores in a data set differ from the center point, that is, how tight or spread out those scores are from the center point.

Measures of Central Tendency

We seem to be fascinated in the United States with "the typical." As Weisberg (1992) explains, "We want to know what typical people do and think, perhaps so that we can be sure that we ourselves are not unusual in our actions and attitudes" (p. 1).

Researchers, too, are interested in what is "typical" about a set of quantitative data. They seek a summary statistic that provides the "typical" or "average" point in a data set, the one score that best represents the entire distribution of data. Intuitively, it makes sense that the most representative point would be somewhere toward the middle of the data set, as opposed to being closer to either of the extremes. Thus, for example, if a researcher measured 100 organizational employees on the quality of their communication with their supervisor (say on a 5-point scale that ranges from very high to very low), the highest score wouldn't be a very good indicator of the "typical" employee's communication, and neither would the lowest score. Either extreme would give an unrepresentative view of that communication. A better indicator of the typical employee's communication is somewhere toward the middle or center of all the scores. The researcher would want to use this "middle" score to best represent the "central tendency" of the distribution. Hence, **measures of central tendency** (also called **representative values**) describe the center point of a distribution of quantitative data.

There are a number of measures of central tendency, but the three most common types are the mode, median, and mean. Each is a summary statistic that identifies the center point of an **array** of quantitative data, an *ordered* display of numerical measurements (e.g., the distribution 5, 3, 10, 7 becomes an array of data when put in either an *ascending order*, beginning with the lowest number and moving to the highest number—3, 5, 7, 10—or a *descending order*, beginning with the highest number and moving to the lowest number—10, 7, 5, 3). Which measure of central tendency is used depends on the type of data collected. Remember from Chapter 4 that there are four types of measurement scales: (a) nominal scales, which classify a variable into different categories; (b) ordinal scales, which rank order categories along some dimension; (c) interval scales, which establish equal distance between each of the adjacent points along the scale and have an arbitrary zero point; and (d) ratio scales, which are like interval scales but establish an absolute zero point where the variable being measured ceases to exist. Let's examine each of the three measures of central tendency and the type of data for which they are most useful.

Mode.   The **mode (*Mo*),** the simplest measure of central tendency, indicates which score or value in a distribution occurs most frequently. It literally points out the category or numerical score that is most typical in terms of the number of times it appears.

The mode is an appropriate measure of central tendency when describing a set of nominal data. Because nominal data are in the form of categories, no mathematical analyses (such as computing the mean, the arithmetic average, discussed below) can be done; all one can do is indicate which category occurred the most.

For example, as part of an attempt to understand more fully the important problem of peer sexual harassment, Ivy and Hamlet (1996) asked 163 students to indicate which behaviors from a list of 15 (identified from previous research) did or did not constitute sexual harassment (by answering "yes" or "no"). The researchers counted the actual number of "yes" and "no" answers for each behavior (see Figure 11.1), As you see, the category of "sexual assault" received the most amount of "yes" responses and, correspondingly, the least amount of "no" responses. Because that category occurred most frequently, it is the mode for this distribution. It is the category that is most typical of this data set. (By the way, the category of "humor and joke" is the **antimode,** Vogt, 1999, because it received the least amount of "yes" responses and, correspondingly, the most amount of "no" responses. The antimode is often helpful for knowing, for example, what people least prefer.)

FIGURE 11.1   Perceptions of sexually harassing behaviors

BEHAVIOR	FREQ. "YES"	FREQ. "NO"
Suggestive or insulting vocal sounds	127	35
Whistling in a suggestive manner	93	69
Repeatedly being asked out on a date, even after saying no	109	54
Humor & jokes about sex or about women and/or men, in general	76	83
Sexual propositions, invitations, or other pressures for sexual activity	146	16
Continual compliments of a personal and/or sexual nature	123	37
Staring	93	69
Making obscene gestures	140	21
Questions about personal and/or sexual life	125	35
Implied or overt sexual threats	146	15
Patting, stroking, pinching, & other similar forms of touch	147	14
Brushing up against the body	124	36
Attempted or actual kissing	132	29
Sexual assault	151	10
Forced sexual intercourse	149	12

Source: Adapted from Diana K. Ivy and Stephen Hamlet, "College Students and Sexual Dynamics: Two Studies of Peer Sexual Involvement," *Communication Education*, 45 (2), p. 159. Copyright by the National Communication Association. 1996. Reprinted by permission of the publisher.

Whereas the mode is the appropriate measure of central tendency for a set of nominal data, it is not usually very useful when applied to ordinal data and is of very limited use for describing the center of a set of interval/ratio data. For example, in a race among nine horses, let's assume one horse finishes first, another finishes second, and so on, down to the horse that finishes ninth. Because each rank only appears once in this set of ordinal data, each rank is the mode. The mode, in this case, thus, is meaningless. Even if two horses tied for fifth, that mode would not tell much, although if two horses tied for first, it would. (Notice, however, that if the data were the number of times a horse finished in first place, second place, and so forth, this would be nominal data, and the mode, the category that occurred most frequently, would be the appropriate summary statistic for describing the central tendency of this data set.)

The mode can also be applied to interval/ratio data to describe the score that occurs the most amount of time. Suppose, for example, that a researcher wants to know how much information people recall from a public service announcement (PSA) about the adverse effects of tobacco. The researcher shows seven people a PSA that contains 25 important pieces of information, and then asks them one hour later to recall that information. The researcher counts the number of correct pieces of information recalled (and, thereby, produces ratio data, as there is an absolute zero point), and finds the following distribution for the seven participants:

P_1	P_2	P_3	P_4	P_5	P_6	P_7
20	12	11	9	5	5	3

In this distribution, the mode is "5" because it occurs more than any other score. As you can see, the mode does not appear to be a very good expression of the center of this distribution. If we had to choose one number from this distribution to describe the central tendency, the number "9" would appear to be a much better choice. And if either extreme score (20 or 3) occurred three times, then it would be the mode and, of course, an even weaker description of the central tendency than the number "5," since the new mode would also be the most extreme point in the distribution.

Thus, it usually makes little sense to use the mode with a set of ordinal, interval, or ratio data. As one final example, consider the amount of money people make in the neighborhood where you live. The mode could be used to describe the central tendency of this data set, but no two people may make the exact amount so there may be no mode. Or suppose two people make exactly the same amount and that happens to be the lowest pay in the neighborhood. In that case, the mode would be a poor measure of the typical income of people living in that neighborhood. For reasons like this, the mode is seldom used to describe the central tendency of ordinal, interval, or ratio data.

Another problem with the mode for nominal, interval, or ratio data is that there may be more than one category or score that occurs the same amount of times. For example, if there were two 20s and two 5s in the PSA information recall data, there would be two modes. Such a distribution is called **bimodal,** in contrast to a **unimodal distribution** in which there is only one mode. And if there were two 20s, two 12s, and two 5s, it is a **multimodal distribution.** In such cases, although the mode still helps us to understand the data, it provides even less useful information about the center point of the data. Mercifully, multimodal data are seldom reported in academic literature.

In summary, the mode is an appropriate measure of the central tendency of a set of nominal data that tells researchers which category occurs the most. The mode, however, cannot be used to describe the center point of a set of ordinal data (when each rank only occurs once), and typically is not a very effective measure of the center point of a set of interval/ratio data.

Median.   The **median (*Md* or *Mdn*)** divides a distribution of quantitative data exactly in half. It is the score above which and below which half the observations fall. It literally locates the middle case, which is why it sometimes is referred to as a *location, positional,* or *order* measure (Weisberg, 1992).

The median is very appropriate for describing the center point of a set of ordinal (rank-ordered) data and often is effective for describing the center point of interval/ratio data. In the case of ordinal data, dividing the possible ranks at the midpoint does, indeed, give us the center of the data. In the horse race example above, the horse that finished fifth out of nine horses is the median, as four horses finished above it and four finished below it.

This same logic and utility applies to a set of interval/ratio data. In the distribution about information recall presented earlier, the median is 9, because half the distribution falls above this score and half below it. (Now we see why that number appeared so tempting when we were talking about the mode.)

In a set of ordinal or interval/ratio data that contains an odd number of scores, the median is an actual score in the distribution (e.g., the number "9" is an actual score in the information recall distribution). When there are an even number of observations, the median is found by taking the two middle numbers, adding them together, and dividing by 2. Thus, for example, if the number 9 is removed from the PSA recall information distribution (leaving 20, 12, 11, 5, 5, 3), the median is found by taking the two middle numbers (11 and 5), adding them together (16), and dividing by 2, which equals 8. So 8 is the median of this distribution. Hence, when there are an even number of scores in a distribution, the median is not a value that appears in the distribution. It is a calculated value halfway between the two middle scores.

The median often makes good sense as an indicator of the central tendency of interval/ratio data. One advantage the median has over the mode in this case is that it takes into account the entire set of scores in a distribution, rather than only one or a few scores, as does the mode. The median considers the entire set of scores and divides it at the halfway point.

A more important advantage is that the median is not swayed by extreme scores, or what are called **outliers.** For example, the score of 20 in the PSA information recall scores seems to be a pretty extreme score as compared to the other scores in that distribution. But this doesn't affect the median per se. Or, let's suppose there are 100 possible pieces of information in the PSA and all the scores remained the same, except that the high score was 80 instead of 20. The median (9) would still be the same. Some measures of central tendency, such as the mean (discussed below), are greatly affected by extreme scores, but the median is not, and is, therefore, considered to be a *resistant* statistic (Weisberg, 1992).

The median, thus, is a very useful measure of central tendency when a set of interval/ratio data contain very extreme scores. For example, the U.S. Census Bureau (1999b) reported that the median household income for 1997 was $37,303. The government uses the median to describe the "average" household income because the few billionaires and millionaires in the population would drive the mean sky-high, maybe to $100,000 or even much

higher. This figure, however (and unfortunately), just doesn't describe very well the "typical" or "average" household income. Hence, government officials divide the distribution of all reported household incomes at the halfway point and use this median to describe the "average" household income.

This example also shows that the term "average" is used as a synonym for any measure of central tendency. Most people think of an "average" as the arithmetic average (the mean) of a set of data, but in statistics, "average" means the "typical" or "most representative" category or score that describes the central tendency of a distribution. Thus, the mode, median, and mean are each an "average." So the next time the term "average" is used as statistical evidence in an argument, check to see which measure of central tendency is being used.

The ability of the median to resist being influenced by extreme scores, however, is also its primary weakness, at least in comparison to the mean. For example, if the score of 20 in the information recall distribution is changed to 19, the median is still 9. But as we will see below, the mean would change. The median, therefore, is not sensitive to changes in the scores that comprise the data set.

In summary, the median is usually the appropriate measure of central tendency for a set of ordinal data. It is also often quite useful for describing interval/ratio data, especially when the distribution has an extreme score(s) that would lead the mean to not represent the center point very well.

Mean. The **mean ($\bar{X}$; sample mean, M; population mean, μ)** is the arithmetic average, and is computed by adding all the scores in a distribution of interval/ratio data and dividing by the total number of scores. The scores can be added together and divided in this manner because the points on an interval/ratio measurement scale are of equal distance (e.g., there is the same amount of difference between 4 and 5 as there is between 27 and 28). In the PSA information recall (ratio) data above, the mean is found by adding up all the scores (20 + 12 + 11 + 9 + 5 + 5 + 3 = 65) and dividing this total by the number of scores on which it is based (7), which equals 9.29. (Typically, means are reported using either one or two decimal points, and are rounded off to the nearest figure; the mean is actually 9.285, so it is rounded off, in this case up to 9.29.)

The mean usually is the most appropriate and effective measure of central tendency of a set of interval/ratio data precisely because it is sensitive to every change in the data. For example, if the number 20 is changed to 19, the total is now 64 and the mean is 9.14. The mean, therefore, changes if *any* number in a distribution changes; the mode and median, as we have seen, don't have this property. The mean, therefore, is considered to be a *nonresistant* statistic (nonresistant to extreme scores), in contrast to the resistant statistic of the median (Weisberg, 1992).

Of course, as explained previously, the mean's sensitivity to all scores in a distribution is a problem when there are extreme scores that lead the mean to be an atypical or unrepresentative middle point (such as in the example of household income). In such cases, the median is used to describe the central tendency, although there are some types of means (other than the arithmetic average) and procedures that can be used to deal with extreme scores (e.g., a **trimmed mean** removes the most extreme scores entirely and **winsorizing** the data changes the most extreme scores to the next less extreme scores). It should also be pointed out that there are other types of means appropriate for particular kinds of ratio data (e.g., **geometric mean** for measuring relative change and **harmonic mean** when averaging rates) (see Weisberg, 1992).

One more minor caution about the mean. As you see from the calculations here, the mean most often results in a fractional value (e.g., 9.29 rather than 9). This is a potential problem only to the extent that it causes difficulties in interpreting statistical information. For example, the U.S. Census Bureau (1999a) reported that the average size of a household in the United States in 1998 was 2.62 people. While we might suspect that some members of households "aren't all there," it isn't physically possible to have a .62 person living in a house!

In summary, the mean is the most sensitive and, therefore, the most useful measure of central tendency for a set of interval/ratio data. This is true

as long as the data don't contain an extreme case(s) that throws off the mean too much, making it unrepresentative of the center point of the data.

Measures of Dispersion

Measures of central tendency describe the middle or central point of a distribution of quantitative data. When the data are in the form of ordinal, interval, or ratio measurements, the mode, median, and mean try to tell us the typical or most representative score of the distribution.

But just giving the central tendency summary statistic by itself can be misleading. For example, suppose we ask four married couples, divided on the basis of whether they are young (say 18–35) or middle-aged (say 36–65), how satisfied they are with the communication in their relationship on a 5-point scale, where 1 = extremely dissatisfied, 2 = dissatisfied, 3 = neither dissatisfied nor satisfied, 4 = satisfied, and 5 = extremely satisfied. The following scores are obtained:

Young Couples	Middle-Aged Couples
Couple A: 3	Couple C: 5
3	1
Couple B: 3	Couple D: 1
3	5

If the mean of each group is calculated, we arrive at the same exact number (3). If we just relied on the mean, we would have to conclude that these groups are equivalent and that the couples are neither satisfied nor unsatisfied with the communication in their relationship.

But clearly, these two groups are *not* equivalent. In the case of the two young couples, each partner is moderately satisfied, whereas one person in each of the two middle-aged couples is extremely satisfied while the other is extremely dissatisfied. Just using the mean to describe each group overlooks an important difference: that the *dispersion* or *spread* of the scores of the middle-aged couples from their distribution's center point (the mean) is much greater than the *dispersion* or *spread* of the scores of the young couples from their distribution's center point. (By the way, researchers used to calculate couple's satisfaction by averaging individuals' scores, but now they tend to use the lowest score, reasoning that if one partner is dissatisfied, the relationship should be classified as dissatisfying.)

Measures of central tendency, therefore, while identifying the typical or most representative score, tell us nothing about how the scores in a distribution differ or vary from this representative score. This is fine as long as all the scores within a distribution are exactly the same (such as with the young couples above). But variety is the spice of life, and the same is true of distributions—they contain scores that vary from the center point.

What would be most helpful, then, is some indication of how typical (or representative) the typical score actually is. Once again, it usually isn't feasible to describe how each individual score in a large data set varies from the center point, so researchers use summary statistics to describe the extent to which the scores as a set vary from the center point of that distribution. **Measures of dispersion** (also called **measures of variability**) report how much scores vary from each other or how far they are spread around the center point of a data set and across that distribution.

Measures of dispersion typically are applied to ordinal, interval, and ratio data because these scales use ordered numbers that vary. There is a measure of dispersion for nominal data, called the **variation ratio,** but it only indicates the relative frequency of the nonmodal scores in a distribution (e.g., if the relative frequency of the modal score, the proportion of total scores in a distribution accounted for by the modal category out of 1.00 or 100%, is .30, the variation ratio is .70) and, thus, is not used very much. While there are a number of measures of dispersion that apply to scales that use ordered numbers, three common measures are the range, variance, and standard deviation.

Range. The **range** (or **span**), the simplest measure of dispersion, reports the distance between the highest and lowest scores in a distribution. The range, therefore, is calculated by subtracting the lowest number from the highest number in a distri-

bution (these are called **extreme values**). For example, the range for the PSA information recall data discussed earlier (20, 12, 11, 9, 5, 5, 3) is found by subtracting 3 from 20, which equals 17. This can also be expressed as "a range from 3 to 20."

The range gives a general sense of how much the data spread out across a distribution, which can be helpful for understanding whether a study included a lot of variability or whether it drew from a narrow spectrum. For example, if a researcher intends to study a communication variable across a wide range of age groups, a sample of people aged 18–21 (range = 3) is not very diverse, whereas a sample of people aged 12–70 (range = 58) potentially is. We say "potentially" because diversity, in this case, would depend on whether there are people represented throughout that age spectrum. A sample of people aged 12, 13, 14, 15, 16, 17, and 70, although it has a range of 58, obviously is not very diverse, whereas a sample of people aged 12, 27, 35, 48, 52, 63, and 70, which also has a range of 58, is far more diverse.

Researchers sometimes report the range for the variables studied as this can potentially be helpful for evaluating the validity of research. For example, Barnett, Chang, Fink, and Richards (1991) examined seasonal patterns of television viewing, believing that people watched more television during the winter (where it is cold in much of the United States) than during the summer. To test this prediction, Barnett et al. used the Nielson Television Index of the average daily viewing hours (the number of hours television sets are turned on) per household, given at monthly intervals from September, 1950, to December, 1988. The range for this distribution of data was, thus, 38 years and 4 months, quite a large range. They also gathered data on the average monthly temperature and the total monthly precipitation from publications by the National Oceanic and Atmospheric Administration, and they calculated the number of minutes of daylight on the basis of sunrise and sunset for the 15th of each month as reported by the *St. Louis Post-Dispatch* newspaper. As Figure 11.2 shows, there are large differences between the maximum and the minimum scores for each of these four variables. The range for each of these variables is: (a) television viewing = 267, (b) daylight = 322, (c) temperature = 53.6, and (d) precipitation = 3.61. The large ranges suggest that these researchers examined a diverse set of scores for each variable, although, as the previous example about age showed, we would need more specific information before this could be concluded.

Knowing the range can also provide a general understanding of how the scores of two groups of people vary. For example, in the communication satisfaction scores given above for young and middle-aged couples, the range of scores is 0 for the young couples and 4 for the middle-aged couples. This summary statistic of dispersion confirms what we saw when we eyeballed the data—that these two groups of couples are not equally satisfied.

The problem with the range is that it is a *non-resistant* measure that is overly sensitive to extreme scores. Hence, one or two extreme scores make a distribution look more dispersed that it actually is. For example, in the information recall distribution of 20, 12, 11, 9, 5, 5, 3, the range is 17, but suppose the PSA contained 100 pieces of information, and while the other scores remained the same, the person who scored 20 scored 100. The range is now 97, but this is misleading, for there aren't any actual cases in between the scores of 12 and 100. Equally important, the range is not sensitive to differences between scores *within* a distribution. Any score other than the highest and lowest scores can change without the range changing. So the range is not a very sensitive measure of dispersion.

To compensate for these problems, researchers can divide a distribution at the median (the halfway point) and calculate the range of values between the median and the lowest score, called the **lowspread,** and the range of scores between the median and the highest score, called the **highspread.** It is more common, however, to divide a distribution at the 25th percentile (the point below which 25% of the scores fall) and at the 75th percentile (the point above which 25% of the scores fall). Calculating the distance between these two percentiles yields the **interquartile range** (IQR; also called the **quartile deviation** or **midspread**), the point in the distribution that divides the scores at the 25th and 75th percentile and is called the lower and upper *hinge,* respectively. This summary statistic represents the range of scores for the middle half of a distribution. The IQR, therefore, is less affected by extreme cases, making it a more resistant measure of dispersion than the range per se. And if finer gradations are desired, researchers can divide the interquartile range exactly in half to produce the **semi-interquartile range** or divide the distribution into **deciles,** 10 equal parts.

The range and its variations are a good first step toward understanding the amount of disper-

---

FIGURE 11.2   Reporting of the range

DESCRIPTIVE STATISTICS FOR TELEVISION VIEWING AND ENVIRONMENTAL DATA

Variable	Mean	SD	Maximum	Minimum
Television viewing	351.552	60.086	478.20	211.20
Daylight	727.478	111.745	900.00	578.00
Temperature	52.940	15.288	76.40	22.80
Precipitation	2.419	0.561	4.15	0.54

Source: George A. Barnett, Hsui-Jung Chang, Edward L. Fink, and William D. Richards, Jr., "Seasonality in Television Viewing: A Mathematical Model of Cultural Processes," *Communication Research, 18*(6), p. 760, copyright © 1991 by Sage Publications. Used by Permission of Sage Publications.

NOTE: N = 460. All variables reflect monthly averages for the United States. See text for complete description and data sources.

sion or variance in a set of ordered measurements and, in fact, are the only measure of dispersion that can be applied meaningfully to ordinal (rank-ordered) data. But the range is also limited in describing the amount of dispersion in a set of interval/ratio data. It is similar to the median in that way: Just as the median is fairly limited as a measure of central tendency of interval/ratio data, so too is the range (and its variations) fairly limited as a measure of dispersion of interval/ratio data, for it only gives researchers a global picture of the amount of dispersion. What is needed are measures of dispersion that are as sensitive as the mean is as a measure of central tendency; that is, a measure of dispersion that takes into account all the individual scores in a distribution. For this, researchers turn to the measures of dispersion known as *variance* and *standard deviation.*

Variance.   **Variance (sample variance, S^2, s^2; population variance, σ^2,** pronounced "sigma squared") is a mathematical index of the average distance of the scores in a distribution of interval/ratio data from the mean, in squared units. That definition probably doesn't make much sense, so let's walk through it and make it clear.

We'll use an easier example (one that doesn't contain a mean with a fraction) to explain variance and standard deviation. Suppose a researcher asks all five campaign managers at a public relations firm to keep track of the number of positive local newspaper reports written about their campaigns over the course of a month. At the end of that month, the five managers (P_s) report the following numbers of positive newspaper reports:

P_1	P_2	P_3	P_4	P_5
10	7	5	2	1

Figure 11.3 shows how variance is calculated for this distribution, using both the definitional formula and an easier computational formula. Walking through the calculation for the definitional formula will help to get a handle on it.

Common sense tells us that each individual score differs from the mean (once in a while, as in this distribution, one or more scores are the same as

the mean, but the other scores differ from it). The amount that one score differs from the mean is called its **deviation score** (**deviate**). For these five scores, the mean is 5; the amount each score differs from this mean, therefore, is its deviation score. The first score of 10 deviates from the group mean of 5 by +5 points. The deviation scores for all the raw scores (starting with 10 and working down) are: +5, +2, 0, –3, –4. (Note that we indicate whether the deviation score is greater or less than the mean by using positive and negative signs.)

So far, so good, but here's the problem. Add up all the deviation scores and you get zero, because the negative scores below the mean equal the positive scores above it. This is always the case for deviation scores in any distribution. So we cannot sum the positive and negative scores to obtain an overall deviation score, because that would make it look like no variation exists. But you can clearly see that the scores do indeed vary from the mean.

The best way to handle this is quite simple; we *square* the deviation scores (that is, multiply the deviation score by itself) and add up the squared scores. Squaring the deviation scores accomplishes two things. First, it converts all deviation scores to positive numbers (a negative number multiplied by itself becomes a positive number). Second, it preserves the original information about deviation and keeps the differences between scores intact. We can now sum the squared deviations in the distribution. The resulting total (54) is called the **sum of squares (SS).**

The catch is that the sum of squares score is both cumulative and expressed in squared units. To find out how much the scores as a set deviate "on the average" from the mean, we must divide the sum of squares score (54) by the number of scores (5) in the distribution. The result (10.8) is the average, or mean, of the squared deviations, which is called the *variance*. (Note: When calculating the variance or standard deviation for a population, as we did, the sum of squares score is divided by the total number of scores [N]. When calculating the variance or standard deviation for a sample drawn from a population, the sum of squares is divided by the total number of scores minus one [$n - 1$].

FIGURE 11.3 Calculating variance

(A) Definitional Formula $\sigma^2 = \dfrac{\Sigma(X - \bar{X})^2}{N}$

STEPS:

1. Find the mean for the group of scores (equals 5).
2. Subtract the mean from each score, noting whether the score is greater or less than the mean by using positive and negative signs. This yields the *deviation score.*
3. Square each deviation score (multiply it by itself) and add the squared scores to get the *sum of squares* (equals 54).
4. Divide the sum of squares score by the number of scores ($N = 5$) to get the *variance* (equals 10.8). (Note: Use the number of scores when calculating variance for a population; use the number of scores minus one when calculating the variance for a sample.)

Scores (X)	Score – Mean $(X - \bar{X})$ (Deviation Scores)	(Score – Mean)² $(X - \bar{X})^2$ (Deviation Scores Squared)
10	+5	25
7	+2	4
5	0	0
2	−3	9
1	−4	16
$\bar{X} = 5$		$\Sigma(X - \bar{X})^2 = 54$
		(Sum of Squares)

Variance = 54 ÷ 5 = 10.8

(B) Computational Formula $\qquad \sigma^2 = \dfrac{\Sigma X^2}{N} - \bar{X}^2$

STEPS:

1. Square each score and add up the squared scores to get the sum of squares (179). Divide this sum of squares by the number of scores ($N = 5$) to get the first part of the equation (equals 35.8)
2. Find the mean for the group of scores (equals 5), and square this mean score (equals 25) to get the second part of the equation.
3. Subtract the value obtained from step 2 (25) from the value obtained for step 1 (35.8) to get the variance (equals 10.8).

Scores (X)	Squared Scores $(X)^2$
10	100
7	49
5	25
2	4
1	1
$\bar{X} = 5$	$\Sigma X^2 = 179$ (Sum of Squares)
$\bar{X}^2 = 25$	$\dfrac{\Sigma X^2}{N} = 179 \div 5 = 35.8$

Variance = 35.8 − 25 = 10.8

Capital *N* is used for a population; lowercase *n* is used for a sample.)

A high variance tells researchers that most scores are far away from the mean; a low variance indicates that most scores cluster tightly about the mean. But a variance score is confusing because it is expressed in units of *squared deviations about the mean,* which are not the same as the original unit of measurement. (We now see that if the definition for variance sounded like "double-talk," that's because it literally is!) What is needed is a measure of dispersion expressed in the same units as the original measurement. For that, we turn to the measure of dispersion known as *standard deviation.*

Standard Deviation. **Standard deviation** (**SD;** **sample standard deviation,** *s;* **population standard deviation,** σ) is a measure of dispersion that explains how much scores in a set of interval/ratio data vary from the mean, expressed *in the original unit of measurement.* The standard deviation of a distribution is found by taking the square root of the variance; that is, the number that when multiplied by itself equals the variance.

In the example of the five newspaper coverage scores (see Figure 11.3), the standard deviation of this population (σ) equals the square root of 10.8, or 3.29. This figure can be thought of as the average amount and, therefore, the best description of the dispersion of this distribution (most managers had between 1.71 and 8.29 positive newspaper reports; the mean minus and plus one standard deviation), just as the mean (5 reports) is the average score and, therefore, the best description of the central tendency of this distribution (although this analogy is not precisely correct).

The mean and standard deviation are the measures of central tendency and dispersion reported most frequently by researchers when analyzing interval/ratio data. They are often reported in a table, which is helpful when scores for different conditions or groups of people are compared. Mongeau and Carey (1996), for example, investigated how initiation of a first date influences people's expectations about the occurrence of sexual activity on that date. They first randomly assigned men and

women to read one of three initiation scenarios: (a) female asks (the female asked the male out on a date to a movie they had discussed), (b) female hints (the female indicated her interest in seeing the movie, followed immediately by the male asking her on the date), or (c) male asks (the male asked the female on the date without a preceding hint). Half the male and female participants then evaluated the male target and the other half evaluated the female target. Part of that evaluation included a 12-item scale that assessed sexual expectations for the date, ranging from 0 (wants no sexual or physical activity to occur on the date) to 12 (wants to engage in sexual intercourse on the date). The researchers, thus, conducted a 3 (initiation) X 2 (gender of target) X 2 (gender of participant) experiment, creating 12 conditions in all (see Chapter 7). As part of the analysis and reporting of the data, Mongeau and Carey included a table that presents the means and standard deviations (along with the number of participants) for these 12 conditions (see Figure 11.4). This table makes it easy to see some of the differences among the conditions, such as the way males approach a first date with heightened sexual expectations, especially when a female initiates the date.

DESCRIBING DATA IN STANDARD SCORES

Calculating the mean and standard deviation for a set of interval/ratio measurements allows for an interesting and important manipulation of data. Researchers often report how many standard deviations a particular score is above or below the mean of its distribution; this type of score is called a **standard score** (or **standard normal deviates**). Standard scores provide a common unit of measurement that indicates how far any particular score is away from its mean.

There are many types of standard scores (e.g., *T*-scores and stanine scale; see Jaeger, 1990). One that is used frequently by researchers is the *z*-score. The formula for *z*-scores is:

$$z = \frac{(X - \bar{X})}{SD}$$

FIGURE 11.4   Table of means and standard deviations

THE IMPACT OF INITIATION TYPE, GENDER OF TARGET, AND GENDER OF PARTICIPANT ON PERCEPTIONS OF SEXUAL INTEREST ON THE DATE

	Male Participant		Female Participant	
	Male Target	Female Target	Male Target	Female Target
Female Asks	M = 7.56 SD = 4.69 n = 18	M = 2.68 SD = 2.19 n = 22	M = 2.96 SD = 3.02 n = 23	M = 2.58 SD = 2.21 n = 24
Female Hints	M = 4.46 SD = 3.73 n = 24	M = 2.91 SD = 2.56 n = 22	M = 3.04 SD = 3.26 n = 21	M = 1.53 SD = 0.96 n = 19
Male Asks	M = 4.19 SD = 3.75 n = 26	M = 2.75 SD = 1.83 n = 20	M = 2.52 SD = 1.36 n = 21	M = 2.11 SD = 1.07 n = 28

Source: Paul A. Mongeau and Colleen M. Carey, "Who's Wooing Whom II? An Experimental Investigation of Date-Initiation and Expectancy Violation," *Western Journal of Communication, 60(3)*, p. 204, copyright © 1996 by the Western States Communication Association. Used by permission of the Western States Communication Association.

NOTE: Scores can range from 0 (wants no sexual or physical activity to occur on the date) to 12 (wants to engage in sexual intercourse on the date).

The formula says that a *z*-score can be computed for any score in a distribution by dividing its deviation score (how much the individual score differs from the mean) $(X - \bar{X})$ by the standard deviation for the distribution (SD). Using the data presented earlier on number of positive newspaper reports (10, 7, 5, 2, 1), dividing the deviation scores (+5, +2, 0, –3, –4, respectively) by the standard deviation (3.29) produces *z*-scores of +1.52, +.61, 0, –.91, and –1.22, respectively. Each *z*-score indicates how many standard deviations that score is from the mean of this distribution. If you calculate the mean of this set of *z*-scores, it equals zero, which is why it is called a "*z*"-score.

Standard scores, like *z*-scores, are used by researchers in some important ways. First, researchers can meaningfully interpret an individual score within a distribution by showing how many standard deviations it is away from the mean of that distribution. For example, a standard score of –1.96 tells researchers that the individual score in question is almost two standard deviations below the mean. In the next chapter, when we discuss normal distributions, the significance of this will become clear, for it means that, under normal conditions, only 2.5% of the population score this badly.

One of the best-known examples of using standard scores in this way is the *deviation-IQ* scale, which is used with many group-administered intelligence (IQ) tests (see Jaeger, 1990). On the basis of numerous national samples, this scale is designed to have a mean score of 100 and a standard deviation of 15. So a person who scores 115 has a standard score +1.00, while a person who scores 85 has a standard score of –1.00. One advantage of these standard IQ scores is that because the percentage of people who achieve any particular standard score is known (which, again, we will explain in Chapter 12 when talking about normal distributions), the percentile rank can be calculated for any standard score. For example, a person who has a +1.00 standard score is in the 84th percentile, because 50% of people score below the mean and approximately another 34% score between the mean and +1.00SD.

For this reason, IQ scores, and many other types of scores, are often reported using standard scores instead of the original unit of measurement.

Another use of standard scores has to do with the fact that different people sometimes do not use the same measurement scale in the same way. For example, suppose three trained judges use a 10-point scale, ranging from poor (1) to excellent (10), to evaluate all 10 public speeches of the same type given at a forensics tournament (a competitive tournament for undergraduates where various types of public speeches are performed and evaluated). As Figure 11.5 shows, the three judges tend to use different portions of the same scale. Judge A tends to use the top portion of the scale (M = 7.3), judge B typically uses the middle portion (M = 4.7), and judge C uses the lower portion (M = 3.0). These public speeches, thus, appear to have been evaluated very differently by these three judges, even though they used the same 10-point scale. But notice how converting these ratings to z-scores reveals some important similarities. For example, speech 7, which received a rating of 7 from judge A and a 4 from judge B have just about the same z-score from both judges (−.21 versus −.22, respectively). So this speech is actually evaluated pretty much the same way by these two judges when standard scores are used. And these standard scores can also help to differentiate the speeches from one another. For example, suppose the forensics tournament organizers want to honor the highest rated speech of this type with a "Top Speech Award." If only mean ratings across the three judges are used, speeches 6 and 9 are tied as the best speech (M = 7.33). But when the ratings are converted to z-scores, and a mean z-score is calculated across the three judges' z-scores, speech 6 (mean z-score = +1.54) is superior to speech 9 (mean z-score = +1.48) and should receive the award. Thus, even though the same (valid and reliable) measurement scale may be used, relying on raw scores may not tell the whole story about the data. For this reason, some researchers first convert raw scores into standard scores, or even **transformed standard scores** (such as multiplying each z-score by 100 to eliminate the decimal point), and then perform subsequent analyses on the standard scores. Data kept in their original unit of measurement and not converted to standard scores are referred to as **raw** or **unstandardized scores.**

Standard scores also allow comparisons between scores on different types of scales for the same individual or for different people. Here's an example of the first. Say you present a speech in a

---

FIGURE 11.5   Comparing z-scores to original units of measurement

Speech	JUDGE A Rating	JUDGE A z-score	JUDGE B Rating	JUDGE B z-score	JUDGE C Rating	JUDGE C z-score	ACROSS JUDGES Mean Rating	ACROSS JUDGES Mean z-score
1	5	−1.62	3	−.78	1	−1.29	3.00	−1.23
2	6	−.92	4	−.22	3	0.00	4.33	−.38
3	7	−.21	5	+.33	2	−.65	4.67	−.18
4	8	+.49	3	−.78	4	+.65	5.00	+.12
5	9	+1.20	5	+.33	3	0.00	5.67	+.51
6	10	+1.90	7	+1.44	5	+1.29	7.33	+1.54
7	7	−.21	4	−.22	2	−.65	4.33	−.36
8	6	−.92	2	−1.33	1	−1.29	3.00	−1.18
9	8	+.49	8	+2.00	6	+1.94	7.33	+1.48
10	7	−.21	3	−.78	3	0.00	4.33	−.33
Mean	7.3		4.4		3.0			
SD	1.42		1.80		1.55			

public speaking (PS) class and write a paper in an organizational communication (ORG) class. Each professor uses a 100-point scale to evaluate the work, although the criteria used to award points are probably very different for a speech and a paper, so these are two different scales. Furthermore, both professors intend to curve the grades given on the basis of all the scores obtained (e.g., the highest score becomes the upper range for a grade of "A"). In the PS class, you score 85 on the speech and in the ORG class you score 80 on the paper. In which class did you do better? Intuitively, you might say the PS class because the score of 85 is higher than the score of 80 in the ORG class, and both are out of a possible 100 points. And you might be right. But what if the score of 85 was actually the lowest score in the PS class, while the score of 80 was the highest in the ORG class? In that case, you clearly did much better in the ORG class, and this would be apparent if these scores were converted to z-scores. The score of 80 in the ORG class will have a positive z-score, whereas the score of 85 in the PS class will have a negative z-score. And because the grades in each class are curved to the distribution of scores in that particular class, your grades will reflect this important difference.

Finally, people say you can't compare apples and oranges (although this isn't the best analogy since both are fruits), but standard scores actually allow comparisons between different people's scores on different types of measurements. Suppose a sports agent has two clients, a major league starting baseball pitcher and an NFL starting football quarterback, and wants to determine who is more valuable, so that the agent can put the most energy into making the best deal for the best client. Now sports enthusiasts probably would agree that an important "stat" for a baseball pitcher is the number of strikeouts recorded per game, while the number of completions per game is an important "stat" for football quarterbacks. The agent, however, can't compare these two "stats" directly. After all, the most amount of strikeouts a pitcher could have in a 9-inning game (assuming the game doesn't go into extra innings) is 27 (9 innings X 3 outs per inning). But the football quarterback can

potentially have a lot more than 27 completions in a game (e.g., by throwing short passes on virtually every play). So these two statistics are like apples and oranges; you can't compare them directly.

The agent, however, can compare these two clients' statistics by converting their number of strikeouts and completions to standard scores. That is, the agent calculates the mean and standard deviation of strikeouts per game for starting baseball pitchers and does the same for completions per game for starting football quarterbacks (assuming all the necessary information for doing so is available). The agent then calculates a z-score for each athlete (see Figure 11.6). The agent can now directly compare the two clients and see that the football quarterback is a better quarterback (z-score = −1.29) than the baseball pitcher is a pitcher (z-score = −2.00), although neither is doing particularly well (both have high negative z-scores). It might be time for the agent to get some new clients!

We just used a kind of "apples and oranges" case (two types of sports statistics) to illustrate the

---

FIGURE 11.6 Using z-scores to compare different distributions

BASEBALL PITCHER

1. Mean (M) number of strikeouts per game for all pitchers = 6.0
2. Standard deviation (SD) of strikeouts per game for all pitchers = 1.5
3. This pitcher's strikeouts per game = 3.0
4. Subtract specific pitcher's strikeouts per game from the mean = −3.0
5. Divide step 4 by the SD = −2.00

FOOTBALL QUARTERBACK

1. Mean (M) number of completions per game for all quarterbacks = 15.0
2. Standard deviation (SD) of completions per game for all quarterbacks = 6.2
3. This quarterback's completions per game = 7.0
4. Subtract specific quarterback's completions/ game from the mean = −8.0
5. Divide step 4 by the SD = −1.29

---

point, but the principle applies to comparing *most* types of measurements, even if they are very different, such as comparing a baseball pitcher's strikeouts with the quality of a person's public speeches. But two cautions are warranted. First, in making such comparisons, researchers and practitioners (like sports agents) have to be confident that the statistics being used address some important, common "dimension," that they are ones on which a comparison ought to be based. Strikeouts by a pitcher and completions by a quarterback seem pretty important and even comparable in that they both address throwing a ball in their respective sport. Using other statistics, such as number of strikeouts and number of fumbles, may not be a meaningful way to compare these athletes. And when very different comparisons are made, this caution is even more important. We're not sure, for example, what the basis would be for comparing strikeouts by a pitcher with the quality of a person's public speeches. Second, comparisons for the purposes of evaluating complex processes and outcomes, such as job performance, should be made on the basis of more than one variable. To compare these two athletes more fully, many variables besides strikeouts and completions would need to be taken into account.

In closing, converting scores on a measurement scale to standard scores that measure how far away they are from the mean of their distribution is an important tool for describing data. We will return later to the principle of seeing how many standard deviations data are from a mean, for it is the cornerstone of the inferential statistics covered in the next three chapters.

DESCRIBING DATA THROUGH VISUAL DISPLAYS

We said earlier that measures of central tendency and dispersion are used to summarize relatively large data sets because it's too difficult to verbally share and process all the data. It's also often helpful to describe data sets through visual means. Remember from the examples that opened this chapter how the colleague at work used charts and

figures to show sales over the past few months. And notice how we have used visual figures in this chapter to help explain summary statistics.

Researchers, educators, and other professionals alike often use tables, figures, graphs, and other forms to visually display distributions of data. These visual displays can highlight important information in the data and/or make complex data more understandable. Wallgren, Wallgren, Persson, Jorner, and Haaland (1996) argue that "good charts *are* information" (p. 3) that help people see both main features of the data (the forest), as well as specific details (the trees). While perhaps overstating the claim, "a good visual display says more than a thousand words." Of course, the reverse is also true in that "bad charts convey disinformation" (Wallgren et al., 1996, p. 6).

Constructing good visual displays of data is as much an art as it is a science. To construct such displays and realize their benefits, one must know what types of visual displays are possible, how to construct them, and when to use them.

There are a wide variety of visual forms that can be used to display quantitative data, although most are variations on a few basic principles. Here, we examine six common types used by researchers and others to visually display quantitative data, and provide examples of each from communication research studies: frequency tables, pie charts, bar charts, line graphs, frequency histograms, and frequency polygons. As you might suspect by now, the choice of which visual display to use is influenced by the type of data one seeks to portray. The first four visual displays are particularly useful for showing differences between the groups (categories) that comprise a nominal independent variable, while frequency histograms and frequency polygons are useful for showing relationships between an ordered independent variable and other variables.

Frequency Tables

In one way or another, most visual displays are attempts to describe **frequency distributions,** a tally of the number of times particular values on a measurement scale occur in a data set. The most basic way is to visually display the **absolute frequency** of the data obtained, the actual number of times each category or measurement point occurs in a distribution, in a **frequency table,** a visual display in table form of the frequency of each category or measurement point on a scale for a distribution of data. Another way is to visually display the **relative frequency** of the data, the proportion of times each category or measurement point occurs (found by dividing the number of cases for a particular category or measurement point by the total number of cases for the entire distribution). Some displays even include the **cumulative frequency (CF),** the total frequency up to and including any particular category or measurement point.

We've already seen a communication research example of a frequency table in Figure 11.1, but let's examine a few more. Hirokawa and Keyton (1995) were interested in the factors that members of organizational work teams believe facilitate and inhibit effective group performance. They studied groups of 4–8 members composed of school principals, teachers, and school resource personnel (e.g., nurses, counselors, and psychologists) from nine different schools. The groups had been designated as student assistance groups within an ongoing drug and alcohol abuse prevention program implemented by the school system. As preparation for their participation in the team, all group members had to attend an intensive two-day workshop conducted by health care experts. Each group was responsible for an on-site, student-directed drug and alcohol abuse prevention program, and each group's primary task during the workshop was to evaluate potential "at-risk" students, find a source of appropriate assistance for them, and follow up on the effectiveness of the recommended assistance. To identify the factors members believed affected their group's task progress, members were asked two open-ended questions about what aspect(s) of their group helped (facilitative factors) and hindered (inhibitive factors) their group's progress. A content-analytic scheme was developed and used to code the answers (see Chapter 9). In presenting the results, the researchers constructed two frequency

tables, one that summarized the facilitative factors, and one for the inhibitive factors (see Figure 11.7).

Frequency tables are used quite often in this way to describe the frequency of occurrence of categories, such as the number of times the categories associated with facilitative and inhibitive factors are mentioned. As Figure 11.7 also illustrates, fre-

---

FIGURE 11.7   Frequency tables

TABLE 1: SUMMARY OF FACILITATIVE FACTORS

Factor	Frequency	Percentage
Organizational assistance	9	19
Compatible work schedules	18	38
Information resources	10	21
Interested/motivated group members	15	32
Good group leadership	9	19
Clear organizational expectations	5	11
No organizational interference	7	15

TABLE 2: SUMMARY OF INHIBITIVE FACTORS

Factor	Frequency	Percentage
Insufficient time	22	47
Information resources	10	21
Procedural conflicts	3	6
Poor group leadership	5	11
Uninterested/unmotivated members	7	15
No organizational assistance	5	11
No financial compensation	6	13
Changing organizational expectations	4	9

Source: Randy Y. Hirokawa and Joann Keyton, "Perceived Facilitators and Inhibitors of Effectiveness in Organizational Work Teams," *Management Communication Quarterly,* 8(4), pp. 438–439, copyright © 1995 by Sage Publications, Inc. Reprinted by Permission of Sage Publications, Inc.

NOTE: *N* = 47. Percentages do not sum to 100% because participants could identify multiple factors.

quency tables usually include both the absolute frequency and relative frequency (e.g., dividing the actual count of 9 for organizational assistance by the 47 total participants studied yields a percentage of 19).

Frequency tables are very effective for highlighting which categories are used most often, and they can also be helpful for comparing at a glance the frequency of different categories for two or more groups. For example, as part of their study, Hirokawa and Keyton (1995) asked group members to rate (on a 3-point scale) the extent to which they had established five facets of data collection and evaluation procedures and three aspects of their communication with external constituents. On the basis of the cumulative average scores in these two areas, groups that fell in the bottom third of the range were labeled "low-effective" while groups that fell in the upper third of the range were identified as "high-effective." In discussing the differences between low- and high-effective groups on the facilitative and inhibitive factors identified previously, the researchers constructed two additional frequency tables (see Figure 11.8). These tables allow one to eyeball differences between these two groups. (The researchers actually identify statistically significant differences between low- and high-effective groups in the table through the use of asterisks and in the accompanying note. We examine principles of statistical significance testing in Chapter 12 and particular statistical tests of differences between groups in Chapter 13.)

Frequency tables are also helpful for showing changes over short or long periods of time. Sapolsky (1982), for example, conducted a two-year (1978–1979) content analysis of the frequency of sexual incidents on prime-time network television shows. The findings, reported in a frequency table, showed that, when gender of the initiator and marital status of partners were combined, the total number of noncriminal sex acts increased from 141 in 1978 to 247 in 1979, with the largest increase involving unmarried partners (22 in 1978 to 138 in 1979). To illustrate long-term change, Bogart (1985) studied changes in the content of United States newspapers over a 20-year period, compar-

ing the percentage of newspapers carrying particular types of features (70 topics in all) at least once a week in 1963, 1974, 1979, and 1983. The findings, reported in a frequency table, showed that while categories such as health and medicine stayed relatively the same over the 20 years (68%, 71%, 66%, 63%, respectively), other categories such as science steadily decreased (34%, 24%, 14%, 9%) and such new categories as "people" emerged (no instances until 50% in 1983). In both studies, the researchers used frequency tables to report some of the data. The next step, of course, would be to make sense of the changes found. For example, what might the steady decline in science articles and the sudden emergence of "people" articles say about our culture?

Frequency tables are an important way for researchers to visually display data. They are, however, fairly simple drawings, in that they do not rely on such graphics as shaded areas or connected lines. The next five visual displays do.

Pie Charts

One way to visually illustrate the frequency of categories using shaded areas is through **pie charts,** which are circles divided into segments proportional to the percentage of the circle that represents the frequency count for each category. Pie charts are a favorite way of visually presenting information in the popular media, such as on television and in newspapers and magazines (*USA Today* seems to have a pie chart virtually every day). They are also frequently employed in business presentations, and even some politicians use them. Ross Perot, for example, used pie charts extensively in his television infomercials during the 1992 presidential campaign, and they became a standard feature of comedic portrayals of him.

Although pie charts are used infrequently in scholarly research reports, they have been used to provide descriptive information about a research data set. Allman (1998), for example, studied physicians' self-disclosure about medical mistakes. Thirty-nine internists and family medicine physicians completed a questionnaire about a medical

FIGURE 11.8   Frequency tables comparing two groups

TABLE 3: FACILITATIVE FACTORS FOR LOW- AND HIGH-EFFECTIVENESS GROUPS

Factor	Low-Effective		High-Effective	
	Frequency	Percent	Frequency	Percent
Organizational assistance	1	10	8	31
Compatible work schedules	2	20	15	58*
Information resources	0	—	8	31**
Motivated members	2	20	13	50*
Good leadership	0	—	8	31**
Clear expectations	1	10	4	15
No interference	0	—	3	12
	(n = 10)		(n = 26)	

TABLE 4: INHIBITIVE FACTORS FOR LOW- AND HIGH-EFFECTIVE GROUPS

Factor	Low-Effective		High-Effective	
	Frequency	Percent	Frequency	Percent
Time availability	9	90	11	42**
Information resources	7	70	2	8***
Procedural conflicts	3	30	0	—**
Poor leadership	5	50	0	—***
Uninterested members	5	50	2	8**
No organizational assistance	5	50	0	—***
No financial compensation	5	50	1	4**
Changing expectations	4	40	0	—**
	(n = 10)		(n = 26)	

Source: Randy Y. Hirokawa and Joann Keyton, "Perceived Facilitators and Inhibitors of Effectiveness in Organizational Work Teams," *Management Communication Quarterly, 8*(4), pp. 439–440, copyright © 1995 by Sage Publications, Inc. Reprinted by Permission of Sage Publications, Inc.

NOTE: Percentages do not sum to 100% because participants could identify multiple factors. *denotes difference in proportion that is significant at the .05 level; **denotes difference in proportion that is significant at the .01 level; ***denotes difference in proportion that is significant at the .001 level.

error they had made at some point after completing their residency. One of the questions asked them to indicate to whom they disclosed the medical error. Allman created a pie chart to visually show the recipients of this self-disclosure (see Figure 11.9). As the pie chart shows, physicians discussed their error primarily with another physician (36%), followed by a significant other (23%), and then the patient or patient's family (21%). Seldom were such mistakes disclosed to other medical person-

nel (12%), risk management or quality assurance personnel (4%), personal attorney or counselor (3%), or a nonmedical friend (1%).

Pie charts can also be very helpful for visually showing differences between groups. A. Rodriguez (1996), for example, analyzed the production of *Noticiero Univision,* the nightly national newscast of the largest Spanish language television network in the United States. Part of this study included an extensive comparative content analysis

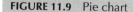

FIGURE 11.9 Pie chart

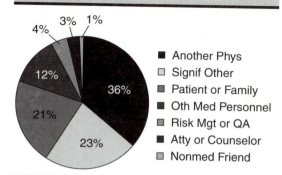

- Another Phys
- Signif Other
- Patient or Family
- Oth Med Personnel
- Risk Mgt or QA
- Atty or Counselor
- Nonmed Friend

Source: Joyce Allman, "Bearing the Burden or Baring the Soul: Physicians Self-Disclosure and Boundary Management Regarding Medical Mistakes," *Health Communication, 10*(2), p. 185, copyright © 1998 by Lawrence Erlbaum Associates, Inc. Reprinted by permission of Lawrence Erlbaum Associates, Inc.

FIGURE 11.10 Pie charts comparing two groups

UNIVISION TOPICS

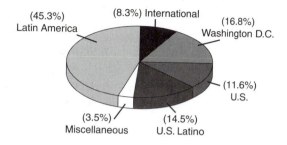

ABC TOPICS

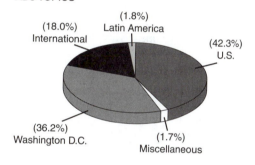

Source: America Rodriguez, "Objectivity and Ethnicity in the Production of the *Noticiero Univision*," *Critical Studies in Mass Communication, 13*(1), p. 67. Copyright by the National Communication Association. 1996. Reprinted by permission of the publisher.

of the stories presented by *Noticiero Univision* and ABC's *World News Tonight with Peter Jennings.* Two pie charts (see Figure 11.10) illustrate "with broad strokes the most obvious differences between these two national newscasts" (Rodriguez, 1996, p. 66). Clearly, *Noticiero Univision* presents a social world, that of Latino communities in the United States and Latin America, rarely seen on mainstream commercial television. But Rodriguez's naturalistic (ethnographic) research also showed that *Noticiero Univision* embraces many of the same structural features as mainstream telecasts, such as "journalistic objectivity." Rodriguez concluded that "in its simultaneous embrace of journalistic objectivity and U.S. Latino panethnic identity, this newscast is a resource for Latinos in their acculturation to U.S. society" (p. 76).

Bar Charts

Bar charts are a common and relatively simple visual depiction that use shaded "blocks" (rectangles and/or squares) to show the frequency counts for the groups that comprise a nominal independent variable. Bar charts typically are drawn using vertical blocks; that is, the independent variable groups are presented on the *abscissa,* the horizon-

tal (or *x*) axis (a line used to construct a graph) (which is why the independent variable is sometimes called the *X variable*), and the frequency of occurrence on the dependent variable (*Y variable*) is presented on the *ordinate,* the vertical (or *y*) axis, so that the blocks rise vertically up the page. (The *y* axis in a three-dimensional visual display references the vertical height axis; the *z* axis references the vertical depth axis.) **Horizontal bar charts,** with blocks running horizontally from left to right, sometimes are used when the categories have long names or when there are many categories (say 10 or 20) (see Wallgren et al., 1996).

Bar charts are especially helpful for visually depicting differences between groups on a variable.

For example, Lang, Geiger, Strickwerda, and Sumner (1993) tested differences between related and unrelated cuts on television viewers' attention, processing capacity, and memory for the information contained in television messages. Participants watched a videotape that contained 12 segments, separated by black, of regularly occurring network television shows. Six segments contained related cuts, those occurring between scenes that were related either by visual or audio information (e.g., a cut from one camera to another in the same visual scene), and six segments contained unrelated cuts, those occurring between scenes that were completely unrelated to one another (e.g., a cut from a scene in one program to a scene in a different program). The percentage of correct scores to a multiple-choice instrument was used to measure participants' information recall. The researchers used a bar chart to visually show the information recall difference between participants in the two conditions on this variable (see Figure 11.11). As you can see, and as predicted, participants remembered more information surrounding related than unrelated cuts.

A very common use of bar charts is to visually show differences between the groups formed from the combination of two or more independent variables, and these are called **grouped** or **segmented bar charts.** As Wallgren et al. (1996) explain, "The different categories are represented by different bars in the same chart with common axes. In order to distinguish the categories we use different patterns of shading and a legend" (p. 26). For example, Le Poire (1994) studied differences in how people respond to gay males and persons with AIDS (PWAs). In one study, 95 participants interacted with a male confederate. They were told to assume that they would like to get to know this person better, and a 22-item self-disclosure sheet was used to guide the interactions. The confederate was trained to answer all questions identically, and did so, except for one question, which read "My greatest fear is...." For this question, the confederate responded in one of three ways: (a) "not getting a job after graduation" (nonstigmatized condition), (b) "that my family will find out I am gay" (gay

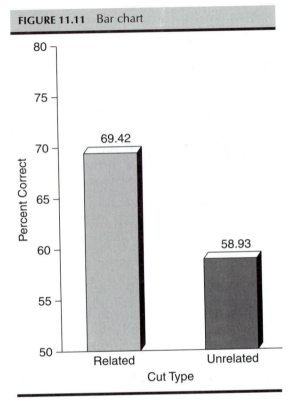

FIGURE 11.11   Bar chart

Source: Annie Lang, Seth Geiger, Melody Strickwerda, and Janine Sumner, "The Effects of Related and Unrelated Cuts on Television Viewers' Attention, Processing Capacity, and Memory," *Communication Research, 20*(4), p. 21, copyright © 1993 by Sage Publications, Inc. Used by Permission of Sage Publications, Inc.

stigmatization condition), or (c) "that the HIV test I just took may be positive" (PWA stigmatization condition). Afterwards, participants were asked to rate their desire for future interaction with the confederate on a four-item, 7-point semantic differential; the four items were combined and a mean score computed, with a higher score indicating more desire. Because Le Poire suspected that participants' gender made a difference, she also analyzed differences between male and female participants' desire for future interaction within each confederate condition. She displayed those results in a grouped bar chart that uses different shading for males and females (explained in a legend) in the three conditions (see Figure 11.12). As you see, and as statistical analyses revealed, there is a very different pattern for females and males in the three conditions. While females desired the most amount of future interaction with the PWA, followed by the gay male, and then by the nonstigmatized male, males desired the most amount of future interaction with the nonstigmatized male, followed by the PWA, followed by the gay male. How would you interpret these findings?

Line Graphs

A final type of visual display particularly useful for showing differences between independent variable groups is **line graphs,** which use a single

FIGURE 11.12   Grouped bar chart

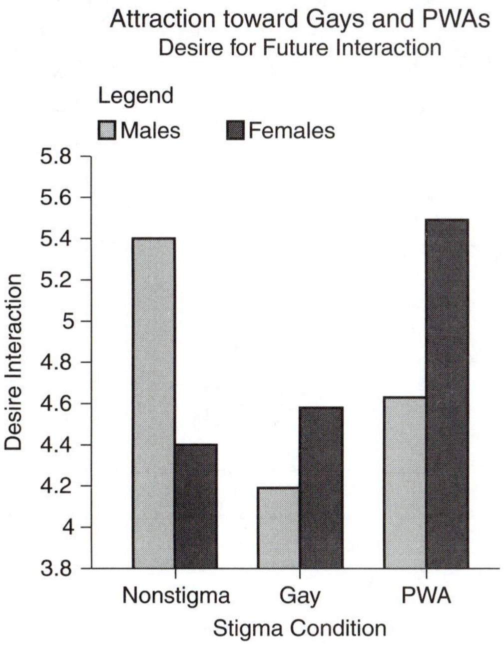

Attraction toward Gays and PWAs
Desire for Future Interaction

Source: Beth A. Le Poire, "Attraction toward and Nonverbal Stigmatization of Gay Males and Persons With AIDS: Evidence of Symbolic over Instrumental Attitudinal Structures," *Human Communication Research,* *21*(2), p. 254, copyright © 1994 by Sage Publications, Inc. Reprinted by Permission of Sage Publications, Inc.

point to represent the frequency count on a dependent variable for each of the groups and then connect these points with a single line.

The simplest type of line graph compares two groups with respect to a dependent variable. For example, Weiss, Imrich, and Wilson (1993), assessed the impact of two desensitization exposure strategies on children's emotional reactions to a frightening movie scene. Young boys and girls either were exposed to a live earthworm demonstration (live exposure condition) or received no such exposure (no live exposure condition). In the live exposure condition, the boys and girls watched an experimenter reach into a bowl of worms, pick one up, and hold it for all to see and, thereby, show them that they weren't harmful. All the children then viewed a frightening scene from the PG-rated movie *Squirm,* in which a man and woman are fishing in a boat, a container of worms tips over and they spill out, and as the man moves toward the woman, he falls over and the worms begin to attack his face. The boat capsizes, and the scene ends with the man running out of the water. Immediately after viewing this segment, the children were asked how scared they felt while watching it, using a scale that ranged from 0 (not scared at all) to 4 (very very scared). The percentage of boys and girls expressing fear in the two conditions was shown in a line graph (see Figure 11.13). As you see, and as statistical analyses revealed, the percentage of boys expressing fear after seeing the live worms (34%) was much less than the percentage of boys who had not seen the live worms (59%). Such exposure, however, had no impact on girls, as 70% who had live exposure expressed fear compared to 60% who did not have such exposure. The researchers posit that the desensitization procedure could not overcome girls' general dislike for insects, reptiles, and snakes.

Line graphs are particularly useful for showing changes in groups over two or more points in time. For example, Mares and Cantor (1992) examined the effects of two types of portrayals of old age on the emotional responses of aging viewers. Two hundred and fifty aging participants (M = 75.1, SD = 5.0) were measured with regard to their

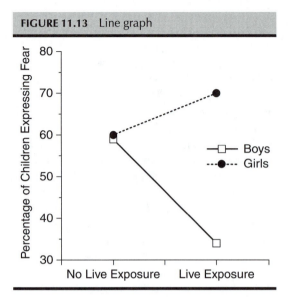

FIGURE 11.13 Line graph

Source: Audrey J. Weiss, Dorothy J. Imrich, and Barbara J. Wilson, "Prior Exposure to Creatures From a Horror Film: Live Versus Photographic Representations," *Human Communication Research, 20*(1), p. 55, copyright © 1993 by Sage Publications, Inc. Reprinted by Permission of Sage Publications, Inc.

degree of loneliness. Those falling in the top or bottom 20% of the scores (designated as lonely and nonlonely, respectively) were shown one of two 9-minute videotapes. One tape portrayed an aging man as isolated (e.g., his wife had just died and he described his loneliness), whereas the other tape portrayed the man as integrated (e.g., he was successful and happy, living with his wife, and had many friends). Both before and after viewing the stimulus tape, participants' degree of affect was measured through the Multiple Adjective Affect Checklist (MAACL), which asks people to say how they feel by selecting from positive words (e.g., agreeable) and negative words (e.g., unhappy); the score ranges from 0 (maximum positive mood) to 43 (maximum negative mood). The researchers used a line graph to show the differences among the four groups from pre-viewing to post-viewing (see Figure 11.14). As you see, lonely people had more negative affect than non-

lonely people prior to viewing the tape, but after watching the tape, the nonlonely/isolated group increased their negative affect substantially (and statistically significantly), whereas the lonely/isolated group actually decreased (statistically significantly) their negative affect. The finding that lonely people feel better after watching a negative program is actually predicted by Social Comparison Theory, in that people are assumed to feel better after seeing another person's misery. Most important, the findings suggest that emotional responses to media content are complex and related to viewers' prior emotional states.

Frequency Histograms and Frequency Polygons

Pie charts, bar charts, and line graphs are very useful for visually showing differences between nom-

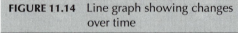

FIGURE 11.14 Line graph showing changes over time

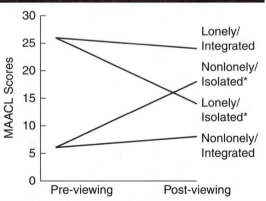

Source: Marie-Louise Mares and Joanne Cantor, "Elderly Viewers' Responses to Televised Portrayals of Old Age: Empathy and Mood Management Versus Social Comparison," *Communication Research, 19*(4), p. 473, copyright © 1992 by Sage Publications Inc. Reprinted by Permission of Sage Publications Inc.

NOTE: The higher the MAACL score, the greater the negative affect.

*p < .05.

inal independent variable groups with regard to a dependent variable. When an independent variable is measured using an interval or ratio scale, tables could be constructed to show the frequency counts for each of the measurement points, but these would sometimes be so big (e.g., a table with 100 rows to show percentages) that they would be overwhelming and confusing. So instead, researchers typically illustrate these frequency distributions visually. Two procedures used to show such frequency distributions are frequency histograms and frequency polygons.

Frequency histograms, like bar graphs, use blocks to show how frequently each point on an interval/ratio scale occurs. However, because an interval/ratio scale has equal distances between the points on the scale, the blocks touch. For example, mass communication scholars are interested in identifying factors that influence "looks," those periods where people watching television look at and then away from the screen. J. J. Burns and Anderson (1993) studied looks by applying the theory of attentional inertia, which argues that "if a medium of information has held a person's attention for a period of time, a generalized tendency develops to sustain attention to that medium" (p. 778). The researchers tested hypotheses derived from the theory by videotaping male and female students watching an episode of the television show *Magnum P. I.* followed by an episode of *Cagney and Lacy.* The videotapes were coded for looks using a computer-assisted coding system. Participants were then tested on their recognition of 232 separate items shown in the videotapes. To see the shape of the data, the researchers constructed a frequency histogram of look lengths on the basis of 1-second intervals, and provided a typical example for a single female viewer (see Figure 11.15). Running along the *x*-axis is the look length in seconds; running along the *y*-axis is the frequency for the 200/232 items where the looks were separated by pauses of 3 seconds' duration or less. You can see that the scores are skewed to the left (see Chapter 12 for a discussion of distribution skewness), a shape

actually predicted by one of the hypotheses derived from the theory.

Frequency polygons are similar to line graphs, except that a line connects the points representing the frequency counts for each point on the interval/ratio scale used to measure the independent variable (rather than each group of a nominal independent variable, as in line graphs). For example, the Lang et al. (1993) study described earlier talked about the effects of related and unrelated TV cuts on viewers' attention, processing capacity, and memory. The researchers predicted that both related and unrelated cuts would elicit orienting responses, an involuntary, automatic response elicited by changes in the environment. To test this hypothesis, they attached electrodes to participants' forearms while they watched the television segments to collect heart rate data. The

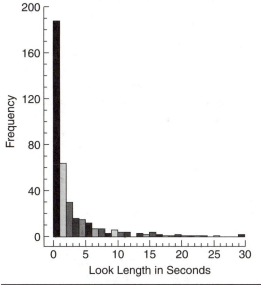

FIGURE 11.15 Frequency histogram

Source: John J. Burns and Daniel R. Anderson, "Attentional Inertia and Recognition Memory in Adult Television Viewing," *Communication Research, 20*(6), p. 792, copyright © 1993 by Sage Publications, Inc. Reprinted by Permission of Sage Publications, Inc.

FIGURE 11.16   Frequency polygon

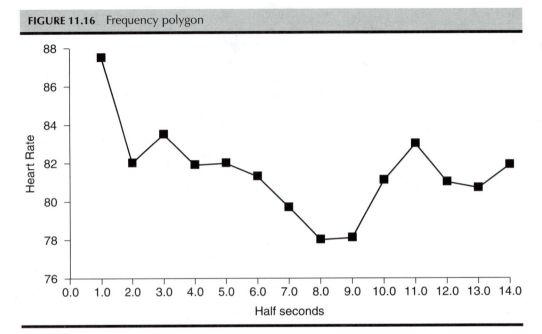

Source: Annie Lang, Seth Geiger, Melody Strickwerda, and Janine Sumner, "The Effects of Related and Unrelated Cuts on Television Viewers' Attention, Processing Capacity, and Memory," *Communication Research, 20*(1), p. 19, copyright © 1993 by Sage Publications, Inc. Adapted by Permission of Sage Publications, Inc.

frequency polygon, with half seconds on the *x*-axis and heart rate on the *y*-axis (see Figure 11.16), and statistical analyses provided support for the hypothesis, as there was a deceleration of heart rate for the first 4 seconds (8 half seconds) after a cut, followed by an acceleration.

CONCLUSION

The statistics discussed in this chapter explain various ways in which researchers attempt to describe the data they have acquired. The first step in analyzing a set of data is to understand its characteristics. Once important characteristics have been determined, it is possible to go beyond description

to infer conclusions about the data. Go back to the examples that started this chapter and you will see that the final three attempt to infer conclusions from the relevant data. The television newscaster concluded from the poll results that the election was all but over. The newspaper claimed, on the basis of percentages, that there exists an "important" difference between men and women in the standard of living in the first year after divorce. And in the final example, the television program concluded, on the basis of a statistical analysis, that there is a "substantial" relationship between eating a particular food and heart disease. To find out how researchers and others draw such conclusions, we now examine inferential statistics.

CHAPTER 12

INFERRING FROM DATA: ESTIMATION AND SIGNIFICANCE TESTING

Suppose you are the owner of a relatively large chain of grocery stores across the United States that employs many people and want to know how satisfied employees are with the communication they have with their immediate supervisor. Suppose, too, that you believe there might be differences in employees' communication satisfaction depending on whether their supervisor is of the same gender or not. Moreover, you suspect that there is a relationship between employees' satisfaction with their supervisor's communication and employees' motivation to perform, such that the more satisfied employees are, the more motivated they are to perform.

Because of the large size of the company, it's certainly not possible to ask every employee of every store to fill out a questionnaire about their gender, the gender of their supervisor, and that measured the two variables of communication satisfaction and motivation. Instead, you (or, more likely, a firm you hire) would need to use survey research procedures (see Chapter 8) to randomly select (see Chapter 5) a sample of employees who are representative of the company and ask them to complete the questionnaire. The statistics examined in the last chapter could then be used to describe the communication satisfaction data, as well as the motivation data, by calculating the summary statistics of measures of central tendency (e.g., the mean) and measures of dispersion (e.g. the standard deviation). The data for each scale could even be converted into standard scores (e.g., z-scores) to avoid the problem of employees using the same scale in very different ways. A bar graph could even be constructed as a visual representation to show the different amount of communication sat-

isfaction when the supervisor is and is not of the same gender as the employee.

But your interests don't lie just with describing the data for these particular employees. You're also interested in using the answers received from this sample of employees to draw conclusions about all your employees. You want to know the general communication satisfaction and motivation of all the employees, whether supervisor-employee gender similarity makes a difference in general, and whether the suspected relationship between satisfaction and motivation to perform exists in the entire population of employees.

What you are doing in each of these cases is going beyond descriptions of the data acquired from particular people to infer conclusions about a much larger group of people. To do so, we need **inferential statistics** (also called **inductive statistics**), which is the "set of statistical procedures that allows a researcher to go beyond the group that has been measured, and make statements about the characteristics of a much larger group" (Jaeger, 1983, p. 12).

Inferential statistics, as mentioned at the beginning of Chapter 11, accomplish two purposes: (a) **estimation** is used to generalize the results obtained from a sample to its parent population, and (b) **significance testing** examines how likely differences between groups and relationships between variables occur by chance. In this chapter, we first explore estimation and then focus on principles of significance testing that apply to both difference and relationship analysis. In the next two chapters, we examine specific procedures used to test for significant differences between groups and significant relationships between variables.

ESTIMATION

The best way to measure any characteristic of a population is, of course, to study every member, so researchers prefer to conduct a census if they can (see Chapter 5). But as the example at the start of this chapter shows, the size of most populations usually makes it too difficult or impossible to conduct a census, so researchers must study a sample(s) drawn from a targeted population and use the results from that sample to describe the population. The ultimate purpose for many researchers is to generalize the results found for a sample back to its parent population. Survey research—like predicting how people in a state will vote in an upcoming election on the basis of asking a few hundred people, or a company deciding whether to invest substantial money in a public relations health campaign on the basis of a survey of some communities—is conducted expressly for the purpose of inferring characteristics of a large population from characteristics found in a relatively small sample. Experimental researchers and some textual analysts also sometimes generalize from the research participants/texts studied to the population they represent. Researchers, therefore, often *estimate* population characteristics (called **parameters**) on the basis of characteristics found in a sample (called *statistics*). (So here's another use of the term *statistics*.) Hence, estimation procedures are often referred to as **parametric statistics.** The statistics computed are called **estimates** and the formulas used to compute estimates are called **estimators** (Vogt, 1999).

Estimates of population parameters from sample statistics are possible as long as two assumptions are met: (a) the variable(s) of interest is assumed to be distributed "normally" in the population being studied, and (b) a random sample has been selected from that population. We shall explain these two assumptions before proceeding.

The Normal Distribution

Estimation procedures start with the assumption that scores on the variable(s) of interest in the population being studied are distributed in the shape of a symmetrical bell (see Figure 12.1). This type of distribution is called a **normal distribution, normal curve,** or, because of its symmetrical geometric shape, a **bell-shaped curve.**

In a normal distribution, the center point is in the exact middle of the distribution and is the highest point of the curve. The center point, therefore, is the mean, median, and mode of the distribution. The shape of the scores on the right and left sides of the center point, with units expressed in standard deviations (SD) away from the mean (+1SD, –1SD, +2SD, –2SD, etc.) are symmetrical; two halves of a bell shape.

Because of the shape of a normal distribution, researchers know the proportion of scores that falls within any particular area of the curve (see F. Williams, 1992). In a normal distribution, 34.13% of scores fall in the area between the center point and +1SD, and 34.13% of scores fall between the center point and –1SD. Together, these two areas account for 68.26% of all the scores in a normal distribution. The area between +1SD and +2SD contains 13.59% of the scores, and the same is true for the area between –1SD and –2SD. And 2.14% of all scores fall in the area between +2SD and +3SD, as

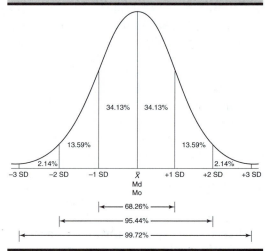

FIGURE 12.1   A normal distribution (normal curve, bell-shaped curve)

well as in the area between –2SD and –3SD. If you count up these percentages, 99.72% of the scores in a normal distribution are accounted for in the area from +3SD to –3SD. As you also see, the curve continues to run on (theoretically forever; a curve that runs on like this, getting ever closer to the line but never touching it is called **asymptotic**), and the few remaining scores will be accounted for at some point. For our purposes, however, we only need to talk about the area from +3SD to –3SD away from the center point of the distribution.

Scores on most variables are assumed to be distributed in the population of interest in this "normal" fashion, unless shown to be otherwise. It doesn't matter whether we are talking about physical strength, intelligence, or any other variable; the distribution of all possible scores in a population typically is assumed to have this shape. Communication variables are no exception; they, too, typically are assumed to be distributed normally throughout a population.

An example of a communication variable may help to understand the normal distribution. Say we are talking about the distribution of student scores at a large university on a communication apprehension scale, "an individual's level of fear or anxiety associated with either real or anticipated communication with another person or persons" (McCroskey, 1977, p. 78). The assumption is that if every student at that university were measured on this scale, a visual display of the scores would look like the normal distribution depicted in Figure 12.1.

Some hypothetical numbers can help make this more concrete. Let's say scores on the communication apprehension scale range from 0 (no apprehension) to 20 (high apprehension). After measuring every single student at that university on this scale, the mean is found to be 10, and the standard deviation is 2. If the population scores are distributed in a normal manner, then 34.13% of scores fall between the mean (10) and +1SD (12), and 34.13% of scores fall between the mean (10) and –1SD (8). The 68.26% of people whose scores fall between +1SD and –1SD could be labeled "average" with regard to communication apprehension. There are 13.59% of scores between +1SD

(12) and +2SD (14), and this group of people could be labeled "above average" on communication apprehension. The same percentage of scores (13.59%) falls between –1SD (8) and –2SD (6), in the "below average" communication apprehension group. Finally, 2.14% of scores fall between +2SD (14) and +3SD (16), which could be called the "high" communication apprehension group, and 2.14% of scores fall between –2SD (6) and –3SD (4), and constitutes the "low" communication apprehension group.

The normal distribution, thus, tells researchers the relative probability of a score falling in any given area of the curve. We now see one advantage of converting raw scores into standard scores and, thereby, creating a distribution with a mean of 0 and a standard deviation of 1 (see Chapter 11). Remember that some concepts, such as intelligence (IQ), are reported in standard scores. Hence, if a person's IQ is +2.75SD, we know this score is quite unique, as only 2.14% of the population scores fall between +2SD and +3SD. Consequently, we might label this person a "genius." After all, a person is only a genius in relation to how his or her IQ score compares to the distribution of all IQ scores in the population to which he or she belongs. The labels we would use to describe the scores of other people in that population (e.g., average intelligence, above average, below average, and so forth) are also, of course, determined on the basis of how they compare against others.

Sometimes a set of data can be manipulated or structured to form a normal distribution, or close to it. One example with which students are all too familiar is the curving of test examination scores. A teacher, for example, could compute the mean and standard deviation for a set of test scores, and then use .5SD (or some other appropriate cut-off point) to determine the different grades: The grade of "C" is given to scores between –.5SD and +.5SD; the grade of "B" to scores between +.5SD and +1SD and the grade of "D" to scores between –.5SD and –1SD; and the grade of "A" to scores greater than +1SD and the grade of "F" to scores lower than –1SD. In this way, a normal distribution of grades could be created that has about one-third of the grades above "C," with only a few "A's," and about one-third of the grades below "C," with only a few "F's."

We said above that the assumption of a normal distribution applies to most variables. There are, of course, variables that are known not to be normally distributed. Household income in the United States, for example, is undoubtedly not normally distributed, which probably explains why the government reports the median rather than the mean when referring to the average household income (see Chapter 11).

Distributions not in the shape of a normal curve can be described using two characteristics: kurtosis and skewness (see Figure 12.2). **Kurtosis** refers to how pointed or flat is the shape of a distribution of scores. The shape of the normal curve, with the center point being the highest peak and the two tails leveling off in a similar way, is called **mesokurtic,** which comes from the words "meso" meaning "middle" and "kurtic" meaning "peakedness." In contrast, a curve that is tall and sharply pointed, with scores clustered around the middle, is called a **peaked** or **leptokurtic distribution** (Figure 12.2a). If scores do not cluster around the middle but are dispersed rather evenly across the distribution, making the curve flat and more spread out, the curve is said to be a **flat** or **platykurtic distribution** (Figure 12.2b).

Skewness means that the majority of scores are toward one end of a distribution and the curve tails off (becomes pointy, like a skewer) across the rest of the distribution, which creates an asymmetric distribution. A **positively skewed distribution** (Figure 12.2c) occurs when the tail runs to the right side of the curve (we saw an example from communication research in Figure 11.15); a **negatively skewed distribution** (Figure 12.2d) occurs when the tail runs to the left side of the curve.

Use of Random Sampling

The second assumption that informs estimation procedures is the selection of a random sample from the population being studied. Remember from Chapter 5 that if researchers intend to infer the results from a sample to its population, the sample must be representative of that population. The best assurance of a representative sample is random selection of population members, such that each population member has an equal chance of being selected for the sample.

The reason a random sample is representative of a population is that it is probable that if a population is normally distributed on a variable, then a random sample drawn from that population will also be normally distributed on that variable. This principle does not hold true for a nonrandom sample; it may or may not be normally distributed on that, or any other, variable.

We also need to point out a very important principle of inference that is related to sampling: the **Central Limits Theorem.** According to Norusis (1991), "the Central Limits Theorem says that for samples of a sufficiently large size, the real distribution of means is almost always approximately normal. The original variable can have any distribution. It doesn't have to be bell-shaped in the least" (p. 198). Kerlinger (1973) is even more specific about the Central Limits Theorem:

> If samples are drawn from a population at random, the means of the samples will tend to be normally distributed. *The larger the* n*'s the more this is so. And the shape and kind of distribution of the origi-*

FIGURE 12.2   Shapes of nonnormal distributions curve, bell-shaped curve)

(a) Peaked (Leptokurtic)

(b) Flat (Platykurtic)

(c) Positively Skewed

(d) Negatively Skewed

nal population makes no difference. That is, the population distribution does not have to be normally distributed. (p. 207)

The Central Limits Theorem doesn't contradict what we said about the normal distribution of variables; it addresses two important points about the samples selected. First, larger samples give more accurate results than do smaller samples. In fact, if the sample is quite large, researchers can treat the data as normally distributed, even if the data actually are distributed in a perfect rectangle (see Kerlinger, 1986). Second, random samples are where it is at as far as inference is concerned. As one of the authors of this textbook is fond of saying in class, "Random samples allow researchers to operate safely under the normal curve." The second point is probably more important than the first; hence, if researchers ever have to choose between a random and a nonrandom sample, they go with the random sample, even if they have to use a somewhat smaller sample size.

The reason we made such a big deal about normally distributed variables is that researchers often do not deal with very large sample sizes or, unfortunately, are not able to select random samples. Should a researcher not do a study if the samples are small or nonrandom? Of course not, because some very important issues would get ignored. For example, researchers shouldn't give up studying sexual harassment communication just because they can't get a complete list of those who have been harassed and, therefore, can't draw a random sample. Knowing to watch for normal distributions of variables is important, but when researchers are able to select large or random samples, the matter is taken care of. When using smaller samples, and particularly nonrandom samples, it is up to the researcher to check that a normal distribution has been obtained.

Inferring from a Random Sample to a Population

With these two assumptions in hand, we can now explain the process of inferring from a sample to a population. While the process is a bit complex, we'll try to keep it as simple as possible, posing

questions and giving answers along the way. Let's use the example of communication apprehension discussed above to illustrate the process.

Suppose, again, that a researcher is interested in knowing the mean level of communication apprehension in a student population at a large university. Imagine that the researcher draws a large number of random samples from this population (say 100 samples), and that each sample has 100 students, and the researcher then calculates the mean communication apprehension score for each of those 100 random samples.

Treating the 100 random sample means as a distribution of data creates what is called a **sampling distribution.** (Sampling distributions can also be formed of other values, such as percentages or median scores.) The mean of this hypothetical sampling distribution (the grand mean of the 100 random sample means) can then be calculated. Let's be consistent with the example before and say that the grand mean of this sampling distribution equals 10. The standard deviation (see Chapter 11) of this sampling distribution can also be calculated. If we divide that standard deviation figure by the square root of the size of the samples, we have what is called the **standard error of the mean (SE_M).** The standard error of the mean tells researchers how much these random sample means are likely to differ from the grand mean of the sampling distribution. In this case, let's say the SD of the sampling distribution is, again, 2, which, when divided by 10 (the square root of 100, the size of each of the random samples selected), equals an SE_M of .2.

Now, if the frequency of occurrence of these 100 random sample means were displayed visually, what shape do you think the distribution would take? Would it demonstrate skewness by being positively or negatively skewed? Would it show kurtosis by being flat or peaked? The answer is "No" to both questions. Why?

Remember that researchers assume that any characteristic normally distributed in a population (scores on the communication apprehension measure, in this case) will also be normally distributed in a random sample selected from that population. So the sampling distribution of these 100 random samples means also forms a normal distribution. It would look like Figure 12.1 (except that it now is a sampling distribution composed of 100 random sample means, and instead of SD units, there are SE_M units, and these units are much smaller than the SD units because they were calculated by dividing the SD by the square root of the sample size).

Returning to the goal of estimating the population mean from these 100 random sample means, what is the researcher's best estimate of the "true" population mean? That is, if one score from the distribution of 100 random sample means had to be picked as the best guess of the population mean, which score would it be? The answer, as you probably figured out, is the score that is the center point (the grand mean) of the sampling distribution. Thus, in this example, the best estimate of the population mean is 10.

Of course, only some of the 100 random sample means may be the same as this best estimate of the population mean. The majority of the sample means deviate from this sampling distribution grand mean. So what if the researcher used the best estimate of the population mean of 10, but said that the true population mean is between 9.8 and 10.2? What percentage of the 100 random sample means would be accounted for by this range? The answer is 68.26%, because that is the proportion of the 100 random sample means covered from $-1SE_M$ (9.8) to $+1SE_M$ (10.2) away from the mean.

But saying that 68.26% of the time the population mean is between 9.8 and 10.2 also means this estimate is wrong 31.74% of the time. That is, 31.74% of the time, the true population mean would probably not be between 9.8 and 10.2; it might be 9.7 or 10.4, or some other number. Being wrong almost one-third of the time is a high amount of error, and researchers don't like to be wrong that much of the time. As Jaeger (1990) claims, "Statisticians pride themselves on being right, 'on the average'" (p. 147).

So what if the researcher used the best estimate of the population mean of 10, but claimed that the true population mean ranged from 9.6 to 10.4 (that is, plus or minus .4)? In that case, 95.44% of the 100 random sample means would be accounted for,

because that is the proportion of the 100 random sample means that is between $-2SE_M$ and $+2SE_M$ away from the grand mean of the sampling distribution. This now means the estimate is wrong only 4.56% of the time, which is much better than being wrong a third of the time. To reduce even further the chances of being wrong, the researcher could say the population mean is 10, plus or minus .6, which covers the random sample means that fall in the area from +3SD to –3SD away from the mean, or 99.72% of the 100 random sample means.

The percentage of random sample means (or other statistics) in a sampling distribution covered by the estimate of a population parameter is called the **confidence level** (also called the **confidence coefficient**). The confidence level is the degree of assurance that an actual mean in a sampling distribution accurately represents the true population mean. Covering the random sample means from $-1SE_M$ to $+1SE_M$ produces a 68.26% confidence level; covering the means from $-2SE_M$ to $+2SE_M$ equals a 95.44% confidence level; and covering the means from $-3SE_M$ to $+3SE_M$ equals a 99.72% confidence level.

The range of the scores of the random sample means (or other statistics) associated with a confidence level is called the **confidence interval (CI).** In this example, an estimate of the population mean of 10 at a 68.26% confidence level has a confidence interval of plus or minus .2 (meaning a range 9.8–10.2 in actual random sample mean scores on the communication apprehension scale); an estimate of 10 at a 95.44% confidence level has a confidence interval of plus or minus .4 (a range of 9.6–10.4); and an estimate of 10 at a 99.72% confidence level has a confidence interval of plus or minus .6 (a range of 99.4–10.6).

The only question remaining is how confident a researcher should be when estimating population parameters from a sampling distribution. The answer depends on the purpose of any particular estimation and, more importantly, the potential consequences of being wrong. In the social sciences (which includes public opinion polls), researchers and pollsters generally agree to use a 95% confidence level, meaning they are inaccurate

5% of the time. Applying this to the example of communication apprehension scores, a researcher would say that the population mean is 10, plus or minus .39, which is the confidence interval from $-1.96SE_M$ to $-1.96SE_M$ away from the sampling distribution grand mean that corresponds to the 95% confidence level.

The 95% confidence level is an arbitrary level accepted by those in the social sciences. In other disciplines, different rules about confidence levels apply. For example, a 95% confidence level may not be acceptable in pharmaceutical research. If researchers are estimating the effect of a new drug on a population on the basis of findings from random samples (following the procedures we just explained), a 95% confidence level could mean that the new drug might kill 5% of the people taking it, or 1 out of every 20! Thus, a much more stringent confidence level would be used, such as 99.99%, which means that the estimate is inaccurate only one time out of 10,000.

We just explained the process of estimation, but we were speaking in theory, using a hypothetical sampling distribution composed of 100 random sample means. The fact is that those who do estimation don't draw 100 random samples. Indeed, most don't draw more than *one* random sample. So how can they estimate a population parameter from only one random sample?

The answer is that they use a single random sample to stand for the large number of random samples (e.g., 100) that should have selected. That is, they select a random sample, calculate the mean and the standard error of the mean (or other appropriate statistics), and use the mean from that one sample to represent the sampling distribution mean (e.g., the grand mean for the hypothetical 100 random samples) and the standard error of the mean for that one sample to represent the sampling distribution's standard error of the mean. Thus, in actual practice, researchers select a random sample, calculate the mean and standard error of the mean (or other statistics), move out $-1.96SE_M$ and $+1.96SE_M$ away from the mean so that they are 95% confident, and use that range of scores as the confidence interval (the actual values of the upper and lower limits

of a confidence interval is called the **confidence limits** or **confidence bounds**), or, as it typically is called, the "margin of error" or "sampling error."

It should be pointed out that, ideally, the goal is to make the confidence interval as small as possible. After all, it doesn't tell us much about who will win an election if one candidate is found in a sample to be preferred over another 45% to 55% with a margin of error (confidence interval) of +/–15%!

The size of the confidence interval is influenced by three things: (a) the variability that exists on the topic in the population being studied, (b) the confidence level employed, and (c) the size of the random sample. There isn't much that can be done about the variability that exists in a population. If most people in a population are undecided about an upcoming election, then there will be a large confidence interval, or margin of error, attached to any estimate inferred from a sample of that population. Reducing the size of the confidence interval can, of course, be accomplished by decreasing the confidence level. As we saw in the example of communication apprehension scores, the confidence interval is much lower when using a 68.26% confidence level (.2 in that example) than when using a 95% confidence level (.39 in that example). But that's hardly a fair trade-off, because the chances of the population estimate being wrong have now increased substantially to almost one-third of the time.

The best way to reduce the size of the confidence interval is to increase the size of the random sample selected, for a confidence interval depends partly on sample size because the square root of the sample size is used to calculate the standard error of the mean. Hence, the smaller the size of a random sample, the less accurately it approximates a true population parameter. The general rule, therefore, known as the **Law of Large Numbers,** is that the larger the size of a random sample, the more it approximates the true population and the smaller the amount of error (and, thus, a smaller confidence interval). This is only true, however, up to about 1,600–2,000 people; after that, the reduction in error (and, hence, the size of the confidence interval) is often too small to justify sampling additional people. For this reason, national random samples conducted by pollsters, such as Gallup and Harris, or by ratings companies, such as Arbitron and Nielsen, often use approximately 1,600–2,000 people (although many use multiple random samples rather than just one random sample).

Most researchers (especially academic researchers) rely on much smaller samples and accept larger confidence intervals (or error) in their population estimates. There are formulas that tell approximately how many people are needed in a random sample to reduce the size of the confidence interval. Using one of those formulas, Figure 12.3 provides estimates of the minimum number of people that need to be randomly selected from small populations, ranging from 200 to 100,000, to produce confidence intervals (margin of error) of +/– 3%, 5%, and 10% at the 95% confidence level. (If a population is less than 200, a census should be conducted. If the population is between 200 and 1,000, and the desired confidence level is +/–3% or if the population is between 200 and 400 and the desired

FIGURE 12.3   Minimum sample sizes for selected small populations

	95% CONFIDENCE LEVEL		
	Confidence Interval (Margin of Error)		
Population Size (N)	+/–3%	+/–5%	+/–10%
200*	100a	100a	65
300	150a	150a	72
400	200a	200a	78
500	250a	218	81
750	325a	255	86
1,000	500a	278	88
1,250	576	294	90
1,500	624	306	91
1,750	664	316	92
2,000	696	323	92
2,250	724	329	93
2,500	748	334	93
3,000	788	341	94
3,500	818	347	94
4,000	843	351	94
4,500	863	354	94
5,000	880	357	95
7,500	935	366	95
10,000	965	370	96
15,000	997	375	96
20,000	1,014	377	96
50,000	1,045	382	96
75,000	1,053	383	96
100,000	1,056	383	96

Source: Adapted from Jack E. Edwards, Marie D. Thomas, Paul Rosenfeld, and Stephanie Booth-Kewley, *How to Conduct Organizational Surveys: A Step-by-Step Guide,* p. 63, © 1997 by Sage Publications, Inc. Reprinted by Permission of Sage Publications, Inc.

NOTES: *If the population is less than 200, the entire group should be used.

a. Population size for which the assumption of a normal distribution does not apply. In such cases, the sample size should be 50% of the population size (Rea & Parker, 1992).

confidence level is 5%, the assumption of a normal distribution does not hold, and half of the population should be selected.) Thus, if a researcher studies a population of 100,000 people, a random sample of 1,056 should be selected if a confidence interval of +/–3% is desired (at the 95% confidence level). If the researcher is willing to accept +/–5% as the confidence interval, then 383 persons can be selected. And if the researcher is willing to accept +/–10% as the confidence interval (the largest margin of error that should be tolerated, according to Rea & Parker, 1992), only 96 people need to be selected. These figures are the actual number of people that have to be in the random sample. In practice, researchers typically have to draw a larger random sample than the number recommended to account for those who do not respond or are ineligible (e.g., they weren't available at the time the sample was drawn) (see Henry, 1990, for a formula that corrects for ineligibles and nonresponses).

One final point deserves mention. We just examined the process of inferring population parameters from sample statistics using the example of means on an interval/ratio communication apprehension scale. But we mentioned that other statistics can also be used to estimate population parameters. Most of the population estimates reported in the media, for example, are based on percentages of people who respond to variables measured at the nominal level, such as choosing between two or more candidates, answering "yes" or "no" to a question, or some similar variation. In such cases, the hypothetical sampling distribution scores are percentages, ranging from 0 to 100 percent, and the confidence interval (margin of error) is reported in terms of plus or minus percentage points.

Here's a recent example of an opinion poll that assessed the general public's view of the First Amendment, which is near and dear to the hearts of communication researchers because it guarantees freedom of speech. A poll conducted by the *Chicago Tribune* revealed the following results:

1. 27% of people thought the First Amendment "goes too far in the rights it guarantees," 55%

thought the guarantees "about right," 8% said "not far enough," and 11% answered "don't know."
2. 58% thought radio personalities who use implicit or explicit sexual expressions "should not be allowed" on the air, while 35% believed they "should be allowed," and 7% answered "don't know."
3. 49% thought that militia group/white supremacists/skinheads/Nazis "should not be allowed" to protest in a community like theirs, 42% believed they "should be allowed," and 4% answered "don't know." (Madigan & Secter, 1997, Sect. 1, p. 1)

The newspaper reported that these poll results were obtained on the basis of a (random) survey of 1,001 adults and that the margin of error was +/–3% points.

We trust you did not have any trouble understanding the explanation of the poll or its results, and you probably even noticed that the confidence level was not reported. The media, unfortunately, often do not report the confidence level. In such cases, you should assume that the 95% confidence level agreed on in the social sciences is being used. You should now be able to interpret any population parameter estimates from sample statistics the next time you see them.

SIGNIFICANCE TESTING

The term *significant* is defined in the *New World Dictionary of the English Language* as "important," "monumentous," and "an observed departure from a hypothesis too large to be reasonably attributed to chance [a statistically *significant* difference]." The first two meanings are quite common in everyday conversation. People often claim to have a "significant" (meaning important) point to make during an argument or have "significant" (meaning monumentous) news to share with another person. People even sometimes use the term in ways that suggest the third definition, for example, when they claim that there are significant differences between groups of people (such as lifestyle differences between members of one generation and another) or significant relationships between variables (such as the oft-cited relationship between smoking tobacco and lung cancer). But most people wouldn't be able to recite that third definition, let alone explain what it means. This section of the chapter explains this third use of the term "significant" by exploring the principles that guide the statistical testing of significant differences between groups and significant relationships between variables.

Because you now understand estimation procedures, it will be relatively easy to understand significance testing, for both are attempts to generalize from a sample to a population. The difference has to do with their intended purpose. Remember from Chapter 2 that communication research serves at least two general purposes. The first purpose is to describe communication behavior by answering the general question, "What is the nature of communication behavior 'X'?" Estimation seeks to answer this question by describing population characteristics (the nature of communication behavior "X," such as communication apprehension in a population of students at a university) on the basis of characteristics found in a sample selected from that population.

The second purpose is to understand relationships between communication variables and other variables by answering the general question, "How is communication variable 'X' related to other variables?" Significance testing seeks to answer this question by inferring relationships between variables within a population on the basis of relationships found in a sample selected from that population.

Remember, too, that variables are differentiated with regard to the values researchers assign to them or the kind of "scale" used to measure them. Nominal variables (such as gender) are differentiated on the basis of type or category (men and women), whereas ordered variables (for example age) can be assigned numerical values that indicate how much of the concept is present (10 years old, 28, 54, 72, etc.). When an independent variable is nominal, researchers pose a research question (a question) or a hypothesis (a prediction) about the difference between the categories of the independent variable with regard to the dependent variable. When an independent variable is ordered, researchers pose a research question or hypothesis about the type of relationship between the independent and dependent variables.

Estimation and significance testing, therefore, serve different purposes, although both are attempts to generalize from a sample to a population. Unlike estimation, however, not all significance tests assume that the variable(s) being studied is normally distributed in the population of interest. Significance tests that do assume this are, once again, called *parametric statistics;* significance tests that do not assume this are called **nonparametric statistics** (or **distribution-free statistics**).

When conducting significance testing, a random sample, should, of course, be selected from the population of interest. Sometimes researchers practice what is preached, but quite often they don't randomly sample from the targeted population. In some cases, this may be because they can't afford the time and/or expense. In other cases, researchers may not be able to get a complete list of everyone in a population, such as all people who watch a particular television show or people who give lots of public speeches. In addition, many researchers in university settings use college students to represent the general population, a questionable assumption at best. (College students are much smarter and kinder than most people!)

Technically, if a random sample has not been selected, inferences about the population should not be made. In practice, however, researchers often use a small, nonrandom sample, proceed to test for significant differences and relationships in that sample, and, then, in the discussion section of a journal article, generalize the results to the population. Next time you read a research study, you should be able to judge for yourself whether the sample is representative of the population being studied and, therefore, whether the results obtained from that sample can be generalized to the population.

The Logic of Significance Testing

The best way to explain the logic underlying significance testing is through two hypothetical examples, one about differences between groups and one about relationships between variables. We'll use the two examples from Chapter 2 (see Figure 2.7), when we explained research questions and hypotheses: (a) the difference between males and females with respect to self-disclosure, and (b) the relationship between age and self-disclosure.

Let's first work with testing hypotheses and then we'll come back and talk about answering research questions. Remember that a one-tailed hypothesis about differences between groups predicts the direction of the suspected difference. Hence, a one-tailed hypothesis about self-disclosure differences between males and females takes the form of "Males self-disclose more than females" or "Males self-disclose less than females." (These categories can, of course, also be reversed to read, "Females self-disclose more than males" or "Females self-disclose less than males.") (A two-tailed hypothesis, "Males and females self-disclose differently," predicts a difference but does not specify its direction. We'll return to two-tailed hypotheses later in this discussion.)

A one-tailed hypothesis about a relationship between variables predicts the direction of the suspected relationship as being either *positive* (meaning that as scores increase on one variable, scores increase on the other variable) or *negative* (as scores increase on one variable, scores decrease on the other variable). Hence, a one-tailed hypothesis about the relationship between age and self-disclosure takes the form of "There is a positive relationship between age and self-disclosure" or "There is a negative relationship between age and self-disclosure." (A two-tailed hypothesis, "Age and self-disclosure are related," predicts a relationship, but does not specify its direction.)

Testing a Null Hypothesis.   Here's the first important step to understanding significance testing. You might think that researchers are trying to "prove" the research hypothesis, but this isn't the case. Researchers cannot prove a prediction by testing *all* possible instances in which it might apply—there might be millions. However, if researchers find a situation in which the idea does *not* work, they know the hypothesis (and in the case of theory testing, the theory from which it is derived) is incorrect.

Researchers, therefore, actually test a **null hypothesis** (H_0), an implicit statement (you typically won't see it explicitly specified in published research studies) that underlies every hypothesis and predicts that there is *no* difference between the groups or *no* relationship between the variables being studied. (Technically, this is the null hypothesis that underlies a two-tailed hypothesis. For a one-tailed hypothesis, the null hypothesis says that the predicted difference or relationship does not exist, meaning that it takes into account *both* no difference and the opposite type of difference—for example, that women may disclose more than men in the case of a one-tailed hypothesis that predicts that men disclose more than women—or *both* no relationship and the opposite type of relationship—that there may be a negative relationship between age and self-disclosure in the case of a one-tailed hypothesis that predicts a positive relationship between these variables. For the sake of explaining significance testing, however, we first use the null hypothesis of no difference or no relationship, even when talking about one-tailed hypotheses, and then once this foundation is laid, we explain the specific difference between testing one-tailed and two-tailed hypotheses and research questions.) **Significance testing,** then, is the process of analyzing quantitative data for the purpose of testing whether a null hypothesis is *probably* either *correct* or *false*. Some people, therefore, refer to significance testing as **hypothesis testing.**

The null hypothesis represents chance occurrence—that the difference or relationship occurred simply by chance. Researchers obviously need to reject chance differences or relationships before inferring patterned or stable ones. Thus, if a null hypothesis is shown to probably be correct, researchers accept that there is no significant difference or relationship. If, however, a null hypothesis is shown to probably be false, researchers can reject it and, assuming there isn't another likely explanation (such as threats to the validity of the findings; see Chapter 5 and the discussion below), accept its logical alternative, the research hypothesis of a significant difference or relationship. In the case of theory-testing research, acceptance of the research hypothesis does not, of course, prove a theory; it merely offers one piece of support for it.

It should also be noted that, on rare occasions, researchers may actually predict no significant difference or relationship, in which case the null hypothesis serves as a research hypothesis. The logic of testing this null hypothesis remains the same as that explained below, but the probabilities are different.

Every research hypothesis, thus, has a corresponding null hypothesis. In our first example, the research hypothesis (H_1) and its corresponding null hypothesis (H_0) are:

H_1: Males self-disclose more than females.

H_0: There is no difference between males and females with respect to self-disclosure.

In our second example, the research hypothesis (H_1) and its corresponding null hypothesis (H_0) are:

H_1: There is a positive relationship between age and self-disclosure.

H_0: There is no relationship between age and self-disclosure.

Thus, researchers actually test null hypotheses to see whether they are probably correct or false. Testing the null, as opposed to the research, hypothesis is analogous to the way a defendant (the accused) is treated in a criminal trial. A defendant in a criminal trial is assumed, at least in theory, to be innocent until proven guilty (perhaps a better way of saying it is that a person is innocent until shown to be "not innocent") beyond a reasonable doubt. The defendant does not have to demonstrate his or her innocence; in fact, the person doesn't even have to testify if he or she chooses not to. It's up to the prosecutor to show that the defendant is not innocent beyond a reasonable doubt. If the jury is persuaded that the defendant is not innocent beyond a reason-

able doubt, then it can convict him or her. (Note that we are talking about criminal and not civil trials. In a civil trial, a defendant must testify. That's why O. J. Simpson didn't have to testify at his criminal trial, but did have to at his civil trial.)

The logic of the criminal courtroom applies well to significance testing. Groups of people (like men and women) are assumed to be innocent of any difference, unless a difference can be shown to exist beyond a reasonable doubt. Similarly, variables (such as age and self-disclosure) are assumed to be innocent of any relationship, unless a relationship can be shown to exist beyond a reasonable doubt.

Rejecting a Null Hypothesis.   The only thing left to explain is the concept of "beyond a reasonable doubt." In the courtroom, this is the point at which the evidence suggests that the jury can reject a plea of innocence (the null hypothesis, if you will) as being false and accept the alternative that the person is not innocent (or guilty). Similarly, in research, this is the point at which the evidence suggests that a researcher can reject a null hypothesis of no difference or no relationship as being false and accept the most likely alternative explanation, the research hypothesis that predicts a difference or relationship. Of course, there are a number of other potential explanations for finding a null hypothesis in research to be false—all the validity threats discussed in Chapter 5. Thus, the null hypothesis might be false because of one of the threats posed by researchers (e.g., the researcher unintentional expectancy effect), the way the study was conducted (e.g., a lack of procedure validity), or because of the research participants studied (e.g., the Hawthorne effect). However, if a researcher conducts a study in such a way as to confidently rule out or sufficiently minimize these validity threats, then the most likely explanation for the null hypothesis being false is the suspected difference between the groups or the relationship between the variables predicted by the research hypothesis.

At this point, to understand when a researcher can reject a null hypothesis, we have to talk a little about mathematical probability. Let's use another, relatively simple example to illustrate the decision about when a null hypothesis can be rejected. Suppose one of your friends wants to bet you on whether a coin tossed into the air will come up heads or tails, and lets you make the call while it is being tossed. Would you bet on heads or tails? While you might have a gut feeling that the coin is going to come up heads (or tails), the actual probability of it coming up either heads or tails, as we are sure you know, is 50%. That is, in theory, the coin should come up heads 50% of the time and tails 50% of the time. Hence, it doesn't really matter which way you bet; there is an equal chance of either side of the coin coming up.

Now let's say that your friend tossed the coin five times in a row, and heads came up every single time. Which way would you bet on the sixth toss? While it might be tempting to say tails, thinking that somehow tails is "due" so that the theoretical 50–50 balance begins to be reestablished, the fact is that there is still a 50% chance of the sixth coin toss being either heads or tails, regardless of what happened before. That's because the six coins tosses are independent of, or unrelated to, one another. This means whatever happened before doesn't affect the sixth coin flip. (This is in contrast to instances of *conditional probability,* where a preceding occurrence does, in fact, influence a subsequent occurrence, such as the odds of being dealt a diamond after already having been dealt four diamonds from a deck of playing cards.)

Taking it a step further, what if your friend tossed the coin 10 times in a row and it came up heads all 10 times. What would you bet on the 11th time? We know this may sound counterintuitive, but again, there is a 50% chance of either heads or tails coming up, so it really doesn't matter which way you bet. (One of the authors' students gave an impassioned speech on a conditional probability "system" for winning bets like this. Mistakenly thinking that independent events are conditional is known appropriately as the *gambler's fallacy,* Vogt, 1999.)

Now let's make the circumstances really extreme. Suppose your friend tossed the coin 1000 times, and it came up heads every single time. What would you bet on the next coin flip? If every-

thing is fair, there is still a 50% chance of it being heads or tails on the next flip. But the authors of this textbook, while not encouraging you to gamble and bet, recommend that if you are going to bet in this situation, bet the farm on heads, because we suspect there is something very wrong with the coin. The most likely explanation is that it's a two-headed coin, although perhaps it's possible that your friend somehow mastered coin tossing in such a way that heads always comes up. (It was actually a custom in some places for a friend to give an impending groom/bride a two-headed coin so that when he or she gets into arguments with his or her partner about who should do something, like cleaning the dishes, he or she can flip the coin for it, and call heads!)

In addition to the point that each independent flip has a 50% chance of being heads or tails, this coin-tossing example also illustrates that we assume the coin is just fine, until it reaches a certain point where one side has come up so often that we suspect it is crooked. The coin is, thus, assumed to be "innocent" until shown beyond a reasonable doubt to be crooked ("guilty").

This is the same logic that guides significance testing. Researchers assume that the null hypothesis of no difference or no relationship (analogous to a coin being considered fine or not crooked) is true, until a certain point is reached where the difference or relationship has occurred so often that they must conclude something is crooked—that there is an actual difference or relationship that seems to exists (the coin is crooked).

Deciding on the Probability Level.   The probability level (p value) researchers set for rejecting a null hypothesis is called the **significance level.** The significance level establishes a point at which a researcher is confident enough of a statistical difference or relationship to reject a null hypothesis. The specific significance level set by a researcher for rejecting a null hypothesis prior to conducting a study and analyzing the data is referred to as a **decision rule.** While the significance level depends somewhat on the purposes of the research and/or the consequences of being wrong (see the discussion below), those who study human behavior, including communication researchers, typically want to be at least 95% confident that the null hypothesis is false, the same level of probability used for the confidence level in estimation procedures discussed earlier in this chapter. In significance testing, the 95% confidence level is referred to as the .05 significance level, which references the probability of the difference or relationship being significant. That is, a significant difference or relationship found at the .05 level of probability means that researchers are 95% confident that the difference or relationship is not due to chance or error. Put another way, this means that the result is only likely to happen by chance 5 out of 100 times.

A .05 significance level is a very stringent requirement for rejecting a null hypothesis. Think about it with regard to coin tossing. This would mean that a coin has to come up heads (or tails) 95 times out of 100 (or 19 out of 20) before judging it to be crooked. Try flipping a coin and seeing whether you can get it to come up heads (or tails) this many times out of 100 tosses. It will only happen if the coin is crooked, or because of the small probability (5%) of it occurring by chance alone. Thus, researchers set the significance level quite high to minimize reporting a significant difference or relationship that occurs due to chance. Just as our society doesn't want to find an innocent person guilty and, thus, makes it very difficult to reject the assumption of innocence, researchers too don't want to find groups or variables "guilty" when they are actually "innocent" of a difference or relationship. Therefore, they make it very difficult to reject the null hypothesis.

The .05 significance level is, as we explained before, an arbitrary level commonly used in social science research. (Interestingly enough, although not too surprising given the general consensus of using a 95% confidence level/.05 significance level in studying human behavior, del Carmen, 1991, explains that the same degree of certainty is theoretically required in criminal proceedings to convict a defendant.) However, in some cases, for example,

medical research, this level of confidence is not considered stringent enough, because a .05 significance level, as explained before, might mean that a new drug kills people 5% of the time. Hence, medical researchers typically make it much more difficult to reject the null hypothesis by setting the significance level much higher (meaning more stringent), such as .0001, which means the null hypothesis is probably wrong only one time out of 10,000. Even social scientists will sometimes use a more stringent significance level, especially when they conduct many significance tests in the same study. This is because of the threat to validity that results from *additive error.* Hence, if a researcher conducts 20 significance tests of differences and/or relationships, each with a 5% probability of error, there is much more than 5% additive chance of error. (It would not reach 100%, but it is much greater than 5%.) And in the case of a relatively large sample, statistical differences are likely to be found using the .05 significance level, because it's easier to find such differences when one observes a lot, as opposed to a small number, of people. Researchers can guard against finding a spurious or relatively unimportant difference or relationship under these circumstances by using a .01 significance level, or an even more stringent one. Garlick and Mongeau (1993), for example, assessed the influence of minority group members' status characteristics (e.g., physical attractiveness and expertise) on their ability to persuade others. Because of the relatively large size of their sample (480 participants), they were concerned that "small and uninteresting mean differences are likely to be significant at the .05 level" (p. 296). Therefore, they used the more stringent .01 significance level.

It should also be pointed out that occasionally social science researchers use a less stringent significance level, such as .10, which means they are 90% confident of rejecting the null hypothesis. This sometimes is used in exploratory or pilot research, where researchers wish to see whether the suspected difference or relationship is worth pursuing in more detailed, follow-up studies. Some researchers also talk about a finding at the .10 level of probability (or between .10 and .05) as being a *trend* or, if it is very close to .05, as *marginally significant.* Ultimately, social scientists' decision to employ a significance level other than the agreed-on .05 level has to be argued for persuasively on the basis of the purposes of the research and, most importantly, the potential consequences of being wrong.

In summary, researchers always begin the significance testing process by assuming there are no differences between groups or no relationships between variables (the null hypothesis). If the null hypothesis can be shown to be false at the 95% level of probability, it can be rejected and the research hypothesis can be accepted (assuming no other likely explanation exists). Put another way, the research hypothesis is supported (we urge you to use this word and to avoid words such as "proven" or "proved") at the .05 level of probability when the difference or relationship has less than a 5% chance of occurring due to chance or error. In such cases, a researcher can reject the null hypothesis and adopt its alternative, the research hypothesis.

The Practice of Significance Testing

We just explained the theory behind significance testing, so now let's look at actual practice. There are essentially three steps involved in inferring significant differences between groups or relationships between variables on the basis of the results obtained from a single study.

Step 1: Posing a research question or hypothesis and a null hypothesis. The first step, as we saw above, is for a researcher to pose a research question or hypothesis about a difference between groups or a relationship between variables (see Chapter 2). Research questions typically are posed when a researcher doesn't have enough evidence, after reviewing the relevant literature, to make a prediction, or when the literature reveals conflicting evidence. A hypothesis is posed when a researcher has enough evidence from theory, relevant literature, or sometimes logic and/or observations from everyday life to make a prediction.

Step 2: Conducting the study. The researcher conducts a study to investigate the suspected difference between groups or relationship between variables. The researcher might conduct an experiment or a survey, or use textual-analytic methods, such as content analysis or interaction analysis. The researcher identifies the population of interest and, in theory, randomly selects from it the necessary sample size.

Step 3: Testing the null hypothesis. The researcher analyzes the data to determine whether there is a significant difference between groups or relationship between variables. To do so, the researcher uses an appropriate statistical technique (see Chapters 13 and 14) to test whether the null hypothesis of no difference between groups or no relationship between variables is probably correct or incorrect. Testing the null hypothesis entails three things: (a) setting the significance level, (b) computing the calculated value, and (c) comparing the calculated value to the critical value needed to reject the null hypothesis.

Setting the Significance Level. As explained above, communication researchers most often set the significance level at .05, so that the probability of mistakenly rejecting the null hypothesis is only 5%. However, a more stringent and sometimes a less stringent significance level may be justified.

Computing the Calculated Value. There are many types of significance-testing procedures (e.g., chi-square, *t* test, *F* test, *r* correlation); their use depends on such things as the number of groups or variables being studied and whether the independent and dependent variables are measured using nominal, ordinal, interval, and/or ratio scales. The specific procedures for calculating a critical value are discussed in the next two chapters. Each significance-testing procedure, however, results in a final number, a numerical value called the **calculated value.** This calculated value is then assessed in terms of the probability of its occurrence.

Comparing the Calculated Value to the Critical Value.

The calculated value is assessed in terms of the probability of it occurring by chance by consulting an appropriate table for the particular significance test being used (see Appendices B through E). If the calculated value has a 5% or less probability of occurrence by chance, the researcher can reject the null hypothesis and accept the research hypothesis. However, if the calculated value occurs more than 5% of the time due to chance, the researcher must accept the null hypothesis.

The table for each statistical significance test is constructed on the basis of the potential distribution of calculated scores for that particular statistical test. Researchers, therefore, can assess the probability of obtaining the calculated value they found for the data analyzed from any particular study.

This is done by first locating the **critical value** that corresponds to the .05 significance level (or whatever significance level is set) needed to reject the null hypothesis. For example, turn to Appendix C, which is a table of critical values for the *t* test, a significance test examined in the next chapter that is used to compare two groups (like males and females) on an interval/ratio dependent variable (such as number of topics disclosed). Running across the top of the table are probabilities (.05, .025, .01, etc.; note that this table lists probabilities for both one-tailed and two-tailed hypotheses/significance tests). If a .05 significance level is set for a one-tailed hypothesis, the researcher is interested in the critical values identified in the first column of this table.

Running down the side of the table (the rows) are what are called **degrees of freedom (df),** which means the number of scores that are "free to vary." For example, if we know that combining three scores equals 10, the first two are free to vary, but the third is not. Hence, if the first two numbers are 4 and 3, the third must be 3 and, therefore, is not free to vary.

In research, degrees of freedom usually are computed on the basis of sample size (or sometimes on the number of categories employed). Degrees of freedom generally equal either N-1, the number of people sampled minus 1 or the number of categories employed minus 1, or N–2, the number of people sampled minus two.

Researchers determine how likely it is that the calculated value occurred by chance or error (at the .05 significance level) by comparing it to the critical value indicated in the appropriate row and column of the table. If the calculated value does not reach the critical value (that is, it occurs more than 5% of the time due to chance, say .25), it falls into the **region of acceptance,** and the null hypothesis of no difference or no relationship is accepted. If, however, the calculated value reaches or exceeds the critical value (it is equal to or less than .05, say .03), it falls into the **region of rejection** (also called the **critical region**), and the null hypothesis can be rejected. If the null hypothesis is rejected, and assuming there are no competing explanations for the findings, the research hypothesis that there is a significant difference or relationship can be accepted.

For example, suppose a researcher uses a *t* test (see Chapter 13) to test the one-tailed hypothesis that males disclose more topics to strangers than do females, and finds a calculated value of 1.700, with a sample size of 46 people (23 males and 23 females). The researcher looks down the first column of this table (corresponding to the .05 significance level for a one-tailed test) to the row closest to the degrees of freedom of 45 (in this case, N–1, the number of people minus one, is used to determine degrees of freedom), which is the row that starts with 30. The intersection of this column and row reveals a critical value of 1.697. This is the critical value needed for rejecting the null hypothesis. If the calculated value is equal to or exceeds this critical value, then the null hypothesis can be rejected and the research hypothesis accepted. If, however, the calculated value is less than the critical value, then the null hypothesis must be accepted. In this particular example, the calculated value of 1.700 exceeds the critical value of 1.697, so the null hypothesis of no difference between males and females on number of topics disclosed to strangers is rejected, and the research hypothesis that males self-disclose more topics than do females is accepted (as long as the mean scores for both groups show that this is, indeed, the case; a researcher must always check the scores to determine that the direction is, in fact, the one predicted).

You probably noticed that as you move down the first column of this *t* table, the size of the critical value needed to reject the null hypothesis becomes smaller. When degrees of freedom are tied to sample size, the larger the degrees of freedom, the smaller the critical value needed for rejecting the null hypothesis. So here's another reason why researchers typically want to sample more rather than less people.

Finally, the critical value needed for accepting or rejecting a null hypothesis also depends on whether a *one-tailed hypothesis, two-tailed hypothesis,* or *research question* is posed. As Figure 12.4 shows, using the example above, there are two extreme possibilities concerning self-disclosure dif-

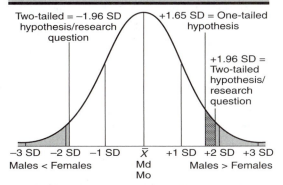

FIGURE 12.4   Critical values needed for rejecting the null hypothesis associated with a one-tailed hypothesis, two-tailed hypothesis, and research question

Two-tailed = −1.96 SD hypothesis/research question

+1.65 SD = One-tailed hypothesis

+1.96 SD = Two-tailed hypothesis/ research question

−3 SD   −2 SD   −1 SD $\bar{X}$ +1 SD   +2 SD   +3 SD

Males < Females

Md Mo

Males > Females

▨ = Region of rejection for the null hypothesis for a one-tailed research hypothesis

▢ = Region of rejection for the null hypothesis for a two-tailed research hypothesis

ferences between males and females: (a) males self-disclose more than females (the right side of the distribution), or (b) males self-disclose less than females (the left side). (The middle corresponds to no difference whatsoever between males and females.) When a one-tailed hypothesis is advanced, such as males self-disclose more than females, a researcher is only interested in knowing whether the calculated value reaches the critical value on that side (the right side, in this case) of the normal distribution that corresponds to the .05 significance level. The other side of the distribution (that males self-disclose less than females) does not need to be taken into account, since that wasn't predicted. In the case of a one-tailed hypothesis, to reach the .05 significance level, the calculated value must, thus, be at least +1.65SD away from the mean.

However, when no direction can be predicted, a researcher advances a two-tailed hypothesis, such as "Men and women self-disclose differently," or a research question, such as "Is there a difference between men and women with regard to self-disclosure?" In both cases, both sides of the normal distribution must be considered. That is, it is possible that *either* males self-disclose significantly more than females or that males self-disclose significantly less than females. Both possibilities must be taken into account for a two-tailed hypothesis or a research question. Hence, the .05 significance level must be divided in half (.025) to account for both sides of the normal distribution (which is why this is sometimes called a *double-tailed test*). This means that to reach the .025 significance level, the calculated value must be at least +/−1.96SD away from the mean. In the example we have been using, had a two-tailed hypothesis been advanced, the researcher would consult the second column of the table in Appendix C, which corresponds to the .05 significance level for a two-tailed test (.025 for a one-tailed test). Assuming the same number of people sampled (46), the critical value needed to reject the null hypothesis for the appropriate row (of 50) is now 2.009. Thus, if the researcher advanced a two-tailed hypothesis or a research question and found a calculated value of 1.700, the null hypothesis would have to be accepted. This shows that when researchers advance two-tailed hypotheses or research questions and divide the .05 significance level in half, a higher calculated value is needed to reject the null hypothesis. For this reason, many researchers prefer to advance a one-tailed hypothesis, as they need a smaller calculated value to reject the null hypothesis. However, a one-tailed hypothesis should only be advanced if there is sufficient justification for posing one.

It should also be pointed out that researchers often indicate the degree to which a difference or relationship is significant by indicating the actual significance level obtained. (**NS** is often used to signify a result that is *not* [statistically] *significant.*) For example, researchers often construct tables in which they report a great number of differences or relationships, with significant ones marked by one, two, or three asterisks that correspond to different significance levels (e.g., .05, .01, .001; see, for instance, Figure 11.8). As Mohr (1990) points out, this technically is not proper, as researchers should set the level of significance prior to conducting any analyses of the data. However, Mohr also argues that while a purist might object to such a procedure,

> the more practical view might be to judge on the basis of whether, in last analysis, the claims being made for the *real*-world *(rather than statistical) significance of the results are overblown or are reasonable, regardless of whether the textbook method was strictly applied. (p. 61)*

The process of significance testing, as explained above, ultimately ends in a decision researchers make about whether to accept or reject the null hypothesis. In most cases, researchers probably make the correct decision, but like a number of decisions made in life, researchers sometimes make **decision errors** about whether to accept or reject the null hypothesis. We now turn our attention to two such errors.

Type I Error and Type II Error

There are two kinds of decision errors researchers might make when employing significance testing.

Type I error (alpha error) occurs when researchers reject a null hypothesis and accept a research hypothesis when, in fact, the null hypothesis is probably true and should have been accepted. **Type II error (beta error, or B, β; also called acceptance error)** is exactly the opposite, and occurs when researchers accept a null hypothesis when, in fact, it is probably false and, thereby, reject a sound research hypothesis. As Figure 12.5 shows, there are, thus, four possible decisions that can be made, two of which are correct, one that results in Type I error, and one that results in Type II error.

Take the example of self-disclosure differences between males and females. If males and females in the sample selected do not differ significantly on self-disclosure scores but the researcher reports that they do (called a "false positive"), Type I error has been committed. If the two groups do differ significantly but the researcher reports that they do not (called a "false negative"), Type II error has been committed.

Type I error (rejecting a null hypothesis that is probably true) means that researchers believe that a difference or relationship is significant when it is not. The chance of committing Type I error is easy to calculate; it is equal to the significance level employed. Thus, if researchers use a .05 significance level to reject a null hypothesis, the chance of committing Type I error is 5%. However, when multiple comparisons are made to test the same hypothesis (e.g., testing significant differences among three groups by comparing two groups at a time), the chance of committing a Type I error can increase (in this example, it would be

FIGURE 12.5   Type I and Type II errors

	H_0 Probably True	H_0 Probably False
Accept H_0	Correct	Type II Error
Reject H_0	Type I Error	Correct

roughly equal to .15 [.05 + .05 + .05]), if appropriate procedures that take this error into account are not used. In this case, the probability of committing a Type I error is called **familywise error** (with "family" meaning a group of related statistical tests) or **experimentwise error** (see Vogt, 1999).

Calculating Type II error is much more complex than calculating Type I error, far too complex to explain here. Suffice it to say that there are many factors that influence Type II error, including:

> *(1) the true value of the parameter in question, (2) the significance level* α *we use to evaluate our working hypothesis* H_0 *and whether we use a one-tailed or two-tailed test, (3) the standard deviation* σ *of the sample population, and (4) the size of our sample* n, *where the latter two factors combine to determine the standard error of the sampling distribution of the statistic in question. (Kashigan, 1986, pp. 169–170)*

Type I error is reduced by making significance testing more stringent or more conservative, which is accomplished by lowering the alpha level and adopting a lower significance level. A .01 significance level, for example yields a 1% chance of committing Type I error. You might think, therefore, that researchers should use more stringent significance levels to guard against making Type I error. But doing so would lead them to be more likely of committing Type II error (accepting a null hypothesis that is probably false, a false negative), meaning that researchers believe a difference or relationship is not significant when, in fact, it is. Type I and Type II errors are, thus, inversely related, such that when researchers use a more stringent significance level (such as .01 or .001), the chance of committing Type I error decreases but the chance of committing Type II error increases. Likewise, if researchers use a more liberal significance level (such as .10), the risk of committing Type II error decreases but the chance of committing Type I error increases.

If a tradeoff between Type I and Type II errors is necessary (e.g., there aren't time and resources to conduct a large sample), then researchers tend to try to reduce the risk of making Type I error, be-

lieving that it's better not to reject a null hypothesis that is probably true than to accept a research hypothesis that is false. In the case of medicine, for example, it's better to err on the side of caution, making sure a drug is safe before releasing it on the market. That's exactly why a very stringent significance level is employed in such research.

Statistical Power

A final factor we want to mention that affects the strength of inferences about significant differences and relationships is **statistical power** (also called **power analysis**), "a gauge of the sensitivity of a statistical test; that is, its ability to detect effects of a specific size, given the particular variance and sample size of a study" (Vogt, 1999, p. 277). D. B. Wright (1997) points out that researchers use statistical power in two important ways: (a) to estimate the probability of rejecting a null hypothesis that is, in fact, probably false and, therefore, should be rejected; and (b) to calculate, before conducting research, the number of research participants needed to have a reasonable chance of rejecting the null hypothesis.

Statistical power is equal to 1 minus the probability of committing a Type II error (failing to reject a false null hypothesis). Hence, the minimum statistical power is 0 and the maximum is 1.0. J. Cohen (1988) suggests that a Type II beta of .20 is reasonable; therefore, Sirkin (1995) points out, statistical power should be .80 at a minimum.

Statistical power is a particularly important concept in the case of studying small samples, because some differences and relationships that actually exist are not likely to be large enough in those samples to yield statistically significant results (see Sirkin, 1995). Increasing the statistical power of a statistical significance test to detect such differences or relationships can be accomplished in a number of ways. Many of these procedures increase statistical power and, therefore, decrease Type II error without having an effect on Type I error (see F. Williams, 1992).

Levy and Steelman (1996) point out at least three ways of increasing statistical power. First, statistical power is increased when the most sensitive statistical test is used to analyze the collected data. As will be shown in the next two chapters, particular statistical tests are more or less appropriate for particular types of data (e.g., nominal, ordinal, or interval/ratio). When the most appropriate test is used, power is increased. Second, testing one-tailed hypotheses is more powerful than testing two-tailed hypotheses and research questions; hence, in line with what we said previously, a one-tailed hypothesis should be advanced whenever it is warranted. Third, one common means of increasing statistical power (as well as reducing the chances of committing Type I or Type II error) is to increase the size of the random sample studied, as the chances of rejecting a null hypothesis that is false are increased when more people are studied. This is true because, as we explained before, large random samples better approximate the targeted population than small random samples, and, thus, reduce sampling error. Increasing sample size means researchers can make what is probably the correct decision most of the time (see Jaeger, 1990). However, as Levy and Steelman (1996) caution, it is a mistake to assume that "any increase in sample size provides a corresponding increase in power;... you will often need a substantial increase in sample size to effect the desired increase in power" (p. 220). And, as D. B. Wright (1997) points out, there is another problem to watch for in the case of extremely large samples: "If we collect a million responses, even the most trivial difference will be *statistically significant*. There is always some effect, however minuscule, that is present in the population" (p. 77).

Because of the problems discussed above with finding statistically significant differences between groups and relationships between variables, many statisticians argue that what is most important is the size of an effect. **Effect size (ES)** is "an estimate of the degree to which a phenomenon is present in a population and/or the extent to which the null hypothesis is false" (Vogt, 1993, p. 79). J. Cohen (1988) identified three types of effect sizes—small, medium, and large—and later (1992) showed that

if the minimum statistic power of .80 is established using a .05 significance level (for a two-tailed hypothesis), the necessary sample sizes for small, medium, and large effects are 393, 64, and 26, respectively.

Effect size is a complicated topic and we will not go into any more detail about it, but it is important to differentiate effect size from statistical significance (see J. Cohen, 1988; Rosenthal, 1993). A statistically significant finding only indicates the extent to which the results are due to chance; it does not reference how "small" or "large" a finding may be. As Dickter and Roznowski (1996) explain, "Results that are significant at $p < .05$ are not necessarily 'large'; similarly, researchers should avoid the temptation to proclaim that an effect that is significant at a smaller probability (e.g., $p < .001$) is 'very large'" (p. 211). Researchers, therefore, look not only at the statistical significance of a finding but also at how large is the effect size. Hopefully, if desired, they find both statistically significant findings and large effect sizes.

Just because an effect size is small, however, does not mean that the findings aren't important. Rosenthal (1990) gives the example of a study of the effects of aspirin that was discontinued because questions were raised about the ethics of the standard practice of giving some research participants placebos (pills containing no aspirin), despite the known positive effects of aspirin in preventing heart attacks. The effect size of the correlation between aspirin and prevention of heart attacks was only .03, but this meant that 3 out of every 100 people who previously were given placebos were now being given aspirin—perhaps helping to save their lives.

CONCLUSION

In this chapter, we explored how researchers infer from a relatively small sample to its parent population. Inferring in this way certainly is not limited to research; it's a common feature of everyday life. Mauro (1992) offers the examples of a chef who judges the flavor of a large pot of soup by stirring it up and tasting a tablespoon, or a doctor who draws a small amount of blood to test for a person's cholesterol level. The chef doesn't need to drink the whole pot to judge its flavor, and fortunately, the doctor doesn't have to draw all of the person's blood to test for cholesterol! Both rely on a small sample to make judgments about the larger unit of interest.

Over the course of time, researchers have developed the inferential processes of estimation and significance testing into a science. Now that the basic principles of inferential statistics are clear, we move on to consider the specific statistical procedures used to examine significant differences between groups and relationships between variables.

CHAPTER 13

ANALYZING DIFFERENCES BETWEEN GROUPS

The French have a saying: "Vive la difference." While we don't always celebrate differences (sometimes perceived differences lead to war), we certainly seem fascinated by them. People often see significant cultural differences between themselves and those from other countries. Members of rival political parties believe that there are deep political differences between the parties. And probably the most popular of them all, which we never seem to grow tired of discussing, are the supposed differences between men and women. As Gray (1992) claims in his popular book, *Men Are from Mars, Women Are from Venus,* while men and women inhabit the same Earth, they're so different that they might have well come from different planets.

The search for differences is so ubiquitous that there is, as Canary and Emmers-Sommer (1997) point out, a popular paradox that says there are two types of people in this world: those who categorize people into one of two groups and those who do not. But all joking aside, some differences really are important. Consider for a moment something that probably is very important to you as a male or female college student: income differences between male and female college dropouts and graduates. McCormick and Press (1997) reported average earned income for males and females in 1979 and 1995 (using 1995 dollars). The data showed that in 1979, female high school dropouts earned $17,093, whereas male dropouts earned $29,723. In 1995, female dropouts earned $16,319, whereas male dropouts earned $23,338. Contrasting these incomes with those who graduated from college, in 1979, male college graduates earned $55,751, and by 1995, they earned $61,717.

Meanwhile, female college graduates earned $30,915 in 1979 and $37,924 in 1995.

There are a number of important differences here that deserve consideration. First, the good news is that over the course of a working life, say 45 years, those with a college degree make approximately $1–2 million more than those who drop out, and that's using the 1995 figures, so the difference is bound to be even more over the next 45 years. Finishing college, therefore, seems like a good idea, at least from a financial perspective (just in case you were thinking about dropping out).

The bad news, unfortunately, is that there appears to still be pay discrimination between men and women. For instance, if the incomes of those who completed college and those who dropped out are combined and averaged, the amount women made in 1995 was $27,122, whereas males earned $42,528. So it appears that for all the talk about equality, females still face unfair pay discrimination. But perhaps that wasn't any surprise to you, especially our female readers.

We've just looked at differences between various combinations of the two variables of education and gender. We could have also looked at differences in incomes between 1975 and 1995, and even more complex differences, such as those between the decades for males versus females or for college dropouts versus graduates, or for all of these variables together.

As you see, there are many important differences in those data that could be analyzed. In each case, we would want to ask whether the difference is statistically significant; that is, whether the difference occurs by chance so rarely that the results are probably due to the real difference that exists (as explained in Chapter 12). In this chapter, we focus on statistical procedures used in communication research to analyze such differences. We walk through some of the more common procedures, explaining the reasons why they are used and providing examples along the way. By the end of this chapter, you should be able to return to the discussion of income and calculate whether there is, for instance, a significant statistical difference between the $37,924 that female college graduates made and the $61,717 that male college graduates earned in 1995.

TYPES OF DIFFERENCE ANALYSIS

Difference analysis examines differences between the categories of an independent variable that has been measured using discrete categories, as on a nominal scale (see Chapter 4). For example, difference analysis is used to see whether there are differences between or among such groups of people as males and females; young, middle-aged, and elderly; and freshmen, sophomores, juniors, and seniors. It is also used to see whether there are differences between or among types of texts, such as pre-1960 and post-1960 films; newspapers, magazines, and books; or written, audio, video, and Internet materials. In each case, the independent variable is measured using a nominal scale, and the research question or hypothesis, as explained in Chapter 2, is about the differences between the nominal categories with respect to some other variable.

That other variable, the dependent variable, may be measured using a nominal, ordinal, interval, or ratio scale. Researchers may want to know, for example, whether two groups of people—say relatively new employees hired within the last year versus those with 10 or more years of service—prefer working face-to-face, via the telephone, or over e-mail. If these employees are asked to choose which medium they prefer, that's nominal data. If, however, they are asked to rank order these three ways of working in terms of preference, that produces ordinal data. If employees are asked to rate on a 5-point scale how much they prefer any or

all of these media (e.g., a lot, much, some, a little, not at all), that's interval data. And if employees are asked how many times a day they would prefer to use any or all of these media, that's ratio data.

So while the independent variable in difference analysis is measured using a nominal scale, the dependent variable may be any of the four types (nominal, ordinal, interval, or ratio). The reason that's important to know is that the particular type of procedure used to determine whether the differences between the categories of the nominal independent variable are statistically significant depends on how the *dependent variable* is measured. Figure 13.1 provides an overview of common procedures used by researchers to test for differences between the categories of the independent variable when there is a single dependent variable that is measured using a nominal, ordinal, or interval/ratio scale. (Multiple dependent variables are discussed at the end of the chapter.) We'll walk through and explain each of these procedures.

Nominal Data

The **chi-square (χ^2) test** examines differences between the categories of an independent variable with respect to a dependent variable measured on a nominal scale. There are two types of chi-square tests: a *one-variable chi-square test* examines differences in the distribution of the categories of a single nominal independent or dependent variable; a *two-variable chi-square test* analyzes differences in the distributions of the categories created from two nominal independent variables or a nominal independent and dependent variable. Below we explain each of these tests.

One-Variable Chi-Square Test. A **one-variable chi-square test** (also known as **one-way** or **single-sample chi-square test**) assesses the statistical significance of differences in the distribution of the categories of a single nominal independent or dependent variable. If researchers want to know, for instance, whether people prefer one type of communication strategy versus another (i.e., differences in the categories of this independent variable

FIGURE 13.1   Some common forms of difference analysis

Difference analysis is used to examine the significance of statistical differences between the categories of a nominal independent variable with respect to a dependent variable. The particular statistical procedure used depends on how the dependent variable is measured. The statistical procedures listed below are used when there is one dependent variable.

A. Nominal Dependent Variable
   1. One-variable chi-square test: Examines differences in the distribution of categories for a single nominal independent or dependent variable.
   2. Two-variable chi-square test: Examines differences in the distribution of categories created from two nominal independent variables or a nominal independent and dependent variable.
B. Ordinal Dependent Variable
   1. Median Test: Examines differences between two groups.
C.   Interval/Ratio Dependent Variable
   1. *t* test: Examines differences between two groups.
   2. One-variable *F* test: Examines differences between two or more groups or measurements.
   3. Factorial *F* test: Examines differences between the conditions created from two or more independent variables.

with respect to the nominal dependent variable of preference) or whether a set of texts contains more of one type of theme than another (i.e., differences in this nominal dependent variable of theme type), they would use the one-variable chi-square test.

As an example from communication research, consider Bruess and Pearson's (1997) study of the types of rituals—"stylized, repetitive, communicative enactments that pay homage to a valued object, person, or phenomenon" (p. 25)—performed in marital and adult friendship dyads. Couples were asked to describe in detail any rituals they en-

acted currently or previously in their marriage and in their joint and/or individual friendships. The 671 rituals occurring in marriages were coded inductively (see Chapter 10) by the researcher and one additional coder. Seven major types of rituals emerged: couple-time rituals, idiosyncratic/symbolic rituals, daily routines and tasks, intimacy expressions, communication rituals, patterns/habits and mannerisms, and spiritual rituals.

The researchers further divided some of these categories. The category of idiosyncratic/symbolic rituals, for instance, was divided into four subcategories: (a) favorites (couple's most preferred places to go, things to eat, etc.); (b) private codes (the repeated use of jointly developed words that have unique, private, and special meaning for a couple); (c) play rituals (intimate fun in the form of kidding and bantering); and (d) celebration rituals (e.g., acknowledging birthdays and other special events). Of the 129 total idiosyncratic/symbolic rituals, there were 48 favorites, 41 private codes, 27 play, and 13 celebration rituals.

If the researchers wanted to see whether there was a significant difference in the distribution of these four categories, they could have used a one-variable chi-square test, as we have done in Figure 13.2. This statistical test begins by noting the frequencies of occurrence for each category, called the **observed frequencies.** Researchers then calculate the **expected frequencies** (also called the **theoretical frequencies**) for each category. The expected frequencies are determined in one of two ways.

First, if researchers know in advance what frequencies to expect, those frequencies are used. For instance, if researchers want to know whether the number of people in a city who watch a television show in two particular months is unusually high, the average viewership for that show from a national sample might serve as the expected frequency.

Most of the time, however, researchers don't know what frequencies to expect. So they assume, in accordance with the null hypothesis, that there are no differences between the categories. For example, if there are 100 responses distributed over four categories and there are no differences among

---

FIGURE 13.2   One-variable chi-square test

STEPS:

1. List the *observed frequency* for each category of the variable.
2. Calculate the *expected frequency* for each category of the variable. If the expected frequencies are known, use them; if not, divide the total number of observations (129) by the total number of categories (4) (equals 32.25).
3. For each category, subtract the expected frequency from the observed frequency. Square this figure and then divide this figure by the expected frequency.
4. Add up the resulting figures for each category to get the *chi-square* (χ^2) *calculated value* (equals 22.40)
5. Calculate the *degrees of freedom,* which equal the number of categories (4) minus 1 (equals 3).
6. Look up the *critical value* needed for rejecting the null hypothesis at the .05 significance level with the appropriate degrees of freedom on the chi-square table (see Appendix B) (equals 7.815).
7. If the calculated value meets or exceeds the critical value, the null hypothesis can be rejected and the research hypothesis accepted. If the calculated value does not meet the critical value, the null hypothesis must be accepted.

	Favorites	Private Codes	Play	Celebrations	Total
Observed frequency (O)	48	41	27	13	129
Expected frequency (E)	32.25	32.25	32.25	32.25	129

$$\chi^2 = \Sigma \frac{(O-E)^2}{E}$$

$$= \frac{(48-32.25)^2}{32.25} + \frac{(41-32.25)^2}{32.25} + \frac{(27-32.25)^2}{32.25} + \frac{(13-32.25)^2}{32.25}$$

$$= \frac{(15.75)^2}{32.25} + \frac{(8.75)^2}{32.25} + \frac{(-5.25)^2}{32.25} + \frac{(-19.25)^2}{32.25} = \frac{248.06}{32.25} + \frac{76.56}{32.25} + \frac{27.56}{32.25} + \frac{370.56}{32.25}$$

$$= 7.69 + 2.37 + .85 + 11.49 = 22.40$$

Degrees of Freedom $= (n-1) = (4-1) = 3$

Critical Value $= 7.815$

$p < .001$

---

the categories, how many responses would be in each category? Twenty-five, right?

The same principle holds for the example given in Figure 13.2. If there were no differences among the four categories of favorites, private codes, play, and celebration rituals for the 129 total responses, the expected frequencies are calculated

by dividing 129 by the four categories, which equals 32.25 per category (typically, two decimal points is enough, rounding up or down, as appropriate, from the third decimal).

Now that both the observed and expected frequencies have been noted, the chi-square calculated value is found by subtracting the expected frequency for each category/cell from the observed frequency, squaring this figure, and dividing by the expected frequency. The resulting figures for each category/cell are then added together to obtain the calculated value. To test whether this calculated value is significant, the researcher consults a chi-square table (a distribution of chi-square values; see Appendix B). The researcher reads across to the column corresponding to the appropriate level of significance (.05 typically in the social sciences, as explained in Chapter 12), and then reads down that column to the row representing the appropriate degrees of freedom.

For a one-variable chi-square test, the degrees of freedom are equal to the number of categories minus 1 (in this example, $4 - 1 = 3$). (Note: On this or any other statistical table, if the specific degrees of freedom are not listed, use the next lowest degrees of freedom listed.) The critical value needed to reject the null hypothesis of no difference among the four categories with 3 degrees of freedom at the .05 significance level is 7.815.

The chi-square calculated value of 22.40 exceeds this critical value. In fact, it exceeds the critical value of 12.267 for the .001 significance level. This means that there is about 1 chance in 1000 that the results are due to chance. Thus, the null hypothesis can be rejected and its alternative, the research hypothesis that there is a significant difference between the rituals identified, can be accepted.

Two-Variable Chi-Square Test. A **two-variable chi-square test** (also called **contingency table analysis, crosstabulation, multiple-sample chi-square test, two-way chi-square test**) examines differences in the distributions of the categories created from two nominal independent variables or a nominal independent and dependent variable. (We'll cover the use of three or more variables later in the chapter.) It can be used to compare differences among the categories created from two nominal independent variables with regard to a nominal dependent variable (such as differences among male and female college graduates and college dropouts in whether they use a proactive information-giving strategy when interviewed for a job) or

to compare differences among the categories of a nominal independent variable with regard to the categories of a nominal dependent variable (such as differences between college graduates and college dropouts in whether they use a proactive or reactive information-giving strategy when interviewed for a job). In each case, researchers are interested in assessing differences among the distributions of the categories of two nominal variables of interest.

To illustrate the potential use of a two-variable chi-square test, let's go back to Bruess and Pearson's (1997) study. In addition to knowing what rituals are used, they were also interested in comparing the rituals used in adult dyadic friendships to those used in marital relationships. They coded the rituals reported in adult friendships using the scheme they had developed for coding rituals reported in marriages. However, some of the rituals reported for marriages didn't hold for friendships. For instance, the category of private codes from the idiosyncratic/symbolic rituals described earlier didn't emerge for friendships, so they were left with the other three rituals of favorites, play, and celebration. They then assessed whether there were differences between marriages and friendships with regard to the reported frequencies of the various rituals.

To show how a two-variable chi-square test is computed, we've pulled out Bruess and Pearson's (1997) reported frequencies for the two variables of idiosyncratic/symbolic rituals (divided into favorites, play, and celebration) and type of relationship (marriage and friendship) and analyzed these data using this test (see Figure 13.3). Essentially, a two-variable chi-square test is computed in the same way as a one-variable chi-square test. One difference, however, is in how the expected frequencies are determined. The expected frequency for any particular cell/category in a two-variable chi-square test is found by multiplying the total frequency count for the respective row by the total frequency count for the respective column and dividing that figure by the grand sum. For example, the expected frequency for the first cell (favorites—marriage) is found by multiplying the total for the favorites row (55) by the total for the marriage column (88)

FIGURE 13.3   Two-variable chi-square test

STEPS:

1. List the *observed frequency* for each category created by the two variables.
2. Find the total for each row (equals 55, 43, and 35) and the total for each column (equals 88 and 45). Add the row totals to get the *grand total* (equals 133). (Add the column totals, too, and make sure that this, like the row total, equals the grand total.)
3. Calculate the *expected frequency* for each category by multiplying the appropriate row total by the appropriate column total and then dividing that figure by the grand total.
4. For each category, subtract the expected frequency from the observed frequency. Square this figure and then divide this figure by the expected frequency.

5. Add up the resulting figures for each category to get the *chi- square(χ^2) calculated value* (equals 24.33)
6. Calculate the *degrees of freedom,* which equal the number of rows minus 1 $(r - 1)$ multiplied by the number of columns $(c - 1)$ (equals 2).
7. Look up the *critical value* needed for rejecting the null hypothesis at the .05 significance level with the appropriate degrees of freedom on the chi-square table (see Appendix B) (equals 5.991).
8. If the calculated value meets or exceeds the critical value, the null hypothesis can be rejected and the research hypothesis accepted. If the calculated value does not meet the critical value, the null hypothesis must be accepted.

	Marriage	Friendship	Row Total	
Favorites				
Observed	48	7	55	
Expected	36.39	18.61		
Play				
Observed	27	16	43	
Expected	28.45	14.55		
Celebrations				
Observed	13	22	35	
Expected	23.16	11.84		
Column Total	88	45	133	Grand Total

$$\chi^2 = \Sigma \frac{(O - E)^2}{E}$$

$$= \frac{(48 - 36.39)^2}{36.39} + \frac{(7 - 18.61)^2}{18.61} + \frac{(27 - 28.45)^2}{28.45} + \frac{(16 - 14.55)^2}{14.55} + \frac{(13 - 23.16)^2}{23.16} + \frac{(22 - 11.84)^2}{11.84}$$

$$= \frac{134.79}{36.39} + \frac{134.79}{18.61} + \frac{2.10}{28.45} + \frac{2.10}{14.55} + \frac{103.23}{23.16} + \frac{103.23}{11.84}$$

$$= 3.70 + 7.24 + .07 + .14 + 4.46 + 8.72 = 24.33$$

Degrees of Freedom $= (r - 1)(c - 1) = (3 - 1)(2 - 1) = (2)(1) = 2$

Critical Value $= 5.991$

$p < .001$

(equals 4840) and dividing that figure by the grand total (133). The expected frequency for this first cell, therefore, is 36.39. The calculation then proceeds using the same formula as for a one-variable chi-square test.

The calculated value is then compared to the critical value needed for rejecting the null hypothesis, using the chi-square table (see Appendix B). Degrees of freedom for a two-variable chi-square test are equal to the number of rows minus 1 $(r - 1)$ multiplied by the number of columns minus 1 $(c - 1)$. For this example, the degrees of freedom equal $(3 - 1)$ multiplied by $(2 - 1)$, which equals 2. Using the .05 significance level with 2 degrees of freedom, a critical value of 5.991 is needed to reject the null hypothesis of no difference between the two conditions of marriage and friendships with regard to the reported frequency of these three rituals.

The calculated value of 24.33 exceeds the critical value. Hence, there are significant differences between the types of rituals reported for marriages and friendships. However, a two-variable chi-square test tells researchers only that a significant difference exists; it does not identify the specific significant difference(s) that exists. Researchers must examine the data carefully to detect the specific difference(s). One way the authors of this study did that was by looking at the percentages for each of the three rituals used in marriages and friendships. Using the figures from Figure 13.3, 54.5% of all the idiosyncratic/symbolic rituals in marriages were favorites, 30.7% were play, and 14.8% were celebrations. In contrast, only 15.6% of those rituals in friendships were favorites, whereas 35.6% were play, and 48.9% were celebrations (note that the percentages for friendships add to 100.1% due to rounding up from the second decimal point). So the difference appears to be that while marriages emphasize favorites and downplay celebration rituals, friendships are the exact opposite, emphasizing celebration rituals and downplaying favorites. The amount of play ritual is relatively equal compared to the differences demonstrated in the other categories.

This example assessed differences between the categories of one variable with regard to the categories of another variable for the same group of people interviewed. The two-variable chi-square test is also used to assess differences between the categories of one nominal independent variable that constitute different groups of people and the categories of a nominal dependent variable. Using the example of rituals, one could assess whether males and females differ in their preference for the idiosyncratic/symbolic rituals of favorites, play, and celebrations.

Ordinal Data

Recall that ordinal measurements not only categorize variables but also rank them along a dimension. Most analyses of data acquired from groups measured on an ordinal dependent variable use relationship analysis to see whether two sets of ordinal measurements are related to one another. If there is no significant relationship between the two sets of measurements, they are significantly different. So most of the discussion of analyzing ordinal data is covered in Chapter 14.

Sometimes researchers examine whether there are significant differences between two groups of people with respect to how they rank a particular variable. For example, suppose that a public relations researcher interested in political campaigns wants to know if there is a statistically significant difference between the voters of the United States and Brazil with respect to the perceived effectiveness of a political campaign strategy that involves attacking the opponent. On the basis of available intercultural communication theory and research, the researcher advances the following one-tailed research hypothesis and its corresponding null hypothesis:

H_1: Voters from the United States perceive an opponent attack campaign strategy to be more effective than do voters from Brazil.

H_0: There is no difference between voters from the United States and Brazil in their perceptions of the effectiveness of an opponent attack campaign strategy.

Suppose the researcher chooses 292 respondents, half from Porto Alegre, Brazil, and half from Indianapolis, Indiana, and asks them to assess an opponent attack campaign strategy in terms of its effectiveness by assigning the strategy a score from 0–100. The researcher decides not to treat the scores obtained as interval data, perhaps

because he or she is not confident that respondents used equal intervals to make this judgment or because the data are badly skewed. Instead, the researcher decides to treat these as ordinal measurements and uses an appropriate statistical procedure to analyze the data.

One statistical procedure that can be used to analyze these data is the **median test** (see Figure 13.4). The test itself is quite simple. The raw scores for all respondents are listed together.

FIGURE 13.4   Median test

STEPS:

1. List all the raw scores for both groups (not shown here).
2. Calculate the *grand median,* the point above which half the raw scores fall and below which the other half fall (not shown here).
3. Determine how many of the raw scores for the first group (United States voters in this case) fall above (90) and below (46) the grand median. Determine how many of the raw scores for the second group (Brazilian voters) fall above (56) and below (100) the grand median.

4. Put these *observed frequencies* into a table that has the two groups as the rows and the above grand mean and below grand mean as the columns.
5. Calculate the *expected frequency* for each cell by dividing the total number of research participants (292 in this case) by the total number of categories (4) (equals 73).
6. Perform a two-variable chi-square test as explained in Figure 13.3.

	Above Grand Median	Below Grand Median
United States Voters		
Observed Frequency	90	46
Expected Frequency	73	73
Brazilian Voters		
Observed Frequency	56	100
Expected Frequency	73	73

$$\chi^2 = \Sigma \frac{(O - E)^2}{E}$$

$$= \frac{(90 - 73)^2}{73} + \frac{(46 - 73)^2}{73} + \frac{(56 - 73)^2}{73} + \frac{(100 - 73)^2}{73}$$

$= 3.96 + 9.99 + 3.96 + 9.99 = 27.90$

Degrees of Freedom $= (r - 1)(c - 1) = (2 - 1)(2 - 1) = (1)(1) = 1$

Critical Value $= 3.841$

$p < .001$

The median for this set of scores, the point at which half the scores fall above and half below (see Chapter 11), is then calculated. The total number of scores in each of the two groups that fall above and below the median are determined and these are placed in a table that has the two groups as rows and the ratings above the grand median and below the grand median as the columns. In this example, suppose 90 scores for the respondents from the United States fell above and 46 fell below the grand median, while 56 scores for the respondents from Brazil fell above the grand median and 100 fell below. So this table now looks like the kind of table used in the two-variable chi-square test. In fact, that's the procedure used to see whether there is a significant difference between the ranks for these two groups. The only difference is that the expected frequencies are determined as in a one-variable chi-square test—by dividing the total number of respondents (292 in this example) by the number of categories (4) (equals 73).

As the results show, this difference is statistically significant, which means that the null hypothesis can be rejected. Looking at the data, the number of voters from the United States who fell above the grand median is much higher than the number of voters from Brazil who did so. Hence, in this hypothetical study, as the research hypothesis predicted, voters from the United States perceive an opponent attack campaign strategy to be more effective than do voters from Brazil.

The median test is simply one statistical procedure used to analyze differences between groups with respect to a dependent variable measured on an ordinal scale. There are other statistical procedures that can be used as well. The **Mann-Whitney U-test,** for instance, is often used to analyze differences between two groups, especially when the data are badly skewed (Bruning & Klintz, 1968), while the **Kruskal-Wallis test** is used to analyze differences between three or more groups.

In each of the cases discussed so far, the assumption is that two different (independent) groups are studied, such as voters from the United States and Brazil. Often, however, researchers obtain scores from one group of people, such as in experiments in which a group of research participants are tested before and after an intervention. Hence, the scores are related. In the case of related ordinal scores, the **Wilcoxon signed-rank test** can be used to examine differences between the rank scores. The difference between independent and related scores is very important, as we will see in the discussion of interval/ratio data.

Interval/Ratio Data

When the dependent variable is measured on an interval or ratio scale, the statistical procedures assess differences between group means and variances (see Chapter 11). These tests essentially compare the variance between the groups (the differences between the groups) to the variance within each group (how the scores cluster around the mean of its group). A significant difference tends to exist when there is both a large difference between the groups (high between-group variance) and comparatively little variation among the research participants within each group (low within-group variance). If, for example, researchers want to know whether there is a significant difference in the quality of communication (measured on an interval scale) between efficient and inefficient teams, with efficiency measured on an interval/ratio scale, a significant difference is likely be found if there is a relatively large difference between the scores of the efficient and inefficient teams coupled with relatively similar scores among the members of the efficient teams and relatively similar scores among the members of the inefficient teams.

Two types of difference analysis commonly are employed to assess differences between groups with respect to an interval/ratio dependent variable: the *t* test and the analysis of variance.

t *Test.* Researchers use a *t* test to examine differences between two groups measured on an interval/ratio dependent variable. Only two groups can be studied at a single time; if there are three or more groups, the analysis of variance procedure (discussed below) is used. There are two types of *t* tests, one that compares differences between two independent groups (samples) and one that compares differences between two related measures.

Independent-Sample t *Test.*   An **independent-sample t test** examines differences between two independent (different) groups. These groups may be natural ones or ones created by researchers. Onwumechili (1996) for example, conducted an exploratory study of organizational culture in Nigeria. Part of the study involved assessing differences between males' and females' perceptions of the various dimensions of organizational culture. Males and females completed an instrument that assessed their strength of preference for organizational cultural values (such as teamwork, supervision, and involvement) using a 5-point scale that ranged from 1 (to a very little extent) to 5 (to a very great extent). Given that there were two independent groups (males and females) and interval data for the dependent variable (strength of preference), an independent-sample *t* test was used to examine where there were any statistical differences. The analysis revealed that there were a number of significant differences. For instance, in contrast to Nigerian women, Nigerian men preferred a supervisor who criticized positively.

To illustrate how an independent-sample *t* test is calculated, let's return to the hypothetical example we used before of looking at differences between voters from the United States and Brazil. Suppose a researcher suspects that there are differences between these two groups of voters with regard to their preference for another political campaign strategy—the strategy of promising things. On the basis of intercultural communication theory and research, the researcher advances the following one-tailed hypothesis and corresponding null hypothesis:

H₁: Voters from Brazil perceive a promise campaign strategy to be more effective than voters from the United States.

H₀: There is no difference between voters from Brazil and the United States in their perceptions of the effectiveness of a promise campaign strategy.

This time the researcher asks 20 voters from Brazil and 20 voters from the United States to answer 10 questions about the effectiveness of a promise campaign strategy using a 5-point Likert agree-disagree scale. Each respondent's answers to the 10 questions are added together to get an overall effectiveness score. Because the data were measured using a Likert scale, they are assumed to be interval data (see Chapter 4). An independent-sample *t* test, therefore, can be used to examine whether there are differences between the two groups of voters' ratings of the effectiveness of the promise campaign strategy (see Figure 13.5).

After performing the calculations, the researcher compares the calculated value of .54 with the critical value needed for rejecting the null hypothesis by consulting the *t* table (a distribution of *t* values; see Appendix C). The .05 significance level is used because the researcher advanced a one-tailed research hypothesis (see Chapter 12). Degrees of freedom for an independent-sample *t* test are equal to the number of participants in the first group minus 1 plus the number of participants in the second group minus 1, or the total number of participants in the study minus 2 (40 − 2 = 38 in this example). The critical *t* value of 1.697 needed to reject the null hypothesis (using the *df* = 30 row in the *t* table) is higher than the calculated *t* value. Therefore, the researcher must accept the null hypothesis that there is no difference between voters in Brazil and the United States in the perceived effectiveness of a promise campaign strategy.

Related-Measures t *Test.*   A **related-measures t test** (also called **matched-sample** or **paired t test**) examines differences between two sets of related measurements. It is used most frequently to examine whether there is a difference in two measurements, such as scores on a pretest and posttest, for the same group of research participants.

For example, M. Burgoon, Cohen, Miller, and Montgomery (1978) wanted to know what makes people resist persuasive attempts. They designed an experiment to study, among other things, whether people induced to evaluate sources negatively and those induced to evaluate arguments negatively demonstrate a different level of attitude change after receiving a second persuasive message. Participants were assigned randomly to conditions in which they were told to focus on the negative characteristics of either the speaker or the arguments advanced. Both groups then received two persuasive messages that urged the legalization of heroin in the United States. Related-measures t tests were used to analyze changes in each group's attitudes from the first persuasive message to the second. The results supported the research hypothesis: Participants in the negative source condition demonstrated a more positive attitude toward legalization of heroin after receiving the second message, whereas participants in the negative argument condition demonstrated no significant attitudinal change.

Analysis of Variance.   When researchers study statistical differences between just two sets of scores, the t test is an appropriate procedure. But what happens if three or more groups or related measurements are compared? It certainly is possible to compare three or more groups by conducting t tests on all the possible pairs of groups or related measurements. So, for example, in the case of three groups, (A, B, and C) that would involve conducting three t tests between groups A and B, A and C, and B and C. But what if there were 10 groups or related measurements? That would mean conducting 45 t tests!

The sheer number of t tests that might have to be computed when there are three or more groups or related measurements is certainly a problem, although computers can easily perform such calculations quickly. But a more serious problem with using multiple t tests in this manner is *additive error.* As R. S. Witte and Witte (1997) explain, "Among other complications, the use of multiple t-tests increases the probability of Type I error (rejecting a true null hypothesis) beyond the value specified by the level of significance" (p. 364). Thus, if researchers conduct too many t tests, they will potentially find themselves not using the .05 level of significance to reject the null hypothesis, but some inflated error rate, such as .10, .15, or

---

FIGURE 13.5   An independent-sample t test

STEPS:

1. Calculate the mean for each group (35 for Brazilian voters; 33 for United States voters).
2. For the first group, subtract the mean from each of the scores to get the *deviation scores.* Do the same for the second group.
3. For the first group, square the deviation scores (d^2) and then add them together to get the *sum of squares* (Σd^2) (equals 2100 for Brazilian voters). Do the same for the second group (equals 3020 for United States voters.)
4. Subtract the mean of group 2 from the mean of group 1 (equals 2).
5. Add together the sum of squares for both groups (equals 5120) and divide by the number of participants minus 2 (38) (equals 134.74).
6. Divide the total number of participants (40) by the number of participants in group 1 (20) multiplied by the number of participants in group 2 (20) ($20 \times 20 = 400$) ($40 \div 400 = .1$).

7. Multiply the result of step 5 (134.74) by the result of step 6 (.1) (equals 13.47).
8. Take the square root of step 7 (equals 3.67).
9. Divide the result of step 4 (2) by step 8 (3.67) to get the *calculated* t value (equals .54).
10. Calculate the *degrees of freedom,* which equal the total number of participants (40) minus 2 for independent samples (equals 38).
11. Look up the *critical value* needed for rejecting the null hypothesis at the .05 significance level with the appropriate degrees of freedom on the t table (see Appendix C) (equals 1.697 for a one-tailed hypothesis).
12. If the calculated value meets or exceeds the critical value, the null hypothesis can be rejected and the research hypothesis accepted. If the calculated value does not meet the critical value, the null hypothesis must be accepted.

FIGURE 13.5

BRAZILIAN VOTERS			UNITED STATES VOTERS		
Score	$(X-\bar{X})$ Deviation	$(X-\bar{X})^2$ Squared Deviation	Score	$(X-\bar{X})$ Deviation	$(X-\bar{X})^2$ Squared Deviation
40	5	25	30	−3	9
30	−5	25	40	7	49
20	−15	225	50	17	289
40	5	25	50	17	289
30	−5	25	40	7	49
10	−25	625	30	−3	9
40	5	25	40	7	49
30	−5	25	30	−3	9
50	15	225	40	7	49
20	−15	225	50	17	289
50	15	225	10	−23	529
40	5	25	40	7	49
30	−5	25	30	−3	9
50	15	225	40	7	49
40	5	25	40	7	49
30	−5	25	30	−3	9
40	5	25	30	−3	9
40	5	25	20	−13	169
40	5	25	10	−23	529
30	−5	25	10	−23	529
$M_1 = 35$		$\Sigma d_1^2 = 2100$ (sum of squares)	$M_2 = 33$		$\Sigma d_2^2 = 3020$ (sum of squares)

$$t = \frac{M_1 - M_2}{\sqrt{\frac{\Sigma d_1^2 + \Sigma d_2^2}{(n_1 + n_2 - 2)} \cdot \frac{n_1 + n_2}{n_1 \cdot n_2}}}$$

$$= \frac{35 - 33}{\sqrt{\frac{2100 + 3020}{(20 + 20 - 2)} \cdot \frac{20 + 20}{(20 \cdot 20)}}} = \frac{2}{\sqrt{\left(\frac{5120}{38}\right)\left(\frac{40}{400}\right)}} = \frac{2}{\sqrt{(134.74)(.1)}} = \frac{2}{\sqrt{13.47}} = \frac{2}{3.67}$$

$= .54$

Degrees of Freedom $= (n_1 + n_2 - 2) = (20 + 20 - 2) = 38$

Critical Value $= 1.697$ (one-tailed)

$p > .05$, NS

even .20. So computing lots of *t* tests is not a good way to analyze differences when there are more than two groups or related measurements.

Instead, researchers use **analysis of variance** (**ANOVA,** or ***F*** **test**) to examine differences between two or more groups or related measurements on an interval/ratio dependent variable. There are two types of analysis-of-variance procedures: one-variable and multiple-variable.

One-Variable Analysis of Variance. **One-variable analysis of variance** (also called **one-way analysis of variance**) examines differences between two or more groups on a dependent interval/ratio variable. In addition, sometimes scores are recorded for the same group at different points in time; for example, before exposing research participants to a first treatment (T_1), between the first and second treatment (T_2), and after the second treatment (T_3). This is called **repeated-measures analysis of variance** and it examines whether there are differences between the measurement time periods.

In both cases, a one-variable ANOVA is in some ways similar to a *t* test. In fact, when examining differences between two groups or related measurements, ANOVA is simply an alternative to a *t* test.

Unlike a *t* test, however, ANOVA can be used to examine differences among three or more groups or related measurements without additive error. For example, S. A. Meyers and Avtgis (1997) studied how people's use of nonverbal immediacy (nonverbal behaviors that reduce psychological and physical distance between people) is related to their sociocommunicative style (the way in which people present themselves to others). After completing a series of questionnaires, respondents were divided into four communicator types: competent, noncompetent, submissive, and aggressive. To examine whether there were differences among these four types with regard to interval ratings on 10 nonverbal immediacy behaviors (such as the use of gestures, smiles, and touch), 10 separate one-variable ANOVAs were computed. Of course, this might raise the issue of additive error, just as when multiple *t* tests are performed.

To illustrate a one-variable ANOVA further, let's suppose that a researcher wants to know whether there are differences in the decision-making performance among small groups that conduct their meetings either face-to-face (FTF), via videoconferencing (VC), or by computer mediation (CM). The researcher advances the following one-tailed research hypothesis and its corresponding null hypothesis:

H_1: Groups that work via FTF have higher decision-making performance than groups that work via VC or CM.

H_0: There are no differences in decision-making performance among groups that work via FTF, VC, or CM.

The researcher randomly assigns research participants to small groups (say five people) that works via FTF, VC, or CM on a decision-making task. At the end of the session, each group's decision-making performance is rated by five expert judges (15 judges in all) on 10 questions using a 5-point Likert agree-disagree scale. Each judge's ratings of the 10 items are added together to obtain an overall decision-making performance score.

Because there are three groups and an interval/ratio dependent variable, the researcher uses a one-variable ANOVA to see whether there are differences among the groups. Computing a one-variable ANOVA is somewhat complex, and such calculations (and the other ones discussed in this and the next chapter) are most often performed by computers using various statistical packages (such as SPSS, the Statistical Package for the Social Sciences). However, we computed one so you can see how it is done (see Figure 13.6).

The formula for a one-variable ANOVA is:

$$F \text{ value} = \frac{MS_b}{MS_w}$$

This formula says that an *F* value is a ratio of the variance among groups (MS_b), also called *systematic variance,* to the variance within groups (MS_w), also called *random variance.* Put another way, an ANOVA tells researchers if the difference among the groups (what researchers really want to know and, thus, could be thought of as "good" variance) is sufficiently greater than the differences within the groups (which brings up the possibility of alternative causality and, thus, could be thought of as "bad" variance) to warrant a claim of a statistically significant difference among the groups. In fact, most advanced statistical procedures operate on the basis of this kind of "partitioning" of variance.

The calculated value ANOVA yields is called an F value and is compared to the critical value needed for rejecting the null hypothesis by consulting an F table (a distribution of F values; see Appendix D). Degrees of freedom for an F value are calculated in two ways. Numerator degrees of freedom (between-group variance), the columns of the F table, are equal to the number of groups minus 1 (equals 2 in this example). Denominator degrees of freedom (within-group variance), the rows, are equal to the number of research participants in the first group minus 1 plus the number of participants in the second group minus 1 plus the number of participants in the third group minus 1, and so on (which equals 12 in this example). Since the calculated F value in this particular example does not meet or exceed the critical value, the null hypothesis must be accepted.

Remember that we said earlier that a *repeated-measures ANOVA* is used to assess differences between two or more related measures for a single group of people. In the example we just used, if the researcher had assigned people to a small group that first met via FTF, then met via VC, and then met via CM, and the order of the treatments received is counterbalanced so as to rule out order effects (see Chapter 7), and assessed group decision-making performance after each treatment, a repeated-measures ANOVA would be used to analyze whether there are differences among the three media with respect to group decision-making performance.

Multiple Comparison Tests. ANOVA is what is called an **omnibus test,** an overall statistical test that tells researchers whether there is any signifi-

cant difference(s) that exists among the groups or related measurements. In the case of a nonsignificant F value, this means there are no differences among the groups or related measurements. But in the case of a significant F value, the researcher only knows that *some* difference exists somewhere. The researcher does not know, in the case of three or more groups or measurements, which specific groups or measurements differ (that difference, of course, is obvious when there are only two groups or measurements). In the example of the three media, a significant F value can mean one of four things: (a) all three groups are significantly different from one another; (b) FTF is significantly different from VC, but not from CM; (c) FTF is significantly different from CM, but not from VC; or (d) VC is significantly different from CM, but not from FTF.

To solve this puzzle, researchers use a **multiple comparison test** as a follow-up procedure (that's why it is often called a **follow-up test, post-hoc comparison,** or **a posteriori comparison**). A multiple comparison test pinpoints the specific significant difference(s) that exists.

Many appropriate multiple comparison tests have been created, ranging from those that are more conservative (leaning toward underestimating significant differences, like the **Scheffe Test**), to those that are moderate (a **Tukey Test**), to those that are more liberal (or lenient, such as the **Least Significant Difference (LSD) Test** which is like doing a series of *t* tests without protecting against additive error due to the multiple comparisons; see Norusis, 1993). Some of these multiple comparison tests use some method to adjust the significance level so as to reduce the chance of making a Type I error, that is, rejecting the null hypothesis when it should have been accepted (see Chapter 12). For example, the **Bonferroni technique** divides the significance level a researcher uses by the number of comparisons that are made.

To illustrate the use of a multiple comparison test, consider Pinkleton's (1998) research on the effects of different kinds of print ads on political decision making and participation. A pretest-posttest experiment was conducted in which research

FIGURE 13.6 One-variable ANOVA

STEPS:

1. Calculate the *total sum of squares* as follows:

   A. Calculate the mean for each group. Sum these group means and divide by the number of groups to get the *grand mean* ($\bar{X}_g$ = 31.33).

   B. (1) Subtract the grand mean from each score to get the *deviation scores* ($d_g = X - \bar{X}_g$). (2) Square these deviation scores (d_g^2). (3) Sum these squared deviation scores for each group. (4) Add these sums of group-squared deviations to get the *total sum of squares* ($\Sigma\, d_g^2$ = 873.35).

2. Calculate the *within-group sum of squares* as follows:

   A. Subtract the group mean from each score to get the *deviation-within scores* (d_w). (b) Square these deviations within (d_w^2). (c) Sum these squared deviation scores for each group. (d) Add these group sums of squared deviations to get the *within-group sum of squares* ($\Sigma\, d_w^2$ = 730).

3. Calculate the *between-groups sum of squares* as follows:

   A. (1) Subtract the grand mean from each group mean to get the *deviation-between scores* (d_b). (2) Square these scores (d_b^2). (3) Multiply the d_b^2 scores by the number in each group (n) (equals 5) to get the *between-group deviations-squared score* for each group (nd_b^2). (4) Sum these to get the *between-group sum of squares* ($\Sigma\, nd_b^2$ = 143.35).

4. Complete the Summary Table and Calculate the *F* value as follows:

   A. The total sum of squares, the between-group sum of squares, and the within-group sum of squares,

go into the summary table. (Note that the between-group and within-group sum of squares must add up to the total sum-of-squares. Use this to double-check your results.)

   B. The between-group degrees of freedom equal the number of groups minus 1 (3 − 1 = 2). The within-group degrees of freedom equal the number of research participants in group 1 minus 1 plus the number of research participants in group 2 minus 1 plus the number of research participants in group 3 minus 1 [(5 − 1) + (5 − 1) + (5 − 1) = 12].

   C. Divide the between-group sum of squares by the between-group degrees of freedom to get the *between-group mean squares* (MS) (equals 71.68).

   D. Divide the within-group sum of squares by the within-group degrees of freedom to get the *within-group mean squares* (equals 60.83).

   E. Divide the between-group mean squares (71.68) by the within-group mean squares (60.83) to get the *F ratio* (1.178).

5. Testing for Statistical Significance

   A. Look up the *critical value* needed for rejecting the null hypothesis at the .05 significance level with the appropriate degrees of freedom on the *F* table (see Appendix D; between-group degrees of freedom are the columns, within-group degrees of freedom are the rows) (equals 3.885).

   B. If the calculated value meets or exceeds the critical value, the null hypothesis can be rejected and the research hypothesis accepted. If the calculated value does not meet the critical value, the null hypothesis must be accepted.

	FTF			VC			CM		
	X Score	$(X - \bar{X}_g)$ d_g	$(X - \bar{X}_g)^2$ d_g^2	X Score	$(X - \bar{X}_g)$ d_g	$(X - \bar{X}_g)^2$ d_g^2	X Score	$(X - \bar{X}_g)$ d_g	$(X - \bar{X}_g)^2$ d_g^2
Total	20	−11.33	128.37	35	3.67	13.47	45	13.67	186.87
Sum of	25	−6.33	40.07	35	3.67	13.47	45	13.67	186.87
Squares	30	−1.33	1.77	30	−1.33	1.77	20	−11.33	128.37
	35	3.67	13.47	40	8.67	75.17	25	−6.33	40.07
	25	−6.33	40.07	30	−1.33	1.77	30	−1.33	1.77
	$M = 27$		$\Sigma d_g^2 = 223.75$	$M = 34$		$\Sigma d_g^2 = 105.65$	$M = 33$		$\Sigma d_g^2 = 543.95$

Grand Mean ($\bar{X}_g$) = 31.33
Total sum of squares (Σd_g^2) = 873.35

FIGURE 13.6

Within-group sum of squares

$(X - \bar{X})$	$(X - \bar{X})^2$
d_w	d_w^2
−7	49
−2	4
3	9
8	64
−2	4
	$\Sigma d_w^2 = 130$

$(X - \bar{X})$	$(X - \bar{X})^2$
d_w	d_w^2
1	1
1	1
−4	16
6	36
−4	16
	$\Sigma d_w^2 = 70$

$(X - \bar{X})$	$(X - \bar{X})^2$
d_w	d_w^2
12	144
12	144
−13	169
−8	64
−3	9
	$\Sigma d_w^2 = 530$

Within-group sum of squares $(\Sigma d_w^2) = 730$

Between-group sum of squares

Group mean	27	34	33
Group mean deviation from grand mean (deviation-between score, d_b)	−4.33	2.67	1.67
Squared deviation (d_b^2)	18.75	7.13	2.79
Group $n \times$ squared deviation (between-group deviation squared score, nd_b^2)	93.75	35.65	13.95

Between-group sum of squares $(\Sigma nd_b^2) = 143.35$

SUMMARY TABLE

Source	SS	df	MS	F Ratio	Prob.
Total	873.55				
Between groups	143.35	2	71.68	1.178	NS
Within groups	730.00	12	60.83		

participants first read some information about a fictional candidate running for a state senate seat in Idaho and completed some pretests measuring such things as liking for the candidate. Participants then were assigned to either a control group or one of three treatment conditions that received a comparative print advertisement that ranged from most negative to moderately negative to least negative depending on the number of statements comparing the desired issue position of the sponsoring candidate with the opposite issue position of the targeted candidate. Following this exposure, participants engaged in a thought-listing exercise and after 4 minutes were reexposed to the print ad and completed the posttest scales again. The change in liking score from the pretest to the posttest was computed and these change scores for the two categories of targeted versus sponsoring candidate for the three advertisement conditions of most negative, moderately negative, and least negative, and the control group, were analyzed using ANOVA. The omnibus F test revealed that significant change-score differences existed. Pinkleton then used **Tukey's Honestly Significant Difference (HSD) Test,** one of the more popular multiple comparison tests, to pinpoint the specific differences. In this case, liking for the targeted candidate was significantly lower in the most negative (–1.23 average change score) and moderately negative (–1.33 average change score) conditions than in the control condition (–.028 average change score).

Factorial Analysis of Variance. **Factorial analysis of variance** is used when researchers examine differences between the conditions created by two or more nominal independent variables with regard to a single interval/ratio dependent variable. For example, previous research has shown that communicators using rebuttal analogy (e.g., challenging an opponent's claims using an analogy, a correspondence between otherwise dissimilar things) are perceived more negatively than communicators using a nonanalogy form of the same argument. Whaley, Nicotera, and Samter (1998) pointed out, however, that this research was limited because it had focused largely on European Americans and excluded other important groups, such as African Americans. They believed that research on African American culture and communication suggested that this finding should, in fact, hold for African Americans, especially African American women. So they conducted an experiment in which African American women were exposed to two different types of print media editorial rebuttals (analogy versus nonanalogy). They also wanted to see whether that finding would hold across various topics, so they included four different topics (legalizing marijuana for medical purposes, using condoms as a safer sex practice, whaling, and logging) that had been used in previous research with European Americans by Whaley (1997). Thus, they conducted a 2 (rebuttal type: analogy and nonanalogy) × 4 (message topic) experiment in which African American women were exposed to one of the eight editorials created from these two independent variables (recall this kind of factorial statement from Chapter 7 and the factorial designs discussed

there). The women then rated the message source on a number of variables (e.g., polite/rude) using interval scales. Because there were two nominal independent variables (rebuttal type and message topic) and an interval dependent variable, the researchers used factorial analysis of variance to examine differences among the ratings made in the eight conditions.

Computing a factorial ANOVA is too complicated to explain here. All factorial ANOVAs, however, yield two types of F values. One type refers to the overall effects of each independent variable, which (as discussed in Chapters 2 and 7) are called *main effects.* The second type refers to the unique combination of the independent variables, called *interaction effects.* Hence, when there are two independent variables, a factorial analysis of variance yields three F values: (a) one for the first independent variable (in the example above, rebuttal type), (b) one for the second independent variable (in this example, message topic), and (c) one for the interaction effect between the two independent variables (e.g., rebuttal type × message topic). When there are three independent variables, a factorial analysis of variance yields seven F values, one for: (a) the first independent variable, (b) the second independent variable, (c) the third independent variable, (d) the two-way interaction effect between the first and second independent variables, (e) the two-way interaction effect between the first and third independent variables, (f) the two-way interaction effect between the second and third independent variables, and (g) the three-way interaction effect among all three independent variables.

It is possible that a factorial ANOVA may reveal a significant main effect but no significant interaction effect. In fact, that's what Whaley et al. (1998) found with respect to African American women's ratings of the message source, depending on whether the communicator used an analogy or nonanalogy rebuttal. The main effect for rebuttal type was significant, $F(1, 192) = 5.16$, $p < .02$, with African American women rating communicators using rebuttal analogy as less polite than those using nonanalogy phrasing. However, neither the

FIGURE 13.7   Advanced difference analysis

Researchers use the following advanced difference analyses when they are appropriate. We give the purpose of each and provide an example of how it has been used in communication research.

1. Log-Linear Analysis: **Log-linear analysis** is an advanced chi-square test that analyzes differences among groups with respect to three or more variables. Kemper (1992) examined whether there were differences between two groups of older adults, a young-old group (60–74 years of age) and an old-old group (75–90), in their use of sentence fragments. Participants produced narratives in response to a request to tell a story, and approximately 1000 utterances were coded as complete sentences, continuations, or fragments. Fragments were classified on three nominal variables (types are in quotation marks): (a) locus (whether they occurred within a sentence "subject" or as part of the sentence "predicate"), (b) level (whether they occurred within a "simple" clause or a "complex" embedded clause), and (c) part of speech (whether they preceded a missing "noun," "verb," or "other," such as an adverb). Kemper used log-linear analysis to examine differences between the two groups on these three nominal variables. One of the results showed a three-way interaction effect among age, locus, and part of speech, such that "the old-old groups' sentences fragmented before nouns in the embedded clauses of sentence predicates, whereas the young-old groups' sentences fragmented before verbs in the embedded clauses of sentence subjects" (pp. 452–453). The author attributes the first type of sentence fragments to word-retrieval problems associated with nouns, which appear to increase with age, while the second type may be due to sentence-planning problems associated with embedded verbs, which seem to decrease with age.

2. Multivariate Analysis of Variance: **Multivariate analysis of variance (MANOVA)** is an extension of ANOVA that analyzes differences among groups on multiple, and related, interval/ratio dependent variables. Mongeau, Hale, and Alles (1994) investigated the types of accounts and attributions people give following an incident of sexual infidelity. They conducted a 2 × 2 × 2 × 2 between-group experi-

ment in which they manipulated (a) intent to commit an infidelity (either low, as in going to a bar and meeting a friend by chance, or high, bar-hopping to try and meet the friend), (b) revenge factor (either present, in that the person's boyfriend or girlfriend had been having a sexual relationship with another person and the infidel went to the bar after a heated argument, or absent/no revenge), (c) gender of infidel, and (d) gender of research participant. After reading a scenario, participants were asked to put themselves in the infidel's place and completed a number of attribution measures, including degree of intent, responsibility, blame, and guilt. Because these dependent measures were significantly correlated, MANOVA procedures were initially employed to determine whether the four independent variables influenced these dependent variables. The omnibus (overall) F test indicated that they did, so the researchers followed this up with ANOVA procedures to analyze the effects of the independent variables on each dependent variable.

3. Analysis of Covariance: **Analysis of covariance (ANCOVA)** is an extension of ANOVA that analyzes differences among groups on a dependent interval/ratio variable while controlling for the effects of potentially confounding variables (covariates). di Battista (1997) used this procedure to see whether the type of lie one tells affects deceivers' response to probing. Participants were induced to tell one of two lies (familiar or unfamiliar) to another person (a confederate), who responded by saying that he or she did not believe what was said based either on the deceiver's (a) facial expressiveness or (b) verbal expressiveness. Modifications in the deceiver's facial and vocal indicators during his or her response to the confederate were videorecorded and coded by judges. di Battista suspected that deceivers differed in their arousal and nervousness while telling the lie, so he measured them on these variables. In analyzing the effects of lie types and response types on each dependent variable, ANCOVA was used to control for the effects of arousal as a covariate. One finding showed that people telling unfamiliar lies, when probed, diverted their eye gaze more than those telling familiar lies. Moreover, the arousal covariate did not have a significant effect, which

(continued)

FIGURE 13.7   Continued

increased the confidence in the independent variable effects found for lie type.

4. Multivariate Analysis of Covariance: **Multivariate analysis of covariance (MANCOVA)** is an extension of ANCOVA that analyzes differences among groups on multiple, and related, interval/ratio dependent variables while controlling statistically for the effects of potentially confounding covariates. Gudykunst et al. (1996) were interested in the effects of individual versus collectivist (I-C) cultural differences on individuals' use of a low-context (LC) communication style (explicit and direct messages that contain the meaning) versus a high-context (HC) communication style (implicit and indirect messages in which the meaning is in the person or sociocultural context). People from two individualistic (United States and Australia) and two collectivist (Japan and Korea) cultures were measured for LC and HC communication. But the researchers suspected that how individuals conceive of themselves might make a difference, so they measured participants' "construal of self," the relative extent to which a person views himself or herself as independent (behavior directed by forces inside a person) versus interdependent (behavior contingent on others' behavior). They then used a MANCOVA to analyze the effects of I-C on LC and HC, while controlling for effects of self-construal as a covariate. As expected, both types of self-construals were found to mediate the effects of I-C on LC and HC.

main effect for message topic, $F (3, 192) = .68$, nor the interaction effect between rebuttal type and message topic, $F (3, 192) = .09$, was significant. Hence, the findings showed that the effect found for European Americans did hold for African American women, regardless of the topic to which they were exposed.

Of course, it can also be the case that there is a significant interaction effect, but there are no significant main effects. There can also be significant main and interaction effects together. In cases when both effects are present, it may be inappropriate to interpret the main effects. First, if the main effect is weak, it may be misleading to interpret that effect in the presence of a significant interaction effect. Second, if the interaction effect is *disordinal,* as opposed to *ordinal,* it is often misleading to interpret the main effect. An **ordinal interaction** is an interaction that, when plotted on a graph, the lines representing the two variables do not intersect, whereas a **disordinal interaction** is one in which the lines cross. For these reasons, when main and interaction effects occur together, researchers usually focus their attention on discussing the interaction effects.

ADVANCED DIFFERENCE ANALYSIS

The difference analyses discussed so far are some of the most common techniques employed by researchers. There are, however, many additional, and more complex, significance tests for analyzing differences between groups. These statistical procedures, which examine two or more independent variables and/or two or more dependent variables at the same time, are referred to as **multivariate analysis.**

Although these advanced difference analyses are too complex to examine within the scope of this text, researchers use them quite frequently. For that reason, in Figure 13.7 we explain the purpose of some of these advanced difference analyses and illustrate how each has been used to study communication behavior.

CONCLUSION

Differences are the spice of life; imagine how boring it would be if everyone were the same. To know whether groups of people or texts are significantly different, researchers use the statistical procedures discussed in this chapter. All of these procedures result in a numerical value(s) that indicates how often the observed difference is likely to occur by chance or error. A finding that is very unlikely to occur by chance is assumed to be due to the actual difference that exists.

You should now be able to go back to the example that started this chapter about the income of male and female college graduates and dropouts and be able to calculate some of the differences between some of these variables. Is there, for instance, a statistically significant difference between the $37,924 that female college graduates earned on the average in 1995 and the $61,717 that male college graduates earned?

We have stressed in this chapter the analysis of differences. But this doesn't mean that similarities between people aren't important; in many cases, it's just as important to know the ways in which people are similar as it is to know how they differ. Remember from Chapter 2 that researchers often ask about the relationship that exists between variables, that is, how variables change in similar or dissimilar ways when studied together. In Chapter 14, we examine the nature of relationship analysis and some of the more common statistical techniques for assessing relationships.

ANALYZING RELATIONSHIPS
BETWEEN VARIABLES

Think for a moment about all the people with whom you do and do not have what you would call a relationship. At one end of the continuum are people with whom you are not associated in any way (other than the fact that you're both human beings); what they do doesn't relate to what you do in any way, and vice versa. At the other end are those with with whom you have a very strong relationship—your family, partner, and close friends—and whose actions relate to what you do, and vice versa. Of course, there are all those relationships in between, ranging from relatively distant to relatively close associations.

In an analogous way, we can talk about relationships between variables. Some variables, in a sense, don't even know one another; they have no relationship of which to speak. Other variables are intimately related because how each of the variables behaves is very much related to how the other variable behaves. And, again, there are all those relationships in between.

This chapter examines how two or more variables may be related. We start by considering the relationship between two variables (**bivariate association**) and then expand to consider more variables. We examine the types of possible relationships between variables, explain how relationships are analyzed statistically, show how relationship analysis is used to make predictions, and introduce some advanced statistical relationship analyses used in communication research.

TYPES OF RELATIONSHIPS

Two variables can be associated in one of three ways: They can be *unrelated, linear,* or *nonlinear.*

Take the example (one that might be very important to college students) of whether the time spent watching television is related to academic performance. Let's operationally define time spent watching television in terms of the average number of hours per day over the course of a given semester, and academic performance as grade point average (GPA) for that semester. If we plot each person's scores on both variables on a graph, called a **scatter plot** (**scattergram** or **scatter diagram**), we get a visual image of the way in which those variables may or may not be related (see Figure 14.1).

Unrelated variables have no systematic relationship (Figure 14.1a). **Linear relationships** between variables can generally be represented and explained by a straight line on a scatter plot (Figures 14.1b and 14.1c). **Nonlinear relationships** between variables can be represented and explained by a line on a scatter plot that is not straight, but curved in some way (Figures 14.1d and 14.1e). Let's examine each of these in turn.

Unrelated Variables

Two variables are unrelated when they vary independently of each other (see Figure 14.1a). This means that there is no systematic relationship between the variables. Changes in one variable simply are not related to the changes in the other variable, and vice versa. In our example, this would mean that the number of hours students spend watching television is not related to their GPA. When two variables are unrelated, knowing how one changes does not give researchers any understanding of how the other variable changes.

FIGURE 14.1   Types of relationships between variables

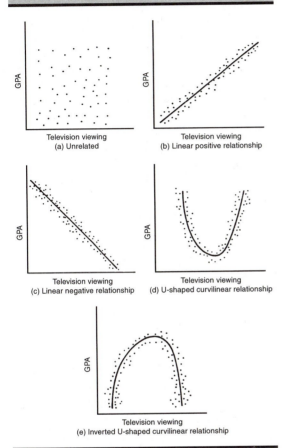

Television viewing
(a) Unrelated

Television viewing
(b) Linear positive relationship

Television viewing
(c) Linear negative relationship

Television viewing
(d) U-shaped curvilinear relationship

Television viewing
(e) Inverted U-shaped curvilinear relationship

For example, most communication scholars (and students) probably think job candidates' communication competence is related to their communication performance during a job selection interview and their tendency to be hired. Spano and Zimmerman (1995) actually tested whether this was the case. They first measured college students' interpersonal communication competence (a global measure of competence), communication flexibility (the ability to create and adapt messages to interaction situations), and rhetorical sensitivity (the ability to adapt to the needs of others in achieving communication goals, such as avoiding rigid communication patterns). Stu-

dents then engaged in a simulated interview with a trained interviewer for a real job in a real organization that the student had identified. To make the interview situation realistic, students were required to supply a Job Description Form, resume, and cover letter before the interview began. After the interview, students were evaluated by the interviewer with respect to their communication performance (e.g., verbal behaviors, such as clarity and conciseness of answers) and the likelihood that the interviewer would hire the applicant. The results showed no relationship between any of three communication competence measures and interviewers' ratings of applicants' communication performance. And there was also no relationship between each of those measures and the likelihood of hiring applicants. Of course, a single study doesn't prove anything (which might give you some comfort if you are hoping your communication skills will help you get a job), but the finding of no relationships raises interesting questions. The authors suggest that perhaps these kinds of global communication competence traits are less important than situation-specific communication skills, such as those that you might learn in an interviewing class. That's certainly worth exploring in future research.

Linear Relationships between Variables

Linear relationships between two variables generally follow a consistent pattern that, when plotted on a graph, forms the general shape of a straight line. There are two types of linear relationships: positive and negative.

As discussed in Chapter 2, a *positive relationship* means that two variables move, or change, in the *same* direction (see Figure 14.1b). If one variable goes up, the other tends to also; if it goes down, the other does too. A positive relationship tells researchers that the type of change in one variable is associated with a similar type of change in another variable. In our example, this would mean that the number of hours of television watched would be related to GPA, such that the more hours spent watching television the higher the GPA.

Do not, however, immediately attribute causation to this relationship. A positive relationship does not necessarily mean that *because* students watch more television their GPAs are higher; it merely means that the two scores are related. There could be a causal relationship; maybe these students watched more educational programs that helped them in their courses (e.g., a program on continental drift helping in a geography course that covered that material). But a positive (or negative) relationship does not mean per se that there is a causal relationship between the variables. We'll return to the issue of causation later in this chapter; for now, keep in mind that we are talking about associations between variables, not necessarily causal connections.

A *negative relationship* means that two variables move, or change, in *opposite* directions, such that if one variable goes up, the other goes down. (see Figure 14.1c). A negative relationship, thus, means that the type of change in one variable is associated with the opposite type of change in another variable. In our example, as might be suspected, a negative relationship would mean that increased number of hours of television watching are associated with lower GPA.

To illustrate positive and negative relationships, even within the context of television viewing, consider the study by Kapoor, Kang, Kim, and Kim (1994) about the relationship between television viewing behavior and perceptions of social reality. As part of their study, Korean viewers were measured with regard to how many hours of television they watched on weekdays and weekends with respect to 11 program types: dramas, action/adventure, imported (United States) programs, movies on television, variety shows, situation comedies, cartoons, game shows, cultural/educational programs, sports, and news. Viewers' beliefs about social reality were also measured, such as their belief in a "mean world." The results showed a positive relationship between viewers' mean world score and the extent of their watching of television dramas, variety shows, sitcoms, and cartoons. By contrast, the amount of movies and sports watched was negatively related to mean world score. Thus, different types of television programs watched

were related in positive and negative ways to people's perceptions of social reality.

Finally, before we leave this discussion of linear relationships, using the example of television viewing and academic performance, we should point out a study by G. B. Armstrong, Biorsky, and Mares (1991) that investigated the effect of background television on cognitive performance. As part of their study, they reported relationships between television viewing variables and academic achievement measures. Overall amount of television viewing was negatively related to scores on the English placement test, college GPA, math GPA, communication GPA, social science GPA, and natural science GPA. However, when broken down further into the time of day that television was watched, these relationships tended to hold for those who watched morning, afternoon, and late night television, but none of the variables were related to watching television during the evening. So if you're going to watch television, it's probably best to do so in the evening, after, of course, your school work is done.

Nonlinear Relationships between Variables

Nonlinear relationships between variables, like linear relationships, follow a pattern, but that pattern is not simple and direct enough to be represented by a straight line. Instead, there is at least one curve, or "hump," in the data (see Figures 14.1d and 14.1e). Take the relationship between amount of talk and having friends. People who talk very little may have few friends, and people who talk a moderate amount probably have more friends. So the two variables seem positively related. But people who talk a lot aren't likely to have even more friends—probably fewer. So the relationship isn't consistently positive. It's more complex and probably best represented by a curved, rather than straight, line.

A **curvilinear relationship** is described by a polynomial equation, which simply means that it takes at least one curve, or turn, to represent the data on a scatter plot. The curvilinear relationships depicted in Figures 14.1d and 14.1e are called **quadratic relationships** because they only have one curve in them, while cubic, quartic, and quintic relationships describe even more complex relationships between variables that need more than one curve to represent them. These more complex relationships are beyond the scope of this book, but it is good to remember that many important relationships between variables in real life cannot be described by a straight line.

As you can see, if there was a quadratic relationship between television watching and GPA, the two variables would be related in one way up to a certain point and then the relationship would reverse. A **U-shaped curvilinear relationship** means that two variables are related negatively until a certain point and then are related positively (see Figure 14.1d). Thus, for some reason, it might be the case that those who watch either only a few hours or a great many hours of television have a high GPA, whereas those who watch a moderate amount have a low GPA.

An **inverted U-shaped curvilinear relationship** means that two variables are related positively to a certain point and then are related negatively (see Figure 14.1e). Thus, a moderate amount of television watching might be associated with a high GPA, whereas a low or high amount of watching might be associated with a low GPA. As a real-life communication example, J. Comstock, Rowell, and Bowers (1995) found an inverted U-shaped curvilinear relationship between teachers' use of nonverbal immediacy (nonverbal behaviors that enhance closeness to and interactions with others) and a variety of student outcomes (such as short-term retention and affect toward the teacher and course material). That is, the outcomes were significantly lower when the teacher was excessively high or low on nonverbal immediacy in comparison to when the teacher was moderately high. As the authors conclude, "In other words, it seems that where teacher nonverbal immediacy is concerned, students can get either too little or too much of a good thing" (p. 262).

CORRELATIONS

Researchers use statistical procedures to assess the relationship between two or more variables. A sta-

tistical relationship between variables is referred to as a **correlation;** a correlation between two variables is sometimes called a **simple correlation** (this term also applies to a correlation for a linear, as opposed to nonlinear, relationship between variables). To determine the statistical correlation between two variables, researchers calculate two things: (a) a *correlation coefficient,* which indicates the type and strength of the relationship between the variables; and (b) a *coefficient of determination,* which indicates how much one variable can be explained by the other variable. (The term **measure of association** is sometimes used to refer to any statistic that expresses the degree of relationship between variables. The term **correlation ratio,** symbolized and commonly known as **eta,** is sometimes used to refer to a correlation between variables that have a curvilinear relationship.)

Correlation Coefficients

A **correlation coefficient** is a numerical summary of the type and strength of a relationship between variables. A correlation coefficient takes the form $r_{ab} = +/-x$, where r stands for the correlation coefficient, a and b represent the two variables being correlated, the plus or minus sign indicates the direction of the relationship between the variables (positive and negative, respectively), and x stands for some numerical value.

A correlation coefficient, thus, has two separate parts. The first part is the sign, which indicates the *direction* of the relationship between the variables of interest. A plus sign (+) means a positive relationship; a negative sign (−) means a negative relationship. It should be pointed out, however, that the plus sign is typically left off when reporting correlation coefficients; if a correlation coefficient doesn't have a minus sign in front of it, you can assume that it is a positive relationship.

The second part is a numerical value that indicates the *strength* of the relationship between the variables. This number is expressed as a decimal value that ranges from +1.00 to −1.00. A correlation coefficient of +1.00 describes a perfect positive relationship in which consistent increases in the units of the measurement scale of one variable are associated with a consistent increase in the number of units of the measurement scale for the other variable. A correlation coefficient of −1.00 describes a perfect negative relationship in which consistent increases in the units of the measurement scale of one variable are associated with a consistent decrease in the number of units of the measurement scale for the other variable. A correlation coefficient of 0.00 means two variables are unrelated, at least in a linear manner (the variables may, in fact, be related in a nonlinear way). Using our example of hours of television watched and grade point average, Figure 14.2 shows some examples of perfect positive relationships of +1.00 and perfect negative relationships of −1.00, as well as an example of no relationship of 0.00.

FIGURE 14.2   Examples of perfect positive and negative relationships and no relationship

A. Perfect Positive Relationships (+1.00)

TV Hours	GPA	TV Hours	GPA	TV Hours	GPA
1	0.00	1	0.50	1	0.00
2	1.00	2	1.00	2	0.75
3	2.00	3	1.50	3	1.50
4	3.00	4	2.00	4	2.25
5	4.00	5	2.50	5	3.00

B. Perfect Negative Relationships (−1.00)

TV Hours	GPA	TV Hours	GPA	TV Hours	GPA
1	4.00	1	2.50	1	3.00
2	3.00	2	2.00	2	2.25
3	2.00	3	1.50	3	1.50
4	1.00	4	1.00	4	0.75
5	0.00	5	0.50	5	0.00

C. No relationship (0.00)

TV Hours	GPA
1	2.00
2	5.00
3	3.00
4	1.00
5	4.00

Interpreting Correlation Coefficients.   Variables are rarely related perfectly to one another, so researchers need to assess the significance of a correlation coefficient. Studies assessing a relationship between two variables begin with a null hypothesis of no relationship and pose a research hypothesis, predicting a positive or negative relationship, or a research question, asking whether there is a positive or negative relationship (see Chapter 12).

Once data are collected and a correlation coefficient has been computed, researchers test whether that correlation coefficient is statistically significant, by comparing it to the critical value listed in the appropriate table for the statistical test performed to see how likely it is that the correlation coefficient occurs by chance. If the calculated value equals or exceeds the critical value for the .05 significance level used in communication research, researchers reject the null hypothesis of no relationship and accept its alternative, the research hypothesis. Just because a relationship between two variables is significant statistically, however, does not mean that it is an *important* relationship. Researchers have to be careful not to report significant but trivial results. Interpreting the importance or strength of a correlation coefficient depends on many things, including the purpose and use of the research and sample size. There are no universal guidelines for interpreting the strength of a statistically significant correlation coefficient, but Guilford (1956) proposes that when the sample size is fairly large, the following criteria can be used:

<.20	Slight, almost negligible relationship
.20–.40	Low correlation, definite but small relationship
.40–.70	Moderate correlation, substantial relationship
.70–.90	High correlation, marked relationship
>.90	Very high correlation, very dependable relationship (p. 145)

Calculating Correlation Coefficients.   Researchers use a variety of statistical procedures to calculate correlation coefficients between two variables. Which statistical procedure is used depends on how the two variables are measured. Here, we explain three procedures that are appropriate when both variables are measured at the ratio/interval, ordinal, and nominal level.

Relationships between Ratio/Interval Variables. The most popular correlational procedure is probably the **Pearson product moment correlation.** This procedure calculates a correlation coefficient for two variables that are measured on a ratio or interval scale (called the **Pearson's correlation coefficient, product-moment correlation,** or, simply, **Pearson's r** or **Pearson** *r*).

For example, we probably have all experienced some form of jealousy in our romantic relationships. There are, of course, many ways to express jealousy, from yelling and shouting to giving our partner the silent treatment. P. A. Andersen et al. (1995) were interested in how different types of communication responses to episodes of jealousy are associated with relational satisfaction. On the basis of previous research, they divided responses to jealousy into six categories: (1) integrative communication (expression of feelings without placing blame on one's partner); (2) distributive communication (negatively valanced responses, such as making accusations); (3) active distancing (such as the silent treatment); (4) expression of negative affect (nonverbally displaying such emotions as anger and frustration); (5) avoidance/denial (pretending not to be jealous); and (6) violent communication threats (such as threatening to physically hurt one's partner). Which do you tend to use when feeling jealous?

P. A. Andersen et al. (1995) predicted that the use of integrative communication to cope with romantic jealousy would be positively associated with relational satisfaction, whereas the other types of communication would be negatively associated with satisfaction. They asked 346 individuals currently involved in dating or marital relationships to complete a questionnaire that used a 5-point scale (ranging from 1 = Never to 5 = Always) to measure their typical responses to jealousy and another interval scale to measure relational satisfaction.

Because both variables (communication responses and relational satisfaction) were mea-

sured using interval scales, Andersen et al. analyzed the data via the Pearson product moment correlation procedure. They found that integrative communication about jealousy was not, in fact, significantly associated with relational satisfaction (the correlation coefficient was .05). However, all five of the other communication responses were negatively associated with relational satisfaction (with correlations ranging from −.13 to −.44). Thus, while integrative communication may not help in the case of romantic jealously, some other types of responses may well hurt. And keep in mind that this was from the perspective of the person expressing jealousy; imagine how satisfied the other person is when threatened or given the silent treatment!

Figure 14.3 shows an example of how to calculate a Pearson product moment correlation coefficient. We've used the jealousy response of integrative communication and satisfaction (measured on a 5-point scale from 1 = Very Low to 5 = Very High), but we've made up the data just to illustrate how the coefficient is calculated. In our hypothetical example, the positive correlation of +.64 came out to be significant (using a two-tailed test; degrees of freedom equal the number of participants minus 2, which equals 13 in this case). While such a relationship wasn't found by Anderson et al., one can always hope that integrative communication responses to jealousy are, in fact, positively related to relational satisfaction.

The Pearson product moment correlation is the most appropriate and popular correlational procedure when both variables are measured using ratio/interval scales. There are times, however, when researchers measure one variable using a ratio/interval scale and the other variable using a nominal scale. In such cases, they use the **point biserial correlation** (r_{pb}) to analyze the relationship between the two variables. J. Comstock (1994), for example, was interested in patterns of parent-adolescent conflict (mother-daughter, mother-son, father-daughter, and father-son) across early, middle, and late adolescents. Adolescents were given a typical parent-adolescent conflict situation (such as a conflict over how much the adolescent helped

FIGURE 14.3   Pearson product moment correlation

STEPS:

1. Calculate the mean for each set of scores (3 for integrative response; 4 for satisfaction).
2. For each set of scores, subtract the mean from the score to get the *deviation scores* (columns x and y).
3. Square the deviation scores for column x and add these squared deviation scores to get the sum of the x^2 scores (Σx^2) (equals 26). Square the deviation scores for column y and add these squared scores to get the sum of the y^2 scores (Σy^2) (equals 32).
4. Multiply each score in column x by its respective score in column y, and add these scores together to get the sum of the xy scores (Σxy) (equals 18).
5. Multiply the Σx^2 score (26) by the Σy^2 score (32) (equals 832), and take the square root of this value (equals 28.84).

6. Divide the Σxy score (18) by the result of step 5 (28.84) to get the Pearson product moment correlation (equals +.62).
7. Look up the *critical value* needed for rejecting the null hypothesis at the .05 significance level with the appropriate degrees of freedom ($n - 2$) (equals 13) on the Pearson r table (see Appendix E) (equals .514 for a two-tailed test).
8. If the calculated value (the Pearson r) meets or exceeds the critical value, the null hypothesis can be rejected and the research hypothesis accepted. If the calculated value does not meet the critical value, the null hypothesis must be accepted.

Research Participant	Integrative Response	Satisfaction	Deviation Scores		Squared Deviation Scores		Deviations Multiplied
			x	y	x^2	y^2	xy
1	3	3	0	−1	0	1	0
2	2	5	−1	1	1	1	−1
3	3	5	0	1	0	1	0
4	1	1	−2	−3	4	9	6
5	1	2	−2	−2	4	4	4
6	2	5	−1	1	1	1	−1
7	4	5	1	1	1	1	1
8	5	5	2	1	4	1	2
9	5	5	2	1	4	1	2
10	2	1	−1	−3	1	9	3
11	4	5	1	1	1	1	1
12	3	4	0	0	0	0	0
13	5	5	2	1	4	1	2
14	2	5	−1	1	1	1	−1
15	3	4	0	0	0	0	0
	$M = 3$	$M = 4$			$\Sigma x^2 = 26$	$\Sigma y^2 = 32$	$\Sigma xy = 18$

$$r = \frac{\Sigma xy}{\sqrt{\Sigma x^2 \cdot \Sigma y^2}}$$

$$= \frac{18}{\sqrt{26 \times 32}} = \frac{18}{\sqrt{832}} = \frac{18}{28.84} = +.62$$

Degrees of Freedom = $(n - 2) = 13$

Critical Value = .514 (two-tailed)

$p < .02$

around the house) and asked to script how this type of conflict is played out between them and the parent with whom they have the most conflict. The scripts were coded into conflict strategies and each parent's and adolescent's scripted behavior was classified as cooperative, competitive, or avoidance. To examine the relationships between each of the four parent-adolescent relationship categories for early, middle, and late adolescents (a nominal variable) with the number of cooperative, competitive, or avoidance conflicts experienced (a ratio/interval variable), Comstock used the point biserial correlation procedure. Thus, for example, as predicted, cooperative mother-daughter conflict patterns characterized middle and late adolescents (.50 and .44 correlations, respectively, which were both statistically significant), but not early adolescents (a .28 correlation, which was not statistically significant).

Relationships between Ordinal Variables.   When two variables are measured on an ordinal (or rank-order) scale, researchers can calculate the correlation coefficient using the **Spearman correlation coefficient (rho).** Researchers might use this procedure to compare two sets of ranked scores for the same group of research participants, or the ranked scores of various items by two different groups might be compared.

Sugimoto (1997), for example, compared United States and Japanese styles of apologizing. Two hundred U.S. students from the University of Illinois at Urbana-Champaign and 181 Japanese students at Tokai University were asked to complete a questionnaire that presented several interpersonal situations—such as breaking a friend's Sony Walkman and not being ready for a movie previously planned for—that had been selected from actual instances reported as requiring apology during pretests conducted in the two countries. One of the questions asked participants to write exactly what the offender would say or do to the victim. Every segment—the smallest meaningful unit of utterance—of the 144 messages generated was coded, in its original language, into 11 categories of accounts.

As part of the data analysis, Sugimoto listed each category of strategy in terms of its frequency of occurrence for United States and Japanese students. To analyze the data, he converted the frequencies into rankings (as we do in Figure 14.4). As you can see, the relative rankings appear to be quite similar, with the first four most commonly used categories exactly the same. To test whether there was a significant relationship between the ranked categories, Sugimoto used the Spearman correlation coefficient (see Figure 14.4). The correlation between the reported ranks was .90, a statistically significant correlation. (Note: p is the symbol for rho; r_s is frequently used to avoid confusion with procedures involving population correlations.) Thus, these results suggest that similar basic norms of apology exist in these two cultures.

In some cases, **Kendall's correlation (tau),** which actually refers to three measures of association, is used in place of Spearman correlation coefficient. This procedure is typically used when a researcher has a pair of ranks for each of several individuals (such as two judges rank ordering each of eight speakers), and is also considered better than the Spearman correlation coefficient when there are a number of tied ranks (Vogt, 1999). Like the Spearman correlation coefficient, Kendall's correlation shows the degree of relationship between two ordinal variables.

Relationships between Nominal Variables.   Finally, researchers can assess the relationship between two variables that are both measured on a nominal scale. For example, a researcher might want to assess the relationship between different types of organizational members (e.g., managers versus line workers) and the types of strategies they used to acquire information.

The procedures for computing a correlation coefficient between two nominal variables are based on the chi-square value associated with the two-variable chi-square test discussed in Chapter 13. For instance, a procedure used commonly for this purpose, especially when there are different sample sizes and different numbers of cells (see Vogt,

FIGURE 14.4   Spearman correlation coefficient (*rho*)

STEPS:

1. Take the difference between the two rankings for each item/research participant.
2. Square each difference score and add these scores to get the total squared difference score (ΣD^2) (equals 22).
3. Multiply the total squared difference score (22) by 6 (equals 132).
4. Multiply the number of items/research participants (11) by itself and subtract 1 (equals 120), and then multiply this figure by the number of items/research participants (equals 1320).
5. Divide step 3 (132) by step 2 (1320) (equals .10).
6. Subtract the figure from Step 5 (.10) from 1.00 to get the Spearman correlation coefficient (equals .90).

7. Look up the *critical value* needed for rejecting the null hypothesis at the .05 significance level with the appropriate degrees of freedom (number of pairs − 2) (equals 9) on the Spearman *rho* table (see Appendix E) (equals .683 for a two-tailed test).
8. If the calculated value (the Spearman correlation coefficient) meets or exceeds the critical value, the null hypothesis can be rejected and the research hypothesis accepted. If the calculated value does not meet the critical value, the null hypothesis must be accepted.

Type of Apology	U.S. Ranking	Japanese Ranking	Difference	Squared Difference
Statement of remorse	1	1	0	0
Accounts	2	2	0	0
Descriptions of damage	3	3	0	0
Reparation	4	4	0	0
Compensation	5	6	−1	1
Explicit statement of responsibility	6	8	−2	4
Request for forgiveness	7	5	2	4
Gratitude	8	10	−2	4
Self-castigation	9	9	0	0
Promise not to repeat the same offense	10	7	3	9
Contextualization	11	11	0	0
				$\Sigma D^2 = 22$

$$r_s = 1 - \frac{6\Sigma D^2}{N(N^2 - 1)}$$

$$= 1 - \frac{6(22)}{11(11^2 - 1)} = 1 - \frac{132}{1320} = 1 - .10 = .90$$

Degrees of Freedom = $(N - 2) = 9$

Critical Value = .683 (two-tailed)

$p < .01$

1999), is **Cramer's V;** the resulting correlation coefficient ranges from 0 to 1. The formula for Cramer's V is:

$$V = \sqrt{\frac{\chi^2}{N \times S}}$$

where N is the grand sum of observed frequencies associated with the contingency table and S is the smaller of $(R - 1)$ and $(C - 1)$, the rows and columns, respectively, of the chi-square table.

Correlation Matrices.   Researchers often study the relationships among numerous variables. In such cases, they compute correlation coefficients for all the possible pairs of variables. They often report these paired correlation coefficients by depicting them visually on a **correlation matrix** that lists all the relevant variables both across the top and down the left side of a matrix. Where the respective rows and columns meet, researchers indicate the **bivariate correlation coefficient** for those two variables and whether it is significant, typically by using stars (such as one star for significance at the .05 level, two stars for significance at the .01 level) or in a note that accompanies the matrix. The diagonal line from the top left to the bottom right of the matrix is usually left blank, since the relationship between a variable and itself is +1.00. The bottom left half or top right half of the matrix is also typically left blank because it simply would be a reflection of the other half.

Barbato and Perse (1992), for example, contrasted the contribution of chronological age and contextual age (categorized into physical health, life satisfaction, economic security, mobility, social activity, and interpersonal interaction) with regard to elders' motives for communicating interpersonally with others. They asked adults over 55 years of age to complete questionnaires that measured their contextual and chronological age and a number of motives they had for communicating interpersonally with others, such as pleasure, comfort, affection, and control. As part of the analysis, the researchers reported the correlation coefficients for each of the possible pairs of variables using a correlation matrix (see Figure 14.5). The correlation matrix shows clearly the degree to which the variables are correlated and the note explains which correlations are significant at the .05, .01, and .001 (using a two-tailed test, because these relationships were not part of their hypotheses per se). Note, for instance, that life satisfaction is positively correlated with the motives of pleasure and affection: the greater the elders' life satisfaction, the greater their interpersonal communication motives of pleasure and affection. The researchers also included the demographic variables of age, gender, household size, and education at the bottom of the correlation matrix (these are covariates, see Chapter 7, so the researchers weren't interested per se in the relationships among them and, therefore, didn't include them on the top half of the matrix).

Causation and Correlation.   As mentioned earlier, a correlation coefficient only indicates whether two variables are related and if so, how much. It does not tell researchers per se how changes in one variable *produce* changes in another. Causation, thus, cannot necessarily be inferred from a correlation coefficient. Correlation, of course, is one of the three criteria used to determine causation (see Chapter 7), but by itself, a correlation is extremely susceptible to alternate causality arguments—multiple explanations for why the observed relationship occurred. For example, two variables may vary together not because one causes the other but because a third variable causes both of them to vary (see Chapter 7).

The following Chinese fable illustrates that, even in ancient times, people recognized the danger of confusing correlation with causation.

While hunting for prey, a tiger caught a fox. The fox thought quickly and said, "You can't eat me! The Emperor of Heaven appointed me king of the beasts. If you eat me, you'll be disobeying his orders. If you don't believe me, follow me. You'll soon see whether the other animals run away at the sight of me or not."

Agreeing to this, the tiger accompanied him. Every beast who saw them coming dashed away. Not realizing they were afraid of him, the tiger believed they were afraid of the fox.

FIGURE 14.5   Correlation matrix

	Pleasure	Comfort	Affection	Control	Physical Health	Life Satisfaction	Economic Security	Mobility	Social Activity	Interpersonal Interaction
Comfort	.10									
Affection	.12	.03								
Control	.00	.04	−.02							
Physical health	.10	−.31	.07	−.21						
Life satisfaction	.25	−.11	.31	−.01	.43					
Economic security	.18	−.06	.09	.04	.32	.42				
Mobility	.05	−.37	.04	−.15	.51	.37	.29			
Social activity	.19	.03	.20	.11	.36	.47	.37	.40		
Interpersonal interaction	.17	−.04	.32	−.10	.38	.61	.28	.27	.48	
Age	.07	.19	−.11	.01	−.21	−.10	.02	−.37	−.20	−.18
Gender	.13	.25	.13	−.24	.02	−.07	−.09	−.26	−.05	.09
Household size	−.06	−.01	−.01	−.04	.08	.08	.01	.07	.00	.15
Education	.00	−.23	.02	.08	.19	.12	.24	.40	.23	.10

Source: Carole A. Barbato and Elizabeth M. Perse, "Interpersonal Communication Motives and the Life Position of Elders," *Communication Research, 19*(4), p. 523, copyright © 1992 by Sage Publications, Inc. Used by Permission of Sage Publications, Inc.

NOTE: $r = .11$, $p < .05$; $r = .14$, $p < .01$; $r = .20$, $p < .001$ (two-tailed).

Researchers must, therefore, refrain from immediately inferring causation from correlation. For example, suppose that researchers found a very high positive correlation between increased advertising and increased sales of a particular product. Would it be safe to assume that increasing advertising *causes* the increased sales? Maybe, maybe not. What if the increased advertising and the increased sales were both due to a once-a-year clearance sale during which prices were cut in half and two-thirds of the year's advertising budget was spent to promote that sale?

Although a correlation coefficient does not indicate whether one variable causes a change in another variable, researchers can sometimes use the sequencing of events in time to infer causation (a second of the three criteria for inferring causation). It wouldn't make much sense, for example, to suggest that a high correlation between heart attacks and dying is due to dying causing heart attacks!

Another problem with interpreting correlation coefficients is assuming that just because two variables are correlated, they are related *meaningfully.* *Mad* magazine once "proved" that baseball causes juvenile delinquency because more than 90% of juvenile delinquents played baseball! Similarly, suppose that people's height correlates positively with how much television they watch. Does any theoretical or logical rationale suggest that a meaningful relationship exists between these two variables? It seems safe to assume that this correlation occurs because of chance and is, therefore, not meaningful. As explained in Chapter 7, variables that correlate statistically but are not related meaningfully are referred to as *spurious relationships.*

The problem of confusing correlation with causation is well illustrated in the recent controversy about intelligence (IQ), race, and social policies engendered by Herrnstein and Murray's (1994) now-infamous book, *The Bell Curve: Intel-*

ligence and Class Structure in American Life, Herrnstein and Murray claimed to show that IQ (measured via a number known as *g*) is innate and that people of certain races or ethnic groups (specifically, African Americans) are inferior to others (e.g., Caucasians) when it comes to innate intelligence. Unfortunately, lots of people have tried to make and support this ridiculous claim. But let's take it apart to show the problem with not differentiating causation from correlation.

Let's assume for the moment that the IQ test is a valid measurement of intelligence (although many people argue otherwise; see, for example, Gould, 1995). Herrnstein and Murray did find some low correlations between race and intelligence (a point we will return to in a moment), and they acknowledge the difference between correlation and causation, but they then:

> *consistently use language of causation when they have merely demonstrated a correlation. They show a statistical correlation between IQ and various social maladies, but they repeatedly describe low IQ as a "factor in," "a significant determinant of," and "a strong precursor of" various social maladies.*
>
> *[Herrnstein and Murray's] confusion of correlations with causes reaches a point of absurdity when they suggest that raising society's average IQ score will reduce crime, unemployment, and poverty…. This kind of crackpot utopianism is based upon mistaking a correlation with a cause. It's like arguing that because people with long noses happen to be more intelligent, we could produce a race of geniuses by breeding Pinochios. (Judis, 1995, p. 127)*

Coefficient of Determination

A correlation coefficient tells researchers whether and how strongly variables are related. It does not indicate, however, how much changes in one variable can be explained by changes in the other variable. For example, say the amount of watching television is negatively correlated with GPA at –.91. This is obviously a significant and very strong positive correlation.

This correlation, however, does not tell researchers how much of the differences between students' GPA can be explained by the amount of television viewing they do. To know this, researchers calculate a **coefficient of determination,** a numerical indicator that tells how much of the variance in one variable is associated, explained, or determined by another variable.

The coefficient of determination (*r*-squared, r^2) is a decimal value ranging from 0.00 to 1.00 that is found simply by squaring the correlation coefficient. For the example of the relationship between watching television and GPA, squaring the correlation coefficient of –.91 yields a coefficient of determination of .83. Venn diagrams are useful for illustrating graphically the information contained in a coefficient of determination (see Figure 14.6). The two circles represent the amount of time spent watching television and GPA. The shaded area of overlap shows that the two variables share 83% of their variance. Put another way, about 83% of the variance in GPA is explained by the amount of time spent watching television. This does not mean that watching television necessarily *causes* a lower GPA; it could be that as students get lower GPAs, they turn on the television more!

The coefficient of determination is very important for understanding relationships between

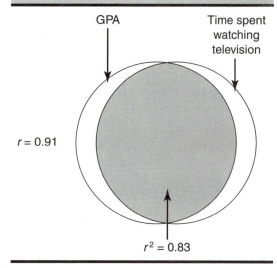

FIGURE 14.6   Variance explained by a coefficient of determination (r^2)

GPA   Time spent watching television

$r = 0.91$

$r^2 = 0.83$

variables. Let's return to Herrnstein and Murray's (1994) supposed "demonstration" of the innate intelligence of certain races over others. Gould (1995) rightly points out that

> most of Herrnstein and Murray's correlations are very weak—often in the 0.2 to 0.4 range. Now, 0.4 may sound respectably strong, but—and this is the key point—…a 0.4 correlation yields an R-squared of only .16. In Appendix 4, one discovers that the vast majority of the conventional measures of R^2, excluded from the main body of the text, are less than .01….
>
> These very low values of R^2 expose the true weaknesses, in any meaningful vernacular sense, of nearly all of the relationships that form the meat of The Bell Curve. (p. 20)

Researchers, therefore, must pay careful attention to the correlation of determination when interpreting the results of the correlation coefficients found in their studies. The reason is clear when we look at how quickly the amount that one variable is explained by the other decreases as the correlation coefficient decreases:

Correlation Coefficient	*Coefficient of Determination*
.90	.81
.80	.64
.70	.49
.60	.36
.50	.25
.40	.16
.30	.09
.20	.04
.10	.01

Let's return to the example of television watching and GPA. The coefficient of determination may help to put in context G. B. Armstrong et al.'s (1991) finding of a negative correlation of –.32 (which was significant at the .001 level) between overall television viewing and college GPA. This means that approximately 10% of GPA can be explained by television viewing (or that 10% of television watching can be explained by GPA). Ninety percent of each variable is left unexplained by the other. What other variables do you think account for GPA or watching television for that matter?

Multiple Correlation

Because communication processes are complex, researchers are often interested in the relationships among more than two variables. For example, say a researcher wants to know how GPA is related to amount of studying and amount of communication students have with professors outside of the classroom about coursework. Computing the relationships among each of the possible pairs of variables (GPA and studying, GPA and teacher-student communication, studying and teacher-student communication) would not reveal how GPA is related to the *combination* of studying and teacher-student communication working together.

Researchers compute **multiple correlations** when they want to assess the relationship between the variable they wish to explain, the **criterion variable,** and two or more other independent variables working together. Multiple correlations yield two types of statistics: a multiple correlation coefficient and a coefficient of multiple determination.

Multiple Correlation Coefficient. A **multiple correlation coefficient (R)** is just like a correlation coefficient, except that it tells researchers how two or more variables *working together* are related to the criterion variable of interest. A multiple correlation would, thus, show how studying and teacher-student communication working together are related to GPA (the criterion variable).

A multiple correlation coefficient indicates both the direction and the strength of the relationship between a criterion variable and the other variables. A multiple correlation coefficient takes the form $R_{a.bc} = +/- x$, read, "The multiple correlation of variables *b* and *c* with variable *a* (the criterion variable) is…." For example, an observed multiple correlation coefficient of +.60 might mean that GPA is positively related with the amount of studying students do combined with the amount of their teacher-student communication outside of the classroom about coursework.

Researchers can of course consider any of the variables the criterion variable, as long as there is good reason for doing so. For example, GPA (b) and studying (c) could be related to the criterion variable of teacher-student communication (a), if there were good reasons for doing so.

Coefficient of Multiple Determination.

A **coefficient of multiple determination (R-squared, R^2)** expresses the amount of variance in the criterion variable that can be explained by the other variables acting together. A coefficient of multiple determination is computed simply by squaring the multiple correlation coefficient, just as a coefficient of determination is computed by squaring the correlation coefficient.

In the hypothetical example of the relationship of GPA, studying, and teacher-student communication, $R^2_{a.bc} = .60^2 = .36$. If this correlation were actually the case, it would mean that 36% of the variance in GPA could be explained by studying and teacher-student communication working together. Of course, that still leaves 64% of GPA left unexplained by these two variables (.64 is called the **coefficient of nondetermination,** that part of the variance in the criterion variable that is left unexplained by the independent variables, symbolized and calculated as $1 - R^2$.) What other variables, then, would you add to explain GPA?

Partial Correlation

A multiple correlation assesses the relationship among multiple variables, but it does not inform researchers about the relationship between two variables when the effects of another variable(s) are removed. A **partial correlation** (called **partial** for short) explains the relationship between two variables while statistically controlling for (rule out, remove, hold constant, residualize, or "partial out") the influence of one or more other variables (sometimes called **effects analysis** or **elaboration**). A partial correlation coefficient takes the form $r_{ab.c} = +/- x$, read, "The partial correlation coefficient between variable *a* and variable *b* with variable *c* controlled for is…." A **first-order partial correlation** controls for one other variable; a **higher-order partial correlation** controls for two or more variables (i.e., second-order partial correlation, third-order partial correlation, etc.); and a **zero-order correlation** is a correlation between two variables with no variable controlled for.

For example, television executives believe that on-air promotions (promos) are important in attracting viewers to new series and one-time-only programs, such as made-for-TV movies (see Cowles & Klein, 1991). Eastman and Newton (1999) examined more than 600 promos carried within or immediately before/after all situation comedies aired by ABC, CBS, Fox, and NBC networks during a week each in April, May, October, and November of 1994. The salience of the promos was coded by the researchers in a number of ways, including their location within a spot break and the total number of elements in the promo. They were interested in the relationship between the promos' salience and viewership of the programs being advertized, so they obtained the viewership ratings of those programs. However, they suspected that the lead-in ratings of the program that preceded the one being promoted might make a difference, so they obtained the viewership ratings of the lead-in program as well. In assessing the relationships between the viewership ratings of the program promoted and the various salience measures, the researchers controlled for, "partialed out," the effects of the lead-in ratings. They found, for instance, using partial correlation procedures, that the more desirable location of a promo as first or last within a spot break was positively associated with outcome ratings for the program, whereas the amount of clutter contained in the promo was negatively related to outcome ratings. Partial correlations, thus, allow researchers to assess a relationship while eliminating the influence of a potentially confounding variable.

Researchers also sometimes conduct **semipartial correlations** (also called **part correlation**) that partial out a variable from one of the other variables being correlated. A semipartial correlation coefficient takes the form $r_{a(b.c)} = +/- x$, read, "The semipartial correlation coefficient of variables *a* and *b* after variable *c* has been partialed out from variable *b* is…."

REGRESSION ANALYSIS

Besides investigating whether variables are related, many researchers wish to *predict or explain* how people are likely to score on a criterion, or outcome, variable on the basis of their scores on another variable, called a **predictor variable** (also called a **regressor**). Statistical procedures used to make such predictions are referred to as **regression analysis.** When applied to the study of linear relationships between variables, regression analysis takes the form of *linear regression* or *multiple linear regression* depending on how many predictor variables are studied.

Linear Regression

Linear regression (also called **simple regression**) is used to predict or explain scores on a criterion variable on the basis of obtained scores on a predictor variable and knowledge of the relationship between the two variables. For example, universities often use linear regression to evaluate applicants. Universities over the years collect, for instance, their students' scores on the SAT examination and their overall GPA once they graduate from the university, and can compute the relationship between these two sets of scores. They then use that known relationship to predict a particular high school applicant's future college cumulative GPA on the basis of his or her particular SAT score. Some organizations use known relationships between certain screening instruments and employee success to predict the likelihood that a particular applicant will be successful. In each case, a person's score on one variable is used to predict or explain scores on another variable on the basis of the known relationship between the two variables.

To understand linear regression, let's suppose a researcher is interested in predicting a person's tendency toward violence (the criterion variable) on the basis of how much television he or she watches (the predictor variable). The researcher collects data on the number of hours a large group of people spend watching television per day and uses an instrument to measure their tendency toward violence (say on a scale from 0 to a high of 100). The researcher plots these individuals' scores on a scatter plot (see Figure 14.7). The researcher then attempts to fit a straight line through the data that minimizes the distance between each

observed score and the line. In regression analysis, this straight line is referred to as the **regression line** (or **line of best fit**). The researcher can then locate a person's score on the horizontal or *x*-axis of the line of best fit (the number of hours spent watching television per day) and find the corresponding point on the vertical or *y*-axis (tendency toward violence) to predict the score on that variable. For example, if a person watched 2 hours of television per day, the researcher would find this point on the *x*-axis, move up to the line of best fit, and then follow a straight line across to the *y*-axis to predict the person's tendency toward violence score. In this case, the best prediction of his or her tendency toward violence score would be about 33.

Now let's formalize the procedure a bit. Regression analysis is actually accomplished by constructing a **regression equation** (also called a **prediction equation** or **regression model**), which is an algebraic equation expressing the relationship between variables. The regression line is, thus, a visual representation of a regression equation. The typical regression equation for two variables is:

$$y = a + bx$$

where *y* is the criterion variable, *a* is the *intercept*, *b* is the *slope*, and *x* is the predictor variable.

The **intercept** (also called **y intercept**) is how far up the *y*-axis the regression line crosses—intercepts—it, when the value on the *x*-axis is zero. The **slope,** which depends on the correlation be-

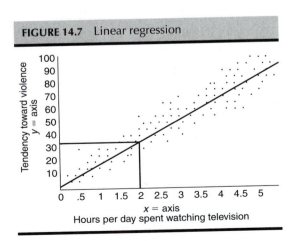

FIGURE 14.7   Linear regression

tween the two variables, is "how many units the variable Y is increasing for every unit increase in X" (Williams, 1992, p. 152). Figure 14.7 helps to make these two concepts more clear. Notice that the intercept is at about 3 on the *y*-axis. This means that even those who watch no television would have some small tendency toward violence. People who watch half-an-hour (.5) of television per day, for example, would score about 10 on the tendency toward violence measure, a difference of 7, which is explained largely by the intercept. People who watch 5 hours per day of television news, however, can be expected to score about 90 on tendency toward violence, a difference of 80. The difference between hours watched and tendency toward violence is now far greater than the intercept. This is because the slope, in this case, tells the reader that increases in tendency toward violence goes up much faster than increases in television watching time.

So we can predict tendency toward violence by multiplying the number of television hours watched by the slope (amount of change in score per watching hour) and adding the initial intercept point to this product, just as the regression equation formula suggests. Linear regression analysis, thus, uses a known score and the slope and intercept of the regression line to predict what another score is likely to be without having to actually measure that other score.

It should be pointed out that the stronger the correlation between the two variables being studied, the more accurate the prediction. A **regression coefficient,** which is part of a regression equation, is a statistical measure of the relationship between the variables (in this case, it is called a **bivariate regression coefficient** because only two variables are involved). In addition, significance tests are applied to a regression equation to determine whether the predicted variance is statistically significant. One common procedure, for example, is to use an *F* test to see whether the predicted variance is significantly greater than the unpredicted variance. And the extent to which any model or equation, such as a regression line, summarizes or "fits" the data is referred to as the **goodness of fit.**

As we pointed out before, linear regression analysis is used in many different types of businesses. It is, for example, the procedure used by insurance companies to determine rates for automobile drivers on the basis of their age. They use available data on past customers' age and, for instance, number of accidents to determine the likelihood of an accident for a person of a particular age and then determine the appropriate rate. In fact, Vogt (1999) points out that statisticians who specialize in probability theory, especially with regard to calculating risks for insurance companies, called **actuaries,** were historically among the earliest professional statisticians. That's why a new, 16-year-old male driver pays more for insurance than a 40-year-old male driver or than a female driver of the same age, all other things being equal. Although this may at first seem unfair (for there are undoubtedly conscientious 16-year-old male drivers), as Lauden (1997) explains, they are actually getting a pretty good deal:

> Consider that a 16 year-old male driver is about 40 times more dangerous on the highways than a 40 year-old woman. The truth is that the high added premiums usually charged to teenage drivers, especially males, do not begin to reflect how dangerous they are. Everyone else is paying extra premiums to subsidize this group's notoriously bad driving record. (p. 149)

Of course, the determination of insurance premiums for any group of people typically is not done on the basis of making a prediction from a single variable, for instance, the likelihood of an accident. Such a determination is typically made on the basis of building a predictive model that includes numerous variables (such as the type of car one drives and whether one lives in a crowded city or the open countryside). To do that, multiple linear regression is needed.

Multiple Linear Regression

Multiple linear regression allows researchers to predict or explain scores on a criterion variable on the basis of obtained scores on two or more predictor variables and knowledge of the relationships among all the variables. For example, multiple linear regression could be used to predict a person's GPA on the basis of how much time he or she spends watching television and how much time he or she spends studying *combined,* if the relationships among these variables are known. The procedure is essentially the same as linear regression; however, because two or more predictor variables are involved, multiple linear regression involves using a weighted combination of these variables to predict scores on the criterion variable.

As with most other statistics, but especially complex ones like this, multiple linear regression is performed using a computer. There are a number of ways to do multiple linear regression with respect to how the predictor variables are entered into the regression analysis to see how much variance they explain in the criterion variable. In **hierarchical regression analysis,** the researcher determines, on the basis of previous theory and research, the order of the variables entered into the regression equation; in **stepwise regression,** the computer is instructed to enter the predictor variables in various combinations and orders until a "best" equation is found.

Regardless of the process, a multiple linear regression provides researchers with at least three important pieces of information. First, it yields a *multiple correlation coefficient (R)* that tells researchers the relationship between the criterion variable and all the predictor variables. Second, it yields a *coefficient of multiple determination (R^2)* that expresses the amount of variance in the criterion variable that can be explained by the predictor variables acting together. Some researchers use an **adjusted R^2 (*R^2)** that takes into account the number of independent variables studied. Third, it tells researchers how much *each* of the predictor variables contributes toward explaining the criterion variable. It does this by providing a *regression coefficient,* a **beta coefficient** (often called a **beta weight, regression weight,** or sometimes **standardized regression coefficient**), that indicates the extent to which, or relative weight that, each predictor variable contributes to explaining the scores on the criterion variable, while controlling

for the other predictor variables. A beta coefficient actually provides a measure of the difference in the criterion variable "associated with an increase (or decrease) of one standard deviation in an independent [predictor] variable—while controlling for the effects of the other independent [predictor] variables" (Vogt, 1999, p. 22). So it is a type of standardized score (see Chapter 12) and, as such, allows for the comparison of the relative effects in explaining the criterion variable of predictor variables that use different types of measurements scales. Researchers, however, must be aware of the potential problem of **collinearity** (or **multicollinearity**), which refers to the extent to which the predictor variables are correlated with one another (a correlation between independent/predictor variables is called an **intercorrelation,** as compared to a correlation between an independent/predictor and dependent/criterion variable). If the variables are highly correlated, "it is very easy to believe that a certain result comes from variable A, when in fact it is due to variable Z, with which A happens to be correlated" (Sowell, 1995, p. 77).

To illustrate the use of multiple linear regression, consider Desmond, Singer, Singer, Calam, and Colimore's (1985) study of the extent to which family communication mediates children's comprehension of television. They showed kindergarten and first-grade children a 15-minute edited version of an episode of the TV show *Swiss Family Robinson.* After seeing the program, the children were asked to recall what happened in the show—a measure of their comprehension of what they saw. The children also completed a series of questionnaires that measured such things as their general television knowledge and knowledge of their parents' specific rules about watching television. Finally, the researchers asked the children's parents to complete a number of questionnaires that measured how they communicated with their children in general and about television in particular.

The researchers used multiple linear regression to show how the criterion variable of television comprehension could be explained by the various communication predictor variables. The regression analysis showed that comprehension could be predicted by three variables ($R = .367$, $R^2 = .135$), listed in order of their predictive strength. As the researchers explain:

> When television comprehension is examined as a function of family variables, television-specific rules, a report of positive communication between mother and child, and a pattern of explanation of television content by parents are associated with children who gain knowledge from a television plot. (p. 476)

Multiple linear regression, thus, showed how television comprehension could be explained by these three predictor variables.

Explaining and predicting complex events demands taking numerous variables into account. Because multiple linear regression assesses the relationships between numerous predictor variables and a criterion variable, researchers frequently use this procedure to capture the complexity of events, including communication processes. It should also be pointed out that there are regression procedures, called **polynomial regression analysis** (or **curvilinear regression**), that are used to predict variables that have a nonlinear relationship.

How successful are these procedures at predicting a criterion variable? Consider that an acquaintance of one of the authors, who, until recently, worked for a large investment company,

specializes in building regression models that predict how to invest in the stock market. Building a regression model about something this complex demands taking into account literally hundreds of predictor variables. But when built well, such models can be very successful. Indeed, one year, and it was not an uncommon year, this person, who made a healthy six-figure salary, received a Christmas bonus of $16 million, and there was someone else in the firm who received $21 million. Imagine how much money they must have generated from these regression models to justify such a bonus. And you thought knowledge of statistics didn't pay!

ADVANCED RELATIONSHIP ANALYSIS

Up to this point we have discussed the most common relationship analysis techniques employed by researchers. There are, however, more complex *multivariate analytic procedures* that assess relationships among three or more variables.

These advanced relational analyses are too complex for this text but they are quite common in communication research. Figure 14.8 provides short explanations of several of these advanced relationship analyses and illustrates how each has been used to study communication behavior.

FIGURE 14.8 Advanced relationship analysis

Researchers use the following advanced relationship analyses when they are appropriate. We explain the purpose of each procedure and provide an example of how it has been used in communication research.

1. Canonical Correlation Analysis: **Canonical correlation analysis** (R_c) is a form of regression analysis used to examine the relationship between multiple independent and dependent variables by determining which set of the independent variables is more closely associated with which set of the dependent variables. Each set is called a **canonical variate** and the canonical correlation coefficient, called a **canonical,** ranges, like other correlation coefficients, from

$+1.00$ to -1.00. Weider-Hatfield and Hatfield (1996) used canonical correlation to examine relationships between three conflict management strategies used by managers (collaborating, forcing, and accommodating) and four types of rewards that subordinates might experience at work (system, job, performance, and interpersonal). The analysis showed a significant relationship between a set that was largely defined by collaborating and less so by forcing (negatively related) and a set defined largely by interpersonal rewards and performance rewards. As the authors concluded, "That collaborating and forcing emerged as predictors of both interpersonal rewards and performance rewards suggests that the conflict management strategies selected by managers have

(continued)

FIGURE 14.8   Continued

significant import for superior-subordinate relationships, as well as the outcomes related to job performance experienced individually by subordinates" (p. 203).

2. Path Analysis: **Path analysis** examines hypothesized relationships among multiple variables (usually independent, mediating, and dependent) for the purpose of helping to establish causal connections and inferences by showing the "paths" the causal influences take. The total effect of an independent variable on the dependent variable in a path analysis is called an **effect coefficient;** the correlation coefficient between pairs of variables is called a **path coefficient.** The results of path analysis typically are portrayed in a graphic representation, called a **path diagram.** W. J. Brown and Basil (1995) wanted to know the effects of media exposure to celebrities (in this case, "Magic" Johnson) on people's health-related beliefs, attitudes, and behavior (HIV/AIDS awareness and prevention). They advanced a path-analytic model in which the influence of prior media exposure (television and print exposure)—with some demographic variables (e.g., gender, culture, and

sexual experience) included as covariates—was hypothesized to lead to knowledge of Magic, which, in turn, should lead to emotional involvement with him, which should then lead to various outcomes (including personal concern about AIDS, perceived personal risk of HIV infection, concern about risk of AIDS to heterosexuals, intention to change sexual behavior, and intentions to take an HIV blood test). The first path analysis conducted, which did not include the variable of involvement with Magic, showed that while media exposure influenced knowledge of Magic, that knowledge did not affect any of the outcomes. However, as the following path diagram shows, when involvement with Magic was included, the path analysis confirmed the predictions, as media exposure to Magic produced both knowledge of and involvement with him, and that involvement was positively related to perceptions of AIDS risks and intentions to reduce high-risk sexual behavior. The authors concluded that "involvement with a celebrity through media exposure is an important mediating variable in persuasive communication, and celebrities can effectively endorse health-related messages" (p. 345).

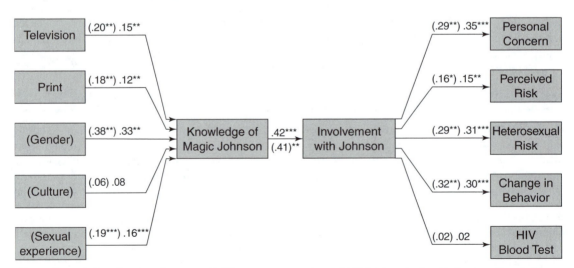

Effects of knowledge of and involvement with Johnson on perceptions of AIDS risk and related behaviors. Correlation coefficients are in parentheses. Regression coefficients from path analyses are beside correlations. **$p<.01$. ***$p<.001$.

Source: Willam J. Brown and Michael D. Basil, "Media Celebrities and Public Health: Responses to 'Magic' Johnson's HIV Disclosure and Its Impact on AIDS Risk and High-Risk Behaviors" *Health Communication, 7*(4), p. 363, copyright © 1995 by Lawrence Erlbaum Associates. Used by permission of Lawrence Erlbaum Associates.

FIGURE 14.8

3. Discriminant Analysis: **Discriminant analysis** is a form of regression analysis that classifies, or discriminates, individuals on the basis of their scores on two or more ratio/interval independent variables into the categories of a nominal dependent variable. Rosenfeld, Richman, and Bowen (1998) used discriminant analysis to see whether middle-school children who did or did not receive each of eight types of social support (such as listening support and emotional support) could be discriminated with respect to four sources of support (parents, teachers, friends, and neighbors) and five school variables (such as school satisfaction and grades). (The authors also compared students considered "at-risk" of poor school performance with students not identified "at-risk.") Students first were divided into two groups on the basis of whether they indicated receiving or not receiving each type of social support—the dependent variable in the analysis. These two groups then were discriminated from each other on the basis of the four sources of support—the independent variables—with the sources of support entered into each discriminant analysis as potential discriminating variables. The same thing was then done for each type of social support using the five school variables as potential discriminating variables. The results showed that the discriminant analyses were highly successful in discriminating students who received social support from students who did not.

4. Factor Analysis: **Factor analysis** examines whether a large number of variables can be reduced to a smaller number of factors (a set of variables). It typically is used to see whether items of a measurement instrument can be reduced to one or more common dimensions or factors (i.e., whether an instrument measures a unidimensional or multidimensional construct; see Chapter 5), and which items best correlate with ("load on" and, thus, called **factor loadings**) which factor. **Confirmatory factor analysis** is used to identify factors that a researcher expects to find on the basis of theory and/or research; **exploratory factor analysis** identifies factors without such expectations. Frymier, Shulman, and Houser (1996) used factor analysis to develop an instrument to measure learner empowerment, students' feelings of "responsibility, personal meaningfulness, ownership, self-efficacy, and intrinsic motivation to learn" (p. 183). Students completed a 38-item Likert-type instrument designed to measure empowerment. A factor analysis revealed that the items measured three factors: (a) 16 items loaded on impact (perceiving that one can make a difference, such as the item "I can make a difference in the learning that goes on in this class"), (b) 10 items loaded on meaningfulness (the value of learning in relation to one's beliefs, ideals, and standards, such as "The tasks required of me in this class are valuable to me"), and (c) 9 items loaded on competence (feeling qualified to perform the activities to reach the intended goal, such as "I possess the necessary skills to perform successfully in class").

5. Cluster Analysis: **Cluster analysis** explains whether multiple variables or elements are similar enough to be placed together into meaningful groups or clusters that have not been predetermined by the researcher. Poole and Holmes (1995) used cluster analysis in their study of how a new technology, a group decision support system (GDSS) that combines communication, computer, and decision technologies to support group work, affects group decisions developed over time. Forty groups of 3–4 persons each used a GDSS to solve a task, and their interactions were videotaped, transcribed, and coded to identify the series of phases that occurred during group discussion. Cluster analysis was used to cluster the 40 groups on the basis of similarity in their decision paths. The analysis revealed seven clusters. For instance, one cluster (consisting of six groups) engaged mostly in orientation, with solution development occurring near the end, whereas another cluster (composed of six groups) engaged in more solution- and criteria-related phases, with orientation interspersed throughout. Once these clusters were identified, similarities and differences in their group processes (such as the orderliness of their decision paths) and outcomes (such as perceived decision quality) were then assessed.

6. Multidimensional Scaling: **Multidimensional scaling (MDS)** plots variables or elements in two or

(continued)

FIGURE 14.8   Continued

more dimensions to see the statistical similarities and differences between and among them. E. L. Fink and Chen (1995) examined the relationship between communication and convergence of views regarding organizational climate among a group of university faculty members. Faculty members completed questionnaires measuring their views of eight topics related to their organizational climate (e.g., Ideal University) in relation to themselves, other faculty, and a common referent point (University Today). The researchers used the Galileo multidimensional scaling model to provide a description of the faculty climate at the university studied. For instance, as the following diagram shows, the two concepts that were farthest away from the attributes of University Today were Ideal University and Quality Education, which suggests some serious climate problems at this university. The researchers also found that individuals' climate space was related to their communication behavior; for example, their climate space was more similar to the space of the group with which they maintained strong communication ties as compared to the space of the group with which they did not communicate much.

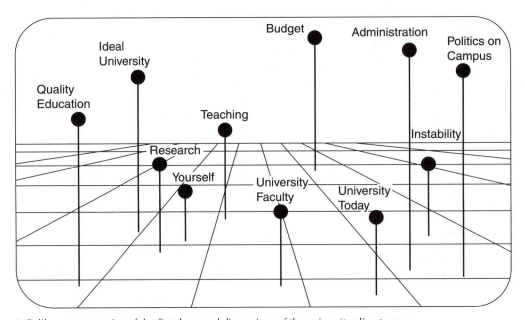

A Galileo representation of the first three real dimensions of the university climate space.

Source: Edward J. Fink and Shih-Shin Chen, "A Galileo Analysis of Organizational Climate," *Human Communication Research, 21*(4), p. 506, copyright © 1995 by Sage Publications, Inc. Used by Permisssion of Sage Publications, Inc.

CONCLUSION

We started this chapter by drawing an analogy between the relationships people have—such as parent-child, husband-wife, and boss-employee—and the relationships that variables have. Like the relationships that exist between people, relationships between variables range from positive to neutral to negative.

But also as with real-life relationships, such as among members of a large family, relationships among variables quickly become numerous and complex, especially when the goal is to make a prediction about something. Sorting out those relationships, much as in some of our personal relationships, is not always easy. But if we are to fully understand something as complex as communication behavior, we have to try.

Finally, we caution you once again about the difference between correlation and causation. As before, the analogy to real-life relationships helps to make this point clear. When relational partners quarrel, each presumes to know who "started it." Actually, one can usually say with certainly only that the two parties were in each other's presence throughout the argument and that their behaviors are related. Likewise, researchers and readers of research must be careful interpreting statistical relationships between variables. Remember that variables must be related meaningfully and that correlation does not equal causation.

PART FIVE

RECONCEPTUALIZING COMMUNICATION RESEARCH

CHAPTER 15

EPILOGUE: CONCLUDING RESEARCH

An excerpt from a poem by T. S. Eliot expresses the process of research well:

> We shall not cease from our exploration
> And the end of all our exploring
> Will be to arrive where we started
> And know the place for the first time

Research studies are indeed cyclical: Each ends by returning to the issues introduced at the start, ideally with greater understanding. Reports of research are, thus, usually structured in an "hourglass" shape. Researchers begin by addressing a broad issue about some aspect of the communication process. As a study progresses, the perspective is narrowed; precise research questions are answered or hypotheses are tested with a particular population or sample in a specific context. At the end, the perspective widens again as the researchers discuss the meaning of the results, relating what they have found to other research literature, identifying the social applications to which their findings might be put and suggesting directions for future research. This chapter deals with the expansive phase that completes the research process when researchers return to broader issues that are at the heart of the concluding "so what?" portion of a research project. This chapter is, thus, concerned with the *reconceptualization* that occurs when researchers rethink the topic of inquiry as a result of the systematic processes associated with conceptualization, planning and designing research, using methodologies to gather data, analyzing the data, and, finally, interpreting research findings.

DISCUSSING RESEARCH FINDINGS

The "Results" section of a research article is a straightforward report of the analysis of the data gathered in a study; this section presents, as Sergeant Friday of the television show *Dragnet* used to say, "Just the facts, Ma'am." Authors are usually careful here to cover only what the analyses of the data examined in that study revealed.

In the final section of a research article, however, often called "Discussion" or "Conclusion," researchers expound on the findings and place what they found in a larger context. In many ways, this is one of the most important parts of the written study, for it gives researchers the opportunity to discuss, and readers the chance to learn about, the larger meaning of the study in terms of the conclusions that can be drawn. Typically, researchers do three things in this section: (a) interpret the meaning or significance of the research findings, (b) identify limitations of the study, and (c) suggest directions for future research.

Interpreting the Meaning of Research Findings

Researchers usually begin the discussion section by examining the meaning or significance of the research findings. We're not talking about statistical significance here (as we did in Chapters 12–14) but, instead, about **substantive significance** (sometimes called **scientific significance,** Vogt, 1999), that is, the theoretical and/or practical significance of the findings. Take the case of statistical versus *practical significance,* the question of whether a research finding can be put to good use (see Figure 15.1). The most meaningful findings clearly are those that are both statistically and practically significant. It may well be the case, however, that a statistically significant finding (e.g., a significant difference between groups or relationship between variables) is not all that important pragmatically. Suppose, for example, that a researcher finds a statistically significant difference between female and male managers' levels of communication competence, with females demonstrating a mean of 48 and males a mean of 44 on a 50-point scale (with 50 being the highest communication competence score). What's more important, the fact that statistically, such a difference would not occur by chance alone more than 5% of the time, or that both female and male managers scored high on communication competence? The latter appears to be the more meaningful finding. Hence, the difference between the two groups' communication competence scores seems less important than their similarity. Although a researcher might still suggest that something be done to narrow this gap, such as providing male managers with a communication competence training program, this doesn't seem to be an urgent problem that needs to be immediately addressed. Suppose, however, that the researcher finds a statistically

significant difference between female and male managers, but both groups have a mean communication competence score of 10. Although there is no statistical significance, there certainly is practical significance to the finding, as there appears to be an urgent need to do something to help all the managers become more competent communicators. Finally, there undoubtedly are cases where research findings demonstrate no statistical nor practical significance. Fortunately, that type of research is rarely published.

Researchers, therefore, look long and hard at the results from their studies to identify the meanings that can be attributed. To describe the larger meaning of the results, researchers often relate findings to theory, previous research, and expectations, and explain how the findings may be applied in relevant contexts.

Relating Findings to Theory. Many research studies are *theory-based;* that is, they are attempts to disprove a concise statement (a theory) that purports to explain a wide range of human behavior. (Yes, we said "disprove," not "prove." As explained in Chapter 2, theories are valid only if they hold up despite scholars' attempts to disprove them.) After the findings from a theory-based study have been determined, researchers relate

---

FIGURE 15.1   The relationship between statistical and practical significance

		PRACTICAL SIGNIFICANCE	
		Yes	*No*
STATISTICAL SIGNIFICANCE	*Yes*	A reliable and important finding	A reliable but not important finding
	No	A potentially important but not reliable finding; more data should be collected	A finding that is neither reliable nor important

Source: Adapted from John R. Hayes, Richard E. Young, Michele L. Matchett, Maggie McCaffrey, Cynthia Cochran, and Thomas Hajduk, "Chapter 2: Reading Research Reports," in John R. Hayes, Richard E. Young, Michele L. Matchett, Maggie McCaffrey, Cynthia Cochran, and Thomas Hajduk (Eds.), *Reading Empirical Research Studies: The Rhetoric of Research,* p. 16, copyright © 1992 by Lawrence Erlbaum Associates. Adapted by permission of Lawrence Erlbaum Associates.

them to the theory being tested. If the findings are consistent with the theory, the validity of that theory is strengthened. If the findings are inconsistent, the theory may need to be modified or replaced with an alternative theoretical explanation for what occurred.

In most cases, the theory or model being tested is essentially supported. That's because researchers start out with good reasons to believe that it is valid, and their predictions, as expected, are borne out. As an example, Hummert's (1994) Stereotype-Sensitive Model, derived from the Predicament of Aging Model (see E. B. Ryan, Giles, Bartolucci, & Henwood, 1986) and Communication Accommodation Theory (see Giles, Mulac, Bradac, & Johnson, 1987), argues that the way people communicate with older persons—the type of accommodations they make in their speech acts—depends on how they categorize an older person as a particular type, as opposed to being based on the categorization of a person as older per se, as some other theories assert. The model predicts, for instance, that patronizing communication, or "elderspeak" as G. Cohen and Faulkner (1986) called it—characterized by simplification and clarification strategies, such as slow speech and careful articulation, a demeaning emotional tone, and a low, superficial quality of talk (see Hummert & Shaner, 1994)—should be more likely to occur when negative, as opposed to positive, aging stereotypes have been activated. A series of studies by Hummert and colleagues (Hummert, Garstka, & Shaner, 1995; Hummert & Shaner, 1994; Hummert, Shaner, Garstka, & Henry, 1998) provided support for this model by showing that young, middle-aged, and older respondents evaluated and responded differently to older targets who varied in terms of positive and negative stereotypes of older adults (e.g., Golden Ager versus Despondent, respectively). As predicted, people did use significantly more patronizing messages (such as overly nurturing communication) with negative than with positive targets.

Occasionally, however, a prediction derived from a theory and, therefore, the underlying theory is disconfirmed. Such an outcome places an explanatory burden on the researcher. Why would a reasonable prediction not be fulfilled; what other explanation applies? The unsupported theory might, thus, need to be reconceptualized.

For example, the Yerkes-Dodson Law (Yerkes & Dodson, 1908) predicts that learning is an inverse curvilinear (an inverted U-shaped; see Chapter 14) function of anxiety (or drive or motivation). That is, people at either extreme—those either very low or very high in anxiety—learn less well than people with moderate levels of anxiety. S. Booth-Butterfield (1988a), however, found that the greater the communication apprehension of students he studied, the less they recalled what a teacher said—a linear relationship. At the end of his study, he explained the inconsistency between his findings and the Yerkes-Dodson Law by suggesting that the latter relates primarily to "state" anxiety, the assumption that anxiety is context-specific; that is, people are anxious in some situations but not others. In contrast, Booth-Butterfield argued that he measured "trait" anxiety, the assumption that anxiety is personality-based; that is, some people are more anxious than others, regardless of the situation. So he reconceptualized the theory in relation to communication behavior by identifying a limitation in the range it explained. Revising a theory by redefining its range of coverage and application is a common way in which unexpected findings are explained.

Some researchers conduct research with the expressed purpose of revising a theory so that it accounts for a wider range of phenomena. For example, communication scholars have often drawn on Brown and Levinson's (1978, 1987) Politeness Theory to explain compliance-gaining strategies (communication designed to get others to behave in accordance with one's request). The theory maintains that attempts to change another person's behavior are inherently face (ego) threatening, so communicators often use politeness to save the other person's face when requesting compliance. S. R. Wilson et al. (1998) pointed out, however, that the theory "neither predicts the conditions under which seeking compliance will create multiple face threats nor explains how such threats arise within specific contexts" (p. 64). So they conducted a study to explore some of the specific contextual factors that affect face threats. As they discovered:

> The degree of intrinsic threat to the target's autonomy as well as a variety of other potential face threats depend on the specific influence goal. Giving advice creates one set of potential face threats for the message source and target; asking favors creates another. (p. 92)

Their study, thus, fleshes out and extends Politeness Theory by identifying an important additional factor that needs to be taken into account when using the theory to explain influence strategies.

Sometimes researchers compare two theories that appear to be contradictory or mutually exclusive, and their findings are used to lend support to one theory or the other. For example, some personality theories, such as Sigmund Freud's, presume that all people are fundamentally alike, whereas others, such as Carl Jung's, posit that people differ in fundamental ways and, moreover, that those ways can be condensed into basic types (four in Jung's theory). If the latter theory is correct, people should perceive and communicate with people of their own type better than they do with people of different types. Motley and Smith (1989) found that after a job interview, interviewers were more likely to offer positions to candidates similar to their own temperament than they were to candidates of dissimiliar temperament. They argued that this finding lends support to Jung's theory. Using findings to argue for the greater validity of one theory over another is another common way in which research results are tied to theory testing.

Finally, some communication research is oriented toward the development of new theories. One way this is done is by applying a theoretical concept to a field of study that has heretofore lacked theoretical explanation. For example, in studying plan-based communication (interaction guided by organized intentions and schemes), Jordan (1998) applied the concept of "executive cognitive control" processes—the mental processes through which "individuals plan and direct, select and or-

chestrate the various cognitive structures and processes available to them for attaining some goal" (Schumacher, 1987, p. 109). The results from Jordan's studies document, among other things, how efficiency in people's executive cognitive control processes is positively related to their involvement in interaction, self-monitoring (paying attention to their actions), and correspondence between their plans and behavior. In discussing the significance of the study, Jordan claimed:

> This research represents the first efforts by researchers in communication to incorporate the concept of executive cognitive control into a theory of communication. This strategy represents an opportunity to move beyond the current atheoretical approaches to communication competence. Years of research on competence have told us little beyond the self-evident conclusion that effective communicators exhibit contextually appropriate actions. We know little about how these skills are developed, and thus, we are limited in how we can teach people to become better communicators. (p. 31)

Other communication researchers, using naturalistic methods (as explained in Chapter 10), develop theory from the "ground up," letting it emerge from the data collected. K. B. Wright (1997), for example, used the grounded theory approach to explore the nature and effects of shared ideology espoused by members of Alcoholic Anonymous (AA). On the basis of in-depth interviews and participant observation, Wright identified five major categories (e.g., sense of belonging to the group) and three major subcategories (e.g., trust of group motives) that he then used to articulate a theoretical model of the shared ideological action/interaction strategies that help members manage difficulties in various stages of the AA recovery process.

Relating Findings to Previous Research. Researchers invariably compare their findings to those from *other research*. Research is a cooperative enterprise; hence, researchers attempt to interrelate their study with what others have done and, thereby, build on others' work. If the findings from two or more studies are consistent, the strength of both studies is bolstered.

Not surprisingly, researchers often verify what other scholars have previously found. Mayer (1998), for example, studied behaviors that lead to more effective decisions by members of small groups working in organizations. One finding, as might be expected, was that negative socioemotional communication behaviors (e.g., sarcastic comments or personal attacks) were perceived by respondents to decrease the effectiveness of group decision making, whereas positive socioemotional behaviors (e.g., encouraging member participation and listening) were perceived to improve decision-making effectiveness. In the discussion section, Mayer related this finding to previous research conducted on organizational groups that found similar results (e.g., Couch & Yetton, 1987; Gladstein, 1984; Harrison, 1985; Tjvosvold & Dumes, 1980; Tjvosvold, Wedley, & Field, 1986). Such consistency across studies suggests that the findings from Mayer's study (as well as the other studies) are meaningful and not due to idiosyncrasies in the research methods he (or the other researchers) used or in the phenomena being studied.

Comparisons to findings from other studies can also help researchers to explain their own findings. O'Hair, Cody, Goss, and Krayer (1988), for example, asked people to judge the honesty of candidates they observed in videotaped job interviews. They found that candidates' attentiveness affected observers' judgments: attentive people seemed honest; inattentive people seemed dishonest. Such results don't explain, however, *why* observers made these inferences. The authors provided an explanation by relating their finding to another study by Zuckerman, DePaulo, and Rosenthal (1981) that reported that deception takes more "cognitive processing" time. Presumably, research participants in O'Hair et al.'s study inferred that inattentive interviewees were conjuring up, or cognitively processing, deceptive answers.

Researchers, of course, don't always obtain findings harmonious with what was learned in other studies. On occasion, their results are inconsistent with what others have found. The discrepancy must be explained: Was one finding inaccurate, or does a variable that was previously overlooked account for the difference?

N. L. Harper and Hirokawa (1988), for example, found that the female managers they studied tended to use different methods to influence female and male employees. They pointed out that this finding contradicted an earlier study by Rossi and Todd-Mancillas (1984) that showed that female managers treat male and female employees alike. Harper and Hirokawa attributed the discrepancy to differences in social conditions that prevailed when the two studies were conducted, five years apart. They maintained that during the intervening years,

> [i]ncreased numbers of women in management should tend to…reduce any tendency women managers may have had to avoid "male" behaviors and to bring to the ranks of women in management the same range of diversity that exists among men in management. (p. 166)

Relating Findings to Expectations.   After analyzing the data collected for a study, researchers occasionally obtain results that are *surprising* or *contradict their expectations.* When that happens, they attempt to offer an explanation or a rationale that takes these unanticipated findings into account.

For example, Vangelisti and Crumley (1998) examined how relational context (the relationship between two people) affects the way people react to messages that hurt their feelings. They were surprised to find that such relational qualities as closeness, contact, satisfaction, and similarity did not predict the use of seemingly "invulnerable" reactions, such as ignoring the message, laughing, and being silent, to hurtful messages. They suggested that perhaps invulnerable reactions depend on the situation: they may be used more when the hurtful remark is made in public than in private (the context examined in their study). The researchers also found that invulnerable responses were used more with low levels of hurtfulness (the degree of hurt elicited by a message). They speculated that perhaps people use these reactions when they "are not willing to perceive a remark as extremely hurtful—individuals may try to dismiss the remark by denigrating its importance (or the importance of the relationship)" (p. 190). Alternatively, they noted that invulnerable responses may be "non-threatening ways to reciprocate the sting of a hurtful message and regain a degree of relational balance" (p. 190). Based on what you've seen when people are hurt by a message (perhaps even one you've sent), when and why do they respond with invulnerable reactions?

In still other cases, the findings actually run counter to researchers' expectations and necessitate some explanation. In studying television channel changing using the remote control device, Perse (1998) hypothesized that negative affective reactions to a television program would lead to increased channel changing. But the results demonstrated otherwise: "Instead of turning away from programs that made them feel angry, fearful, worried, and the like, viewers paid more attention to the programs and thought about them more" (p. 64). Perse offered three potential explanations for this unexpected finding. First, the arousal of fear created by magazine and news program stories that report problems may lead people to protect themselves by paying even more attention to these stories to learn how to avoid the problems (and Perse referred readers to K. Witte, 1994, for indirect support). Second, Perse pointed out that her findings are in line with studies that show that some negative affective reactions, such as anger, lead people to ruminate and search for explanations (e.g., Weiner, 1982), so people may pay more attention to television programs that trigger such emotions. Third, the findings support previous research that shows that people remember negative news (e.g., Lang, Newhagen, & Reeves, 1996; Newhagen & Reeves, 1992). As Perse concluded, "Negative videos seem to compel attention, engage mental resources, and arouse viewers" (p. 64). Thus, she advanced tentative explanations for the unexpected findings and used previous research to support those explanations. It will be up to future researchers to explore more fully why negative reactions may cause some people to watch these television programs more intently, whereas others turn away.

In the most extreme case, the results are so startling that they force researchers to completely reconsider their original expectations. For instance, there has been a lot of concern expressed about "trash TV," especially daytime television talk shows that focus on sensational stories (e.g., "I Married My Brother"), such as the Jerry Springer show. Many critics contend that these shows have negative effects, especially on younger viewers. So Davis and Mares (1998) were pretty sure when they began their study that these shows would affect in some negative ways adolescent viewers' beliefs about social reality. Specifically, they hypothesized that adolescent viewers of these shows would, among other things, become desensitized to the suffering of others and trivialize the importance of social issues. Instead, their survey of 282 high school students revealed that viewers were not desensitized and that, among some age groups, talk show viewing was actually positively related to the perceived importance of social issues. Such startling and unexpected results led the researchers to rethink their original position and to contest the popular image of these shows:

> Overall, we conclude that the sweeping condemnation of talk show viewing is rather extreme. Although talk shows may offend some people, these data do not suggest that the youth of the U.S. is corrupted by watching them.... We suggest that the primary value of this study lies in taking a piece of conventional wisdom (i.e., talk shows are harmful) that has been bandied about by people with considerable power, and testing it. As usual, it appears that conventional wisdom is overly pessimistic and much too simplistic. (pp. 84–85)

Finally, even if the findings of a study are as expected and consistent with prior research, more than one conclusion may be drawn from them. Researchers can legitimately interpret the same research findings differently. Researchers must, therefore, consider *alternative explanations* for their results.

Alberts (1988), for example, examined how couples voice complaints and found that, compared to unhappy couples, happy couples phrase their complaints more in behavioral terms, express more positive feelings when discussing complaints, and respond to spouses' complaints more often by agreeing. As she concluded, "The implications of this study seem clear: Couples' feelings about their relationship are connected to their complaint behavior" (p. 193). But she wisely added, "What is not clear is whether the differences in complaint behavior preceded or followed the couples' feelings about their partners" (p. 193). That is, did their level of satisfaction influence how they talked about problems, or vice versa—which came first? Further research will be needed to determine which of these alternative explanations best applies.

Applying Findings. Communication research always has some potential practical application (see Chapter 2), leading researchers to *suggest practical uses* for their findings in the discussion section and, thereby, exploring the implications that their results may have for how others can operate more effectively. There are a number of audiences to which such practical suggestions are directed.

Sometimes research findings have the potential to benefit virtually everyone. For example, everyone, at one time or another, experiences some form of stress and must find ways to relieve it. One way people frequently do that is by watching television, at least according to Mood Management Theory (see Bryant & Zillman, 1984; Zillman, 1982; Zillman & Bryant, 1985). The social isolation experienced and the tendency to lose one's self while watching television is thought to help alleviate stress. D. R. Anderson, Collins, Schmitt, and Jacobvitz (1996) conducted three studies to test this theory and generally found support for it. In discussing the implications of their findings, the authors raised the issue of whether people should, in fact, use television in this manner:

> *Is TV viewing a useful or positive way for adults to cope with stress? The answer is not a simple yes or no. Mood management theory suggests that TV is used in part to block thoughts that cause anxiety. For many stress-inducing life events, however, a long-term coping strategy requires thought about the events and active problem solving to deal with them (Pennebaker & Susman, 1988). If television is used as a way of chronically avoiding such thinking, then it may delay or hinder positive coping*

> *strategies.... On the other hand, TV viewing may be an appropriate and positive coping strategy to temporarily reduce stress and anxiety. This may be especially true for stressors over which the individual has no control. (pp. 256–257)*

So if you're experiencing temporary, relatively low-level stress (like the kind you get on a daily basis from attending school), then Anderson et al. appear to be encouraging you to turn on the television and "veg out" for a little while. But if you're experiencing major stress (including long-term academic problems), television may be part of the problem, not the solution.

Most research, of course, is conducted about a particular issue, in a particular context, and with a particular group of people, so the suggestions offered by researchers in the discussion section most often focus appropriately on that issue, setting, and people. For example, the process of socializing new employees into an organization is an important issue that can have long-term consequences for both employees and organizations. In studying the organizational socialization of new faculty members in communication departments across the United States, Cawyer and Friedrich (1998) found that the amount of time spent in orientation activities was the best predictor of new employees' satisfaction with their university. This finding, as well as comments from respondents, led the researchers to recommend that university administrators should offer more opportunities for newcomers to socialize, establish formal mentoring programs, and provide adequate information on policies and procedures—good advice for all organizational planners.

Perhaps the group that benefits the most from practical suggestions that researchers offer are practitioners, those who apply the knowledge researchers produce, such as educators, media personnel, and those involved in various communication campaigns. As explained in Chapter 2, many practitioners try to stay up-to-date on what the latest research shows, so they rely on researchers to point out the pragmatic implications of their findings for professional practice.

Educators, for example, frequently benefit from communication research; indeed, there is an entire field of scholarship devoted to communication education. An example of an issue that has received a lot of attention from communication education researchers is the assessment of negative effects due to communication apprehension (CA), fear of communicating, on students' cognitive and affective learning, and ways of combating those effects. Dwyer (1998), for example, found that learning style preferences (e.g., Analytic Evaluators who learn best when the learning environment is thought-provoking versus Hands-on Experimenters who learn primarily by doing and need the learning environment to be highly task oriented) were significantly related to high CA for women, but not for men. In a subsection of the discussion section, Dwyer spelled out some instructional implications of these findings, most of which involve teachers adopting instructional strategies to meet the needs of specific types of women learners who demonstrate high CA. For example, she recommended that Hands-on Experimenters need more application-type exercises and coaching to understand more effectively the material covered in courses, whereas Analytic Evaluators need opportunities to reflect on and evaluate the material.

Much communication research is directed toward studying the media, and the findings from such research often lead scholars to make recommendations to those who work in the media. Liebes and Ribak (1994), for example, found that the television framing practices of partisan journalists who belonged to one side or the other in the Arab-Israeli conflict reinforced viewers' tendencies to attribute dispositional (i.e., personal) motives to aggression committed by the other side (Palestinian uprisers, in this case) and situational reasons for violence on their own side (i.e., Israeli soldiers). The authors argued that that because most viewers "regard the news as a window to reality" (p. 123), the study has important implications for journalists and news producers:

> The authors propose, therefore, that journalists strive for constructing a balanced picture, that they seek to equalize the presentation of pain and human suffering, and that they make the voices of both sides evenly heard.... [I]t is unrealistic to expect journalists to form artificial identification with what is, after all, a party to the conflict.... It is possible, however, to require that they be consciously aware of the possibility of bias, that they attempt to remedy an unbalanced picture by confirming and contextualizing information, and that they permit minority reporters and alternative reports. News producers should also encourage reflexivity in meta-news programs where coverage, conventions, and constraints are exposed and deconstructed and their weight in the news text assessed. (p. 123)

Such advice makes good sense, but one wonders how readily it will be accepted and put into practice by journalists and news producers. Recognizing that "this may be too much to ask" (p. 123), Liebes and Ribak also pointed to the need to teach media literacy in the school curriculum so that the general public becomes more media savvy.

Many communication practitioners are involved in various types of communication campaigns, such as health promotion campaigns, and researchers will assess the relative effectiveness of these campaigns and suggest modifications in the intervention programs. Smaglik et al. (1998), for example, examined differences in HIV-infected individuals who did and did not improve their quality of life after using an interactive health software package called CHESS (Comprehensive Health Enhancement Support System), which provides information and support in a variety of ways, including a discussion group and chat-line. They found that although the discussion group accounted for the majority of people's use of CHESS and time spent with the system, those whose quality of life improved were among the most involved in using CHESS's information tools. This finding led the authors to conclude:

> Although discussion groups or chat-line functions are easy to provide, are often enormously popular, and can stimulate interest and user loyalty, they may not be sufficient to achieve many needed changes. Systems should probably also include a mix of information tools to help individuals take control of and improve their quality of life. (p. 67)

They recommended that designers of these systems need to find ways to link online discussion groups with information tools and perhaps even monitor users' patterns so they can suggest productive options to people who aren't making use of the information tools. Of course, as they also pointed out, this is "uncharted territory and will demand careful thought during design and experimental testing" (p. 67).

Finally, communication researchers sometimes point out important implications their findings have for public policy. While many of these policies probably make good sense, there are many competing values at the societal level that influence whether suggested policies can and will be enacted. For example, on the basis of a meta-analysis (see Chapter 3) of the research literature on television and viewer aggression, Hogben (1998) concluded that the research showed that "a reduction in the amount of exposure to televised aggression should result in reductions in viewer aggression" (p. 241). One implication of this finding that Hogben acknowledged is the need for television to be regulated, perhaps above and beyond the warning labels that currently are used. However, he was quick to point out that further regulation in the United States in the foreseeable future is unlikely because of First Amendment rights. He believes that other alternatives should be sought. "Perhaps the best way to combat the effects of televised aggression," he argued, "is not to ban it but rather to make sure that viewers, particularly children, think about what they are watching" (p. 242).

On rare occasions, however, communication researchers do have significant impact on public policy. C. Ryan, Carragee, and Schwerner (1998), members of the Media Research and Action Project, an organization that assists marginalized groups to employ news as a political resource, documented their work with a Massachusetts-based coalition that included activists from groups marginalized in the mainstream news media—workers, women, and communities of color—to launch a media-centered public information campaign to influence policy formation and public attitudes concerning women's reproductive rights in the workplace. The campaign stemmed from a United States Supreme Court case, in which

United Autoworkers sued Johnson Controls, a lead battery producer, on the grounds of discrimination because the company excluded fertile females from working in high-lead areas. Johnson Controls argued that it was attempting to protect the unborn from serious birth defects that might be caused by exposure to lead. The coalition garnered significant attention from local newspapers in the Boston area, and the Supreme Court, which concluded that Johnson Controls's fetal protection policy constituted sex discrimination under the terms of the Civil Rights Act of 1964, stressed in its majority opinion some of the media frames highlighted by this coalition during the campaign.

Identifying Limitations of the Research

Besides commenting on the content of their findings, researchers discuss the *limitations or flaws* in their studies. (This is sometimes done in a separate "Limitations" subsection in the discussion section.) Ethical researchers make a point of being self-critical (see Chapter 1), explaining all aspects of their study that limit the validity of the findings (although they also often offer rationales that attempt to mitigate those limitations). Research findings have limited utility when studies are compromised by too many threats to internal and external validity (see Chapter 5).

Limitations Due to Internal Validity Threats. Remember that criteria of internal validity must be met for a study to obtain accurate conclusions for the people or texts studied. When research is plagued by the internal validity threats discussed in Chapter 5, little confidence in the conclusions is warranted.

Researchers assess the internal validity of their findings in a number of ways. They, will, for example, report any limitations or flaws in the study's *design.* D. H. Solomon (1997), for example, advanced a developmental model to explain changes in the explicitness of requests for a date with a member of the opposite sex. She hypothesized a curvilinear relationship (see Chapter 14) between intimacy and request explicitness, such that requests are highly explicit when intimacy is either low (e.g., so as to initiate a relationship) or high (e.g., because partners feel very comfortable with one another) and less explicit when there is moderate intimacy (a somewhat difficult period when there may be uncertainty about the status of the relationship). Support for this hypothesis and, therefore, the developmental model was found. Solomon cautioned, however, that

> a developmental model suggests over-time changes in behavior that are not directly testable within a cross-sectional design. Although intimacy presumably influences the degree of explicitness manifested in request strategies, conclusions regarding causal relations can only be speculative in the absence of longitudinal data. The present study highlights the particular stages during which the negotiation of intimacy appears to be most troubling; therefore, these results indicate that longitudinal investigations should focus on the transition to mutual commitment within dating relationships. (p. 115)

There are often problems or limitations with the *methodological procedures* researchers use. J. K. Burgoon, Buller, Dillman, and Walther (1995), for example, studied interpersonal deception and detection by designing an experiment that was supposed to "permit participants to engage in 'normal' interaction behavior lasting long enough to reveal dynamic changes and to register the influence of both actual and perceived suspicion on each person's behavior" (p. 170). Basically, participants who had been assigned to a low-, moderate- or high-suspicion condition (i.e., based on how much they were told to expect lying) were videotaped interacting in a living-room-style laboratory in an open-ended interview during which a friend or stranger answered either truthfully or deceptively (the person began lying on all questions after the fifth question asked). Although most of the hypotheses were confirmed, the researchers acknowledged a problem with the experimental task and the laboratory setting that potentially threaten the internal (as well as external) validity of the findings:

> Whereas friends were highly animated with each other before the experiment began, they frequently became wooden and restrained once the taping started. This creates a real quandary about whether interpersonal deception research, if conducted in a semicontrolled environment, will yield artificial results and prevent one from truly unmasking the deception process. (p. 190)

In the case of textual analysis, such as content analysis, internal validity problems may result from the methodological procedures used to select the texts. For example, in their study of the effects of a number of social characteristics of a homicide (e.g., race and gender of the people involved) on newspapers' coverage of homicides, Pritchard and Hughes (1997) content analyzed the coverage by two Milwaukee newspapers of 100 homicides occurring between January 1, 1994 and March 1, 1995. But as they pointed out:

> Our relatively small sample size of 100 meant that an effect had to be fairly large to be significant at the .05 level. There is a risk that an analysis based on such a small sample is not sufficiently sensitive to detect subtle, but nonetheless important, effects. (p. 65)

Of course, as the authors explained, this also meant that "the effects we found with a sample of only 100, however, make us confident that those effects are meaningful" (p. 65). So what they lost in terms of the ability to detect significant findings because of sample size was compensated by the confidence they had in the significant findings they did discover.

Researchers also point out shortcomings in the *measurement techniques* used to gather data for their study and how these might potentially limit or jeopardize the findings. Poole and Roth (1989) tested a model of the factors that influence groups to follow various paths as they make decisions. They employed three judges to rate group discussions on such task-related variables as openness, goal clarity, expertise, and novelty. At first, there was relatively low interobserver reliability (see Chapter 5), so they allowed the observers to discuss disagreements on codings to increase the reliability of the ratings. The researchers pointed out in the discussion section, however, that this initial low reliability renders questionable some reported relationships between the independent and dependent variables affected.

Some measurement techniques need to be modified to compensate for shortcomings, and researchers will point out these modifications when discussing the results. Darling (1989), for example, conducted research in several classrooms using an already established category system to record how students signal to their teachers that they don't understand something being explained. She found that only 88% of the relevant comments could be classified into one of the system's categories, so she created an additional category that covered the other 12% of the comments. Thus, part of her findings included assessing and improving a measurement instrument.

One common methodological limitation in communication research, and most other social-scientific research, is the measurement of behavior through *self-report methods.* As discussed in Chapter 4, self-report methods are a valid form of measurement, but they have important limitations as well, especially when used to measure behavior (as saying so doesn't necessarily make it so). Researchers who use self-report methods, therefore, frequently point out these potential limitations.

For example, Fiebig and Kramer (1998) studied how people manage their emotions in organizational contexts. Respondents completed a questionnaire that asked them, among other things, to describe positive and negative organizational incidents, their feelings and thoughts during the incidents, and the communication they expressed. Their findings yielded a rich understanding of the role of emotions in organizational contexts, especially with regard to disguising or expressing emotions. But they were quick to point out (indeed, it is the first sentence in the limitations subsection) that one limitation was the use of self-report methods to collect the data. While the self-reports probably validly assessed respondents' thoughts and feelings during the incidents (after all, people are the best judge of their thoughts and feelings), the communication respondents said they expressed may not be what

they actually expressed. Therefore, as Fiebig and Kramer suggested:

> *Future research should examine the role of emotions in organizations by using more in-depth, probing methods for data collection. For example, observation along with intensive follow-up interviews, that is, stimulated recall, might provide a richer data set than the present study. (p. 567)*

Finally, in discussing their findings, researchers often point out how *unobserved or intervening variables* may have confounded the results. In contrasting the effectiveness of face-to-face (FTF) communication versus computer-mediated communication (CMC) for teaching group dynamics and group decision making in educational settings, Olaniran, Savage, and Sorenson (1996) gave students opportunities to complete semistructured tasks in both types of groups. The results showed that students perceived FTF groups to be more effective, easier to use, and more satisfying than CMC groups. While it might be tempting to recommend on the basis of these findings that students only work in FTF groups, before throwing the "baby out with the bath water," Olaniran et al. pointed out that they did not assess students' predispositions toward working in CMC and FTF groups prior to doing so. That's important to acknowledge, for such predispositions might have influenced how participants responded to these conditions; after all, people often get what they expect. Given that CMC is a relatively new medium and people probably don't have a lot of experience with it, it may take some time to develop favorable attitudes toward using it. Of course, we should also keep in mind that perceptions don't always equal reality. In this study, although students preferred FTF groups, they actually produced more ideas working in CMC groups.

Limitations Due to External Validity Threats. Remember that external validity asks whether the findings from a particular research study can be generalized to other people/texts, places, and/or times. Most research is externally limited in some way, so conscientious researchers identify the context-bound limitations of their results. They might comment on the people, texts, or events sampled; the ecological validity of the procedures used; and/or the need to replicate the research findings before they are fully accepted (see Chapter 5).

Many internally valid conclusions drawn from communication studies are not necessarily generalizable. The primary reason is due to the *sampling procedures*, the way in which the subset of the population that is studied is selected. Even more specifically, the problem is often a result of using nonrandom samples drawn from the college population. Convenience samples of college students are used so frequently in social-scientific research, including communication research, that McNemar (1960) argued that such research was basically "a science of the behavior of sophomores." Rosenthal and Rosnow (1969) narrowed this even further to "a science of just those sophomores who volunteer to participate in research and who also keep their appointment with the investigator" (p. 110).

Little has changed over the years concerning the use of college students as research participants. Rossiter (1976) and Applebaum and Phillips (1977) found, respectively, that 75% and 77% of the participants studied in communication research were college students. A decade later, Applebaum (1985) found that 65.5% of published communication research still used samples drawn from the college population. Similarly, L. R. Frey (1988) noted in a review of group communication research published during the 1980s that 72.3% of studies relied on students. Lest this be thought to be an indictment solely of communication research, Frey's (1994e) content analysis of articles published during the early 1990s in the interdisciplinary journal *Small Group Research* showed that 66.1% of studies used students.

Significant differences exist, however, between college and noncollege populations on such variables as intelligence, age, and social-class background (Applebaum & Phillips, 1977). College students majoring in different disciplines also vary in their patterns of attitudes, values, and interests (Jung, 1969). Generalizing findings from student samples or from majors in any one department or area of study to the general popula-

tion, therefore, is questionable. Recognizing this problem, researchers who rely on nonrandom samples of college students are quick to point out the limited external validity of their sample.

Many communication researchers do sample from "real-world" populations (see the examples in Chapter 8), but this doesn't necessarily solve the problem of acquiring representative samples. Krcmar (1996), for example, studied how family communication patterns are related to children's television-viewing behavior. Although the results revealed a number of important findings, she started the limitations subsection by describing important features of the sample and their potential effects on the external validity of the findings:

> *First, the sample represents only middle-class families in a midsized city. Therefore, caution should be used in generalizing from these findings to families of more diverse socioeconomic backgrounds. In addition, this study looked only at fairly traditional family forms: Nuclear, intact families and some reconstituted families made up most of the sample. Generalizability is limited in this way, too. (p. 274)*

Virtually every sample is limited in terms of generalizability, but some samples are better than others. So whenever possible, researchers point out how their sampling procedures may have reduced any potential bias and, thereby, increased the external validity of their findings. For example, to study the perceived importance of the media by individuals in satisfying fundamental human goals, Skumanich and Kintsfather (1998) surveyed 1,500 customers of a major television home shopping network, selected from the customer data base of all people who made at least one purchase during a 3-month period. They surveyed "real" users, but pointed out that the sample was from a single home shopping network and not from a nationwide pool of all television home shoppers. Although this might potentially limit the generalizability of the findings, the researchers argued that because at that time, "there are only three major television national shopping networks and more than 75% of the respondents in this survey cross-view networks, this bias may be minimal" (p. 216).

Similar types of problems, of course, occur in the sampling of texts for textual analysis. The representativeness of the texts selected may be called into question. van Driel and Richardson (1988), for example, content analyzed articles about new religious movements (NRMs) reported in four newspapers, *The New York Times, Washington Post, Los Angeles Times,* and *San Francisco Chronicle,* and three news weeklies, *Newsweek, Time,* and *U.S. News and World Report.* The authors acknowledged, however, that this "elite" sample might be biased:

> *The limiting of our sample to nationally known and respected newspapers and three national newsweeklies may, of course, have consequences for the analysis. A majority of the population does not regularly read a newspaper or newsweekly of the quality of those selected.... Moreover, Shupe and Bromley [1980] found that most anticult stories were printed in small community newspapers. (p. 39)*

However, the authors did follow that point up by arguing that because they primarily were interested in understanding the newspaper reporting that had the "most significant impact on the tense dialogue between NRMs and society, then the choice of nationally acclaimed media representatives is justified" (p. 39).

In other cases, analysts work with relatively unidentified texts in terms of who produced them, which raises concerns about their representativeness. Opt (1998), for example, content analyzed 144 messages left in a suggestion box at a two-year, senior-level state university branch campus as a form of upward organizational communication, as well as the reflection of the American myth of the individual making a difference. Although the university respondents' affiliation (faculty, staff, student, or unknown) was indicated, Opt noted that one limitation was not knowing who contributed the messages. It could be that just a few people contributed a lot of them. If that happened, the generalizability of the results might be compromised.

Sometimes research is externally limited because of the particular event or point in time studied. Pfau et al. (1997), for example, investigated the influence of five communication modalities (interpersonal communication, political talk radio, print news, television news, and political advertisements) on voters' perceptions of candidates during the final week of the 1996 New Hampshire Republican presidential primary campaign. The researchers were quick to point out in the discussion section that the "most serious limitation of this investigation concerns the uniqueness of the 1996 Republican primary campaign, which affects the generalizability of the results" (p. 21). They documented how this campaign was different from others in terms of widespread media disinterest (as demonstrated by lower network news coverage) and voter apathy. The results obtained in this study, therefore, may not be generalizable to other presidential primary or general election campaigns. Only more research along the same lines with other campaigns will answer that question.

A second external validity threat that researchers often discuss concerns the *ecological validity* of the methodological procedures used, that is, the extent to which the procedures mirror real-life situations. Sometimes the tasks that research participants are asked to perform are just not indicative of what they normally encounter in real life. For example, to study the effects of people's communication abilities (e.g., person-centered verbal ability) on verbal and nonverbal performance during persuasive dyadic conversations, Woods (1998) used a typical procedure of pairing students who did not know each other on the basis of a previous measurement—in this case, their disagreement about what they would say to regulate the behavior of an offending roommate. Even though this task situation had been pretested and employed in a number of studies (see Applegate, 1982; Applegate & Delia, 1980; Applegate & Woods, 1991; Woods, 1996), the author readily admitted that "the nature of the interaction task is a potential limitation, as it may not be representative of the frequent interpersonal encounters that respondents have with people they do not know very well" (p. 175).

Ecologically invalid procedures may lead people to distort their behavior, overemphasizing things they typically wouldn't do or suppressing their normal ways of behaving. The latter appears to have been the case in Jansma, Linz, Mulac, and Imrich's (1997) study of men's interactions with women after viewing a sexually explicit film to see whether the degradation of women made a difference. Some men watched a 15-minute degrading sexual film segment, some watched a nondegrading sexual segment, and others watched a nonsexual film segment (control group). They then interacted with a woman and completed a problem-solving task. No effects for film exposure alone were found with respect to women's ratings of the men's sexual interest, dominance, and their own feelings of degradation during the interaction. The researchers suspected, however, that the artificiality of watching the film in a laboratory setting limited or diminished the men's responses. They argued that "the responses of participants in this study may have been more negative toward women in a natural setting in which they viewed the films for purposes of diversion or partner substitution" (p. 21). Moreover, they asserted:

> Further limitations of the experimental setting include those on participants' degree of arousal compared to a natural setting.… Thus, when men watch sexual films in an environment in which they are more likely to become aroused, differences in their evaluations of women may be more pronounced than in a laboratory setting. (p. 22)

Clearly, then, future research is needed to discover whether the findings from this study (or lack thereof, in this case) were, in fact, due to the potentially problematic ecological validity of the procedures used in the laboratory setting.

A third feature of external validity is *replication*. Researchers are well aware that a single study does not "prove" anything; that many studies need to be conducted before conclusion can be fully accepted. Researchers will, thus, urge that the findings from their study be replicated. Typically, such calls are part of the suggestions offered for future research.

Suggesting Directions for Future Research

The final element discussed in concluding a study is an agenda for future research. Most studies end with what might be labeled "MRNTBD," the call

for "more research needs to be done." Specific suggestions for future research take a number of forms (and, as we have seen, are often linked with the limitations identified), including posing follow-up research questions and hypotheses, suggesting new or refined methodological procedures, arguing for the transfer of findings from the laboratory to the field and the extension of the explanatory range of the findings, and proposing new topics to be explored.

Virtually all researchers identify *follow-up research questions or hypotheses* worth posing about the topic being explored. Reeves, Lang, Thorson, and Rothschild (1989), for example, studied how positive and negative television scenes influenced hemispheric differences in cortical arousal. In line with their predictions, they found greater cortical arousal for negative than positive scenes. They went on to suggest in the discussion section that future researchers should investigate three features of television scenes: luminance, movement, and picture complexity. They suspected that negative scenes cause more emotional responses than positive scenes because they are darker, show less movement, and use more simple visual patterns, and encouraged researchers to test this hypothesis.

Researchers also often suggest *new or refined methodological procedures* that can be used to study the same topic. For example, Yang and Linz's (1990) content analysis of the amount of sexual violence portrayed against women in X-rated and R-rated videos showed that although sexually violent episodes lasted longer in X-rated videos, R-rated videos actually contained more sexually (as well as nonsexually) violent episodes on a percentage basis. They coded the episodes in a number of useful ways, including the gender of the characters portrayed and whether they were an "initiator," recipient," or "mutual participant," but they also recommended an improvement in future coding procedures and a reason for it:

> A more refined analysis of the portrayals of male and female characters in R-rated versus X-rated videos would include more subtle indicators of power relations. Our suspicion from viewing these materials, for example, is that females are portrayed nude more often than males in R-rated vid-

eos, are more likely than men to remain nameless in sex scenes in R-rated videos, and are more likely to be found in the "traditional" sexual position (on the bottom) in R-rated materials than in the X-rated videos. (p. 40)

One frequent call for future research is to *transfer findings* from laboratory experiments to the "real world." For instance, Bavelas, Black, Chovil, Lemery, and Mullett (1988) conducted a laboratory experiment to study motor mimicry behavior during dyadic conversations by having a confederate manipulate her leaning behavior and observing whether research participants mimicked the behavior. The results from three separate experiments showed that motor mimicry functions primarily as a nonverbal message that indicates that the observer is aware of and concerned about the situation, rather than as a way of taking the role of the other or of "feeling oneself into" the other person. The researchers cautioned, however, that "we cannot know about the communicative function of a nonverbal behavior unless we study it in a communicative setting rather than in experimentally isolated individuals" (p. 297).

In a similar vein, researchers call for *extending the explanatory range of the findings*. Dupagne (1997), for example, showed that the introduction of color television, cable television, and the videocassette recorder had a significant effect on the overall level of mass media expenditures over time in Belgium. He urged researchers to "extend this analysis to other technologies, such as personal computers, CD players, and cordless phones" (p. 65).

Finally, researchers propose *new topics* to explore. For example, in comparing the preferred linguistic forms for first- and second-attempt requests by people of different cultural orientations, M-S. Kim, Shin, and Cai (1998) found, among other things, that people's cultural orientation affected the degree to which they perceived silence as effective and likely to be used in both attempted requests. They argued that silence is a neglected variable in communication research, but their results suggested that it should be studied more, especially in intercultural communication research. As they concluded, "Neither sociolinguistics nor

the study of goal-oriented communication have attributed much importance to silence as a communication strategy. We should view silence as itself a valid object of investigation, bounded by cultural orientations" (p. 63).

This discussion of future research truly completes the research cycle. The mission of research is fulfilled in three essential steps: (a) making a contribution to the reservoir of communication knowledge that scholars, professionals, and the general public can call on to explain, understand, and potentially influence communication events; (b) identifying important limitations that need to be kept in mind about the research findings; and (c) raising meaningful new questions for future communication researchers to pursue. This final phase of research, thus, serves a *heuristic function* of encouraging future investigation.

CONCLUSION

Researchers are like pioneers venturing into unexplored territory. When they begin their investigations, what is to be investigated is relatively unknown yet intriguing. Setting off down "the road less traveled" involves entering an area of life where clear paths have yet to be charted. To do research requires a restless spirit and a willingness to devote oneself to a long-term, demanding journey. Biologist Albert Szent-Gyorgyi (1971) wrote:

Research means going out into the unknown with the hope of finding something new to bring home. If you know in advance what you are going to do, or even to find there, then it is not research at all. (p. 1)

Doing research is a challenging endeavor—to succeed seems at times to require taking it on as a way of life. Indeed, we might say that the process of research takes a practitioner through a full life cycle.

Researchers, when they begin, must call on the curiosity, creativity, and love of adventure they had as children, for when they operate on the cutting edge of knowledge, they are in the same frightening yet exhilarating position children are in when first exposed to new experiences. They must comprehend for themselves something unfamiliar, something no one else can explain to them.

At first, they may explore simply in an impromptu fashion, as children do, playfully feeling their way around in the new domain. Once they believe they sense intuitively the lay of the land, have investigated some of the maps others have drawn, and know with some precision what they want to map, they bring out their scientific instruments and measure the territory. We have tried to provide some of those instruments—in the form of ideas, skills, and tools—in this book.

The number of instruments needed may appear overwhelming. Because there are so many different approaches to doing research, few people are equally adept at them all. In fact, one of the hardest aspects of being a researcher—an aspect we can't teach you—is making choices: what topic to study, what research questions or hypotheses to pose, in what context to study the phenomena, using what methods to gather and analyze the data, and drawing what inferences and conclusions from the results. Research, thus, involves a long series of decisions.

So researchers must quickly lose their innocence and assume the adult position of making difficult personal and professional choices. And they must carry out their work thoroughly, responsibly, and ethically if what they do is to be worthwhile.

Moreover, when they have something to report about the object of their study, they age once again. They become elders or teachers to their peers, practitioners, and the general public. Their task becomes that of providing a full description of their explorations and what they have found so that others may share their discoveries.

However, as Veblen (1919) suggests, the outcome of research is the generation of more research questions. No sooner do researchers shed some light on what they have studied than the next areas of darkness—which they might never have known existed had they not done their research— calls out for exploration. And the life cycle is resumed once again.

Research is, thus, a spiral, looping endlessly, and evading full resolution. Yet knowledge grows continually. More and more of human life, including communication, is understood, problems can be addressed more skillfully, and people can treat each other more compassionately—*nam et ipsa scientia potestas est:* For knowledge itself is power.

The researchers of one generation pass on what they've learned to the next so that they may live with greater understanding and fulfill their intentions in life. What you have learned in your communication courses, and in most of your formal education, is knowledge contributed by the efforts of researchers.

Recall a moment when you felt increased insight or personal power from an idea encountered when reading or listening in class. After reading this book, you have a much better idea of the activities from which that idea was derived and, consequently, a greater appreciation of the industry and intelligence of the people who did the research. We hope you also have a better ability to eliminate the "middle-people"—the teachers and textbook authors (like us) who have paraphrased researchers' writings for you. You now should be able to read, understand, and, dare we say, enjoy researchers' reports in their original form, "hot off the presses" in the journals and scholarly texts in which they are published.

Finally, you can make an informed choice regarding whether to incorporate the practices of research into your own life. With the knowledge you have gained from this book, you can now personally experience the excitement of exploration firsthand. Through your own research efforts, you can discover, and pass along to the generation of students that will follow you, new information about what now is unknown about communication. In doing so, you will enrich their lives as countless researchers have enriched your life. We hope you will.

COLUMNS

Row	1–3	4–6	7–9	10–12	13–15	16–18	19–21	22–24	25–27	28–30	31–33	34–36	37–39
1	318	627	204	014	302	833	519	776	969	017	220	314	648
2	989	953	621	950	703	395	318	887	920	450	663	537	904
3	292	001	125	919	351	167	872	447	257	508	742	597	090
4	572	080	091	638	502	966	876	692	455	253	102	098	593
5	804	305	226	990	758	928	618	782	321	929	986	019	570
6	741	026	148	109	433	053	130	719	520	310	387	654	579
7	550	696	174	503	107	625	729	244	977	353	777	458	758
8	373	374	252	896	781	701	886	378	562	369	366	496	994
9	254	035	974	487	089	846	373	333	532	866	802	169	515
10	866	893	607	299	995	325	608	436	136	294	280	924	347
11	473	910	087	319	422	903	153	794	837	835	977	615	070
12	574	686	899	104	236	483	288	356	588	463	753	214	319
13	654	914	798	555	039	730	604	080	591	436	067	560	449
14	486	590	291	534	191	900	561	883	985	417	030	824	826
15	432	165	832	016	516	035	930	062	897	423	548	397	158
16	153	822	663	466	118	739	074	879	293	758	476	858	320
17	195	078	225	126	748	695	997	990	067	156	731	741	107
18	870	878	106	893	158	129	100	411	807	294	311	773	343
19	879	392	433	495	882	404	580	705	674	871	123	262	796
20	105	683	663	628	884	931	411	083	831	445	608	345	332
21	028	444	707	759	498	577	849	097	861	205	048	768	741
22	179	988	322	273	113	771	387	625	609	884	534	879	678
23	097	685	709	661	033	491	114	820	891	970	510	546	155
24	196	019	258	425	951	306	392	729	501	440	838	664	023
25	008	465	374	393	467	687	819	250	956	173	317	947	876
26	220	375	324	137	106	749	384	134	418	245	600	693	821
27	952	047	034	174	249	622	780	698	229	294	442	217	549
28	710	177	794	634	438	645	787	960	497	132	217	617	141
29	449	882	780	095	477	559	682	866	169	807	643	590	054
30	194	467	356	266	768	892	605	300	032	284	650	959	719
31	644	139	081	197	331	724	816	567	075	953	330	619	187
32	203	853	355	725	927	016	790	047	655	132	910	574	267
33	871	468	653	813	746	698	075	678	895	766	680	763	588
34	447	413	280	504	065	692	862	989	766	504	809	359	024
35	452	034	574	148	348	069	196	352	275	343	007	225	922
36	248	838	513	607	203	520	772	139	209	023	944	219	564
37	753	783	650	121	633	331	249	483	866	370	381	036	309
38	218	836	318	513	040	049	021	322	207	757	944	270	847
39	489	967	037	446	392	029	383	414	879	894	487	389	003
40	189	774	081	384	008	046	028	014	535	113	961	306	527
41	278	920	103	973	396	160	816	898	891	347	752	231	320
42	393	582	806	524	574	024	747	423	959	990	409	507	506
43	448	080	547	268	321	821	079	309	897	821	705	092	821
44	890	898	856	097	794	015	532	830	905	178	964	402	734

APPENDIX B   Chi-Square Table

df	ALPHA					
	.10	.05	.02	.01	.002	.001
1	2.706	3.841	5.412	6.635	9.550	10.828
2	4.605	5.991	7.824	9.210	12.430	13.816
3	6.251	7.815	9.837	11.345	14.796	16.267
4	7.779	9.488	11.668	13.277	16.924	18.468
5	9.236	11.071	13.388	15.086	18.908	20.516
6	10.645	12.592	15.033	16.812	20.792	22.459
7	12.017	14.067	16.622	18.475	22.601	24.323
8	13.362	15.507	18.168	20.090	24.353	26.124
9	14.684	16.919	19.679	21.666	26.056	27.877
10	15.987	18.307	21.161	23.209	27.722	29.588
11	17.275	19.675	22.618	24.725	29.354	31.264
12	18.549	21.026	24.054	26.217	30.957	32.909
13	19.812	22.362	25.472	27.688	32.535	34.528
14	21.064	23.685	26.873	29.141	34.091	36.123
15	22.307	24.996	28.259	30.578	35.628	37.697
16	23.542	26.296	29.633	32.000	37.146	39.252
17	24.769	27.587	30.995	33.409	38.648	40.790
18	25.989	28.869	32.346	34.805	40.136	42.312
19	27.204	30.144	33.687	36.191	41.610	43.820
20	28.412	31.410	35.020	37.566	43.072	45.315
21	29.615	32.671	36.343	38.932	44.522	46.797
22	30.813	33.924	37.659	40.289	45.962	48.268
23	32.007	35.172	38.968	41.638	47.391	49.728
24	33.196	36.415	40.270	42.980	48.812	51.179
25	34.382	37.652	41.566	44.314	50.223	52.620
26	35.563	38.885	42.856	45.642	51.627	54.052
27	36.741	40.113	44.140	46.963	53.023	55.476
28	37.916	41.337	45.419	48.278	54.411	56.892
29	39.087	42.557	46.693	49.588	55.792	58.301
30	40.256	43.773	47.962	50.892	57.167	59.703
50	63.167	67.505	72.613	76.154	83.657	86.661
100	118.498	124.342	131.142	135.807	145.577	149.449
500	540.930	553.127	567.070	576.493	595.882	603.446

Source: Mary B. Harris, *Basic Statistics for Behavioral Science Research* (2nd ed.), p. 526, copyright © 1998 by Allyn and Bacon. Used by permission of Allyn and Bacon.

APPENDIX C   *t* Table

	LEVEL OF SIGNIFICANCE FOR ONE-TAILED TEST					
	.05	.025	.01	.005	.001	.0005
	LEVEL OF SIGNIFICANCE FOR TWO-TAILED TEST					
df	.10	.05	.02	.01	.002	.001
1	6.314	12.706	31.820	63.657	318.309	636.619
2	2.920	4.303	6.965	9.925	22.327	31.599
3	2.353	3.182	4.541	5.841	10.215	12.924
4	2.132	2.776	3.747	4.604	7.173	8.610
5	2.015	2.571	3.365	4.032	5.893	6.869
6	1.943	2.447	3.143	3.707	5.208	5.959
7	1.895	2.365	2.998	3.499	4.785	5.408
8	1.860	2.306	2.896	3.355	4.501	5.041
9	1.833	2.262	2.821	3.250	4.297	4.781
10	1.812	2.228	2.764	3.169	4.144	4.587
11	1.796	2.201	2.718	3.106	4.025	4.437
12	1.782	2.179	2.681	3.055	3.930	4.318
13	1.771	2.160	2.650	3.012	3.852	4.221
14	1.761	2.145	2.624	2.977	3.787	4.140
15	1.753	2.131	2.602	2.947	3.733	4.073
16	1.746	2.120	2.583	2.921	3.686	4.015
17	1.740	2.110	2.567	2.898	3.646	3.965
18	1.734	2.101	2.552	2.878	3.610	3.922
19	1.729	2.093	2.539	2.861	3.579	3.883
20	1.725	2.086	2.528	2.845	3.552	3.850
21	1.721	2.080	2.518	2.831	3.527	3.819
22	1.717	2.074	2.508	2.819	3.505	3.792
23	1.714	2.069	2.500	2.807	3.485	3.768
24	1.711	2.064	2.492	2.797	3.467	3.745
25	1.708	2.060	2.485	2.787	3.450	3.725
26	1.706	2.056	2.479	2.779	3.435	3.707
27	1.703	2.052	2.473	2.771	3.421	3.690
28	1.701	2.048	2.467	2.763	3.408	3.674
29	1.699	2.045	2.462	2.756	3.396	3.659
30	1.697	2.042	2.457	2.750	3.385	3.646
50	1.676	2.009	2.403	2.678	3.261	3.496
100	1.660	1.984	2.364	2.626	3.174	3.390
∞	1.645	1.960	2.326	2.576	3.090	3.291

Source: Mary B. Harris, *Basic Statistics for Behavioral Science Research* (2nd ed.), p. 517, copyright © 1998 by Allyn and Bacon. Used by permission of Allyn and Bacon.

df*	p	DF FOR NUMERATOR				
		1	2	3	4	5
1	.05	161.447	199.500	215.707	224.583	230.162
	.01	4052.176	4999.492	5403.344	5624.574	5763.641
2	.05	18.513	19.000	19.164	19.247	19.296
	.01	98.502	99.000	99.166	99.249	99.299
	.001	998.500	999.000	999.166	999.250	999.299
3	.05	10.128	9.552	9.277	9.117	9.013
	.01	34.116	30.816	29.457	28.710	28.237
	.001	167.029	148.500	141.108	137.100	134.580
4	.05	7.709	6.944	6.591	6.388	6.256
	.01	21.198	18.000	16.694	15.977	15.522
	.001	74.137	61.246	56.177	53.436	51.712
5	.05	6.608	5.786	5.409	5.192	5.056
	.01	16.258	13.274	12.060	11.392	10.967
	.001	47.181	37.122	33.202	31.085	29.752
6	.05	5.987	5.143	4.757	4.534	4.387
	.01	13.745	10.925	9.780	9.148	8.746
	.001	35.507	27.000	23.703	21.924	20.803
7	.05	5.591	4.737	4.347	4.120	3.972
	.01	12.246	9.547	8.451	7.847	7.460
	.001	29.245	21.689	18.772	17.198	16.206
8	.05	5.318	4.459	4.066	3.838	3.687
	.01	11.259	8.649	7.591	7.006	6.632
	.001	25.415	18.494	15.829	14.392	13.485
9	.05	5.117	4.256	3.863	3.633	3.482
	.01	10.561	8.022	6.992	6.422	6.057
	.001	22.857	16.387	13.902	12.560	11.714
10	.05	4.965	4.103	3.708	3.478	3.326
	.01	10.044	7.559	6.552	5.994	5.636
	.001	21.040	14.905	12.553	11.283	10.481
11	.05	4.844	3.982	3.587	3.357	3.204
	.01	9.646	7.206	6.217	5.668	5.316
	.001	19.687	13.812	11.561	10.346	9.578
12	.05	4.747	3.885	3.490	3.259	3.106
	.01	9.330	6.927	5.953	5.412	5.064
	.001	18.643	12.974	10.804	9.633	8.892
13	.05	4.667	3.806	3.411	3.179	3.025
	.01	9.074	6.701	5.739	5.205	4.862
	.001	17.815	12.313	10.209	9.073	8.354
14	.05	4.600	3.739	3.344	3.112	2.958
	.01	8.862	6.515	5.564	5.035	4.695
	.001	17.143	11.779	9.729	8.622	7.922
15	.05	4.543	3.682	3.287	3.056	2.901
	.01	8.683	6.359	5.417	4.893	4.556
	.001	16.587	11.339	9.335	8.253	7.567

*For denominator.

APPENDIX D

df*	p	DF FOR NUMERATOR 6	7	8	10	15	20
1	.05	233.986	236.768	238.882	241.882	245.950	248.013
	.01	5858.977	5928.348	5981.062	6055.836	6157.273	6208.719
2	.05	19.330	19.353	19.371	19.396	19.429	19.446
	.01	99.333	99.356	99.374	99.399	99.432	99.449
	.001	999.333	999.356	999.375	999.399	999.433	999.449
3	.05	8.941	8.887	8.845	8.786	8.703	8.660
	.01	27.911	27.672	27.489	27.229	26.872	26.690
	.001	132.847	131.583	130.619	129.247	127.374	126.418
4	.05	6.163	6.094	6.041	5.964	5.858	5.803
	.01	15.207	14.976	14.799	14.546	14.198	14.020
	.001	50.525	49.648	48.996	48.053	46.761	46.100
5	.05	4.950	4.876	4.818	4.735	4.619	4.558
	.01	10.672	10.456	10.289	10.051	9.722	9.553
	.001	28.834	28.163	27.649	26.917	25.911	25.395
6	.05	4.284	4.207	4.147	4.060	3.938	3.874
	.01	8.466	8.260	8.102	7.874	7.559	7.396
	.001	20.030	19.463	19.030	18.411	17.559	17.120
7	.05	3.866	3.787	3.726	3.637	3.511	3.445
	.01	7.191	6.993	6.840	6.620	6.314	6.155
	.001	15.521	15.019	14.634	14.083	13.324	12.292
8	.05	3.581	3.500	3.438	3.347	3.218	3.150
	.01	6.371	6.178	6.029	5.814	5.515	5.359
	.001	12.858	12.398	12.046	11.540	10.841	10.480
9	.05	3.374	3.293	3.230	3.137	3.006	2.936
	.01	5.802	5.613	5.467	5.257	4.962	4.808
	.001	11.128	10.698	10.368	9.894	9.238	8.898
10	.05	3.217	3.135	3.072	2.978	2.845	2.774
	.01	5.386	5.200	5.057	4.849	4.558	4.405
	.001	9.926	9.517	9.204	8.754	8.129	7.804
11	.05	3.095	3.012	2.948	2.854	2.719	2.646
	.01	5.069	4.886	4.744	4.539	4.251	4.099
	.001	9.047	8.655	8.355	7.922	7.321	7.008
12	.05	2.996	2.913	2.849	2.753	2.617	2.544
	.01	4.821	4.640	4.499	4.296	4.010	3.858
	.001	8.379	8.001	7.710	7.292	6.709	6.405
13	.05	2.915	2.832	2.767	2.671	2.533	2.459
	.01	4.620	4.441	4.302	4.100	3.815	3.665
	.001	7.856	7.489	7.206	6.799	6.231	5.934
14	.05	2.848	2.764	2.699	2.602	2.463	2.388
	.01	4.456	4.278	4.140	3.939	3.656	3.505
	.001	7.436	7.077	6.802	6.404	5.848	5.557
15	.05	2.790	2.707	2.641	2.544	2.403	2.328
	.01	4.318	4.142	4.004	3.805	3.522	3.372
	.001	7.092	6.741	6.471	6.081	5.535	5.248

(continued)

APPENDIX D   Continued

		DF FOR NUMERATOR				
df^*	p	1	2	3	4	5
16	.05	4.494	3.634	3.239	3.007	2.852
	.01	8.531	6.226	5.292	4.773	4.437
	.001	16.120	10.971	9.006	7.944	7.272
17	.05	4.451	3.592	3.197	2.965	2.810
	.01	8.400	6.112	5.185	4.669	4.336
	.001	15.722	10.658	8.727	7.683	7.022
18	.05	4.414	3.555	3.160	2.928	2.773
	.01	8.285	6.013	5.092	4.579	4.248
	.001	15.379	10.390	8.487	7.459	6.808
19	.05	4.381	3.522	3.127	2.895	2.740
	.01	8.185	5.926	5.010	4.500	4.171
	.001	15.081	10.157	8.280	7.265	6.622
20	.05	4.351	3.493	3.098	2.866	2.711
	.01	8.096	5.849	4.938	4.431	4.103
	.001	14.819	9.953	8.098	7.096	6.461
21	.05	4.325	3.467	3.072	2.840	2.685
	.01	8.017	5.780	4.874	4.369	4.042
	.001	14.587	9.772	7.938	6.947	6.318
22	.05	4.301	3.443	3.049	2.817	2.661
	.01	7.945	5.719	4.817	4.313	3.988
	.001	14.380	9.612	7.796	6.814	6.191
23	.05	4.279	3.422	3.028	2.796	2.640
	.01	7.881	5.664	4.765	4.264	3.939
	.001	14.195	9.469	7.669	6.696	6.078
24	.05	4.260	3.403	3.009	2.776	2.621
	.01	7.823	5.614	4.718	4.218	3.895
	.001	14.028	9.339	7.554	6.589	5.977
25	.05	4.242	3.385	2.991	2.759	2.603
	.01	7.770	5.568	4.675	4.177	3.855
	.001	13.877	9.223	7.451	6.493	5.885
26	.05	4.225	3.369	2.975	2.743	2.587
	.01	7.721	5.526	4.637	4.140	3.818
	.001	13.739	9.116	7.357	6.406	5.802
27	.05	4.210	3.354	2.960	2.728	2.572
	.01	7.677	5.488	4.601	4.106	3.785
	.001	13.613	9.019	7.272	6.326	5.726
28	.05	4.196	3.340	2.947	2.714	2.558
	.01	7.636	5.453	4.568	4.074	3.754
	.001	13.498	8.931	7.193	6.253	5.656
29	.05	4.183	3.328	2.934	2.701	2.545
	.01	7.598	5.420	4.538	4.045	3.725
	.001	13.391	8.849	7.121	6.186	5.593
30	.05	4.171	3.316	2.922	2.690	2.534
	.01	7.562	5.390	4.510	4.018	3.699
	.001	13.293	8.773	7.054	6.125	5.534

*For denominator.

APPENDIX D

| | | \multicolumn{6}{c}{DF FOR NUMERATOR} |
df*	p	6	7	8	10	15	20
16	.05	2.741	2.657	2.591	2.494	2.352	2.276
	.01	4.202	4.026	3.890	3.691	3.409	3.259
	.001	6.805	6.460	6.195	5.812	5.274	4.992
17	.05	2.699	2.614	2.548	2.450	2.308	2.230
	.01	4.102	3.927	3.791	3.593	3.312	3.162
	.001	6.562	6.223	5.962	5.584	5.054	4.775
18	.05	2.661	2.577	2.510	2.412	2.269	2.191
	.01	4.015	3.841	3.705	3.508	3.227	3.077
	.001	6.355	6.021	5.763	5.390	4.866	4.590
19	.05	2.628	2.544	2.477	2.378	2.234	2.155
	.01	3.939	3.765	3.631	3.434	3.153	3.003
	.001	6.175	5.845	5.590	5.222	4.704	4.430
20	.05	2.599	2.514	2.447	2.348	2.203	2.124
	.01	3.871	3.699	3.564	3.368	3.088	2.938
	.001	6.019	5.692	5.440	5.075	4.562	4.290
21	.05	2.573	2.488	2.420	2.321	2.176	2.096
	.01	3.812	3.640	3.506	3.310	3.030	2.880
	.001	5.881	5.557	5.308	4.946	4.437	4.167
22	.05	2.549	2.464	2.397	2.297	2.151	2.071
	.01	3.758	3.587	3.453	3.258	2.978	2.827
	.001	5.758	5.438	5.190	4.832	4.326	4.058
23	.05	2.528	2.442	2.375	2.275	2.128	2.048
	.01	3.710	3.539	3.406	3.211	2.931	2.781
	.001	5.649	5.331	5.085	4.730	4.227	3.961
24	.05	2.508	2.423	2.355	2.255	2.108	2.027
	.01	3.667	3.496	3.363	3.168	2.889	2.738
	.001	5.550	5.235	4.991	4.638	4.139	3.873
25	.05	2.490	2.405	2.337	2.236	2.089	2.007
	.01	3.627	3.457	3.324	3.129	2.850	2.699
	.001	5.462	5.148	4.906	4.555	4.059	3.794
26	.05	2.474	2.388	2.321	2.220	2.072	1.990
	.01	3.591	3.421	3.288	3.094	2.815	2.664
	.001	5.381	5.070	4.829	4.480	3.986	3.723
27	.05	2.459	2.373	2.305	2.204	2.056	1.974
	.01	3.558	3.388	3.256	3.062	2.783	2.632
	.001	5.308	4.998	4.759	4.412	3.920	3.658
28	.05	2.445	2.359	2.291	2.190	2.041	1.959
	.01	3.528	3.358	3.226	3.032	2.753	2.602
	.001	5.241	4.933	4.695	4.349	3.859	3.598
29	.05	2.432	2.346	2.278	2.177	2.027	1.945
	.01	3.499	3.330	3.198	3.005	2.726	2.574
	.001	5.179	4.873	4.636	4.292	3.804	3.543
30	.05	2.421	2.334	2.266	2.165	2.015	1.932
	.01	3.473	3.304	3.173	2.979	2.700	2.549
	.001	5.122	4.817	4.581	4.239	3.753	3.493

(continued)

APPENDIX D Continued

df*	p	DF FOR NUMERATOR				
		1	2	3	4	5
40	.05	4.085	3.232	2.839	2.606	2.449
	.01	7.314	5.179	4.313	3.828	3.514
	.001	12.609	8.251	6.595	5.698	5.128
50	.05	4.034	3.183	2.790	2.557	2.400
	.01	7.171	5.057	4.199	3.720	3.408
	.001	12.222	7.956	6.336	5.459	4.901
60	.05	4.001	3.150	2.758	2.525	2.368
	.01	7.077	4.977	4.126	3.649	3.339
	.001	11.973	7.768	6.171	5.307	4.757
70	.05	3.978	3.128	2.736	2.503	2.346
	.01	7.011	4.922	4.074	3.600	3.291
	.001	11.799	7.637	6.057	5.201	4.656
80	.05	3.960	3.111	2.719	2.486	2.329
	.01	6.963	4.881	4.036	3.563	3.255
	.001	11.671	7.540	5.972	5.123	4.582
90	.05	3.947	3.098	2.706	2.473	2.316
	.01	6.925	4.849	4.007	3.535	3.228
	.001	11.573	7.466	5.908	5.064	4.526
100	.05	3.936	3.087	2.696	2.463	2.305
	.01	6.895	4.824	3.984	3.513	3.206
	.001	11.495	7.408	5.857	5.017	4.482
120	.05	3.920	3.072	2.680	2.447	2.290
	.01	6.851	4.787	3.949	3.480	3.174
	.001	11.380	7.321	5.781	4.947	4.416
150	.05	3.904	3.056	2.665	2.432	2.274
	.01	6.807	4.749	3.915	3.447	3.142
	.001	11.267	7.236	5.707	4.879	4.351
200	.05	3.888	3.041	2.650	2.417	2.259
	.01	6.763	4.713	3.881	3.414	3.110
	.001	11.154	7.152	5.634	4.812	4.287
300	.05	3.073	3.026	2.635	2.402	2.244
	.01	6.720	4.677	3.848	3.382	3.079
	.001	11.044	7.069	5.562	4.746	4.225
400	.05	3.865	3.018	2.627	2.394	2.237
	.01	6.699	4.659	3.831	3.366	3.063
	.001	10.989	7.028	5.527	4.713	4.194
500	.05	3.860	3.014	2.623	2.390	2.232
	.01	6.686	4.648	3.821	3.357	3.054
	.001	10.957	7.004	5.506	4.693	4.176
1000	.05	3.851	3.005	2.614	2.381	2.223
	.01	6.660	4.626	3.801	3.338	3.036
	.001	10.892	6.956	5.464	4.655	4.139
∞	.05	3.841	2.996	2.605	2.372	2.214
	.01	6.635	4.605	3.782	3.319	3.017
	.001	10.828	6.908	5.422	4.617	4.103

*For denominator.

APPENDIX D							

		DF FOR NUMERATOR					
df*	p	6	7	8	10	15	20
40	.05	2.336	2.249	2.180	2.077	1.924	1.839
	.01	3.291	3.124	2.993	2.801	2.522	2.369
	.001	4.731	4.436	4.207	3.874	3.400	3.145
50	.05	2.286	2.199	2.130	2.026	1.871	1.784
	.01	3.186	3.020	2.890	2.698	2.419	2.265
	.001	4.512	4.222	3.998	3.671	3.204	2.951
60	.05	2.254	2.167	2.097	1.993	1.836	1.748
	.01	3.119	2.953	2.823	2.632	2.352	2.198
	.001	4.372	4.086	3.865	3.541	3.078	2.827
70	.05	2.231	2.143	2.074	1.969	1.812	1.722
	.01	3.071	2.906	2.777	2.585	2.306	2.150
	.001	4.275	3.992	3.773	3.452	2.991	2.741
80	.05	2.214	2.126	2.056	1.951	1.793	1.703
	.01	3.036	2.871	2.742	2.551	2.271	2.115
	.001	4.204	3.923	3.705	3.386	2.927	2.677
90	.05	2.201	2.113	2.043	1.938	1.779	1.688
	.01	3.009	2.845	2.715	2.524	2.244	2.088
	.001	4.150	3.870	3.653	3.336	2.879	2.629
100	.05	2.191	2.103	2.032	1.927	1.768	1.676
	.01	2.988	2.823	2.694	2.503	2.223	2.067
	.001	4.107	3.829	3.612	3.296	2.840	2.591
120	.05	2.175	2.087	2.016	1.910	1.750	1.659
	.01	2.956	2.792	2.663	2.472	2.192	2.035
	.001	4.044	3.767	3.552	3.237	2.783	2.534
150	.05	2.160	2.071	2.001	1.894	1.734	1.641
	.01	2.924	2.761	2.632	2.441	2.160	2.003
	.001	3.981	3.706	3.493	3.179	2.727	2.479
200	.05	2.144	2.056	1.985	1.878	1.717	1.623
	.01	2.893	2.730	2.601	2.411	2.129	1.971
	.001	3.920	3.647	3.434	3.123	2.672	2.424
300	.05	2.129	2.040	1.969	1.862	1.700	1.606
	.01	2.862	2.699	2.571	2.380	2.099	1.940
	.001	3.860	3.588	3.377	3.067	2.618	2.371
400	.05	2.121	2.032	1.962	1.854	1.691	1.597
	.01	2.847	2.684	2.556	2.365	2.084	1.925
	.001	3.830	3.560	3.349	3.040	2.592	2.344
500	.05	2.177	2.028	1.957	1.850	1.686	1.592
	.01	2.838	2.675	2.547	2.356	2.075	1.915
	.001	3.813	3.542	3.332	3.023	2.576	2.328
1000	.05	2.108	2.019	1.948	1.840	1.676	1.581
	.01	2.820	2.657	2.529	2.339	2.056	1.897
	.001	3.778	3.508	3.299	2.991	2.544	2.297
∞	.05	2.099	2.010	1.938	1.880	1.831	1.752
	.01	2.802	2.639	2.511	2.407	2.321	2.185
	.001	3.743	3.475	3.266	3.097	2.959	2.742

APPENDIX E Pearson *r* Table

	LEVEL OF SIGNIFICANCE FOR ONE-TAILED TEST					
	.05	.025	.01	.005	.001	.0005
	LEVEL OF SIGNIFICANCE FOR TWO-TAILED TEST					
df	.10	.05	.02	.01	.002	.001
1	0.988	0.997	1.000	1.000	1.000	1.000
2	0.900	0.950	0.980	0.990	0.998	0.999
3	0.805	0.878	0.934	0.959	0.986	0.991
4	0.729	0.811	0.882	0.917	0.963	0.974
5	0.669	0.754	0.833	0.875	0.935	0.951
6	0.621	0.707	0.789	0.834	0.905	0.925
7	0.582	0.666	0.750	0.798	0.875	0.898
8	0.549	0.632	0.715	0.765	0.847	0.872
9	0.521	0.602	0.685	0.735	0.820	0.847
10	0.497	0.576	0.658	0.708	0.795	0.823
11	0.476	0.553	0.634	0.684	0.772	0.801
12	0.458	0.532	0.612	0.661	0.750	0.780
13	0.441	0.514	0.592	0.641	0.730	0.760
14	0.426	0.497	0.574	0.623	0.711	0.742
15	0.412	0.482	0.558	0.606	0.694	0.725
16	0.400	0.468	0.543	0.590	0.678	0.708
17	0.389	0.456	0.529	0.575	0.662	0.693
18	0.378	0.444	0.516	0.561	0.648	0.679
19	0.369	0.433	0.503	0.549	0.635	0.665
20	0.360	0.423	0.492	0.537	0.622	0.652
21	0.352	0.413	0.482	0.526	0.610	0.640
22	0.344	0.404	0.472	0.515	0.599	0.629
23	0.337	0.396	0.462	0.505	0.588	0.618
24	0.330	0.388	0.453	0.496	0.578	0.607
25	0.323	0.381	0.445	0.487	0.568	0.597
26	0.317	0.374	0.437	0.479	0.559	0.588
27	0.311	0.367	0.430	0.471	0.550	0.579
28	0.306	0.361	0.423	0.463	0.541	0.570
30	0.296	0.349	0.409	0.449	0.526	0.554
40	0.257	0.304	0.358	0.393	0.463	0.490
50	0.231	0.273	0.322	0.354	0.419	0.443
60	0.211	0.250	0.295	0.325	0.385	0.408
80	0.183	0.217	0.257	0.283	0.336	0.357
100	0.164	0.195	0.230	0.254	0.303	0.321
200	0.116	0.138	0.164	0.181	0.216	0.230
500	0.073	0.088	0.104	0.115	0.138	0.146

Source: Mary B. Harris, *Basic Statistics for Behavioral Science Research* (2nd ed.), p. 512, copyright © 1998 by Allyn and Bacon. Used by permission of Allyn and Bacon.

APPENDIX F   Spearman *rho* Table

		LEVEL OF SIGNIFICANCE FOR ONE-TAILED TEST			
		.05	.025	.01	.005
		LEVEL OF SIGNIFICANCE FOR TWO-TAILED TEST			
N	df	.10	.05	.02	.01
5	3	.900	1.000	1.000	—
6	4	.829	.886	.943	1.000
7	5	.714	.786	.893	.929
8	6	.643	.738	.833	.881
9	7	.600	.683	.783	.833
10	8	.564	.648	.746	.794
12	10	.506	.591	.712	.777
14	12	.456	.544	.645	.715
16	14	.425	.506	.601	.665
18	16	.399	.475	.564	.625
20	18	.377	.450	.534	.591
22	20	.359	.428	.508	.562
24	22	.343	.409	.485	.537
26	24	.329	.392	.465	.515
28	26	.317	.377	.448	.496
30	28	.306	.364	.432	.478

Source: Mary B. Harris, *Basic Statistics for Behavioral Science Research* (2nd ed.), p. 513, copyright © 1998 by Allyn and Bacon. Used by permission of Allyn and Bacon.

N = number of pairs

abscissa The horizontal (or *x*) axis of a graph; generally used to display the values of the independent variable. *Compare* ordinate.

absolute frequency The display in a frequency table of the actual number of times each category or measurement point occurs in a distribution (as opposed to its relative frequency or the proportion of times it occurs). *Compare* cumulative frequency; relative frequency.

abstract A (typically one-paragraph) summary of the important points in a scholarly journal article.

academic freedom The ability to teach and research topics that professors consider to be important. *See* tenure.

academic library A library attached to a university/college that supports its research and teaching needs. *Compare* public library; special-use library.

accelerated longitudinal design A design that combines cross-sectional and longitudinal studies in research on individuals over time.

acceptance error (*See* Type II error)

accidental error (*See* random error)

accidental sample (*See* convenience sample)

account analysis An in-depth naturalistic inquiry interview that asks people to account for what a researcher observed. *Compare* critical incident technique; episode analysis; ethnomethodological interview; key informant; life story interview; long interview; oral history; protocol analysis.

acquiescent response style A response style (set) tendency of some respondents to be agreeable and say "yes" to whatever question is asked. *Compare* quarrelsome response style; social desirability bias.

action research A form of applied communication research that involves "a collaborative approach to *inquiry* or *investigation* that provides people with the means to take systematic *action to resolve specific problems*" (Stringer, 1996, p. 15).

active variable (*See* manipulated variable)

actuaries Statisticians who specialize in probability theory, especially with regard to calculating risks for insurance companies; historically among the earliest professional statisticians (see Vogt, 1999).

adjusted R² (*r²) A multiple correlation coefficient that takes into account the number of independent variables studied.

advertising readership study Market research conducted regularly by companies to identify differences in demographic characteristics between readers and nonreaders, and to identify those who read advertisements for specific products. *Compare* broadcast audience survey; contextual inquiry; editorial content readership survey; usability testing.

aggregate data Data about groups, rather than about individuals.

agreement coefficient A measure of the relation of a single item on an instrument to the rest of the instrument.

alpha coefficient (*See* Cronbach alpha coefficient method)

alpha error (*See* Type I error)

alternate causality argument (alternate hypothesis) Occurs when some variable other than the one researchers study in an experiment causes the changes observed in the dependent variable.

alternate hypothesis (*See* alternate causality argument)

alternative procedure method A multiple-administration reliability technique that assesses the temporal stability of instruments at two or more points in time by having the same people complete another, equivalent instrument at the second administration; comparing scores on these two instruments is then the basis for making claims about the reliability of the first instrument. *See* coefficient of equivalence.

analysis of covariance (ANCOVA) A multivariate difference analysis that is an extension of analysis of variance used to analyze differences among groups on a dependent interval/ratio variable while controlling for the effects of potentially confounding variables (covariates). *Compare* analysis of covariance; log-linear analysis; multivariate analysis of covariance.

analysis of variance (ANOVA, or *F* Test) A statistical procedure that examines differences between the conditions created from two or more independent variables with respect to an interval/ratio dependent variable. *See* analysis of covariance; factorial analysis of variance; one-variable analysis of variance; multiple comparison tests; multiple-variable analysis of variance; multivariate analysis of covariance; multivariate analysis of variance; omnibus tests; repeated-measures analysis of variance. *Compare* chi-square test; *t* test.

analytic induction In naturalistic inquiry, inferring meanings from the data collected, rather than imposing such meanings on the data from another source (such as a theory). *See* grounded theory.

anonymity Protection of research participants' right to privacy that exists when researchers cannot connect responses to the individuals who provided them. *Compare* confidentiality.

antimode The score or value in a distribution that occurs the least. *Compare* mode.

a posteriori comparison (*See* multiple comparison tests)

appeals to tradition, custom, and faith A type of everyday way of knowing that involves believing something simply because most people in a society assume it is true (tradition), because it has always been done that way (custom), or a belief that does not rest on logical proof or material evidence (faith). *Compare* authority; intuition; magic, superstition, and mysticism; personal experience.

applied communication research Research conducted for the purpose of solving a "real-world," socially relevant communication problem. *See* action research; social justice communication research. *Compare* basic communication research.

applied research Research designed to solve a practical problem. *See* applied communication research. *Compare* basic research.

archival communication research Research that involves describing and evaluating communication embedded in existing records of human behavior kept in archives. *See* archive.

archive A place where primary source materials, original records and documents, are housed. *See* primary source materials.

array An ordered display of numerical measurements (e.g., the distribution 5, 3.3, 10, 7.5 becomes an array of data when put in either an *ascending order,* beginning with the lowest number and moving to the highest number—3.3, 5, 7.5, 10—or a *descending order,* beginning with the highest number and moving to the lowest number—10, 7.5, 5, 3.3).

asymptotic A curve on a graph, like the normal curve, that runs on, theoretically forever, getting ever closer to the line but never touching it.

attribute variable A trait or characteristic of people, such as age or gender. *See* background variable.

attrition (*See* mortality)

authority A type of everyday way of knowing that involves believing something because of trust in the person who said it. *Compare* appeals to tradition, custom, and faith; intuition; magic, superstition, and mysticism; personal experience.

autobiography The story of one's own life, of which autoethnography is one form. *See* autoethnography.

autoethnography (personal ethnography) A form of naturalistic inquiry in which researchers examine their own life experiences and fieldwork. *Compare* critical ethnography; ethnography; ethnomethodology.

axiological assumption Assumptions about the role of values in the research process. *Compare* epistemological assumption; methodological assumption; ontological assumption; rhetorical assumption.

axis A line (horizontal or vertical) used to construct a graph. *See* abscissa; ordinate.

background variable (classification, individual-difference, organismic, subject variable) An aspect of "subjects' [research participants'] 'backgrounds' that may influence other variables but will not be influenced by them" (Vogt, 1993, p. 16), such as gender and ethnicity. *See* attribute variable.

backward telescoping The tendency for people to think that past events occurred longer ago than they did. *Compare* forward telescoping.

bar chart A visual display that uses shaded "blocks" (rectangles and/or squares), usually arranged vertically, to show the frequency counts in each category of a nominal independent variable. *See* grouped bar chart; horizontal bar chart. *Compare* frequency histogram; frequency polygon; line graph; pie chart.

basement effect (*See* floor effect)

basic communication research Research designed to increase knowledge about communication phenomena by testing, refining, and elaborating theory. *Compare* applied communication research.

basic research Research designed to test and refine theory. *See* basic communication research. *Compare* applied research.

before-after designs Experimental designs that involve a pretest and a posttest.

bell-shaped curve (*See* normal distribution)

beta coefficient (beta weight, regression weight, standardized regression coefficient) In multiple linear regression, a coefficient that indicates the extent to which, or relative weight that, each predictor variable explains the scores on the criterion variable, while controlling for the other predictor variables.

beta error (*See* Type II error)

beta weight (*See* beta coefficient)

between-group design (between-subjects design) A research design in which one group of research participants receives one level of an independent variable (such as a treatment) and are compared to another group that receives another level (such as no treatment). *Compare* within-group design.

between-subjects design (*See* between-group design)

bimodal distribution A distribution of data that has two modes. *Compare* multimodal distribution; unimodal distribution.

binomial variable (*See* dichotomized variable; dichotomous variable)

biographical studies A form of historical criticism that examines public and private texts of prominent, influential, or otherwise remarkable individuals. *Compare* historical case studies; oral histories; social movement studies.

bivariate association A statistical relationship between two variables.

bivariate correlation coefficient A correlation coefficient between two variables.

bivariate regression coefficient In linear regression analysis, a statistical measure of the relationship between two variables only.

blank experiment Introducing an irrelevant treatment in experimental research to keep participants from guessing the true purpose of the experiment or becoming automatic in their responses.

blind review The process used by most scholarly journals today, whereby reviewers are not told the name or institutional affiliation of the person(s) who submitted the manuscript; the goal is to judge the work on its merits, not on the reputation of the institutional affiliation of the researcher(s).

Bonferroni technique A method used in multiple comparison tests that adjusts the significance level so as to reduce the chance of making a Type I error, that is, rejecting the null hypothesis when it should have been accepted; in this case, by dividing the significance level used by the number of comparisons that are made. *Compare* Least Significant Difference Test; Scheffe Test; Tukey's Honestly Significant Difference Test; Tukey Test.

boolean operators In electronic searches, words that allow one to narrow or broaden the search or to link related terms (such as *and, or, not*). *Compare* positional operators.

broadcast audience survey Market research conducted to identify the size and composition of the audience that different television and radio programs and stations reach. *Compare* advertising readership study; contextual inquiry; editorial content readership survey; usability testing.

calculated value The numerical value that results from a statistical significance-testing procedure, which is then assessed in terms of the probability of its occurrence. *Compare* critical value.

call number The unique number assigned to each book in a library by some type of cataloguing system, such as the Dewey Decimal System or the Library of Congress System.

canonical The correlation coefficient in canonical correlation analysis.

canonical correlation analysis (R_c) A multivariate relationship analysis that is a form of regression analysis used to examine the statistical relationship between multiple independent and dependent variables by determining which set of the independent variables are more closely associated with which set of the dependent variables. *See* canonical; canonical variate. *Compare* cluster analysis; discriminant analysis; factor analysis; multidimensional scaling; path analysis.

canonical variate A set of variables in canonical correlation analysis.

card catalogue A centralized file in libraries that contains cards for each book in the holdings that are cross-referenced in three ways: by author, title of work, and subject area.

case study The findings from naturalistic inquiry reported in the form of a detailed examination of a single subject, group, or phenomenon.

cataloguing system The system libraries use to organize their holdings. *See* call number; card catalogue; Dewey Decimal System; Library of Congress System.

categorical variable (*See* nominal variable)

causal relationship A relationship between variables in which changes in the independent variable cause changes in the dependent variable. *See* nonrecursive causal model; recursive causal model. *Compare* noncausal relationship.

CD-ROM Stands for "compact disk-read-only memory"; databases are often stored on these disks.

ceiling effect Occurs when research participants have scores that are at the upper limit ("ceiling") of a variable, making it difficult to tell whether a treatment has any effect. *Compare* floor effect.

cell Each possible combination of the independent variables in a study.

cell suppression A process used with statistical disclosure limitation methods by which an agency that collects data that will be shared with the public defines a cell as "sensitive" because the number of responses in it is less than some specified number (e.g., 10) and then does not publish information about sensitive cells to protect the identity of these respondents.

census Studying every member of a population or universe. *Compare* sample.

central limits theorem "For samples of a sufficiently large size, the real distribution of means is almost always approximately normal. The original variable can have any distribution. It doesn't have to be bell shaped in the least" (Norusis, 1991, p. 194).

chance error (*See* random error)

character units (*See* referential units)

chi-square (χ^2) test A statistical procedure that examines differences between the categories of an independent variable with respect to a dependent variable measured on a nominal scale. *See* expected frequencies; log-linear analysis; observed frequencies; one-variable chi-square test; two-variable chi-square test. *Compare* analysis of variance; *t* test.

claim An assertion or conclusion. *Compare* evidence; warrant.

classical rhetoric Early rhetorical theory and criticism developed by the Greeks and Romans that examined the characteristics and effects of persuasive public speaking, such as how political speeches enlisted support for a specific leader or helped establish and maintain social order. *Compare* contemporary rhetorical criticism.

classification variable (*See* background variable)

classificatory variable (*See* nominal variable)

closed question A question that provides respondents with a limited number of predetermined responses from which to choose. *Compare* open question.

cluster analysis A multivariate relationship analysis that explains whether multiple variables or elements are similar enough to be placed together into meaningful groups or clusters that have not been predetermined by the researcher. *Compare* canonical correlation analysis; discriminant analysis; factor analysis; multidimensional scaling; path analysis.

cluster sample A random sample drawn by means of a procedure that selects units (clusters) randomly from a population. *See* multistage sampling. *Compare* simple random sample; stratification sample; systematic sample.

coders In content analysis, trained observers who identify the appropriate category for each unit.

coding scheme A classification system that describes the nature or quantifies the frequency of particular communication behaviors, either during or after the observations take place.

coefficient alpha (*See* Cronbach's alpha coefficient method)

coefficient of determination (r-squared, r^2) A numerical indicator that tells how much of the variance in one variable is associated, explained, or determined by another variable; computed by squaring the correlation coefficient. *Compare* coefficient of multiple determination; coefficient of nondetermination; correlation coefficient.

coefficient of equivalence The statistical measure of reliability for the alternative procedure method. *Compare* coefficient of stability.

coefficient of multiple determination (R-squared, R^2) A numerical indicator that expresses the amount of variance in the criterion variable that can be explained by the independent variables acting together; computed by squaring the multiple correlation coefficient. *Compare* coefficient of determination; coefficient of nondetermination.

coefficient of nondetermination That part of the variance in the criterion variable that is left unexplained by an/the independent variable(s); symbolized and calculated as $1 - R_2$. *Compare* coefficient of determination; coefficient of multiple determination.

coefficient of stability The statistical measure of reliability for the test-retest method. *Compare* coefficient of equivalence.

cognitive conservatism In intuition, a proclivity to hold onto conclusions people reach even when presented with contradictory information.

cohort effects Effects due to membership in a cohort (a particular group). *See* generation effects; period effects.

cohort study A longitudinal survey in which responses from specific subgroups of a population, usually divided on the basis of age, are identified and compared over time. *See* cohort effects; generation effects; period effects.

collinearity (multicollinearity) In multiple linear regression, the extent to which the predictor variables are correlated with one another.

combination purposive sample (mixed purposive sample) A purposive sample used in naturalistic inquiry that combines purposive sampling methods; allows triangulation and meets multiple interests and needs.

communication The processes by which verbal and nonverbal messages are used to create meaning.

community structure approach A form of quantitative content analysis that focuses on the ways in which key characteristics of communities (such as cities) are related to the content coverage of newspapers in those communities.

comparison group Any group in an experiment against which another group is compared, such as two treatment groups. *See* control group.

complete observer An observational role in naturalistic inquiry in which a researcher does not interact with the people being observed. *Compare* complete participant; observer-participant; participant-observer.

complete participant An observational role in naturalistic inquiry in which a researcher is fully involved in a social setting and does not let people know they are being studied. *Compare* complete observer; observer-participant; participant-observer.

computer-assisted personal interviewing (CAPI) A form of survey interviewing in which "the question text appears on the screen, with possible response categories or indication of what sort of answer is required. The interviewer reads out the question and enters the response and the next question appears automatically" (J. Martin & Manners, 1995, p. 52). *Compare* computer-assisted telephone interviews.

computer-assisted telephone interviews (CATI) A form of survey interviewing in which respondents are automatically selected and called, interviewers are cued to the questions to ask, and the computer records, codes, and processes responses. *See* touch-tone data entry; voice recognition entry. *Compare* computer-assisted personal interviewing.

conceptual definition A statement that describes what a concept means by relating it to other abstract concepts. *See* conceptual fit. *Compare* operational definition.

conceptualization The first phase of research, which involves forming an idea about what needs to be studied. *Compare* operationalization; reconceptualization.

conceptual fit The preservation of meaning between a conceptual definition and an operational definition.

conceptual replication A replication that examines the same issue as a previous study but uses entirely different procedures, measurement instruments, sampling procedures, and/or data-analytic techniques for the purpose of seeing if the same results can be obtained with very different research procedures. *Compare* exact replication; partial replication.

concomitant variable (*See* control variable)

concurrent validity (convergent validity) A form of criterion-related validity that is established when the results from a new measurement instrument agree (concur) with those from an existing, known-to-be-valid criterion. *Compare* predictive validity.

conditioning effects (*See* interaction effects)

conditions (groups) Groups in an experiment that receive differential exposure to the independent variable. *See* level.

confederate A person who pretends to be a research participant to help a researcher.

conference paper A manuscript presented at a scholarly convention/conference. *Compare* scholarly journal; scholarly text.

confessional tale A tale told in reporting naturalistic inquiry that focuses primarily on the researcher and his or her experiences during the fieldwork. *Compare* critical tale; formal tale; impressionistic tale; jointly told tale; literary tale; realist tale.

confidence coefficient (*See* confidence level)

confidence interval (CI; margin of error) In estimation, the range of the scores of the random sample means (or other statistics) associated with a confidence level. *See* confidence level; confidence limits.

confidence level (confidence coefficient) In estimation, the percentage of random sample means (or other statistics) in a sampling distribution covered by the estimate of a population parameter.

confidence limits (confidence bounds) The upper and lower values of a confidence interval. *See* confidence interval.

confidentiality The protection of research participants' right to privacy that exists when researchers know who said what, but promise not to reveal that information publicly. *See* Federal Certificate of Confidentiality. *Compare* anonymity.

confirmatory factor analysis A type of factor analysis used to identify factors that a researcher expects to find on the basis of theory and/or research. *Compare* exploratory factor analysis.

confirming and disconfirming case sample A purposive sample used in naturalistic inquiry of people who can confirm or disconfirm researchers' expectations; used to elaborate and deepen initial analysis and test variation. *Compare* criterion sample; critical case sample; extreme case sample; homogeneous sample; intensity sample; maximum variation sample; opportunistic sample; politically important case sample; random purposive sample; stratified purposive sample; theoretical sample; typical case sample.

confounded When the separate effects of two or more variables cannot be determined. *See* confounding variable.

confounding variable A variable that obscures the effects of another variable. *See* confounded; extraneous variable; intervening variable; reinforcer variable; suppressor variable.

consistency effect A question order effect that occurs when respondents believe that questions answered later must be consistent with answers to earlier questions. *Compare* fatigue effect; redundancy effect.

constant comparative method A data-analytic method used in grounded theory in naturalistic inquiry to create and compare exhaustive categories that explain the data.

construct validity A form of measurement validity that is established on the basis of the extent to which scores on a measurement instrument are related in logical ways to other established measures. *Compare* content validity; criterion-related validity.

contact rate The percentage of phone calls in survey research that result in contact with an English-speaking interviewee. *Compare* cooperation rate; surveyed rate.

contemporary rhetorical criticism A wide range of philosophical, theoretical, and methodological perspectives used to study the persuasive impact of many different types of texts and messages. *Compare* classical rhetoric.

content analysis A form of textual analysis used to identify, enumerate, and analyze occurrences of specific messages and message characteristics embedded in relevant texts. *See* coders; qualitative content analysis; quantitative content analysis; unitizing. *Compare* interaction analysis; performance studies; rhetorical criticism.

content validity A form of measurement validity that argues via face validity and/or a panel approach that a measurement instrument measures the attributes (or content) of the concept being investigated. *See* face validity; panel approach. *Compare* construct validity; criterion-related validity.

context-bound findings Findings that apply to the particular people, situation, and/or time period studied. *Compare* context-free generalizations.

context-free generalizations Conclusions that can be generalized to other people, situations, and/or time periods than the ones studied. *Compare* context-bound findings.

contextual inquiry Market research that involves studying customers' use of a product at their place of work. *Compare* advertising readership study; broadcast audience survey; editorial content readership survey; usability testing.

contingency effects (*See* interaction effects)

contingency table analysis (*See* two-variable chi-square test)

continuous variable (metric variable, numerical variable) A variable measured on an interval or ratio measurement scale. *Compare* nominal variable; ordered variable.

control In experimental research, when a researcher "tries systematically to rule out variables that are possible 'causes' of the effects he [or she] is studying other than the variable that he [or she] has hypothesized to be 'causes'" (Kerlinger, 1973, p. 4).

control group A condition (group) in an experiment that does not get the independent variable manipulation or any other manipulation (such as a placebo); a no-treatment comparison group. *See* comparison group. *Compare* placebo group; treatment group.

controlled variable (*See* manipulated variable)

controlling for environmental influences A form of procedure validity and reliability that involves keeping the setting in which a study is done as consistent as possible. *Compare* treatment validity and reliability.

control variable A variable for which researchers try to control. *See* covariate.

convenience sample (accidental sample, haphazard sample) A nonrandom sample in which respondents are selected on the basis of availability.

Compare network sample; purposive sample; quota sample; volunteer sample.

convergent validity (*See* concurrent validity)

conversation analysis A form of naturalistic ethnomethodological research that involves the study of interaction using qualitative methods. *Compare* formal ethnomethodology; interaction analysis.

cooperation rate The percentage of phone calls in survey research in which interviewees agree to participate. *Compare* contact rate; surveyed rate.

correlation A statistical relationship between variables. *See* correlation coefficient; correlation matrix; correlation ratio; Cramer's V; criterion variable; intercorrelation; Kendall's correlation; measure of association; multiple correlation; multiple correlation coefficient; partial correlation; Pearson product moment correlation; point biserial correlation; predictor variable; simple correlation; Spearman correlation coefficient.

correlational design A research strategy that assesses all of the variables of interest at one point in time to describe the relationships among those variables.

correlation coefficient A numerical summary of the type and strength of a statistical relationship between variables; takes the form $r_{ab} = +/-x$, where r stands for the correlation coefficient, a and b represent the two variables being correlated, the plus or minus sign indicates the direction of the relationship between the variables, and x stands for some numerical value. *Compare* coefficient of determination.

correlation matrix A visual depiction of paired correlation coefficients that lists all the relevant variables both across the top and down the left side of a matrix; where the respective rows and columns meet, researchers indicate the bivariate correlation coefficient for those two variables and whether it is significant. *See* bivariate correlation coefficient.

correlation ratio (eta) A type of correlation that is used with variables that have a curvilinear relationship.

counterbalance In a repeated-measures design, when all possible orders of the treatments are administered.

covariate Any variable whose effects are controlled for statistically. *See* control variable.

Cramer's V A correlational procedure used when two variables are measured on a nominal scale that is based on the chi-square value associated with the two-variable chi-square test; used frequently when there are different sample sizes and different numbers of cells. *Compare* Kendall's correlation; Pearson product moment correlation; point biserial correlation; Spearman correlation coefficient.

criterion-related validity A form of measurement validity, established via concurrent validity and/or predictive validity, which shows that a measurement technique is related to another instrument or behavior (called the *criterion,* or, in the case of a group of people, the *criterion group*) already known to be valid; if scores on a measurement technique are associated with scores on this well-established standard, it is considered valid. *See* concurrent validity; predictive validity. *Compare* construct validity; content validity.

criterion sample A purposive sample used in naturalistic inquiry of people who meet some criterion, such as children abused in a treatment facility, to produce a quality assurance sample. *Compare* confirming and disconfirming case sample; critical case sample; extreme case sample; homogeneous sample; intensity sample; maximum variation sample; opportunistic sample; politically important sample; random purposive sample; stratified purposive sample; theoretical sample; typical case sample.

criterion variable A variable that researchers wish to explain when using correlational procedures. *Compare* predictor variable.

critical case sample A purposive sample used in naturalistic inquiry in which an exemplar is chosen that permits logical generalization and maximum application of information to other people because what is true of this person is likely to be true of other people. *Compare* confirming and disconfirming case sample; criterion sample; extreme case sample; homogeneous sample; intensity sample; maximum variation sample; opportunistic sample; politically important case sample; random purposive sample; stratified purposive sample; theoretical sample; typical case sample.

critical ethnography A form of naturalistic inquiry designed to promote emancipation and reduce oppression. *Compare* autoethnography; ethnography; ethnomethodology.

critical incident technique Flanagan's (1954) in-depth interview used in naturalistic inquiry that asks for "people's most memorable positive and negative experiences within a specific, social context" (Query & Kreps, 1993, p. 64). *Compare* account analysis; episode analysis; ethnomethodological interview; key informant; life story interview; long interview; oral history; protocol analysis.

critical region (*See* region of rejection)

critical tale A tale told in reporting naturalistic inquiry that critiques problematic social structures through the perspective of those who are disadvantaged. *Compare* confessional tale; formal tale; impressionistic tale; jointly told tale; literary tale; realist tale.

critical value The numerical value that corresponds to the statistical significance level set for rejecting a null hypothesis. *Compare* calculated value.

Cronbach's alpha coefficient method (alpha coefficient, coefficient alpha, A, α) A single-administration reliability technique that uses the overall statistical relationship among the answers on a measurement instrument as the reliability coefficient for the instrument.

crossed factor design A factorial design in which every level of one factor appear with every level of the other factor. *Compare* mixed design; nested factor design.

cross-level inferences Drawing conclusions about one level of analysis (e.g., family units) from data acquired from another level (e.g., individual family members). *See* ecological fallacy.

cross-sectional survey A survey that studies respondents at one point in time. *Compare* longitudinal survey.

crosstabulation (*See* two-variable chi-square test)

cumulative frequency (CF) The display in a frequency table of the total frequency up to and including any particular category or measurement point. *Compare* absolute frequency; relative frequency.

curvilinear regression (*See* polynomial regression analysis)

curvilinear relationship A relationship between variables described by a polynomial equation, which means that there is at least one curve, or turn, in the data. *See* correlation ratio; inverted U-shaped curvilinear relationship; quadratic relationship; U-shaped curvilinear relationship.

data analysis The process of examining what data mean to researchers. *See* qualitative data analysis; statistical data analysis.

database Information stored in machine-readable form that can be retrieved by a computer located in a library or elsewhere. *See* CD-ROM; online database.

data triangulation The use of a number of data sources to study the same phenomenon. *Compare* methodological triangulation; researcher triangulation; theoretical triangulation.

debriefing Interactions between researchers and research participants after a study has been completed in which researchers explain the full purpose of the study, clear up any deception used, seek feedback from participants to learn how they perceived the research, and provide an opportunity for participants to ask questions and offer unsolicited observations. *See* dehoaxing; desensitizing.

decile One of the parts of a frequency distribution that has been divided into 10 equal parts.

decision error An error made when deciding whether to accept or reject a null hypothesis. *See* Type I error; Type II error.

decision rule The specific statistical significance level set by a researcher for rejecting a null hypothesis prior to conducting a study and analyzing the data.

deduction Moving from the general (tentative explanation) to the specific (evidence). *Compare* induction.

degrees of freedom (df) The number of scores that are "free to vary"; in significance testing, degrees of freedom are usually based on sample size (or sometimes on the number of categories employed), and generally equal either $N - 1$, the number of research participants sampled minus 1 or the number of categories employed minus 1, or $N - 2$, the number of research participants sampled minus two.

dehoaxing A type of debriefing in which research participants who have been deceived must be convinced that they actually have been deceived so as to "eliminate any undesirable effects the deception might have had" (Vogt, 1993, p. 65). *Compare* desensitizing.

deliberate sample (*See* purposive sample)

dependent variable (DV, Y) A variable that is thought to be changed by another (independent) variable; changes in it are dependent on changes in the other variable. It sometimes is called the *criterion variable* or *outcome variable* in nonexperimental research. *Compare* extaneous variable; independent variable; intervening variable; lurking variable.

descriptive statistical data analysis Statistical data-analytic procedures used to construct simple descriptions about the characteristics of a set of quantitative data, including: (a) numerical indicators that summarize the data, called *summary statistics;* (b) converting raw scores into what are called *standard scores;* and (c) constructing visual displays of data. *See* bar chart; frequency histogram; frequency polygon; frequency table; measures of central tendency; measures of dispersion pie chart; standard scores; summary statistic. *Compare* inferential statistical data analysis.

desensitizing A form of debriefing in which research participants may need help coping with negative information they may have acquired about themselves as a result of a research study. *Compare* dehoaxing.

design diagram A visual representation of a factorial design. *See* design statement; factorial design.

design statement A summary of a factorial design using a series of numbers, one for each independent variable in the study, separated by a multiplication sign (X); the numbers represent the total number of levels for each independent variable. *See* design diagram; factorial design; N-by-M design; two-by-two design.

deviant case sampling (*See* extreme case sampling)

deviate (*See* deviation score)

deviation score (deviate) The amount one score/value differs from the mean of its distribution.

Dewey Decimal System A cataloguing system that originated in the nineteenth century by Melvil Dewey, and used most frequently in public libraries, that employs 10 numbered categories as general headings, subdivided as many times as necessary to assign a unique call number to each book. *See* call number. *Compare* Library of Congress System.

dialectical analysis A qualitative data-analytic technique used in naturalistic inquiry that explores the tensions produced from seemingly contradictory elements within a system. *Compare* fantasy theme analysis; metaphor analysis.

dichotomized variable (binomial variable) An ordered variable that has been divided into two categories. *Compare* dichotomous variable.

dichotomous variable (binomial variable) A nominal variable that can only be divided into two categories (e.g., gender). *Compare* dichotomized variable.

difference score (gain score) The score found by subtracting a pretest score from a posttest score.

diffusion effect (*See* diffusion of treatment)

diffusion of treatment (diffusion effect) A form of interparticipant bias that results when research participants tell other participants about an experimental treatment.

directional hypothesis (*See* one-tailed hypothesis)

directive questionnaire or interview A questionnaire or interview that presents respondents with a predetermined sequence of questions. *Compare* nondirective questionnaire or interview.

direct observation Observing people engaging in communication behavior as it occurs. *Compare* indirect observation.

direct relationship (*See* positive relationship)

discrete variable (*See* nominal variable)

discriminant analysis A multivariate relationship analysis that is a form of regression analysis that classifies, or discriminates, individuals on the basis of their scores on two or more interval/ratio independent variables into the categories of a nominal dependent variable. *Compare* canonical correlation analysis; cluster analysis; factor analysis; multidimensional scaling; path analysis.

disordinal interaction An interaction effect in which, when plotted on a graph, the lines representing two variables cross. *Compare* ordinal interaction.

distribution-free statistics (*See* nonparametric statistics)

double-barreled question A question that asks about several issues at once.

double-blind procedure A procedure used in experimental research to ensure that those who administer different independent variable manipulations and those who receive them do not know (are "blind to") which participants are getting which manipulation.

dramatistic criticism A form of rhetorical criticism that primarily analyzes texts according to philosopher Kenneth Burke's (1945, 1950, 1966) view that all communication can be viewed in terms of five elements (act, purpose, agent, agency, and scene) that comprise a dramatic event (called *pentadic analysis*). *Compare* fantasy theme criticism; feminist criticism; genre criticism; historical criticism; metaphoric criticism; narrative criticism; neo-Aristotelian criticism.

ecological fallacy A cross-level inference error that exists when data collected from survey respondents representing one unit of analysis do not describe accurately the larger unit of analysis.

ecological validity In external validity, the extent to which procedures used in a research study mirror what actually occurs in real-life circumstances.

editorial content readership survey Market research conducted to determine which articles newspaper and magazine subscribers like and don't like, and what topics they would like to see covered in the publication. *Compare* advertising readership study; broadcast audience survey; contextual inquiry; usability testing.

effect coefficient In path analysis, the total effect of an independent variable on the dependent variable.

effects analysis (*See* partial correlation)

effect size (ES) "An estimate of the degree to which a phenomenon is present in a population and/or the extent to which the null hypothesis is false" (Vogt, 1993, p. 79); has a large impact on statistical power.

elaboration (*See* partial correlation)

emergent design A design in which researchers plan out their research but then take advantage of opportunities that present themselves during the research process; used in naturalistic inquiry. *Compare* static design.

emic A relatively close observational role in naturalistic inquiry. *Compare* etic.

episode analysis An in-depth interview used in naturalistic inquiry that asks a person to reconstruct a scene, complete with lines of dialogue, that represents a recurring pattern in a relationship. *Compare* account analysis; critical incident technique; ethnomethodological interview; key informant; life story interview; long interview; oral history; protocol analysis.

epistemological assumption Assumptions concerning the relationship of the researcher to that which is being researched. *Compare* axiological assumption; methodological assumption; ontological assumption; rhetorical assumption.

error score component In an observed measurement, the amount of deviation from the true value; comprised of measurement error and random error. *See* measurement error; random error. *Compare* true score component.

estimates Statistics computed using estimation procedures for a population on the basis of the results obtained from a sample. *Compare* estimators.

estimation Inferential statistics used to generalize the results obtained from a sample to its parent population. *See* confidence interval; confidence limits; confidence level; estimates; estimators.

estimators Formulas used in estimation procedures to compute estimates. *Compare* estimates.

ethics Moral principles and recognized rules of conduct regarding a particular class of human action. *See* research ethics.

ethnography A type of naturalistic inquiry in which a researcher examines a culture by immersion in a cultural context, exploring the patterned interactions and significant symbols of specific groups to identify the cultural norms (rules) that direct their behaviors and the meanings that people ascribe to their own and each other's behavior. *Compare* autoethnography; critical ethnography; ethnomethodology.

ethnomethodological indifference A posture assumed in ethnomethodology that leads researchers to abstain from judging people's actions.

ethnomethodological interview An in-depth interview used in naturalistic inquiry that follows ethnomethodological procedures. *Compare* account analysis; critical incident technique; episode analysis; key informant; life story interview; long interview; oral history; protocol analysis.

ethnomethodology A type of naturalistic inquiry that involves "the empirical study of methods that individuals use to give sense to and at the same time to accomplish their daily actions: communicating, making decisions, and reasoning" (Coulon, 1995, p. 15). *See* conversation analysis; ethnomethodological indifference; experimental breaching; formal ethnomethodology. *Compare* autoethnography; critical ethnography; ethnography.

etic A relatively distant observational role in naturalistic inquiry. *Compare* emic.

evaluation research Public opinion research used to assess the performance of specific programs, products, and/or organizations. *See* formative evaluation; need analysis; network analysis; organizational feedback surveys and audits; summative evaluation. *Compare* market research; political poll.

everyday ways of knowing The acceptance of information at face value, relying on knowledge that we have not questioned or tested. *See* appeals to tradition, custom, and faith; authority; intuition; magic, superstition, and mysticism; personal experience. *Compare* pseudoresearch; research.

evidence A reason for a claim. *Compare* claim.

exact replication A replication that duplicates a research study as closely as possible, with the exception of different research participants. *Compare* conceptual replication; partial replication.

exit poll A poll taken after voters have cast their ballots.

expected frequencies (theoretical frequencies) In a chi-square test, the frequencies of occurrence that are expected for each category. *Compare* observed frequencies.

experiment A controlled test of a cause-and-effect relationship that researchers suspect exists. *See* field experiment; full experiment; laboratory experiment; natural experiment; preexperiment; quasi-experiment. *Compare* naturalistic inquiry; survey method; textual analysis.

experimental breaching In ethnomethodology, deliberately upsetting patterned routines to reveal the rules participants use to organize experiences.

experimental group (*See* treatment group)

experimenter effects A potential internal validity threat that can occur in experimental research when different experimenters consistently administer different manipulations of the independent variable.

experimentwise error (*See* familywise error)

explanatory variable (*See* independent variable)

exploratory factor analysis A type of factor analysis used to identify factors without prior expectations on the part of a researcher. *Compare* confirmatory factor analysis.

external validity The generalizability of the findings from a research study. *See* ecological validity; population validity; replication. *Compare* internal validity.

extraneous variable A variable that is not the main focus of attention in an experiment but which can have an effect on the variables being studied and potentially compromise any causal relationship found between the independent and dependent variables. *See* confounding variable; intervening variable.

extreme case sample (deviant case sample) A purposive sample used in naturalistic inquiry in which people are chosen on the basis of extreme characteristics, such as top-of-the-class students. *Compare* confirming and disconfirming case sample; criterion sample; critical case sample; homogeneous sample; intensity sample; maximum variation sample; opportunistic sample; politically important case sample; random purposive sample; stratified purposive sample; theoretical sample; typical case sample.

extreme values The lowest and highest scores in a distribution.

face validity A form of content validity based on logical or conceptual validity in which researchers generate items for a measurement instrument that "on the face of it" seem to accurately reflect the concept being investigated. *Compare* panel approach.

factor An independent variable in a study that has more than one independent variable. *See* factorial designs.

factor analysis A multivariate relationship analysis that examines whether a large number of variables can be reduced to a smaller number of factors (a set of variables); typically used to see whether items of a measurement instrument can be reduced to one or more common dimensions or factors (i.e., whether an instrument measures a unidimensional or multidimensional construct), and which items best corre-

late with ("load on") which factor. *See* confirmatory factor analysis; exploratory factor analysis; factor loadings. *Compare* canonical correlation analysis; cluster analysis; discriminant analysis; multidimensional scaling; path analysis.

factorial analysis of variance A type of analysis of variance that examines differences between the conditions created by two or more nominal independent variables with regard to a single interval/ratio dependent variable. *Compare* multivariate analysis of variance; one-variable analysis of variance.

factorial designs Studies in which there is more than one independent variable. *See* crossed factor design; design diagram; design statement; factor; mixed design; nested factor design; unbalanced design.

factor loadings In factor analysis, the correlation of items with factors.

false drops (*See* false hits)

false hits (false drops) Records accessed during free-text electronic searches that are not relevant to one's interest.

familywise error (experimentwise error) The probability that a Type I error has been committed when multiple comparisons are performed using related statistical tests.

fantasy theme analysis/criticism A form of rhetorical criticism and naturalistic inquiry, based on the work of Ernest Bormann (1972, 1973, 1982), that examines the common images used to portray narrative elements of situations described in a text with respect to four symbolic categories (fantasy themes, fantasy types, rhetorical visions, and rhetorical communities). *Compare* dramatistic criticism; dialectical analysis; feminist criticism; genre criticism; historical criticism; metaphor analysis; metaphoric criticism; narrative criticism; neo-Aristotelian criticism.

fatigue effect A question order effect that occurs when respondents grow tired after answering many questions and don't provide accurate information to later items. *Compare* consistency effect; redundancy effect.

Federal Certificate of Confidentiality A government document that authorizes the legal withholding of information by researchers conducting sensitive research.

feminist criticism A form of rhetorical criticism that analyzes how conceptions of gender are produced and maintained in persuasive messages. *Compare* dramatistic criticism; fantasy theme criticism; genre criticism; historical criticism; metaphoric criticism; narrative criticism; neo-Aristotelian criticism.

field experiment An experiment conducted in research participants' natural setting. *Compare* laboratory experiment.

field notes A naturalistic researcher's way of keeping track of observations in the form of written or audiorecorded records of what occurred.

file drawer problem A potential problem affecting meta-analyses and literature reviews that results because studies that yield nonsignificant results are often not published (they're put in researchers' drawers), so the significant effects found may seem to happen more often than they actually do.

first-order explanation In naturalistic inquiry, an explanation by research participants of their own attitudes, behaviors, and so forth. *Compare* second-order explanation.

first-order interaction effect An interaction effect between two variables when there are three or more variables in a study. *Compare* second-order interaction effect.

first-order partial correlation A partial correlation that controls for one other variable. *Compare* higher-order partial correlation; zero-order correlation.

flat distribution (platykurtic distribution) The shape of a distribution in which scores do not cluster around the middle but are dispersed rather evenly across the distribution, making the curve flat and more spread out. *Compare* mesokurtic distribution; peaked distribution.

floor effect (basement effect) Occurs when people have scores at the lower range ("floor") of a variable, which makes it difficult to tell whether any treatment has an effect. *Compare* ceiling effect.

focus group interview An interview in which a facilitator leads a small group of people (usually five to seven members) in a relatively open discussion about a specific product or program.

follow-up test (*See* multiple comparison test)

footnotes Explanations of material mentioned in the body of a text (e.g., scholarly journal article) that are elaborated on at the end of the text for interested readers.

formal ethnomethodology A form of ethnomethodological naturalistic inquiry that involves "a series of single case studies focusing on the social construction of everyday events within a variety of set-

tings" (Beach, 1982, pp. 314–315). *Compare* conversation analysis.

formal tale A tale told in reporting naturalistic inquiry that follows the rules of a particular theory or analytic procedure, such as semiotics or conversational analysis. *Compare* confessional tale; critical tale; impressionistic tale; jointly told tale; literary tale; realist tale.

formative evaluation Evaluation research conducted while a program or product is in the process of being developed to identify ways to refine it. *Compare* summative evaluation.

forward telescoping The tendency for people to think that past events occurred more recently than they did. *Compare* backward telescoping.

free-text searching (keyword searching) Electronic searches for key words, regardless of where they appear in a record. *See* boolean operators; false hits; positional operators.

frequency distribution A tally of the number of times particular values on a measurement scale occur in a data set. *See* frequency histogram; frequency polygon; frequency table.

frequency histogram A visual display of a frequency distribution of interval/ratio data that uses blocks that touch one another to show how frequently each point on the scale occurs. *Compare* bar chart; frequency polygon; line graph; pie chart.

frequency polygon A visual display of a frequency distribution of interval/ratio data that uses a single point to represent the frequency counts for each point on the scale. *Compare* bar chart; frequency histogram; line graph; pie chart.

frequency table A visual display in table form of the frequency of each category or measurement point on a scale for a distribution of data. *See* absolute frequency; cumulative frequency; relative frequency.

frugging Fund-raising attempts under the guise of a survey. *Compare* sugging.

full experiment The type of experiment with the highest degree of control because the independent variable is manipulated by the researcher (as opposed to being observed) and research participants are randomly assigned to two or more conditions to create equivalent conditions. *See* pretest-posttest equivalent groups design; posttest-only equivalent groups design; Solomon four-group designs. *Compare* preexperiment; quasi-experiment.

funnel format A question format in which broad, open questions are used to introduce the questionnaire/

interview, followed by narrower, closed questions that seek more specific information. *Compare* inverted funnel format; tunnel format.

garbology A measure of accretion that involves researchers gathering, sifting through, identifying, and categorizing refuse (garbage) as a way of determining people's behavior.

general consent plus proxy consent A form of voluntary informed consent in which a researcher first obtains the general consent of a person to participate in a study that may involve extreme procedures, and empowers a friend to serve as a proxy, who examines the details of the specific procedures in advance and makes a judgment as to whether the person would have consented to it given the choice.

generation effects Cohort effects due to being a member of the same generation or age group. *Compare* period effects.

genre criticism A form of rhetorical criticism that rejects using a single set of criteria to evaluate all persuasive messages, arguing, instead, that standards vary according to the particular type, or *genre,* of text being studied. *Compare* dramatistic criticism; fantasy theme criticism; feminist criticism; historical criticism; metaphoric criticism; narrative criticism; neo-Aristotelian criticism.

geometric mean An appropriate mean for measuring relative change. *Compare* mean; harmonized mean.

goodness of fit The extent to which any model or equation, such as a regression line, summarizes or "fits" the data.

grant money Money awarded by public institutions (e.g., government bodies) or private individuals and organizations for the purpose of promoting research.

grounded theory A form of analytic induction in which generalizations are grounded in or inferred from the data collected. *See* constant comparative method.

grouped bar chart (segmented bar chart) A bar chart that shows the frequency of occurrence in two or more categories for two or more groups.

groups (*See* conditions)

halo effect An observational bias that occurs when observers make multiple judgments of the same person over time and typically overrate (which is why it is called a "halo" effect, although it can apply to underrating as well) a research participant's performance because that participant did well (or poorly) in an earlier rating.

haphazard sample (*See* convenience sample)

harmonized mean An appropriate mean when averaging rates. *Compare* geometric mean; mean.

Hawthorne effect An internal validity threat due to research participants that occurs when any change in research participants' behavior is due primarily to the fact that they know they are being observed. *See* John Henry effect. *Compare* interparticipant bias; maturation; mortality; selection; statistical regression.

hierarchical regression analysis A form of multiple linear regression in which a researcher determines, on the basis of previous theory and research, the order of the variables entered into the regression equation. *Compare* stepwise regression.

higher-order interaction effect (*See* second-order interaction effect)

higher-order partial correlation A partial correlation that controls for two or more variables (i.e., second-order partial correlation controls for two variables, third-order partial correlation controls for three variables, etc.). *Compare* first-order partial correlation; zero-order correlation.

highspread The range of values between the median and the highest score of a distribution. *Compare* lowspread.

historical case studies A form of historical criticism that examines texts related to a single, salient historical event to understand the role played by communication. *Compare* biographical studies; oral histories; social movement studies.

historical criticism A form of rhetorical criticism that examines how important past events shape and are shaped by rhetorical messages. *See* biographical studies; historical case studies; oral histories; social movement studies. *Compare* dramatistic criticism; fantasy theme criticism; feminist criticism; genre criticism; metaphoric criticism; narrative criticism; neo-Aristotelian criticism.

history An internal validity threat related to the way research is conducted that occurs when changes in the environment external to a study influence people's behavior within the study. *Compare* procedure validity and reliability; sensitization; sleeper effect.

homogeneous sample A purposive sample used in naturalistic inquiry of similar types of people; used to focus, reduce, and simplify analysis, and facilitate interviewing. *Compare* confirming and disconfirming case sample; criterion sample; critical case sample; extreme case sample; intensity sample; maximum variation sample; opportunistic sample;

politically important case sample; random purposive sample; stratified purposive sample; theoretical sample; typical case sample.

horizontal bar chart A bar chart with blocks running horizontally from left to right, sometimes used when the categories have long names or when there are many categories (say 10 or 20).

humanities The study of the achievements of creative people and/or those who produce creative products, such as in the academic disciplines of music, art, and literature. *Compare* physical sciences; social sciences.

human sciences (*See* social sciences)

hypothesis A tentative statement about the relationship between independent and dependent variables. *See* null hypothesis; one-tailed hypothesis; two-tailed hypothesis. *Compare* research question.

hypothesis testing (*See* significance testing)

implied consent Consent that is implied by research participants' behavior, such as the completion and return of the questionnaire itself in large-scale surveys.

impressionistic tale A tale told in reporting naturalistic inquiry that blends the realist and confessional tales to provide an account of the participants and the researcher as central characters in an unfolding drama. *Compare* confessional tale; critical tale; formal tale; jointly told tale; literary tale; realist tale.

incidence In a stratified sample, the frequency with which respondents can be obtained from the stratified populations.

independent-sample *t* test A type of *t* test that examines differences between two independent (different) groups. *Compare* related-measures *t* test.

independent variable (IV, X) A variable that is thought to influence changes in another (dependent) variable. It sometimes is called an *explanatory variable;* in nonexperimental research, a *predictor variable. Compare* dependent variable; extraneous variable; intervening variable; lurking variable.

in-depth interview A naturalistic inquiry interview that typically proceeds inductively, using an unstructured format consisting of open questions. *See* critical incident technique; episode analysis; ethnomethodological interview; key informant; life story interview; long interview; oral history; protocol analysis.

indirect observation Examining communication artifacts, texts produced by people (such as recordings/transcripts or products people produce, such as

books), as opposed to live communication events. *Compare* direct observation.

indirect relationship (*See* negative relationship)

individual-difference variable (*See* background variable)

induction Moving from the specific (the evidence) to the general (tentative explanations). *Compare* deduction.

inductive statistics (*See* inferential statistics)

inferential statistical data analysis Statistical data-analytic procedures used for estimation and significance testing. *See* estimation; significance testing. *Compare* descriptive statistical data analysis.

inferential statistics (inductive statistics) "The set of statistical procedures that allows a researcher to go beyond the group that has been measured, and make statements about the characteristics of a much larger group" (Jaeger, 1983, p. 12).

informants In naturalistic inquiry, people who can provide unique insight into the culture, people, and communication behavior being studied. *See* key informants.

institutional review boards (IRBs) A committee mandated by the National Research Act passed by Congress that reviews research proposals to make sure that research participants are not harmed, have been informed of the benefits and risks, and have given informed consent.

instrument A specific, formal measurement tool researchers use to gather data about research variables.

intensity sample A purposive sample used in naturalistic inquiry of information-rich people who manifest the phenomenon intensely, but not extremely, such as good students/poor students, above average/below average students. *Compare* confirming and disconfirming case sample; criterion sample; critical case sample; extreme case sample; homogeneous sample; maximum variation sample; opportunistic sample; politically important case sample; random purposive sample; stratified purposive sample; theoretical sample; typical case sample.

interaction analysis A form of textual analysis that involves the use of quantitative methods to study interaction. *Compare* content analysis; conversation analysis; performance studies; rhetorical criticism.

interaction effects (conditioning effect, contingency effect, joint effect, moderating effect) Effects due to the unique combination of the independent variables that make a difference on the dependent variable(s); sometimes called *multiplicative* *relations* in nonexperimental research. *See* disordinal interaction; first-order interaction effect; ordinal interaction; second-order interaction effect. *Compare* main effects.

intercept (*y* intercept) In a regression equation, how far up the *y*-axis the regression line crosses—intercepts—it, when the value on the *x*-axis is zero. *Compare* slope.

intercoder reliability (*See* interobserver reliability)

intercorrelation A correlation between independent/predictor variables.

intermediary variable (*See* intervening variable)

internal consistency A form of measurement reliability that references the extent to which items on a measurement instrument give similar results.

internal validity The accuracy of the conclusions drawn from a particular research study. *See* Hawthorne effect; history; interparticipant bias; maturation; measurement validity and reliability; mortality; procedure validity and reliability; researcher observational biases; researcher personal attribute effect; researcher unintentional expectancy effect; selection; sensitization; sleeper effect; statistical regression. *Compare* external validity.

Internet A global network of computers connected to each other. *See* World Wide Web.

interobserver reliability (interrater reliability, intercoder reliability) A measurement reliability method for assessing the reliability of observations by calculating the percentage of agreement between the observations of independent coders.

interparticipant bias (intersubject bias) An internal validity threat due to research participants that occurs when the people being studied influence one another. *See* diffusion of treatment. *Compare* Hawthorne effect; maturation; mortality; selection; statistical regression.

interpretive The assumption in naturalistic inquiry that "the researcher, while trying to see the situation from the point of view of those who are being studied, cannot escape from providing his or her own interpretation of the situation" (Potter, 1996, p. 43). *Compare* naturalism; phenomenology.

interquartile range (quartile deviation/midspread) The range of scores between the 25th percentile (the point below which 25% of the scores fall) and the 75th percentile (the point above which 25% of the scores fall); the point in a distribution that divides the scores at the 25th and 75th percentile is called a *hinge* (lower and upper hinge, respectively). *Compare* semi-interquartile range.

interrater reliability (*See* interobserver reliability)

interrupted time series quasi-equivalent groups design (multiple time series design) A quasi-experimental design in which research participants are nonrandomly assigned to one of (at least) two conditions (such as a treatment or control group) and are measured on a series of pretests and posttests. *Compare* pretest-posttest quasi-equivalent groups design; single-group interrupted time series design.

intersubject bias (*See* interparticipant bias)

interval measurement scale A measurement scale that categorizes a variable, rank orders it along some dimension that has equal distances between each of the adjacent points along the measurement scale, and has an arbitrary zero point. *See* Likert scale; Likert-type scale; semantic differential scale; Thurstone scale. *Compare* nominal measurement scale; ordinal measurement scale; ratio measurement scale.

intervening variable (intermediary variable, mediating variable) A variable that intervenes between an independent and dependent variable to explain the relationship between the two variables. *See* confounding variable; extraneous variable; lurking variable.

interview The presentation of spoken questions to evoke spoken responses from people. *See* directive interview; focus group interview; in-depth interview; interviewee; interviewer; nondirective interview. *Compare* questionnaire; observation.

interviewee A person who is interviewed. *Compare* interviewer.

interviewer A person who conducts an interview. *Compare* interviewee.

interview schedule (protocol) The list of questions that guide an interview. *See* semistructured interview; structured interview; unstructured interview.

intuition A type of everyday way of knowing that involves believing something is true or false simply because it "makes sense." *See* cognitive conservatism; pareidolia; tunnel effect. *Compare* appeals to tradition, custom, and faith; authority; magic, superstition, and mysticism; personal experience.

inverted funnel format A question format that begins with narrow, closed questions and builds to broader, open questions. *Compare* funnel format; tunnel format.

inverted U-shaped curvilinear relationship A curvilinear relationship in which two variables are related positively to a certain point and then are related negatively. *Compare* U-shaped curvilinear relationship.

ipsative scale An ordinal measurement scale in which a particular rank can only be used once. *Compare* normative scale.

John Henry effect A type of Hawthorne effect that occurs when research participants in a control group take the experiment as a challenge and exert more effort than they otherwise would.

joint effects (*See* interaction effects)

jointly told tale A tale told in reporting naturalistic inquiry by researchers and participants working together. *Compare* confessional tale; critical tale; formal tale; impressionistic tale; literary tale; realist tale.

judgment sample (*See* purposive sample)

junk science (*See* pseudoresearch)

Kendall's correlation (*tau*) A correlational procedure, which actually refers to three measures of association, that is used in place of the Spearman correlation coefficient when a researcher has a pair of ranks for each of several individuals; considered better than the Spearman procedure when there are a number of tied ranks. *Compare* Cramer's V; Pearson product moment correlation; point biserial correlation; Spearman correlation coefficient.

key informants "Well-informed informants" (J. C. Johnson, 1990, p. 31) who can enlighten a naturalistic researcher conducting in-depth interviews on what and whom he or she should know. *Compare* account analysis; critical incident technique; episode analysis; ethnomethodological interview; life story interview; long interview; oral history; protocol analysis.

keyword searching (*See* free-text searching)

Kruskal-Wallis test A statistical procedure used to analyze differences among three or more groups with respect to a dependent variable measured on an ordinal scale. *Compare* Mann-Whitney U-Test; median test; Wilcoxon signed-rank test.

Kurtosis How pointed or flat is the shape of a frequency distribution. *See* flat distribution; mesokurtic distribution; peaked distribution.

laboratory experiment An experiment that takes place in a setting created by a researcher. *Compare* field experiment.

Law of Large Numbers The principle that the larger the size of a random sample, the more it approximates the population from which it is drawn.

Least Significant Difference (LSD) Test The most liberal multiple comparison test that is like doing a series of *t* tests without protecting against additive error because of multiple comparisons (see Norusis, 1993). *Compare* Bonferroni technique; Scheffe Test; Tukey's Honestly Significant Difference Test; Tukey Test.

leptokurtic distribution (*See* peaked distribution)

level A condition of an independent variable in an experiment; applies to both nominal and ordered variables.

Library of Congress System A cataloguing system created by the Library of Congress that uses letters to designate major categories and a combination of letters and numbers to divide each category so that each book is assigned a unique call number. *See* call number. *Compare* Dewey Decimal System.

life story interview An in-depth interview used in naturalistic inquiry that asks people to construct in their own words their entire life as a story or narrative, starting from the time a person is born to the present day, as well as hopes and visions for the future. *Compare* account analysis; critical incident technique; episode analysis; ethnomethodological interview; key informant; long interview; oral history; protocol analysis.

Likert scale An interval measurement scale, developed by psychologist Rensis Likert (1932), that identifies the extent of a person's beliefs, attitudes, or feelings toward some object by asking him or her to indicate the extent to which he or she agrees or disagrees with a statement on a 5-point scale that ranges from "strongly agree" to "strongly disagree." *Compare* Likert-type scale; semantic differential scale; Thurstone scale.

Likert-type scale (Likert-like scale) An adaptation of Likert scales that uses different answer categories than agree-disagree or different number of answers (e.g., 6-point, 7-point scales, etc.). *Compare* Likert scale; semantic differential scale; Thurstone scale.

linear regression (simple regression) A regression analysis used to predict or explain scores on a criterion variable on the basis of obtained scores on a predictor variable and knowledge of the statistical relationship between the two variables. *See* bivariate regression coefficient; regression line. *Compare* multiple linear regression; polynomial regression analysis.

linear relationship A statistical relationship between variables that can generally be represented and explained by a straight line on a scatter plot. *See* negative relationship; positive relationship. *Compare* nonlinear relationship.

line graph A visual display for showing differences between groups/categories of an independent variable that uses a single point to represent the frequency count for each of the categories and then connect these points with a single line. *Compare* bar chart; frequency histogram; frequency polygon; pie chart.

line of best fit (*See* regression line)

literary tale A tale told in reporting naturalistic inquiry using a novelist's sense of narration. *Compare* confessional tale; critical tale; formal tale; impressionistic tale; jointly told tale; realist tale.

loaded question A question that leads people to respond in certain ways.

log-linear analysis A multivariate difference analysis that is an advanced chi-square test used to analyze differences between groups with respect to three or more variables. *Compare* analysis of covariance; multivariate analysis of covariance; multivariate analysis of variance; one-variable chi-square; two-variable chi-square.

long interview McCraken's (1988) in-depth interview used in naturalistic inquiry that employs a questionnaire to ensure that the same topics are covered in the same order for each interviewee to create a "sharply focused, rapid, highly intensive interview process that seeks to diminish the indeteminancy and redundancy that attends more unstructured research processes" (p. 7). *Compare* account analysis; critical incident technique; episode analysis; ethnomethodological interview; key informant; life story interview; oral history; protocol analysis.

longitudinal survey A survey that studies respondents at several points in time. *See* panel study; trend study. *Compare* cross-sectional survey.

lowspread The range of values between the median and the lowest value of a distribution. *Compare* highspread.

lurking variable A variable that causes both the independent and dependent variable, lurking there "like the troll under the bridge, an unpleasant surprise when discovered" (Vogt, 1999, p. 165). *See* confounding variable; extraneous variable.

magic, superstition, mysticism A type of everyday way of knowing that rests on mystery as the explanation for an otherwise unexplainable event. *Compare* appeals to tradition, custom, and faith; authority; intuition; personal experience.

main effects The effects of an independent variable on a dependent variable. *Compare* interaction effects.

manipulated variable (active variable, controlled variable) An independent variable that is manipulated by a researcher in an experiment by controlling when or how much of it research participants receive. *Compare* observed variable.

manipulation check A procedure used in experimental research to make sure that a treatment given to research participants is reliable and valid.

Mann-Whitney U-Test A statistical procedure used to analyze differences between two independent groups measured on an ordinal dependent variable; used especially when the data are badly skewed (Bruning & Kintz, 1968). *Compare* Kruskal-Wallis Test; median test; Wilcoxon Signed-Rank Test.

marginally significant Sometimes used to describe a statistical finding that is almost significant at the .05 level.

margin of error (*See* confidence interval)

market research Public opinion research conducted to describe consumers' attitudes and product preferences. *See* advertising readership study; broadcast audience survey; contextual inquiry; editorial content readership survey; usability testing. *Compare* evaluation research; political poll.

matched-pairs design (participant matching, subject matching) An experimental design in which research participants are matched in pairs on some important characteristic and then one member of each pair is randomly assigned to the first condition and the other partner is assigned to the second condition.

maturation An internal validity threat due to research participants that refers to internal changes that occur within people over the course of a study that explain their behavior. *Compare* Hawthorne effect; interparticipant bias; mortality; selection; statistical regression.

maximum variation sample A purposive sample used in naturalistic inquiry of people who vary in how they adapt to particular conditions; used to identify important common patterns that cut across variations. *Compare* confirming and disconfirming case sample; criterion sample; critical case sample; extreme case sample; homogeneous sample; intensity sample; opportunistic sample; politically important case sample; random purposive sample; stratified purposive sample; theoretical sample; typical case sample.

mean ($\overline{X}$; sample mean, M; population mean, μ) A measure of central tendency that is the arithmetic average, computed by adding all the scores in a distribution of interval/ratio data and dividing by the total number of scores. *See* geometric mean; harmonic mean; trimmed mean; winsorizing. *Compare* median; mode.

meaning units In unitizing in content analysis, units that involve symbolic meaning. *See* propositional units; referential units; syntactical units; thematic units. *Compare* physical units.

measurement The process of determining the existence, characteristics, size, and/or quantity of changes or differences in a variable through systematic recording and organization of observations.

measurement error The amount of error due to faulty measurement procedures. *Compare* random error.

measurement reliability Measuring something in a consistent and stable manner. *See* internal consistency; interobserver reliability; multiple-administration techniques; single-administration techniques. *Compare* measurement validity.

measurement scale "A specific scheme for assigning numbers or symbols to designate characteristics of a variable" (Williams, 1986, p. 14). *See* interval measurement scale; nominal measurement scale; ordinal measurement scale; ratio measurement scale.

measurement validity How well researchers measure what they intend to measure; made up of construct, content, and criterion-related validity. *See* construct validity; content validity; criterion-related validity. *Compare* measurement reliability.

measure of association Any statistic that expresses the degree of a statistical relationship between variables.

measures of accretion Measures that show how physical traces build up over time. *See* garbology. *Compare* measures of erosion.

measures of central tendency (representative values) Measures that describe the center point of a distribution of quantitative data. *See* mean; median; mode. *Compare* measures of dispersion.

measures of dispersion (measures of variability) Measures that report how much scores on ordinal, interval, and ratio data vary from each other or how far they are spread around the center point of the data and across the distribution. *See* range; standard deviation; variance. *Compare* measures of central tendency.

measures of erosion Measures that show how physical objects are worn down by use over time. *Compare* measures of accretion.

measures of variability (*See* measures of dispersion)

median (Md or Mdn) A measure of central tendency that divides a distribution of quantitative data at the 50th percentile, or exactly in half; the score above which and below which half the observations fall. *Compare* mean; mode.

median test A statistical procedure used to analyze differences between two independent groups measured on an ordinal dependent variable. *Compare* Kruskal-Wallis Test; Mann-Whitney U-Test; Wilcoxon Signed-Rank Test.

mediating variable (*See* intervening variable)

member checks A procedure in naturalistic inquiry that involves giving a draft of the research report to participants, or people similar to them, for feedback.

mesokurtic distribution The shape of a normal distribution; comes from "meso" meaning "middle" and "kurtic" meaning "peakedness." *Compare* flat distribution; peaked distribution.

meta-analysis (metaanalysis) A procedure used to identify patterns in findings across multiple studies that examine the same research topic or question. *See* file drawer problem.

metaphor analysis A qualitative data-analytic technique used in naturalistic inquiry that looks for people's use of *metaphors,* figures of speech in which a word or phrase that denotes one object is applied to another. *See* metaphoric criticism.

metaphoric criticism A form of rhetorical criticism that involves identifying and evaluating how rhetors use metaphors to help create a shared reality for an audience. *See* metaphor analysis. *Compare* dramatistic criticism; fantasy theme criticism; feminist criticism; genre criticism; historical criticism; narrative criticism; neo-Aristotelian criticism.

methodological assumption Assumptions concerning the process of research. *Compare* axiological assumption; epistemological assumption; ontological assumption; rhetorical assumption.

methodological triangulation The use of multiple methods to study the same phenomenon. *Compare* data triangulation; researcher triangulation; theoretical triangulation.

metric variable (*See* continuous variable)

midspread (*See* interquartile range)

mixed design A factorial design in which the number of levels for each factor are not equal. *Compare* crossed factor design; nested factor design.

mixed purposive sample (*See* combination purposive sample)

mode (Mo) A measure of central tendency that indicates which score or value in a distribution occurs most frequently. *See* bimodal distribution; multimodal distribution; unimodal distribution. *Compare* antimode; mean; median.

moderating effects (*See* interaction effects)

mortality (attrition) An internal validity threat due to research participants that results from the (differential) loss of participants from the beginning to the end of a research study. *Compare* Hawthorne effect; interparticipant bias; maturation; selection; statistical regression.

multicollinearity (*See* collinearity)

multidimensional concept A concept measured by a series of scale items that assess more than one factor. *See* factor analysis. *Compare* unidimensional concept.

multidimensional scaling (MDS) A multivariate relationship analysis that plots variables or elements in two or more dimensions to see the statistical similarities and differences between and among them. *Compare* canonical correlation analysis; cluster analysis; discriminant analysis; factor analysis; path analysis.

multimodal distribution A distribution of data that has three or more modes. *Compare* bimodal distribution; unimodal distribution.

multiple-administration techniques Measurement reliability techniques that assess the temporal stability of instruments at two or more points in time. *See* alternative procedure method; test-retest method. *Compare* single-administration techniques.

multiple comparison tests (follow-up tests, post-hoc comparison, a posteriori comparison) Follow-up procedures to the omnibus test in the analysis of variance that pinpoint the specific significant difference(s) that exists. *See* Bonferroni technique; Least Significant Difference (LSD) Test; Scheffe Test; Tukey's Honestly Significant Difference (HSD) Test; Tukey Test.

multiple correlation The statistical relationship between a variable to be explained (the criterion variable) and two or more other independent variables working together. *See* coefficient of multiple determination; multiple correlation coefficient. *Compare* partial correlation; simple correlation.

multiple correlation coefficient (R) A correlation coefficient that explains how two or more variables working together are related to a criterion variable; takes the form $R_{a.bc} = +/- x$, read, "The multiple correlation of variables b and c with variable a (the criterion variable) is…." *See* adjusted R^2. *Compare* coefficient of multiple determination; partial correlation.

multiple linear regression A form of regression analysis used to predict or explain scores on a criterion variable on the basis of obtained scores on two or more predictor variables and knowledge of the relationships of all the variables. *See* Adjusted R^2; beta coefficient; collinearity; hierarchical regression analysis; stepwise regression. *Compare* linear regression; polynomial regression analysis.

multiple-sample chi-square test (*See* two-variable chi-square test)

multiple time series design (*See* interrupted time series quasi-equivalent groups design)

multiplicative relations (*See* interaction effects)

multiplicity sample (*See* network sample)

multistage sampling A cluster sample procedure for selecting a sample in two or more stages, in which successively smaller clusters are picked randomly. One form is *area probability sampling* (also called *block sampling*), which is used for studying large geographical areas.

multivariate analysis Statistical procedures that examine three or more independent variables and/or two or more dependent variables at the same time.

multivariate analysis of covariance (MANCOVA) A multivariate difference analysis that is an extension of analysis of covariance that analyzes differences among groups on multiple, and related, interval/ratio dependent variables while controlling statistically for the effects of potentially confounding covariates. *Compare* analysis of covariance; log-linear analysis; multivariate analysis of variance.

multivariate analysis of variance (MANOVA) A multivariate difference analysis that is an extension of analysis of variance that analyzes differences among groups on multiple, and related, interval/ratio dependent variables. *Compare* factorial analysis of variance; analysis of covariance; log-linear analysis; multivariate analysis of covariance; one-variable analysis of variance.

narrative criticism A form of rhetorical criticism that involves analyzing the stories rhetors tell and evaluating how effective they are at shaping an audience's perception of reality. *Compare* dramatistic criticism; fantasy theme criticism; feminist criticism; genre criticism; historical criticism; metaphoric criticism; neo-Aristotelian criticism.

natural experiment A naturally occurring experiment involving no manipulation of an independent variable by the researcher in which one group is exposed to one level of the independent variable and another group is exposed to another level or does not receive it.

naturalism The assumption in naturalistic inquiry that phenomena should be studied in their natural context. *Compare* interpretive; phenomenology.

naturalistic inquiry The study of how people behave when they are absorbed in genuine life experiences in natural settings. *See* autoethnography; case study; critical ethnography; emergent design; emic; ethnography; ethnomethodology; etic; field notes; first-order explanation; in-depth interview; informants; interpretive; member checks; naturalism; natural setting; observational role; phenomenology; purposive sample; qualitative data; qualitative data analysis; qualitative measurement; qualitative methods; second-order explanation; tale. *Compare* experiment; survey method; textual analysis.

naturalistic paradigm The family of philosophies characterized by a focus on the socially constructed nature of reality. *See* context-bound findings; induction; naturalistic inquiry; natural setting; qualitative methods. *Compare* positivist paradigm.

natural setting A setting in which people's behavior normally takes place, not a setting created and controlled by a researcher. *Compare* researcher-controlled setting.

N-by-M designs Factorial designs that have more than two independent variables. *Compare* two-by-two design.

need analysis The use of surveys to identify both specific problems experienced by a target group, usually by comparing what exists with what would be preferred, as well as potential solutions to those problems. *Compare* network analysis; organizational feedback surveys and audits.

negative relationship (inverse relationship) A relationship between variables in which increases in one variable, such as an independent variable, are associated with decreases in another variable, such as a dependent variable. *Compare* positive relationship.

negatively skewed distribution A skewed distribution in which the tail runs to the left side of the curve. *Compare* positively skewed distribution.

neo-Aristotelian criticism A form of rhetorical criticism that evaluates whether the most appropriate and effective means, as articulated in the specific set of criteria given in Aristotle's *Rhetoric,* were used to create the rhetorical text(s) intended to influence a particular audience. *Compare* dramatistic criticism; fantasy theme criticism; feminist criticism; genre criticism; historical criticism; metaphoric criticism; narrative criticism.

nested factor design A factorial design in which levels of one factor only appear (are "nested") within a single level of another factor. *Compare* crossed factor design; mixed factor design.

network analysis Use of the survey method to examine patterns of interaction among members of a social network. *Compare* need analysis; organizational feedback surveys and audits.

network sample (multiplicity sample) A nonrandom sample in which respondents are asked to refer a researcher to other respondents; these people are contacted and, in turn, are asked for the names of additional respondents, who are contacted, and asked for additional names, and so forth. This type of procedure is sometimes called the *snowball technique;* just as a snowball rolling down a hill picks up more and more snow, so too does a network sample become larger as a researcher contacts people who have been referred by other respondents. *Compare* convenience sample; purposive sample; quota sample; volunteer sample.

nominal measurement scale A measurement scale that classifies a variable into qualitatively different categories. *Compare* interval measurement scale; ordinal measurement scale; ratio measurement scale.

nominal variable (categorical variable, classificatory variable, discrete variable) A variable that can be differentiated only on the basis of type. *See* dichotomized variable; dichotomous variable; polytomous variable. *Compare* continuous variable; ordered variable.

noncausal relationship A relationship between variables in which changes in variables are associated, or occur together, without one necessarily causing changes in the other. *Compare* causal relationship.

nondirectional hypothesis (*See* two-tailed hypothesis)

nondirective questionnaire or interview A questionnaire or interview in which respondents' initial responses determine what will be asked next. *Compare* directive questionnaire or interview.

nonlinear relationship A relationship between variables that can generally be explained by a line through the data on a scatter plot that is not straight, but curved in some way. *See* curvilinear relationship. *Compare* linear relationship.

nonparametric statistics (distribution-free statistics) Statistical significance tests that do not assume that the variables of interest are normally distributed in a population. *Compare* parametric statistics.

nonprobability sampling (*See* nonrandom sampling)

nonrandom sampling (nonprobability sampling) Samples drawn in such a way that they do not ensure that each member of a population or universe has an equal chance of being selected. *See* convenience sample; network sample; purposive sample; quota sample; volunteer sample. *Compare* random sampling.

nonreactive measures (*See* unobtrusive measures)

nonrecursive causal model A model of causality in which a causal relationship between variables is reciprocal or two-way, in that a variable can be both a cause and an effect. *Compare* recursive causal model.

nonresponse bias A bias that occurs when nonrespondents are different in important ways from those who responded, which potentially jeopardizes the validity of the results.

nonsense correlations (*See* spurious relationships)

normal curve (*See* normal distribution)

normal distribution (bell-shaped curve, normal curve) A distribution in which scores are distributed in the shape of a symmetrical bell, such that the center point is in the exact middle of the distribution and is the highest point of the curve (it is the mean, median, and mode of the distribution), and the shape of the scores on the right and left sides of the center point, with units expressed in standard deviations away from the mean, are exactly the same; two halfs of a bell-shape. Because of the symmetrical shape of a normal distribution, researchers know the proportion of scores that fall within any particular area of the curve.

normative scale An ordinal, as well as interval and ratio, measurement scale, in which a particular rank or rating can be used more than once (creating ties in ranked items). *Compare* ipsative scale.

NS Stands for "not (statistically) significant."

null hypothesis An implicit statement that underlies every hypothesis and indicates that there is *no* difference between the groups or *no* relationship between the variables being studied.

numerical variable (*See* continuous variable)

observation The systematic inspection and interpretation of communication phenomena. *See* direct observation; indirect observation. *Compare* others' reports; self-reports.

observational role The observational role a researcher assumes in naturalistic inquiry. *See* complete observer; complete participant; observer-participant; participant-observer.

observed frequencies In a chi-square test, the frequencies of occurrence for each category. *Compare* expected frequencies.

observed variable An independent variable in an experiment that is observed, rather than manipulated, by the researcher. *Compare* manipulated variable.

observer bias A researcher observational bias that occurs when observers' knowledge of the research (e.g., its purpose or hypotheses) influences their observations. *Compare* observer drift.

observer drift A researcher observational bias that occurs when observers become inconsistent in the criteria used to make and record observations. *Compare* observer bias.

observer-participant An observational role in naturalistic inquiry in which a researcher primarily observes and only participates to a limited extent. *Compare* complete observer; complete participant; participant-observer.

omnibus test An overall statistical test, such as an analysis of variance, that tells researchers whether there is any significant difference(s) that exists between or among the groups or related measurements. *See* multiple comparison tests.

one-group pretest-posttest design A preexperimental design in which a single group is given a pretest, exposed to the independent variable, and then given a posttest. *See* before-after designs. *Compare* one-group posttest-only design; posttest-only nonequivalent groups design.

one-group posttest-only design A preexperimental design in which a single group is exposed to the independent variable and then given a posttest. *Compare* one-group pretest-posttest design; posttest-only nonequivalent groups design.

one-tailed hypothesis (directional hypothesis) A hypothesis that predicts the specific nature of the relationship between variables. *Compare* two-tailed hypothesis.

one-variable analysis of variance (one-way analysis of variance) A type of analysis of variance that examines differences between two or more groups on an interval/ratio dependent variable or two or more interval/ratio measurements for a single group. *See* repeated-measures analysis of variance. *Compare* factorial analysis of variance; multivariate analysis of variance.

one-variable chi-square test (one-way chi-square test, single-sample chi-square test) A type of chi-square test that assesses the statistical significance of differences in the distribution of the categories of a single nominal independent or dependent variable. *Compare* log-linear analysis; two-variable chi-square test.

one-way chi-square test (*See* one-variable chi-square test)

online database A database that is stored on the mainframe of a large computer center, such as a university computer center. *See* CD-ROM.

ontological assumption Assumptions about the nature of reality. *Compare* axiological assumption; epistemological assumption; methodological assumption; rhetorical assumption.

open question (open-ended question, unstructured item) A question that asks respondents to use their own words in answering questions. *Compare* closed question.

open-ended question (*See* open question)

operational construct sample (*See* theoretical sample)

operational definition A statement that describes a concept in terms of its observable characteristics or behaviors. *See* conceptual fit. *Compare* conceptual definition.

operationalization The process of determining the observable characteristics associated with a concept or variable. *See* operational definition. *Compare* conceptualization.

opportunistic sample A purposive sample used in naturalistic inquiry that involves following new leads during fieldwork, taking advantage of unexpected opportunities to interview people. *Compare* confirming and disconfirming case sample; criterion sample; critical case sample; extreme case sample; homogeneous sample; intensity sample; maximum variation sample; politically important case sample; random purposive sample; stratified purposive sample; theoretical sample; typical case sample.

oral history A form of historical criticism and naturalistic inquiry that obtains narratives of personal experiences via in-depth interviews to understand more fully what happened in the past. *Compare* account analysis; biographical studies; critical incident technique; episode analysis; ethnomethodological interview; historical case studies; key

informant; life story interview; long interview; protocol analysis; social movement studies.

ordered variable A variable that can be assigned meaningful numerical values that indicate how much of the concept is present. *See* dichotomized variable. *Compare* continuous variable; nominal variable.

ordinal interaction An interaction effect in which, when plotted on a graph, the lines representing the two variables do not intersect. *Compare* disordinal interaction.

ordinal measurement scale A measurement scale that not only classifies a variable into nominal categories, but also rank orders those categories along some "greater than" and "less than" dimension. *See* ipsative scale; normative scale. *Compare* interval measurement scale; nominal measurement scale; ratio measurement scale.

ordinal sampling (*See* systematic sample)

ordinate The vertical (or *y*) axis of a graph; generally used to display the values of the dependent variable. *Compare* abscissa.

organizational feedback surveys and audits Use of the survey method in which members of organizations and representatives of relevant organizational publics are questioned about current or potential opportunities and constraints facing an organization. *Compare* need analysis; network analysis.

organismic variable (*See* background variable)

others' reports A measurement method for assessing whether people demonstrate particular characteristics/behavior by asking people to comment on other people. *Compare* observation; self-reports.

outcome variables (*See* dependent variable)

outlier An extreme score in a distribution.

outputs of communication Messages produced by communicators themselves, including written artifacts (such as letters, graffiti, and books), works of art (such as paintings, statues, and films), and other symbolic outputs (such as footprints and refuse), often studied in textual analysis. *Compare* transcripts of communication.

panel approach A procedure for establishing the content validity of a measurement instrument whereby qualified people are recruited to describe the aspects of that variable or to agree that an instrument taps the concept being measured. *Compare* face validity.

panel study (prospective study) A longitudinal survey in which responses from the same people over time are obtained to learn how their beliefs, attitudes, and/or behaviors change; the loss of respondents from a panel study is called *panel attrition. Compare* trend study.

paradigm Worldviews; a set of basic assumptions or beliefs to which proponents subscribe. *See* axiological assumption; epistemological assumption; methodological assumption; naturalistic paradigm; positivist paradigm; ontological assumption; rhetorical assumption.

pareidolia In intuition, a type of misperception or illusion that occurs when one perceives meaning in the face of meaningless objects or stimuli, such as discernible images in clouds. *Compare* tunnel effect.

parameter In estimation, an estimated population characteristic.

parametric statistics Statistical estimates of population parameters from estimation and significance testing that assume the variables of interest are normally distributed in the population being studied. *See* estimates; estimator; parameters. *Compare* nonparametric statistics.

part correlation (*See* semipartial correlation)

partial (*See* partial correlation)

partial correlation (effects analysis, elaboration, partial) The analysis of the statistical relationship between two variables while statistically controlling for (rule out, remove, hold constant, residualize, or "partial out") the influence of one or more other variables; takes the form $r_{ab.c} = +/- x$, read, "The partial correlation coefficient of variable *a* and variable *b* with variable *c* controlled for is…" *See* first-order partial correlation; higher-order partial correlation; zero-order correlation. *Compare* correlation; multiple correlation; semipartial correlation; simple correlation.

partial replication A replication that duplicates a previous research study by changing one procedure while keeping the rest of the procedures the same. *Compare* conceptual replication; exact replication.

participant matching (*See* matched-pairs design)

participant-observer An observational role in naturalistic inquiry in which a researcher becomes involved as fully as possible in a social setting where people know they are being studied. *Compare* complete observer; complete participant; observer-participant.

path analysis A multivariate relationship analysis that examines hypothesized relationships among multiple variables (usually independent, mediating, and dependent) for the purpose of helping to establish

causal connections and inferences by showing the "paths" the causal influences take. *See* effect coefficient; path coefficient; path diagram. *Compare* canonical correlation analysis; cluster analysis; discriminant analysis; factor analysis; multidimensional scaling.

path coefficient In path analysis, the correlation coefficient between pairs of variables.

path diagram In path analysis, a graphic representation of the results.

peaked distribution (leptokurtic distribution) The shape of a distribution that is tall and sharply pointed, with scores clustered around the middle. *Compare* flat distribution; mesokurtic distribution.

pearson product moment correlation Probably the most popular statistical procedure used to calculate a correlation coefficient for two variables that are measured on an interval or ratio scale. *See* Pearson's correlation coefficient. *Compare* Cramer's V; Kendall's correlation; point biserial correlation; Spearman correlation coefficient.

Pearson *r* (*See* Pearson's correlation coefficient)

Pearson's correlation coefficient (product-moment correlation, Pearson's *r*, or Pearson *r*) The correlation coefficient for the Pearson product moment correlation.

Pearson's *r* (*See* Pearson's correlation coefficient)

peer review The process of having colleagues in a field review manuscripts submitted for publication in scholarly journals, which became institutionalized in the mid-twentieth century (Burnham, 1990). *See* blind review.

performance studies A form of textual analysis that involves "[t]he process of dialogic engagement with one's own and others' aesthetic communication through the means of performance" (Pelias, 1992, p. 15). *See* performance vision. *Compare* content analysis; interaction analysis; rhetorical criticism.

performance vision In performance studies, a reading that a performance researcher attempts to enact.

period effects Cohort effects due to the influence of a particular era or time period. *Compare* generation effects.

periodicity A biased systematic sample that occurs when every *n*th person/text in a population possesses a characteristic that the other people do not, and these people are selected.

personal ethnography (*See* autoethnography)

personal experience A type of everyday way of knowing that involves experiencing something firsthand. *Compare* appeals to tradition, custom, and faith; authority; intuition; magic, superstition, and mysticism.

phenomenology The assumption in naturalistic inquiry that "the object of interest be examined without any preconceived notions or a priori expectations" (Potter, 1996, p. 43). *Compare* interpretive; naturalism.

physical sciences The study of the physical and natural world, as represented by such academic disciplines as physics, chemistry, and biology. *Compare* humanities; social science.

physical units In unitizing in content analysis, the space and time devoted to content, such as the number of particular items or amount of space devoted to them in the texts. *Compare* meaning units.

pie chart A visual display of the frequency of nominal categories that uses circles divided into segments proportional to the percentage of the circle that represents the frequency count for each category. *Compare* bar chart; frequency histogram; frequency polygon; line graph.

pilot study A preliminary study that tests the procedures to be used to make sure they are as effective as possible before the main study starts.

placebo group A condition in an experiment where research participants believe they are getting the independent variable being studied but do not. *See* placebo effect. *Compare* control group; treatment group.

placebo effect Any change in a placebo group.

platykurtic distribution (*See* flat distribution)

point biserial correlation (r_{pb}) A correlational procedure used when one variable is measured on a interval/ratio scale and the other variable is measured on a nominal scale. *Compare* Cramer's V; Kendall's correlation; Pearson product moment correlation; Spearman correlation coefficient.

politically important case sample A purposive sample used in naturalistic inquiry of politically important people; used to attract public attention to the study (or avoid attracting undersired attention by purposefully eliminating from the sample politically sensitive cases). *Compare* confirming and disconfirming case sample; criterion sample; critical case sample; extreme case sample; homogeneous sample; intensity sample; maximum variation sample; opportunistic sample; random purposive sample; stratified purposive sample; theoretical sample; typical case sample.

political poll Public opinion research conducted to describe public opinion on political issues and potential voting behavior. *See* exit poll. *Compare* evaluation research; market research.

polynomial regression analysis (curvilinear regression) A form of regression analysis used to predict variables that have a nonlinear relationship. *Compare* linear regression analysis; multiple regression analysis.

polytomous variable A nominal variable that can be divided into more than two categories (e.g., ethnicity).

population (universe) All the people/texts who/that possess a particular characteristic of interest. *See* census; sample; sample frame; target group.

population validity The extent to which a sample is representative of the population from which it is drawn.

positional operators In electronic searches, words that can be used to make sure that records are searched with regard to particular word orders (e.g., *adj*). *Compare* boolean operators.

positive relationship (direct relationship) A relationship between variables in which increases in a variable, an independent variable, are associated with increases in another variable, a dependent variable. *Compare* negative relationship.

positively skewed distribution A skewed distribution in which the tail runs to the right side of the curve. *Compare* negatively skewed distribution.

positivism (*See* positivist paradigm)

positivist paradigm (positivism) The "family of philosophies characterized by an extremely positive evaluation of science and scientific method" (W. L. Reese, 1980, p. 450). *See* context-free generalizations; deduction; quantitative methods; researcher-controlled setting. *Compare* naturalistic paradigm.

posthoc comparison (*See* multiple comparison test)

posttest In experiments, a measurement of relevant variables that occurs after the manipulation of an independent variable. *Compare* pretest.

posttest-only control group design (*See* posttest-only equivalent groups design)

posttest-only equivalent groups design (posttest-only control group design) A full experimental design in which research participants are randomly assigned to one of at least two conditions (such as a treatment and a control group) and then given a posttest. *Compare* pretest-posttest equivalent groups design; posttest-only nonequivalent groups design; Solomon four-group design.

posttest-only nonequivalent groups design (static group comparison design) A preexperimental design in which research participants are nonrandomly assigned to one of two conditions (such as a treatment or a control group) and then given a posttest. *Compare* one-group pretest-posttest design; one-group posttest-only design; posttest-only equivalent groups design.

power analysis (*See* statistical power)

practice effects (*See* sensitization)

predictive validity A form of criterion-related validity that refers to how well a measurement instrument forecasts or predicts an outcome. *Compare* concurrent validity.

predictor variable (regressor) In regression analysis, the independent variable, or the variable whose scores are being used to predict the score on a criterion variable. *See* independent variable. *Compare* criterion variable.

preexperiment The least controlled type of experiment in which an independent variable is manipulated or observed and there may be one or more conditions; when there are multiple conditions, neither random assignment nor pretests are used to rule out initial differences between the conditions, which creates nonequiavlent conditions; when there is only one condition, a single pretest, at most, is used and, therefore, no baseline comparison is established. *See* one-group posttest-only design; one-group pretest-posttest design; posttest-only nonequivalent groups design. *Compare* full experiment; quasi-experiment.

pretest In experiments, a measurement of research participants on relevant variables that need to be accounted for *before* exposing the treatment group to the manipulation of the independent variable. *Compare* posttest.

pretest-posttest control group design (*See* pretest-posttest equivalent groups design)

pretest-posttest equivalent groups design (pretest-posttest control group design) A full experimental design in which research participants are randomly assigned to one of at least two conditions (such as a treatment or a control group), and a pretest and posttest are given. *Compare* pretest-posttest quasi-equivalent groups design; posttest-only equivalent groups design; Solomon four-group design.

pretest-posttest quasi-equivalent groups design A quasi-experimental design that nonrandomly assigns research participants to two different conditions (such as a treatment or control group), measures them on a pretest, manipulates the independent variable, and then measures both conditions again on a posttest. *Compare* interrupted time series design; pretest-posttest equivalent groups design; single-group interrupted time series design.

pretest sensitizing (*See* sensitization)

primary research report The first reporting of a research study by the person(s) who actually conducted the study; technically, a subset of primary source materials. *Compare* secondary research report.

primary source materials Original records and documents. *See* archive; primary research report.

probability sampling (*See* random sampling)

procedure validity and reliability Conducting research accurately and consistently; a potential internal validity threat related to the way research is conducted. *See* controlling for environmental influences; treatment validity and reliability. *Compare* history; sensitization; sleeper effect.

product-moment correlation (*See* Pearson's correlation coefficient)

proportional stratified random sample A stratification sample in which respondents from the categories are selected in proportion to their representation in the population.

propositional units In unitizing in content analysis, meaning units that place content into a consistent structure, such as assertions about an object. *Compare* referential units; syntactical units; thematic units.

proprietary research Research conducted for a specific audience and not necessarily shared beyond that audience. *Compare* scholarly research.

prospective study (*See* panel study)

protocol Step-by-step procedures in a study. *See* interview schedule.

protocol analysis An in-depth interview used in naturalistic inquiry that asks people to verbalize their intentions, thoughts, and feelings as they engage in an event or activity. *See* stimulated recall. *Compare* account analysis; critical incident technique; episode analysis; ethnomethodological interview; key informant; life story interview; long interview; oral history.

pseudoresearch (junk science) "Claims dressed up in the form of serious science but lacking serious empirical and conceptual credentials" (Huber, 1991, p. 223). *Compare* everyday ways of knowing; research.

public library A municipal library operated by a city, town, or local government that is accessible to the general public.

public opinion research Applied survey research conducted to measure public opinion; comprised of evaluation research, market research, and political polls. *See* evaluation research; market research; political poll.

purposeful sample (*See* purposive sample)

purposive sample (deliberate, judgment, purposeful, strategic sample) A nonrandom sample in which respondents are selected nonrandomly on the basis of a particular characteristic. *See* combination purposive sample; confirming and disconfirming case sample; criterion sample; critical case sample; extreme case sample; homogeneous sample; intensity sample; maximum variation sample; opportunistic sample; politically important case sample; random purposive sample; stratified purposive sample; theoretical sample; typical case samples. *Compare* convenience sample; network sample; quota sample; volunteer sample.

Pygmalion effect (*See* unintentional expectancy effect)

quadratic relationship A curvilinear relationship between two variables in which there is only one curve.

qualitative content analysis A form of content analysis in which researchers are more interested in the meanings associated with messages than with the number of times message variables occur. *Compare* quantitative content analysis.

qualitative data Data using symbols other than meaningful numbers. See qualitative measurement. *Compare* quantitative data.

qualitative data analysis The analysis of data that indicates the meanings (other than relative amounts) people have of something. See analytic induction; dialectical analysis; fantasy theme analysis; grounded theory; metaphor analysis; *Compare* statistical data analysis.

qualitative measurement Measurement that employs symbols (words, diagrams, and nonmeaningful numbers) to indicate the presence or absence of something or to categorize things into different types. *See* qualitative data; qualitative data analysis. *Compare* quantitative measurement.

qualitative methods Research methods that focus on the acquisition of data that take the form of symbols other than meaningful numbers. See qualita-

tive data; qualitative data analysis; qualitative measurement. *Compare* quantitative methods.

quantitative content analysis A form of content analysis that involves the "systematic and replicable examination of symbols of communication, which have been assigned numeric values according to valid measurement rules, and the analysis of relationships involving those values using statistical methods, in order to describe the communication, draw inferences about its meaning, or infer from the communication to its context, both of production and consumption" (Riffe et al., 1998, p. 20). *See* community structure approach. *Compare* qualitative content analysis.

quantitative data Data in the form of meaningful numbers. *See* quantitative measurement. *Compare* qualitative data.

quantitative measurement Measurement that employs sequential numerical indicators to ascertain the relative amount of something. *See* quantitative data; statistical data analysis. *Compare* qualitative measurement.

quantitative methods Research methods that focus on the collection of data in the form of meaningful numbers. *See* quanitative data; quantitative measurement. *Compare* qualitative methods; statistical data analysis.

quarrelsome response style A response style (set) tendency for people to disagree or say "no" to whatever question is asked. *Compare* acquiescent response style; social desirability bias.

quartile deviation (*See* interquartile range)

quasi-experiment A moderately controlled experiment in which the independent variable is either manipulated or observed and has one or more conditions; when there are multiple conditions, research participants are not randomly assigned to them, but quasi-equivalent conditions are created by using pretests to assess whether there are important differences between the conditions; when there is only one condition, multiple pretests and posttests are used as baseline measures to assess changes within those same participants before and after an experimental treatment. *See* single-group interrupted time series design; pretest-posttest quasi-equivalent groups design; interrupted time series quasi-equivalent groups design. *Compare* full experiment; preexperiment.

question format The strategic sequence of queries on survey instruments. *See* funnel format; inverted funnel format; tunnel format.

questionnaire The presentation of written questions to evoke written responses from people. *Compare* interview; observation.

question order effect An effect that occurs when responses to earlier questions influence how people respond to later questions. *See* consistency effect; fatigue effect; redundancy effect.

quota sample A nonrandom sample in which respondents are selected nonrandomly on the basis of their known proportion in a population. *Compare* convenience sample; network sample; purposive sample; volunteer sample.

random assignment (randomization) A procedure used in experimental research in which each research participant has an equal chance of being assigned to any particular condition of an experiment. *Compare* random sampling.

random-digit dialing Survey research method in which a computer generates randomly all possible combinations of telephone numbers in a given exchange.

random error (accidental error, chance error) Error that is not or cannot be predicted or controlled and is assumed to equal out over time. *Compare* measurement error; true score component.

randomization (*See* random assignment)

random number table A table of numbers that has been generated by a computer in a nonpurposive way (each number had an equal chance of being selected), which means there is no predetermined relationship whatsoever among the numbers on the table; sometimes used in random sampling to select a sample.

random purposive sample A purposive sample used in naturalistic inquiry that involves selecting people from a small sample such that each has an equal chance of being selected; used to add credibility to the sample when potential purposive sample is larger than one can handle. *Compare* confirming and disconfirming case sample; criterion sample; critical case sample; extreme case sample; homogeneous sample; intensity sample; maximum variation sample; opportunistic sample; politically important case sample; stratified purposive sample; theoretical sample; typical case sample.

random sampling (probability sampling) Selecting a sample in such a way that each person/text in the population/universe of interest has an equal chance of being included. *See* cluster sample; simple random sample; stratification sample; systematic samples. *Compare* nonrandom sampling; random assignment.

range (span) A measure of dispersion that reports the distance between the highest and lowest scores in a distribution. *See* extreme values; highspread; interquartile range; lowspread; semiquartile range. *Compare* standard deviation; variance.

ratio measurement scale A measurement scale that categorizes a variable, rank orders it along some dimension with standard equal distances between the adjacent points on the scale, and has an absolute, or true, zero point where the variable being measured ceases to exist. *Compare* interval measurement scale; nominal measurement scale; ordinal measurement scale.

raw scores (unstandardized scores) Data kept in their original unit of measurement and not converted to standard scores. *Compare* standard scores.

readability analysis An analysis, sometimes used in survey research and content analysis, of how easy or difficult it is to read a particular passage that tells the educational grade level needed to comprehend the passage on the basis of such things as word and sentence length.

realist tale A tale told in reporting naturalistic inquiry from the point of view of the people studied; the goal is to capture as fully as possible the ways in which the participants make sense of their world, and the researcher is removed from the tale, which is told in documentary style. *Compare* confessional tale; critical tale; formal tale; impressionistic tale; jointly told tale; literary tale.

reconceptualization The concluding phase of the research process that occurs when researchers rethink the topic of inquiry as a result of the systematic processes associated with conceptualization, planning and designing research, using methodologies to gather data, analyzing the data, and interpreting research findings. *Compare* conceptualization.

recursive causal model A model of causality in which the causal relationship between variables is one-way in that the one variable influences another but not the other way around; that is, one is the cause and the other is the effect. *Compare* nonrecursive causal model.

redundancy effect A question order effect that occurs when respondents breeze over questions that repeat previous questions. *Compare* consistency effect; fatigue effect.

references A complete and accurate list of all sources cited in a text (e.g., primary or secondary research report). *See* footnotes.

referential units (character units) In unitizing in content analysis, meaning units that "involve some physical or temporal unit (e.g., event, people, objects, etc.) referred to or alluded to within content…. Referential units can be used to measure the meaning attached to a particular person, event, or issue" (Riffe et al., 1998, p. 66). *Compare* propositional units; syntactical units; thematic units.

region of acceptance The region of a normal distribution of a statistical significance test that indicates that the calculated value does not meet or exceed the critical value and, therefore, the null hypothesis of no difference or no relationship must be accepted. *Compare* region of rejection.

region of rejection (critical region) The region of a normal distribution of a statistical significance test that indicates that the calculated value does meet or exceed the critical value and, therefore, the null hypothesis of no difference or no relationship can be rejected and the hypothesis of a difference or relationship accepted. *Compare* region of acceptance.

regression analysis Statistical procedures used to make predictions. *See* goodness of fit; linear regression; multiple linear regression; polynominal regression analysis; regression coefficient; regression equation; regression line.

regression artifact (*See* regression effect)

regression coefficient In regression analysis, a statistical measure of the relationship between the variables. *See* bivariate regression coefficient.

regression effect (regression artifact) A finding that is due to statistical regression.

regression equation (prediction equation, regression model) An algebraic equation expressing the statistical relationship between variables; the typical regression equation for two variables is: $y = a + bx$, where y is the criterion variable, a is the intercept, b is the slope, and x is the predictor variable. *See* intercept; slope.

regression line (line of best fit) In linear regression, a straight line fit through the data that minimizes the distance between each observed score and the line.

regression toward the mean (*See* statistical regression)

regression weight (*See* beta coefficient)

regressor (*See* predictor variable)

reinforcer variable A variable that increases a causal relationship between variables. *Compare* suppressor variable.

related-measures *t* test (matched-sample or paired *t* test) A type of *t* test that examines differences between two sets of related measurements for the same group. *Compare* independent-sample *t* test.

relative frequency The display in a frequency table of the proportion of times each category or measurement point occurs (found by dividing the number of cases for a particular category or measurement point by the total number of cases for the entire distribution). *Compare* absolute frequency; cumulative frequency.

reliability Consistency/stability. *See* measurement reliability.

reliability coefficient A numerical indicator of the extent to which a measurement is reliable, or free of error.

repeated-measures analysis of variance A type of analysis of variance that examines differences between two or more interval/ratio measurements obtained from a single group.

repeated-measures design A within-group design in which the same research participants are given multiple levels (multiple treatments) of the independent variable and measured after each exposure. *See* counterbalance; treatment carryover effect; treatment order effect.

replication Conducting a study that repeats or duplicates in some systematic manner a previous study. *See* conceptual replication; exact replication; partial replication; replication battery.

replication battery A research project that contains multiple replications of a previous study, such as a study that includes an exact replication and one that is a partial or conceptual replication.

representative values (*See* measures of central tendency)

research The form of disciplined inquiry that involves studying something in a planned manner and reporting it so that other inquirers can potentially replicate the process if they choose. *See* proprietary research; research methods; scholarly research. *Compare* everyday ways of knowing; pseudo-research.

researcher-controlled setting A research setting created and controlled by a researcher. *See* laboratory. *Compare* natural setting.

researcher effects The influence of a researcher on the people/texts being studied. *See* experimenter effects; researcher observational biases; researcher personal attribute effect; researcher unintentional expectancy effect.

researcher observational biases An internal validity threat due to researcher effects that occurs whenever researchers, their assistants, or the people they employ to observe research participants demonstrate inaccuracies during the observational process. *See* halo effect; observer bias; observer drift. *Compare* researcher personal attribute effect; researcher unintentional expectancy effect.

researcher personal attribute effect An internal validity threat due to researcher effects that occurs when particular characteristics of a researcher influence people's behavior. *Compare* researcher observer bias; researcher unintentional expectancy effect.

researcher triangulation The use of multiple researchers to collect and analyze data. *Compare* data triangulation; methodological triangulation; theoretical triangulation.

researcher unintentional expectancy effect (Rosenthal effect, Pygmalion effect) An internal validity threat due to researcher effects that occurs when researchers influence research participants' responses by inadvertently letting them know the behavior they desire. *Compare* researcher observer bias; researcher personal attribute effect.

research ethics Moral principles and recognized rules of conduct governing the activities of researchers. *See* anonymity; confidentiality; institutional review boards; voluntary informed consent.

research methods The strategies researchers use to solve puzzling mysteries about the world; they are the means used to collect evidence necessary for building or testing explanations about that which is being studied.

research participants The particular persons, groups of people, or texts in a study. *See* informants; respondents; subjects; texts.

research question A formal question posed to guide research. *Compare* hypothesis.

research topic The novel idea that researchers consider worth studying and hope to understand better.

respondents Research participants who answer survey questions. *See* research participants; subjects.

response rate The number of usable responses in survey research divided by the total number of people sampled. *See* nonresponse bias.

response set (response style) The tendency to answer questions the same way automatically (such as using only one side of a scale) rather than thinking about each individual question. *See* acquiescent response style; quarrelsome response style.

response style (*See* response set)

rhetorical assumption Assumptions about how research reports are to be written. *Compare* axiological assumption; epistemological assumption; methodological assumption; ontological assumption.

rhetorical criticism A form of textual analysis that involves a systematic method for describing, analyzing, interpreting, and evaluating the persuasive force of messages embedded within texts. *See* classical rhetoric; contemporary rhetorical criticism; dramatistic critcism; fantasy theme critcism; genre critcism; historical critcism; metaphoric critcism; narrative critcism; neo-Aristotelian criticism. *Compare* content analysis; interaction analysis; performance studies.

Rosenthal effect (*See* unintentional expectancy effect)

sample A subgroup selected from a population or universe. *Compare* census.

sampling error A number that expresses how much the characteristics of a sample probably differ from the characteristics of its population.

sampling distribution A (hypothetical) distribution formed from statistics (e.g., means, medians, and proportions) collected on a large number (e.g., 100) random samples. *See* standard error; standard error of the mean.

sampling frame A list of the population from which researchers sample.

sampling rate The interval used in a systematic sample to choose every nth person/text.

scatter diagram (*See* scatter plot)

scattergram (*See* scatter plot)

scatter plot (scattergram, scatter diagram) A plotting of two variables on a graph.

Scheffe Test A conservative multiple comparison test that leans toward underestimating significant differences. *Compare* Bonferroni technique; Least Significant Difference Test; Tukey's Honestly Significant Difference Test; Tukey Test.

scholarly journal A periodical publication that prints scholarly essays and studies; the most important source for locating primary research reports. *See* blind review; peer review. *Compare* conference paper; scholarly text.

scholarly research Research conducted to promote public assess to knowledge. *Compare* proprietary research.

scholarly text A text authored or edited by a scholar that is intended primarily for other scholars to read. *Compare* conference paper; scholarly journal.

scientific significance (*See* substantive significance)

secondary data analysis Reanalysis by one scholar of data collected by someone else.

secondary research report A report of a research study by someone other than the person who conducted the study or a later report by the person who conducted the study that cites or uses the primary report that has already appeared elsewhere. *Compare* primary research report.

second-order explanation In naturalistic inquiry, an explanation of participants' attitudes, behaviors, and other things, as seen through the researcher's eyes. *Compare* first-order explanation.

second-order interaction effect (higher-order interaction effect) An interaction effect among three or more variables. *Compare* first-order interaction effect.

secular trend A long-term trend, as opposed to a short-term fluctuation.

segmented bar chart (*See* grouped bar chart)

selection An internal validity threat due to research participants that results from the process of choosing people or texts for a study. *See* self-selection bias. *Compare* Hawthorne effect; inter-participant bias; maturation; mortality; statistical regression.

self-reports A measurement method for assessing whether people demonstrate particular characteristics/behavior by asking them to comment on themselves; their answers are then taken as a measurement of the operationally defined concept. *Compare* observation; others' reports.

self-selection bias A problem that can occur when comparisons are made between groups of people that have been formed on the basis of self-selection.

semantic differential scale An interval measurement scale, developed by Osgood, Suci, and Tannenbaum (1957), that measures the meanings people create in response to a specific stimulus by presenting the stimulus item at the top of a list of (usually) 7-point scales representing polar opposites and asking people to choose a single point on each scale that expresses their perception of the stimulus object. *Compare* Likert scale; Likert-type scale; Thurstone scale.

semi-interquartile range The interquartile range divided in half. *Compare* interquartile range.

semipartial correlation (part correlation) A partial correlation that partials out a variable from one of the other variables being correlated; takes the form $r_{a(b.c)} = +/- x$, read, "The semipartial correlation coefficient of variables a and b after variable c has been partialed out from variable b is…" *Compare* partial correlation.

semistructured interview An interview schedule in which interviewers ask the specific primary questions on the interview schedule but can also ask probing secondary questions, usually to gather specific details or more complete answers. *Compare* structured interview; unstructured interview.

sensitization (practice effects, pretest sensitizing, testing) An internal validity threat related to the way research is conducted that occurs when there is a tendency for an initial measurement in a research study to influence a subsequent measurement. *Compare* history; procedure validity and reliability; sleeper effect.

significance level The probability level (p value) researchers set for rejecting a null hypothesis. *See* decision rule; marginally significant.

significance testing (hypothesis testing) Inferential statistics that examine how likely differences between groups and relationships between variables occur by chance by testing whether a null hypothesis is probably either correct or false. *See* critical value; decision error; decision rule; degrees of freedom; NS; region of acceptance; region of rejection.

simple correlation A correlation between two, as opposed to more, variables, or a correlation for a linear, as opposed to nonlinear, relationship. *Compare* multiple correlation.

simple random sample A random sample drawn from a population in which each person/text is assigned a consecutive number and then the sample is selected from these numbers such that each number has an equal chance of being chosen until the desired sample size is obtained. *Compare* cluster sample; stratified sample; systematic sample.

simple regression (*See* linear regression)

single-administration techniques Measurement reliability techniques that involve testing the internal consistency of an instrument on the basis of a single administration of it. *See* agreement coefficient; Cronbach's alpha coefficient method; split-half reliability. *Compare* multiple-administration techniques.

single-group interrupted time series design (time series design) A quasi-experimental design that involves giving a series of pretests to a single group prior to an independent variable manipulation, followed by a series of posttests. *Compare* interrupted time series quasi-equivalent groups design; pretest-posttest quasi-equivalent groups design.

single-sample chi-square test (*See* one-variable chi-square test)

skewness A distribution in which the majority of scores are toward one end of a distribution and the curve tails off across the rest of the distribution. *See* negatively skewed distribution; positively skewed distribution.

sleeper effect An internal validity threat related to the way research is conducted that involves an effect that is not immediately apparent but becomes evidenced over the course of time. *Compare* history; procedure validity and reliability; sensitization.

slope In a regression equation, "How many units the variable Y is increasing for every unit increase in X" (Williams, 1992, p. 152), which depends on the correlation between the two variables. *Compare* intercept.

social desirability bias The tendency for people to answer in socially desirable ways. *Compare* acquiescent response style; quarrelsome response style.

social justice communication research A form of applied communication research that deals with and contributes to the well-being of people who are economically, socially, politically, and/or culturally underresourced and disenfranchised.

social movement studies A form of historical criticism that examines persuasive strategies used to influence the historical development of specific campaigns and causes. *Compare* biographical studies; historical case studies; oral histories.

social sciences (human sciences) The application of scientific methods to the study of human behavior, such as the academic disciplines of anthropology, psychology, and sociology. *See* naturalistic paradigm; positivist paradigm. *Compare* humanities; social science.

Solomon four-group design A full experimental design that combines the pretest-posttest equivalent groups design and the posttest-only equivalent groups design by randomly assigning research participants to one of four conditions: in the first condition, they receive a pretest, treatment, and posttest; in the second condition, they receive the pretest, no

treatment, and posttest; in the third condition, they receive the treatment and posttest; and in the fourth condition, they receive no treatment and the posttest. *Compare* pretest-posttest equivalent groups design; posttest-only equivalent groups design.

span (*See* range)

Spearman correlation coefficient (rho) A correlational procedure used when two variables are measured on an ordinal scale. *Compare* Cramer's V; Kendall's correlation; Pearson product moment correlation; point biserial correlation.

special-use library A library that contains materials that meet specific needs. *See* archive. *Compare* academic library; public library.

split-half reliability A single-administration reliability technique that assesses reliability by separating people's answers on an instrument into two parts (half the questions in one part and half in the other) and then comparing the two halves.

spurious relationships (nonsense correlations) Patterns of statistical, but meaningless occurrence.

standard deviation (SD; sample standard deviation, S; population standard deviation, σ) A measure of dispersion that explains how much scores in a set of interval/ratio data vary from the mean, expressed in the original unit of measurement; found by taking the square root of the variance. *Compare* range; variance.

standard error The standard deviation of a sampling distribution.

standard error of the mean (SE_M) The standard deviation of a sampling distribution of means.

standard normal deviates (*See* standard scores)

standard scores (standard normal deviates) Scores that report how many standard deviation units a particular score is above or below the mean of its distribution. *See* transformed standard scores, z-score. *Compare* raw score.

standardized regression coefficient (*See* beta coefficient)

static design A design in which the specific research procedures are all worked out ahead of time and the researcher sticks to that plan carefully and conscientiously; used in experimental research, survey research, content analysis, and interaction analysis. *Compare* emergent design.

static group comparison design (*See* posttest-only nonequivalent groups design)

statistics Any numerical indicator of a set of data; the application of procedures that result in a statistic;

the reasoning about and arguments developed from statistical techniques and products; and/or characteristics found in a sample.

statistical data analysis The process of examining what quantitative data mean to researchers. *See* descriptive data analysis; inferential data analysis. *Compare* qualitative data analysis.

statistical disclosure control procedures (*See* statistical disclosure limitation methods)

statistical disclosure limitation methods (statistical disclosure control procedures) Statistical methods used to limit the disclosure of statistical information by agencies that collect data that will be shared with the public. *See* cell suppression.

statistical laws "Assert that a specified antecedent condition will be followed by a given event a certain percentage of the time, and they predict the percentage within specific limits" (Bowers & Courtright, 1984, p. 19). *Compare* universal laws.

statistical power (power analysis) The probability of rejecting a null hypothesis that is, in fact, probably false and, therefore, should be rejected; equal to 1 minus the probability of Type II error and, hence, the minimum statistical power is 0 and the maximum is 1.0. *See* effect size.

statistical regression (regression toward the mean) An internal validity threat due to research participants that results from the tendency for people selected on the basis of initial extreme scores on a measurement instrument to behave less atypically on the second and subsequent times on that instrument. *See* regression artifact. *Compare* Hawthorne effect; interparticipant bias; maturation; mortality; selection.

stepwise regression A form of multiple linear regression in which a computer is instructed to enter the predictor variables in various combinations and orders until a "best" equation is found. *Compare* hierarchical regression analysis.

stimulated recall A technique sometimes used in naturalistic in-depth interviews with protocol analysis to first record a conversation and then play back the tape for the conversational partners to stimulate their recall of the episode.

strategic sample (*See* purposive sample)

stratification variable In a stratification sample, the characteristic along which a population is stratified.

stratified purposive sample A purposive sample used in naturalistic inquiry of particular subgroups that share a characteristic; used to facilitate compari-

sons. *Compare* confirming and disconfirming case sample; criterion sample; critical case sample; extreme case sample; homogeneous sample; intensity sample; maximum variation sample; opportunistic sample; politically important case sample; random purposive sample; theoretical sample; typical case sample.

stratified sample A random sample that categorizes a population with respect to a characteristic important to the research and then samples randomly from each category. *See* incidence; proportional stratified random sample; stratification variable. *Compare* cluster sample; simple random sample; systematic sample.

structured interview An interview schedule that lists all the questions an interviewer is supposed to ask, and interviewers are expected to follow that schedule conscientiously so that interviews by different interviewers and with different respondents are conducted in the same way. *Compare* semistructured interview; unstructured interview.

subject matching (*See* matched-pairs design)

subject variable (*See* background variable)

subjects A term used by many researchers when referring to research participants, but it can also be used to reference other units, such as cities and organizations. *See* research participants; respondents.

substantive significance (scientific significance) The theoretical and/or practical value of research findings.

sugging Selling under the guise of a survey. *Compare* frugging.

summated scale A measurement scale made up of items that measure the same concept that can be summed to obtain an overall score.

summary statistic A numerical indicator that best summarizes the data set.

summative evaluation Evaluation research conducted after a program or product is completed to learn its overall effectiveness, usually to determine whether to continue or discontinue it. *Compare* formal evaluation.

sum of squares (SS) The sum of the deviation scores for a distribution.

suppressor variable A variable that conceals or reduces (suppresses) a relationship between an independent and dependent variable. *Compare* reinforcer variable.

surveyed rate The percentage of phone calls in survey research in which respondents have been surveyed too frequently to qualify for the survey. *Compare* contact rate; cooperation rate.

survey method A research method that asks questions about the beliefs, attitudes, and behaviors of respondents for the purpose of describing both the characteristics of those respondents and the population(s) they were chosen to represent. *See* accelerated longitudinal design; cohort study; contact rate; cooperation rate; correlational design; cross-sectional survey; frugging; longitudinal survey; public opinion research; response rate; surveyed rate. *Compare* experiment; naturalistic inquiry; textual analysis.

syntactical units In unitizing in content analysis, meaning units that consist of discrete units of language, such as individual words, sentences, and paragraphs. *Compare* propositional units; referential units; thematic units.

systematic sample (ordinal sampling) A random sample that chooses every *n*th person/text from a complete list of a population after starting at a random point. *See* periodicity; sampling rate. *Compare* cluster sample; simple random sample; stratified sample.

target group The particular population of interest to a researcher.

tale In naturalistic inquiry, a story told by a member of one culture about another culture (or his or her own culture) to the members of his or her own culture. *See* confessional tale; critical tale; formal tale; impressionistic tale; jointly told tale; literary tale; realist tale.

tenure The guarantee of lifetime faculty appointment at a particular institution, except in the most drastic circumstances. *See* academic freedom.

testing (*See* sensitization)

test-retest method A multiple-administration reliability technique that involves administering the same measurement procedure to the same group of people at different times. *See* coefficient of stability.

texts Recorded or visual messages.

textual analysis The method communication researchers use to describe and interpret the characteristics of a recorded or visual message. *See* content analysis; interaction analysis; outputs of communication; performance studies; rhetorical criticism; texts; transcripts of communication. *Compare* experiment; naturalistic inquiry; survey method.

thematic units In unitizing in content analysis, meaning units that reference topics contained within messages. *Compare* propositional units; referential units; syntactical units.

theoretical frequencies (*See* expected frequencies)

theoretical sample (operational construct sample, theory-based sample) A purposive sample used in naturalistic inquiry in which people are selected because they possess salient characteristics that, on the basis of theory and/or previous research, may make a difference. *Compare* confirming and disconfirming case sample; criterion sample; critical case sample; extreme case sample; homogeneous sample; intensity sample; maximum variation sample; opportunistic sample; politically important case sample; random purposive sample; stratified purposive sample; typical case sample.

theoretical triangulation The use of multiple theories and/or perspectives to interpret the same data. *Compare* data triangulation; methodological triangulation; researcher triangulation.

theory A generalization about a phenomenon, an explanation of how or why something occurs.

theory-based sample (*See* theoretical sample)

threshold effect An effect that occurs where changes in a dependent variable may not occur until the independent variable reaches a certain level (threshold).

Thurstone scale An interval measurement scale, developed by L. L. Thurstone, that attempts to ensure that the distances between the points on the scale are equal. A researcher first generates many statements, usually several hundred, related to the referent being investigated, and then asks a large number of judges, usually 50 to 300, to independently categorize the statements into 11 categories, ranging from "extremely favorable" to "extremely unfavorable." The researcher selects those statements, usually about 20, that consistently have been coded into a particular category by all the judges, and assigns a value based on the mean rating by all the judges. The instrument that incorporates these statements is then assumed to provide interval measurements, such that a score of 4.2 is assumed to be twice as much as a score of 2.1. *Compare* Likert scale; Likert-type scale; semantic differential scale.

time series design (*See* single-group interrupted time series design)

touchtone data entry (TDE) A computer-assisted telephone interview in which a computer reads questions and respondents answer by punching in the appropriate number on their touchtone telephone. *Compare* voice recognition entry.

trace measures The assessment of behavior by studying physical evidence, such as footprints or hair left behind; comprised of measures of erosion and measures of accretion. *See* measures of accretion; measure of erosion.

transcripts of communication Verbatim recordings of actual communication, such as written transcripts of courtroom behavior made by a court stenographer or audio/audiovisual recordings of group meetings, often studied in textual analysis. *Compare* outputs of communication.

transformed standard scores Transformations performed on standard scores (such as multiplying each *z*-score by 100 to eliminate the decimal point).

treatment carryover effect An effect that occurs in a repeated-measures design when the effects of each treatment have not passed before exposing participants to subsequent treatments. *Compare* treatment order effect.

treatment group (experimental group) A group in an experiment that receives a manipulation of the independent variable. *Compare* control group; placebo group.

treatment order effect An effect that occurs in a repeated-measures design if the order in which the treatments are presented in a within-group experiment makes a difference. *Compare* treatment carryover effect.

treatment validity and reliability A form of procedure validity and reliability that involves making sure that any treatment the study is investigating is what it purports to be every time it is administered. *See* manipulation check. *Compare* controlling for environmental influences.

trend study A longitudinal survey that measures people's beliefs, attitudes, and/or behaviors at two or more points in time to identify changes or trends. *See* secular trend. *Compare* panel study.

triangulation Studying something in multiple ways within a single study. *See* data triangulation; methodological triangulation; researcher triangulation; theoretical triangulation.

trimmed mean A procedure used when there are extreme scores that lead the mean to be an atypical or unrepresentative middle point, and involves removing the most extreme scores from the distribution. *See* winsorizing.

true score component In theory, the actual score if researchers could measure something perfectly. *Compare* error score component.

***t* test** A statistical procedure used to examine differences between two groups measured on an interval/ratio dependent variable. *See* independent-sample *t* test; related-measures *t* test. *Compare* analysis of variance; chi-square test.

Tukey's Honestly Significant Difference (HSD) Test A popular multiple comparison test used by researchers. *Compare* Bonferroni technique; Least Significant Difference Test; Scheffe Test; Tukey Test.

Tukey Test A moderate multiple comparison test used by researchers. *Compare* Bonferroni technique; Least Significant Difference Test; Scheffe Test; Tukey's Honestly Significant Difference Test.

tunnel effect In intuition, a perceptual trick of the mind in which the "mind enters a tunnel in its reasoning" (Piatelli-Palmarini, 1994, p. 24), such as seeing the figure of a man in the moon. *Compare* pareidolia.

tunnel format A question format in which respondents are asked a straight series of similarly organized questions. *Compare* funnel format; inverted funnel format.

two-by-two design A factorial design that has two independent variables. *Compare* N-by-M designs.

two-direction hypothesis (*See* two-tailed hypothesis)

two-tailed hypothesis (nondirectional hypothesis, two-direction hypothesis) A hypothesis that predicts a relationship between variables without specifying the nature of that relationship. *Compare* one-tailed hypothesis.

two-variable chi-square test (contingency table analysis, crosstabulation, multiple-sample chi-square test, two-way chi-square test) A type of chi-square test that examines differences in the distributions of the categories created from two nomical independent variables or a nominal independent and dependent variable. *Compare* log-linear analysis; one-variable chi-square test.

two-way chi-square test (*See* two-variable chi-square test)

Type I error (alpha error) A decision error that occurs when researchers reject a null hypothesis and accept a research hypothesis when, in fact, the null hypothesis is probably true and should have been accepted. *See* familywise error. *Compare* Type II error.

Type II error (acceptance error, beta error, β) A decision error that occurs when researchers accept a null hypothesis when, in fact, it is probably false, leading them to reject a perfectly sound research hypothesis. *Compare* Type I error.

typical case sample A purposive sample used in naturalistic inquiry of typical, normal, or average people. *Compare* confirming and disconfirming case sample; criterion sample; critical case sample; extreme case sample; homogeneous sample; intensity sample; maximum variation sample; opportunistic sample; politically important case sample; random purposive sample; stratified purposive sample; theoretical sample.

unbalanced design (nonorthogonal design) A study that includes an unequal number of research participants in each cell.

unidimensional concept A concept that is measured by a set of multiple indicators on an instrument that can be added together equally to derive an overall score. *See* factor analysis; summated scale. *Compare* multidimensional concept.

unimodal distribution A distribution of data that has only one mode. *Compare* bimodal distribution; multimodal distribution.

unitizing In content analysis, identifying the appropriate message unit to be coded. *See* meaning units; physical units; propositional units; referential units; syntactical units; thematic units.

universal laws "Suggest that a consequent event or condition will always follow a given antecedent" (Bowers & Courtright, 1984, p. 19). *Compare* statistical laws.

universe (*See* population)

unobtrusive measures (nonreactive measures) Indirect observational methods, as well as covert direct observation where people don't know they are being observed, that are relatively "clean" or "nonreactive" ways to gather data because they don't intrude into people's lives and, therefore, eliminate many of the problems associated with asking people questions via questionnaires and interviews (e.g., not telling the truth).

unrelated variables Variables that have no systematic relationship to one another.

unstandardized scores (*See* raw scores)

unstructured interview An interview schedule in which interviewers are provided with a list of topics but have maximum freedom to decide what questions (usually nondirective, open questions) to ask and how to phrase them. *Compare* semi-structured interview; structured interview.

unstructured item (*See* open question)

usability testing Market research that involves watching potential users interact with a new product under carefully controlled conditions, such as in a laboratory. *Compare* advertising readership study; broadcast audience survey; contextual inquiry; editorial content readership survey.

U-shaped curvilinear relationship A curvilinear relationship in which two variables are related negatively until a certain point and then are related positively. *Compare* inverted U-shaped curvilinear relationship.

validity Accuracy. *See* internal validity; external validity.

variable Any concept that can have two or more values. *See* attribute variable; background variable; binomial variable; confounding variable; continuous variable; control variable; dependent variable; dichotomized variable; dichotomous variable; extraneous variable; independent variable; intervening variable; lurking variable; manipulated variable; nominal variable; observed variable; ordered variable; polytomous variable; reinforcer variable; stratification variable; suppressor variable.

variance (sample variance, S^2, s^2; population variance, σ^2, pronounced "sigma squared") A measure of dispersion that is a mathematical index of the average distance of the scores in a distribution of interval/ratio data from the mean in squared units. *See* deviation score; sum of squares. *Compare* range; standard deviation.

variation ratio A measure of dispersion for nominal data that indicates the relative frequency of the nonmodal scores in a distribution (e.g., if the relative frequency of the modal score is .30, the variation ratio is .70).

voluntary informed consent In research ethics, research participants voluntarily agreeing to participate only after they have been fully informed about the study; if for legal reasons participants cannot grant consent, it is obtained from the legal guardian or agency. *See* general consent plus proxy consent; implied consent.

voice recognition entry (VRE) A computer-assisted telephone interview in which a computer reads questions and respondents answer by speaking directly into the telephone and the computer recognizes the numeric answers. *Compare* touchtone data entry.

volunteer sample A nonrandom sample in which respondents choose to participate in a study. *Compare* convenience sample; network sample; purposive sample; quota sample.

warrant A statement that logically connects a claim and evidence. *Compare* claim; evidence.

Web (*See* World Wide Web)

Wilcoxon Signed-Rank Test A statistical procedure used to analyze differences between two sets of related ordinal measurements. *Compare* Kruskal-Wallis Test; Mann-Whitney U-Test; median test.

Winsorizing A procedure used where there are extreme scores that lead the mean to be an atypical or unrepresentative middle point that involves changing the most extreme scores to the next less extreme score.

within-group design (within-subjects design) A design in which one group of research participants' scores on two or more measurements are compared and there is no comparison group, or one in which the same participants are given multiple levels (multiple treatments) of the independent variable and measured after each exposure. *See* repeated-measures design; treatment order effect; treatment carryover effect. *Compare* between-group design.

within-subjects design (*See* within-group design)

World Wide Web (Web, WWW) A portion of the Internet that uses hypertext language to combine text, graphics, audio, and video (Courtright & Perse, 1998).

y **intercept** (*See* intercept)

zero-order correlation A correlation between two variables with no variable controlled for. *Compare* first-order partial correlation; higher-order partial correlation.

z-**score** The standard score used most frequently by researchers.

Abelson, R. P. (1995). *Statistics as principled argument.* Hillsdale, NJ: Lawrence Erlbaum.

Adams, R. C. (1989). *Social survey methods for mass media research.* Hillsdale, NJ: Lawrence Erlbaum.

Adams, R. J., & Parrott, R. (1994). Pediatric nurses' communication of role expectations to parents of hospitalized children. *Journal of Applied Communication Research, 22,* 36–47.

Adelman, M. B. (1989). Social support and AIDS. *AIDS & Public Policy Journal, 4,* 31–39.

Adelman, M. B., & Frey, L. R. (1994). The pilgrim must embark: Creating and sustaining community in a residential facility for people with AIDS. In L. R. Frey (Ed.), *Group communication in context: Studies of natural groups* (pp. 3–21). Hillsdale, NJ: Lawrence Erlbaum.

Adelman, M. B., & Frey, L. R. (1997). *The fragile community: Living together with AIDS.* Mahwah, NJ: Lawrence Erlbaum.

Adelman, M. B., Frey, L. R., & Budz, T. (1994). Keeping the community spirit alive. *Journal of Long-Term Care Administration, 22*(2), 4–7.

Adelman, M. B. (Producer), & Schultz, P. (Director). (1991). *The pilgrim must embark: Living in community* [Videotape]. (Available from Lawrence R. Frey, 2266 Washington Avenue, Memphis, TN 38104)

Aden, R. C., Rahoi, R. L., & Beck, C. S. (1995). "Dreams are born on places like this": The process of interpretive community formation at the *Field of Dreams* site. *Communication Quarterly, 43,* 368–380.

Adler, P. A., & Adler, P. (1987). *Membership roles in field research.* Newbury Park, CA: Sage.

Adler, P. A., & Adler, P. (1993). Ethical issues in self-censorship: Ethnographic research on sensitive topics. In C. M. Renzetti & R. M. Lee (Eds.), *Researching sensitive topics* (pp. 249–266). Newbury Park, CA: Sage.

Afifi, W. A., & Reichert, T. (1996). Understanding the role of uncertainty in jealousy experience and expression. *Communication Reports, 9,* 93–104.

Ahern, T. C., & Durrington, V. (1995). Effects of anonymity and group saliency on participation and interaction in a computer-mediated small-group discussion. *Journal of Research on Computing in Education, 28,* 133–147.

Aitkin, J. E., & Neer, M. R. (1993). College student question-asking: The relationship of classroom communication apprehension and motivation. *Southern Communication Journal, 59,* 73–81.

Alberts, J. K. (1988). An analysis of couples' conversational complaints. *Communication Monographs, 55,* 184–197.

Alberts, J. K., Kellar-Guenther, Y., & Corman, S. R. (1997). That's not funny: Understanding recipients' responses to teasing. *Western Journal of Communication, 60,* 337–357.

Albrecht, T. L., Adelman, M. B., & Associates. (1987). *Communicating social support.* Newbury Park, CA: Sage.

Alcalay, R., & Bell, R. A. (1996). Ethnicity and health knowledge gaps: Impact of the California *Wellness Guide* on poor African American, Hispanic, and non-Hispanic White women. *Health Communication, 8,* 303–329.

Alder, G. S., & Tompkins, P. K. (1997). Electronic performance monitoring: An organizational justice and concertive control perspective. *Management Communication Quarterly, 10,* 259–288.

Alderton, S. (1980). Attributions of responsibility for socially deviant behavior in decision-making discussions as a function of situation and locus of control of attributor. *Central States Speech Journal, 31,* 117–127.

Alderton, S. M. (1982). Locus of control-based argumentation as a predictor of group polarization. *Communication Quarterly, 30,* 381–387.

Alderton, S. M., & Frey, L. R. (1983). Effects of reactions to arguments on group outcomes: The case of group polarization. *Central States Speech Journal, 34,* 88–95.

Alderton, S. M., & Frey, L. R. (1986). Argumentation in small group decision-making. In R. Y. Hirokawa & M. S. Poole (Eds.), *Communication and group decision-making* (pp. 154–174). Newbury Park, CA: Sage.

Aldrich, J. H., Niemi, R. G., Rabinowitz, G., & Rhode, D. W. (1982). The measurement of public opinion about public policy: A report on some new question formats. *American Journal of Political Science, 26,* 391–414.

Aldridge, H., & Carlin, D. B. (1993). The rap on violence: A rhetorical analysis of rapper KRS-One. *Communication Studies, 44,* 102–116.

Alexander, V. D. (1994). The image of children in magazine advertisements from 1905 to 1990. *Communication Research, 45,* 20–39.

Allen, J., Livingstone, S., & Reiner, R. (1997). The changing generic location of crime in film: A content analysis of film synopses, 1945–1991. *Journal of Communication, 47*(4), 88–101.

Allen, M. (1991). Meta-analysis comparing the persuasiveness of one-sided and two-sided messages. *Western Journal of Speech Communication, 55,* 390–404.

Allen, M. (1998). Comparing the persuasive effectiveness of one- and two-sided messages. In M. Allen & R. W. Preiss (Eds.), *Persuasion: Advances through meta-analysis* (pp. 87–98). Cresskill, NJ: Hampton Press.

Allen, M., Berkowitz, S., Hunt, S., & Louden, A. (1999). A meta-analysis of the impact of forensics and communication education on critical thinking. *Communication Education, 48,* 18–30.

Allen, M., & Bourhis, J. (1996). The relationship of communication apprehension to communication behavior: A meta-analysis. *Communication Quarterly, 44,* 214–226.

Allen, M., Bourhis, J., Emmers-Sommer, T., & Sahlstein, E. (1998). Reducing data anxiety: A meta-analysis. *Communication Reports, 11,* 49–56.

Allen, M., D'Alessio, D., & Brezgel, K. (1995). A meta-analysis summarizing the effects of pornography II: Aggression after exposure. *Human Communication Research, 22,* 258–283.

Allen, M., Emmers, T., Gebhardt, L., & Giery, M. (1995). Pornography and the acceptance of rape myths. *Journal of Communication, 45*(2), 5–27.

Allen, M., Mabry, E. A., Banski, M., Stoneman, M., & Carter, P. (1990). A thoughtful appraisal of measuring cognition using the role category questionnaire. *Communication Reports, 3,* 49–57.

Allen, M., & Preiss, R. W. (1990). Using meta-analysis to evaluate curriculum: An examination of selected college textbooks. *Communication Education, 39,* 103–116.

Allen, M., & Preiss, R. W. (1997). Comparing the persuasiveness of narrative and statistical evidence using meta-analysis. *Communication Research Reports, 14,* 125–131.

Allen, M., & Stiff, J. B. (1998). An analysis of the sleeper effect. In M. Allen & R. W. Preiss (Eds.), *Persuasion: Advances through meta-analysis* (pp. 175–188). Cresskill, NJ: Hampton Press.

Allen, M. W., & Brady, R. M. (1997). Total quality management, organizational commitment, perceived organizational support, and intraorganizational communication. *Management Communication Quarterly, 10,* 316–341.

Allen, M. W., Gotcher, J. M., & Seibert, J. H. (1993). A decade of organizational communication research: Journal articles 1980–1991. In S. A. Deetz (Ed.), *Communication yearbook 16* (pp. 252–330). Newbury Park, CA: Sage.

Allman, J. (1998). Bearing the burden or baring the soul: Physicians' self-disclosure and boundary management regarding medical mistakes. *Health Communication, 10,* 175–197.

Altheide, D. L. (1996). *Qualitative media analysis.* Thousand Oaks, CA: Sage.

Altman, L. K. (1981, Winter). Cheating in science and publishing. *CBE Views, 4,* 19–24.

American Psychological Association. (1994). *Publication manual of the American Psychological Association* (4th ed.). Washington, DC: Author.

American Psychological Association. (1999a, August 2). PsycLIT[R] on CD-ROM: Psychological research made easy for all [Online Website]. Available Internet: http://www.apa.org/psycinfo/psyclit.html

American Psychological Association. (1999b, August 2). What is PsycINFO? [Online Website]. Available Internet: http://www.apa.org/psycinfo/whatis.html

Amir, Y., & Sharon, I. (1991). Replication research: A "must" for the scientific advancement of psychology. In J. W. Neuliep (Ed.), *Replication research in the social sciences* (pp. 51–69). Newbury Park, CA: Sage.

Andersen, J. F. (1979). Teacher immediacy as a predictor of teaching effectiveness. In D. Nimmo (Ed.), *Communication yearbook 3* (pp. 543–559). New Brunswick, NJ: Transaction Books.

Andersen, J. W. (1989). Unobtrusive measures. In P. Emmert & L. L. Barker (Eds.), *Measurement of communication behavior* (pp. 249–266). White Plains, NY: Longman.

Andersen, P. A., Eloy, S. V., Guerrero, L. K., & Spitzberg, B. H. (1995). Romantic jealousy and relational satisfaction: A look at the impact of jealous experience and expression. *Communication Reports, 8,* 77–85.

Anderson, C. M., & Martin, M. M. (1995). The effects of communication motives, interaction involvement, and loneliness on satisfaction: A model of small groups. *Small Group Research, 26,* 118–137.

Anderson, D. R., Collins, P. A., Schmitt, K. L., & Jacobvitz, R. S. (1996). Stressful life events and television viewing. *Communication Research, 23,* 243–260.

Anderson, J. A. (1987). *Communication research: Issues and methods.* New York: McGraw-Hill.

Anderson, J. A. (1996). *Communication theory: Epistemological foundations.* New York: Guilford Press.

Anderson, J. C., Rungtusanatham, M., & Schroeder, R. G. (1994). A theory of quality management underlying the Deming Management Method. *Academy of Management Review, 19,* 472–509.

Andreski, S. (1972). *Social sciences as sorcery.* New York: St. Martin's Press.

Andrews, J. R. (1983). *The practice of rhetorical criticism.* New York: Macmillan.

Appel, E. C. (1997). The rhetoric of Dr. Martin Luther King, Jr.: Comedy and context in tragic collision. *Western Journal of Communication, 61,* 376–402.

Applebaum, R. L. (1985). Subject selection in speech communication research: A reexamination. *Communication Quarterly, 33,* 227–235.

Applebaum, R. L., & Phillips, S. (1977). Subject selection in speech communication research. *Communication Quarterly, 25,* 18–22.

Applegate, J. L. (1982). The impact of construct system development on communication and impression formation in persuasive contexts. *Communication Monographs, 49,* 277–299.

Applegate, J. L., & Delia, J. G. (1980). Person-centered speech, psychological development, and the contexts of language usage. In R. St. Clair & H. Giles (Eds.), *The social and psychological contexts of language* (pp. 245–282). Hillsdale, NJ: Lawrence Erlbaum.

Applegate, J. L., & Woods, E. (1991). Construct system development and attention to face wants in persuasive situations. *Southern Communication Journal, 56,* 24–31.

Argyris, C. (1995). Knowledge when used in practice tests theory: The case of applied communication research. In K. N. Cissna (Ed.), *Applied communication research in the 21st century* (pp. 1–19). Mahwah, NJ: Lawrence Erlbaum.

Argyris, C., Putnam, R., & Smith, M. C. (1985). *Action science: Concepts, methods, and skills for research and intervention.* San Francisco: Jossey-Bass.

Armstrong, G. B., Biorsky, G. A., & Mares, M-L. (1991). Background television and reading performance. *Communication Monographs, 58,* 235–253.

Armstrong, J. S., & Lusk, J. (1987). Return postage in mail surveys: A meta-analysis. *Public Opinion Quarterly, 51,* 233–248.

Armstrong, J. S., & Overton, T. S. (1977). Estimating nonresponse bias in mail surveys. *Journal of Marketing Research, 14,* 396–402.

Arnston, P., Mortensen, C. D., & Lustig, M. W. (1980). Predispositions toward verbal behavior in task-oriented interaction. *Human Communication Research, 6,* 239–252.

Aronson, E., & Carlsmith, J. M. (1968). Experimentation in social psychology. In G. Lindzey & E. Aronson (Eds.), *Handbook of social psychology: Vol. 2. Research methods* (2nd ed., pp. 1–79). Reading, MA: Addison-Wesley.

Artz, L. (1998). African-Americans and higher education: An exigence in need of applied communication. *Journal of Applied Communication Research, 26,* 210–231.

Ashmore, T. M. (1987). The prisoner's dilemma: A computer adaptation. *Western Journal of Speech Communication, 51,* 117–126.

Atkinson, R. (1998). *The life story interview.* Thousand Oaks, CA: Sage.

Aune, K. S., Buller, D. B., & Aune, R. K. (1996). Display rule development in romantic relationships: Emotion management and perceived appropriateness of emotions across relationship stages. *Human Communication Research, 23,* 115–145.

Ausmus, W. A. (1998). Pragmatic uses of metaphor: Models and metaphor in the nuclear winter scenario. *Communication Monographs, 65,* 67–82.

Austin, D. A. (1996). Kaleidoscope: The same and different. In C. Ellis & A. P. Bochner (Eds.), *Composing ethnography: Alternative forms of qualitative writing* (pp. 206–230). Walnut Creek, CA: Altamira Press.

Austin, E. W., & Nach-Ferguson, B. (1995). Sources and influences of young and school-age children's general and brand-specific knowledge about alcohol. *Health Communication, 7,* 1–20.

Austin, J. L. (1962). *How to do things with words.* Oxford, England: Oxford University Press.

Auto safety tests slanted, groups say. (1991, October 29). *Chicago Tribune,* Sect. 1, p. 17.

Ayres, D. M., Ayres, J., & Hopf, T. (1995). Reducing communication apprehension among at-risk children. *Communication Reports, 9,* 178–198.

Ayres, J., Ayres, F. E., Baker, A. L., Colby, N., De Blasi, C., Dimke, D., Docken, L., Grubb, J., Hopf, T., Mueller, R. D., Sharp, D., & Wilcox, K. (1993).

Two empirical tests of a videotape designed to reduce public speaking anxiety. *Journal of Applied Communication Research, 21,* 132–147.

Azrin, N. H., Holtz, W., Ulrich, R., & Goldiamond, I. (1961). The control of the content of conversation through reinforcement. *Journal of the Experimental Analysis of Behavior, 4,* 25–30.

Babbie, E. (1967, January). A religious profile of Episcopal churchwomen. *Pacific Churchman,* pp. 6–8, 12.

Babbie, E. (1973). *Survey research methods.* Belmont, CA: Wadsworth.

Babbie, E. (1992). *The practice of social research* (6th ed.). Belmont, CA: Wadsworth.

Babbie, E. (1995). *The practice of social research* (7th ed.). Belmont, CA: Wadsworth.

Bach, T. E., Blair, C., Nothstine, W. L., & Pym, A. L. (1996). How to read "How to Get Published." *Communication Quarterly, 44,* 399–422.

Badzinski, D. M., & Pettus, A. B. (1994). Nonverbal involvement and sex: Effects on jury decision making. *Journal of Applied Communication Research, 22,* 309–321.

Baesler, E. J., & Burgoon, J. K. (1994). The temporal effects of story and statistical evidence on belief change. *Communication Research, 21,* 582–602.

Baglan, T., Lalumia, J., & Bayless, O. L. (1986). Utilization of compliance-gaining strategies: A research note. *Communication Monographs, 53,* 290–293.

Bales, R. F. (1950). *Interaction process analysis: A method for the study of small groups.* Reading, MA: Addison-Wesley.

Ball, M. S., & Smith, G. W. H. (1992). *Analyzing visual data.* Newbury Park, CA: Sage.

Balon, R. E. (1981). Measuring station audiences by telephone. In J. E. Fletcher (Ed.), *Handbook of radio and TV broadcasting* (pp. 54–71). New York: Van Nostrand Reinhold.

Bamber, E. M., Watson, R. T., & Hill, M. C. (1996). The effects of group support system technology on audit group decision making. *Auditing: A Journal of Practice and Theory, 15,* 122–134.

Baran, S. J., & Davis, D. K. (1995). *Mass communication theory: Foundations, ferment, and future.* Belmont, CA: Wadsworth.

Barbato, C. A., & Perse, E. M. (1992). Interpersonal communication motives and the life position of elders. *Communication Research, 19,* 516–531.

Barbee, A. P., & Cunningham, M. R. (1995). An experimental approach to social support communica-tions: Interactive coping in close relationships. In B. R. Burleson (Ed.), *Communication yearbook 18* (pp. 381–413). Thousand Oaks, CA: Sage.

Barber, T. X. (1976). *Pitfalls in human research: Ten pivotal points.* Elmsford, NY: Pergamon Press.

Barker, J. R. (1993). Tightening the iron cage: Concertive control in self-managing teams. *Administrative Science Quarterly, 38,* 408–437.

Barker, J. R., Melville, C. W., & Pacanowsky, M. E. (1993). Self-directed teams at XEL: Changes in communication practices during a program of cultural transformation. *Journal of Applied Communication Research, 21,* 297–312.

Barker, J. R., & Tompkins, P. K. (1994). Identification in the self-managing organization: Characteristics of target and tenure. *Human Communication Research, 21,* 223–240.

Barker, L. L. (1989). Evaluating research. In P. Emmert & L. L. Barker (Eds.), *Measurement of communication behavior* (pp. 68–83). White Plains, NY: Longman.

Barnes, J. A., & Hayes, A. F. (1995a). Integration of the language arts and teaching training: An examination of speech communication instruction in high school English classrooms. *Communication Education, 44,* 307–320.

Barnes, J. A., & Hayes, A. F. (1995b). Language arts practices in the instruction of oral communication in California high schools. *Communication Reports, 8,* 61–68.

Barnett, G. A., Chang, H-J., Fink, E. L., & Richards, W. D., Jr. (1991). Seasonality in television viewing: A mathematical model of cultural processes. *Communication Research, 18,* 755–772.

Barnett, G. A., & Danowski, J. A. (1992). The structure of communication: A network analysis of the International Communication Association. *Human Communication Research, 19,* 264–285.

Barnlund, D. C. (1968). *Interpersonal communication: Survey and studies.* Boston: Houghton Mifflin.

Barnlund, D. C. (1988). Communication in a global village. In L. A. Samovar & R. E. Porter (Eds.), *Intercultural communication: A reader* (5th ed., pp. 4–15). Belmont, CA: Wadsworth.

Baron, R. A. (1996). "La vie en rose" revisited: Contrasting perceptions of informal upward feedback among managers and subordinates. *Management Communication Quarterly, 9,* 338–348.

Basil, M. D., Schooler, C., Altman, D. G., Slater, M., Albright, C. L., & Maccoby, N. (1991). How cigarettes are advertised in magazines: Special messages for special markets. *Health Communication, 3,* 75–91.

Baumeister, R. F., Reis, H. T., & Delespaul, P. (1995). Subjective and experiential correlates of guilt in daily life. *Personality and Social Psychology Bulletin, 21,* 1256–1268.

Baumeister, R. F., Stillwell, A., & Heatherton, T. F. (1994). Guilt: An interpersonal approach. *Psychological Bulletin, 115,* 243–267.

Baumeister, R. F., Stillwell, A., & Heatherton, T. F. (1995). Interpersonal aspects of guilt: Evidence from narrative studies. In J. P. Tangney & K. W. Fischer (Eds.), *Self-conscious emotions: The psychology of shame, guilt, embarrassment, and pride* (pp. 255–273). New York: Guilford Press.

Baumrin, B. H. (1970). The immortality of irrelevance: The social role of science. In F. F. Korten, S. W. Cook, & J. I. Lacey (Eds.), *Psychology and the problems of society* (pp. 73–83). Washington, DC: American Psychological Association.

Baumrind, D. (1979). IRBs and social science research: The costs of deception. *IRB: A Review of Human Subjects Research, 1,* 1–4.

Bausell, R. B. (1994). *Conducting meaningful experiments: 40 steps to becoming a scientist.* Thousand Oaks, CA: Sage.

Bavelas, J. B., Black, A., Chovil, N., Lemery, C. R., & Mullett, J. (1988). Form and function in motor mimicry: Topographic evidence that the primary function is communicative. *Human Communication Research, 14,* 275–300.

Bavelas, J. B., Black, A., Chovil, N., & Mullet, J. (1990a). *Equivocal communication.* Newbury Park, CA: Sage.

Bavelas, J. B., Black, A., Chovil, N., & Mullet, J. (1990b). Truth, lies, and equivocations: The effects of conflicting goals on discourse. *Journal of Language and Social Psychology, 9,* 135–161.

Bavelas, J. B., & Chovil, N. (1986). How people disqualify: Experimental studies of spontaneous written disqualification. *Communication Monographs, 53,* 70–74.

Bavelas, J. B., & Smith, B. J. (1982). A method for scaling verbal disqualification. *Human Communication Research, 8,* 214–227.

Baxter, L. A. (1979). Self-disclosure as a relationship disengagement strategy. *Human Communication Research, 5,* 215–222.

Baxter, L. A. (1982). Strategies for ending relationships: Two studies. *Western Journal of Speech Communication, 46,* 223–241.

Baxter, L. A. (1984). An investigation of compliance-gaining as politeness. *Human Communication Research, 10,* 427–456.

Baxter, L. A. (1993). "Talking things through" and "putting it in writing": Two codes of communication in an academic institution. *Journal of Applied Communication Research, 21,* 313–326.

Baxter, L. A., & Dindia, K. (1990). Marital partners' perceptions of marital maintenance strategies. *Journal of Social and Personal Relationships, 7,* 651–675.

Baxter, L. A., & Goldsmith, D. (1990). Cultural terms for communication events among some American high school student adolescents. *Western Journal of Speech Communication, 54,* 377–394.

Baxter, L. A., & Simon, E. P. (1993). Relationship maintenance strategies and dialectical contradictions in personal relationships. *Journal of Social and Personal Relationships, 10,* 225–242.

Beach, W. A. (1982). Everyday interaction and its practical accomplishment: Progressive developments in ethnomethodological research. *Quarterly Journal of Speech, 68,* 314–327.

Beach, W. A. (1996). *Conversations about illness: Family preoccupations with bulemia.* Mahwah, NJ: Lawrence Erlbaum.

Beatty, M. J., & Behnke, R. R. (1991). Effects of public speaking trait anxiety and intensity of speaking task on heart rate during performance. *Human Communication Research, 18,* 147–187.

Beatty, M. J., & Payne, S. K. (1984). Loquacity and quantity of constructs as predictors of social perspective-taking. *Communication Quarterly, 32,* 207–210.

Beatty, M. J., & Payne, S. K. (1985). Is construct differentiation loquacity? A motivational perspective. *Human Communication Research, 11,* 605–612.

Becker, C. S. (1987). Friendship between women: A phenomenological study of best friends. *Journal of Phenomenological Psychology, 18,* 59–72.

Becker, H. S. (1954). Field notes and techniques: A note on interviewing tactics. *Human Organization, 12*(4), 31–32.

Beentjes, J. W. J., Koolstra, C. M., & van der Voort, T. H. A. (1996). Combining background media with doing homework: Incidence of background media use and perceived effects. *Communication Education, 45,* 59–72.

Bell, E., & Forbes, L. C. (1994). Office folklore in the academic paperwork empire: The interstitial space of gendered (con)texts. *Text and Performance Quarterly, 14,* 181–196.

Bell, R. A. (1985). Conversational involvement and loneliness. *Communication Monographs, 52,* 218–235.

Bell, R. A. (1987). Social involvement. In J. C. McCroskey & J. A. Daly (Eds.), *Personality and interpersonal communication* (pp. 195–242). Newbury Park, CA: Sage.

Bell, R. A., Abrahams, M. F., Clark, C. L., & Schlatter, C. (1996). The door-in-the-face compliance strategy: An individual differences analysis of two models in an AIDS fundraising context. *Communication Quarterly, 44,* 107–124.

Bell, R. A., & Daly, J. A. (1984). The affinity-seeking function of communication. *Communication Monographs, 51,* 91–115.

Bell, R. A., & Daly, J. A. (1985). Some communicator correlates of loneliness. *Southern Speech Communication Journal, 50,* 121–142.

Bell, R. A., & Roloff, M. E. (1991). Making a love connection: Loneliness and communication competence in the dating marketplace. *Communication Quarterly, 39,* 58–74.

Bell, R. A., Tremblay, S. W., & Buerkel-Rothfuss, N. L. (1987). Interpersonal attraction as a communication accomplishment: Development of a measure of affinity-seeking competence. *Western Journal of Speech Communication, 51,* 1–18.

Bello, R. (1996). A Burkean analysis of the "political correctness" confrontation in higher education. *Southern Communication Journal, 61,* 243–252.

Bem, S. L. (1979). The measurement of psychological androgeny. *Journal of Consulting and Clinical Psychology, 42,* 155–162.

Beniger, J. R. (1987). The future of public opinion: A symposium. *Public Opinion Quarterly, 51,* S173–191.

Benoit, P. L., & Benoit, W. L. (1994). Anticipated future interaction and conversational memory using participants and observers. *Communication Quarterly, 42,* 274–286.

Benoit, W. L. (1998). Forewarning and persuasion. In M. Allen & R. W. Preiss (Eds.), *Persuasion: Advances through meta-analysis* (pp. 130–154). Cresskill, NJ: Hampton Press.

Benoit, W. L., Benoit, P. J., & Wilkie, J. (1988, May). *Observers' memory for conversational behavior.* Paper presented at the meeting of the International Communication Association, New Orleans, LA.

Benoit, W. L., & Hanczor, R. S. (1994). The Tonya Harding controversy: An analysis of image restoration strategies. *Communication Quarterly, 42,* 416–433.

Benoit, W. L., Pier, P. M., & Blaney, J. R. (1997). "Sustainable development" in visual imagery: A functional approach to televised political spots: Attacking, acclaiming, defending. *Communication Quarterly, 45,* 1–20.

Bentham, J. (1995). *The Panopticon writings* (M. Bozovic, Ed.). New York: Verso.

Berdayes, L. C., & Berdayes, V. (1998). The information highway in contemporary magazine narrative. *Journal of Communication, 48*(2), 109–124.

Berg, B. L. (1998). *Qualitative research methods for the social sciences* (3rd ed.). Boston: Allyn & Bacon.

Berger, C. R. (1989). Goals, plans, and discourse comprehension. In J. J. Bradac (Ed.), *Message effects in communication science* (pp. 75–101). Newbury Park, CA: Sage.

Berger, C. R., & Bell, R. A. (1988). Plans and the initiation of social relationships. *Human Communication Research, 15,* 217–235.

Berger, C. R., & Calabrese, R. J. (1975). Some explorations in initial interactions and beyond: Toward a developmental theory of interpersonal communication. *Human Communication Research, 1,* 99–112.

Berger, C. R., & di Battista, P. (1992). Communication failure and plan adaptation: If at first you don't succeed, say it louder and slower. *Communication Monographs, 59,* 220–238.

Berger, C. R., & di Battista, P. (1993). Information seeking and plan elaboration: What do you need to know to know what to do. *Communication Monographs, 60,* 368–387.

Berger, C. R., & Jordan, J. M. (1992). Planning sources, planning difficulty and verbal fluency. *Communication Monographs, 59,* 130–149.

Berger, C. R., Karol, S. H., & Jordan, J. M. (1989). When a lot of knowledge is a dangerous thing: The debilitating effects of plan complexity on verbal fluency. *Human Communication Research, 16,* 91–119.

Berger, C. R., Knowlton, S. W., & Abrahams, M. F. (1996). The hierarchy principle in strategic communication. *Communication Theory, 6,* 111–142.

Berlo, D. K. (1955). Problems in communication research. *Central States Speech Journal, 7,* 3–7.

Berlo, D. K., Lemert, J. B., & Mertz, R. J. (1971). Dimensions for evaluating the acceptability of message sources. *Public Opinion Quarterly, 33,* 563–576.

Berne, E. (1972). *What do you say after you say hello? The psychology of human destiny.* New York: Grove Press.

Berry, S. H., & Kanouse, D. E. (1987). Physician response to a mailed survey: An experiment in timing of payment. *Public Opinion Quarterly, 51,* 102–114.

Berscheid, E., Baron, R. S., Dermer, M., & Lebman, M. (1973). Anticipating informed consent: An empirical approach. *American Psychologist, 28,* 913–925.

Beville, H. M., Jr. (1988). *Audience ratings: Radio, television, and cable* (Rev. ed.). Hillsdale, NJ: Lawrence Erlbaum.

Biagioli, M. (1993). *Galileo, courtier: The practice of science in the culture of absolutism.* Berkeley: University of California Press.

Bikson, T. K. (1996). Groupware at the World Bank. In C. U. Ciborra (Ed.), *Groupware and teamwork: Invisible aid or technical hindrance?* (pp. 145–183). Chichester, England: John Wiley & Sons.

Billiet, J., & Loosveldt, G. (1988). Improvement of the quality of responses to factual survey questions by interviewer training. *Public Opinion Quarterly, 42,* 190–211.

Bingham, S. G. (1994). *Conceptualizing sexual harassment as discursive practice.* Westport, CT: Praeger.

Bird, S. E. (1992). Travels in nowhere land: Ethnography and the "impossible" audience. *Critical Studies in Mass Communication, 9,* 250–260.

Black, E. (1965). *Rhetorical criticism: A study in method.* New York: Macmillan.

Black, E. (1994). Gettysburg and silence. *Quarterly Journal of Speech, 80,* 21–36.

Blair, C., Brown, J. R., & Baxter, L. A. (1994). Disciplining the feminine. *Quarterly Journal of Speech, 80,* 383–409.

Blair, C., Jeppeson, M. S., & Pucci, E., Jr. (1991). Public memorializing in postmodernity: The Vietnam veterans memorial as prototype. *Quarterly Journal of Speech, 77,* 263–288.

Bochner, S. (1979). Designing unobtrusive field experiments in social psychology. In L. Sechrest (Ed.), *Unobtrusive measurement today* (pp. 33–46). San Francisco: Jossey-Bass.

Bogart, L. (1985). How U.S. newspaper content is changing. *Journal of Communication, 35*(2), 82–90.

Bolls, D. B., Tan, A., & Austin, E. (1997). An exploratory comparison of Native American and Caucasian students' attitudes toward communicative behavior and toward school. *Communication Education, 46,* 198–202.

Bolner, M. S., & Poirier, G. A. (1997). *The research process: Books and beyond* (Rev. ed.). Dubuque, IA: Kendall/Hunt.

Booth-Butterfield, M., & Booth-Butterfield, S. (1990). Conceptualizing affect as information in communication production. *Human Communication Research, 16,* 451–476.

Booth-Butterfield, M., & Booth-Butterfield, S. (1994). The affective orientation to communication: Conceptual and empirical distinctions. *Communication Quarterly, 42,* 331–344.

Booth-Butterfield, M., & Booth-Butterfield, S. (1998). Emotionality and affective orientation. In J. C. McCroskey, J. A. Daly, M. M. Martin, & M. J. Beatty (Eds.), *Communication and personality: Trait perspectives* (pp. 171–189). Cresskill, NJ: Hampton Press.

Booth-Butterfield, S. (1988a). Inhibition and student recall of instructional messages. *Communication Education, 37,* 312–324.

Booth-Butterfield, S. (1988b). A meta-analysis of the cross-situational consistency of communication apprehension. *Communication Research Reports, 5,* 64–70.

Booth-Butterfield, S., & Booth-Butterfield, M. (1991). Individual differences in the communication of humorous messages. *Southern Communication Journal, 56,* 205–218.

Booth-Kewley, S., Rosenfeld, P., & Edwards, J. E. (1993). Computer-administered surveys in organizational settings: Alternatives, advantages, and applications. In P. Rosenfeld, J. E. Edwards, & M. D. Thoms (Eds.), *Improving organizational surveys: New directions, methods, and applications* (pp. 73–101). Newbury Park, CA: Sage.

Bourhis, J., & Allen, M. (1992). Meta-analysis of the relationship between communication apprehension and cognitive performance. *Communication Education, 41,* 68–76.

Bormann, E. G. (1972). Fantasy and rhetorical vision: The rhetorical criticism of reality. *Quarterly Journal of Speech, 58,* 396–407.

Bormann, E. G. (1973). The Eagleton affair: A fantasy theme analysis. *Quarterly Journal of Speech, 59,* 143–159.

Bormann, E. G. (1980). The paradox and promise of small group research revisited. *Central States Communication Journal, 31,* 214–220.

Bormann, E. G. (1982). Colloquy I. Fantasy and rhetorical vision: Ten years later. *Quarterly Journal of Speech, 68,* 288–305.

Bormann, E. G., Bormann, E., & Harty, K. C. (1995). Using symbolic convergence theory and focus group interviews to develop communication designed to stop teenage use of tobacco. In L. R. Frey (Ed.), *Innovations in group facilitation: Applications in natural settings* (pp. 200–232). Cresskill, NJ: Hampton Press.

Bornstein, R. F., (1990). Manuscript review in psychology: An alternative model. *American Psychologist, 45,* 672–673.

Bornstein, R. F. (1991). Publication politics, experimenter bias and the replication process in social science research. In J. W. Neuliep (Ed.), *Replication research in the social sciences* (pp. 71–81). Newbury Park, CA: Sage.

Bostdorff, D. M. (1992). Idealism held hostage: Jimmy Carter's rhetoric on the crisis in Iran. *Communication Studies, 43,* 14–28.

Boster, F. J., & Stiff, J. B. (1984). Compliance-gaining message selection behavior. *Human Communication Research, 10,* 539–556.

Bostrom, R. N., & Harrington, N. G. (1999). An exploratory investigation of characteristics of compulsive talkers. *Communication Education, 48,* 73–80.

Botan, C. (1996). Communication work and electronic surveillance: A model for predicting panoptic effects. *Communication Monographs, 63,* 293–313.

Botan, C. H., & Frey, L. R. (1983). Do workers trust labor unions and their messages? *Communication Monographs, 50,* 233–244.

Bourque, L. B., & Fielder, E. P. (1995). *How to conduct self-administered and mail surveys.* Thousand Oaks, CA: Sage.

Bowers, D. L. (1995). A place to stand: African-Americans and the first of August platform. *Southern Communication Journal, 60,* 348–361.

Bowers, J. W., & Courtright, J. A. (1984). *Communication research methods.* Glenview, IL: Scott, Foresman.

Bowers, J. W., & Ochs, D. J. (1971). *The rhetoric of agitation and control.* Reading, MA: Addison-Wesley.

Boyer, E. L. (1990). *Scholarship reconsidered: Priorities of the professoriate.* Princeton, NJ: Carnegie Foundation for the Advancement of Teaching.

Bozarth, J. D., & Roberts, R. R. (1972). Signifying significant significance. *American Psychologist, 27,* 774–775.

Braaten, D. O., Cody, M. J., & DeTienne, K. B. (1993). Account episodes in organizations: Remedial work and impression management. *Management Communication Quarterly, 6,* 219–250.

Bracey, G. W. (1987, March 25). The time has come to abolish research journals: Too many are writing too much about too little. *Chronicle of Higher Education,* p. 44.

Bradburn, N. M., Sudman, S., & Associates. (1979). *Improving interview method and questionnaire design.* San Francisco: Jossey-Bass.

Braithwaite, D. O. (1991). "Just how much did that wheelchair cost?": Management of privacy boundaries by persons with disabilities. *Western Journal of Speech Communication, 55,* 254–274.

Braithwaite, D. O. (1995). Ritualized embarrassment at "coed" wedding and baby showers. *Communication Reports, 8,* 145–157.

Brandt, A. M. (1978, December). Racism and research: The case of the Tuskegee syphilis study. *Hasting Center Report,* 21–29.

Brashers, D. E., Adkins, M., & Meyers, R. A. (1994). Argumentation in computer-mediated decision making. In L. R. Frey (Ed.), *Communication in context: Studies of natural groups* (pp. 262–283). Hillsdale, NJ: Lawrence Erlbaum.

Brenner, M. (1985). Intensive interviewing. In M. Brenner (Ed.), *The research interview* (pp. 147–162). London: Academic Press.

Brentar, J. E., Neundorf, K. A., & Armstrong, G. B. (1994). Exposure effects and affective responses to music. *Communication Monographs, 61,* 160–181.

Brinberg, D., & McGrath, J. E. (1985). *Validity and the research process.* Newbury Park, CA: Sage.

Brinson, S. L., & Benoit, W. L. (1996). Dow Corning's image repair strategies in the breast implant crisis. *Communication Quarterly, 44,* 29–41.

Broadhead, R. S., & Rist, R. C. (1976). Gatekeepers and the social control of social research. *Social Problems, 23,* 325–336.

Brogdan, W. J. (1951). Animal studies of learning. In S. S. Stevens (Ed.), *Handbook of experimental psychology* (pp. 568–612). New York: Wiley.

Brookey, R. A. (1996). A community like Philadelphia. *Western Journal of Communication, 60,* 40–56.

Brooks, K., Callicoat, J., & Siegerdt, G. (1979). The ICA communication audit and perceived communication effectiveness changes in 16 audited organizations. *Human Communication Research, 5,* 130–137.

Bross, I. B. J. (1953). *Design for decisions.* New York: Macmillan.

Brouwer, D. (1998). The precarious visibility politics of self-stigmatization: The case of HIV/AIDS tattoos. *Text and Performance Quarterly, 18,* 114–136.

Brown, B. R. (1970). Face-saving following experimentally induced embarrassment. *Journal of Experimental Social Psychology, 48,* 231–246.

Brown, M. H. (1985). That reminds me of a story: Speech action in organizational socialization. *Western Journal of Speech Communication, 49,* 27–42.

Brown, P., & Levinson, S. (1978). Universals in language usage: Politeness phenomena. In E. Goody (Ed.), *Questions and politeness: Strategies in social interaction* (pp. 256–289). Cambridge, MA: Harvard University Press.

Brown, P., & Levinson, S. C. (1987). *Politeness: Some universals in language usage.* Cambridge, United Kingdom: Cambridge University Press.

Brown, W. J., & Basil, M. D. (1995). Media celebrities and public health: Responses to "Magic" Johnson's HIV disclosure and its impact on AIDS risk and high-risk behaviors. *Health Communication, 7,* 345–370.

Brown, W. J., & Cody, M. J. (1991). Effects of a prosocial television soap opera in promoting women's status. *Human Communication Research, 18,* 114–142.

Bruess, C. J. S., & Pearson, J. C. (1997). Interpersonal rituals in marriage and adult friendship. *Communication Monographs, 64,* 25–46.

Brugchardt, C. R. (1980). Two faces of American communism: Phamplet rhetoric of the third period and the popular front. *Quarterly Journal of Speech, 66,* 375–391.

Bruning, J. L., & Kintz, B. L. (1968). *Computational handbook of statistics.* Glenview, IL: Scott, Foresman.

Bryant, J., & Zillman, D. (1984). Using television to alleviate boredom and stress: Selective exposure as a function of induced excitational states. *Journal of Broadcasting, 28,* 1–20.

Buerkel-Rothfuss, N. L., & Bell, R. A. (1987). Validity of the affinity-seeking instrument. *Communication Research Reports, 4,* 24–30.

Buller, D. B., & Burgoon, J. K. (1994). Deception: Strategic and nonstrategic communication. In J. A. Daly & J. M. Wiemann (Eds.), *Strategic interpersonal communication* (pp. 191–223). Hillsdale, NJ: Lawrence Erlbaum.

Buller, D. B., & Hall, J. R. (1998). The effects of distraction during persuasion. In M. Allen & R. W. Preiss (Eds.), *Persuasion: Advances through meta-analysis* (pp. 155–173). Cresskill, NJ: Hampton Press.

Bullis, C. (1991). Communication practices as unobtrusive control: An observational study. *Communication Studies, 42,* 254–271.

Bullis, C., & Horn, C. (1995). Get a little closer: Further examination of nonverbal comforting strategies. *Communication Reports, 8,* 10–17.

Bulmer, M. (1979). Concepts in the analysis of qualitative data. *Sociological Review, 27,* 651–677.

Bulmer, M. (1982a). Ethical problems in social research: The case of covert participation. In M. Bulmer (Ed.), *Social research ethics: An examination of the merits of covert participant observation* (pp. 3–12). New York: Holmes & Meier.

Bulmer, M. (1982b). The merits and demerits of covert participant observation. In M. Bulmer (Ed.), *Social research ethics: An examination of the merits of covert participant observation* (pp. 217–251). New York: Holmes & Meier.

Burgoon, J. K. (1976). Unwillingness-to-communicate scale: Development and validation. *Communication Monographs, 43,* 60–69.

Burgoon, J. K. (1982). Privacy and communication. In M. Burgoon (Ed.), *Communication yearbook 6* (pp. 206–249). Beverly Hills, CA: Sage.

Burgoon, J. K. (1994). Nonverbal signals. In M. L. Knapp & G. R. Miller (Eds.), *Handbook of interpersonal communication* (2nd ed., pp. 229–285). Thousand Oaks, CA: Sage.

Burgoon, J. K., Buller, D. B., Dillman, L., & Walther, J. B. (1995). Interpersonal deception: IV. Effects of suspicion on perceived communication and nonverbal behavior dynamics. *Human Communication Research, 22,* 163–196.

Burgoon, J. K., Buller, D. B., Guerrero, L. K., Afifi, W. A., & Feldman, C. M. (1996). Interpersonal deception: XII. Information management dimensions underlying deceptive and truthful messages. *Communication Monographs, 63,* 50–69.

Burgoon, J. K., & Le Poire, B. A. (1993). Effects of communication expectancies, actual communication, and expectancy disconfirmation on evaluations of communicators and their communication behavior. *Human Communication Research, 20,* 67–96.

Burgoon, M., Cohen, M., Miller, M. D., & Montgomery, C. L. (1978). An empirical test of a model of resistance to persuasion. *Human Communication Research, 5,* 27–39.

Burgoyne, J. G., & Hodgson, V. E. (1984). An experimental approach to understanding managerial action. In J. G. Hunt, D. Hosking, C. Shriesheim, & R. Stewart

(Eds.), *Leaders and managers: International perspectives on managerial behavior and leadership* (pp. 163–178). Elmsford, NY: Pergamon Press.

Burke, K. (1945). *A grammar of motives.* Englewood Cliffs, NJ: Prentice-Hall.

Burke, K. (1950). *A rhetoric of motives.* Englewood Cliffs, NJ: Prentice-Hall.

Burke, K. (1966). *Language as symbolic action.* Berkeley: University of California Press.

Burleson, B. R. (1984). Comforting communication. In H. Sypher & J. Applegate (Eds.), *Communication by children and adults* (pp. 63–104). Beverly Hills, CA: Sage.

Burleson, B. R. (1997). Introduction. In B. R. Burleson (Ed.), *Communication yearbook 20* (pp. ix–xv). Thousand Oaks, CA: Sage.

Burleson, B. R., Albrecht, T. L., & Sarason, I. G. (Eds.). (1994). *Communication of social support: Messages, interactions, relationships, and community.* Thousand Oaks, CA: Sage.

Burleson, B. R., & Caplan, S. E. (1998). Cognitive complexity. In J. C. McCroskey, J. A. Daly, M. M. Martin, & M. J. Beatty (Eds.), *Communication and personality: Trait perspectives* (pp. 233–286). Cresskill, NJ: Hampton Press.

Burleson, B. R., & Goldsmith, D. J. (1998). How the comforting process works: Alleviating emotional distress through conversationally induced reappraisals. In P. A. Andersen & L. K. Guerrero (Eds.), *Handbook of communication and emotion: Theory, research, application, and contexts* (pp. 245–280). San Diego, CA: Academic Press.

Burnham, J. C. (1990). The evolution of editorial peer review. *Journal of the American Medical Association, 263,* 1323–1329.

Burns, D. (1991). Cold fusion's tale of intrigue, paranoia, scandal and farce [Review of the book *Too hot to handle: The race for cold fusion*]. *Chicago Tribune,* Sect. 14, pp. 3–4.

Burns, J. J., & Anderson, D. R. (1993). Attentional inertia and recognition memory in adult television viewing. *Communication Research, 20,* 777–799.

Burrell, N. A., & Koper, R. J. (1998). The efficacy of powerful/powerless language on attitudes and source credibility. In M. Allen & R. W. Preiss (Eds.), *Persuasion: Advances through meta-analysis* (pp. 203–215). Cresskill, NJ: Hampton Press.

But should we believe it? (1994, October 17). *Time,* p. 70.

Buttney, R. (1993). *Social accountability in communication.* London: Sage.

Buzzanell, P. M. (1995). Reframing the glass ceiling as a socially constructed process: Implications for understanding and change. *Communication Monographs, 62,* 327–354.

Buzzanell, P. M., Burrell, N. A., Stafford, R. S., & Berkowitz, S. (1997). When I call you up and you're not there: Application of communication accommodation theory to telephone answering machine messages. *Western Journal of Communication, 60,* 310–336.

Byerly, C. M., & Warren, C. A. (1996). At the margins of the center: Organized protest in the newsroom. *Critical Studies in Mass Communication, 13,* 1–23.

Cai, D., Giles, H., & Noels, K. (1998). Elderly perceptions of communication with older and younger adults in China: Implications for mental health. *Journal of Applied Communication Research, 26,* 32–51.

Campbell, D. T., & Stanley, J. C. (1963). *Experimental and quasi-experimental designs for research.* Skokie, IL: Rand McNally.

Campbell, J. P., Daft, R. L., & Hulin, C. L. (1982). *What to study: Generating and developing research questions.* Newbury Park, CA: Sage.

Campbell, K. K. (1995). Gender and genre: Loci of invention and contradiction in the earliest speeches by U.S. women. *Quarterly Journal of Speech, 81,* 479–495.

Canary, D. J., Brossman, J. E., Brossman, B. G., & Weger, H., Jr. (1995). Toward a theory of minimally rational argument: Analyses of episode-specific effects of argument structures. *Communication Monographs, 62,* 183–212.

Canary, D. J., Brossman, B. G., & Seibold, D. R. (1987). Argument structures in decision-making groups. *Southern Speech Communication Journal, 53,* 18–37.

Canary, D. J., Cunningham, E. M., & Cody, M. J. (1988). Goal types, gender, and locus of control in managing interpersonal conflict. *Communication Research, 15,* 426–446.

Canary, D. J., & Emmers-Sommer, T. M. (with Faulkner, S.). (1997). *Sex and gender differences in personal relationships.* New York: Guilford Press.

Canary, D. J., & Spitzberg, B. H. (1987). Appropriateness and effectiveness perceptions of conflict strategies. *Human Communication Research, 14,* 93–118.

Canary, D. J., & Spitzberg, B. H. (1989). A model of the perceived competence of conflict strategies. *Human Communication Research, 15,* 630–649.

Canary, D. J., & Spitzberg, B. H. (1990). Attribution biases and associations between conflict strategies and competence outcomes. *Communication Monographs, 56,* 139–151.

Canary, D. J., & Stafford, L. (1992). Relational maintenance strategies and equity in marriage. *Communication Monographs, 59,* 243–267.

Canary, D. J., Stafford, L., Hause, K. S., & Wallace, L. A. (1993). An inductive analysis of relational maintenance strategies: Comparisons among lovers, relatives, friends, and others. *Communication Research Reports, 10,* 5–14.

Cannell, C. F., & Kahn, R. L. (1968). Interviewing. In G. Lindzey & E. Aronson (Eds.), *Handbook of social psychology: Vol. II. Research methods* (2nd ed., pp. 526–595). Reading, MA: Addison Wesley.

Cappella, J. N., & Jamieson, K. H. (1994). Broadcast adwatch effects: A field experiment. *Communication Research, 21,* 342–365.

Cappella, J. N., & Planalp, S. (1981). Talk and silence sequences in informal conversations (III): Interspeaker influence. *Human Communication Research, 7,* 117–132.

Cardello, L. L., Ray, E. B., & Pettey, G. R. (1995). The relationship of perceived physician communicator style to patient satisfaction. *Communication Reports, 8,* 27–37.

Carlson, A. C. (1992). Creative casuistry and feminist consciousness: A rhetoric of moral reform. *Quarterly Journal of Speech, 78,* 16–32.

Carlson, A. C., & Hocking, J. E. (1988). Strategies of redemption at the Vietnam veterans' memorial. *Western Journal of Speech Communication, 52,* 203–215.

Carmines, E. G., & Zeller, R. A. (1979). *Reliability and validity assessment.* Newbury Park, CA: Sage.

Carrell, L. J., & Willmington, S. C. (1998). The relationship between self-report measures of communication apprehension and trained observers' ratings of communication competence. *Communication Reports, 1,* 73–86.

Caspi, D. (1984). On the control of media by politicians: A new perspective. *Political Communication and Persuasion, 2,* 263–269.

Cawyer, C. S., Bystrom, D., Miller, J., Simonds, C., O'Brien, M., & Storey-Martin, J. (1994). Communicating gender equity: Representation and portrayal of women and men in introductory communication textbooks. *Communication Studies, 45,* 325–331.

Cawyer, C. S., & Friedrich, G. W. (1998). Organizational socialization: Processes for new communication faculty. *Communication Education, 47,* 234–245.

Cawyer, C. S., & Smith-Dupré, A. (1995). Communicating social support: Identifying supportive episodes in an HIV/AIDS support group. *Communication Quarterly, 43,* 243–358.

Cegala, D. J. (1981). Interaction involvement: A cognitive dimension of communicative competence. *Communication Education, 30,* 109–121.

Cegala, D. J., McNeilis, K. S., McGee, D. S., & Jonas, A. P. (1995). A study of doctors' and patients' perceptions of information processing and communication competence during the medical interview. *Health Communication, 7,* 179–203.

Chaffee, S. H., Nass, C. I., Yang, S-M. (1990). The bridging role of television in immigrant political socialization. *Human Communication Research, 7,* 266–288.

Chapanis, A. (1963). Engineering psychology. *Annual Review of Psychology, 14,* 285–318.

Chapman, S. (1997, January 30). Avoiding the 2nd Amendment. *Chicago Tribune,* Sect. 1, p. 19.

Chatham-Carpenter, A., & DeFrancisco, V. (1997). Pulling yourself up again: Women's choices and strategies for recovering and maintaining self-esteem. *Western Journal of Communication, 61,* 164–187.

Chen, G. (1993). Self-disclosure and Asian students' abilities to cope with social difficulties in the United States. *Journal of Psychology, 127,* 602–610.

Chen, G-M., & Starosta, W. J. (1996). Intercultural communication competence. In B. R. Burleson (Ed.), *Communication yearbook 19* (pp. 353–383). Thousand Oaks, CA: Sage.

Chen, V., & Pearce, W. B. (1995). Even if a thing of beauty, can a case study be a joy forever? A social constructionist approach to theory and research. In W. Leeds-Hurwitz (Ed.), *Social approaches to communication* (pp. 135–154). New York: Guilford Press.

Cheney, G. (1982). *Identification as process and product: A field study.* Unpublished master's thesis, Purdue University, West Lafayette, IN.

Cherry, K. (1995). The best years of their lives: A portrait of a residential home for people with AIDS. *Symbolic Interaction, 18,* 463–486.

Chesebro, J. W. (1991). Communication, values, and popular television series—A seventeen-year assessment. *Communication Quarterly, 39,* 197–225.

Chesebro, J. W. (1993). How to get published. *Communication Quarterly, 41,* 373–382.

Chirban, J. T. (1996). *Interviewing in depth: The interactive-relational approach.* Thousand Oaks, CA: Sage.

Chovil, N. (1994). Equivocation as an interactional event. In W. R. Cupach & B. H. Spitzberg (Eds.), *The dark side of interpersonal communication* (pp. 105–123). Hillsdale, NJ: Lawrence Erlbaum.

Christensen, C. J., & Menzel, K. E. (1998). The linear relationship between student reports of teacher immediacy behaviors and perceptions of state motivation, and of cognitive, affective, and behavioral learning. *Communication Education, 47,* 82–90.

Christenson, P. G., & Peterson, J. B. (1988). Genre and gender in the structure of music preference. *Communication Research, 15,* 282–301.

Christiansen, A. E., & Hanson, J. J. (1996). Comedy as cure for tragedy: ACT UP and the rhetoric of AIDS. *Quarterly Journal of Speech, 82,* 157–170.

Chubin, D. E., & Hackett, E. J. (1990). *Peerless science: Peer review and U.S. science policy.* Albany: State University of New York Press.

Cicchetti, D. V. (1991). The reliability of peer review for manuscript and grant submissions: A cross disciplinary investigation. *Behavioral and Brain Sciences, 14,* 119–135.

Cicourel, A. V. (1980). Three models of discourse analysis: The role of social structure. *Discourse Processes, 3,* 101–132.

Cissna, K. N. (1982). Editor's note: What is applied communication research? *Journal of Applied Communication Research, 10* (Editorial Statement).

Cissna, K. N., & Anderson, R. (1990). The contributions of Carl R. Rogers to a philosophical praxis of dialogue. *Western Journal of Speech Communication, 54,* 125–147.

Cissna, K. N., Cox, D., & Bochner, A. (1990). The dialectic of marital and parental relationships within the stepfamily. *Communication Monographs, 57,* 44–61.

Citro, C. F. (1997). Windows on Washington. *Change, 10*(4), 26–31.

Clair, R. P. (1997). Organizing silence: Silence as voice and voice as silence in the narrative exploration of the Treaty of New Echota. *Western Journal of Communication, 61,* 315–337.

Clair, R. P. (1993). The use of framing devices to sequester organizational narratives: Hegemony and harassment. *Communication Monographs, 60,* 113–116.

Clair, R. P., & Thompson, K. (1996). Pay discrimination as a discursive and material practice: A case concerning extended housework. *Journal of Applied Communication Research, 24,* 1–20.

Clark, A. L., & Wallin, P. (1964). The accuracy of husbands' and wives' reports of the frequency of marital coitus. *Population Studies, 18,* 165–173.

Clark, E. C., Hyde, M. J., & McMahan, E. M. (1980). Communication in the oral history interview: Investigating problems of interpreting oral data. *International Journal of Oral History, 1,* 28–40.

Clark, J. N. (1992). Cancer, heart disease, and AIDS: What do the media tell us about these diseases? *Health Communication, 4,* 105–120.

Clark, R. A., & Delia, J. G. (1997). Individuals' preferences for friends' approaches to providing support in distressing situations. *Communication Reports, 10,* 115–122.

Clayman, S. E. (1995). Defining moments, presidential debates, and the dynamics of quotability. *Journal of Communication, 45*(3), 118–146.

Clayton, R., & Harrel, L. J. (1989). Developing a cost model for alternative data collection methods: Mail, CATI and TDE. *American Statistical Association Proceedings,* 264–269.

Cline, R. J., & Boyd, M. F. (1993). Communication as threat and therapy: Social support and coping with HIV infection. In E. B. Ray (Ed.), *Case studies in health communication* (pp. 131–147). Hillsdale, NJ: Lawrence Erlbaum.

Cody, M. J., Kersten, L., Braatan, D. O., & Dickson, R. (1992). Coping with relational dissolutions: Attributions, account credibility, and plans for resolving conflict. In J. H. Harvey, T. L. Orbuch, & A. L. Weber (Eds.), *Attributions, accounts, and close relationships* (pp. 93–115). New York: Springer-Verlag.

Coffman, S. L. (1992). Staff problems with geriatric care in two types of health care organizations. *Journal of Applied Communication Research, 20,* 292–307.

Cohen, G., & Faulkner, D. (1986). Does "elderspeak" work?: The effect of intonation and stress on comprehension and recall of spoken discourse in old age. *Language & Communication, 6,* 91–98.

Cohen, J. (1988). *Statistical power analysis for the behavioral sciences* (2nd ed.). Hillsdale, NJ: Lawrence Erlbaum.

Cohen, J. (1992). A power primer. *Psychological Bulletin, 112,* 155–159.

Coleman, C.-L. (1993). The influence of mass media and interpersonal communication on societal and personal risk judgments. *Communication Research, 20,* 611–628.

Coleman, D. (1997). Electronic meetings as today's presentations. In D. Coleman (Ed.), *Groupware: Collaborative strategies for corporate LANs and intranets* (pp. 183–191). Upper Saddle River, NJ: Prentice-Hall.

Coltheart, M., Hull, E., & Slater, D. (1975). Sex differences in imagery and reading. *Nature, 253,* 438–440.

Comer, D. R. (1991). Organizational newcomers' acquisition of information from peers. *Management Communication Quarterly, 5,* 64–89.

Comeraux, P. (1995). The impact of an interactive distance learning network on classroom communication. *Communication Education, 44,* 353–361.

Communication Studies 298. (1997). Fragments of self at the postmodern bar. *Journal of Contemporary Ethnography, 26,* 251–292.

Comstock, G. (1975). *Television and human behavior: The key studies.* Santa Monica, CA: Rand Corporation.

Comstock, J. (1994). Parent-adolescent conflict: A developmental approach. *Western Journal of Communication, 58,* 263–282.

Comstock, J., Rowell, E., & Bowers, J. W. (1995). Food for thought: Teacher nonverbal immediacy, student learning, and curvilinearity. *Communication Education, 44,* 251–266.

Conquergood, D. (1988). Health theatre in a Hmong refugee camp: Performance, communication, and culture. *TDR: Journal of Performance Studies, 32,* 174–208.

Conquergood, D. (1991a). "For the nation!": How street gangs problematic patriotism. In R. Troester (Ed.), *Peacemaking through communication* (pp. 8–21). Annandale, VA: Speech Communication Association.

Conquergood, D. (1991b). Rethinking ethnography: Towards a critical cultural politics. *Communication Monographs, 58,* 179–194.

Conquergood, D. (1992). Life in Big Red: Struggles and accommodations in a Chicago polyethnic tenement. In L. Lamphere (Ed.), *Structuring diversity: Ethnographic perspectives on the new immigration* (pp. 95–144). Chicago: University of Chicago Press.

Conquergood, D. (1994). Homeboys and hoods: Gang communication and cultural space. In L. R. Frey (Ed.), *Group communication in context: Studies of natural groups* (pp. 23–55). Hillsdale, NJ: Lawrence Erlbaum.

Conquergood, D. (1995). Between rigor and relevance: Rethinking applied communication. In K. N. Cissna (Ed.), *Applied communication in the 21st century* (pp. 79–96). Mahwah, NJ: Lawrence Erlbaum.

Conquergood, D. (Producer), & Siegel, T. (Producer & Director). (1985). *Between two worlds: The Hmong shaman in America* [Videotape]. (Available from Filmmakers Library, 124 E. 40th St., Suite 901, New York, NY 10016)

Conquergood, D. (Producer), & Siegel, T. (Producer & Director). (1990). *The heart broken in half* [Videotape]. (Available from Filmmakers Library, 124 E. 40th St., Suite 901, New York, NY 10016)

Conrad, C. (1991). Communication in conflict: Style-strategy relationships. *Communication Monographs, 58,* 135–155.

Cook, T. D., & Campbell, D. T. (1979). *Quasi-experimentation: Design and analysis issues for field settings.* Boston: Houghton Mifflin.

Cooks, L., & Descutner, D. (1993). Different paths from powerlessness to empowerment: A dramatistic analysis of two eating disorder therapies. *Western Journal of Communication, 57,* 494–514.

Cooper, E., & Allen, M. (1998). A meta-analytic examination of the impact of student race on classroom interaction. *Communication Research Reports, 15,* 151–161.

Cornett-DeVito, M. M., & Friedman, P. G. (1995). Communication processes and merger success: An exploratory study of four financial institution mergers. *Management Communication Quarterly, 9,* 46–77.

Couch, A., & Yetton, P. (1987). Manager behavior, leadership style, and subordinate performance: An empirical extension of the Vroom-Yetton conflict rules. *Organizational Behavior and Human Decision Processes, 39,* 384–396.

Coughlin, E. K. (1989, February 15). Concerns about fraud, editorial bias prompt scrutiny of journal practices. *Chronicle of Higher Education,* pp. A4–7.

Coulon, A. (1995). *Ethnomethodology.* Thousand Oaks, CA: Sage.

Courtright, J. A., & Perse, E. M. (1998). *Communicating online: A guide to the Internet.* Mountain View, CA: Mayfield.

Cox, S. A., & Kramer, M. W. (1995). Communication during employee dismissals: Social exchange principles and group influences on employee exit. *Management Communication Quarterly, 9,* 156–190.

Cowles, M. (1980). *Statistics in psychology: An historical perspective.* Hillsdale, NJ: Lawrence Erlbaum.

Cowles, S. B., & Klein, R. A. (1991). Network television promotion. In S. T. Eastman & R. A. Klein (Eds.), *Promotion & marketing for broadcasting & cable* (pp. 168–185). Prospect Heights, IL: Waveland Press.

Cozby, P. C. (1973). Self-disclosure: A literature review. *Psychological Bulletin, 79,* 73–91.

Crabtree, R. D. (1998). Mutual empowerment in cross-cultural participatory democracy and service learning: Lessons in communication and social justice from projects in El Salvador and Nicaragua. *Journal of Applied Communication Research, 26,* 182–209.

Cragan, J. F., & Shields, D. C. (1995). Using SCT-based focus group interviews to do applied communication research. In L. R. Frey (Ed.), *Innovations in group facilitation: Applications in natural settings* (pp. 233–256). Cresskill, NJ: Hampton Press.

Craig, J. R., & Reese, S. C. (1973). Retention of raw data: A problem revisited. *American Psychologist, 28,* 723.

Craig, R. T. (1989). Communication as a practical discipline. In B. Dervin, L. Grossberg, B. J. O'Keefe, & E. Wartella (Eds.), *Rethinking communication: Vol. 1. Paradigm issues* (pp. 97–122). Newbury Park, CA: Sage.

Craig, R. T. (1995). Applied communication research in a practical discipline. In K. N. Cissna (Ed.), *Applied communication in the 21st century* (pp. 147–155). Mahwah, NJ: Lawrence Erlbaum.

Craig, R. T., & Tracy, K. (1995). Grounded practical theory: The case of intellectual discussion. *Communication Theory, 5,* 248–272.

Craig, R. T., Tracy, K., & Spisak, F. (1986). The discourse of requests: Assessment of a politeness approach. *Human Communication Research, 12,* 437–468.

Crandall, C. S., & Coleman, R. (1992). AIDS-related stigmatization and the disruption of social relationships. *Journal of Social and Personal Relationships, 9,* 163–177.

Crawford, L. (1986). Reluctant communitarians: Personal stories and commune behavior. *Communication Quarterly, 34,* 286–305.

Crawford, L. (1996). Personal ethnography. *Communication Monographs, 63,* 158–170.

Cresswell, J. W. (1994). *Research design: Qualitative & quantitative approaches.* Thousand Oaks, CA: Sage.

Crewdson, J. (1991, December 31). In bid to claim AIDS test, U.S. concealed evidence. *Chicago Tribune,* Sect. 1, pp. 1, 12.

Crewdson, J. (1992, December 31). U.S. criticizes AIDS researcher: Gallo found guilty of misconduct. *Chicago Tribune,* Sect. 1, pp. 1, 4.

Crewdson, J. (1994a, March 22). Breast cancer data in doubt: Agency admits further review of flawed studies is needed. *Chicago Tribune,* Sect. 1, pp. 1, 16.

Crewdson, J. (1994b, March 13). Fraud in breast cancer study: Doctor lies on data for decade. *Chicago Tribune,* Sect. 1, pp. 1, 16.

Crockett, W. H. (1965). Cognitive complexity and impression formation. In B. A. Maher (Ed.), *Progress in experimental personality research* (Vol. 2, pp. 47–90). New York: Academic Press.

Cronbach, L. J. (1951). Coefficient alpha and the internal structure of tests. *Psychometrika, 16,* 297–334.

Cronbach, L. J., & Meehl, P. E. (1955). Construct validity in psychological tests. *Psychological Bulletin, 52,* 281–302.

Crossen, C. (1994). *Tainted truth: The manipulation of fact in America.* New York: Touchstone.

Crow, B. K. (1988). Conversational performance and the performance of conversation. *The Drama Review: TDR, 32,* 23–54.

Cruz, M. G. (1998). Explicit and implicit conclusions in persuasive messages. In M. Allen & R. W. Preiss (Eds.), *Persuasion: Advances through meta-analysis* (pp. 217–230). Cresskill, NJ: Hampton Press.

Cuklanz, L. M. (1995). "Shrill squawk" or strategic innovation: A rhetorical reassessment of Margaret Sanger's *Woman Rebel. Communication Quarterly, 43,* 1–19.

Cupach, W. R., & Metts, S. (1986). Accounts of relational dissolution: A comparison of marital and non-marital relationships. *Communication Monographs, 53,* 331–334.

Cupach, W. R., & Metts, S. (1990). Remedial processing in embarrassing predicaments. In J. A. Anderson (Ed.), *Communication yearbook 13* (pp. 323–352). Newbury Park, CA: Sage.

Cupach, W. R., & Metts, S. (1992). The effects of type of predicament and embarrassability on remedial responses to embarrassing situations. *Communication Quarterly, 40,* 149–161.

Cupach, W. R., Metts, S., & Hazleton, V., Jr. (1986). Coping with embarrassing predicaments: Remedial strategies and their perceived utility. *Journal of Language and Social Psychology, 5,* 181–200.

Cupach, W. R., & Spitzberg, B. H., (Eds.). (1994). *The dark side of interpersonal communication.* Hillsdale, NJ: Lawrence Erlbaum.

Cutrona, C. E., & Suhr, J. A. (1992). Controllability of stressful events and satisfaction with spouse support behaviors. *Communication Research, 19,* 154–174.

Dainton, M., Stafford, L., & Canary, D. J. (1994). Maintenance strategies and physical affection as predictors of love, liking, and satisfaction in marriage. *Communication Reports, 7,* 88–98.

Dalkey, N. C., Rourke, D. L., Lewis, R., & Snyder, D. (1972). *Studies in the quality of life.* Lexington, MA: Lexington Books.

Dallinger, J. M., & Hample, D. (1994). The effect of gender on compliance gaining strategy endorsement and suppression. *Communication Reports, 7,* 43–49.

Daly, J. A., Vangelisti, A. L., & Daughton, S. M. (1987). The nature and correlates of conversational sensitivity. *Human Communication Research, 14,* 167–202.

Dance, F. E. X. (1982). Essays in human communication theory: A comparative overview. In F. E. X. Dance (Ed.), *Human communication theory: Comparative essays* (pp. 286–299). New York: Harper & Row.

Dance, F. E. X., & Larson, C. E. (1976). *The functions of human communication: A theoretical approach.* New York: Holt, Rinehart and Winston.

Darling, A. L. (1989). Signalling non-comphrensions in the classroom: Toward a descriptive typology. *Communication Education, 38,* 34–40.

Darsey, J. (1991). From "gay is good" to the scourge of AIDS: The evolution of gay liberation rhetoric, 1977–1990. *Communication Studies, 42,* 43–66.

David, P. (1998). News concreteness and visual-verbal association: Do news pictures narrow the recall gap between concrete and abstract news? *Communication Monographs, 25,* 180–201.

Davis, S., & Mares, M-L. (1998). Effects of talk show viewing on adolescents. *Journal of Communication, 48*(3), 69–86.

Dawes, R. M., & Smith, T. L. (1985). Attitude and opinion measurement. In G. Lindzey & E. Aronson (Eds.), *Handbook of social psychology: Vol. 1. Theory and methods* (3rd ed., pp. 509–566). New York: Random House.

Deakins, A. H., Osterink, C., & Hoey, T. (1987). Topics in same sex and mixed sex conversations. In L. B. Nadler, M. J. Nadler, & W. R. Todd-Mancillas (Eds.), *Advances in gender and communication re-*

search (pp. 89–108). Lanham, MD: University Press of America.

Dean, G. (with Mather, A.). (1977). *Recent advances in natal astrology: A critical review 1900–1976.* Rockport, MA: Para Research.

Dean, J. W., Jr., & Bowen, D. E. (1994). Management theory and total quality: Improving research and practice through theory development. *Academy of Management Review, 19,* 392–418.

Deetz, S. A. (1982). Critical interpretive research in organizational communication. *Western Journal of Speech Communication, 46,* 131–149.

DeFrancisco, V. L. (1991). The sounds of silence: How men silence women in marital relations. *Discourse and Society, 2,* 413–423.

Delbecq, A. L., Van de Ven, A. H., & Gustafson, D. H. (1975). *Group techniques for program planning: A guide to nominal group and Delphi processes.* Glenview, IL: Scott, Foresman.

del Carmen, R. (1991). *Criminal laws & practice* (2nd ed.). Belmont, CA: Brooks/Cole.

Delgado, F. P. (1995). Chicano movement rhetoric: An ideographic interpretation. *Communication Quarterly, 43,* 446–455.

Delgado, F. P. (1998). Chicano ideology revisited: Rap music and the (re)articulation of Chicanismo. *Western Journal of Communication, 62,* 95–113.

Della-Piana, C. K., & Anderson, J. A. (1995). Performing community: Community service as cultural conversation. *Communication Studies, 46,* 187–200.

Denzin, J. N. (1970). *The research act: A theoretical introduction to sociological methods.* Hawthorne, NY: Aldine.

Denzin, N. K. (1978). *The research act: A theoretical introduction to sociological methods* (2nd ed.). New York: McGraw-Hill.

Denzin, N. K. (1997). *Interpretive ethnography: Ethnographic practices for the 21st century.* Thousand Oaks, CA: Sage.

Denzin, N. K., & Lincoln, Y. S. (Eds.). (1994). *Handbook of qualitative research.* Thousand Oaks, CA: Sage.

Department of Health and Human Services. (1989). Code of Federal Regulations (45 CFR 46). *Protection of human subjects.* Washington, DC: National Institutes of Health, Office for Protection from Research Risks.

Derber, C. (1979). *The pursuit of attention: Power and individualism in everyday life.* Boston: G. K. Hall.

Desmond, R., Singer, J. L., Singer, D. G., Calam, R., & Colimore, K. (1985). Family mediation patterns and television viewing: Young children's use and grasp of the medium. *Human Communication Research, 11,* 461–480.

deTurck, M. A., Freeley, T. H., & Roman, L. A. (1998). Vocal and visual cue training in behavioral lie detection. *Communication Research Reports, 15,* 249–259.

deTurck, M. A., & Miller, G. R. (1985). Deception and arousal: Isolating the behavioral correlates of deception. *Human Communication Research, 12,* 181–202.

DeVellis, R. F. (1991). *Scale development: Theory and applications.* Newbury Park, CA: Sage.

di Battista, P. (1994). Effects of planning on performance of trust-violating versus tactful, white lies: How are familiar speech acts cognitively represented? *Communication Studies, 45,* 174–186.

di Battista, P. (1997). Deceivers' responses to challenges of their truthfulness: Difference between familiar lies and unfamiliar lies. *Communication Quarterly, 45,* 319–334.

Dickter, D. N., & Roznowski, M. (1996). Basic statistical analysis. In F. T. L. Leong & J. T. Austin (Eds.), *The psychology research handbook: A guide for graduate students and research assistants* (pp. 208–218). Thousand Oaks, CA: Sage.

Dillard, J. P., & Hale, J. L. (1992). Prosocialness and sequential request compliance techniques: Limits to the foot-in-the-door and the door-in-the-face? *Communication Studies, 43,* 220–232.

Dillard, J. P., Kinney, T. A., & Cruz, M. G. (1996). Influence, appraisals, and emotions in close relationships. *Communication Monographs, 63,* 105–130.

Dillard, J. P., Plotnick, C. A., Godbold, L. C., Freimuth, V. S., & Edgar, T. (1996). The multiple affective outcomes of AIDS PSAs: Fear appeals do more than scare people. *Communication Research, 23,* 44–72.

Dimmick, J. W., Sikand, J., & Patterson, S. J. (1994). The gratifications of the household telephone. *Communication Research, 21,* 643–663.

Dindia, K. (1987). The effects of sex of subject and sex of partner on interruptions. *Human Communication Research, 13,* 345–371.

Dindia, K., & Allen, M. (1992). Sex differences in self-disclosure: A meta-analysis. *Psychological Bulletin, 112,* 106–124.

Dindia, K., & Baxter, L. A. (1987). Strategies for maintaining and repairing marital relationships. *Journal of Social and Personal Relationships, 4,* 143–158.

Di Pietro, C. (1995). Meetingware and organizational effectiveness. In D. Coleman & R. Khanna (Eds.), *Groupware: Technology and applications* (pp. 434–473). Upper Saddle River, NJ: Prentice-Hall.

DiSanza, J. R. (1995). Bank teller organizational assimilation in a system of contradictory practices. *Management Communication Quarterly, 9,* 191–218.

Divorce researcher admits statistics flawed: Data on standard of living influenced shift in child-support laws. (1996, May 17). *Chicago Tribune,* Sect. 1, p. 6.

Dollar, N. J., & Zimmers, B. G. (1998). Social identity and communicative boundaries: An analysis of youth and young adult street speakers in a U.S. American community. *Communication Research, 25,* 596–617.

Donnellon, A., Gray, B., & Bongon, M. G. (1986). Communication, meaning, and organized action. *Administrative Science Quarterly, 31,* 43–55.

Donohue, W. A., & Roberto, A. J. (1993). Relational development as negotiated order in hostage negotiation. *Human Communication Research, 20,* 175–198.

Dordick, H. S., & Wang, G. (1993). *The information society: A retrospective view.* Newbury Park, CA: Sage.

Dorsey, L. G. (1995). The frontier myth in presidential rhetoric: Theodore Roosevelt's campaign for conservatism. *Western Journal of Communication, 59,* 1–19.

Dorst, J. D. (1989). *The written suburb: An American site, an ethnographic dilemma.* Philadelphia: University of Pennsylvania Press.

Douglas, J. D. (1985). *Creative interviewing.* Newbury Park, CA: Sage.

Douglas, W. (1987). Affinity-testing in initial interactions. *Journal of Social and Personal Relationships, 3,* 323–336.

Douglas, W. (1994). The acquaintanceship process: An examination of uncertainty, information seeking, and social attraction during initial conversation. *Communication Research, 21,* 154–176.

Dovring, K. (1954–1955). Quantitative semantics in 18th century Sweden. *Public Opinion Quarterly, 18,* 389–394.

Dow, B. J. (1989). The function of epideictic and deliberative strategies in presidential crisis rhetoric. *Western Journal of Speech Communication, 53,* 294–310.

Dow, B. J., & Tonn, M. B. (1993). "Feminine style" and political judgement in the rhetoric of Ann Richards. *Quarterly Journal of Speech, 79,* 286–302.

Downs, C. W. (1988). *Communication audits.* Glenview, IL: Scott, Foresman.

Du Bois, C. N. (1963). *Time* magazine's fingerprints study. *Proceedings: 9th Conference, Advertising Research Foundation.* New York: Advertising Research Foundation.

Duffy, M. (1997). High stakes: A fantasy theme analysis of the selling of riverboat gambling in Iowa. *Southern Communication Journal, 62,* 117–132.

Duncan, O. D. (1984). *Notes on social measurement: Historical and critical.* New York: Russell Sage.

Dupagne, M. (1997). Effect of three communication technologies on mass media in Belgium. *Journal of Communication, 47*(4), 54–68.

Duran, R. L. (1983). Communicative adaptability: A measure of social communicative competence. *Communication Quarterly, 31,* 320–326.

Duran, R. L. (1992). Communicative adaptability: A review of conceptualization and measurement. *Communication Quarterly, 40,* 253–268.

Dwyer, K. K. (1998). Communication apprehension and learning style preference: Correlations and implications for teaching. *Communication Education, 47,* 137–150.

Eadie, B. (1999, January 20). NCA journal acceptance rates. *CRTNET News* [Online]. National Communication Association.

Eastman, S. T., & Newton, G. D. (1999). Hitting promotion hard: A network response to channel surfing. *Journal of Applied Communication Research, 27,* 73–85.

Eaves, M. H., & Leathers, D. G. (1991). Context as communication: McDonald's vs. Burger King. *Journal of Applied Communication Research, 19,* 263–289.

Eberley, S., & Warner, W. K. (1990). Fields or subfields of knowledge: Rejection rates and arguments in peer review. *American Sociologist, 25,* 217–230.

Edgar, T., Fitzpatrick, M. A., & Freimuth, V. S. (Eds.). (1992). *AIDS: A communication perspective.* Hillsdale, NJ: Lawrence Erlbaum.

Edgar, T., Freimuth, V. S., Hammond, S. L., McDonald, D. A., & Fink, E. L. (1992). Strategic sexual communication: Condom use resistance and response. *Health Communication, 4,* 83–104.

Edwards, A. L. (1953). The relationship between judged desirability of a trait and the probability that the trait will be endorsed. *Journal of Applied Psychology, 2,* 90–93.

Edwards, J. E., Thomas, M. D., Rosenfeld, P., & Booth-Kewley, S. (1997). *How to conduct organizational surveys: A step-by-step guide.* Thousand Oaks, CA: Sage.

Edwards, J. L. (1998). The very model of a modern major (media) candidate: Colin Powell and the rhetoric of public opinion. *Communication Quarterly, 46,* 163–176.

Egland, K. I., Spitzberg, B. H., & Zormeier, M. M. (1996). Flirtation and conversational competence in cross-sex platonic and romantic relationships. *Communication Reports, 9,* 105–119.

Eichler, M. (1988). *Nonsexist research methods: A practical guide.* Boston: Allen & Unwin.

Elasmar, M. G., & Hunter, J. E. (1997). The impact of foreign TV on a domestic audience: A meta-analysis. In B. R. Burleson (Ed.), *Communication yearbook 20* (pp. 47–69). Thousand Oaks, CA: Sage.

Ellis, B. H., & Miller, K. I. (1993). The role of assertiveness, personal control, and participation in the prediction of nurse burnout. *Journal of Applied Communication Research, 21,* 327–342.

Ellis, C., & Bochner, A. P. (Eds.). (1996). *Composing ethnography: Alternative forms of qualitative writing.* Walnut Creek, CA: Altamira Press.

Elwood, W., Dayton, C. A., & Richard, A. J. (1995). Ethnography and illegal drug users: The efficacy of outreach as HIV prevention. *Communication Studies, 46,* 261–275.

Emerson, R. M., Fretz, R. I., & Shaw, L. L. (1955). *Writing ethnographic fieldnotes.* Chicago: University of Chicago Press.

Emmers, T. M., & Hart, R. D. (1996). Romantic relationship disengagement and coping rituals. *Communication Research Reports, 13,* 8–18.

Emmert, P. (1989). Attitude measurement. In P. Emmert & L. L. Barker (Eds.), *Measurement of communication behavior* (pp. 134–153). New York: Longman.

Engelberg, M., Flora, J. A., & Nass, C. I. (1995). AIDS knowledge: Effects of channel involvement and interpersonal communication. *Health Communication, 7,* 73–91.

Erickson, K., & Stull, D. (1998). *Doing team ethnography: Warnings and advice.* Thousand Oaks, CA: Sage.

Erlandson, D. A., Harris, E. L., Skipper, B. L., & Allen, S. D. (1993). *Doing naturalistic inquiry: A guide to methods.* Newbury Park, CA: Sage.

Ethical Principles of Psychologists and Code of Conduct. (1992). *American Psychologist, 47,* 1597–1611.

Everett, D. R., & Ahern, T. C. (1994). Computer-mediated communication as a teaching tool: A case study. *Journal of Research on Computing in Education, 26,* 336–357.

Fabj, V. (1993). Motherhood as political voice: The rhetoric of the Mothers of Plaza de Mayo. *Communication Studies, 44,* 1–18.

Fabj, V. (1998). Intolerance, forgiveness, and promise in the rhetoric of conversion: Italian women defy the mafia. *Quarterly Journal of Speech, 84,* 190–208.

Fairhurst, G. T. (1993). Echoes of the vision: When the rest of the organization talks total quality. *Management Communication Quarterly, 6,* 331–371.

Farrow, J. M., Farrow, B. J., Lohss, W. E., & Taub, S. I. (1975). Intersubject communication as a contaminating factor in verbal conditioning. *Perceptual and Motor Skills, 40,* 975–982.

The father of the Web. (1997, March). *Wired,* pp. 140–141.

Feingold, A. (1982). Measuring humor ability: Revision and construct validation of the Humor Perceptiveness Test. *Perceptual and Motor Skills, 56,* 159–166.

Ferguson, S. M., & Dickson, F. C. (1995). Children's expectations of their single parents' dating behaviors: A preliminary investigation of emergent themes relevant to single parent dating. *Journal of Applied Communication Research, 23,* 308–324.

Ferraris, C., Carveth, R., & Parrish-Sprowl, J. (1993). Interface precision benchmarks: A case study in organizational identification. *Journal of Applied Communication Research, 21,* 343–357.

Few Americans doubt Holocaust: Poll finds 1% deny Nazis slaughtered Jews in WWII. (1994, July 8). *Chicago Tribune,* Sect. 1, p. 6.

Fiebig, G. V., & Kramer, M. W. (1998). A framework for the study of emotions in organizational contexts. *Management Communication Quarterly, 11,* 536–572.

Fielding, N. G., & Lee, R. M. (1998). *Computer analysis and qualitative research.* Thousand Oaks, CA: Sage.

Fienberg, S. E. (1971). Randomization and social affairs: The 1970 draft lottery. *Science, 171,* 255–261.

Filsted, W., Reich, W., Parrella, D., & Rossi, J. (1985). *Using electronic pagers to monitor the process of recovery in alcoholics and drug abusers.* Paper presented at the meeting of the International Congress on Alcohol, Drug Abuse and Tobacco, Edmonton, Alberta.

Fink, A. (1995a). *How to ask survey questions.* Thousand Oaks, CA: Sage.

Fink, A. (1995b). *The survey handbook.* Thousand Oaks, CA: Sage.

Fink, A., & Kosecoff, J. (1985). *How to conduct surveys: A step-by-step guide.* Beverly Hills, CA: Sage.

Fink, A., & Kosecoff, J. (1998). *How to conduct surveys: A step-by-step guide* (2nd ed.). Thousand Oaks, CA: Sage.

Fink, E. L., & Chen, S-H. (1995). A Galileo analysis of organizational climate. *Human Communication Research, 21,* 494–521.

Fitch, K. L. (1991). The interplay of linguistic universals and cultural knowledge in personal address: Columbian *madre* terms. *Communication Monographs, 58,* 254–272.

Fitch, K. L. (1994). A cross-cultural study of directive sequences and some implications for compliance-gaining research. *Communication Monographs, 61,* 185–209.

Fitzpatrick, M. A., & Ritchie, L. D. (1994). Communication schemata within the family: Multiple perspectives on family interaction. *Human Communication Research, 20,* 275–301.

Flanagan, J. C. (1954). The critical incident technique. *Psychological Bulletin, 51,* 327–357.

Fleming, J. (1999). Antigone in Argentina: Griselda Gambaro's *Antigona Furiosa. Text and Performance Quarterly, 19,* 74–90.

Flesch, R. (1949). *The art of readable writing.* New York: Collier.

Fletcher, J. E., & Martin, E., Jr. (1981). Message and program testing. In J. E. Fletcher (Ed.), *Handbook of radio and TV broadcasting* (pp. 137–160). New York: Van Nostrand Reinhold.

Floyd, K., & Morman, M. T. (1997). Affectionate communication in nonromantic relationships: Influences of communicator, relational, and contextual factors. *Western Journal of Communication, 61,* 279–298.

Floyd, K., & Parks, M. R. (1995). Manifesting closeness in the interactions of peers: A look at siblings and friends. *Communication Reports, 8,* 69–76.

Fontaine, G. (1996). The experience of experiential training exercises: The role of a sense of presence and other states. *Communication Reports, 13,* 52–57.

Ford, L. A., & Ellis, B. H. (1988). A preliminary analysis of memorable support and nonsupport messages received by nurses in acute care settings. *Health Communication, 10,* 37–63.

Ford, W. S. Z. (1995). Evaluation of the indirect influence of courteous service on customer discretionary behavior. *Human Communication Research, 22,* 65–89.

Foss, S. K. (1989). *Rhetorical criticism: Exploration & practice.* Prospect Heights, IL: Waveland Press.

Foss, S. K. (1994). A rhetorical schema for the evaluation of visual imagery. *Communication Studies, 45,* 213–224.

Foucault, M. (1977). *Discipline and punish: The birth of prison* (A. Sheridan, Trans.). New York: Pantheon Books. (Original work published 1975)

Fowler, F. J., Jr. (1993). *Survey research methods* (2nd ed.). Newbury Park, CA: Sage.

Fox, K. V. (1996). Silent voices: A subversive reading of child sexual abuse. In C. Ellis & A. P. Bochner (Eds.), *Composing ethnography: Alternative forms of qualitative writing* (pp. 330–356). Walnut Creek, CA: Altamira Press.

Fox, R. J., Crask, M. R., & Kim, J. (1988). Mail survey response rate: A meta-analysis of selected techniques for inducing response. *Public Opinion Quarterly, 52,* 467–491.

Frankel, M. R., & Frankel, L. R. (1987). Fifty years of survey sampling in the United States. *Public Opinion Quarterly, 51,* S127–138.

Franzosi, R. (1990). Computer-assisted coding of textual data. *Sociological Methods and Research, 19,* 225–257.

Franzosi, R. (1995). Computer-assistent content analysis of newspapers: Can we make an expensive research tool more efficient? *Quality & Quantity, 29,* 157–172.

Freimuth, V. S., Hammond, S. L., Edgar, T., & Monahan, J. L. (1990). Reaching those at risk: A content-analytic study of AIDS PSAs. *Communication Research, 17,* 775–791.

Freitas, F. A., Meyers, S. A., & Avtgis, T. (1998). Student perceptions of instructor immediacy in conventional and distributed learning classrooms. *Communication Education, 47,* 366–372.

French, J. R. P., & Raven, B. G. (1959). The basis of social power. In D. Cartwright (Ed.), *Studies in social power* (pp. 150–167). Ann Arbor, MI: Institute of Social Research.

Frey, J. H. (1983). *Survey research by telephone.* Newbury Park, CA: Sage.

Frey, J. H. (1989). *Survey research by telephone* (2nd ed.). Newbury Park, CA: Sage.

Frey, J. H., & Oishi, S. M. (1995). *How to conduct interviews by telephone and in person.* Thousand Oaks, CA: Sage.

Frey, L. R. (1988, November). *Meeting the challenges posed during the 70s: A critical review of small group communication research during the 80s.* Paper presented at the meeting of the Speech Communication Association, New Orleans, LA.

Frey, L. R. (1994a). The call of the field: Studying communication in natural groups. In L. R. Frey (Ed.), *Group communication in context: Studies of natural groups* (pp. ix–xiv). Hillsdale, NJ: Lawrence Erlbaum.

Frey, L. R. (1994b). Call and response: The challenge of conducting research on communication in natural groups. In L. R. Frey (Ed.), *Group communication in context: Studies of natural groups* (pp. 293–304). Hillsdale, NJ: Lawrence Erlbaum.

Frey, L. R. (Ed.). (1994c). *Group communication in context: Studies of natural groups.* Hillsdale, NJ: Lawrence Erlbaum.

Frey, L. R. (1994d). Introduction: Revitalizing the study of small group communication. *Communication Studies, 45,* 1–6.

Frey, L. R. (1994e). The naturalistic paradigm: Studying small groups in the postmodern era. *Small Group Research, 25,* 551–557.

Frey, L. R. (Ed.). (1995). *Innovations in group facilitation: Applications in natural settings.* Cresskill, NJ: Hampton Press.

Frey, L. R. (1996). Remembering and "re-membering": A history of theory and research on communication and group decision making. In R. Y. Hirokawa & M. S. Poole (Eds.), *Communication and group decision making* (2nd ed., pp. 19–51). Thousand Oaks, CA: Sage.

Frey, L. R. (Ed.). (in press). *Group communication in context: Studies of bona fide groups* (2nd ed.). Mahwah, NJ: Lawrence Erlbaum.

Frey, L. R., & Adelman, M. B. (1993). Building community life: Understanding individual, group, and organizational processes. In S. J. Miller, K. I. Ward, & R. Rybicki (Eds.), *Handbook for assisted living* (pp. 31–39). Chicago: Bonaventure House.

Frey, L. R., Adelman, M. B., Flint, L. J., & Query, J. L., Jr. (in press). Weaving meanings together in an AIDS residence: Communicative practices, perceived health outcomes, and the symbolic construction of community. *Journal of Health Communication.*

Frey, L. R., Adelman, M. B., & Query, J. L., Jr. (1996). Communication practices in the social construction of health in an AIDS residence. *Journal of Health Psychology, 1,* 383–397.

Frey, L. R., & Botan, C. H. (1988). The status of instruction in introductory undergraduate communication research methods. *Communication Education, 37,* 249–256.

Frey, L. R., Botan, C. H., Friedman, P. G., & Kreps, G. L. (1992). *Interpreting communication research: A case study approach.* Englewood Cliffs, NJ: Prentice-Hall.

Frey, L. R., Pearce, W. B., Pollock, M. A., Artz, L., & Murphy, B. A. O. (1996). Looking for justice in all the wrong places: On a communication approach to social justice. *Communication Studies, 47,* 110–127.

Frey, L. R., Query, J. L., Jr., Flint, L. J., & Adelman, M. B. (1998). Living together with AIDS: Social support processes in a residential facility. In V. J. Derlega & A. P. Barbee (Eds.), *HIV infection and social interactions* (pp. 129–146). Thousand Oaks, CA: Sage.

Fried, J. P. (1984, April 8). Judge protects waiter's notes on fire inquiry. *New York Times,* p. A47.

Frymier, A. B., & Shulman, G. M. (1995). "What's in it for me?": Increasing content relevance to enhance students' motivation. *Communication Education, 44,* 40–50.

Frymier, A. B., Shulman, G. M., & Houser, M. (1996). The development of a learner empowerment measure. *Communication Education, 45,* 181–199.

Fulk, J., Schmitz, J., & Ryu, D. (1995). Cognitive elements in the social construction of communication technology. *Management Communication Quarterly, 8,* 259–288.

Funkhouser, E. T. (1996). The evaluative use of citation analysis for communication journals. *Human Communication Research, 22,* 563–574.

Fuoss, K. W. (1999). Lynching performances, theatres of violence. *Text and Performance Quarterly, 19,* 1–37.

Furnham, A. (1986). Response bias, social desirability and assimilation. *Personality and Individual Difference, 7,* 385–400.

Gaines, B. R. (1996). Dimensions of electronic journals. In T. M. Harrison & T. Stephen (Eds.), *Computer networking and scholarly communication in the twenty-first-century university* (pp. 315–334). Albany: State University of New York Press.

Gallup, G. H., Jr., & Newport, F. (1991). Belief in paranormal phenomena among adult Americans. *Skeptical Inquirer, 15,* 137–147.

Gallup, G. H., & Rae, S. F. (1940). *The pulse of democracy: The public opinion poll and how it works.* New York: Simon and Schuster.

Gans, H. J. (1962). *The urban villagers: Group and class in the life of Italian-Americans.* New York: Free Press of Glencoe.

Gao, G., & Gudykunst, W. B. (1995). Attributional confidence, perceived similarity, and network involvement in Chinese and American romantic relationships. *Communication Quarterly, 43,* 431–445.

Gardner, W. L., III, & Gundersen, D. E. (1995). Information system training, usage, and satisfaction: An exploratory study of the hospitality industry. *Management Communication Quarterly, 9,* 78–114.

Garfinkel, H. (1967). *Studies in ethnomethodology.* Englewood Cliffs, NJ: Prentice-Hall.

Garlick, R., & Mongeau, P. A. (1993). Argument quality and group member status as determinants of attitudinal minority influence. *Western Journal of Communication, 57,* 289–308.

Garside, C. (1996). Look who's talking: A comparison of lecture and group discussion teaching strategies in developing critical thinking skills. *Communication Education, 45,* 212–227.

Gayle, B. M., Preiss, R. W., & Allen, M. (1998). Another look at the use of rhetorical questions. In M. Allen & R. W. Preiss (Eds.), *Persuasion: Advances through meta-analysis* (pp. 189–201). Cresskill, NJ: Hampton Press.

Geertz, C. (1988). *Works and lives: The anthropologist as author.* Stanford, CA: Stanford University Press.

Geist, P., & Dreyer, J. (1993). The demise of dialogue: A critique of medical encounter ideology. *Western Journal of Communication, 57,* 233–246.

Gephart, R. P., Jr. (1988). *Ethnostatistics: Qualitative foundations for quantitative research.* Newbury Park, CA: Sage.

German, K. M. (1995). Invoking the glorious war: Framing the Persian Gulf conflict through directive language. *Southern Communication Journal, 60,* 292–302.

Gibson, D. C. (1994). J. Edgar Hoover's four-baggers: An analysis of rhetorical functions. *Southern Communication Journal, 59,* 284–293.

Gibson, R., & Zillmann, D. (1994). Exaggerated versus representative exemplification in news reports: Perceptions of issues and personal consequences. *Communication Research, 21,* 603–624.

Giffin, K. (1968). *The trust differential.* Unpublished manuscript, University of Kansas, Lawrence.

Giffin, K. (1969). *The conceptualization and measurement of interpersonal trust.* Unpublished manuscript, University of Kansas, Lawrence.

Gilbert, C., Cox, J. L., Kashima, H., & Eberle, K. (1996). Survey biases: When does the interviewer's race matter? *Change, 9*(4), 23–25.

Giles, H., Mulac, A., Bradac, J. J., & Johnson, P. (1987). Speech accommodation theory: The last decade and beyond. In M. L. McLaughlin (Ed.), *Communication yearbook 10* (pp. 13–48). Newbury Park, CA: Sage.

Gilsdorf, J. W. (1992). Writing corporate policy on communicating: A Delphi survey. *Management Communication Quarterly, 5,* 316–347.

Girden, E. R. (1996). *Evaluating research articles: From start to finish.* Thousand Oaks, CA: Sage.

Gladstein, D. L. (1984). Groups in context: A model of task group effectiveness. *Administrative Science Quarterly, 29,* 499–517.

Glaser, B. G., & Strauss, A. L. (1967). *The discovery of grounded theory: Strategies for qualitative research.* Chicago: Aldine.

Glass, G., McGraw, B., & Smith, M. L. (1981). *Meta-analysis in social research.* New York: Holt, Rinehart & Winston.

Goetz, J. P., & Le Compte, M. D. (1984). *Ethnography and qualitative design in educational research.* Orlando, FL: Academic Press.

Goffman, E. (1959). *The presentation of self in everyday life.* Garden City, NY: Doubleday.

Goffman, E. (1989). On fieldwork. *Journal of Contemporary Ethnography, 18,* 123–132.

Gold, R. L. (1958). Roles in sociological field observations. *Social Forces, 36,* 317–323.

Goldhaber, G., & Rogers, D. (with Lesniak, R., & Porter, D. T.). (1979). *Auditing organizational communication systems: The ICA communication audit.* Dubuque, IA: Kendall-Hunt.

Goldsmith, D. (1990). A dialectical perspective on the expression of autonomy and connection in romantic relationships. *Western Journal of Speech Communication, 54,* 537–556.

Goldsmith, D. (1992). Managing conflicting goals in supportive interaction: An integrative theoretical framework. *Communication Research, 19,* 264–286.

Goldzwig, S. R., & Dionisopoulos, G. N. (1995). Legitimating liberal credentials for the presidency: John F. Kennedy and *The Strategy of Peace. Southern Communication Journal, 60,* 312–331.

Goldzwig, S. R., & Sullivan, P. A. (1995). Post-assassination newspaper editorial eulogies: Analysis and assessment. *Western Journal of Communication, 59,* 126–150.

Goss, B. (1991). A test of conversational listening. *Communication Research Reports, 8,* 19–22.

Gould, S. J. (1995). Curveball. In S. Fraser (Ed.), *The bell curve wars: Race, intelligence, and the future of America* (pp. 11–22). New York: Basic Books.

Gouran, D. S., & Hirokawa, R. Y. (1996). Functional theory and communication in decision-making and problem-solving groups: An expanded view. In R. Y. Hirokawa & M. S. Poole (Eds.), *Communication and group decision making* (2nd ed., pp. 55–80). Thousand Oaks, CA: Sage.

Gouran, D. S., Hirokawa, R. Y., & Martz, A. E. (1986). A critical analysis of factors related to decisional processes involved in the Challenger disaster. *Central States Speech Journal, 37,* 119–135.

Graham, E. E., Barbato, C. A., & Perse, E. M. (1993). The interpersonal communication motives model. *Communication Quarterly, 41,* 172–186.

Graham, E. E., Papa, M. J., & Brooks, G. P. (1992). Functions of humor in conversation: Conceptualization and measurement. *Western Journal of Communication, 56,* 161–183.

Granovetter, M. S. (1976). Network sampling: Some first steps. *American Journal of Sociology, 81,* 1287–1303.

Gray, J. (1992). *Men are from Mars, women are from Venus: A practical guide for improving communication and getting what you want in your relationship.* New York: HarperCollins.

Greenbaum, T. (1997). *The handbook for focus group research.* Thousand Oaks, CA: Sage.

Greenwald, A. G. (1975). Consequences of prejudice against the null hypothesis. *Psychological Bulletin, 82,* 1–20.

Grice, H. P. (1975). Logic and conversation. In P. Cole & J. L. Morgan (Eds.), *Speech acts* (pp. 41–58). New York: Academic Press.

Grice, P. (1989). *Studies in the way of words.* Cambridge, MA: Harvard University Press.

Griffin, C. L. (1994). Rhetoricizing alienation: Mary Wollstonecraft and the rhetorical construction of women's oppression. *Quarterly Journal of Speech, 80,* 293–312.

Griffin, E. (1997). *A first look at communication theory* (3rd ed.). New York: McGraw-Hill.

Griffin, J. H. (1961). *Black like me.* Boston: Houghton Mifflin.

Grob, L. M., Meyers, R. A., & Schuh, R. (1997). Powerful/powerless language use in group interactions: Sex differences or similarities? *Communication Quarterly, 45,* 282–303.

Gross, A. G. (1990). Rhetoric of science is epistemic rhetoric. *Quarterly Journal of Speech, 76,* 304–306.

Grosvernor, D., & Grosvernor, G. (1996, April). Ceylon. *National Geographic,* pp. 447–497.

Groves, R. M. (1987). Research on survey data quality. *Public Opinion Quarterly, 51,* S156–172.

Guba, E. G. (1990). The alternative paradigm dialog. In E. G. Guba (Ed.), *The paradigm dialogue* (pp. 15–27). Newbury Park, CA: Sage.

Guba, E. G., & Lincoln, Y. S. (1994). Competing paradigms in qualitative research. In N. K. Denzin & Y. S. Lincoln (Eds.), *Handbook of qualitative research* (pp. 105–117). Thousand Oaks, CA: Sage.

Gudykunst, W. B., Matsumoto, Y., Ting-Toomey, S., Nishida, T., Kim, K., & Heyman, S. (1996). The influence of cultural individualism-collectivism, self construals, and individual values on communication styles across cultures. *Human Communication Research, 22,* 510–543.

Guedon, J-C. (1996). Electronic academic journals: From disciplines to "seminars"? In T. M. Harrison & T. Stephen (Eds.), *Computer networking and scholarly communication in the twenty-first-century university* (pp. 335–350). Albany: State University of New York Press.

Guerrero, L. K. (1996). Attachment-style differences in intimacy and involvement: A test of the four-category model. *Communication Monographs, 63,* 269–292.

Guerrero, L. K., Andersen, P. A., Jorgensen, P. F., Spitzberg, B. H., & Eloy, S. V. (1995). Coping with the green-eyed monster: Conceptualizing and measuring communicative responses to romantic jealousy. *Western Journal of Communication, 59,* 270–304.

Guerrero, L. K., & Burgoon, J. K. (1996). Attachment styles and reactions to nonverbal involvement change in romantic dyads: Patterns of reciprocity and compensation. *Human Communication Research, 22,* 335–370.

Guest, L. (1947). A study of interviewer competence. *International Journal of Opinion and Attitude Research, 1,* 17–30.

Guilford, J. P. (1956). *Fundamental statistics in psychology and education* (3rd ed.). New York: McGraw-Hill.

Gunter, B. (1994). The question of media violence. In J. Bryant & D. Zillman (Eds.), *Media effects: Advances in theory and research* (pp. 163–211). Hillsdale, NJ: Lawrence Erlbaum.

Gunther, A. C. (1995). Overrating the X-rating: The third-person perception and support for censorship of pornography. *Journal of Communication, 45*(1), 27–38.

Hacker, D. A., & Hansen, A. A. (1974). The Manzanar riot: An ethnic perspective. *Amerasia Journal, 2,* 112–157.

Hacker, K. L., Howl, L., Scott, M., & Steiner, R. (1996). Uses of computer-mediated political communication in the 1992 presidential campaign: A content analysis of the Bush, Clinton, and Perot computer lists. *Communication Research Reports, 13,* 138–146.

Hale, J. L., & Dillard, J. P. (1991). The uses of meta-analysis: Making knowledge claims and setting research agendas. *Communication Monographs, 59,* 388–396.

Hall, C. S., & Lindzey, G. (1970). *Theories of personality* (2nd ed.). New York: Wiley.

Hallstein, D. L. O. (1996). Feminist assessment of emancipatory potential and Madonna's contradictory gender practices. *Quarterly Journal of Speech, 82,* 125–141.

Hamel, J. (with Defour, S., & Fortin, D.). (1993). *Case study methods.* Newbury Park, CA: Sage.

Hamilton, M. A., & Hunter, J. E. (1998a). The effect of language intensity on receiver evaluations of message, source, and topic. In M. Allen & R. W. Preiss (Eds.), *Persuasion: Advances through meta-analysis* (pp. 99–138). Cresskill, NJ: Hampton Press.

Hamilton, M. A., & Hunter, J. E. (1998b). A framework for understanding: Meta-analysis of the persuasion literature. In M. Allen & R. W. Preiss (Eds.), *Persuasion: Advances through meta-analysis* (pp. 1–28). Cresskill, NJ: Hampton Press.

Hample, D., & Dalliner, J. M. (1987a). Individual differences in cognitive editing standards. *Human Communication Research, 14,* 123–144.

Hample, D., & Dallinger, J. M. (1987b). Self-monitoring and the cognitive editing of argument. *Central States Speech Journal, 38,* 152–165.

Hanke, R. (1998). The "mock-macho" situation comedy: Hegemonic masculinity and its reiteration. *Western Journal of Communication, 62,* 74–93.

Hansen, A. A. (Ed.). (1991). *Japanese American World War II evacuation project: Part I. Internees.* Westport, CT: Meckler.

Hansen, A. A. (1994). A riot of voices: Racial and ethnic variables in interactive oral history interviewing. In E. M. McMahan & K. L. Rogers (Eds.), *Interactive oral history interviewing* (pp. 107–139). Hillsdale, NJ: Lawrence Erlbaum.

Hansen, A. A., & Mitson, B. E. (Eds.). (1974). *Voices long silent: An oral inquiry into the Japanese American evacuation.* Fullerton: Japanese American Project, Oral History Program, California State University.

Hansen, M. (1996, February). Out of the blue. *ABS Journal,* pp. 50–55.

Hansen, M. H., Hurwitz, W. N., Marks, E. S., & Maudlin, W. P. (1951). Response errors in surveys. *Journal of the American Statistical Association, 46,* 147–190.

Harding, S. (1987a). Conclusion: Epistemological questions. In S. Harding (Ed.), *Feminism & methodology* (pp. 181–190). Bloomington: Indiana University Press.

Harding, S. (1987b). Introduction: Is there a feminist method? In S. Harding (Ed.), *Feminism & methodology* (pp. 1–14). Bloomington: Indiana University Press.

Harding, S. (1990). Feminism, science, and the anti-enlightement critiques. In J. Nicholson (Ed.), *Feminism/postmodernism* (pp. 83–106). New York: Routledge.

Harper, D. (1989). Visual sociology: Expanding sociological vision. In G. Blank, J. L. McCartney, & E. Brent (Eds.), *New technology in sociology: Practical applications in research and work* (pp. 81–97). New Brunswick, NJ: Transaction Books.

Harper, N. L., & Hirokawa, R. Y. (1988). A comparison of persuasive strategies used by female and male managers I: An examination of downward influence. *Communication Quarterly, 36,* 157–168.

Harré, R., & Secord, P. F. (1973). *The explanation of social behavior.* Totowa, NJ: Littlefield, Adam.

Harrington, A. (1997). Introduction. In A. Harrington (Ed.), *The placebo effect: An interdisciplinary exploration* (pp. 1–11). Cambridge, MA: Harvard University Press.

Harrison, T. M. (1985). Communication and participative decision making: An exploratory study. *Personnel Psychology, 38,* 93–116.

Hart, D., & Damon, W. (1986). Developmental trends in self-understanding. *Social Cognition, 4,* 388–407.

Hart, R. D., & Williams, D. E. (1995). Able-bodied instructors and students with physical disabilities: A relationship handicapped by communication. *Communication Education, 44,* 140–154.

Hart, R. P., & Burks, D. M. (1972). Rhetorical sensitivity and social interaction. *Speech Monographs, 39,* 75–91.

Hart, R. P., Carlson, R. E., & Eadie, W. F. (1980). Attitudes toward communication and the assessment of rhetorical sensitivity. *Communication Monographs, 47,* 1–22.

Hartman, J. J., & Hedblom, J. H. (1979). *Methods for the social sciences: A handbook for students and non-specialists.* Westport, CT: Greenwood Press.

Hartnett, S. (1998). Lincoln and Douglas meet the abolitionist David Walker as prisoners debate slavery: Empowering education, applied communication, and social justice. *Journal of Applied Communication Research, 26,* 232–253.

Hasian, M., Jr., & Flores, L. A. (1997). Children of the stones: The Intifada and the mythic creation of the Palestinian state. *Southern Communication Journal, 62,* 89–106.

Havick, J. (1997). Determinants of national media attention. *Journal of Communication, 47*(2), 97–111.

Hawes, L. C. (1975). *Pragmatics of analoguing: Theory and model construction in communication.* Reading, MA: Addison-Wesley.

Hayano, D. M. (1979). Auto-ethnography. *Human Organization, 38,* 99–104.

Hayden, S. (1997). Re-claiming bodies of knowledge: An exploration of the relationship between feminist theorizing and feminine style in the rhetoric of the Boston Women's Health Book Collective. *Western Journal of Communication, 61,* 127–163.

Health official blocks survey on teenage sex. (1991, July 21). *Chicago Tribune,* Sect. 1, p. 18.

Hearold, S. (1986). A synthesis of 1043 effects of television on social behavior. In G. Comstock (Ed.), *Public communication and behavior* (Vol. 1, pp. 65–133). Orlando, FL: Academic Press.

Hecht, M. L., Boster, F. J., & LaMer, S. (1989). The effect of extroversion and differentiation on listener-adapted communication. *Communication Reports, 2,* 1–8.

Hecht, M. L., Collier, M. J., & Ribeau, S. A. (1993). *African American communication: Ethnic identity and cultural interpretation.* Newbury Park, CA: Sage.

Hecht, M. L., Larkey, L. K., & Johnson, J. N. (1992). African American and European American perceptions of problematic issues in interethnic communication effectiveness. *Human Communication Research, 19,* 209–236.

Helmer, J. (1993). Storytelling in the creation and maintenance of organizational tension and stratification. *Southern Communication Journal, 59,* 34–44.

Henderson, R. W. (1988). EVENTLOG: A tool for observational research. *Academic Computing, 2,* 36, 47.

Hendrick, C. (1991). Replications, strict replications, and conceptual replications: Are they important? In J. W. Neuliep (Ed.), *Replication research in the social sciences* (pp. 41–49). Newbury Park, CA: Sage.

Henriksen, L. (1996). Naive theories of buying and selling: Implications for teaching critical-viewing skills. *Journal of Applied Communication Research, 24,* 93–109.

Henry, G. T. (1990). *Practical sampling.* Newbury Park, CA: Sage.

Heritage, J. (1989). Current developments in conversation analysis. In D. Roger & P. Bull (Eds.), *Conversation: An interdisciplinary perspective* (pp. 21–47). Clevedon, England: Multilingual Matters.

Herndon, S. L. (1993). Using focus group interviews for preliminary investigation. In S. L. Herndon & G. L. Kreps (Eds.), *Qualitative research: Applications in organizational communication* (pp. 39–46). Cresskill, NJ: Hampton Press.

Herndon, S. L., & Kreps, G. L. (Eds.). (1993). *Qualitative research: Applications in organizational communication.* Cresskill, NJ: Hampton Press.

Heron, J., & Reason, P. (1997). A participatory inquiry paradigm. *Qualitative Inquiry, 3,* 274–294.

Herrett-Skjellum, J., & Allen, M. (1996). Television programming and sex stereotyping: A meta-analysis. In B. R. Burleson (Ed.), *Communication yearbook 19* (pp. 157–186). Thousand Oaks, CA: Sage.

Herrnstein, R. J., & Murray, C. (1994). *The bell curve: Intelligence and class structure in American life.* New York: Free Press.

Hersen, M., & Barlow, D. (1976). *Single case experimental designs: Strategies for studying behavior change.* New York: Pergamon Press.

Hershey, N., & Miller, R. (1976). *Human experimentation and the law.* Germantown, MD: Aspen Systems.

Hertog, J. K., & Fan, D. P. (1995). The impact of press coverage on social beliefs: The case of HIV transmission. *Communication Research, 22,* 545–574.

Hickson, M., III. (1983). Ethnomethodology: The promise of applied communication research? *Southern Speech Communication Journal, 48,* 183–195.

Hickson, M., III, Scott, R. K., & Vogel, R. (1995). A content analysis of local television news in a top 50 market. *Communication Research Reports, 12,* 71–79.

Hickson, M., III, Stacks, D. W., & Amsbary, J. H. (1993). Active prolific scholars in communication studies: Analysis of research productivity, II. *Communication Education, 42,* 224–233.

Hill, F. (1972). Convention wisdom—traditional form: The president's message of November 3, 1969. *Quarterly Journal of Speech, 58,* 373–386.

Hill, M. R. (1993). *Archival strategies and techniques.* Newbury Park, CA: Sage.

Hiltz, S. R., Turoff, M., & Johnson, K. (1989). Experiments in group decision making, 3: Disinhibition, deindividuation, and group process in pen name and real name computer conferences. *Decision Support Systems, 5,* 217–232.

Hines, S. C. (1992, November). *Succinctness as a measure of construct system development: A preliminary assessment of construct validity.* Paper presented at the meeting of the Speech Communication Association, Chicago.

Hines, S. C. (1994, November). *The Role Category Questionnaire: Why it is plausible to view as a referential communication task but not as a construct system development measure.* Paper presented at the meeting of the Eastern Communication Association, Washington, DC.

Hines, S. C. (1995). Referential skill or construct system development: Testing alternative explanations for role category questionnaire-based measures. *Communication Research Reports, 12,* 15–24.

Hines, S. C., Badzek, L., & Moss, A. H. (1997). Informed consent among chronically ill elderly: Assessing its (in)adequacy and predictors. *Journal of Applied Communication Research, 25,* 151–169.

Hirokawa, R. Y. (1985). Decision procedures and decision-making performance: A test of a functional perspective. *Human Communication Research, 12,* 203–224.

Hirokawa, R. Y., Gouran, D. S., & Martz, A. E. (1988). Understanding the sources of faulty group decision-making: A lesson from the Challenger disaster. *Small Group Behavior, 19,* 411–433.

Hirokawa, R. Y., & Keyton, J. (1995). Perceived facilitators and inhibitors of effectiveness in organizational work teams. *Management Communication Quarterly, 8,* 424–446.

Hirokawa, R. Y., & Salazar, A. J. (1999). Task-group communication and decision-making performance. In Frey, L. R. (Ed.), Gouran, D. S., & Poole, M. S. (Assoc. Eds.), *The handbook of group communication theory and research* (pp. 167–191). Thousand Oaks, CA: Sage.

Hirsch, E. D., Jr. (1967). *Validity in interpretation.* New Haven, CT: Yale University Press.

Hoffner, C., Cantor, J., & Thorson, E. (1988). Children's understanding of a televised narrative: Developmental differences in processing video and audio content. *Communication Research, 15,* 227–245.

Hoffner, C., & Haefner, M. J. (1997). Children's comforting of frightened coviewers: Real and hypothetical television-viewing situations. *Communication Research, 24,* 136–152.

Hofstetter, C. R., Sticht, T. G., & Hofstetter, C. H. (1999). Knowledge, literacy, and power. *Communication Research, 26,* 58–80.

Hogan, J. M. (1997). George Gallup and the rhetoric of scientific discovery. *Communication Monographs, 64,* 161–179.

Hogben, M. (1998). Factors moderating the effect of televised aggression on viewer behavior. *Communication Research, 25,* 220–247.

Hollihan, T. A., & Riley, P. (1987). The rhetorical power of a compelling story: A critique of a "Toughlove" parental support group. *Communication Quarterly, 35,* 13–25.

Hollingshead, A. B. (1996). Information suppression and status persistence in group decision making: The effects of communication media. *Human Communication Research, 23,* 193–219.

Holstein, J. A., & Gubrium, J. F. (1995). *The active interview.* Thousand Oaks, CA: Sage.

Holsti, O. R. (1969). *Content analysis for the social sciences and humanities.* Reading, MA: Addison-Wesley.

Honigmann, J. J. (1970). Sampling in ethnographic field work. In R. Naroll & R. Cohen (Eds.), *A handbook of method in cultural anthropology* (pp. 266–281). Garden City, NY: Natural History Press.

Hopper, R. (1981). The taken-for-granted. *Human Communication Research, 7,* 195–211.

Hopper, R. (1992). *Telephone conversations.* Bloomington: Indiana University Press.

Hormuth, S. (1986). The sampling of experiences in situ. *Journal of Personality, 54,* 262–293.

Hornsby-Smith, M. (1993). Gaining access. In N. Gilbert (Ed.), *Researching social life* (pp. 52–67). London: Sage.

Hosman, L. A. (1991). The relationships among need for privacy, loneliness, conversational sensitivity, and interpersonal communication motives. *Communication Reports, 4,* 73–80.

Hosman, L. A. (1997). The relationship between locus of control and the evaluative consequences of powerful and powerless speech styles. *Journal of Language and Social Psychology, 16,* 70–78.

Hosman, L. A., & Siltanen, S. A. (1995). Relationship intimacy, need for privacy, and privacy restoration behaviors. *Communication Quarterly, 43,* 64–74.

Houck, D. W. (1993). "By any means necessary": Rereading Malcolm X's MECCA conversion. *Communication Studies, 44,* 285–298.

Houck, D. W. (1997). Reading the body in the text: FDR's 1932 speech to the Democratic National Convention. *Southern Communication Journal, 63,* 20–36.

Houston, M. J., & Nevin, J. R. (1977). The effects of source and appeal on mail survey response patterns. *Journal of Marketing Research, 14,* 374–378.

Howard, G. S., Maxwell, S. E., Wiener, R. L., Boynton, K. S., & Rooney, W. M. (1980). Is a behavioral measure the best estimate of behavioral parameters? Perhaps not. *Applied Psychological Measurement, 4,* 293–311.

Howard, L. A., & Geist, P. (1995). Ideological positioning in organizational change: The dialectic of control in a merging organization. *Communication Monographs, 62,* 110–131.

Howze, E. H., Broyden, R. R., & Impara, J. C. (1992). Using informal caregivers to communicate with women about mammography. *Health Communication, 4,* 227–244.

Hsia, H. J. (1988). *Mass communications research methods: A step-by-step approach.* Hillsdale, NJ: Lawrence Erlbaum.

Huber, P. W. (1991). *Galileo's revenge: Junk science in the courtroom.* New York: Basic Books.

Huberman, A. M., & Miles, M. B. (1994). Data management and analysis methods. In N. K. Denzin & Y. S. Lincoln (Eds.), *Handbook of qualitative research* (pp. 428–444). Thousand Oaks, CA: Sage.

Huck, S. W., Cormier, W. H., & Bounds, W. G., Jr. (1974). *Reading statistics and research.* New York: Harper & Row.

Huff, D. (1954). *How to lie with statistics.* New York: Norton.

Hummert, M. L. (1994). Stereotypes for the elderly and patronizing speech. In M. L. Hummert, J. M. Wiemann, & J. F. Nussbaum (Eds.), *Interpersonal communication in older adulthood: Interdisciplinary research* (pp. 162–184). Thousand Oaks, CA: Sage.

Hummert, M. L., Garstka, T. A., & Shaner, J. L. (1995). Beliefs about language performance: Adults' perceptions about self and elderly targets. *Journal of Language and Social Psychology, 14,* 235–239.

Hummert, M. L., & Shaner, J. L. (1994). Patronizing speech to the elderly: Relationship to stereotyping. *Communication Studies, 45,* 145–158.

Hummert, M. L., Shaner, J. L., Garstka, T. A., & Henry, C. (1998). Communication with older adults: The influence of age stereotypes, context, and communicator age. *Human Communication Research, 25,* 124–151.

Humphreys, L. (1970). *Tearoom trade: Impersonal sex in public places.* Chicago: Aldine.

Hunt, R. G. (1970). *Strategic selection: A purposive sampling design for small numbers research, program evaluation, and management.* Buffalo: State University of New York Press.

Hunter, J., & Schmidt, F. (1990). *Methods of meta-analysis: Correcting error and bias in research findings.* Newbury Park, CA: Sage.

Hutchby, I. (1996). *Confrontation talk: Arguments, asymmetries, and power on talk radio.* Mahwah, NJ: Lawrence Erlbaum.

Hyman, H. H. (1954). *Interviewing in social research.* Chicago: University of Chicago Press.

Ice, R. (1991). Corporate public and rhetorical strategies: The case of Union Carbide's Bhopal crisis. *Management Communication Quarterly, 4,* 341–362.

Ifert, D. E., & Bearden, L. (1998). The influence of argumentativeness and verbal aggression on responses to refused requests. *Communication Reports, 11,* 145–154.

Ifert, D. E., & Roloff, M. E. (1996). Responding to refusals of requests: The role of requester sex on persistence. *Communication Reports, 9,* 119–126.

An immoral study. (1972, July 30). *St. Louis Post-Dispatch,* p. 2D.

Imrich, D. J., Mullin, C., & Linz, D. (1995). Measuring the extent of prejudicial pretrial publicity in major American newspapers: A content analysis. *Journal of Communication, 45*(3), 94–117.

Infante, D. A. (1981). Trait argumentativeness as a predictor of communicative behavior in situations requiring argument. *Central States Communication Journal, 32,* 265–272.

Infante, D. A. (1995). Teaching students to understand and control verbal aggression. *Communication Education, 44,* 51–63.

Infante, D. A., Hartley, K. C., Martin, M. M., Higgins, M. A., Bruning, S. D., & Hur, G. (1992). Initiating and reciprocating verbal aggression: Effects on credibility and credited valid arguments. *Communication Studies, 43,* 182–190.

Infante, D. A., & Rancer, A. S. (1982). A conceptualization and measure of argumentativeness. *Journal of Personality Assessment, 46,* 72–80.

Infante, D. A., & Rancer, A. S. (1996). Argumentativeness and verbal aggressiveness: A review of recent theory and research. In B. R. Burleson (Ed.), *Communication yearbook 19* (pp. 319–351). Thousand Oaks, CA: Sage.

Infante, D. A., Rancer, A. S., & Jordan, F. F. (1996). Affirming and nonaffirming style, dyad sex, and the perception of argumentation and verbal aggressiveness in an interpersonal dispute. *Human Communication Research, 22,* 315–334.

Infante, D. A., Rancer, A. S., & Womack, D. F. (1996). *Building communication theory* (3rd ed.). Prospect Heights, IL: Waveland Press.

Infante, D. A., Trebing, J. D., Shepherd, P. E., & Seeds, D. E. (1984). The relationship of argumentativeness to verbal aggression. *Southern Speech Communication Journal, 50,* 67–77.

Inhuman experiment. (1972, July 31). *Oregonian,* p. 16.

Ivy, D. K., & Hamlet, S. (1996). College students and sexual dynamics: Two studies of peer sexual harassment. *Communication Education, 45,* 149–166.

Jackson-Beeck, M., & Kraus, S. (1980). Political communication theory and research: An overview, 1978–1979. In D. D. Nimmo (Ed.), *Communication yearbook 4* (pp. 449–465). New Brunswick, NJ: Transaction Books.

Jacobs, S. (1989). Speech acts and arguments. *Argumentation, 3,* 345–365.

Jacobs, S., Brashers, D., & Dawson, E. J. (1996). Truth and deception. *Communication Monographs, 63,* 98–103.

Jacobs, S., Dawson, E. J., & Brashers, D. (1996). Information manipulation theory: A replication and assessment. *Communication Monographs, 63,* 70–82.

Jacobs, S., & Jackson, S. (1981). Argument as a natural category: The routine grounds for arguing in conversation. *Western Journal of Speech Communication, 45,* 111–117.

Jacobs, S., & Jackson, S. (1982). Conversational argument: A discourse analytic approach. In J. R. Cox & C. A. Willard (Eds.), *Advances in argument theory and research* (pp. 205–237). Carbondale: Southern Illinois University.

Jaeger, R. M. (1983). *Statistics: A spectator sport.* Newbury Park, CA: Sage.

Jaeger, R. M. (1990). *Statistics: A spectator sport* (2nd ed.). Newbury Park, CA: Sage.

James, F. (1997, July 9). Panel rejects pleas to add "multiracial" as official category. *Chicago Tribune,* Sect. 1, p. 3.

Janis, I. L., & Feshbach, S. (1953). Effects of fear-arousing communications. *Journal of Abnormal and Social Psychology, 48,* 78–92.

Jansma, L. L., Linz, D. G., Mulac, A., & Imrich, D. J. (1997). Men's interactions with women after viewing sexually explicit films: Does degradation make a difference? *Communication Monographs, 64,* 1–24.

Jefferson, G. (1978). Sequential aspects of storytelling in conversation. In J. Schenkein (Ed.), *Studies in the organization of conversational interaction* (pp. 219–248). Orlando, FL: Academic Press.

Jensen, R. J., & Hammerback, J. C. (1998). "Your tools are really the people": The rhetoric of Robert Parris Moses. *Communication Monographs, 65,* 126–140.

Jensen, R. J., & Lichtenstein, A. (1995). From yippie to yuppie: Jerry Rubin as rhetorical icon. *Southern Communication Journal, 60,* 332–347.

Johannesen, R. L. (1986). An ethical assessment of the Reagan rhetoric, 1981–1982. In K. R. Sanders, L. L. Kaid, & D. Nimmo (Eds.), *Political communication yearbook 4* (pp. 226–241). Carbondale: Southern Illinois University.

Johannesen, R. L. (1995). The ethics of plagiarism reconsidered: The oratory of Martin Luther King, Jr. *Southern Communication Journal, 60,* 185–194.

Johnson, C., & Larson, R. (1982). Bulemia: An analysis of moods and behavior. *Psychometric Medicine, 44,* 341–351.

Johnson, D., & Sellnow, T. (1995). Deliberative rhetoric as a step in organizational crisis management: Exxon as a case study. *Western Journal of Communication, 8,* 54–60.

Johnson, G. M., Staton, A. Q., & Jorgensen-Earp, C. R. (1995). An ecological perspective on the transition of new university freshman. *Communication Education, 44,* 336–352.

Johnson, J. C. (1990). *Selecting ethnographic informants.* Newbury Park, CA: Sage.

Johnson, J. D. (1987). Development of the communication and physical environment scale. *Communication Studies, 38,* 35–43.

Johnson, J. D., & Meischke, H. (1993). A comprehensive model of cancer-related information seeking applied to magazines. *Human Communication Research, 19,* 343–367.

Johnson, J. D., Meischke, H., Grau, J., & Johnson, S. (1992). Cancer-related channel selection. *Health Communication, 4,* 183–196.

Johnston, D. D. (1995). Adolescents' motivations for viewing graphic horror. *Human Communication Research, 21,* 522–552.

Johnston, D. D., Stinski, M., & Meyers, D. (1993). Development of an alexithymia instrument to measure the diminished communication of affect. *Communication Research Reports, 10,* 149–160.

Johnstone, C. L. (1995). Reagan, rhetoric, and the public philosophy: Ethics and politics in the 1984 campaign. *Southern Communication Journal, 60,* 93–108.

Jones, J. H. (1981). *Bad blood: The Tuskegee syphilis experiment.* New York: Free Press.

Jones, J. L. (1996). The self as other: Creating the role of Joni the ethnographer for *Broken Circles. Text and Performance Quarterly, 16,* 131–145.

Jones, T. S., & Bodtker, A. (1998). A dialectical analysis of a social justice process: International collaboration in South Africa. *Journal of Applied Communication Research, 26,* 357–373.

Jones, W. H., Kugler, K., & Adams, P. (1995). You always hurt the one you love: Guilt and transgressions against relationship partners. In J. P. Tangney & K. W. Fischer (Eds.), *Self-conscious emotions: The psychology of shame, guilt, embarrassment, and pride* (pp. 301–321). New York: Guilford Press.

Jones, W. H., & Lang, J. R. (1980). Sample composition bias and response bias in mail survey: A comparison of inducement methods. *Journal of Marketing Research, 17,* 69–76.

Jones, W. H., & Linda, G. (1978). Multiple criteria effects in a mail survey experiment. *Journal of Marketing Research, 15,* 280–284.

Jordan, J. M. (1994). Plan monitoring in conversations: An exploration of on-line cognitive activity. *Communication Studies, 45,* 159–173.

Jordan, J. M. (1998). Executive cognitive control in communication: Extending plan-based theory. *Human Communication Research, 25,* 5–38.

Jorgensen, D. L. (1989). *Participant observation: A methodology for human sciences.* Newbury Park, CA: Sage.

Jorgensen-Earp, C. R., & Lanzilotti, L. A. (1998). Public memory and private grief: The construction of shrines at the sites of public tragedy. *Quarterly Journal of Speech, 84,* 150–170.

Jourard, S. M. (1971). *The transparent self.* New York: Van Nostrand Reinhold.

Judge to researchers: Treat rats humanely. (1992, January 9). *Chicago Tribune,* Sect. 1, p. 12.

Judis, J. B. (1995). Hearts of darkness. In S. Fraser (Ed.), *The bell curve wars: Race, intelligence, and the future of America* (pp. 124–129). New York: Basic Books.

Jung, J. (1969). Current practices and problems in the use of college students for psychological research. *Canadian Psychologist, 10,* 280–290.

Jurma, W. E. (1982). Moderate movement leadership and the Vietnam memorial committee. *Quarterly Journal of Speech, 68,* 262–272.

Kahneman, D., & Tversky, S. (1972). Subjective probability: A judgment of representativeness. *Cognitive Psychology, 3,* 430–454.

Kahneman, D., & Tversky, S. (1973). On the psychology of prediction. *Psychological Review, 80,* 237–251.

Kahneman, D., & Tversky, A. (1982). On the study of statistical intuitions. *Cognition, 11,* 237–251.

Kaid, L. L., & Wadsworth, A. J. (1989). Content analysis. In P. Emmert & L. L. Barker (Eds.), *Measurement of communication behavior* (pp. 197–217). White Plains, NY: Longman.

Kalbfleisch, P. J., & Bach, B. W. (1998). The language of mentoring in a health care environment. *Health Communication, 10,* 373–392.

Kalbleisch, P. J., & Davies, A. (1993). An interpersonal model for participation in mentoring relationships. *Western Journal of Communication, 57,* 399–415.

Kampmeier, R. H. (1972). The Tuskegee study of untreated syphilis. *Southern Medical Journal, 65,* 1247–1251.

Kaplan, A. (1964). *The conduct of inquiry.* New York: Harper & Row.

Kapoor, S., Kang, J. G., Kim, W. Y., & Kim, K. (1994). Televised violence and viewers' perceptions of social reality: The Korean case. *Communication Research Reports, 11,* 189–200.

Kapoor, S., Wolfe, A., & Blue, J. (1995). Universal values structures and individualism-collectivism: A U.S. test. *Communication Research Reports, 12,* 112–123.

Karan, V., Kerr, D. S., Murthy, U. S., & Vinze, A. S. (1996). Information technology support for collaborative decision making in auditing: An experimental investigation. *Decision Support Systems, 16,* 181–194.

Karp, D. A. (1986). "You can take the boy out of Dorchester, but you can't take Dorchester out of the boy": Toward a psychology of social mobility. *Symbolic Interaction, 9,* 19–36.

Kashigan, S. K. (1986). *Statistical analysis: An interdisciplinary introduction to univariate and multivariate methods.* New York: Radius Press.

Katriel, T. (1997). *Performing the past: A study of Israeli settlement museums.* Mahwah, NJ: Lawrence Erlbaum.

Katriel, T., & Shenhar, A. (1990). Tower and stockade: Dialogic narration in Israeli settlement ethos. *Quarterly Journal of Speech, 76,* 359–380.

Katz, J. E. (1994). Empirical and theoretical dimensions of obscene phone calls to women in the United States. *Human Communication Research, 21,* 155–182.

Kaufmann, B. J. (1992). Feminist facts: Interview strategies and political subjects in ethnography. *Communication Theory, 2,* 187–206.

Kazoleas, D. C. (1993). A comparison of the persuasive effectiveness of qualitative versus quantitative evidence: A test of explanatory hypotheses. *Communication Quarterly, 41,* 40–50.

Kellerman, K., & Shea, B. C. (1996). Threats, suggestions, hints, and promises: Gaining compliance efficiently and politely. *Communication Quarterly, 44,* 145–165.

Kelly, C. W., Chase, L. J., & Tucker, R. K. (1979). Replication in experimental communication research: An analysis. *Human Communication Research, 5,* 338–342.

Kelly, H. H. (1950). The warm-cold variable in first impressions of persons. *Journal of Personality, 18,* 431–439.

Kelly, H. H. (1967). Attribution theory in social psychology. *Nebraska Symposium on Motivation, 15,* 192–238.

Kelly, J. W. (1985). Storytelling in high tech organizations: A medium for sharing culture. *Journal of Applied Communication Research, 13,* 45–58.

Kelman, H. C. (1967). Humane use of human subjects: The problem of deception in social psychological experiments. *Psychological Bulletin, 67,* 1–11.

Kelso, J. A. (1980). Science and the rhetoric of reality. *Central States Speech Journal, 31,* 17–29.

Kemper, S. (1992). Adults' sentence fragments: Who, what, when, where, and why. *Communication Research, 19,* 444–458.

Kennedy, C. W., & Camden, C. T. (1983). A new look at interruptions. *Western Journal of Speech Communication, 47,* 45–58.

Kennedy, J. A., & Benoit, W. L. (1997). The Newt Gingrich book deal controversy: Self-defense rhetoric. *Southern Communication Journal, 62,* 197–216.

Kennedy, J. W. (1952). An evaluation of extra-sensory perception. *Proceedings of the American Philosophical Society, 96,* 513–518.

Kerlinger, F. N. (1973). *Foundations of behavioral research* (2nd ed.). New York: Holt, Rinehart and Winston.

Kerlinger, F. N. (1986). *Foundations of behavioral research* (3rd ed.). New York: Holt, Rinehart and Winston.

Ketrow, S. M. (1991). Nonverbal communication and client satisfaction in computer-assisted transactions. *Management Communication Quarterly, 5,* 192–219.

Keyton, J. (1996). Sexual harassment: A multidisciplinary synthesis and critique. In B. R. Burleson (Ed.), *Communication yearbook 19* (pp. 93–155). Thousand Oaks, CA: Sage.

Kidder, L. H. (1981). *Selltiz, Wrightsman and Cook's research methods in social relations* (4th ed.). New York: Holt, Rinehart and Winston.

Kiesler, S., & Sproull, L. S. (1986). Response effects in the electronic survey. *Public Opinion Quarterly, 50,* 402–413.

Killingsworth, M. J., & Palmer, J. S. (1992a). *Ecospeak: Rhetoric and environmental politics.* Carbondale: Southern Illinois University Press.

Killingsworth, M. J., & Palmer, J. S. (1992b). How to save the world: The greening of instrumental discourse. *Written Communication, 9,* 385–403.

Killingsworth, M. J., & Palmer, J. S. (1995). The discourse of "environmental hysteria." *Quarterly Journal of Speech, 81,* 1–19.

Kim, K., & Barnett, G. A. (1996). The determinants of international news flow: A network analysis. *Communication Research, 23,* 323–352.

Kim, M., Hunter, J. E. (1993a). Attitude-behavior relations: A meta-analysis of attitudinal relevance. *Journal of Communication, 43*(1), 101–142.

Kim, M., & Hunter, J. E. (1993b). Relationships among attitudes, behavioral intentions, and behaviors: A meta-analysis of past research, part 2. *Communication Research, 20,* 331–364.

Kim, M-S., Shin, H-C., & Cai, D. (1998). Cultural influences on the preferred forms of requesting and re-requesting. *Communication Monographs, 65,* 47–66.

Kimmel, A. J. (1988). *Ethics and values in applied social research.* Newbury Park, CA: Sage.

Kinsey, A. C., Pomeroy, W. B., Martin, C. E., & Gebhard, P. H. (1953). *Sexual behavior in the human female.* Philadelphia: Saunders.

Kirkwood, W. G. (1992). Narrative and the rhetoric of possibility. *Communication Monographs, 59,* 30–47.

Kish, L. (1970). Statistical problems in research design. In D. E. Morrison & R. E. Henkel (Eds.), *The significance test controversy: A reader* (pp. 127–141). Hawthorne, NY: Aldine.

Kish, L., & Slater, C. W. (1960). Two studies of interviewer variance of socio-psychological variables. *Proceedings of the American Statistical Association, Social Science Section* (pp. 66–70). New York: American Statistical Association.

Kiss your browser goodbye: The radical future of media beyond the Web. (1997, March). *Wired,* pp. 1, 12–23.

Knapp, M. L., & Comadena, M. E. (1979). Telling it like it isn't: A review of theory and research on deceptive communication. *Human Communication Research, 5,* 270–285.

Knapp, M. L., & Daly, J. A. (1993). *A guide to publishing in scholarly communication journals.* Austin, TX: International Communication Association.

Knapp, M. L., Hart, R. P., & Dennis, H. (1974). An exploration of deception as a communication construct. *Human Communication Research, 1,* 15–29.

Knapp, M. L., Hart, R. P., Friedrich, G. W., & Shulman, G. M. (1973). The rhetoric of goodbye: Verbal and nonverbal correlates of human leave-taking. *Speech Monographs, 40,* 182–198.

Koch, N. (1992, April 19). She lives! She dies! Let the audience decide. *The New York Times,* Sect. H, pp. 11, 18.

Koch, S., & Deetz, S. (1981). Metaphor analysis of social reality in organizations. *Journal of Applied Communication Research, 9,* 1–15.

Kohn, A. (1990). *You know what they say: The truth about popular beliefs.* New York: HarperCollins.

Komter, M. L. (1998). *Dilemmas in the courtroom: A study of violent crime in the Netherlands.* Mahwah, NJ: Lawrence Erlbaum.

Koolstra, C. M., & van der Voort, T. H. A. (1996). Longitudinal effects of television on children's leisure-time reading: A test of three explanatory models. *Human Communication Research, 23,* 4–35.

Kopfman, J. E., & Smith, S. W. (1996). Understanding the audiences of a health communication campaign: A discriminant analysis of potential organ donors based on intent to donate. *Journal of Applied Communication Research, 24,* 33–49.

Kopfman, J. E., Smith, S. W., Ah Yun, J. K., & Hodges, A. (1998). Affective and cognitive reactions to narrative versus statistical evidence organ donation messages. *Journal of Applied Communication Research, 26,* 279–300.

Kramer, M. W. (1989). Communication during intraorganizational job transfers. *Management Communication Quarterly, 3,* 213–248.

Kramer, M. W. (1995). A longitudinal study of superior-subordinate communication during job transfers. *Human Communication Research, 22,* 39–64.

Krcmar, M. (1996). Family communication patterns, discourse behavior, and child television viewing. *Human Communication Research, 23,* 251–277.

Kreps, G. L. (1986). *Organizational communication.* White Plains, NY: Longman.

Kreps, G. L. (Ed.). (1993). *Sexual harassment: Communicative implications.* Cresskill, NJ: Hampton Press.

Kreps, G. L. (1994). Gender differences in the critical incidents reported by elderly health care residents: A narrative analysis. In H. Sterk & L. Turner (Eds.), *Differences that make a difference: Examining the assumptions of research in communication, language, and gender* (pp. 27–34). Westport, CT: Bergin and Garvey.

Kreps, G. L. (1995). Using focus group discussions to promote organizational reflexivity: Two applied communication field studies. In L. R. Frey (Ed.), *Innovations in group facilitation: Applications in natural settings* (pp. 177–199). Cresskill, NJ: Hampton Press.

Kreps, G. L., Frey, L. R., & O'Hair, D. (1991). Applied communication research: Scholarship that can make a difference. *Journal of Applied Communication Research, 19,* 71–87.

Kreps, G. L., & Lederman, L. C. (1985). Using the case study method in organizational communication education: Developing students' insight, knowledge, and creativity through experience-based learning and systematic debriefing. *Communication Education, 34,* 358–364.

Krippendorf, K. (1980). *Content analysis: An introduction to its methodology.* Newbury Park, CA: Sage.

Krivonos, P. D., & Knapp, M. L. (1975). Initiating communication: What do you say when you say hello? *Central States Speech Journal, 26,* 115–125.

Krizek, R. L., Hecht, M. L., & Miller, M. (1993). Language as an indicator of risk in the prevention of drug use. *Journal of Applied Communication Research, 21,* 245–262.

Krosnick, J. A., & Berent, M. K. (1993). Comparisons of party identification and policy preferences: The impact of survey question format. *American Journal of Political Science, 37,* 941–964.

Krueger, R. A. (1994). *Focus groups: A practical guide for applied research* (2nd ed.). Newbury Park, CA: Sage.

Kubey, R., Larson, R., & Csikszentmihalyi, M. (1996). Experience sampling method applications to communication research questions. *Journal of Communication, 46*(2), 99–120.

Kuhn, T. S. (1970). *The structure of scientific revolutions.* Chicago: University of Chicago Press.

Kuiper, K. (1996). *Smooth talkers: The linguistic performance of auctioneers and sportscasters.* Mahwah, NJ: Lawrence Erlbaum.

Kunin, T. (1955). The construction of a new type of attitude measure. *Personnel Psychology, 8,* 65–78.

Kunkel, D., & Gantz, W. (1992). Children's television advertising in the multichannel environment. *Journal of Communication, 42*(3), 134–152.

Kuypers, J. A., Young, M. J., & Launer, M. K. (1994). Of mighty mice and meek men: Contextual reconstruction of the Iranian airbus shootdown. *Southern Communication Journal, 59,* 294–306.

Kvale, S. (1996). *InterViews: An introduction to qualitative research interviewing.* Thousand Oaks, CA: Sage.

Labov, W., & Fanshel, D. (1977). *Therapeutic discourse: Psychotherapy as conversation.* New York: Free Press.

Lacy, S., Fico, F., & Simon, T. F. (1991). Fairness and balance in the prestige press. *Journalism Quarterly, 12,* 46–57.

Ladd, E. C. (1994, July/August). The Holocaust poll error. *Public Perspective,* pp. 3–5.

LaFollette, M. C. (1992). *Stealing into print: Fraud, plagiarism, and misconduct in scientific publishing.* Berkeley: University of California Press.

Lamal, P. A. (1991). On the importance of replication. In J. W. Neuliep (Ed.), *Replication research in the social sciences* (pp. 31–35). Newbury Park, CA: Sage.

Landis, M. H., & Burtt, H. E. (1924). A study of conversations. *Journal of Comparative and Physiological Psychology, 4,* 81–89.

Lang, A., Geiger, S., Strickwerda, M., & Sumner, J. (1993). The effects of related and unrelated cuts on television viewers' attention, processing, capacity, and memory. *Communication Research, 20,* 4–29.

Lang, A., Newhagen, J., & Reeves, B. (1996). Negative video as structure: Emotion, attention, capacity, and memory. *Journal of Broadcasting & Electronic Media, 40,* 460–477.

Lange, J. I. (1993). The logic of competing information campaigns: Conflict over old growth and the spotted owl. *Communication Monographs, 60,* 239–257.

Larson, L. H., & Bell, N. J. (1988). Need for privacy and its effect upon interpersonal attraction and interaction. *Journal of Social and Clinical Psychology, 6,* 1–10.

Larson, M. S. (1991). Health-related messages embedded in prime-time television entertainment. *Health Communication, 3,* 175–184.

Larson, S. G. (1991). Television's mixed messages: Sexual content on *All My Children. Communication Quarterly, 39,* 156–163.

Larzelere, R. E., & Houston, T. L. (1980). The Dyadic Trust Scale: Toward understanding interpersonal trust in close relationships. *Journal of Marriage and the Family, 42,* 595–604.

Laslo, J. P., & Rosenthal, R. (1971). Subject dogmatism, experimenter status, and experimenter expectancy effects. *Personality, 1,* 11–23.

Latham, A. J. (1997). Performance, ethnography, and history: An analysis of displays by female bathers in the 1920s. *Text and Performance Quarterly, 17,* 170–181.

Lauden, L. (1997). *Danger ahead: The risks you really face on life's highway.* New York: John Wiley & Sons.

Laumann, E., Michael, R., Gagnon, J., & Michaels, S. (1994). *The social organization of sexuality: Sexual practices in the United States.* Chicago: University of Chicago Press.

Lee, B. S. (1988). Holocaust survivors and internal struggles. *Journal of Humanistic Psychology, 28,* 67–96.

Lee, R. E. (1991). The rhetorical construction of time in Martin Luther King, Jr.'s "Letter from Birmingham Jail." *Southern Communication Journal, 56,* 279–288.

Lee, R. E. (1995a). Electoral politics and visions of community: Jimmy Carter, virtue, and the small town myth. *Western Journal of Communication, 59,* 39–60.

Lee, R. (1995b). Humility and the political servant: Jimmy Carter's post-presidential rhetoric of virtue and power. *Southern Communication Journal, 60,* 120–130.

Leeds-Hurwitz, W., & Sigman, S. J. (1996). Editor's preface. In C. M. K. Lum, *In search of a voice: Karoke and the construction of identity in Chinese America* (pp. ix–x). Mahwah, NJ: Lawrence Erlbaum.

Leeman, R. W. (1995). Spatial metaphors in African-American discourse. *Southern Communication Journal, 60,* 165–180.

Lees, D., & Berkowitz, S. (1981). *The movie business.* New York: Vintage Books.

Legge, N. J., & Rawlins, W. K. (1992). Managing disputes in young adult friendships: Modes of convenience, cooperation, and commitment. *Western Journal of Communication, 56,* 226–247.

Leichty, G., & Applegate, J. L. (1991). Social-cognitive and situational influences on the use of face-saving persuasive strategies. *Human Communication Research, 17,* 451–484.

Le Poire, B. A. (1994). Attraction toward and nonverbal stigmatization of gay males and persons with AIDS: Evidence of symbolic over instrumental attitudinal structures. *Human Communication Research, 21,* 241–279.

Le Poire, B. A., Burgoon, J. K., & Parrott, R. (1992). Status and privacy restoring communication in the workplace. *Journal of Applied Communication Research, 20,* 419–436.

Lesch, C. L. (1994). Observing theory in practice: Sustaining consciousness in a coven. In L. R. Frey (Ed.), *Group communication in context: Studies of natural groups* (pp. 57–82). Hillsdale, NJ: Lawrence Erlbaum.

Lessl, T. M. (1985). Science and the sacred cosmos: The ideological rhetoric of Carl Sagan. *Quarterly Journal of Speech, 71,* 175–187.

Lessl, T. M. (1999). The Galileo legend as scientific folklore. *Quarterly Journal of Speech, 85,* 146–168.

Leventhal, H. (1970). Findings and theory in the study of fear communications. In L. Berkowitz (Ed.), *Advances in experimental social psychology* (Vol. 5, pp. 119–186). New York: Academic Press.

Levin, J., & Arluke, A. (1987). *Gossip: The inside scoop.* New York: Plenum Press.

Levine, H. G. (1985). Principles of data storage and retrieval for use in qualitative evaluations. *Educational Evaluation and Policy Analysis, 7,* 169–186.

Levine, R. J. (1986). *Ethics and regulations of clinical research* (2nd ed.). Baltimore, MD: Urban and Schwarzenberg.

Levine, T. R., King, G., III, & Popoola, J. K. (1994). Ethnic and gender differences in opening lines. *Communication Research Reports, 11,* 143–151.

Levine, T. R., & McCornack, S. A. (1991). The dark side of trust: Conceptualizing and measuring types of communicative suspicion. *Communication Quarterly, 39,* 325–340.

Levine, T. R., McCornack, S. A., & Avery, P. B. (1992). Sex differences in emotional reactions to discovered deception. *Communication Quarterly, 40,* 289–296.

Levine, T. R., & Wheeless, L. R. (1990). Cross-situational consistency and use/nonuse tendencies in compliance-gaining tactic selection. *Southern Communication Journal, 56,* 1–11.

Levy, P. E., & Steelman, L. A. (1996). Using advanced statistics. In F. T. L. Leong & J. T. Austin (Eds.), *The psychology research handbook: A guide for graduate students and research assistants* (pp. 219–228). Thousand Oaks, CA: Sage.

Levy-Leboyer, C. (1988). Success and failure in applying psychology. *American Psychologist, 43,* 779–785.

Lewin, K. (1947). Group decision and social change. In T. M. Newcomb & E. L. Hartley (Eds.), *Readings in social psychology* (pp. 330–344). New York: Holt, Rinehart and Winston.

Lewin, K. (1951). *Field theory in social science: Selected theoretical papers* (D. Cartwright, Ed.). New York: Harper & Row.

Lewin, M. (1979). *Understanding psychological research: The student researcher's handbook.* New York: Wiley.

Lewis, L. K., & Seibold, D. R. (1996). Communication during intraorganizational innovation adoption: Predicting users' behavioral coping responses to innovations in organizations. *Communication Monographs, 63,* 131–157.

Li, X., & Crane, N. B. (1993). *Electronic style: A guide to citing electronic information.* Westport, CT: Meckler.

Liebes, T., & Ribak, R. (1992). The contribution of family culture to political participation, political outlook, and its reproduction. *Communication Research, 19,* 618–641.

Liebes, T., & Ribak, R. (1994). In defense of negotiated readings: How moderates on each side of the conflict interpret Infada news. *Journal of Communication, 44*(2), 108–124.

Likert, R. (1932). A technique for the measurement of attitudes. *Archives of Psychology, 140,* 1–55.

Lim, T-S., & Bowers, J. W. (1991). Face-work: Solidarity, approbation, and tact. *Human Communication Research, 17,* 415–450.

Lin, C. A. (1993). Modeling the gratification-seeking process of television viewing. *Human Communication Research, 20,* 224–244.

Lincoln, Y. S., & Guba, E. G. (1985). *Naturalistic inquiry.* Beverly Hills, CA: Sage.

Lind, R. A. (1997). Ethical sensitivity in viewer evaluations of a TV news investigative report. *Human Communication Research, 23,* 535–561.

Lindholm-Romantschuk, Y. (1998). *Scholarly book reviewing in the social sciences and humanities: The flow of ideas within and among disciplines.* Westport, CT: Greenwood Press.

Lindkvist, K. (1981). Approaches to textual analysis. In K. E. Rosengren (Ed.), *Advances in content analysis* (pp. 23–42). Newbury Park, CA: Sage.

Lindlof, T. R. (1995). *Qualitative communication research methods.* Thousand Oaks, CA: Sage.

Lineham, M., & Nielsen, S. (1981). Assessment of suicide ideation and parasuicide: Hopelessness and social desirability. *Journal of Consulting and Clinical Psychology, 49,* 773–775.

Lipset, S. M., Trow, M. A., & Coleman, J. S. (1970). Statistical problems. In D. E. Morrison & R. E. Henkel (Eds.), *The significance test controversy: A reader* (pp. 81–86). Hawthorne, NY: Aldine.

Lipsey, M. W. (1990). *Design sensitivity: Statistical power for experimental research.* Newbury Park, CA: Sage.

Littlejohn, S. W. (1996). *Theories of human communication* (5th ed.). Belmont, CA: Wadsworth.

Lofland, J. (1971). *Analyzing social settings: A guide to qualitative observation and analysis.* Belmont, CA: Wadsworth.

Lofland, J. (1976). *Doing social life.* New York: Wiley.

Loftus, E. F. (1979). *Eyewitness testimony.* Cambridge, MA: Harvard University Press.

Lombard, T. C. (1999). *Social science research: A cross section of journal articles for discussion* (2nd ed.). Los Angeles: Pyrczak.

Looney, R. (1991). Pollsters fret as Americans learn to say no. *Chicago Tribune,* Sect. 5, p. 1.

Lower Working Phone Rate in Areas. (1997, November). *The Frame,* p. 1.

Lowry, D. T., & Towles, D. E. (1989). Soap opera portrayals of sex, contraception, and sexually transmitted diseases. *Journal of Communication, 39*(2), 76–83.

Lucaites, J. L., & Condit, C. M. (1990). Reconstructing <equality>: Culturetypal and counter-cultural rhetorics in the martyred black vision. *Communication Monographs, 57,* 5–24.

Lum, C. M. K. (1996). *In search of a voice: Karoke and the construction of identity in Chinese America.* Mahwah, NJ: Lawrence Erlbaum.

Lunt, P., & Livingstone, S. (1996). Rethinking the focus group in media and communication research. *Journal of Communication, 46*(2), 79–98.

Lyne, J., & Howe, H. F. (1986). "Punctuated equilibria": Rhetorical dynamics of a scientific controversy. *Quarterly Journal of Speech, 72,* 132–147.

Lyne, J., & Howe, H. F. (1990). The rhetoric of expertise: E. O. Wilson and sociobiology. *Quarterly Journal of Speech, 76,* 134–151.

MacIntyre, P. D. (1994). Variables underlying willingness to communicate: A causal analysis. *Communication Research Reports, 11,* 135–142.

Mackay, A. L. (1977). *The harvest of a quiet eye: A selection of scientific quotations.* London: Institute of Physics.

Madigan, C. M., & Secter, B. (1997, July 4). Second thoughts on free speech. *Chicago Tribune,* Sect. 1, pp. 1, 18.

Mahoney, M. J. (1985). Open exchange and the epistemic process. *American Psychologist, 73,* 753–772.

Maibach, E., Flora, J. A., & Nass, C. (1991). Changes in self-efficacy and health behavior in response to a minimal contact community health campaign. *Health Communication, 3,* 1–15.

Maibach, E. W., Kreps, G. L., & Bonaguro, E. W. (1993). Developing strategic communication campaigns for HIV/AIDS prevention. In S. Ratzan (Ed.), *AIDS: Effective health communication for the 90s* (pp. 15–35). Washington, DC: Taylor and Francis.

Maier, M. H. (1991). *The data game: Controversies in social science statistics.* Armonk, NY: M. E. Sharpe.

Maione, M., & McKee, J. (1987). AIDS: Implications for counselors. *Journal of Humanistic Education and Development, 26,* 120–123.

Makoul, G., & Roloff, M. E. (1998). The role of efficacy and outcome expectations in the decision to withhold relational complaints. *Communication Research, 25,* 5–29.

Mandelbaum, J. (1987). Couples sharing stories. *Communication Quarterly, 35,* 144–170.

Manusov, V. (1995). Reacting to changes in nonverbal behaviors: Relational satisfaction and adaptation patterns in romantic dyads. *Human Communication Research, 21,* 456–477.

Manusov, V., Cody, M. J., Donohue, W. A., & Zappa, J. (1994). Accounts in child custody mediation sessions. *Journal of Applied Communication Research, 22,* 1–15.

Marcus, A. (1991, December 16). Stopping big science's big slide. *Chicago Tribune,* Sect. 1, p. 23.

Marcus, G. E., & Fischer, M. M. J. (1986). *Anthropology as cultural critique: An experimental moment in the human sciences.* Chicago: University of Chicago Press.

Mares, M-L., & Cantor, J. (1992). Elderly viewers' responses to televised portrayals of old age: Empathy and mood management versus social comparison. *Communication Research, 19,* 459–478.

Marin, M. J., Sherblom, J. C., & Shipps, T. B. (1994). Contextual influences on nurses's conflict management strategies. *Western Journal of Speech Communication, 58,* 201–228.

Markel, N., Long, J., & Saine, T. (1976). Sex effects in conversational interaction: Another look at male dominance. *Human Communication Research, 2,* 356–364.

Marshall, A. A., Smith, S. W., & McKeon, J. K. (1995). Persuading low-income women to engage in mammography screening: Source, message, and channel preferences. *Health Communication, 7,* 283–299.

Marshall, A. A., & Stohl, C. (1993). Participating as participation: A network analysis. *Communication Monographs, 60,* 137–157.

Marshall, C., & Rossman, G. B. (1989). *Designing qualitative research.* Newbury Park, CA: Sage.

Martin, J., & Manners, T. (1995). Computer-assisted personal interviewing in survey research. In R. M. Lee (Ed.), *Information technology for the social scientist* (pp. 52–71). London: VCL Press.

Martin, M. M., Anderson, C. M., Burant, P. A., & Weber, K. (1997). Verbal aggression in sibling relationships. *Communication Quarterly, 45,* 304–317.

Martin, M. M., Anderson, C. M., & Hovarth, C. L. (1996). Feelings about aggression: Justifications for sending and hurt from receiving verbally aggressive messages. *Communication Research Reports, 13,* 19–26.

Martindale, C., & McKenzie, D. (1995). On the utility of content analysis in author attribution: *The Federalist. Computers and the Humanities, 29,* 259–270.

Marwell, G., & Schmitt, D. R. (1967). Dimensions of compliance-gaining behavior: An empirical analysis. *Sociometry, 30,* 350–364.

Mascheter, C., & Harris, L. M. (1986). From divorce to friendship: A study of dialectic relationship development. *Journal of Social and Personal Relationships, 3,* 177–189.

Massey, A. P., & Clapper, D. L. (1995). Element finding: The impact of a group support system on a crucial phase of sense making. *Journal of Management Information Systems, 11,* 149–176.

Matlon, R. J. (Ed.), & Ortiz, S. P. (Assoc. Ed.). (1997). *Index to journals in communication studies through 1995.* Annandale, VA: National Communication Association.

Mauro, R. (1992). *Statistical deception at work.* Hillsdale, NJ: Lawrence Erlbaum.

Mayer, M. E. (1998). Behaviors leading to more effective decisions in small groups embedded in organizations. *Communication Reports, 11,* 123–132.

McCarthy, P. (1989). Psuedoteachers. *Omni, 11*(10), 74.

McClearey, K. E. (1994). "A tremendous awakening": Margaret H. Sanger's speech at Fabian Hall. *Western Journal of Communication, 58,* 182–200.

McComb, M. (1995). Becoming a travelers aid volunteer: Communication in socialization and training. *Communication Studies, 46,* 297–316.

McCormick, J., & Press, A. (1997, June 16). Pomp and promises. *Newsweek,* pp. 44–46.

McCornack, S. A. (1992). Information manipulation theory. *Communication Monographs, 59,* 1–16.

McCornack, S. A., Levine, T. R., Morrison, K., & Lapinski, M. (1996). Speaking of information manipulation: A critical rejoinder. *Communication Monographs, 63,* 83–92.

McCornack, S. A., Levine, T. R., Solowczuk, K. A., Torres, H. I., & Campbell, D. M. (1992). When the alteration of information is viewed as deception: An empirical test of information manipulation theory. *Communication Monographs, 59,* 17–29.

McCornack, S. A., & Parks, M. R. (1990). What women know that men don't: Sex differences in determining the truth behind deceptive messages. *Journal of Social and Personal Relationships, 7,* 107–118.

McCracken, G. (1988). *The long interview.* Newbury Park, CA: Sage.

McCroskey, J. C. (1977). Oral communication apprehension: A summary of recent theory and research. *Human Communication Research, 4,* 78–96.

McCroskey, J. C. (1992). Reliability and validity of the willingness to communicate scale. *Communication Quarterly, 40,* 16–25.

McCroskey, J. C., Andersen, J. F., Richmond, V. P., & Wheeless, L. R. (1981). Communication apprehension of elementary and secondary students and teachers. *Communication Education, 30,* 122–132.

McCroskey, J. C., & Richmond, V. P. (1987). Willingness to communicate. In J. C. McCroskey & J. A. Daly (Eds.), *Personality and interpersonal communication* (pp. 129–156). Newbury Park, CA: Sage.

McCroskey, J. C., & Richmond, V. P. (1989). Bipolar scales. In P. Emmert & L. L. Barker (Eds.), *Measurement of communication behavior* (pp. 154–167). New York: Longman.

McCroskey, J. C., & Richmond, V. P. (1990). Willingness to communicate: A cognitive view. *Journal of Social Behavior and Personality, 5*(2), 19–37.

McCroskey, J. C., & Richmond, V. P. (1993). Identifying compulsive communicators: The talkaholic scale. *Communication Research Reports, 10,* 107–114.

McCroskey, J. C., & Richmond, V. P. (1995). Correlates of compulsive communication: Quantitative and qualitative characteristics. *Communication Quarterly, 43,* 39–52.

McCroskey, J. C., & Richmond, V. P. (1998). Willingness to communicate. In J. C. McCroskey, J. A. Daly, M. M. Martin, & M. J. Beatty (Eds.), *Communication and personality: Trait perspectives* (pp. 119–131). Cresskill, NJ: Hampton Press.

McCroskey, J. C., Richmond, V. P., Sallinen, A., Fayer, J. M., & Barraclough, R. A. (1995). A cross-cultural and multi-behavioral analysis of the relationship between nonverbal immediacy and teacher evaluation. *Communication Education, 44,* 281–291.

McCroskey, J. C., Sallinen, A., Fayer, J. M., Richmond, V. P., & Barraclough, J. C. (1996). Nonverbal immediacy and cognitive learning: A cross-cultural investigation. *Communication Education, 45,* 200–211.

McDiarmid, J. (1937). Presidential inaugural addresses: A study in verbal symbols. *Public Opinion Quarterly, 1,* 79–82.

McGuire, M., Stilborne, L., McAdams, M., & Hyatt, L. (1997). *The Internet handbook for writers, researchers, and journalist.* New York: Guilford Press.

McHenry, L., & Bozik, M. (1995). Communicating at a distance: A study of interaction in a distance education classroom. *Communication Education, 44,* 362–371.

McIntyre, B. T. (1995). VCR use in Hong Kong. *Communication Research Reports, 12,* 61–70.

McLaughlin, M. L. (1984). *Conversation: How talk is organized.* Newbury Park, CA: Sage.

McLaughlin, M. L., & Cody, M. J. (1982). Awkward silences: Behavioral antecedents and consequences of the conversational lapse. *Human Communication Research, 8,* 299–316.

McLaughlin, M. L., Cody, M. J., Kane, M. L., & Robey, C. S. (1981). Sex differences in story receipt and story sequencing behaviors in dyadic conversations. *Human Communication Research, 7,* 99–116.

McLaughlin, M. L., Cody, M. J., & O'Hair, H. D. (1983). The management of failure events: Some contextual determinants of accounting behavior. *Human Communication Research, 9,* 220–224.

McLaughlin, M. L., Cody, M. J., & Robey, C. S. (1980). Situational influences on the selection of strategies to resist compliance-gaining attempts. *Human Communication Research, 7,* 14–36.

McLaughlin, M. L., Cody, M. J., & Rosenstein, N. E. (1983). Account sequences in conversations between strangers. *Communication Monographs, 50,* 102–125.

McLeod, J. M., Daily, K., Guo, Z., Eveland, W. P., Jr., Bayer, J., Yang, S., & Wang, H. (1996). Community integration, local media use, and democratic processes. *Communication Research, 23,* 179–209.

McMahan, E. M., & Rogers, K. L. (Eds.). (1994a). *Interactive oral history interviewing.* Hillsdale, NJ: Lawrence Erlbaum.

McMahan, E. M., & Rogers, K. L. (1994b). Preface. In E. M. McMahan & K. L. Rogers (Eds.), *Interactive oral history interviewing* (pp. vii–ix). Hillsdale, NJ: Lawrence Erlbaum.

McMillan, J. J., & Northern, N. A. (1995). Organizational codependency: The creation and maintenance of closed systems. *Management Communication Quarterly, 9,* 6–45.

McNemar, Q. (1960). Opinion-attitude methodology. *Psychological Bulletin, 53,* 289–374.

McOmber, J. B. (1996). Silencing the patient: Freud, sexual abuse, and "the etiology of hysteria." *Quarterly Journal of Speech, 82,* 343–363.

McPhee, R. D., & Corman, S. R. (1995). An activity-based theory of communication networks in organizations, applied to the case of a local church. *Communication Monographs, 62,* 132–151.

McQuarrie, E. F. (1996). *The market research toolbox: A concise guide for beginners.* Thousand Oaks, CA: Sage.

McQuillen, J. S. (1986). The development of listener-adapted compliance-resisting strategies. *Human Communication Research, 12,* 354–375.

Mechling, E. W., & Mechling, J. (1994). The Jung and the restless: The mythopoetic men's movement. *Southern Communication Journal, 59,* 97–111.

Medhurst, M. J. (1994). Reconceptualizing rhetorical history: Eisenhower's farewell address. *Quarterly Journal of Speech, 80,* 195–218.

Menzel, K. E., & Carrell, L. J. (1994). The relationship between preparation and performance in public speaking. *Communication Education, 43,* 17–26.

Merskin, D. L., & Huberlie, M. (1995). A content analysis of faculty position announcements. *Journalism & Mass Communication Educator, 50,* 79–85.

Metts, S. (1989). An exploratory investigation of deception in close relationships. *Journal of Social and Personal Relationships, 6,* 159–180.

Metts, S. (1991). *Instructor's manual* to accompany *Investigating communication: An introduction to research methods* (1st ed.). Englewood Cliffs, NJ: Prentice Hall.

Metts, S., & Cupach, W. R. (1986). Accounts of relational dissolution: A comparison of marital and non-marital relationships. *Communication Monographs, 53,* 311–334.

Metts, S., Cupach, W. R., & Imahori, T. T. (1992). Perceptions of sexual compliance-resisting messages in three types of cross-sex relationships. *Western Journal of Communication, 56,* 1–17.

Metts, S., & Spitzberg, B. H. (1996). Sexual communication in interpersonal contexts: A script-based approach. In B. R. Burleson (Ed.), *Communication yearbook 19* (pp. 49–91). Thousand Oaks, CA: Sage.

Meyer, J. C. (1995). Tell me a story: Eliciting organizational values from narratives. *Communication Quarterly, 43,* 210–224.

Meyer, J. R. (1994a). Effect of situational features on the likelihood of addressing face needs in requests. *Southern Communication Journal, 59,* 240–254.

Meyer, J. R. (1994b). Formulating plans for requests: An investigation of retrieval processes. *Communication Studies, 45,* 131–144.

Meyer, M. (with Bede-Fabbamila, B. O.). (1997). Ifa and me: A divination of ethnography. *Text and Performance Quarterly, 17,* 33–57.

Meyers, R. A., & Brashers, D. E. (1998). Argument in group decision making: Explicating a process model and investigating the argument-outcome link. *Communication Monographs, 65,* 261–281.

Meyers, R. A., Seibold, D. R., & Brashers, D. (1991). Argument in initial group decision-making discussions: Refinement of a coding scheme and a descriptive quantitative analysis. *Western Journal of Speech Communication, 55,* 47–68.

Meyers, S. A., & Avtgis, T. A. (1997). The association of socio-communicative style and relational type on perceptions of nonverbal immediacy. *Communication Research Reports, 14,* 339–349.

Miall, C. E. (1986). The stigma of involuntary childlessness. *Social Problems, 33,* 268–279.

Mienczakowski, J. (1996). An ethnographic act: The construction of consensual theatre. In C. Ellis & A. P. Bochner (Eds.), *Composing ethnography: Alternative forms of qualitative writing* (pp. 244–264). Walnut Creek, CA: Altamira Press.

Miles, E. W., & Leathers, D. G. (1984). The impact of aesthetic and professionally-related objects on credibility in the office setting. *Southern Speech Communication Journal, 49,* 361–379.

Miles, M. B., & Huberman, A. M. (1994). *Qualitative data analysis: An expanded sourcebook* (2nd ed.). Thousand Oaks, CA: Sage.

Milgram, S. (1963). Behavioral study of obedience. *Journal of Abnormal and Social Psychology, 67,* 371–378.

Milinki, A. K. (1999). *Cases in qualitative research: A casebook with questions for discussion.* Los Angeles: Pyrczak.

Millar, F. E., Rogers, L. E., & Bavelas, J. B. (1984). Identifying patterns of verbal conflict in interpersonal dynamics. *Western Journal of Speech Communication, 48,* 231–246.

Miller, D. C. (1991). *Handbook of research design and social measurement* (5th ed.). Newbury Park, CA: Sage.

Miller, G. R. (1995). "I think my schizophrenia is better today," said the communication researcher unanimously: Some thoughts on the dysfunctional dichotomy between pure and applied communication research. In K. N. Cissna (Ed.), *Applied communication in the 21st century* (pp. 47–55). Mahwah, NJ: Lawrence Erlbaum.

Miller, G. R., & Boster, F. J. (1989). Data analysis in communication research. In P. Emmert & L. L. Barker (Eds.), *Measurement of communication behavior* (pp. 18–39). White Plains, NY: Longman.

Miller, K., Birkholt, M., Scott, C., & Stage, C. (1995). Empathy and burnout in human service work: An extension of a communication model. *Communication Research, 22,* 123–147.

Miller, K., Scott, C. R., Stage, C., & Birkholt, M. (1995). Communication and coordination in an interorganizational system: Service provision for the urban homeless. *Communication Research, 22,* 679–699.

Miller, K. I., Stiff, J. B., & Ellis, B. H. (1988). Communication and empathy as precursors to burnout among human service workers. *Communication Monographs, 55,* 250–265.

Miller, M. (1995). An intergenerational case study of suicidal tradition and mother-daughter communication. *Journal of Applied Communication Research, 23,* 247–270.

Miller, S. (1997). The woven gender: Made for a woman, but stronger for a man. *Southern Communication Journal, 62,* 217–228.

Mitchell, R. G., Jr. (1993). *Secrecy and fieldwork.* Newbury Park, CA: Sage.

Mitofsky, W. J. (1998). The polls—a review: Was 1996 a worse year for polls than 1948? *Public Opinion Quarterly, 62,* 230–249.

Mohr, L. B. (1990). *Understanding significance testing.* Newbury Park, CA: Sage.

Mokros, H. B., & Deetz, S. (1996). What counts as real?: A constitutive view of communication and the disenfranchised in the context of health. In E. B. Ray (Ed.), *Communication and disenfranchisement: Social health issues and implications* (pp. 29–44). Mahwah, NJ: Lawrence Erlbaum.

Molitor, F. (1993). Accuracy in science news reporting by newspapers: The case of aspirin for the prevention of heart attacks. *Health Communication, 5,* 209–224.

Monahan, J. L. (1995). Information processing differences of conversational partners and observers: The effects of self-presentation concerns and cognitive load. *Communication Monographs, 62,* 265–281.

Mongeau, P. A. (1998). Another look at fear-arousing persuasive appeals. In M. Allen & R. W. Preiss (Eds.), *Persuasion: Advances through meta-analysis* (pp. 53–68). Cresskill, NJ: Hampton Press.

Mongeau, P. A., & Carey, C. M. (1996). Who's wooing whom II? An experimental investigation of date-initiation and expectancy violation. *Western Journal of Communication, 60,* 195–213.

Mongeau, P. A., Hale, J. L., & Alles, M. (1994). An experimental investigation of accounts and attributions following sexual infidelity. *Communication Monographs, 61,* 326–344.

Moon, Y., & Nass, C. (1996). How "real" are computer personalities? Psychological responses to personality types in human-computer interaction. *Communication Research, 23,* 651–674.

Mooney, H. W. (1962). *Methodology in two California health surveys* (Public Health Monograph No. 70). Washington, DC: Government Printing Office.

Moore, A., Masterson, J. T., Christophel, D. M., & Shear, K. A. (1996). College teacher immediacy and student ratings of instruction. *Communication Education, 45,* 29–39.

Moore, C. M. (1987). *Group techniques for idea building.* Newbury Park, CA: Sage.

Moore, H. T. (1922). Further data concerning sex differences. *Journal of Abnormal Social Psychology, 17,* 210–214.

Moore, M. P. (1996). From a government of the people, to a people of the government: Irony as rhetorical strategy in presidential campaigns. *Quarterly Journal of Speech, 82,* 22–37.

Moore, M. P. (1997). Rhetorical subterfugre and "The principle of perfection," part II: Bob Packwood's Senate resignation. *Southern Communication Journal, 63,* 37–55.

Morgan, D. L. (1993). (Ed.). *Successful focus groups: Advancing the state of the art.* Newbury Park, CA: Sage.

Morgan, D. L. (1997). *Focus groups as qualitative research* (2nd ed.). Thousand Oaks, CA: Sage.

Morgan, D. L., & Kruger, R. A. (Eds.). (1997). *The focus group kit* (6 vols.). Thousand Oaks, CA: Sage.

Morgan, M., & Shanahan, J. (1997). Two decades of cultivation research: An appraisal and meta-analysis. In B. R. Burleson (Ed.), *Communication yearbook 20* (pp. 1–45). Thousand Oaks, CA: Sage.

Morin, R. (Guest). (1999, January 17). *Washington Journal.* Washington, DC: C-Span.

Morse, J. M. (1998). The contracted relationship: Ensuring protection of anonymity and confidentiality. *Qualitative Health Research, 8,* 301–303.

Motley, M. T., & Reeder, H. M. (1995). Unwanted escalation of sexual intimacy: Male and female perceptions of connotations and relational consequences of resistance messages. *Communication Monographs, 62,* 355–382.

Motley, M. T., & Smith, N. L. (1989). Effects of temperament upon hiring decisions: A preliminary examination of global personality traits and communicator compatibility. *Communication Reports, 2,* 22–29.

Muhr, T. (1991). ATLAS/ti: A prototype for the support of text interpretation. *Qualitative Sociology, 14,* 349–371.

Mullin, C., Imrich, D. J., & Linz, D. (1996). The impact of acquaintance rape stories and case-specific pre-trial publicity on juror decision making. *Communication Research, 23,* 100–135.

Murphy, J. M. (1994). Republicanism in the modern age: Adlai Stevenson in the 1952 presidential campaign. *Quarterly Journal of Speech, 80,* 313–328.

Murphy, J. T. (1980). *Getting the facts: The fieldwork guide for evaluators and policy analysts.* Santa Monica, CA: Goodyear.

Nadesan, M. H., & Sotirin, P. (1998). The romance and science of "breast is best": Discursive considerations and contexts of breast-feeding choices. *Text and Performance Quarterly, 18,* 217–232.

Neikirk, W., & James, F. (1997, May 17). An apology for a "moral wrong." *Chicago Tribune,* Sect. 1, pp. 1, 18.

Nelson, E. J. (1991). "Nothing ever goes well enough": Mussolini and the rhetoric of perpetual struggle. *Communication Studies, 42,* 22–42.

Neuliep, J. W., & Crandall, R. (1991). Editorial bias against replication research. In J. W. Neuliep (Ed.), *Replication research in the social sciences* (pp. 85–90). Newbury Park, CA: Sage.

Newhagen, J. E. (1994). Self-efficacy and call-in political television show use. *Communication Research, 21,* 366–379.

Newhagen, J. E., Cordes, J. W., & Levy, M. R. (1995). Nightly@nbc.com: Audience scope and the perception of interactivity in viewer mail on the Internet. *Journal of Communication, 45*(3), 164–175.

Newhagen, J. E., & Reeves, B. (1992). The evening's bad news: Effects of compelling negative television news images on memory. *Journal of Communication, 42*(2), 25–41.

Nicotera, A. M. (1993). Beyond two dimensions: A grounded theory model of conflict-handling behavior. *Management Communication Quarterly, 6,* 282–306.

Nicotera, A. M. (1996). An assessment of the argumentativeness scale for social desirability bias. *Communication Reports, 9,* 23–35.

Nicotera, A. M., & Rancer, A. S. (1994). The influence of sex and self-perceptions and social stereotyping of aggressive communication predispositions. *Western Journal of Communication, 58,* 283–307.

Nicotera, A. M., Smilowitz, M. S., & Pearson, J. C. (1990). Ambiguity tolerance, conflict management style and argumentativeness as predictors of innovativeness. *Communication Research Reports, 7,* 125–131.

Nisbett, R. E., & Ross, L. (1980). *Human inference: Strategies and shortcomings of social judgment.* Englewood Cliff, NJ: Prentice-Hall.

Nofsinger, R. E. (1975). The demand ticket: A conversational device for getting the floor. *Speech Monographs, 42,* 1–9.

Norusis, M. N. (1991). *SPSS/PC+ studentware plus.* Chicago: Statistical Package for the Social Sciences.

Norusis, M. N. (1993). *SPSS for Windows system users guide release 6.0.* Chicago: Statistical Package for the Social Sciences.

Notz, W., Staw, B. M., & Cook, T. S. (1971). Attitude toward troop withdrawal from Indochina as a function of draft number: Dissonance or self-interest? *Journal of Personality and Social Psychology, 20,* 118–126.

Novek, E. M. (1995). West Urbania: An ethnographic study of communication practices in inner-city youth culture. *Communication Studies, 46,* 169–186.

Nunnally, J. C. (1978). *Psychometric theory* (2nd ed.). New York: McGraw-Hill.

Nussbaum, J. F., Hummert, M. L., Williams, A., & Harwood, J. (1996). Communication and older adults. In B. R. Burleson (Ed.), *Communication yearbook 19* (pp. 1–47). Thousand Oaks, CA: Sage.

Objections to astrology. (1975). *The Humanist, 35,* 4–6.

Oetzel, J. G. (1998). Explaining individual communication processes in homogeneous and heterogeneous groups through individualism-collectivism and self-construal. *Human Communication Research, 25,* 202–224.

Official inhumanity. (1972, July 27). *Los Angeles Times,* Sect. II, p. 6.

O'Hair, H. D., & Cody, M. J. (1994). Deception. In W. R. Cupach & B. H. Spitzberg (Eds.), *The dark side of interpersonal communication* (pp. 181–213). Hillsdale, NJ: Lawrence Erlbaum.

O'Hair, H. D., Cody, M. J., Goss, B., & Krayer, K. (1988). The effect of gender, deceit, orientation and communicator style on macro-assessments of honest. *Communication Quarterly, 36,* 77–93.

Olaniran, B. A., Savage, G. T., & Sorenson, R. L. (1996). Experimental and experiential approaches to teaching face-to-face and computer-mediated group discussion. *Communication Education, 45,* 244–259.

Olaniran, B. A., & Walther, J. B. (1997, May). *Pseudonym vs. real-name in computer-mediated communication brainstorming.* Paper presented at the meeting of the International Communication Association, Montreal, Canada.

O'Leary, K. D., & Kent, R. N. (1973). Behavior modification for social action: Research tactics and problems. In L. A. Hamerlynck, L. C. Handy, & E. J. Marsh (Eds.), *Behavior change: Methodology, concepts, and practice* (pp. 69–96). Campaign, IL: Research Press.

O'Leary, K. D., Kent, R. N., & Kanowitz, J. (1975). Shaping data collection congruent with experimental hypotheses. *Journal of Applied Behavioral Analysis, 8,* 43–51.

Oliver, M. B. (1993). Exploring the paradox and enjoyment of sad films. *Human Communication Research, 19,* 315–342.

Oliver, M. B. (1994). Portrayals of crime, race, and aggression in "reality-based" police shows: A content analysis. *Journal of Broadcasting & Electronic Media, 38,* 179–192.

Olson, K. M., & Goodnight, G. T. (1994). Entanglements of consumption, cruelty, privacy, and fashion: The social controversy over fur. *Quarterly Journal of Speech, 80,* 249–276.

Olson, K. M., & Olson, C. D. (1994). Judges' influence on trial outcomes and jurors' experiences of justice: Reinscribing existing hierarchies through the sanctuary trial. *Journal of Applied Communication Research, 22,* 16–35.

O'Mara, J., Allen, J. L., Long, K. M., & Judd, B. (1996). Communication apprehension, nonverbal immediacy, and negative expectations for learning. *Communication Research Reports, 13,* 109–128.

Onwumechili, C. (1996). Organizational culture in Nigeria: An exploratory study. *Communication Research Reports, 13,* 239–249.

Oppliger, P. A., & Sherblom, J. C. (1990). David Letterman, his audience, his jokes, and their relationship. *Communication Research Reports, 7,* 15–19.

Oppliger, P. A., & Sherblom, J. C. (1992). Humor: Incongruity, disparagement, and David Letterman. *Communication Research Reports, 9,* 99–108.

Opt, S. (1998). Confirming and disconfirming American myth: Stories within the suggestion box. *Communication Quarterly, 46,* 75–87.

Orbe, M. P. (1994). "Remember, it's always whites' ball": Descriptions of African American male communication. *Communication Quarterly, 42,* 287–300.

Osgood, C. E., Suci, C. J., & Tannenbaum, P. H. (1957). *The measurement of meaning.* Urbana: University of Illinois Press.

Oskamp, S. (1991). *Attitudes and opinions* (2nd ed.). Englewood Cliffs, NJ: Prentice Hall.

Owen, W. F. (1990). Delimiting relational metaphors. *Communication Studies, 41,* 35–53.

Pacanowsky, M. (1988). Slouching towards Chicago. *Quarterly Journal of Speech, 74,* 453–467.

Paik, H., & Comstock, G. (1994). The effects of television violence on antisocial behavior: A meta-analysis. *Communication Research, 21,* 516–546.

Palmer, M. T., & Simmons, K. B. (1995). Communicating intentions through nonverbal behaviors: Conscious and nonconscious encoding of liking. *Human Communication Research, 22,* 128–160.

Pan, Z., & Kosicki, G. M. (1996). Assessing news media influences on the formation of Whites' racial policy preferences. *Communication Research, 23,* 147–148.

Paoletti, I. (1997). *Being an older woman: A study in the social production of identity.* Mahwah, NJ: Lawrence Erlbaum.

Papa, L. (1999). "We gotta make up our minds": *Waiting for Lefty,* workers' theatre performance and audience identification. *Text and Performance Quarterly, 19,* 57–73.

Papa, M. J., & Natalle, E. J. (1989). Gender, strategy selection, and discussion satisfaction in interpersonal conflict. *Western Journal of Speech Communication, 53,* 260–272.

Parry-Giles, S. J. (1993). The rhetorical tension between propaganda and democracy: Blending competing conceptions of ideology and theory. *Communication Studies, 44,* 117–131.

Patten, M. L. (1998). *Questionnaire research: A practical guide.* Los Angeles: Pyrczak.

Patterson, B. R., & Beckett, C. S. (1995). A re-examination of relational repair and reconciliation: Impact of socio-communicative style on strategy selection. *Communication Research Reports, 12,* 235–240.

Patterson, B. R., & Bettini, L. (1993). Age, depression, and friendship: Development of a general friendship inventory. *Communication Research Reports, 10,* 161–170.

Patterson, B. R., Bettini, L., & Nussbaum, J. F. (1993). The meaning of friendship across the life-space: Two studies. *Communication Quarterly, 41,* 145–160.

Patterson, B. R., & O'Hair, D. (1992). Relational reconciliation: Toward a more comprehensive model of relational development. *Communication Research Reports, 9,* 119–129.

Patterson, M. L., & Ritts, V. (1997). Social and communicative anxiety: A review and meta-analysis. In B. R. Burleson (Ed.), *Communication yearbook 20* (pp. 263–303). Thousand Oaks, CA: Sage.

Patton, M. Q. (1990). *Qualitative evaluation and research methods* (2nd ed.). Newbury Park, CA: Sage.

Pauley, G. E. (1997). Presidential rhetoric and interest group politics: Lyndon B. Johnson and the Civil Rights Act of 1964. *Southern Communication Journal, 63,* 1–19.

Pauley, G. E. (1998). Rhetoric and timeliness: An analysis of Lyndon B. Johnson's voting rights address. *Western Journal of Communication, 62,* 26–53.

Pauley, J. L., II. (1998). Reshaping public persona and the prophetic *ethos:* Louis Farrakhan at the million man march. *Western Journal of Communication, 62,* 512–536.

Paulos, J. A. (1988). *Innumeracy: Mathematical illiteracy and its consequences.* New York: Vintage Books.

Pavitt, C., Whitchurch, G. G., McClurg, H., & Petersen, N. (1995). Melding the objective and subjective sides of leadership: Communication and social judgments in decision-making groups. *Communication Monographs, 62,* 243–264.

Pearce, W. B. (1995). *Public dialogue & democracy: A guide for the discussion leader.* Chicago: Loyola University Chicago.

Pearce, W. B. (1996). *Research methods: A systemic communication approach.* Woodside, CA: Pearce-Walters.

Pelias, R. J. (1992). *Performance studies: The interpretation of aesthetic texts.* New York: St. Martin's Press.

Pelias, R. J. (1999). *Writing performance: Poeticizing the researcher's body.* Carbondale: Southern Illinois University Press.

Pelto, P. J., & Pelto, G. H. (1975). Intra-cultural diversity: Some theoretical issues. *American Ethnologist, 2,* 1–18.

Pennebaker, J. W., & Susman, J. R. (1988). Disclosure of traumas and psychosomatic processes. *Social Sciences and Medicine, 26,* 327–332.

Penner, M., & Penner, S. (1994). Publicizing, politicizing, and neutralizing homelessness: Comic strips. *Communication Research, 21,* 766–781.

Perloff, R. M., & Ray, G. B. (1991). An analysis of AIDS brochures directed at intravenous drug users. *Health Communication, 3,* 113–125.

Perry, S. D., Jenzowsky, S. A., King, C. M., Yi, H., Hester, J., & Gartenschlaeger, J. (1997). Using humorous programs as the vehicle for humorous commercials. *Journal of Communication, 47*(1), 20–39.

Perse, E. M. (1998). Implications of cognitive and affective involvement for channel changing. *Journal of Communication, 48*(3), 49–68.

Peterson, R. A. (1975). An experimental investigation of mail-survey responses. *Journal of Business Research, 3,* 199–209.

Peterson, T. R., Witte, K., Enkerlin-Hoeflich, E., Espericueta, L., Flora, J. T., Florey, N., Loughran, T., & Stuart, R. (1994). Using informant directed interviews to discover risk orientation: How formative evaluations based in interpretive analysis can improve persuasive safety campaigns. *Journal of Applied Communication Research, 22,* 199–215.

Petronio, S. (1990). The use of a communication boundary perspective to contextualize embarrassment. In J. A. Anderson (Ed.), *Communication yearbook 13* (pp. 365–373). Newbury Park, CA: Sage.

Petronio, S., & Bradford, L. (1993). Issues interfering with the use of written communication as a means of relational bonding between absentee, divorced fathers and their children. *Journal of Applied Communication Research, 21,* 163–175.

Petronio, S., Olson, C., & Dollar, N. (1989). Privacy issues in relational embarrassment: Impact on relational quality and communication satisfaction. *Communication Research Reports, 6,* 21–27.

Petronio, S., Reeder, H. M., Hecht, M. L., & Ros-Mendoza, T. M. (1996). Disclosure of sexual abuse by children and adolescents. *Journal of Applied Communication Research, 24,* 181–199.

Pfau, M., & Eveland, W. P., Jr. (1996). Influence of traditional and non-traditional news media in the 1992 election campaign. *Western Journal of Communication, 60,* 214–232.

Pfau, M., Kendall, K. E., Reichert, T., Hellweg, S. A., Lee, W., Tusing, K. J., & Prosise, T. O. (1997). Influence of communication during the distant phase of the 1996 Republican presidential primary campaign. *Journal of Communication, 47*(4), 6–26.

Philipsen, G. (1975). Speaking "like a man" in Teamsterville: Culture patterns of role enactment in an urban neighborhood. *Quarterly Journal of Speech, 62,* 13–22.

Philipsen, G. (1976). Places for speaking in Teamsterville. *Quarterly Journal of Speech, 61,* 13–22.

Philipsen, G. (1989). An ethnographic approach to communication studies. In B. Dervin, L. Grossberg, B. J. O'Keefe, & E. Wartella (Eds.), *Rethinking communication: Vol. 2. Paradigm exemplars* (pp. 258–268). Newbury Park, CA: Sage.

Piatelli-Palmarini, M. (1994). *Inevitable illusions: How mistakes of reason rule our minds* (M. Piatelli-Palmarini & K. Botsford, Trans.). New York: John Wiley & Sons.

Piliavin, I. M., Rodin, J., & Piliavin, J. A. (1969). Good samaritanism: An underground phenomenon? *Journal of Personality and Social Psychology, 13,* 289–299.

Pinkleton, B. E. (1998). Effects of print comparative political advertising on political decision making and participation. *Journal of Communication, 48*(4), 24–36.

Pollard, C. E. (1996). Electronic meeting systems: Specifications, potential, and acquisition strategies. *Journal of Systems Management, 47,* 22–28.

Pollock, J. C. (1995). Comparing city characteristics and newspaper coverage of NAFTA. *Communication Review, 22,* 166–177.

Pollock, J. C. (1997, May). *Priming the agenda-setters: City characteristics and newspaper coverage of HIV/AIDS from Ryan White to 1995.* Paper presented at the meeting of the International communication Association, Montreal, Canada.

Pollock, J. C. (in press). *Newspapers and the evolution of public issues: Media alignment with political and social change.* Cresskill, NJ: Hampton Press.

Pollock, J. C., Coughlin, J., Thomas, J., & Connaughton, T. (1996). Comparing city characteristics and nationwide coverage of Dr. Jack Kevorkian: An archival approach. *Newspaper Research Journal, 17,* 120–133.

Pollock, J. C., & Dantas, G. (1998, July). *Nationwide newspaper coverage of same-sex marriage: A community structure approach.* Paper presented at the meeting of the International Communication Association, Jerusalem, Israel.

Pollock, J. C., Kreuer, B., & Ouano, E. (1997). Comparing city characteristics and nationwide coverage of China's bid to host the 2000 Olympic games: A community structure approach. *Newspaper Research Journal, 18,* 31–49.

Pollock, J. C., & Montero, E. (1998). Challenging the Mandarins: City characteristics and newspaper coverage of the Internet 1993–1995. In E. Bosah (Ed.), *Cyberghetto or cyberutopia: Race, class, and gender on the Internet* (pp. 103–119). Westport, CT: Greenwood Press.

Pollock, J. C., Robinson, J. L., & Murray, M. C. (1978). Media agendas and human rights: The Supreme Court decision on abortion. *Journalism Quarterly, 55,* 544–548, 561.

Pollock, J. C., Shier, L., & Kelly, P. (1995). Newspapers and the "open door" policy toward Cuba: A sample of major U.S. cities—"community structure" approach. *Journal of International Communication, 2,* 67–86.

Pollock, J. C., & Yulis, S. (1999, May). *Nationwide newspaper coverage of physician-assisted suicide: Media alignment with social change.* Paper presented at the meeting of the International Communication Association, San Francisco, CA.

Pollsters pat selves on the back. (1992, November 5). *Chicago Tribune,* Sect. 1, p. 16.

Pomerantz, A., Fehr, B. J., & Ende, J. (1997). When supervising physicians see patients: Strategies used in difficult situations. *Human Communication Research, 23,* 589–615.

Pool, I. de S. (1957). A critique of the twentieth anniversary issue. *Public Opinion Quarterly, 21,* 190–198.

Poole, M. S. (1990). Do we have any theories of group communication? *Communication Studies, 41,* 237–247.

Poole, M. S. (1999). Group communication theory. In L. R. Frey, (Ed.), D. S. Gouran, & M. S. Poole (Assoc. Eds.), *The handbook of group communication theory and research* (pp. 37–70). Thousand Oaks, CA: Sage.

Poole, M. S., DeSanctis, G., Kirsch, L., & Jackson, M. (1995). Group decision support systems as facilitators of quality team efforts. In L. R. Frey (Ed.), *Innovations in group facilitation: Applications in natural settings* (pp. 299–321). Cresskill, NJ: Hampton Press.

Poole, M. S., & Holmes, M. E. (1995). Decision development in computer-assisted group decision making. *Human Communication Research, 22,* 90–127.

Poole, M. S., & McPhee, R. D. (1985). Methodology in interpersonal communication research. In M. L. Knapp & G. R. Miller (Eds.), *Handbook of interpersonal communication* (pp. 100–170). Newbury Park, CA: Sage.

Poole, M. S., & Roth, J. (1989). Decision development in small groups V: Test of a contingency model. *Human Communication Research, 15,* 549–589.

Popper, K. R. (1962). *Conjectures and refutations.* New York: Basic Books.

Potter, W. J. (1996). *An analysis of thinking and research about qualitative methods.* Mahwah, NJ: Lawrence Erlbaum.

Potter, W. J., Cooper, R., & Dupagne, M. (1993). The three paradigms of mass media research in mainstream communication journals. *Communication Theory, 3,* 317–335.

Power, J. G., Murphy, S. T., & Coover, G. (1996). Priming prejudice: How stereotypes and counter-stereotypes influence attribution of responsibility and credibility among ingroups and outgroups. *Human Communication Research, 23,* 36–58.

Powers, W. G. (1993). The effects of gender and consequence upon perceptions of deceivers. *Communication Quarterly, 41,* 328–337.

Powers, W. G., Jordan, W. J., & Street, R. L. (1979). Language indices in the measurement of cognitive complexity: Is complexity loquacity? *Human Communication Research, 6,* 69–73.

Preiss, R. W., & Allen, M. (1998). Performing counterattitudinal advocacy: The persuasive impact of incentives. In M. Allen & R. W. Preiss (Eds.), *Persuasion: Advances through meta-analysis* (pp. 231–242). Cresskill, NJ: Hampton Press.

Prelli, L. F. (1990). Rhetorical logic and the integration of rhetoric and science. *Communication Monographs, 57,* 315–322.

Pritchard, D., & Hughes, K. D. (1997). Patterns of deviance in crime news. *Journal of Communication, 47*(3), 49–67.

Propp, K. M. (1995). An experimental examination of biological sex as a status cue in decision-making groups and its influence on information use. *Small Group Research, 26,* 451–474.

Punch, M. (1986). *The politics and ethics of fieldwork.* Newbury Park, CA: Sage.

Punch, M. (1994). Politics and ethics in qualitative research. In N. K. Denzin & Y. S. Lincoln (Eds.), *Handbook of qualitative research* (pp. 83–97). Thousand Oaks, CA: Sage.

Putnam, L., Van Hoeven, S. A., & Bullis, C. A. (1991). The role of rituals and fantasy themes in teachers' bargaining. *Western Journal of Speech Communication, 55,* 85–103.

Pyrczak, F., & Bruce, R. R. (1992). *Writing empirical research reports: A basic guide for students of the social and behavioral sciences.* Los Angeles: Pyrczak.

Qualis Research Associates. (1990). *The Ethnograph: A program for the computer-assisted analysis of text-based data.* Corvallis, OR: Author.

Query, J. L., Jr., & Kreps, G. L. (1993). Using the critical incident method to evaluate and enhance organizational effectiveness. In S. L. Herndon & G. L. Kreps (Eds.), *Qualitative research: Applications in organizational communication* (pp. 63–78). Cresskill, NJ: Hampton Press.

Ragsdale, J. D. (1996). Gender, satisfaction level, and the use of relational maintenance strategies in marriage. *Communication Monographs, 63,* 354–369.

Rancer, A. S. (1998). Argumentativeness. In J. C. McCroskey, J. A. Daly, M. M. Martin, & M. J. Beatty (Eds.), *Communication and personality: Trait perspectives* (pp. 149–170). Cresskill, NJ: Hampton Press.

Rancer, A. S., Kosberg, R. L., & Baukus, R. A. (1992). The relationship between self-esteem and aggressive communication predispositions. *Communication Research Reports, 9,* 23–32.

Rancer, A. S., Kosberg, R. L., & Silvestri, V. N. (1992). The relationship between self-esteem and aggressive communication predispositions. *Communication Research Reports, 9,* 23–32.

Rancer, A. S., Whitecap, V. G., Kosberg, R. L., & Avtgis, T. A. (1997). Testing the efficacy of a communication training program to increase argumentativeness and argumentative behavior in adolescents. *Communication Education, 46,* 273–286.

Randall, D. M. (1993). Staged replication of naturally-occurring talk: A performer's perspective. *Text and Performance Quarterly, 13,* 197–199.

Rawlins, W. K., & Holl, M. (1987). The communicative achievement of friendship during adolescence: Predicaments of trust and violation. *Western Journal of Speech Communication, 51,* 354–363.

Ray, E. B. (Ed.). (1996a). *Communication and disenfranchisement: Social health issues and implications.* Mahwah, NJ: Lawrence Erlbaum.

Ray, E. B. (Ed.). (1996b). *Case studies in communication and disenfranchisement: Applications to social health issues.* Mahwah, NJ: Lawrence Erlbaum.

Rea, L. M., & Parker, R. A. (1992). *Designing and conducting survey research: A comprehensive guide.* San Francisco: Jossey-Bass.

Reason, P. (1994). Three approaches to participative inquiry. In N. K. Denzin & Y. S. Lincoln (Eds.), *Handbook of qualitative research* (pp. 324–339). Thousand Oaks, CA: Sage.

Reese, H. W., & Fremouw, W. J. (1984). Normal and normative ethics in behavioral sciences. *American Psychologist, 39,* 863–876.

Reese, W. L. (1980). *Dictionary of philosophy and religion: Eastern and Western thought.* Atlantic Highlands, NJ: Humanities Press.

Reeves, B., Lang, A., Thorson, E., & Rothschild, M. (1989). Emotional television scenes and hemispheric specialization. *Human Communication Research, 15,* 493–508.

Reid, L. N., Soley, L. C., & Wimmer, R. D. (1981). Replication in advertising research. *Journal of Advertising, 10,* 3–13.

Reinard, J. C. (1988). The empirical study of the persuasive effects of evidence: The status after fifty years of research. *Human Communication Research, 15,* 3–59.

Reinking, K., & Bell, R. A. (1991). Relationships among loneliness, communication competence, and career success in a state bureaucracy: A field study of the "lonely at the top" maxim. *Communication Quarterly, 39,* 358–373.

Reiss, A. J., Jr. (1979). Governmental regulation of scientific enquiry: Some paradoxical consequences. In C. B. Klockars & F. W. O'Connor (Eds.), *Deviance and decency: The ethics of research with human subjects* (pp. 61–95). Beverly Hills, CA: Sage.

Renzetti, C. M., & Lee, R. M. (Eds.). (1993). *Researching sensitive topics.* Newbury Park, CA: Sage.

Riccillo, S. C. (1989). Physiological measurement. In P. Emmert & L. L. Barker (Eds.), *Measurement of communication behavior* (pp. 267–295). White Plains, NY: Longman.

Richards, T. J., & Richards, L. (1994). Using computers in qualitative research. In N. K. Denzin & Y. S. Lincoln (Eds.), *Handbook of qualitative research* (pp. 445–462). Thousand Oaks, CA: Sage.

Richardson, L. (1994). Writing: A method of inquiry. In N. K. Denzin & Y. S. Lincoln (Eds.), *Handbook of qualitative research* (pp. 516–529). Thousand Oaks, CA: Sage.

Riches, S. V., & Sillars, M. O. (1980). The status of movement criticism. *Western Speech, 44,* 275–287.

Richmond, V. P., & Martin, M. M. (1998). Sociocommunicative style and sociocommunicative orientation. In J. C. McCroskey, J. A. Daly, M. M. Martin, & M. J. Beatty (Eds.), *Communication and personality: Trait perspectives* (pp. 133–148). Cresskill, NJ: Hampton Press.

Riffe, D., Lacy, S., & Fico, F. G. (1998). *Analyzing media messages: Using quantitative content analysis in research.* Mahwah, NJ: Lawrence Erlbaum.

Riffe, D., Lacy, S., Nagovan, J., & Barkum, L. (1996). The effectiveness of simple and stratified sampling in broadcast news content analysis. *Journalism and Mass Communication Quarterly, 73,* 159–168.

Riggs, K. E. (1996). Television use in a retirement community. *Journal of Communication, 46*(1), 144–156.

Riley, P. (1983). A structurationist account of political culture. *Administrative Science Quarterly, 28,* 414–437.

Riley, P. (1985). Spinning on symbolism: The spinning metaphor and dialectical tension. *Journal of Management, 11,* 49–50.

Rintell, E. S., & Pittam, J. (1997). Strangers in a strange land: Interaction management on Internet relay chat. *Human Communication Research, 23,* 507–534.

Ristock, J. L., & Pennell, J. (1996). *Community research as empowerment: Feminist links, postmodern interruptions.* Toronto, Canada: Oxford University Press.

Roberts, C. V. (1984). A physiological validation of the Receiver Apprehension Test. *Communication research Reports, 1,* 126–129.

Robinson, J. D., & Skill, T. (1995). The invisible generation: Portrayals of the elderly on prime-time television. *Communication Reports, 8,* 111–119.

Rodriguez, A. (1996). Objectivity and ethnicity in the production of the Noticiero Univision. *Critical Studies in Mass Communication, 13,* 59–81.

Rodriguez, J., Plax, T. G., & Kearney, P. (1996). Clarifying the relationship between teacher nonverbal immediacy and student cognitive learning: Affective learning as the central causal mediator. *Communication Education, 45,* 293–305.

Roethlisberger, F. J., & Dickson, W. J. (1939). *Management and the worker: An account of a research program conducted by the Western Electric Company, Hawthorne Works, Illinois.* Cambridge, MA: Harvard University Press.

Rogan, R. G., & Hammer, M. R. (1994). Crisis negotiations: A preliminary investigation of facework in naturalistic conflict. *Journal of Applied Communication Research, 22,* 216–231.

Rogan, R. G., & Hammer, M. R. (1995). Assessing message affect in crisis negotiations: An exploratory study. *Human Communication Research, 21,* 553–574.

Roghaar, L. A., & Vangelisti, A. L. (1996). Expressed attributions for academic success and failure by adolescents and young adults. *Western Journal of Communication, 60,* 124–145.

Rosenfeld, L. B., Richman, J. M., & Bowen, G. L. (1998). Supportive communication and school outcomes for academically "at-risk" and other low income middle school students. *Communication Education, 47,* 309–325.

Rosenkrantz, R. D. (1980). Rational information acquisition. In L. J. Cohen & M. Hesse (Eds.), *Applications of inductive logic* (pp. 68–98). Oxford, England: Clarendon Press.

Rosenthal, R. (1965). The volunteer subject. *Human Relations, 18,* 403–404.

Rosenthal, R. (1966). *Experimenter effects in behavioral research.* Norwalk, CT: Appleton & Lange.

Rosenthal, R. (1976). *Experimenter effects in behavioral research* (Enl. ed.). New York: Irvington.

Rosenthal, R. (1984). *Meta-analytic procedures for social research.* Newbury Park, CA: Sage.

Rosenthal, R. (1990). How are we doing in soft psychology? *American Psychologist, 45,* 775–777.

Rosenthal, R. (1991). Replication in behavioral research. In J. W. Neuliep (Ed.), *Replication research in the social sciences* (pp. 1–30). Newbury Park, CA: Sage.

Rosenthal, R. (1993). Cumulating evidence. In C. Keren & C. Lewis (Eds.), *A handbook for data analysis in the behavioral sciences: Methodological issues* (pp. 519–559). Hillsdale, NJ: Lawrence Erlbaum.

Rosenthal, R., & Rosnow, R. L. (1969). The volunteer subject. In R. Rosenthal & R. L. Rosnow (Eds.), *Artifact in behavioral research* (pp. 59–118). Orlando, FL: Academic Press.

Rossi, A. M., & Todd-Mancillas, W. R. (1984, February). *Gender differences in the management of four different personal disputes with male and female employees.* Paper presented at the meeting of the Western Speech Communication Association, Seattle, WA.

Rossiter, C. M. (1976). The validity of communication experiments using human subjects: A review. *Human Communication Research, 2,* 197–206.

Roth, J. A. (1966). Hired hand research. *American Sociologist, 1,* 190–196.

Roth, N. L. (1995). Calendars on the wall: The influence of sexuality on provide/client communication about HIV/AIDS. *Journal of Psychology and Human Sexuality, 7,* 21–39.

Rothenbuhler, E. W. (1991). The process of community involvement. *Communication Monographs, 58,* 63–78.

Rothschild, M. L., Thorsen, E., Reeves, B., Hirsch, J. E., & Goldstein, R. (1986). EEG activity and the processing of television commercials. *Communication Research, 13,* 182–220.

Rountree, J. C., III. (1995). The president as God, the recession as evil: *Actus, status,* and the president's rhetorical bind in the 1992 election. *Quarterly Journal of Speech, 81,* 325–352.

Ruben, B. D. (1993). What patients remember: A content analysis of critical incidents in health care. *Health Communication, 5,* 99–112.

Rubin, A. M. (1993). The effect of locus of control on communication motivation, anxiety, and satisfaction. *Communication Quarterly, 41,* 161–171.

Rubin, R. B. (1990). Communication competence. In G. M. Phillips & J. T. Wood (Eds.), *Speech communication: Essays to commemorate the 75th anniversary of the Speech Communication Association* (pp. 94–129). Carbondale: Southern Illinois University Press.

Rubin, R. B., & Martin, M. M. (1994). Development of a measure of interpersonal communication competence. *Communication Research Reports, 11,* 33–44.

Rubin, R. B., Martin, M. M., Bruning, S. S., & Powers, D. E. (1993). Test of a self-efficacy model of interpersonal communication competence. *Communication Quarterly, 41,* 210–220.

Rubin, R. B., Palmgreen, P., & Sypher, E. (Ed.). (1994). *Communication research methods: A sourcebook.* New York: Guilford Press.

Rubin, R. B., Perse, E. M., & Barbato, C. A. (1988). Conceptualization and measurement of interpersonal communication motives. *Human Communication Research, 14,* 602–628.

Rubin, R. B., & Rubin, A. M. (1992). Antecedents of interpersonal communication motives. *Communication Quarterly, 40,* 305–317.

Rubin, R. B., Rubin, A. M., & Martin, M. M. (1993). The role of self-disclosure and self-awareness in affinity-seeking competence. *Communication Research Reports, 10,* 115–127.

Rubin, R. B., Rubin, A. B., & Piele, L. J. (1990). *Communication research: Strategies and sources* (2nd ed.). Belmont, CA: Wadsworth.

Rudolph, U. (1997). Implicit verb causality: Verbal schemas and covariation information. *Journal of Language and Social Psychology, 16,* 132–158.

Ryan, C., Carragee, K. M., & Schwerner, C. (1998). Media, movements, and the quest for social justice. *Journal of Applied Communication Research, 26,* 165–181.

Ryan, E. B., Giles, H., Bartolucci, G., & Henwood, K. (1986). Psycholinguistic and social psychological components of communication by and with the elderly. *Language & Communication, 6,* 1–24.

Sable, A. (1978). Deception in social science research: Is informed consent possible? *Hastings Center Report, 8,* 40–46.

Sackmann, S. A. (1989). The role of metaphors in organization transformation. *Human Relations, 42,* 463–485.

Salazar, A. J., Becker, S. L., & Daughety, V. (1994). Social support and smoking behavior: The impact of network composition and type of support on cessation and relapse. *Southern Communication Journal, 59,* 153–170.

Salazar, A. J., Hirokawa, R. Y., Propp, K. M., Julian, K. M., & Leatham, G. B. (1994). In search of true causes: Examination of the effect of group potential and group interaction on decision performance. *Human Communication Research, 20,* 529–559.

Salvador, M. (1994). The rhetorical subversion of cultural boundaries: The national consumers' league. *Southern Communication Journal, 59,* 318–332.

Salwen, M. B., & Driscoll, P. D. (1997). Consequences of third-person perceptions in support of press restrictions in the O. J. Simpson trial. *Journal of Communication, 47*(2), 60–78.

Samora, J., Saunders, L., & Larson, R. (1961). Medical vocabulary knowledge among hospital patients. *Journal of Health and Human Behavior, 2,* 83–93.

Sanders, J. A., Wiseman, R. L., & Matz, S. I. (1990). The influence of gender on reported disclosure, interrogation, and nonverbal immediacy in same-sex dyads: An empirical study of uncertainty reduction theory. *Women's Studies in Communication, 11,* 85–108.

Sanjek, R. (1990). A vocabulary for fieldnotes. In R. Sanjek (Ed.), *Fieldnotes: The making of anthropology* (pp. 92–121). Ithaca, NY: Cornell University Press.

Sapolsky, B. S. (1982). Sexual acts and references on prime-time TV: A two-year look. *Southern Speech Communication Journal, 47,* 212–226.

Sarch, A. (1993). Making the connection: Single women's use of the telephone in dating relationships with men. *Journal of Communication, 43*(2), 128–144.

Saris, W. E. (1991). *Computer-assisted interviewing.* Newbury Park, CA: Sage.

Scarpello, V., & Vandenberg, R. J. (1991). Some issues to consider when studying employee opinions. In J. W.

Jones, B. D. Steffy, & D. W. Bray (Eds.), *Applying psychology in business: The handbook for managers and human resource professionals* (pp. 611–622). Lexington, MA: Lexington Books.

Schatzman, L., & Strauss, A. L. (1973). *Field research: Strategies for a natural sociology.* Englewood Cliffs, NJ: Prentice-Hall.

Scheerhorn, D. (1990). Hemophilia in the days of AIDS: Communicative tensions surrounding associated stigma. *Communication Research, 17,* 842–847.

Scheerhorn, D., & Geist, P. (1997). Social dynamics in groups. In L. R. Frey & J. K. Barge (Eds.), *Managing group life: Communicating in decision-making groups* (pp. 81–103). Boston: Houghton Mifflin.

Scheerhorn, D., Warisse, J., & McNeilis, K. S. (1995). Computer-based telecommunication among an illness-related community: Design, delivery, early use, and the functions of HIGHnet. *Health Communication, 7,* 301–325.

Scheibel, D. (1992). Faking identity in clubland: The communicative performance of "fake ID." *Text and Performance Quarterly, 12,* 160–175.

Schely-Newman, E. (1991). *Self and community in historical narratives: Tunisian immigrants in an Israeli moshav.* Unpublished doctoral dissertation, University of Chicago.

Schely-Newman, E. (1993). The woman shot: A communal tale. *Journal of American Folklore, 106,* 285–303.

Schely-Newman, E. (1995). Sweeter than honey: Discourse of reproduction among North-African Israeli women. *Text and Performance Quarterly, 15,* 175–188.

Schely-Newman, E. (1997). Finding one's place: Locale narratives in an Israeli *Moshav. Quarterly Journal of Speech, 83,* 401–415.

Schenkler, B. R. (1985). Introduction: Foundations of the self in social life. In B. R. Schenkler (Ed.), *The self and social life* (pp. 1–21). New York: McGraw-Hill.

Schiavone, N. P. (1984). Guilt by association: The dilemma of phony polls. *Proceedings of the Second Advertising Research Quality Workshop.* New York: Advertising Research Foundation.

Schick, T., Jr., & Vaughn, L. (1995). *How to think about weird things: Critical thinking for a new age.* Mountain View, CA: Mayfield.

Schiffrin, D. (1977). Opening encounters. *American Sociological Review, 42,* 679–691.

Schmitz, J., Rogers, E. M., Phillips, K., & Paschal, D. (1995). The public electronic network (PEN) and

the homeless in Santa Monica. *Journal of Applied Communication Research, 23,* 26–43.

Schneider, D. E., & Beaubien, R. A. (1996). A naturalistic investigation of compliance-gaining strategies employed by doctors in medical interviews. *Southern Communication Journal, 61,* 332–341.

Schommer, J. C. (1994). Effects of interrole congruence on pharmacist-patient communication. *Health Communication, 6,* 297–309.

Schonbach, P. (1980). A category system for account phases. *European Journal of Social Psychology, 10,* 195–200.

Schooler, C., Basil, M. D., & Altman, D. G. (1996). Alcohol and cigarette advertising on billboards: Targeting with social cues. *Health Communication, 8,* 109–129.

Schumacher, G. M. (1987). Executive control in studying. In B. K. Britton & S. M. Glynn (Eds.), *Executive control functions in reading* (pp. 107–144). Hillsdale, NJ: Lawrence Erlbaum.

Schuman, H., Ludwig, J., & Krosnick, J. A. (1986). The perceived threat of nuclear war, salience, and open questions. *Public Opinion Quarterly, 50,* 519–536.

Schuman, H., & Presser, S. (1996). *Questions and answers in attitude surveys: Experiments on question form, wording, and context.* Thousand Oaks, CA: Sage.

Schutt, R. S. (1999). *Investigating the social world: The process and practice of research* (2nd ed.). Thousand Oaks, CA: Pine Forge Press.

Schwartz, H., & Jacobs, J. (1979). *Qualitative sociology: A method to the madness.* New York: Free Press.

Schwartzman, R. (1997). Peer review as the enforcement of disciplinary orthodoxy. *Southern Communication Journal, 63,* 69–75.

Schwichtenberg, C. (1992). Madonna's postmodern feminism: Bringing the margins to the center. *Southern Communication Journal, 57,* 120–131.

Scott, C. R. (1999). Communication technology and group communication. In L. R. Frey (Ed.), D. S. Gouran, & M. S. Poole (Assoc. Eds.), *The handbook of group communication theory and research* (pp. 432–472). Thousand Oaks, CA: Sage.

Scott, C. R., Corman, S. R., & Cheney, G. (1998). Development of a structurational model of identification in the organization. *Communication Theory, 8,* 298–336.

Scott, W. A. (1955). Reliability of content analysis: The case for nominal scale coding. *Public Opinion Quarterly, 19,* 321–325.

Seabrook, C. (1972, July 27). Study genocidal—CDC doctor. *Atlanta Journal,* p. 2A.

Segrin, C. (1990). A meta-analytic review of social skill deficits in depression. *Communication Monographs, 57,* 292–308.

Segrin, C. (1992). Specifying the nature of social skill deficits associated with depression. *Human Communication Research, 19,* 89–123.

Segrin, C. (1993). The effects of nonverbal behavior on outcomes of compliance gaining attempts. *Communication Studies, 44,* 170–187.

Segrin, C., & Dillard, J. (1991). (Non)depressed person's cognitive and affective reactions to (un)successful interpersonal influence. *Communication Monographs, 58,* 115–134.

Segrin, C., & Fitzpatrick, M. A. (1992). Depression and verbal aggressiveness in different marital couple types. *Communication Studies, 43,* 79–91.

Sellnow, D. D. (1996). Rhetorical strategies of continuity and change in the music of popular artists over time. *Communication Studies, 47,* 46–61.

Selvin, H. C. (1970). A critique of tests of significance in survey research. In D. E. Morrison & R. E. Henkel (Eds.), *The significance controversy: A reader* (pp. 94–106). Hawthorne, NY: Aldine.

Sengputa, S. (1996). Understanding less educated smokers' intention to quit smoking: Strategies for anti-smoking communication aimed at less educated smokers. *Health Communication, 8,* 55–72.

Severin, W. J., (with Tankard, J. W., Jr.). (1992). *Communication theories: Origins, methods, and uses in the mass media* (3rd ed.). New York: Longman.

Sharkey, W. F. (1991). Intentional embarrassment: Goal tactics and consequences. In W. R. Cupach & S. Metts (Eds.), *Advances in Interpersonal Communication Research 1991: Proceedings of the Western States Communication Association Interpersonal Communication Interest Group* (pp. 105–128). Normal, IL: Personal Relationships Research Group.

Sharkey, W. F. (1992). Uses and responses to intentional embarrassment. *Communication Studies, 43,* 257–273.

Sharkey, W. F., Kulp, C., Carpenter, B. M., Lee, C., & Rodillas, U. (1997). Embarrassment: The effects of embarrassor and target perceptions. *Communication Research Reports, 14,* 460–480.

Sharkey, W. F., & Stafford, L. (1990). Responses to embarrassment. *Human Communication Research, 17,* 315–342.

Sheatsley, P. B. (1947). Some uses of interviewer-report forms. *Public Opinion Quarterly, 11,* 601–611.

Shedletsky, L. J. (1982). The relationship between sex differences in cerebral organization and nonverbal behavior. *Women's Studies in Communication, 5,* 10–15.

Shedletsky, L. J. (1991). Cognitive style, family handedness, and degree of laterality account for inconsistent sex differences in direction of gaze. In J. W. Neuliep (Ed.), *Replication research in the social sciences* (pp. 391–418). Newbury Park, CA: Sage.

Sheer, V. C. (1995). Sensation seeking predispositions and susceptibility to a sexual partner's appeals for condom use. *Journal of Applied Communication Research, 23,* 212–229.

Sheer, V. C., & Cline, R. J. W. (1995). Individual differences in sensation seeking and sexual behavior: Implications for communication intervention for HIV/AIDS prevention among college students. *Health Communication, 7,* 205–223.

Shefner-Rogers, C. L., Rao, N., Rogers, E. M., & Wayangankar, A. (1998). The empowerment of women dairy farmers in India. *Journal of Applied Communication Research, 26,* 319–337.

Shepherd, G. J., & Condra, M. B. (1988). Anxiety, construct differentiation, and message production. *Central States Speech Journal, 39,* 177–189.

Sheppard, B., Hartwick, J., & Warshaw, P. (1988). The theory of reasoned action: A meta-analysis of past research with recommendations for modifications and future research. *Journal of Consumer Research, 5,* 325–343.

Shermer, M. (1997). *Why people believe weird things.* New York: W. H. Freeman.

Shoham, Y. (1990). Nonmonotonic reasoning and causation. *Cognitive Science, 14,* 213–302.

Should science kill last of smallpox virus? Vials stored in Atlanta, Moscow. (1993, June 22). *Chicago Tribune,* Sect. 1, p. 2.

Shrum, L. J. (1996). Psychological processes underlying cultivation effects: Further tests of construct accessibility. *Human Communication Research, 22,* 482–509.

Shupe, A. D., & Bromley, D. G. (1980). *The new vigilantes: Deprogrammers, anti-cultists, and the new religions.* Beverly Hills, CA: Sage.

Sias, P. M., & Cahill, D. J. (1998). From coworkers to friends: The development of peer friendships in the workplace. *Western Journal of Communication, 62,* 273–299.

Sieber, J. E. (1992). *Planning ethically responsible research: A guide for students and internal review boards.* Newbury Park, CA: Sage.

Sieber, J. E. (1993). The ethics and politics of sensitive research. In C. M. Renzetti & R. M. Lee (Eds.),

Researching sensitive topics (pp. 14–26). Newbury Park, CA: Sage.

Sieber, J. E. (1998). Planning ethically responsible research. In L. Bickman & D. J. Rog (Eds.), *Handbook of applied social research methods* (pp. 127–156). Thousand Oaks, CA: Sage.

Sillars, A. L. (1980). Attribution and communication in roommate conflicts. *Communication Monographs, 47,* 180–200.

Sillars, A. L., Coletti, S. F., Parry, D., & Rogers, M. A. (1982). Coding verbal conflict tactics: Nonverbal and perceptual correlates of the "avoidance-distributive-integrative" distinction. *Human Communication Research, 9,* 83–95.

Silverman, I. (1968). The effects of experimenter outcome expectancy on latency of word association. *Journal of Clinical Psychology, 24,* 718–721.

Simon, E. P., & Baxter, L. A. (1993). Attachment-style differences in relationship maintenance strategies. *Western Journal of Communication, 57,* 416–430.

Simons, H. W. (1970). Requirements, problems, and strategies: A theory of persuasion for social movements. *Quarterly Journal of Speech, 56,* 1–11.

Simons, H. W., Mechling, E. A., & Schreier, H. N. (1984). The functions of human communication in mobilizing for collective action from the bottom up: The rhetoric of social movements. In C. C. Arnold & J. W. Bowers (Eds.), *Handbook of rhetorical and communication theory* (pp. 792–867). Boston: Allyn and Bacon.

Singer, E. T. (1996). *Action research: A handbook for practitioners.* Thousand Oaks, CA: Sage.

Sirkin, R. M. (1995). *Statistics for the social sciences.* Thousand Oaks, CA: Sage.

Skow, L. M., & Dionisopoulus, G. N. (1997). A struggle to contextualize photographic images: American print media and the "burning monk." *Communication Quarterly, 45,* 393–409.

Skumanich, S. A., & Kintsfather, D. P. (1998). Individual media dependency relations within television shopping programming: A causal model reviewed and revised. *Communication Research, 25,* 200–219.

Slagell, A. R. (1991). Anatomy of a masterpiece: A close textual analysis of Abraham Lincoln's second inaugural address. *Communication Studies, 42,* 155–171.

Slagle, R. A. (1995). In defense of Queer Nation: From *identity politics* to a *politics of difference. Western Journal of Communication, 59,* 85–102.

Smaglik, P., Hawkins, R. P., Pingree, S., Gustafson, D. H., Boberg, E., & Bricker, E. (1998). The quality of interactive computer use among HIV-infected individuals. *Journal of Health Communication, 3,* 53–68.

Smith, C. R. (1995). Dan Quayle on family values: Epideictic appeals in political campaigns. *Southern Communication Journal, 60,* 152–164.

Smith, G. (1997). Do statistics test scores regress toward the mean? *Change, 10*(4), 42–45.

Smith, K. A. (1988). Effects of coverage on neighborhood and community concerns. *Newspaper Research Journal, 9,* 35–48.

Smith, L. J., & Malandro, L. A. (1985). *Courtroom communication strategies.* New York: Kluwer.

Smith, N. L. (1985). Introduction: Moral and ethical problems in evaluation. *Evaluation and Program Planning, 8,* 1–3.

Smith, R., & Eisenberg, E. (1987). Conflict at Disneyland: A root-metaphor analysis. *Communication Monographs, 54,* 367–380.

Smith, R. F. (1989). How design and color affect reader judgment of newspapers. *Newspaper Research Journal, 10,* 526–537.

Smith, S. W., Morrison, K., Kopfman, J., & Ford, L. A. (1994). The influence of prior thought and intent on the memorability and persuasiveness of organ donation message strategies. *Health Communication, 6,* 1–20.

Smith, V., Siltanen, S. A., & Hosman, L. A. (1998). The effects of powerful and powerless speech styles and speaker expertise on impression formation and attitude change. *Communication Research Reports, 15,* 27–35.

Smith-Dupre´, A. A., & Beck, C. S. (1996). Enabling patients and physicians to pursue multiple goals in health care encounters: A case study. *Health Communication, 8,* 73–90.

Smythe, M-J. (1995). Talking bodies: Body talk at Bodyworks. *Communication Studies, 46,* 245–260.

Snyder, M. (1974). Self-monitoring of expressive behavior. *Journal of Personal and Social Psychology, 30,* 526–537.

Snyder, M. (1979). Self-monitoring processes. In L. Berkowitz (Ed.), *Advances in experimental social psychology* (Vol. 12, pp. 85–128). Orlando, FL: Academic Press.

Socha, T. J., & Stamp, G. H. (Eds.). (1995). *Parents, children, and communication: Frontiers of theory and research.* Mahwah, NJ: Lawrence Erlbaum.

Solomon, D. H. (1997). A developmental model of intimacy and date request explicitness. *Communication Monographs, 64,* 100–118.

Solomon, M. (1985). The rhetoric of dehumanization: An analysis of medical reports of the Tuskegee syphilis project. *Western Journal of Speech Communication, 49,* 233–247.

Somers, R. H., Mannheimer, D., Kelman, M., & Mellinger, G. D. (1982). Structured interviews: Technical and ethical problems. In R. B. Smith & P. K. Manning (Eds.), *A handbook of social science methods: Vol. 2. Qualitative methods* (pp. 145–162). Cambridge, MA: Ballinger.

Sorenson, P. S., Hawkins, K., & Sorenson, R. L. (1995). Gender, psychological type and conflict style preference. *Management Communication Quarterly, 9,* 115–126.

Sosik, J. J., Avolio, B. J., & Kahai, S. S. (1998). Inspiring group creativity: Comparing anonymous and identified electronic brainstorming. *Small Group Research, 29,* 3–31.

Sowell, T. (1995). Ethnicity and IQ. In S. Fraser (Ed.), *The bell curve wars: Race, intelligence, and the future of America* (pp. 70–79). New York: Basic Books.

Spano, S., & Zimmerman, S. (1995). Interpersonal communication competence in context: Assessing performance in the selection interview. *Communication Reports, 8,* 18–26.

Spears, R., Lea, M., & Lee, S. (1990). De-individuation and group polarization in computer-mediated communication. *British Journal of Social Psychology, 29,* 121–134.

Spencer, N. J., Hartnett, J., & Mahoney, J. (1985). Problems with reviews in the standard editorial practice. *Journal of Social Behavior and Personality, 1,* 21–36.

Spitzberg, B. H., & Canary, D. J. (1985). Loneliness and relationally competent communication. *Journal of Social and Personal Psychology, 2,* 387–402.

Spitzberg, B. H., & Cupach, W. R. (1984). *Interpersonal communication competence.* Beverly Hills, CA: Sage.

Spitzberg, B. H., & Hurt, T. H. (1989). The relationship of interpersonal competence and skills to reported loneliness across time. In M. Hojat & R. Crandall (Eds.), *Loneliness: Theory, research, and applications* (pp. 157–172). Newbury Park, CA: Sage.

Sorenson, P. S., Hawkins, K., & Sorenson, R. L. (1995). Gender, psychological type, and conflict style preference. *Management Communication Quarterly, 9,* 115–126.

Spirek, M. M., & Glascock, J. (1998). Gender analysis of frightening film newspaper advertisements: A 50-year overview (1940–1990). *Communication Quarterly, 46,* 100–108.

Spradley, J. P. (1979). *The ethnographic interview.* New York: Holt, Rinehart and Winston.

Spradley, J. P. (1980). *Participant observation.* New York: Holt, Rinehart and Winston.

Squire, P. (1988). Why the 1936 *Literary Digest* poll failed. *Public Opinion Quarterly, 52,* 125–133.

Stacks, D. W., & Murphy, M. A. (1993). Conversational sensitivity: Further validation and extension. *Communication Reports, 6,* 18–24.

Stafford, L., & Canary, D. J. (1991). Maintenance strategies and romantic relationship type, gender, and relational characteristics. *Journal of Social and Personal Relationships, 8,* 217–242.

Stafford, L., & Kline, S. L. (1996). Women's surnames and titles: Men's and women's views. *Communication Research Reports, 13,* 214–224.

Stake, R. E. (1994). Case studies. In N. K. Denzin & Y. S. Lincoln (Eds.), *Handbook of qualitative research* (pp. 236–247). Thousand Oaks, CA: Sage.

Stamp, G. H., & Banski, M. A. (1992). The communicative management of constrained autonomy during the transition to parenthood. *Western Journal of Communication, 56,* 281–300.

Stamp, G. H., & Sabourin, T. C. (1995). Accounting for violence: An analysis of male spousal abuse narratives. *Journal of Applied Communication Research, 23,* 284–307.

Stamp, G. H., Vangelisti, A. L., & Daly, J. A. (1992). The creation of defensiveness in social interaction. *Communication Quarterly, 40,* 177–190.

Standing Committee on Research. (1993, January). Research paper submissions and acceptance as a function of number of members and number of papers received. *AEJMC News,* p. 18.

Statistical disclosure control. (1998, April). *Amstat News,* p. 4.

Stavitsky, A. G. (1998). Counting the house in public television: A history of ratings use, 1953–1980. *Journal of Broadcasting & Electronic Media, 42,* 520–534.

Steinfatt, T. M. (1987). Personality and communication: Classical approaches. In J. C. McCroskey & J. A. Daly (Eds.), *Personality and interpersonal communication* (pp. 42–126). Newbury Park, CA: Sage.

Sterling, T. D. (1959). Publication decisions and their possible effects on inferences drawn from tests of significance-or vice versa. *Journal of the American Statistical Association, 54,* 30–34.

Stevens, S. S. (1958). Problems and methods of psychophysics. *Psychological Bulletin, 55,* 177–196.

Stewart, C. J. (1991a). The ego function of protest songs: An application of Gregg's theory of protest rhetoric. *Communication Studies, 42,* 240–253.

Stewart, C. J. (1991b). The internal rhetoric of the Knights of Labor. *Communication Studies, 42,* 67–82.

Stewart, C. J. (1997). The evolution of a revolution: Stokely Carmichael and the rhetoric of Black power. *Quarterly Journal of Speech, 83,* 429–446.

Stewart, C. J., Smith, C., & Denton, R. E. (1984). *Persuasion and social movements.* Prospect Heights, IL: Waveland Press.

Stewart, D. W., & Shamdasani, P. N. (1990). *Focus groups: Theory and practice.* Newbury Park, CA: Sage.

Stewart, J. K. (1996a, March 18). Negative polls push ethical boundaries. *Chicago Sun-Times,* p. 43.

Stewart, J. K. (1996b, March 18). Pollsters reap election dividend: Campaigns ice the cake for industry. *Chicago Sun-Times,* pp. 39, 43.

Stiff, J. B., Dillard, J. P., Somera, L., Kim, H., & Sleight, C. (1988). Empathy, communication, and prosocial behavior. *Communication Monographs, 55,* 198–213.

Strauss, A. (1987). *Qualitative analysis for social scientists.* New York: Cambridge University Press.

Strauss, A., & Corbin, J. (1990). *Basics of qualitative research: Grounded theory procedures and techniques.* Newbury Park, CA: Sage.

Stringer, E. T. (1996). *Action research: A handbook for practitioners.* Thousand Oaks, CA: Sage.

Stroman, C. A., & Jones, K. E. (1998). The analysis of television content. In J. K. Asamen & G. L. Berry (Eds.), *Research paradigms, television, and social behavior* (pp. 271–285). Thousand Oaks, CA: Sage.

Stuckey, M. E. (1992). Remembering the future: Rhetorical echoes of World War II and Vietnam in George Bush's public speech on the Gulf War. *Communication Studies, 43,* 246–256.

Stuckey, M. E. (1995). Competing foreign policy visions: Rhetorical hybrids after the cold war. *Western Journal of Communication, 59,* 214–227.

Stucky, N. (1986). Unnatural acts: Performing natural conversation. *Literature in Performance, 8,* 28–39.

Sudman, S. (1986). Do exit polls influence voting behavior? *Public Opinion Quarterly, 50,* 331–339.

Sudman, S., & Bradburn, N. (1974). *Response effects in surveys.* Chicago: Aldine.

Sugimoto, N. (1997). A Japan–U.S. comparison of apology styles. *Communication Research, 24,* 349–369.

Sullivan, P. A. (1993). Women's discourse and political communication: A case study of Congressperson Patricia Schroeder. *Western Journal of Communication, 57,* 530–545.

Sullivan P. A., & Goldzwig, S. R. (1995). A relational approach to moral decision-making: The majority opinion in *Planned Parenthood v. Casey. Quarterly Journal of Speech, 81,* 167–190.

Sunwolf, & Seibold, D. R. (1998). Jurors' intuitive rules for deliberation: A structurational approach to communication in jury decision making. *Communication Monographs, 65,* 282–307.

Surra, C., Chandler, M., & Asmussen, L. (1987). Effects of premarital pregnancy on the development of interdependence in relationships. *Journal of Social and Clinical Psychology, 5,* 123–139.

Surra, C. A., & Ridley, C. A. (1991). Multiple perspectives on interaction: Participants, peers, and observers. In B. M. Montgomery & S. Duck (Eds.), *Studying interpersonal interactions* (pp. 35–55). New York: Guilford Press.

Survey Sampling, Inc. (1990). *A survey researcher's view of the U.S.* [Poster]. Fairfield, CT: Author.

Swartz, O. (1997a). *Conducting socially responsible research.* Thousand Oaks, CA: Sage.

Swartz, O. (1997b). Disciplining the "other": Engaging Blair, Brown, and Baxter. *Southern Communication Journal, 62,* 253–256.

Szent-Gyorgyi, A. (1971). *Perspectives in biology and medicine.* Orlando, FL: Academic Press.

Tackett, M. (1990, December 2). Quake jitters: How a man shook the Midwest. *Chicago Tribune,* Sect. 1, pp. 1, 16.

Tamborini, R., Stiff, J., & Zillman, D. (1987). Preference for graphic horror featuring male versus female victimization. *Human Communication Research, 13,* 529–552.

Tanaka, K. M., & Bell, R. A. (1996). Equivocation in America and Japan: A cross-national comparison of the effects of situational conflict and status. *Communication Research, 23,* 261–296.

Tata, J. (1996). Accounting for untoward managerial actions: The mediating influence of appraisal. *Management Communication Quarterly, 10,* 168–188.

Taub, R. E. (1994). *Reliability for the social sciences: Theory and application.* Thousand Oaks, CA: Sage.

Taylor, B. C. (1992). Elderly identity in conversation: Producing frailty. *Communication Research, 19,* 493–515.

Taylor, R. B. (1994). *Research methods in criminal justice.* New York: McGraw-Hill.

Teboul, JC. B. (1995). Determinants of new hire information-seeking during organizational encounter. *Western Journal of Communication, 59,* 326–346.

Terkel, S. (1970). *Hard times.* New York: Avon Books.

Teven, J. J., & Comadena, M. E. (1996). The effects of office aesthetic quality on students' perceptions of teacher credibility and communicator style. *Communication Research Reports, 13,* 101–108.

Teven, J. J., Martin, M. M., & Newpauer, C. C. (1998). Sibling relationships: Verbally aggressive messages and their effect on relational satisfaction. *Communication Reports, 11,* 179–186.

Teven J. J., & McCroskey, J. C. (1997). The relationship of perceived teacher caring with student learning and teacher evaluation. *Communication Education, 46,* 1–9.

Teven, J. J., McCroskey, J. C., & Richmond, V. P. (1998). Measurement of tolerance for disagreement. *Communication Research Reports, 15,* 209–217.

Theus, K. T. (1993). Organizations and the media: Structures of miscommunication. *Management Communication Quarterly, 7,* 67–94.

Thomas, J. (1993). *Doing critical ethnography.* Thousand Oaks, CA: Sage.

Thompson, C. L., & Pledger, L. M. (1993). Doctor-patient communication: Is patient knowledge of medical terminology improving? *Health Communication, 5,* 89–97.

Thompson, H. (1967). *Hell's angels: A strange and terrible saga.* New York: Ballantine Books.

Thurstone, L. L. (1929). Theory of attitude measurement. *Psychological Bulletin, 36,* 222–241.

Thurstone, L. L. (1931). The measurement of social attitudes. *Journal of Abnormal and Social Psychology, 26,* 249–269.

Thweatt, K. S., & McCroskey, J. C. (1998). The impact of teacher immediacy and misbehaviors on teacher credibility. *Communication Education, 47,* 348–358.

Thyer, B. A. (1994). *Successful publishing in scholarly journals.* Thousand Oaks, CA: Sage.

Tjvosvold, D., & Dumes, D. K. (1980). Effects of controversy within a cooperative or competitive context on organizational decision making. *Journal of Applied Psychology, 65,* 590–595.

Tjvosvold, D., Wedley, W. C., & Field, R. H. G. (1986). Construct controversy, the Vroom-Yetton model, and managerial decision-making. *Journal of Occupational Behaviour, 7,* 125–138.

Tobacco firm concealed '63 research. (1994, May 8). *Chicago Tribune,* Sect. 1, p. 7.

Tolhuizen, J. R. (1989a). Affinity-seeking in developing relationships. *Communication Reports, 2,* 83–91.

Tolhuizen, J. H. (1989b). Communication strategies for intensifying dating relationships: Identification, use and structure. *Journal of Social and Personal Relationships, 6,* 413–434.

Top physicist disputes cold-fusion finding: 2 chemists accused of inventing data. (1991, March 17). *Chicago Tribune,* Sect. 1, p. 16.

Torres, L. (1997). *Puerto Rican discourse: A sociolinguistic study of a New York suburb.* Mahwah, NJ: Lawrence Erlbaum.

Traub, R. E. (1994). *Reliability for the social sciences: Theory and applications.* Thousand Oaks, CA: Sage.

Tracy, S. J., & Tracy, K. (1998). Emotion labor at 911: A case study and theoretical critique. *Journal of Applied Communication Research, 26,* 390–411.

Trenholm, S. (1991). *Human communication theory* (2nd ed.). Englewood Cliffs, NJ: Prentice Hall.

Trent, J. S., & Sabourin, T. (1993). Sex still counts: Women's use of televised advertising during the decade of the 80's. *Journal of Applied Communication Research, 21,* 21–40.

Trujillo, N. (1985). Organizational communication as cultural performance: Some managerial considerations. *Southern Speech Communication Journal, 50,* 201–224.

Trujillo, N. (1992). Interpreting (the work and talk of) baseball: Perspectives on ballpark culture. *Western Journal of Communication, 56,* 350–371.

Trujillo, N. (1993). Interpreting November 22: A critical ethnography of an assassination site. *Quarterly Journal of Speech, 4,* 447–466.

Tucker, R. K., Weaver, R. L., & Berryman-Fink, C. (1981). *Research in speech communication.* Englewood Cliffs, NJ: Prentice-Hall.

Tucker, W. H. (1994). *The science and politics of racial research.* Urbana: University of Illinois Press.

Tukey, J. W. (1969). Analyzing data: Sanctification or detective work? *American Psychologist, 24,* 83–91.

Turner, L. H., Dindia, K., & Pearson, J. C. (1995). An investigation of female/male verbal behaviors in same-sex and mixed-sex conversations. *Communication Research, 8,* 86–96.

U.S. Census Bureau. (1999a, June 12a). Households by type and selected characteristics: 1998. *U.S. Census Bureau* [Online Website]. Available Internet: http://www.census.gov/population/socdemo/hh-fam/98ppla.txt

U.S. Census Bureau. (1999b, June 12). Monthly income in the United States: 1997. *U.S. Census Bureau* [Online Website]. Available Internet: http://www.census.gov/prod/3/98pubs/p60-200.pdf

U.S. Department of Labor. (1991). *What work requires of schools: SCANS report for America 2000.* Washington, DC: Author.

Valacich, J. S., & Schwenk, C. (1995a). Devil's advocacy and dialectical inquiry effects on face-to-face and computer-mediated group decision making. *Organizational Behavior and Human Decision Processes, 63,* 158–173.

Valacich, J. S., & Schwenk, C. (1995b). Structuring conflict in individual, face-to-face, and computer-mediated group decision making: Carping versus objective devil's advocacy. *Decision Sciences, 26,* 369–393.

Valkenburg, P. M., & van der Voort, T. H. A. (1995). The influence of television on children's daydreaming styles: A 1-year panel study. *Communication Research, 22,* 267–288.

Vande Berg, L. R. (1993). *China Beach,* prime time war in the postfeminist age: An example of patriarchy in a different voice. *Western Journal of Communication, 57,* 349–366.

van Driel, B., & Richardson, J. T. (1988). Print media coverage of new religious movements: A longitudinal study. *Journal of Communication, 38*(3), 37–61.

Vangelisti, A. L. (1994a). Couples' communication problems: The counselor's perspective. *Journal of Applied Communication Research, 22,* 106–126.

Vangelisti, A. L. (1994b). Messages that hurt. In W. R. Cupach & B. H. Spitzberg (Eds.), *The dark side of interpersonal communication* (pp. 53–82). Hillsdale, NJ: Lawrence Erlbaum.

Vangelisti, A. L., & Crumley, L. P. (1998). Reactions to messages that hurt: The influence of relational contexts. *Communication Monographs, 65,* 173–196.

Vangelisti, A. L., Daly, J. A., & Rudnick, J. R. (1991). Making people feel guilty in conversations: Techniques and correlates. *Human Communication Research, 18,* 3–39.

Vangelisti, A. L., Knapp, M. L., & Daly, J. A. (1990). Conversational narcissism. *Communication Monographs, 57,* 251–274.

Van Maanen, J. (1979). The fact of fiction in organizational ethnography. *Administrative Science Quarterly, 24,* 535–550.

Van Maanen, J. (1982). Fieldwork on the bear. In J. Van Maanen, J. M. Dabbs, Jr., & R. R. Faulkner (Eds.), *Varieties of qualitative research* (pp. 103–151). Newbury Park, CA: Sage.

Van Maanen, J. (Ed.). (1983). Reclaiming qualitative methods for organizational research: A preface. In J. Van Maanen (Ed.), *Qualitative methodology* (Rev. ed., pp. 9–18). Newbury Park, CA: Sage.

Van Maanen, J. (1988). *Tales of the field: On writing ethnography.* Chicago: University of Chicago Press.

Varallo, S. M., Ray, E. B., & Ellis, B. H. (1998). Speaking of incest: The research interview as social justice. *Journal of Applied Communication Research, 26,* 254–271.

Vaughn, M. A. (1995). Organization symbols: An analysis of their types of functions in a reborn organization. *Management Communication Quarterly, 9,* 219–250.

Vavrus, M. (1998). Working the Senate from the outside in: The mediated construction of a feminist political campaign. *Critical Studies in Mass Communicaion, 15,* 213–235.

Veblen, T. (1919). *The place of science in modern civilization and other essays.* New York: Viking Penguin.

Violanti, M. T. (1996). Hooked on expectations: An analysis of influence and relationships in the Talihook reports. *Journal of Applied Communication Research, 24,* 67–82.

Vogt, W. P. (1993). *Dictionary of statistics and methodology: A nontechnical guide for the social sciences.* Newbury Park, CA: Sage.

Vogt, W. P. (1999). *Dictionary of statistics and methodology: A nontechnical guide for the social sciences* (2nd ed.). Thousand Oaks, CA: Sage.

Vrij, A., Semin, G. R., & Bull, R. (1996). Insight into behavior displayed during deception. *Human Communication Research, 22,* 544–562.

Waitzkin, H., Britt, T., & Williams, C. (1995). Narratives of aging and social problems in medical encounters with older persons. *Journal of Health and Social Behavior, 35,* 322–348.

Waldron, V. R. (1990). Constrained rationality: Situational influences on information acquisition plans and tactics. *Communication Monographs, 57,* 184–201.

Waldron, V. R., & Applegate, J. L. (1994). Interpersonal construct differentiation and conversational planning: An examination of two cognitive accounts for the production of competent verbal disagreement tactics. *Human Communication Research, 21,* 3–35.

Wallgren, A., Wallgren, B., Persson, R., Jorner, U., & Haaland, J-A. (1996). *Graphing statistics & data: Creating better charts.* Thousand Oaks, CA: Sage.

Walsh, J. F., Jr. (1993). Paying attention to channels: Differential images of recruitment in Students for a Democratic Society, 1960–1965. *Communication Studies, 44,* 71–86.

Wanzer, M. B. (1998). An exploratory investigation of student and teacher perceptions of student-generated affinity-seeking behaviors. *Communication Education, 47,* 373–382.

Wanzer, M. B., Booth-Butterfield, M., & Booth-Butterfield, S. (1995). The funny people: A source-orientation to the communication of humor. *Communication Quarterly, 43,* 142–154.

Wanzer, M. B., Booth-Butterfield, M., & Booth-Butterfield, S. (1996). Are funny people popular? An examination of humor orientation, loneliness, and social attraction. *Communication Quarterly, 44,* 42–52.

Warnick, B. (1998). Appearance or reality? Political parody on the Web in campaign '96. *Critical Studies in Mass Communication, 15,* 306–324.

Warren, J. (1993, December 23). Nieman Reports call for more digging on science beat. *Chicago Tribune,* Sect. 5, p. 2.

Wasserman, I. M., Stack, S., & Reeves, J. L. (1994). Suicide and the media: *The New York Times*'s presentation of front-page suicide stories between 1910 and 1920. *Journal of Communication, 44*(2), 64–83.

Watkins, B., Lichtenstein, R., Vest, D., & Thomas, J. W. (1992). HMO advertising and enrollee health status: Marketing medicare plans to seniors. *Health Communication, 4,* 303–322.

Webb, E., Campbell, D. T., Schwartz, R. D., & Sechrest, L. (1973). *Unobtrusive measures: Nonreactive research in the social sciences.* Skokie, IL: Rand McNally.

Weber, M. (1949). *Max Weber on the methodology of the social sciences* (E. A. Shils & H. A. Finch, Trans. & Eds.). Glencoe, IL: Free Press.

Weber, R. P. (1984). Computer-aided content analysis: A short primer. *Qualitative Sociology, 7,* 126–147.

Weber, R. P. (1990). *Basic content analysis* (2nd ed.). Newbury Park, CA: Sage.

Webster, J. G., & Lichty, L. W. (1991). *Ratings analysis: Theory and practice.* Hillsdale, NJ: Lawrence Erlbaum.

Weider-Hatfield, D., & Hatfield, J. D. (1996). Superiors' conflict management strategies and subordinate outcomes. *Management Communication Quarterly, 10,* 189–208.

Weiner, B. (1982). The emotional consequences of causal attributions. In M. S. Clark & S. T. Kiske (Eds.), *Affect and Cognition: The Seventeenth Annual Carnegie Symposium on Cognition* (pp. 185–209). Hillsdale, NJ: Lawrence Erlbaum.

Weintraub, P. (1990). Masters of the universe. *Omni, 12*(6), 42–46, 86–90.

Weisband, S. P., Schneider, S. K., & Connolly, T. (1995). Computer-mediated communication and social information: Status salience and status differences. *Academy of Management Journal, 38,* 1124–1151.

Weisberg, H. F. (1992). *Central tendency and variability.* Newbury Park, CA: Sage.

Weisberg, H. F., Krosnick, J. A., & Bowen, B. D. (1996). *An introduction to survey research, polling, and data analysis* (3rd ed.). Thousand Oaks, CA: Sage.

Weiss, A. J., Imrich, D. J., & Wilson, B. J. (1993). Prior exposure to creations from a horror film: Live versus photographic representations. *Human Communication Research, 20,* 41–66.

Weitzman, E., & Miles, M. B. (1993). *Computer-aided qualitative data analysis: A review of selected software.* New York: Center for Policy Research.

Wenar, C. (1963). *The reliability of developmental histories: Summary and evaluation of evidence.* Philadelphia: University of Pennsylvania Medical School.

Wenner, L. A. (1983). Political news on television: A reconsideration of audience orientations. *Western Journal of Speech Communication, 47,* 380–395.

Weppner, R. S. (1977). *Street ethnography: Selected studies of crimes and drug use in natural settings.* Beverly Hills, CA: Sage.

Werner, O., & Schoepfle, G. M. (1987). *Systematic fieldwork* (2 vols.). Newbury Park, CA: Sage.

Wexler, S. (1990). Ethical obligations and social research. In K. L. Kempf (Ed.), *Measurement issues in criminology* (pp. 78–107). New York: Springer-Verlag.

Whaley, B. B. (1997). Perceptions of rebuttal analogy: Politeness and implications for persuasion. *Argumentation and Advocacy, 33,* 161–169.

Whaley, B. B., Nicotera, A. M., & Samter, W. (1998). African American women's perceptions of rebuttal analogy: Judgments concerning politeness, likability, and ethics. *Southern Communication Journal, 64,* 48–58.

What's justified in fighting AIDS? (1997, October 20). *Chicago Tribune,* Sect. 1, p. 12.

Wheeless, L. R. (1975). An investigation of receiver apprehension and social context dimensions of communication apprehension. *Speech Teacher, 24,* 161–268.

Wheeless, L. R. (1976). Self-disclosure and interpersonal solidarity: Measurement, validation, and relationships. *Human Communication Research, 3,* 47–61.

Wheeless, L. R., & Grotz, J. (1976). Conceptualization and measurement of reported self-disclosure. *Human Communication Research, 3,* 195–213.

Wheeless, L. R., Nesser, K., & McCroskey, J. C. (1986). The relationship of self-disclosure and disclosiveness to high and low communication apprehension. *Communication Research Reports, 3,* 129–134.

Wheeless, L. R., & Parsons, L. A. (1995). What you feel is what you might get: Exploring communication apprehension and sexual communication satisfaction. *Communication Research Reports, 12,* 39–45.

Whitbourne, S. K. (1986). *The me I know: A study of adult identity.* New York: Springer-Verlag.

Who's fault? (1990, December 6). *Chicago Tribune,* Sect. 1, p. 22.

Whyte, W. F. (1955). *Street corner society.* Chicago: University of Chicago Press.

Whyte, W. F. (1984). *Learning from the field: A guide from experience.* Beverly Hills, CA: Sage.

Wicks, R. H., & Kern, M. (1995). Factors influencing decisions by local television news directors to develop news reporting strategies during the 1992 political campaign. *Communication Research, 22,* 237–255.

Wiemann, J. M. (1977). Explication and test of a model of communicative competence. *Human Communication Research, 3,* 195–213.

Wilkins, B. M., & Andersen, P. A. (1991). Gender differences and similarities in management communication: A meta-analysis. *Management Communication Quarterly, 5,* 6–35.

Williams, A., & Giles, H. (1996). Intergenerational conversations: Young adults' retrospective accounts. *Human Communication Research, 23,* 220–250.

Williams, F. (1986). *Reasoning with statistics: How to read quantitative research* (3rd ed.). New York: Holt, Rinehart and Winston.

Williams, F. (1992). *Reasoning with statistics: How to read quantitative research* (4th ed.). Fort Worth, TX: Harcourt Brace Jovanovich.

Williams, M. L., & Goss, B. (1975). Equivocation: Character insurance. *Human Communication Research, 1,* 257–264.

Williams, R. (1988). Reflections on anonymity. *Perceptual and Motor Skills, 67,* 763–766.

Wilson, P. (1996). The rhythm of rhetoric: Jesse Jackson at the 1988 Democratic National Convention. *Southern Communication Journal, 61,* 253–264.

Wilson, S. R., Aleman, C. G., & Leatham, G. B. (1998). Identity implications of influence goals: A revised analysis of face-threatening acts and application to seeking compliance with same-sex friends. *Human Communication Research, 25,* 64–96.

Wimmer, R. D., & Dominick, J. R. (1994). *Mass media research: An introduction* (4th ed.). Belmont, CA: Wadsworth.

Winter, D. L. S., & Clayton, R. L. (1990). *Speech data entry: Results of the first test of voice recognition for data collection.* Washington, DC: Bureau of Labor Statistics.

Wiseman, R. L., & Schenck-Hamlin, W. (1981). A multidimensional scaling validation of an inductively derived set of compliance-gaining strategies. *Communication Monographs, 48,* 251–270.

Witte, K. (1992). Putting the fear back into fear appeals: The extended parallel process model. *Communication Monographs, 59,* 330–349.

Witte, K. (1994). Fear control and danger control: A test of the extended parallel process model (EPPM). *Communication Monographs, 61,* 113–134.

Witte, K., Cameron, K. A., McKeon, J. K., & Berkowitz, J. M. (1996). Predicting risk behaviors: Development and validation of a diagnostic scale. *Journal of Health Communication, 1,* 317–341.

Witte, R. S., & Witte, J. S. (1997). *Statistics* (5th ed.). Fort Worth, TX: Harcourt Brace.

Witteman, H. (1992). Analyzing interpersonal conflict: Nature of awareness, type of initiating event, situational perceptions, and management styles. *Western Journal of Communication, 56,* 248–280.

Wolcott, H. F. (1990). *Writing up qualitative research.* Newbury Park, CA: Sage.

Wolf, F. (1986). *Meta-analysis: Quantitative methods for research synthesis.* Newbury Park, CA: Sage.

Wolins, F. A. (1962). Responsibility for raw data. *American Psychologist, 17,* 657–658.

Wood, J. T. (Ed.). (1992). Telling our stories: Sexual harassment in the communication discipline. *Journal of Applied Communication Research, 20,* 349–418.

Wood, J. T. (1995). Theorizing practice, practicing theory. In K. N. Cissna (Ed.), *Applied communication in the 21st century* (pp. 181–192). Mahwah, NJ: Lawrence Erlbaum.

Woods, E. (1996). Associations of nonverbal decoding ability with indices of person-centered communication ability. *Communication Reports, 9,* 12–22.

Woods, E. (1998). Communication abilities as predictors of verbal and nonverbal performance in persuasive interaction. *Communication Reports, 11,* 167–178.

Wright, D. B. (1997). *Understanding statistics: An introduction for the social sciences.* London: Sage.

Wright, K. B. (1997). Shared ideology in Alcoholics Anonymous: A grounded theory approach. *Journal of Health Communication, 2,* 83–99.

Wright, S. R. (1979). *Quantitative methods and statistics: A guide to social research.* Newbury Park, CA: Sage.

Wuebben, P. L., Straits, B. C., & Schulman, G. I. (1974). *The experiment as a social occasion.* Berkeley, CA: Glendessary Press.

Wyatt, D. F., & Campbell, D. T. (1950). A study of interviewer bias as related to interviewers' expectations and own opinions. *International Journal of Opinion and Attitude Research, 4,* 77–83.

Xioa, X. (1995). China encounters Darwinism: A case of intercultural rhetoric. *Quarterly Journal of Speech, 81,* 83–99.

Yablonsky, L. (1968). *The hippy trip.* New York: Pegasus.

Yagoda, G., & Wolfson, W. (1964). Examiner influence on projective test responses. *Journal of Clinical Psychology, 20,* 389.

Yang, N., & Linz, D. (1990). Movie ratings and the content of adult videos: The sex-violence ratio. *Journal of Communication, 40*(2), 28–42.

Yelsma, P. (1995). Couples' affective orientations and their verbal abusiveness. *Communication Quarterly, 43,* 100–114.

Yerkes, R., & Dodson, J. (1908). The relation of strength of stimulus to rapidity of habit-formation. *Journal of Comparative Neurology and Psychology, 18,* 459–482.

Yin, R. K. (1994). *Case study research: Design and methods* (2nd ed.). Thousand Oaks, CA: Sage.

Young, C. H., Savola, K. L., & Phelps, E. (1991). *Inventory of longitudinal studies in the social sciences.* Newbury Park, CA: Sage.

Yow, V. R. (1994). *Recording oral history: A practical guide for social scientists.* Thousand Oaks, CA: Sage.

Yum, J. O., & Kendall, K. E. (1995). Sex differences in political communication during presidential campaigns. *Communication Quarterly, 43,* 131–141.

Zaeske, S. (1995). The "promiscuous audience" controversy and the emergence of the women's rights movement. *Quarterly Journal of Speech, 81,* 191–207.

Zagacki, K. S. (1995). Eisenhower and the rhetoric of postwar Korea. *Southern Communication Journal, 60,* 233–245.

Zagacki, K. S. (1996). The priestly rhetoric of neoconservatism. *Western Journal of Communication, 60,* 168–187.

Zakahi, W. R., & Duran, R. L. (1985). Loneliness, communicative competence and communication apprehension: Extension and replication. *Communication Quarterly, 33,* 50–60.

Zakahi, W. R., & Goss, B. (1995). Loneliness and interpersonal decoding skills. *Communication Quarterly, 43,* 75–85.

Zaleski, C. (1987). *Otherworld journeys: Accounts of near-death experiences in medieval and modern times.* New York: Oxford University Press.

Zarefsky, D. (1993, October). Rethinking the shape of our discipline. *Spectra,* pp. 2, 4.

Zillman, D. (1982). Television viewing and arousal. In D. Pearl, L. Bouthilet, & J. Lezar (Eds.), *Television and behavior: Ten years of scientific progress and implications for the eighties* (Vol. 2, pp. 53–67). Washington, DC: United States Government Printing Office.

Zillman, D., & Bryant, J. (1985). Affect, mood, and emotion as determinants of selection media exposure. In D. Zillman & J. Bryant (Eds.), *Selective exposure to communication* (pp. 157–190). Hillsdale, NJ: Lawrence Erlbaum.

Ziman, J. (1968). *Public knowledge: The social dimension of knowledge.* Cambridge, England: Cambridge University Press.

Zimmerman, D., & Weider, L. (1977). The diary/diary-interview method. *Urban Life, 5,* 479–498.

Zimmerman, D. H., & West, C. (1975). Sex roles, interruptions and silences in conversations. In B. Thorne & N. Henry (Eds.), *Language and sex: Differences and dominance* (pp. 105–129). Cambridge, MA: Newbury House.

Zimmerman, S. (1995). Perceptions of intercultural communication competence and international student adaptation to an American campus. *Communication Education, 44,* 321–335.

Zorn, T. E. (1993). Motivation to communicate: A critical review with suggested alternatives. In S. A. Deetz (Ed.), *Communication yearbook 16* (pp. 515–549). Thousand Oaks, CA: Sage.

Zorn, T. E., & Violanti, M. T. (1996). Communication abilities and individual achievement in organizations. *Management Communication Quarterly, 10,* 139–167.

Zuckerman, M., DePaulo, B. M., & Rosenthal, R. (1981). Verbal and nonverbal communication of deception. In L. Berkowtiz (Ed.), *Advances in experimental social psychology* (Vol. 4, pp. 1–59). New York: Academic Press.

Zusne, L., & Jones, W. H. (1982). *Anomalistic psychology: A study of extraordinary phenomena of behavior and experience.* Hillsdale, NJ: Lawrence Erlbaum.

NAME INDEX